Chedzoy

Life on the Somerset Levels

John Weeks

Published by Chedzoy 2000 in aid of Chedzoy Village Hall

14 Manor Road, Chedzoy, Bridgwater, Somerset, TA7 8QZ

Chedzoy Village Hall © Maxine Heal

Design, image manipulation, maps and cover by Mark Smith

November 1999

Printed by Bigwood & Staple Ltd., The Mill, Church Street, Bridgwater, Somerset, TA6 5AT

ISBN 0 9537036 0 6

Introduction

Like us, village residents throughout the ages have had their problems as well as their dreams for the future, but through their daily lives and labours they helped to make Chedzoy what it is today.

A sense of belonging to a community is important and helps us to define our identity. As we approach the 21st Century, and in an age when everything is changing so rapidly, it is important that we should not lose sight of our past.

A brief history of Chedzoy and a guide were originally compiled in 1985 by Pauline Clapp, head teacher of the former village school, to interest visitors in the year of the Tercentenary of the Battle of Sedgemoor. My grateful thanks to Pauline for permission to use her format and incorporate her original text into this book. Our thanks to all those who have given freely of their time, skill and knowledge to help in the production of this book.

Every attempt has been made to ensure accuracy but, as so often is the case, sometimes research has only raised more questions than it has answered. Your comments and corrections would be much appreciated.

All proceeds from the sale of this book will be used for improvements to Chedzoy Village Hall.

My sincere thanks go to the staff of the Bridgwater Mercury for their encouragement and support and to the Editor, Mr. Ken Bird, for permission to reproduce the numerous extracts from their archives which have brought village history for the last 150 years to life: this is not intended to be a book of dull facts, but one celebrating the lives of individuals, good and bad.

Thanks are also due to Mark Smith, who has designed and typeset this book and to Maxine Heal for her drawing of Chedzoy Village Hall.

Finally, special thanks to my wife, Maureen, who for 27 years has shared my love of Chedzoy and spent many hours helping me with the research which was necessary.

John Weeks

14 Manor Road, Chedzoy
November 1999

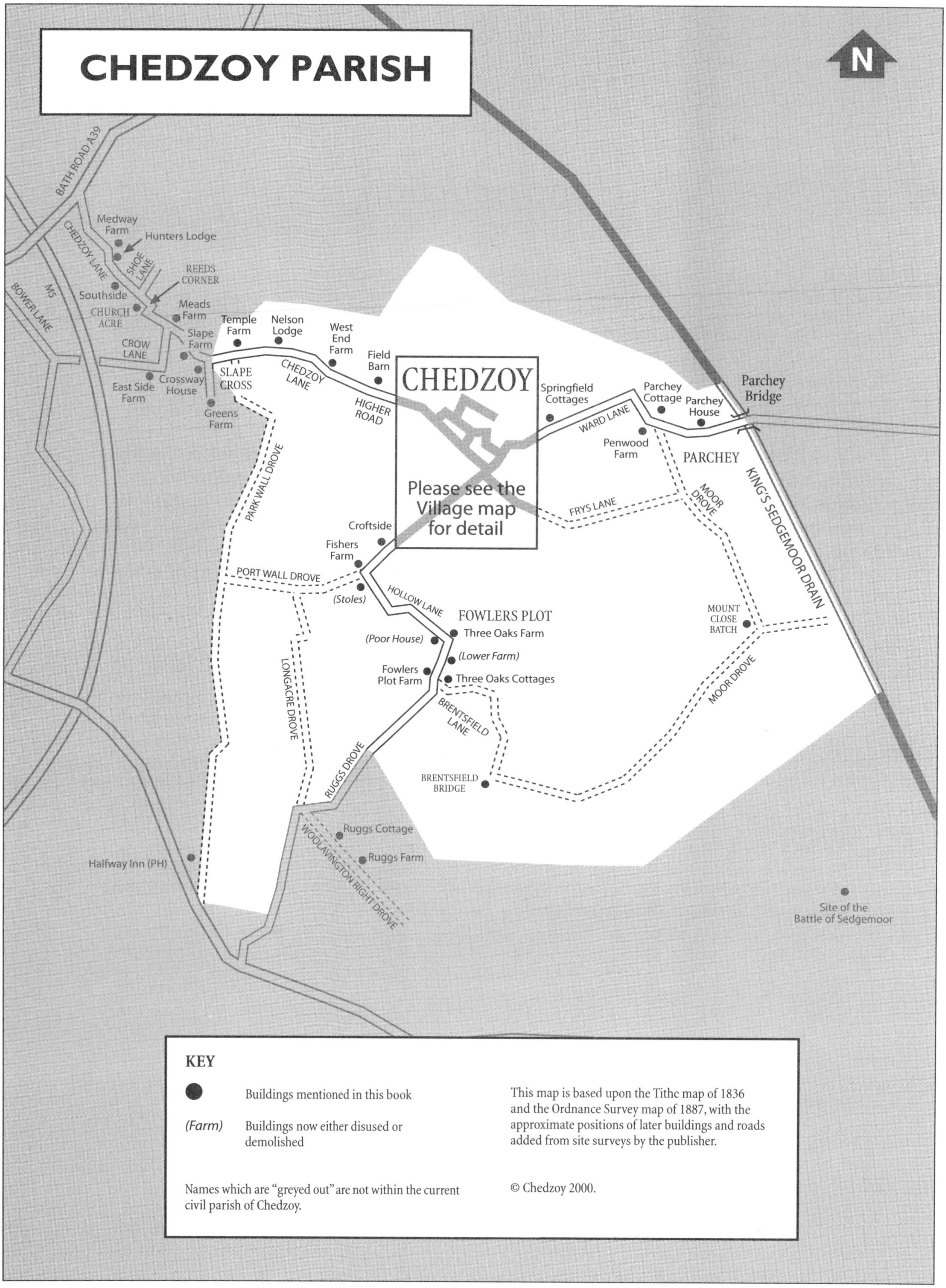

KEY

● Buildings mentioned in this book

(Farm) Buildings now either disused or demolished

Names which are "greyed out" are not within the current civil parish of Chedzoy.

This map is based upon the Tithe map of 1836 and the Ordnance Survey map of 1887, with the approximate positions of later buildings and roads added from site surveys by the publisher.

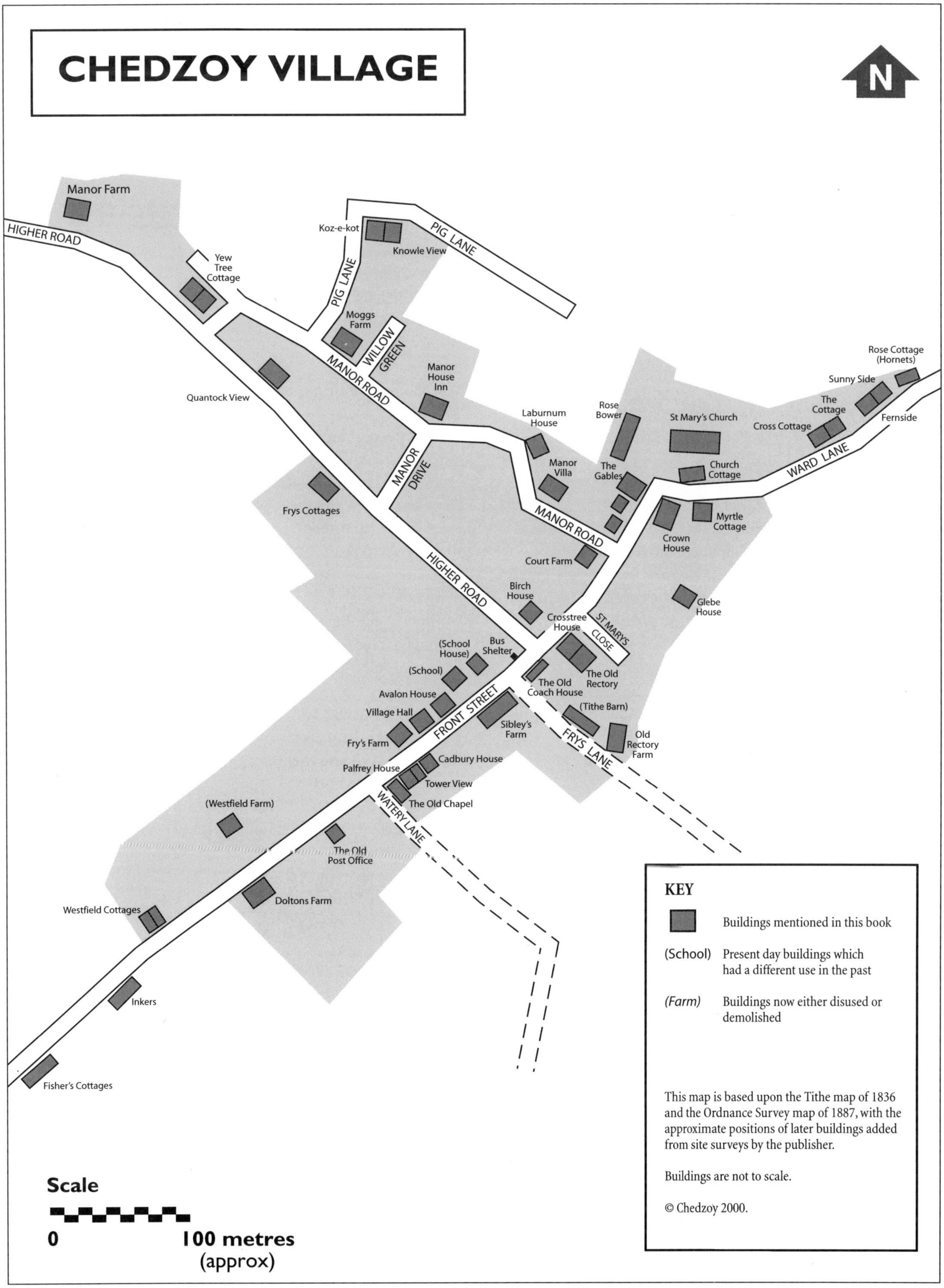
CHEDZOY VILLAGE
N
Manor Farm
HIGHER ROAD
Yew Tree Cottage
Koz-e-kot
Knowle View
PIG LANE
PIG LANE
Moggs Farm
WILLOW GREEN
MANOR ROAD
Quantock View
Manor House Inn
MANOR DRIVE
Laburnum House
Rose Bower
St Mary's Church
Rose Cottage (Hornets)
Sunny Side
The Cottage
Fernside
Cross Cottage
Church Cottage
WARD LANE
Manor Villa
The Gables
Myrtle Cottage
Crown House
Frys Cottages
MANOR ROAD
Court Farm
HIGHER ROAD
Birch House
Glebe House
Crosstree House
ST MARYS CLOSE
(School House)
Bus Shelter
(School)
The Old Rectory
The Old Coach House
Avalon House
Village Hall
FRONT STREET
(Tithe Barn)
Sibley's Farm
Fry's Farm
FRYS LANE
Old Rectory Farm
Cadbury House
Palfrey House
Tower View
The Old Chapel
(Westfield Farm)
WATERY LANE
The Old Post Office
Doltons Farm
Westfield Cottages
Inkers
Fisher's Cottages
Scale
0
100 metres (approx)
KEY
Buildings mentioned in this book
(School) Present day buildings which had a different use in the past
(Farm) Buildings now either disused or demolished
This map is based upon the Tithe map of 1836 and the Ordnance Survey map of 1887, with the approximate positions of later buildings added from site surveys by the publisher.
Buildings are not to scale.
© Chedzoy 2000.

Chedzoy

Away from Chedzoy's pleasant fields,
My steps have wandered wide,
But still my memory oft-times yields,
Views of that countryside.

The ancient church, with her grey walls,
And nave and transept dim,
Embattled ivied tower, still calls,
Her flock to worship 'Him.'

The churchyard, too with well kept sward,
And flower borders gay,
The buttress - scarred of old - when Lord
James Monmouth passed that way.

And if one climbs the tower, not high,
Up narrow staircase steep,
What glorious views await the eye,
From Quantocks to Swain's Leap.

Northwards, the Poldens and Knowle Hill,
With Sedgemoor, easterly,
And in the far-off distance, still
The towers of Othery.

And Middlezoy and Weston, higher,
Whilst to the south and west,
We see St. Mary's graceful spire,
'Midst fields and trees so blest.

And from our vantage point above,
We see the village spread,
Its farms, the roads, the fields we love,
That give our daily bread.

From Westfield Farm to Fowlers Plot,
From Northfield to Park Wall,
From Parchey Bridge to the old spot,
Where stands the Cross Tree tall.

From Manor House to Manor Inn,
Where strongest drinks are sold,
And where, amidst the noise and din,
Tales of the past are told.

From Ward Lane to the Rectory,
Past Court Farm and the school,
Past Watery Lane and Chapelry,
Right down to Derrick's pool.

Across the Three Oaks Farm, by way,
Of Dippits and Ruggs Drove,
Through fertile fields and orchards gay,
Crammed full with treasure trove.

O'er hedgerows lush with berries black,
We quickly cast our eyes,
Long Acres now, and then, alack,
We're back again at Frys.

In Sussex, Kent and Devon County,
Is many a village fine,
But this, I'm sure you will agree,
Chedzoy does them outshine.

Edward J. Brooks (1889-1958)

Christmas 1949

Chedzoy - A Somerset Village

Village History - The Early Years

Like that of many villages of the Somerset Levels, the beginnings of Chedzoy are steeped in mystery. The village is situated on an identifiable sandy island below the Polden Hills to the east of Bridgwater. A Roman coin found in the 1980s on the site of the allotments in Higher Road, and the discovery nearby in the excavation of the deep ditches in the vicinity of King's Sedgemoor Drain, of a Neolithic trackway, suggest that the area was on a trade route at least from very early times. The first mention of the village is as early as 729 when it was at the centre of a three way junction of lanes to the east of Bridgwater. In the early 19th Century William Stradling found a Roman villa, complete with hypocaust, somewhere in the village. Its site has since been lost but is believed to have been in the Slape area.

The derivation of the name Chedzoy is uncertain but probably signified Chad's or Cedd's Island from the Old English suffix *"ey"* or *"iey"* meaning island. Others suggest that it derives from the Old English *"sceat"*, meaning inlet, and *"sae"* and *"weg"*, meaning sea way: "The inlet on the sea way river." This suggests that the village was probably inhabited during Saxon times and the flood-free land exploited for agricultural purposes. In 1327 the name was spelt as *Chedesey* and in the middle-1600's, *Chedfey* or *Chedsey*. As long ago as 1859, Kelly's Directory was noting that the name of the village was at one time spelt as *Chedsea*, something which it repeated for many years, but no supporting evidence for this has been found.

In the Middle Ages the Manor of Chedzoy lay on the edge of the estates of Glastonbury Abbey where they met those of North Petherton and lay in the Hundred of that name. At this time the moors were certainly used for seasonal grazing in the dry summer months. To allow the specified number of beasts permitted to graziers with commoner's rights and to eliminate those of outsiders, a drove or drill was held at least once annually. The cattle were rounded up, impounded and only released on payment of a fine. The names of the droves or unmetalled trackways leading onto the moor from the village point to this practice.

In 1235 Abbot Michael of Glastonbury and William de Monte Acute found a battle in arms to decide the ownership of the moors here. William won, and it was mutually agreed that the Abbot and his tenants of Chedzoy should have common in the marsh for all their animals and flocks. The poundage of stray animals was to be collected by a servant of the Abbot and shared equally between him and William. The pound was to be erected in the middle of the marsh and sustained at the cost of both parties. To the south-west of Chedzoy in the direction of Westonzoyland, the route of Moor Drove linking with Brentsfield Drove in a great semicircle clearly delineates even today the boundary of the agricultural land of Chedzoy Field, as it is still known, and the summer grazing of the moors. A walk along Moor Drove to the point where it turns right towards Brentsfield Drove brings the visitor to a noticeable mound on the right known today as Mill Batch or Mount Close Batch and the site of the Medieval mill. As the visitor looks across from Mill Batch to the scene of the Battle of Sedgemoor, he looks at meadows known as Langmoor in Abbot Michael of Glastonbury's survey of 1234 as having been reclaimed from the moor. During the Middle Ages the outfall of winter floodwater into the River Parrett at Andersea occurred through this gap between the islands of sowy - Westonzoyland, Middlezoy and Othery today - and Chedzoy, much of this part of Sedgemoor being protected from extensive flooding of the Parrett by the erection of walls like Lake Wall to be seen on the road between Westonzoyland and Burroughbridge. Simon de Montacute obtained a Tuesday market and a three day fair in the village in 1314.

John Collinson wrote in his "Histories and Antiquities of Somerset," which was published in 1790,

> "The Manor of Chedzoy is now the property of Robert Mackreth, Esq., and is not set down in the Conqueror's survey (i.e. the Doomsday Book). It was anciently vested in the Crown, and given by Edward I in the 13th year of his reign (1285) to Simon de Montacute, in whole descendants of the name Montacute or Montague, Earls of Salisbury, it continued till the time of Henry VI. When Alice, the only daughter and heir of Thomas Montague, Earl of Salisbury, brought it by marriage to Richard Neville, who was created in her right Earl of Salisbury. After his death it was possessed by William de la Pole, Marquis of Suffolk, and after him by Edward, son of George, Duke of Clarence, upon whose attainder it came to the Crown, and Henry VIII held it till his death."

Attainder was the extinction of a person's civil rights resulting from a sentence of death or outlawry on conviction for treason or felony.

> "Soon after which it was by patent dated 4th Oct. 5 Henry VIII (1514) granted to Margaret, his sister, who was attained in 1539 and thus the Manor, again lapsing to the Crown, was kept there until 7 Edward VI (1554), when that King granted

it to the Earl of Pembroke. The Prior of Brewton (sic) had estates valued in 1293 at ten shillings (50p.).

"In this village Roman coins have been discovered and in 1701 several earthen urns and a fibula were found near the church. The living is a Rectory in the deanery of Bridgwater and in the gift of the Coney family. In 1292 the living was valued at 30 marks.

"Several ministers of notoriety have possessed this benefice. Richard Nikke, LL.D., was Rector thereof in A.D. 1489. In 1492 he was constituted Vicar-General to Richard Fox, Bishop of this Diocese; in 1494 he was Archdeacon of Wells, and in 1496 he was made Canon to Windsor and Registrar of the Order of the Garter. In 1501 he was elected to the bishopric of Norwich, in which dignity he died in 1536 and was buried in his own cathedral.

"In 1620 Walter Raleigh, S.T.P. (Sanctae Theologiae Professor - Professor of Sacred Theology), afterwards Dean of Wells, was presented with the living by William, Earl of Pembroke. He was murdered by the rebels (Roundheads) in 1646. Andrew Paschall, Rector of this Parish in the latter end of the last century, undertook the Exordium of a history of this county, but published only a few fugitive pieces, among which is a letter to Dr. Hooke concerning a slight shock of an earthquake in the village of Chedzoy, and in all the neighbourhood of Bridgwater January 4, 1680," of which more later.

In 1320 the manor had a windmill and, possibly at Slape, a watermill which was probably replaced by a windmill before 1348. By 1330 there were three windmills. One at Slape, described as new, was known as the West Mill in 1363. It was probably one of the two mills which survived in 1529 but which had gone by 1576. The second windmill in 1330 was called South Mill and was still in use in 1342. It probably stood near Fowlers Plot. The third windmill mentioned in 1330 was later called Clos Mill. This was blown down in 1379 but had evidently been rebuilt by 1381 and was in use in 1384. A fourth windmill, mentioned in 1349 and described as the East Mill, may have been replaced by one bought at Barrington and re-erected in 1356. It was sited in the East Field at Mill Batch. Two horse mills, used for grinding malt, were held with the South Mill and Clos Mill. One of them was replaced in 1356 by one bought at Glastonbury and rebuilt. One of them may have gone out of use by 1373. The horse mill at Clos Mill had burnt down by 1485.

Slape was recorded about 1329 as a scattered settlement and said to have had a chapel and the remains of a large Medieval house which may have been those of Cauntelos Manor House. Parchey may be identified with Elney which was mentioned between 1332 and the 15th Century. Fowlers Plot was known by this name by 1373.

In 1331 twenty-five people were presented at the Manor Court for breach of the assize of ale, and a further three for selling ale by unlawful measure. There was an inn or ale house in Chedzoy in 1619 and 1629. Between 1657 and 1690 the Bond family kept an inn which may have remained open until 1738 or later. There is no further record of an inn until 1857 when the Crown was mentioned. A beer house was in business west of the church in 1861 and was known as the Manor House by 1881.

In 1497, after Cornish rebels marched on London, 46 men from Chedzoy were fined for their part in the rebellion.

Nowadays, the moors are drained by King's Sedgemoor Drain and an extensive system of ditches, known locally at rhynes or rhines, the biggest being Chedzoy New Cut, which replaces Bussex and Langmoor Rhynes which existed at the time of the Battle of Sedgemoor and delineates the extent of the allocation of reclaimed common land to those with rights of common who performed drainage maintenance, known as the austre holders. The draining of King's Sedgemoor was first proposed in 1618 by King James I. The moor had belonged to Glastonbury Abbey but, after the dissolution of the monasteries, James claimed it had become Crown property and could be enclosed if drained. The King had insufficient funds for such a project and so turned to speculators and developers for assistance. It was agreed that the King was to have a third of the moor - about 4,000 acres - and that local land owners were to share most of the remainder.

In 1625 James died without any progress having been made. Charles I then took on the scheme but by 1632 decided to sell his share and it was bought by one Jeffrey Kirby of London for the sum of £12,000 plus an annual rent of £100. In the 1770s moves were reinstated but a Bill presented to Parliament in December 1775 was defeated, despite forecasts that drainage would improve land values from 18d. (7½p.) to £1 or 25 shillings (£1.25) per acre. The King's Sedgemoor Drain was eventually built in the years following the 1791 Act for The Draining and Dividing of King's Sedgemoor. The River Cary was diverted at Henley Corner beyond Burrowbridge and a new outfall made into the Parrett at Dunball. The whole system is protected by gates and sluices which control the flow of water. These are known locally as clyses. One may be seen on the boundary between Chedzoy and Stawell at Parchey Bridge: the original was built at the time of the cutting of the Drain and figures, together with Chedzoy New Cut, on the map of King's Sedgemoor Drain in 1796 drawn by William White. The cost of construction was £30,656. Once the drainage had been completed, out of 4,063 claims for a share of the land, just 1,796 were allowed. The drain proved inadequate for its purpose and in 1861 the Chedzoy Internal Drainage District built a small pumping station on the River Parrett in Westonzoyland Parish. The drain was deepened and widened in 1868, widened again in 1939/40 and improved to its present width in 1969/70, having previously been of such a width that, in the early 20th Century, with the aid of a pole, it was possible to vault from one bank to the other.

Enclosures under the Act of 1795 and 1797 gave 344 acres of King's Sedgemoor to Chedzoy. Meadows to the west of the village were enclosed in 1836. Rhynes were introduced to West Sedgemoor in 1816 when the cost of construction was put at 1s. 2d. (one shilling and two pence - 5.8p.) per length, or rope, of twenty feet. It was indicated that rhynes should be eight feet wide at the top, four feet wide at the bottom and five feet deep.

On Sedgemoor, however, the rhynes and their courses have not always been dictated by the geographical needs of drainage. Rights of ownership and the relatively cheap and simple division of pastures by a waterway rather than enclosure by a hedge, play an important part in the pattern of the waterways.

During the English Civil War, Lord Thomas Fairfax made Chedzoy his headquarters during the siege of Bridgwater in 1645. Six regiments of the Parliamentary army camped in the village. During the Commonwealth (1649-1660), Dr. Walter Rawley, nephew of Sir Walter Raleigh, was deprived of the living as he had supported Charles I. He was taken from gaol to gaol and was finally murdered at Wells by a shoemaker named Barrett into whose care he had been entrusted. Old records indicate that Barrett lost his temper and stabbed his prisoner when Dr. Rawley was "attempting to screen from Barrett's impudent curiosity the letter he had written to his wife."

The remaining cob buildings and those retaining vestiges of cob; the size and splendour of the Parish Church of St. Mary and the retention of the Medieval Candle Auction to this day, all point to the village's prosperity and ecclesiastical importance in Medieval and Tudor times.

Sturdy as the village buildings may be, the ground below them has not always been so stable. The Reverend Andrew Paschall wrote a letter to Dr. Robert Hooke in London. It was subsequently published under the heading of "An Earthquake in Somerfetshire dated Jan. 4, 1680 from Chedfey in that County." Using modern spelling it reads as follows:

> "Worthy Sir, Yesterday about seven in the morning, I, being about to rise, took notice of what seemed a smart gust of wind, which was followed with a jog of our house, and that immediately with a very sensible shaking of the house, and particularly the bed in which I lay. I doubted the fall of some large piece of timber, or stonework, and caused the servants to make diligent search all about for the cause of it; though not without suspicion that it might be an earthquake. Before night I became fully satisfied that it was so, for my neighbours, many, observed the like in their houses, though no hurt was done. This day, I hear, that it was in other Parishes, one within a mile of me, lying in the same level; another above four miles from me, lying on the further side of an hill, and which is a firm rock. This afternoon comes a letter from an acquaintance of mine in Bridgwater, (two miles from me, and on the other side of their navigable river) which says thus, 'I suppose you heard of the earthquake, which happened with us this morning about seven o'clock: it shook our strong house so, that I began to look whether the walls were scattered or crazed, with a noise, as if some very great thing had fallen on the ground. One or two in Eastover (a part of town on our side of the river) were ready to leap out of bed upon it, &.' The air was very calm, it being a frosty morning, upon the snow lying, which fell, the day before. It lasted but a very short time. I do not remember, for these eighteen years of my abode here, to have known such a thing."

The Monmouth Rebellion

The village's history in Stuart times is dominated by its close association with the Battle of Sedgemoor. In June 1685 Scotland was invaded by rebel forces under the command of the Marquis of Argyll, whilst Charles II's eldest illegitimate son, James, Duke of Monmouth, landed at Lyme Regis on 11th June. Both leaders had assumed that the country would refuse to obey the Roman Catholic James II, who had succeeded Charles II in February that year, and both had designs on the throne. Both were wrong and their ambitions were soon thwarted by the King's armies. Monmouth and his forces had retreated from Bristol to Bridgwater before the decisive battle. Estimates of those who fought for Monmouth at Sedgemoor vary between 3,200 and 7,000, but court records and similar documents put the number at around 4,000.

The story that the marks to be found on the stone of the south wall of Chedzoy church were made by villagers sharpening their scythes for the Battle of Sedgemoor is almost certainly apocryphal, for the Rector at the time, the Rev. Andrew Paschall, had firmly advised his parishioners against joining the rebellion. However, Rev. Paschall watched the progress of the battle from the church tower and noted the events in detail, accompanying his account with a map which was subsequently passed to the Government in London.

Monmouth had six battalions at his command: the Cavalry with artillery (3 guns) commanded by Lord Grey; the Blues commanded by Monmouth himself and Nathaniel Wade; the Whites commanded by Matthews; the Reds commanded by Holmes; the Yellows under Foulkes and the Greens as reserves. It is known that Monmouth and his rebels were guided across the moors by a farm worker from Chedzoy named Richard Godfrey, who informed him as he watched the enemy from St. Mary's church tower in Bridgwater, that the Royal army was not entrenched in its position at Westonzoyland and therefore encouraged Monmouth in his belief that a surprise attack would succeed.

The King's army of some 1,900 men and 700 cavalry formed five regiments, all of which still exist today, albeit under differing names: Dumbarton's Royal Regiment of Foot (now the Royal Scots); the Duke of Grafton's First Regiment of Foot Guards (Grenadier Guards); Lieutenant Colonel Sackville's Second Regiment of Foot Guards (Coldstream Guards); Trelawney's Queen Consort's Regiment of Foot (The King's) under Lieutenant Colonel Charles Churchill and the Queen's Dowager's Regiment of Foot (The Queen's) under Kirke. The Horse Guards were commanded by Colonel Villiers. The regiments were supported by 18 guns and most camped near Bussex Rhyne, not far from the present site of Bussex Farm, Westonzoyland.

Godfrey led Monmouth's army in the late evening of 5th July in a silent march along the Bristol Road, turning south into Bradney Lane and Marsh Lane, past Peasey Farm, still standing today and visible on a low mound between Chedzoy and Bawdrip, and so around the outskirts of Chedzoy below

Pendon Hill.

Monmouth could not count on the loyalty of the village to his cause, for a patrol of Royalist Horse Guards was stationed in the village. Monmouth's men had been seen by two Chedzoy men at Bradney. They informed the men on watch at the village cross, perhaps at Crosstree in the centre of the village or near the site where the present cross stands in Ward Lane near the church. This watch "from country dullness or slowness" (or, perhaps, more than Godfrey in Chedzoy were aware of Monmouth's intentions) failed to tell the patrolling Horse Guards. As Monmouth's men continued their march, Godfrey at last found the crossing point on the Langmoor Rhyne, and then a pistol shot rang out in the darkness, thought to have been fired by one of Compton's patrolling Horse Guards. The element of surprise was lost.

The troops rode swiftly back to inform their commander in Chedzoy, who immediately dispatched a messenger to warn the royalist camp. The trooper, arriving at the Bussex Rhyne below Westonzoyland rode up and down it, shouting across in desperation,

> "Beat ye drums, the enemy is come! For the Lord's sake, beat ye drums!"

The commander of the Chedzoy patrol, Compton himself, rode out with his troops across Chedzoy Field to intercept and skirmish with Grey's Horse who had been sent by Monmouth into the lead, his task being to cross Bussex Rhyne, put the Royalist infantry to flight and turn the Royalists' own guns against them, so that Monmouth's infantry could cross the rhyne. In this skirmish Compton was wounded and, no doubt, Monmouth's battle plan was further jeopardised. However, his men fought bravely and the account by Andrew Paschall, which gives a vivid description of the dangers of discovery which beset Monmouth as he led his men across the moor, suggests that it was a very close-run battle.

> "The King's men fortuned to give a shout. 'Tis said the enemy had as great a reason to do so, which if they had happened to do, 'tis thought the King's army had been utterly routed."

Once it was daylight, Churchill ordered his men onto the offensive and they crossed Bussex Rhyne. By seven o'clock the battle was all but over as the King's army pursued the rebels in the direction of Bridgwater, slaughtering them as they went. Captain Dummer of the Royal Artillery thought that 700 rebels might have been killed and about 300 taken prisoner, whilst Royal losses were 27 dead and about 200 wounded.

The account written by Andrew Paschall contains several differences from that given by other historians.

> "Upon Sunday, July 5, the King's army, consisting of about 4,000 men, marched from Somerton. About noon they encamped at Zog, in the parish of Chedzoy under Weston, 2,000 foot, in five regiments, lodge in the camp; 500 horse quarter in Weston; 1,500 militia men took up their quarters in Middlesoy, Othery, &c., a mile or two distant from Weston. One of the parish of Bridgwater being in the moor to look after his cattle, saw their coming and manner of incamping, goes into the town to the Duke, tells him all that he had seen, informs him of the way to the camp through North Moor, and was rewarded by the Duke with a guinea (£1 1s.) for his pains. The Duke forthwith goes up to the church tower, views all lying open to him there with a perspective glass. Coming down, he calls a council of war, in which it was agreed upon to assault the King's camp.
>
> "That evening, between nine and ten o'clock, the Duke leads his army out of Bridgwater in great silence. He did not take the nearest way to Weston, which was three miles in length, by which way he went, June 22, but he took the long causeway, and so made his march near five miles long before he could reach the King's camp.
>
> "As for the King's army, care was taken and great diligence used upon their encamping, to set guards and sentinels, not only in the common Road from Weston to Bridgwater, and in several ways and lanes on that side of Chedsey (by which was the nearest passage from Bridgwater through Chedsey to Weston) but also in that very way round about by which the enemy did march. There were also two, and perhaps even more, considerable parties of horse sent out in the afternoon from the King's camp to scout that way, though it was somewhat difficult to explain, how it was possible for one of those parties especially to miss the discovering of the enemy, as they were coming from the long causeway through the lanes onto the moor. A trumpeter is said to have been sent into the town to challenge them forth to fight, or in case they refused, to threaten with firing the town about their ears the next morning.
>
> "The guards on the south side of Chedsey retired to the camp. The horse guard, of about 12 or 16 at Langmoor Stone, accompanied that party of horse which went through North Moor into Baudrip (Bawdrip). And now the camp was all quiet and at rest, as believing no danger near. Only Captain Mackintosh, in the Scots regiment, believed over night, and would have ventured wagers upon it, that the Duke would come. He, in that persuasion, marked out the ground between the tents and the ditch, where all his men should stand in case of an attack, and gave directions that all should be readiness; and it was well he did so; for his regiment being in the right wing was to receive the first assault and main shock, which to give them their due they did with great courage, as also did the rest of those valiant men.
>
> "To return to the Duke's army which we left in North Moor, they had placed 42 waggons in the ascent of Bulden (Polden?) Hill in Bristol Road with orders to drive on to Axbridge. They bring with them now three great guns, and march with great silence. The Lord Grey led the horse supposed to be about 800. When they were come to Langmoor Side or near it, a pistol discharged. Captain Hacker is said to have owned it at his trial, as done by him to give the King's

army notice of their danger near by. Presently a trooper, unknown, rode from them at full speed as is supposed, because seen to come that way from the camp. He, standing on the outside of the ditch, called with all possible earnestness to the Scots regiment to beat up their drums, and tells them the enemy was come, and having repeated 20 times at least, as loud as he could, rides back the same way he came. It was this person, and not the pistol, which gave the alarm.

"Now the camp awakes, runs to arms, gets into as good order as they may, and stands ready to receive the enemy. The horse, which the Lord Grey led, marched towards the upper Plugeon. Missing that passage over the ditch he leads them on the outside, till they come to the Scots regiment, by which 500 of these horse pass, pretending that they were friends, and came from the Duke of Albemarle. At length they are discovered by the other regiments and fired at.

They then wheel off, had a skirmish with their own men, and go back by Langmoor Stone, and thus discouraging the rest of their own army fled. Sir Francis Compton stood a guard at the upper Plugeon. One Jones was commanded with a party of horse to beat him from that passage. He played his part with so much valour, that for the same he was thought not unworthy of a pardon from the General. But Sir Francis, though hard beset and wounded yet kept his post so well, that the rebels horse behind, said to be 300, went backwards on the outside of the ditch towards Sutton Mill (near Sutton Mallet), near which they took up their station to see the issue of the fight. When it appeared how things went, they shifted for themselves. Whether Sir Francis were there before the 500 horse missing their way went down towards the camp, or came to the Plugeon afterwards, and so had his encounter with Jones as belonging to the latter 300 horse, we do not know. To be sure that worthy gentleman did great service, for had the horse gone over there, notwithstanding the alarm, all might have been lost. It was not above half a quarter of an hour, before the foot continuing their march appear to the Scots, first in two bodies, then the third lesser body joins with one of the other two. Of these there were 2,000 of their prime, and principally Taunton men, led by Wade. By those the fight was managed. The King's soldiers gave them the commendation of stout men, 2,000 more, among whom were 1,000 scythe men, stood at a distance between Langmoor Stone and them. These 2,000 came not to the fight. Many are said to have been behind them, who being hindered by the lanes, through which they marched could not come up, before they met cause to run with their fellows. The fight continued not much more above half and hour."

Andrew Paschall states that Monmouth was told by one Benjamin Newton, of Bridgwater Parish, of the "manner of the (Royalist) incamping" that he gave an "account of the way through North Moor and had a guinea for his pains." Was it Benjamin Newton of Bridgwater or Richard Godfrey of Chedzoy who led the Duke to the battle? And what of William Sparks, the Sedgemoor farmer whose spy glass is still preserved in Bridgwater Museum? He is said to have used it to survey the King's army from Chedzoy church and to have sent the farm worker to Monmouth. According to Andrew Paschall it was Godfrey who was the guide to the battlefield. The Gaol Delivery Book for the Western Circuit, 1686, records that Godfrey was presented at the Exeter Assize in March 1686, pardoned and dismissed.

The Parish Register at Westonzoyland contains an account of events at the time of the battle. It was probably written by Richard Alford, a churchwarden whose cousin was Mayor of Lyme Regis when Monmouth landed there. In modern spelling it read as follows:

> "The engagement began between one and two o'clock in the morning. It continued nearly one hour and a half. There was killed upon the spot, of the King's soldiers, sixteen: five of them buried in the church: the rest in the churchyard; and they had all Christian burial. One hundred and more of the King's soldiers wounded, of which wounds many died: of which we have no certain account. There was killed of the rebels upon the spot, about 300: hanged with us, 22 - of which 4 were hanged in gemmaces (chains): about 500 prisoners brought into our church, of which there was 79 wounded, and 5 of them died of their wounds in our church."

The aftermath of the battle hopefully passed by a loyal village like Chedzoy. However, the story of one rebel, Samuel Sweet, is inextricably linked with Brentsfield Bridge on the outskirts of the village. He was condemned to hang but his fiancée pleaded for his life. He was known as the fastest runner in these parts and was set to race against a colt for three parts of a mile from Westonzoyland to the bridge. He literally ran for his life and fell exhausted, having reached the bridge before the horse. But Feversham showed no mercy and had the young man hanged at the Bussex tree. The girl lost her reason as a result, and is said to be the White Lady who haunts the grave mound at Westonzoyland still. Charles Causley, a modern poet, wrote a moving ballad, "The Song of Samuel Sweet" about the story.

Before a general pardon was granted to the rebels in October 1688 the Bloody Assize took place, following which John Whiting, a Quaker prisoner at Ilchester Gaol wrote,

> "There were eight executed, quartered and their bowels burnt on the market place before our prison window"

and he complained about

> "forcing poor men to hale about men's quarters, like horse-flesh or carrion, to boil and hang them up as monuments of their cruelty and inhumanity."

The ghastly task of seething the dismembered bodies of rebels in pitch so that they could be hung as a warning in every parish hereabouts, is said to have been pressed upon an unfortunate ploughman of Chedzoy, surnamed Napper. He was afterwards known as "Tom Boilerman" and made a social pariah. Years later he was struck dead by lightning while sheltering beneath a tree at North Petherton. Chedzoy Parish was required by Kirke, the Royalist Colonel, to pay £2 4s. 1d. (£2.20p) for making gallows and burying rebels in the battlefield at Sedgemoor.

Many rebels who escaped hanging were transported for service in the colonies. There was a thriving market and courtiers with business interests in the West Indies began to make bids for the rebels. Each prisoner was worth between £10 and £15 and a total of 890 such sales are recorded. At least 612 prisoners were shipped from Weymouth and Bristol to the West Indies where the Governor of each colony was required to see that the island assemblies passed a law to ensure their ten-year servitude and to notify the safe arrival and disposal of each prisoner. The Lieutenant-Governor of Barbados recorded the safe disposal of 304 out of 329 men who left Weymouth. Any prisoner caught attempting to escape from servitude was to be branded on the forehead with the letters FT for Fugitive-Traitor. They were theoretically freed after a pardon granted in January 1690 but many chose to remain in the Caribbean.

The following advertisement appeared in the London Gazette for 9th and 13th August 1685: "There was taken the 22 past from the Parsonage House in Chedsey near Bridgwater in Somersetshire, a grey Mare upwards of 14 hands high, and about six or seven years old, worth 14 or 15. Also the same day from King's Sedgemoor old black Mare between 13 and 14 hands high. If any one can give tidings of them at the Parsonage House at Chedsey, or at the Post-House in Bridgwater so they may be recovered, his charges shall be born, and be well rewarded for his pains."

Perhaps some of Paschall's parishioners were not so loyal after all and perhaps someone else had this thought too, for King James II in his progress through the West Country was not convinced of the parishioners' loyalty. He came to Chedzoy on 27th August 1686. The churchwardens spent seven shillings (35p.) at Widow Bund's "when the King was heare." A further two shillings (10p.) was charged for a sort of bridge over a rhyne on the moor so that the King could get to the battlefield more easily. However, legend says that he feared a trap and, disdaining to use the bridge erected in his honour, set his horse to leap the rhyne.

In the way that history has of showing the true consequence of events, this last battle on English soil soon proved to be inconsequential in the greater scheme of things. Three years later in 1688 with the "glorious revolution," in reality a Dutch invasion, the throne of King James II began to topple. The Bishop of London and six laymen - known as the Immortal Seven - had secretly invited James' nephew and son-in-law, William of Orange, to come to England. William landed in the south-west of England on 5th November 1688 and James fled. William became King in 1689.

Reverend Paschall continued to work on his history of Somerset, and became Chancellor of the Cathedral of Wells in 1689, becoming three years later a Canon-Residentiary. However, he held the Rectory of Chedzoy until his death in 1696.

Chedzoy, after the Monmouth Rebellion, returned to the peaceful obscurity of Sedgemoor's habitual rhythm of winter flood and summer sunshine.

In more recent times, it was Miss Elizabeth Winter of Fowlers Plot Farm, Chedzoy who organised the public subscription which paid for the monument of Cornish granite in Graveyard Field at Westonzoyland. It was unveiled on 26th July 1928 by Miss Annie Cole of Arsenal House, Bristol Road, Bridgwater. Miss Winter is said to have been moved to instigate the memorial fund as she wept for her collie dog which had been injured and destroyed. She heard a voice saying, "You weep for your dog, what of my poor lambs lying unmourned and unremembered in your fields?" The inscription on the monument reads

> TO THE GLORY OF GOD AND IN MEMORY OF ALL THOSE WHO DOING THE RIGHT AS THEY GAVE IT FELL IN THE BATTLE OF SEDGEMOOR 6TH JVLY 1685 AND LIE BVRIED IN THIS FIELD OR WHO FOR THEIR SHARE IN THE FIGHT SVFFERED DEATH PVNISHMENT OR TRANSPORTATION PRO PATRIA.

The monument on its own was thought to be incomplete and so in 1929 four corner stones were added. A ceremony took place in September that year when the stones were unveiled by representatives of the Church of England, the Army, the Navy and the Royal Air Force.

A glover was recorded in the village in 1394 and a weaver in 1638. In the 17th Century local crops included peas, beans, barley and wheat. Dairy cows, pigs and poultry were frequently recorded in probate inventories, but only two small flocks of sheep were mentioned. One farmer left 40 cheeses and another four hundredweight - about 200 kg. - of cheese. Clover had been introduced by the mid-18th Century but cattle were still turned into the cornfields from harvest to sowing. In 1747 two men from Pawlett and Dunwear were fined for stocking the common beyond the limit of five sheep per acre.

The life of the moorland villages was affected annually by the flooding of the levels. A woodcut of 1607 shows a baby floating in its crib past what is supposed to be Chedzoy church tower, though with its stunted spire the church in the picture bears a much closer resemblance to Puriton church. It is a fact, however, that cradles made locally were waterproof and capable of floating like a boat and the inhabitants, sitting on the roofs of their houses in winter floods, probably took this as an almost annual matter of course in Chedzoy as elsewhere. In the 1607 floods about 100 square miles and 32 villages were inundated after the sea breached coastal defences near Burnham. In 1811 flooding reached as far as Glastonbury. The cutting of King's Sedgemoor Drain and larger rhynes helped to alleviate the situation at the end of the 18th Century, but in the early 1900s a flood is recorded so bad that the only way to reach Stawell from Chedzoy was by boat or on horseback, a method used by a Chedzoy resident, so the story goes, to reach his lady love in the neighbouring village.

It is recorded in Parish records that in 1731 there were just 14

Chedzoy parishioners who were qualified for jury service: Edward Crane, Joseph Crane, William England, Daniel Franklyn, John Mitchel, John Norris, Thomas Norris, James Rood, William Rood, William Sparke, Edward Stradling, William Walters, George Wood and John Wride. In 1801 the population was 457, although this was for a larger area than the modern parish.

In 1791 the Manor of Chedzoy was sold by John Dawes to Sir Robert Mackreath. He in turn conveyed it to Thomas Potter in 1802 on whose death, in 1815, it passed in turn to his sons William and, on his death in 1821, to Henry, who died in 1858. In 1860 the estate was ordered to be sold. The Lordship was not recorded later. Some of the farms were purchased by tenants, but most were bought by the University of Oxford. The University was blamed for charging rents which ruined some of the tenants.

The Early 19th Century

In 1812 Charity Norris, upon her death, bequeathed the sum of £100 to the Rector and churchwardens of Chedzoy, the interest to be paid annually at Christmas to poor persons not receiving constant relief from the parish providing "that care is taken to give it only to such as have conducted themselves with decency and sobriety." The annual interest was £5 0s. 8d.

Clearly some local residents did not come up to Charity Norris' requirements as they spent time in Taunton Gaol at Wilton, part of which still exists as offices behind the Police Station. In September 1815 George Gilbert, a labourer, was sentenced to six months' imprisonment for selling liquor without a licence. 1822 and 1823 were not good years for the men of the village who had failed to pay maintenance for children they had fathered: the modern Child Support Agency pales into insignificance in comparison. Joel Sparks, aged 21, and Charles Stone, aged 26, were both sentenced to two months' imprisonment with hard labour for failing to pay; perhaps William Arthur owed more as he was given three months' hard labour. Joel Sparks returned to Wilton again in March 1829 when he was sentenced to two months' imprisonment with hard labour for injuring a dog.

The Chedzoy Tithing Book dates from "the year ending 25th March 1823." Although some entries are faded and the handwriting can be difficult to decipher, the brief entries in these accounts provide an interesting insight into life at that time. Payments made to Mr. J.R. Poole in 1824 were for

> "14 hedgehogs at 4d. each, 2 stotes (sic) at 4d. each, one polecat at 4d., 50 dozen and 3 sparrows at 3 shillings a dozen and 9 dozen and 3 wants (a local name for moles) at 2s. 6d. dozen" making a total of £1 4s. 10d.

That same year John Sibley was paid £1 8s. 10$^1/_2$d. (£1.44) for "Cleaning the river and rhines and taking up the sides." In 1827 John Dawbin was paid £5 12s. 4d. (£5.61) for "Cleaning the river and throwing the Rhyne."

In June 1828 Joel Crane was paid for "Cleaning the Rhyne leading to Swiftstream cloise (clyce), 70 ropes at 1d. per rope - 5s. 10d." (29p). for cleaning about 1,400 feet of rhyne. He was paid the same sum in October for repeating the task. An amusing entry that year was "Paid for emptying the poor house privey, 3s. (15p.)"

The Tithing account for 1830 has four interesting entries:

> "13 sheaves of reed to thatch Tanners house at 8d. per sheaf, 8s. 8d.;
> 18th October 1830. Paid for a new bucket for the well at the Poor House, 2s. 6d.;
> 25th October 1830. Paid for taking sand out of the well at the Poor House, 2s.;
> November 1830. Gave two shipwreck'd sailors a pafs (pass), 2s.".

The 1831 account indicates that in June "28 poor men who was sworn in Special Constables, £1 8s." This year also contains one of just two mentions of arrears on Bastardy Orders overdue for the year ending on Lady Day (23rd March) 1833: William Stockham, £5 16s.; Jeffrey Smith, £10 7s.; William Andrews £2 11s.; John Sawtell, £2 18s. and John Bailey, £1 14s. In 1834 "Expenses of apprehending, detaining, convicting, etc. of Fish, a vagrant - 7s. (35p.)"

William Bennett (1800-1858) was a blacksmith in the village and his accounts ledger for the period 1826 to 1843 also provide an insight into the cost of things at that time. The charge for shoeing a horse was 6d. (2.5p.) per shoe, plus a further 2d. if it was necessary to remove an old shoe. The 1999 charge per shoe is £8.75! Being smaller in size, the charge per shoe for a donkey was 4$^1/_2$d. (1.8p.). Other charges made were 3d. to grind a scythe, 1$^1/_2$d. to put a ring in a pig's nose, while teeth for an apple mill were charged at a rate of $^1/_2$d. each. Although he would sell a pick for 1s. 3d. (6.5p.) or dress a plough share for 6d. he also dealt with much larger items: a set of wheel irons for two waggons cost John Rainey £26. William's accounts also show that many clients were reluctant to settle their bills: between April 1828 and July 1829 Richard Stone called upon his services 18 times, running up a bill of £1 14s. 4d. before he eventually paid. Even worse was the account of the Lord of the Manor, Henry Porter who, in over two years between January 1835 and April 1837 ran up a bill of £14 14s. 2d. which was eventually settled in 1840!

The Tithe Map of 1836 indicates that the area of the parish was 1,655 acres, 2 roods, 36 perches, including 29 acres, 12 perches of Glebe (i.e. church) land. The amount due annually to the Rector was £387 5s.

Before going any further this seems to be a suitable point at which to explain some of the names recorded on that map. The parish was divided into three very distinct areas which still

The Tithe Map, 1836.

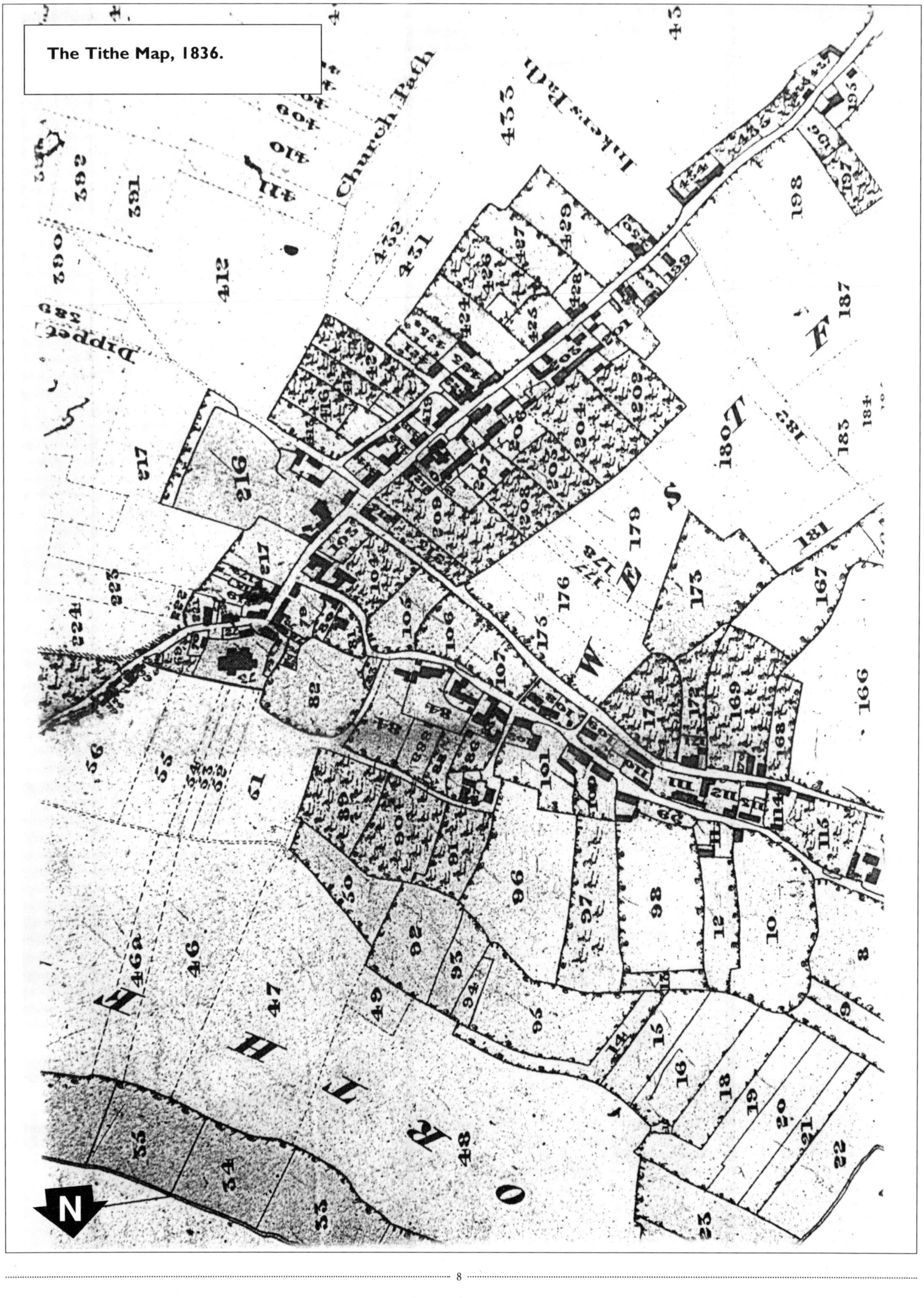

exist to this day. Northfield was the smallest and comprised the area to the north of Chedzoy Lane and Ward Lane from Slape Cross to Parchey Bridge. Westfield was the area bordered by Chedzoy Lane, Front Street and Ruggs Drove out to the parish boundary at Park Wall, the drove which still exists running from opposite Temple Farm on Chedzoy Lane almost through to the Halfway Inn on Westonzoyland Road. By far the largest area was Eastfield, comprising the area south of Ward Lane, Front Street and Ruggs Drove out onto the moor. In addition to this, there were two detached parts of the parish, both on the far side of Westonzoyland Road. The larger comprised, in very general terms, the area opposite Penzoy Farm (on the A372 between the Chedzoy turning and Westonzoyland) and to the east of Bull Horn Drove (the lane running from Westonzoyland Road past Andersea) almost as far as Lake Wall, Westonzoyland. The smaller detached area, known as Fowlers Mead, was near the junction of Westonzoyland Road and the lane to Dunwear. Other parishes also had detached areas: Ruggs Farm was in Woolavington Parish, despite the northern edge of Chedzoy bordering the Parishes of Bawdrip and Cossington.

It seems that having detached parts of the parish caused problems from time to time as this Bridgwater Mercury report of proceedings in the Bridgwater County Police Court in November 1859 illustrates.

> "Mr. H. Lovibond appeared before the magistrates on behalf of the parish of Chedzoy to ask the bench to make an order upon the surveyor of the parish of Westonzoyland for repair of a road called Bull Horn Drove. The road is situated in the parishes of Chedzoy and Westonzoyland, and therefore both parties were bound to keep it in repair. The surveyor of Chedzoy parish had completed his half of the work, and an order was now sought to compel the Westonzoyland surveyor to perform his share. No opposition being offered, the order was granted."

The dispute over maintenance of Bull Horn Drove was resolved in January 1860 when it was reported that

> "Mr. Henry Lovibond made application for the partition of a portion of this road between the parishes of Westonzoyland and Chedzoy, for the purpose of repair. He said he appeared for the surveyors of the two parishes, and that there was no opposition, application being made by mutual consent. The magistrates had the power to make the division under the 58th section of the General Highway Act. Mr. James Ling, surveyor of the highways of the parish of Westonzoyland, stated the partition of the drove which the two parishes were called upon to repair was 1,570 yards in length. He had met Mr. David Brake, surveyor of the parish of Chedzoy, and they had agreed upon a division. They had arranged to apportion half, or 785 yards, to each parish, dividing the road transversely. They had put down boundary stones, and the division was a fair one. The magistrates acceded to the application."

Interestingly, it is the Chedzoy School Board minutes for November 1887 which gives one of the few mentions of the demise of detached parts of the parish. A letter from the Assistant Secretary of the Local Government Board reads

> "Sir, I am directed by the Local Government Board to acknowledge receipt of your letter ... with reference to ... amalgamating two detached parts of Chedzoy with the parish of Westonzoyland ... and the parts of Westonzoyland which were formerly parts of Chedzoy are no longer liable to contribute towards the repayment of the loan raised by the Chedzoy School Board or to any other expenses of that Board."

The first detailed national Census took place in June 1841. The Enumeration District of Chedzoy, which included Horsey and Chedzoy Lane, shows there were 507 residents. Sadly, this census only shows names, ages (rounded down to the nearest five years for those over 15), occupation and whether they had been born in Somerset or "Out of County." No addresses are shown.

Tithing accounts show that on 12th January 1845 Dr. Axford was paid one guinea (£1 1s.) for examining the body of John Waygood. From 1847 onwards the accounts become very brief indeed and the last interesting accounts are for 15th June 1886:

> "To cash paid as per Bill for Expenses incurred in replevin John Rainey's horses and costs of bringing action against Mr. H. Hodges (for having impounded them) in the County Court, Bridgwater when it was decided that the Parish had the right to let Moor Drove: £5 15s. 5d."

On the credit side for 10th August that year,

> "Received from Bridgwater County Court Clerk as money paid by Mr. Henry Hodges for having impounded John Rainey's horses out of the Moor Drove: £2 2s. 6d."

The Bridgewater Times - Bridgwater spelt with an "E" in their pages - was established in 1846 and, although largely featuring national and international news, also carried a few local items. In September that year proceedings at Bridgwater Police Court were reported:

> "George Tutton v. James Gilbert. This was a case of ejectment under the Tenement Act. The parties live at Chedzoy. The Magistrates gave Gilbert twentyone days to seek another house, and in default of so doing ordered that he should be summarily ejected."

Later that year the Bridgewater Times published a series of articles entitled "The Somersetshire Peasantry" written under the pseudonym "Your Inquirer." That published on 29th October 1846 featured Chedzoy, Middlezoy and Westonzoyland and, with the exception of details of individuals in the latter two villages, is repeated here in full as it provides an insight into the hard daily lives of working people at that time.

> "Sir, Since the publication of my last letter I have visited

the villages of Chedzoy, Middlezoy and Westonzoyland. In the village of Chedzoy the peasantry enjoy advantages which are unknown to the labourers of Middlezoy or Westonzoyland. The lord of the manor, Henry Porter, Esq., is patron of a clothing club, to which almost all wives of the working men are members - those having small families pay a single subscription of 1s. 1d. per quarter, of which sum Mr. Porter adds an equal amount, and those having large families pay a subscription for themselves and one of their children, being 2s. 2d. per quarter, which is also doubled by the liberality of the lord of the manor. At Christmas the subscribers receive the value of their doubled subscription in materials for clothes, suitable for either male or female attire, which they themselves make up or employ persons to make up for them. This club is deemed by the people of great advantage, which it undoubtedly is; and there was one universal expression used by the owner at every cottage I visited - 'If it was not for the club, sir, I do not know what we should do for clothing.'

"The cottages here were formerly in the possession of the farmers and relet by them to the poor. Mr. Porter, however, has taken those belonging to him into his own hands, and having reduced the rent, the occupants have been made his tenants. I was informed that their rent since this arrangement has been lowered to full one half its former amount. The clergyman of the parish, the Rev. J.R. Luscombe, jun., also interests himself in the welfare and happiness of his poor parishioners. He has this year caused to be laid out a number of land allotments for spade culture, to be let to the labourers of Chedzoy; the larger containing 40 poles (about 1,010 square metres) at a rental of 20s. (£1), and the smaller containing twenty poles at 10s. per year; the rent to be paid in three instalments - viz., one quarter on the last Monday in March, one-fourth on the last Monday in June, and the remaining half on the last Monday in September. The tenants are subject of course to some salutary regulations, which are conducive alike to the moral deportment of the people and to their domestic comforts.

"In this parish, as in the others I have visited, the farmers let out portions of their land to the labourers for the purpose of growing potatoes. In Chedzoy the rent charged for this ground, for ploughing twice, and also ploughing in the potatoes, amounts to £8 per acre, its being in the occupation of the labourer from about May to October only, and producing for him but one crop. Deducting the ploughing, which is worth about 20s., there remains the enormous sum of £7 an acre for these potato grounds for the period mentioned - equal to double the amount of rental paid by the farmers for the twelve months. Under these circumstances the peasantry will reap a great advantage from the introduction of the allotment system into the parish, as the allotments will be let at a rental of £4 per acre per year, and the persons renting them will have the advantage of a continued possession of the land, providing they conform to the rules under which they take possession, and therefore a greater amount of produce from it - their potato crops can be followed by wheat, and in families where sufficient food is not now to be procured from the miserable reward of labour, their allotment will assist them in obtaining the common necessities of life to which they are now too frequent strangers.

"The village with its church is situated on a gentle elevation, and the roads through it appeared sounder and drier than those of the other two villages to which I shall directly refer; but the land round the neighbourhood is flat and the moor over which I passed for Westonzoyland is cold and wet - on some portions the water was lying in large pools. The houses of the cottagers, though far from comfortable, appeared to be warmer and better than any of the other places I have visited; they would be much benefited by the application of a little whitewash, which would make them more light and cheerful, and add greatly to the health of their inmates.

"I must bear my testimony to the general cleanliness of those whose cases I have below recorded. With all these advantages poverty is evident among the villagers; and when an estimate is made of the few items I have enumerated, such as fuel, soap, &c., and the calculation of what remains out of 7s. (35p.), the weekly wages of the labourer, to maintain each member of the large families of the cases I have instanced, it appears almost an impossibility how these poor creatures subsist. Though the weekly wages of the district are 7s. (one of the farmers rose his men 1s. a week last week), it must be recollected that even that small sum is not earned weekly the year through. From it are to be deducted the many days of bad weather in which the labourer is unable to work, the periods at which he has no employment, and the chances of sickness, when these are considered, it will be readily admitted that his average earnings must be far below even this miserable figure. It appeared to me, sir, a strange anomaly in this parish, that persons who live a life bordering on semi-starvation, should be taxed to maintain the poor, the highway, and the church. Would it not be more just that their humble dwellings should not be rated, and that their more wealthy neighbours should bear the burden of the taxes which are now imposed on them?

"Middlezoy, the next village in which I continued my inquiries is far, very far, below Chedzoy, as regards the social comforts and position of its poor. In the four first cases which I instance in this parish, the people live in poor cabins by the side of filthy roads, ancle-deep (sic) in mud, and their dwellings are of a miserably inconvenient state, bearing the impress of extreme filth and abject poverty. The inmates are also filthy. There is a sick club established in this parish, and on reference to the cases it would appear that, the members when ill receive the amounts of their payments for one month, and at the end of ten years the surplus funds are divided. The intellectual standard of the people is low. I found it difficult to extract an intelligent answer generally to my questions; and it was evident that the depression of their physical powers had tended to depress their mental energies. I was told of no one here who exerted himself to ameliorate the condition of the poor - there was no clothing club, no allotment system - and the people are ill-fed, ill-clothed, ill-housed, and whole families are herded together at night, in many instances in one room. The potato allotments in this parish are let at £9 an acre.

"At Westonzoyland, the people are also ill-clothed and ill-fed, and their houses consist in the cases cited of only two rooms; and in one instance a mud fabric consisted of only one room, in which eight individuals are huddled together, the house being of the most cheerless description. In every instance it will be seen that the whole family sleep in one chamber. In this village there is a sick club, which numbers about forty members. The labourers are exceedingly bad off, scarcely ever tasting animal food, tea or coffee, using as a substitute for the two latter, burnt bread. I cannot too severely animadvert (strongly criticise) on the conduct of a butcher who, in this parish, had some bacon unfit for human food; knowing that he could not exhibit it at market, he offered it at 2d. a pound to the peasantry of Westonzoyland. Many of these poor creatures, seldom able to obtain animal food, purchased some, but after cooking it were unable to eat it. One of them said to me - 'It was too bad, sir, for a dog to eat.' This was an imposition which deserves a severe punishment, but the butcher knew it was only on these poor people that he could impose with impunity. I was much amused at an answer I received from a person to whom I put a question as to the state of the labouring population of this parish, his reply was - 'They are very well off here - they enjoy privileges which are not allowed in other parishes.' And these privileges were - that the farmers let them potato ground at £10 an acre!"

The account then goes on to detail the circumstances of various people who were referred to by initials. The Census returns enable most of them to be identified with a fair degree of certainty.

"J—- P—-, aged 71, has a wife aged 65."

This appears to be John Parish who was born in Chedzoy and lived in Chedzoy Lane.

"He works on the roads, and earns 4s. 6d. (22p) weekly. Lives in a house built by himself, for which he pays 2s. 6d. a year as lord's rent. The house contains two rooms. There is a small piece of garden ground attached, which will bear about a bag of potatoes. He gets some tea, being the only thing he drinks. This man's wife is in the clothing club and pays 4s. 6d. yearly.

"G—- S—- has a wife and six children, the eldest of which is a boy twelve years of age, and the youngest a girl, two years and a half old. The wife expects shortly to be confined with the seventh child."

G.S. was probably George Stone, aged 33 years, an agricultural labourer born in Chedzoy and living somewhere near Cross Cottage in Ward Lane.

"The husband earns 7s. weekly and the eldest boy 4d. (about 1.5p.) a day, when the weather will permit of their working. This man pays 1s. per week rent for his cottage which contains two rooms up and one down stairs. There is a small garden attached to the house sufficient to grow about one or two hundred plants. He also pays the poor, church and highway rates. The family have had nothing but dry bread and one penny-worth of bullock's liver to eat during the last week. Last November one of the children was burned and confined to her bed for seventeen weeks; the parish doctor attended her, and during the last seven weeks of the child's illness the union allowed four loaves of bread weekly. This family never get any tea - they consume one penny-worth of coffee weekly, soap and soda cost 4½ d. weekly, candles 3d. and fire 1s. 3d. The wife pays into the clothing club for herself and one child 8s. 8d. per year. This family, supposing the father and eldest child lose no time from bad weather, after the above payments, have left 10½ d. (less than 4.5p) per week to live on. They have about six willows (baskets) full of potatoes and the wife does not know how they shall get through the winter. The husband is determined to throw himself on the parish - he will, however, work for his family as long as he can, but will not suffer them to be in a worse state of starvation that at present."

The next subject is less certain, but may have been Thomas Conduit who was between 35 and 39 years at the time of the 1841 Census. By the time of the 1851 Census his widow was living near Cross Cottage.

"T—- C—- has a wife and seven children, the eldest of whom is a girl fifteen years of age, the youngest a boy about three months. The wife is generally ill. The husband earns 7s., and one of the children, a boy about twelve years of age, 3d. a day, weather permitting. For their house, which contains two rooms up and one down stairs, £2 is paid for rent; the poor, church and highway rates are also paid by the occupier. This family gets only potatoes and dry bread - they do not taste meat oftener than once a month and sometimes not more than once a quarter. The wife has the tea leaves from the parsonage house, but sometimes when she gets no tea leaves buys an ounce of coffee. Soap, soda, candles and firing cost about 2s. 0½ d. a week. The wife pays to the clothing club for herself and one child. They have about seven willows of potatoes, and when these are consumed, the wife does not know how they will be able to purchase more."

The distinctive initials and occupation leave no doubt that U.M. was Uriah Martin. He was a 37 year old blacksmith who was born at Edington: his wife was born in Chedzoy.

"U—- M—- has a wife and six children, the eldest, a boy of fourteen years of age, is apprenticed to a wheelwright and earns 1d. a day, the youngest is a girl three years of age. The wife, who bore evident signs of ill-health and debility, which I imagined I could trace to want of sufficient sustenance, is unable to earn anything. The man is a smith and earns 12s. (60p.) a week, but is paid only twice a year. The consequence of this is that the family are obliged to live on credit and to deal at a huxter's. The rent of their house is £3 a year, and the occupier is obliged to pay poor, church and highway rates. The family live chiefly on dry bread and occasionally potatoes. Never get any meat. Their soap, soda, candles and fuel cost about 2s. $0\frac{1}{2}$ d. a week. The wife pays into the clothing club for herself and child. The husband rented the past summer half an acre of potato ground, at £8 per acre, and worked three days to get up about twenty willows of potatoes, half of which were bad."

The final description of a Chedzoy family would appear to relate to James Reed who was a 44 year old labourer born in Chedzoy.

"J—- R—- has a wife and eight children, the eldest a boy a 18 years of age, who is almost always ill, and the youngest about six months old. He earns 7s. a week when well, but is not always able to work, being a very unhealthy man. One of the children occasionally earns 2s. a week, but has been as much as six months at a time without earning anything. The rent of the cottage in which this family live is £3 a year, and the payment in taxes about 10s. There is a small piece of ground attached to this house, but it having no fence is entirely useless. The family live on dry bread and sometimes potatoes and salt, and occasionally have a salt herring. The wife has one ounce of coffee a week. Soap, soda, candles and fire cost about 2s. $0\frac{1}{2}$d. This family never taste any meat. The wife pays into the clothing club 8s. 8d. per year for herself and one child. 'If it was not for the club, they would be naked.' This family do not get sufficient food, and the children are frequently put to bed crying with hunger. The poor man last summer had three-quarters of an acre of potato ground, the rent of which was £6. The seed &c., cost £3, and he was obliged to give it all up, not being able to pay the rent. The crop was not worth £3. The wife does not know how they are to meet the coming winter."

After describing the circumstances of eleven similar families in Middlezoy and Westonzoyland, the writer concludes,

"I have already extended my letter, I fear, far beyond the proper limit; and will therefore conclude by merely stating that a general complaint exists in the foregoing parishes, that the bread sold through these districts is invariably short weight - the quartern loaf, in many instances, being a quarter of a pound short. I advised the labourers to resolve among themselves not to purchase, for the future, bread from any baker who refused to weigh it; and informed them that a baker refusing to do so, was subject to a penalty of £5. Would it not be well for some individual of influence in each parish , to see that the bakers who sold bread to the poor did not impose upon them, by selling light bread?"

The Church Rates Dispute

The Western Counties Herald and Bridgwater Mercury, later known as The Bridgwater Mercury and Western News and referred to hereafter as the Bridgwater Mercury was established in 1855 and carried far more local news than the Bridgewater Times: possibly the reason that the latter newspaper eventually ceased publication.

Life in the village was not always orderly. In January 1858 the headline ASSAULT ON A FEMALE preceded this Bridgwater Mercury report of court proceedings.

"John Stone of Chedzoy was charged by Mary Ann Smith, of the same place, with having committed an assault upon her with intent. The charge was substantiated by the evidence adduced: though it was attempted, on behalf of the defendant, to induce the belief that the complainant, by her consent, encouraged him to commit the act alleged. A fine of 40s. and costs was inflicted."

The following month the Bridgwater Mercury noted

"In our obituary we announce the death of Mrs. Dinah Ritchie of Upper Norwood, Surrey. To her immediate relations and friends she has bequeathed handsome legacies, and to the poor of Chedzoy, her natal village, she has ordered the interest of £100 per annum to be expended in the purchase of bread to be distributed annually upon the 24th December for ever." This charity, in common with other minor charities, has since been wound up.

In September 1858 there was concern at the lack of magistrates in the area and at a meeting to discuss the problem it was reported that

"On Monday of last week two men were brought into Bridgwater from Chedzoy on a charge of fowl stealing. Mr.J.L. Sealy was not in town and the prisoners had to consequently be taken to North Petherton where Mr. Broadmead was luckily caught and that gentlemen remanded them for further enquiry."

On another page of the Bridgwater Mercury the details of the case were reported.

"Edwin Perry and James Stevens were brought up on a charge of stealing five fowls, of the value of 7s. 6d., the property of Mr. John Tazewell, yeoman, of Chedzoy. The prosecutor deposed that, on Saturday, the 18th inst., between 12 and 1 o'clock at night, he received information of having lost some fowls. He went downstairs and into his barton (farmyard), and there found that Frederick Giles and Isaac Stone had in their custody both prisoners. Giles had a fowl in his hand, which, on observing, he said, 'That fowl is my property;' Stevens thereupon said, 'It is your fowl, Mr. Tazewell, and I will pay for it.' He then sent for David Brake, parish constable, who came and searched the prisoner Stevens in his presence, and in his pocket found other dead fowls his (prosecutor's) property. On this discovery being made, Stevens said,

'I will give you a £5 note to make it up.' Stevens was sober. Frederick Giles stated that on Saturday night, between the hours of 12 and 1 o'clock, he saw the two prisoners in Mr. Tazewell's barton, and whilst they were there he heard some fowls cry out. He was placed to watch the ground, with Isaac Stone. He then went to the barton, and there saw Perry crouched down by the side of the stall, and Stevens was standing by his side. Stevens said, 'I am come in to lie down.' He asked them to come out; they both came out, and Stevens said, after they had walked a little way, 'Let us lie down,' and he laid down under a barley mow, about four or five yards from the barton. On laying down he (witness) saw him take a white fowl from his pocket which he at once took possession of. The prosecutor then came up, and to him he delivered the fowl. He had seen the prisoners together, at Mr. Sully's public-house (the Crown Inn), between nine and ten o'clock that same evening. Did not hear Perry say anything. Isaac Stone gave corroborative evidence. David Brake spoke of finding four fowls in the possession of the prisoner Stevens. He found nothing on Perry. Stevens offered him a £5 note if he would get Mr. Tazewell to make it up. Mr. P.O.H. Reed, who was retained for the defence, closely cross-examined the witnesses, but elicited nothing favourable to his clients. Mr. Sealey (the magistrate - note the different spelling) declined to decide on the case, preferring to remand the prisoners to the Petty Sessions to be held on the succeeding Thursday."

The following week,

"Edwin Perry and James Stevens, remanded from preceding Thursday, on a charge of stealing four fowls (the previous report says five) at Chedzoy the property of Mr. John Tazewell, were today brought up. Pleading guilty they were sentenced to two months' imprisonment with hard labour in Taunton Gaol. Mr. Reed defended the prisoners and in consequence of having been refused admission to them previous to their examination, applied to the magistrates for their opinion on the subject. The bench ruled that they could not admit any one's having an interview with prisoners previous to their cases being heard."

Children making a nuisance of themselves is sometimes thought of as a modern complaint but, of course, it's nothing new. In February 1859 one of the village children found himself in hot water and the magistrate made his feeling quite clear. The Bridgwater Mercury reported,

"A lad named Levi Day was charged by Edwin Fry, farmer, Chedzoy, with assaulting him. The complainant said that the youth threw a potato at him which 'skeared his eye,' and a second which hit him under the arm. Mr. Evered (one of the magistrates) said he had been told that boys in Chedzoy were very unruly. Mr. King (his colleague) observed that it would have been better to have got the defendant's father to correct him than to have summoned him. Mr. Evered declared it might be necessary to put a stop to such proceedings. Mr. Fry might have had his eye cut out, and such a loss could not be repaired by the boy or any one else. In this instance the boy would be let off with a caution, on paying 4s. 6d. costs. The boy's father paid the money. Mr. King stated that Mr. Fry would have been justified in giving the youth a horsewhipping."

It was not only children but also neighbours who were causing problems in the village. The same court heard another local case in October 1859.

"Percival Bell was summoned by Maria Trott for an assault. The parties reside at Chedzoy."

Only Percival Bell is listed on the 1851 census: he was a 28 year old butcher.

"The alleged assault was caused by the complainant entering the house of a neighbour, who was on the point of leaving, and taking away some potatoes, which the complainant, who is the landlord of the premises, said belonged to her. High words were exchanged, and the defendant in the course of the quarrel put his fist in complainant's face. The woman stated that it was not so much the fault of the defendant as his wife, who was a pest in the neighbourhood. Mr. P.O.H. Reed, who appeared for the defendant, was about to call witnesses for the defence, when he was told that the magistrates thought the best way to settle the matter would be for the defendant to be Bound Over to keep the peace for three months towards the complainant."

The Bridgewater Times for 1st August 1860 reported that

"No little excitement has fallen upon this quiet parish, in consequence of the announcement of the intention of the Lord of the Manor to sell the estate by piecemeal, in suitable lots for farms. The Manor has been offered for sale in one lot, and the owner has now determined upon the above mode of disposing of it."

Copies of an advertisement show that at 2.00 p.m. on 28th August 1860 the auction was to be conducted at the Royal Clarence Hotel, Bridgwater. Offered in one lot the Manor consisted of

"A comfortable residence called The Manor House and 1,563 acres, two roods and 27 perches divided into 10 compact, well arranged farms with convenient farm houses and buildings and 53 dwelling houses and cottages."

Parish records indicate that James Laurie was the Land Steward who lived at the Manor House, Chedzoy, and that the annual rental income was £4,023 1s. 2d.

On 29th August 1860 the Bridgewater Times was able to report,

"The sale of this important Manor was held yesterday (Tuesday), at the Royal Clarence Hotel, Bridgwater. Messrs. Wainwright and Heard, the eminent auctioneers of Shepton Mallet being entrusted with the sale of this valuable property.

1859. P. No. 83.

IN CHANCERY.

PORTER *V.* PORTER.

SOMERSETSHIRE.

PARTICULARS AND CONDITIONS OF SALE

Of the very I[illegible] and Desirable

FREEHOLD ESTATE,

KNOWN AS THE MANOR, OR REPUTED

MANOR OF CHEDZOY,

Three Miles from the

MARKET TOWN AND PORT OF BRIDGEWATER,

In the County of Somerset;

Comprising a Comfortable RESIDENCE, called "The Manor House,"

AND

1,563 Acres, 2r., 27p.,

OF VERY EXCELLENT LAND,

Divided into

10 Compact, Well-arranged Farms,

With Convenient FARM HOUSES and BUILDINGS, and

Fifty-three Dwelling Houses and Cottages,

WHICH WILL BE SOLD BY AUCTION,

Pursuant to an order of the High Court of Chancery, made in the above Cause, (with the approbation of His Honor the Master of the Rolls, the Judge to whose Court the said Cause is attached),

BY MESSRS. WAINWRIGHTS AND HEARD,

(The Persons approved by the said Judge),

AT THE CLARENCE HOTEL, BRIDGEWATER,

On TUESDAY, the 28th of August, 1860, at Two o'clock in the Afternoon.

THE PROPERTY WILL FIRST BE SUBMITTED

IN ONE LOT.

And if not Sold, it will then be offered in the Lots stated in the following Particulars.

The Estate may be viewed on application to Mr. LAURIE, at the Manor House, Chedzoy, aforesaid. Printed Particulars with Plans and Conditions of Sale may be had of GEORGE ANNESLEY, Esq., 64, Lincoln's Inn Fields, London, Solicitor; of CHARLES HENRY MOORE, Esq., 22, Lincoln's Inn Fields, London, Solicitor; of HENSHAW SKINNER RUSSELL, Esq., of Mitre Court Chambers Temple, London, Solicitor; at the Clarence and Railway Hotels, Bridgewater; the Castle Inn, Taunton; at the London Inn, Exeter; of Mr. LAURIE, at Chedzoy; and of WAINWRIGHTS and HEARD, Auctioneers and Surveyors, Shepton Mallet, Somerset.

A. BYRT, PRINTER, "JOURNAL" OFFICE, SHEPTON MALLET.

The attendance was very large. The Manor was first submitted to public competition in one lot, but as the highest sum offered (£110,100) did not reach the reserve price, the auctioneers were instructed to put it up in lots (54) as per catalogue of particulars. 53 of out the number were disposed of and the remaining lot was afterwards sold and thus the Manor realised by piecemeal about £100,000, being less than the sum refused by about £1,100."

The Bridgwater Mercury reported this event in a similar manner.

"The important freehold estate, known as the Manor of Chedzoy, three miles from Bridgwater, containing 1,563 acres, 2 roods and 27 perches of excellent land, divided into 10 compact farms, with convenient farm houses and buildings and 53 dwelling houses and producing an annual rental of £4,022, was sold yesterday (Tuesday) afternoon by Messrs. Wainwright and Heard. The property was first submitted in one lot, and the highest bidding was £110,100. That sum was refused, and the estate then disposed of in 54 lots. The competition for these lots was spirited, the large assembly-room being filled with would-be purchasers. The lots did not realise the original offer, amounting in aggregate to less than £109,000 - a little below £70 per acre."

Popularly, the entire Manor was purchased by the University of Oxford, although this was not the case since only Fowlers Plot Farm, Frys Farm, Lower Farm (at Fowlers Plot), Manor Farm, Sibleys Farm, Three Oaks Farm, West End Farm and Westfield Farm have belonged to the University, the others being privately owned. There does not seem to be any local record as to who paid for the various lots in the sale.

In 1998 the archivist at the University gave some information: Henry Lovibond paid £8,750 for Lot 6 (Westfield Farm and nine cottages), William Brice paid £17,140 for Lots 9 and 38 (Fowlers Plot Farm, the Manor House, Manor Farm and nine cottages), Edwin Fry paid £8,650 for Lots 16 and 19 (Frys Farm and an orchard behind Sibleys Farm) and Elias Porter paid £8,100 for Lot 18 (Sibleys Farm). Each of these persons paid a 10% deposit at the time of the sale. Subsequently the University agreed to purchase possession of these Lots, paying the balance due by 26th April 1861, and also repaid the four original purchasers their deposits.

However, information sent to Norman Fry in 1988 by agents for the University tells a slightly different story. It was noted that Sibleys Farm, Frys Farm and Westfield Farm (South) was acquired by the University from Thomas Baker on 20th June 1861. An hereditament (property capable of being inherited) at Westfield Farm (North) was added on 20th August 1861 from Reginald Porter. Fowlers Plot Farm was purchased in 1877 for £20,600 from the Rt. Hon. Lord Cottesloe and another, whilst West End Farm was conveyed to the University on 10th August 1885 by G. & R.G. Turner.

In March 1862 a sale of livestock and implements took place at Manor Farm. The items were being offered for sale by Mr. Mogg (presumably of Moggs Farm) as he was leaving the estate. James Mogg (1805-1873) at the time of the 1861 Census was a farmer of 155 acres employing five labourers and one boy. The sale particulars provide a fascinating insight as to the inventory of a farm at this time: sadly no report of the sale was published. Amongst the lots were

"47 rare wether (castrated) hogs, 15 excellent dairy cows, some with calves at their side and others forward in calf and in full milk, 4 noble grazing oxen, 6 superior 4 years old working steers, 6 capital 3 years old ditto ditto (sic), 4 improving 2 years old ditto ditto, 1 excellent cross bred bull, 2 powerful draft mares, 1 useful hackney horse 5 years old and good in saddle, 1 ditto mare, excellent in saddle or harness, and 2 valuable fat pigs.

"Implements of husbandry, &c. - 2 strong waggons, 3 useful wheel putts (two wheeled carts), capital turnip drill, 2 excellent turnip cutters, 4 single iron and oak sulls, drags and harrows, superior winnowing machine by Tooze; chaff cutter, 2 American horse rakes, iron cultivator roller, horse hoe, yokes, bows and chains, picks and rakes, ox cribs, winnowing sheet, fan and stand, gate hurdles, waggon lines, 15,000 long and short spars, iron screw cider press, apple mill, 20 empty one, two and three hogshead casks, mow saddles, stocks and covers, &c., &c. The hay, reed, straw, manure and grass - 4 stacks of well made meadow hay, several hundred of reed, several ricks of wheat and barley straw, about 200 loads of manure and the grass of two orchards."

Frederick Giles was born in Chedzoy in 1839 and was a labourer. An incident involving him was reported in the Bridgwater Mercury in November 1862.

"Edward Fry (probably a mistake for Edwin Fry, born in 1820 and a farmer of 252 acres employing seven men and six boys) was summoned by Frederick Giles for an assault. The parties reside at Chedzoy, and Giles stated he went to the premises of the defendant to enquire why he had assaulted his (complainant's) father, and then defendant threatened to kill him, and struck him with a spade, by which his life was endangered. Mr. Lovibond, for the defence, said the complainant's father was seen in possession of a sack, the property of the defendant, and the latter took it from him. The next day the complainant came for the sack, and on defendant saying it was his, the complainant called him 'A b----y liar.' No Englishman could stand for that, and the complainant was ordered to leave the premises. The defendant then put up his spade to push him away, but did not assault him. Mr. Lovibond called two witnesses who swore that the defendant did not assault the complainant, and used the spade to push him off the premises as he would not go. The Bench dismissed the case, each to pay his own costs. The magistrates recommended the parties to be more careful in the use of their language."

Also in November 1862, John Potter, 44 years old and born in Chedzoy, appeared before Bridgwater Police Court. The Bridgwater Mercury reported

"John Potter of Chedzoy was summoned by Mr. James Boulting, Inspector for Weights and Measures for the

Borough, for having unjust scales. The Inspector visited Bridgwater market ... when he found a pair of scales on the defendant's stall. They were incorrect and unjust, and he seized them. In cross-examination, Mr. Boulting said he did not see the scales used, but there were particles of meat showing they had been used that morning. They were one ounce and a half (42 grams) against the purchaser. He did not think an ounce and a half of dirt could be scraped off them. He had examined them before, and they were correct. He accounted for their incorrectness from an accumulation of dirt. He had cautioned Potter several times. The scales were produced and tested in court, which showed them to be one ounce and a half deficient. Superintendent Lear corroborated the evidence of the Inspector. In cross-examination the Superintendent stated that wood scales were affected by damp weather and the juice from the meat weighed. Mr. Lovibond, for the defendant, denied any intention of defrauding the public. It was quite clear that wood scales were affected by the damp, and particles of meat would adhere each time they were used, and it was quite easy to account for an accumulation of one ounce and a half. The defendant was a respectable man and such a thing would not occur again. The Mayor said there was perhaps more neglect than criminality in this case, but still the defendant should take care not to use such scales. He would be fined 5s. (25p.) and costs, or seven days' imprisonment."

Less serious cases also came before the magistrates. In January 1863

"Isaac Stoker pleaded guilty to drunkenness at Chedzoy. Fined 5s. and 5s. 6d. costs."

This seems likely to have been a misprint for Isaac Stokes, a 41 year old agricultural labourer born in the village.

Roads around Chedzoy at that time were very narrow, at least that is the implication of a court report from March 1863:

"John Williams was summoned by Betsy Barnstable for maliciously damaging wheat at Chedzoy. John Wilkins said he saw defendant in complainant's wheat field where he did about threepence (1p) worth of damage. There were thorns on the side of the road and defendant pulled them away. Cross-examined: The road ought to be twelve feet wide. The thorns were about three or four feet from the road. There is only one bound-stone (sic) visible. The case was dismissed."

An old parish record book notes that

"At a meeting held in the School Room in this Parish of Chedzoy the 20th day of Febry. 1863 for the purpose of choosing 3 qualified men for Constable, the following were agreed on: George Parish, James Hook, James Parsons, Wm. Rainey."

After each of the four names it was noted,

"Willing to stand again."

Two years later four Parish Constables were recorded: James Hook (tailor), James Gilbert (market gardener), William Rainey (carpenter) and James Potter (farmer). Other who served in this office in subsequent years were George Winter (farmer) and, for a second time, George Parish (innkeeper).

Another entry is

"28th April 1864. Mr. Derrick having given notice that he required the drove from his house to be put in repair; it was unanimously resolved that Mr. Cary, the Waywarden, be requested to instruct Mr. Hicks, the Surveyor of Roads, to level the uneven parts and pack the wheel tracks in all the droves as far as the gates leading into the different fields."

In August 1863 a report was published in relation to an alleged theft of a purse.

"LOSS AND RECOVERY. Mrs. [Caroline] Jewell (27), a lady now stopping at Chedzoy, and wife of Richard Jewell, a mariner, on the 10th of last month went to Mr. Fry's hayfield, situate in the neighbourhood, in a waggon, and in company with a number of other people. She wore a short jacket, with pockets in front, and in the left-hand pocket she had her purse, containing £4 6s. 6d., and a marked halfpenny (about 1/4 p.). In the waggon, and sitting beside Mrs. Jewell, was a man named Bennett, and he told her of the dangerous situation of her purse, saying, 'It is not much of a place to carry a purse in: you will lose it.' Accordingly she took the purse out, and put it in her right-hand pocket covering it over with her handkerchief. Sitting on this side of her was a lad named Albert Brely (aged 17, born in Chedzoy); a few minutes later after she had altered the position of her purse he picked up her handkerchief out of her pocket; but Mrs. Jewell, thinking it was done in fun, did not say anything to him. She had not been in the field very long, however, before she missed her purse, and she at once told the company of her loss, who began to search for it, but could not find it. After a time the search was abandoned, and the purse and its contents given up as lost. It so happened that in the purse was a marked halfpenny, on one side of which was a cross, and on the other side the letter B. All things remained as before, and nothing was heard of her purse and money until Wednesday week, when this halfpenny was given to Mrs. Jewell by her brother, Francis Conduit, who had received it from a boy named George Newton (a ten year old, born in Chedzoy). The latter, on being questioned, said he had received the coin from the lad Brely, and accordingly Mrs. Jewell paid a visit to this youth, who, however, denied having given Newton anything at all.

"Newton was then sent for, but before he had come, Brely admitted having given him two penny-pieces for a comb and watch-chain. Newton said, in Brely's presence, on being shown the marked coin, 'That is the same halfpenny that I gave your brother, and the same that I received from Albert Brely for a watch-chain.' Brely denied this also, but it so occurred that two other boys, Henry Conduit and Robert Hook (aged 11 and 12 years, both born in Chedzoy), were present when the coin passed; and the former of these on being sent for corroborated the story of Newton, by having observed to Newton, on Brely paying him for the chain, that the halfpenny was bad. Brely then got noisy, and offered £20 to anyone who could prove that the halfpenny had been in his possession. Mrs. Jewell was now convinced that Brely knew something of her purse and its contents, and she handed the coin to P.C. Hiscocks; on the following Monday, and that officer brought Albert Brely up before J.L. Sealy, Esq., at the Town-hall, on Thursday last.

"Mr. P.O.H. Reed defended the prisoner, and elicited from the prosecutrix that he was a native of Chedzoy, and that she didn't suspect him of the robbery, because of his respectability before the discovery of the passing of the halfpenny. Only the evidence of the prosecutrix was now given, and the prisoner was remanded until Thursday, bail being accepted for his appearance. The purse and the remainder of the money had not been traced up to the day of the trial."

The following week a further report was published, repeating and enlarging on the original.

"THE CHARGE OF POCKET-PICKING AT CHEDZOY. Albert Brely, a young man, appeared on remand to answer a charge of stealing £4 6s. 6d. and a portmonie from the jacket-pocket of Caroline Jewell, the wife of a mariner, now residing at Chedzoy, on the 11th of July. Mr. H. Lovibond appeared for the prosecutrix, and Mr. Reed for the defendant. The evidence, taken on the Thursday previous was read over, and in addition to this prosecutrix now stated on cross-examination by Mr. Reed, that after she lost the purse some wild beasts were shown in the parish, and a great many people went to see them. Prisoner was, in her opinion, a highly respectable young man. His parents were also very respectable. - Francis Conduit, a labourer, living at Chedzoy, said he received the halfpenny produced (which was a very peculiar one, and bore several marks) on Tuesday, the 11th, from George Newton, who gave it to him in Mr. Fry's reaping-field. Witness took the coin home and gave it to his sister, the prosecutrix, on the 13th of August. George Newton gave witness the halfpenny because it was a bad one.

"George Newton, a boy ten years of age, said he lived at Chedzoy, and worked for Mr. Fry. He knew the halfpenny produced, and received it from the prisoner on the morning after the shows were exhibited at Chedzoy, which was on the 4th August. Henry Conduit and Robert Hook were present when the prisoner gave witness the halfpenny, and the latter received it in exchange for a watch-guard. Witness afterwards tried to pass it at a shop, but the people would not take it. - Cross-examined by Mr. Reed: I went to the shows, and saw the prisoner there. - Henry Conduit, a labourer, of Chedzoy, recollected seeing prisoner with the halfpenny the morning after the shows. Witness heard prisoner ask the last witness (Newton) if he had a watch-guard to sell him, to which he (Newton) replied he had. The chain was then bought in witness's presence, prisoner giving Newton the halfpenny produced for the same.

"Robert Hook gave similar evidence, and added that he saw the prisoner with a lot of money about a fortnight before the shows were exhibited at Chedzoy. Prisoner took it out of his pocket, and witness saw there were three half-crowns and some small silver; he saw no gold." A half-crown was worth 2s. 6d. (12.5p.). "Prisoner had shown him this money two or three times. - Cross-examined: I know it is the latter part of August now; I can't give any reason for fixing the time I last saw the money. - Francis Bennett identified the halfpenny. He last saw it on the 7th of August. He had before seen it, on the 3rd of July, and on both occasions was in the possession of the prosecutrix. Witness marked the halfpenny about sixteen months ago with a small chisel, cutting out a letter B and a small cross; but he had not seen it since that time until the 3rd July. After he marked the coin he kept it a month, but he did not know to whom he had passed it. He knew the last time he saw it was on the 3rd of July, because it was about a week before the loss of the money by the prosecutrix. In answer to Mr. Trevor (magistrates' clerk), witness stated that he marked it because he had heard that it was lucky to carry a crooked halfpenny - (laughter).

"Elizabeth Conduit (19), living at Chedzoy, deposed that she was the sister to the prosecutrix. She was present when the prosecutrix asked prisoner if he had ever given George Newton a halfpenny, and he replied that he never had. This was last Sunday week, and witness's mother was also present. Afterwards prisoner said he had given Newton two penny-pieces, and this statement he repeated in the presence of Newton, who told prisoner that he had given him the halfpenny in question in the morning after the shows. This the prisoner again denied, and said he would give anyone £20 who could prove that he ever had the coin in his possession. - George Newton, re-called, corroborated this statement bout (sic) the conversation. - Mr. Reed put a question, through the Bench, in answer to which prosecutrix said she would not state that prisoner did not turn out his pockets when the loss was announced.

"P.C. Hiscox (note the different spelling!) deposed having received the halfpenny produced on the 17th August from the prosecutrix. - Cross-examined: I apprehended the prisoner on a warrant, and he said he did not know how he came to be in possession of the halfpenny except that he received it from the shows. - Mr. Reed then addressed the Bench, and said if there was one thing more than another which would entitle his client to favourable consideration, it would be his appearance here; but a stronger claim to their kindly consideration was the testimonials of general good conduct which he was directed to place before them through the vicar of the parish, who had known him from his youth, and from persons for whom he had worked so long as he had been able to work. As to the coin, he had been informed that it was very common to mark coppers, and that the letter B and crosses were considered lucky marks. The learned gentleman was proceeding to offer further remarks on the different points in the evidence, when the Bench interposed by remarking that they did not consider there was sufficient evidence to warrant them in sending the prisoner before a jury. - The accused was therefore discharged, and the result evidently gave satisfaction to a crowded court."

August 1863 also saw another long report in the Bridgwater Mercury in relation to the Harvest Home held in the village.

"The little village of Chedzoy was all astir on Friday last, and for several days previously, in consequence of the celebration of the successful gathering in of the harvest. This was the first year of such a festival here: but it was in every respect a complete success." That was not strictly true, but more of that later. "The more influential farmers of the village, headed by the rector - the Rev. R.H. Mullins - were unanimous in their endeavours to carry out the scheme satisfactorily, and the consequence was that ample funds flowed in. There was not much attempt at decoration in the village, but a flag floated over one of the pinnacles of the church tower, and a string of flags was thrown across the road leading to the scene of the festivity. The bells rang merry peals during the day, and much enlivened the proceedings.

"About eleven o'clock the parishioners, headed by a band of musicians from Bridgwater ... walked to the church where Divine service was performed. ... The service ended, the band headed the procession to a field in the rear of the Parsonage House, in one part of which a large tent had been erected. In this a substantial dinner was speedily served up, to which about 170 persons sat down and did ample justice. The Rev. R.H. Mullins occupied the chair, and there were also present ... Rev. G.O. Mullins (Huish), brother of the rector, ... Messrs. B. Tazewell, Wm. Carey, G. and A. Winter, E. Fry, E. Pollard, W. Barnstable and J. Palfrey, of Chedzoy ..." These were the only Chedzoy residents included on the long guest list. "The dinner was supplied by Mr. Palfrey of the Crown Inn and the tent was decorated with miniature wheat-sheafs, flowers and mottoes, among the latter of which were 'Welcome,' 'God Save the Queen', &c."

It should be noted that the reporter confused two vicars, and spelt their surname incorrectly, in both this and two subsequent reports. Rev. George Oakman Mullens (1830-1895) was Rector of Chedzoy from 1855 to 1891. His brother, Rev. Richard Hubert Mullens (1836-1917), was the Curate at Huish, Devon in 1863.

"On the removal of the cloth, the Chairman rose to propose the toast of 'the Queen.' In doing so he said that at no period had this country been so prosperous or the people so happy as under the present reign. ... The Chairman said that not many years since - indeed, almost within his recollection - a man who knew his right hand from his left was considered of sufficient education for a farmer - (a laugh). But things had changed since then, and the science of agriculture had become as complicated as the science of medicine, and much more agreeable to his own taste - (hear, hear). A man who made two blades of wheat grow where only one grew before was a benefactor to his country, and deserved the best thanks of the community - (hear, hear). The agriculturists of Chedzoy, he was proud to say, were a very enlightened body, and he would propose the health of one whom he though a most excellent farmer, viz., Mr. Benjamin Turner of Lyng Court Farm - (applause). ...

"The Chairman said nothing gave Mrs. Mullins or himself greater pleasure than their being able to add to the happiness of other people - (hear, hear and cheers). This festivity was not got up for their own amusement - although he would not wish to allude to unpleasant circumstances of a statement having been made that this was got up for some selfish motive. A meeting of this kind, in which master and man were brought together promoted mutual benefit, and was not for any selfish object - (hear, hear). ...

"The greater part of the company then retired to join in various games and dancing. A large number of people now arrived from Bridgwater, and the field presented a very gay appearance. In the afternoon the school-children had tea on the same ground, and after satisfying their 'inner man,' disported themselves as they thought fit on the greensward. Between seven and eight o'clock the field was cleared and the assembly dispersed."

However, it is quite clear that not everyone in the village was happy with the Harvest Home as the following week another report appeared.

"It may be remembered that at the dinner on the above occasion, on Friday, the chairman (the Rev. R.H. Mullins), said the whole parish were not exactly unanimous in their desire to carry out the festival. We are now able to state the reasons through which some of them were lukewarm, and a consideration of these might prevent the possibility of there being any opposition on a future occasion. Objections were made by the principal farmers - first, because the harvest was not then more than half gathered in; secondly, because labourers and boys who were not fortunate enough to have tickets given them, and who yet wished to be present at the dinner, had to pay as much for the same as farmers, clergymen, &c.; and, thirdly, because it was decided that the enjoyments of the field should be forbidden to all those who did not attend the dinner, or were not the friends of the subscribers. Besides, a gentleman has informed us that neither he nor another whom he knew - and who were the largest farmers in the neighbourhood - had been asked to assist in the affair. There was, therefore, good reason to object to the celebration as premature. Virtually, it could not be a 'Harvest Home' when a half of the corn was not carried, and farmers could not afford to lose their hands for a half-day, and probably more, in the midst of these important operations, especially in such doubtful weather as they had just experienced. Lastly, no one in the parish should have been prevented from entering into the sports in the field; and it was a poor excuse for this course that 'roughs' might find their way in and do damage, if all parties were indiscriminately allowed to enter. It is hoped that at the next festival all these objections will be met, and that the parishioners may join in the enjoyment of it."

In September 1863 the life of the village was again disturbed, this time by a heated dispute over the payment of church rates. The Bridgwater Mercury reported,

"Hitherto the quiet of this parish has been undisturbed by disputes about church-rates. But the recent sale of the manor in lots has changed the old state of things. About three weeks ago notice was given that a meeting would be held for the purpose of levying a rate. Opposition was talked of, though none was offered; but from a few good-tempered hints, the pro-rate party discovered that their notice was bad. Another notice was therefore given, convening a meeting for Friday last, when an opposition was made at the vestry principally from the parish of Westonzoyland, in the persons of Messrs. Ling, Chapman and Bawden, all of whom are owners and ratepayers in the parish of Chedzoy. The clergyman not being present, Mr. B. Tazewell, churchwarden, was voted to the chair. Mr. Hodges asked for the accounts of the past year to be produced, but the chairman informed him that they were audited and passed at the Easter meeting. Mr. James Ling then requested the chairman to read the entry of the fact in the minute book; but on examination no such entry was to be found. The account book was next called for, and after some time, Mr. Fry fetched it from his house, and in it was found some memorandum made of the accounts having been examined. Mr. Ling now asked for a written estimate setting forth the items of probable expenditure for the ensuing year, saying that there was nothing before the meeting to show that the sum talked of was enough or half enough for the warden's purpose. The chairman said no such estimate had been proposed, but that they would take the expenditure of the past years as their guide. After some talk on the impossibility of deciding upon expenditure for the ensuing year without such account, Mr. James Ling moved the adjournment of the meeting for one month, that the churchwardens might produce it. This motion was carried unanimously. The meeting was well attended, upwards of thirty people being present."

A month later feelings were still running high over this subject.

"On 12th Sept. a vestry meeting was held in the parish school of Chedzoy for the purpose of making a church-rate; but the rate was opposed by several ratepayers who obtained an adjournment of the meeting on the ground that a proper estimate of the ensuing year's probable expenses had not been submitted, and to allow for the preparation of same. The adjourned meeting was therefore held on Friday last, the rector (the rev. R.H. Mullins) (sic) presiding. There were also present Messrs. James Ling, John Ling, Alfred Ling, Guy Ling, Potter (2), Derrick, senr., H. Hodges, W. Carey, Chapman, B. Tazewell, Palfrey, G. Boone, Winter, Dowden, &c. - in all, nearly 30 ratepayers.

"The Chairman having briefly opened the meeting, Mr. Tazewell, one of the churchwardens, handed in an estimate, which was as follows - Estimate of the churchwardens for the parish of Chedzoy for the year 1863-1864:- Repairs to church, £3; sweeping and cleaning same, 7s. 6d.; bell rope, 12s. 3d.; keeping churchyard in order, 5s.; bread and wine for Holy Sacrament, 15s.; washing the surplice, 15s.; visitation fees, 3s. 6d.; new register for the entry of baptisms for the parish priest, 12s. 6d.; clerk's fee, £4; sexton's fee, £2 2s.; repairs of the clock, 10s.; choir mistress, £6; total £19 7s. 9d.

Mr. Tazewell proposed, and Mr. Carey seconded the motion, that this estimate be adopted.

Mr. Ling: You see, gentlemen ...

The Chairman: Order, sir, that I may take down this proposition.

After waiting some time,

Mr. Ling continued: "I find that the estimate sets down the repairs of the church at £3. I want some little better explanation than that - whether it is for the stone-work, plastering, or other kind of work. It may be for the clergyman to build a wine cellar, to put the sacramental wine in, for anything we know.

Mr. Tazewell: The lead on the church wants repairing; the windows are broken; and the seats want repairing.

Mr. Ling: How much will each cost? That is what I want to know.

The Chairman: The churchwardens are not expected to go into so much detail: they are only required by law to give a reasonable estimate.

Mr. Ling: In the absence of some better explanation as to the purpose to which this £3 is to be appropriated, I shall move as an amendment that this item be struck out from the estimate. Mr. John Ling seconded the amendment. The Chairman was going to put the original motion first, but Mr. Ling objected. The Chairman said it was customary at vestry meetings to put the original motion first, and the amendments, one by one, afterwards.

Mr. Ling: I deny that.

The Chairman (obviously starting to lose his temper!): But I have the law here, and it says so. Besides, I am the chairman, and can do as I think fit.

Mr. Ling: You can do as you like, but I shall enter my protest against it. Please enter in the minutes your refusal to put the amendment to the meeting first.

The Chairman (after considering for a minute or two): We will put Mr. Ling's amendment first. But before I do so, I would ask you if you have not too much respect for your parish church - that has now stood for nearly 800 years, and has been kept up with money raised in the parish from time immemorial - to see it brought into that state in which a parish church and churchyard situate not a hundred miles from this place now are, and which are a disgrace to a civilised community. This is the lowest motive I could put it too. I would put it higher, namely, your sense of honour. When you took your farms and bought your farms in this parish, you took them and bought them with certain rates and taxes upon them; and it is just as reasonable for you to try to evade the highway-rate and the poor-rate as to try to evade the church-rate. As a man of honour, I know you will pay your church-rate - (hear, hear). The amendment was then put, and 8 voted for it; for the original motion there were 18 hands held up.

Mr. Ling refused to be beaten.

Mr. Ling: That being the case, I demand a poll upon that item.

The Chairman: I will take the poll now.

Mr. Ling: I beg your pardon. If you do so, how are others in the parish to give their votes? I ask for a poll of the whole parishioners.

The Chairman: Those present represent the whole of the parishioners, and they only have a vote in the matter being here.

Mr. Ling: Now, sir, enter in the book your refusal to take a poll of the whole parish.

The Chairman (clearly getting even more rattled!): I am not here as a lawyer's clerk, but as minister of this parish and chairman of this vestry.

Mr. Ling: Well then; go on with the next item, and remember that you refuse to take a poll of the whole parish.

The Chairman: When a poll is demanded, it may, at the discretion of the chairman, be taken at once, there being no necessity for a poll of the parish, but only those assembled at the vestry meeting.

Mr. Ling: I propose that a poll be taken of the ratepayers of the whole parish, and not only of the ratepayers assembled here."

Both sides were nearing the end of their tethers.

The Chairman (with a nod to Mr. Tazewell): And Mr. Tazewell has proposed, and Mr. Carey seconded, that a poll be taken forthwith on this item.

Mr. Ling: I have not heard that proposed or seconded.

Mr. Hodges: I favour the resolution of Mr. Ling.

The Chairman: Does any one second Mr. Ling's motion?

Mr. Hodges: I beg your pardon; I did.

The Chairman: You only 'favoured' it.

Mr. Hodges: I believe that that is nearly the same. I think that the item for sacramental bread and wine is —-.

The Chairman: But we are not come to that item yet; you are entirely out of order."

A vote was taken and the motion defeated.

"The Chairman: The poll may now be taken on every item. It would be absurd to take the poll of the parish on each item. There has never been any question here about church-rates until now.

Mr. Ling: Hear, hear! Dark and benighted indeed must you have been!

The Chairman: Every man in the parish has too much respect for his place of worship to allow it to go to ruin for want of funds.

Mr. Ling: That's nothing to do with it; you may take a poll of the vestry it you like; but you must take the sense of the parishioners. The object of the law is to prevent a vestry meeting doing what they like - to take a wider range in fact, and ascertain the feelings of the whole parish.

"Mr. Ling then called attention to the next item, 7s. 6d. for sweeping and cleaning something - he did not know what - perhaps it was the minister's surplice.

The Chairman (apparently with one particular person in mind!): The cleaning and sweeping of dirty people out of the parish.

Mr. Ling: Yes, socially and physically dirty, I suppose; but not spiritually dirty, of course, under such a spiritual minister as you are!

Mr. Hodges objected to the item passing, on the ground that his seat had not been swept out for the last month.

Dowden (the parish official): What! Not your seat cleaned! - (loud laughter).

The Chairman said he had no objection to the striking out of this item, to expedite the business, he would second Mr. Hodge's motion. He did this because he intended to pay the man, for cleaning, more that this out of his own pocket.

Mr. Tazewell objected to its being struck out, and proposed an amendment that it be retained, which was seconded by Mr. Winter.

Mr. Ling: Tazewell, don't do the old man out of the chairman's offer!"

The amendment was carried by 18 votes to 5 as was a resolution in relation to the bell ropes.

"The next item was 5s. for keeping the churchyard in good order, and to this Mr. Ling said he could not object, as the churchyard was kept prettier and in better order than any other for miles around. He could not help thinking that if the chairman kept the souls of his flock in as good order as the gardener did the churchyard —-.

The Chairman: We don't allow personalities here! The reason why it is done so cheaply is that my parishioners work for love.

"On the item of 15s. for 'bread and wine for the Holy Communion,' Mr. Ling observed that it was a shame and a positive injustice to make poor people pay for this. Should not their love, their honour, their responsibility - of which their chairman had so much spoken - prompt them to provide it free? The Chairman: We do not make poor people pay for the bread and wine. It is in the power of the minister and churchwardens to exempt any one they deem too poor to pay the church-rate."

Mr. Ling moved that this item be struck out, but it was passed by the same majority.

"Mr. Ling, in referring to the next item, 15s. for washing the rector's surplice, said he should blush to ask the parish to do such a thing - to perpetuate, by wearing it, a practice left by Roman Catholicism, of which probably the chairman was a minister. However, he should not object to it. ... On the subject of the choir-mistress's salary, Mr. Ling said: Next comes an item which looks very much like a provision for theatricals. Did you ever hear of such an item to be taken out of a church-rate? I don't object to it, because it is one of those things that will make the church-rate of Chedzoy ring far and wide as one of the most monstrous ever proposed."

The meeting voted in favour of this item. More debate took place and eventually Mr. Ling said,

"Now, look gentlemen! Just now you defended your estimate, as correct and right; and now you are willing to concede what I have asked for - that this meeting be adjourned for the churchwardens to amend it." The meeting was adjourned and polling took place, but as none of the opposition turned up the estimates were accepted and the meeting further adjourned until the following Friday.

It seems that tempers had still not cooled by the time they met the following week. A very long report was published, broken down here into paragraphs from the one paragraph of the original.

"The adjourned meeting was held on Friday morning at the school-room in the parish of Chedzoy. Mr. B. Tazewell presiding, in the absence of the minister. There were about 40 ratepayers present, and Mr. H. Lovibond, from Bridgwater, professionally advised the church-rate party. It will be remembered that when the estimate was presented at the meeting of last week, it contained an item of £6 as salary for the choir-mistress, and that it was on this item, with one or two others, the opposition party relied to prove the invalidity of the rate after it had been made. Under the advice of Mr. Lovibond, this item was now struck out, and the principal prop of the no-rate party removed.

"The meeting was an adjourned one, for the purpose of taking a poll on several of the items in the estimate which had been objected to, but as we stated last week, the opposition party did not put in an appearance, and the chairman declared that 78 ratepayers had polled, all the votes being in favour of the items objected to. Mr. Turner proposed and Mr. Carey seconded, that the item of £6 for the choir-mistress's salary be struck out. - Mr. Ling remarked that last week they were unanimous - at least those of the meeting who were in favour of the rate - in deciding that the estimate as produced by the churchwardens was right and now they were compelled to eat humble pie, and turn round and say what they did last week was wrong. He (Mr. Ling) thought the item proposed to be struck out was a very proper one to remain.

"But before they began, he would ask them if Mr. Lovibond was a ratepayer.

Mr. Lovibond: I am here to advise the ratepayers and churchwardens.

Mr. Ling: Have you any standing as a lawyer?

Mr. Lovibond: If I had not, I should not be here. - (Hear, hear.)

Mr. Ling: Here's a glaring anomaly - a Radical attorney upholding a Poseyite parson and baptismal regeneration.

Mr. Lovibond: That claptrap is all very fine, Mr. Ling. I am here to advise the churchwardens to do what is legal and necessary for the purpose of making a rate; and now the claptrap you have begun will prevent their doing it. I have told them there is some doubt as to the legality of the item of £6, and advised its erasure.

The Chairman asked if there was any amendment to the motion.

Mr. Ling wished then, first of all, to discuss the presence of Mr. Lovibond. As a friend and a gentleman he did not object to his presence, but he did protest against his being there as a prop to the churchwardens, and for the purpose of awing and intimidating the oppositionists.

Mr. Lovibond: That's all bosh; not all Bridgwater or all the country could do that to you.

Mr. Ling: Perhaps not; but there are others here that might be affected.

Mr. Lovibond: But they come here under your protection. You seem the 'top sawyer' amongst them - (laughter).

Mr. Ling: It is a great compliment to us of the opposition that Mr. Lovibond is here, but by no means a credit to the other party that they cannot get along without a lawyer coming to help them and bringing brains for them.

"The Chairman then put the motion that the estimate with the exception of the £6 be read and adopted.

Mr. Ling moved, as an amendment, that the item of £6 stand as in the original estimate.

Mr. John Ling seconded the amendment, which was lost by an overwhelming majority.

Mr. Ling then demanded a poll of the whole of the parishioners on that item; which Mr. Boone seconded. Mr. Turner proposed and Mr. Potter seconded, that the poll be taken forthwith.

Mr. Ling protested against this, and called it a farce to poll only those present, while the law intended that the opinion of the whole parish should be taken upon any point in dispute.

Mr. Ling: And enter my protest against it in the minutes of this meeting.

Mr. Lovibond (to Mr. Ling): Let me appeal to your common sense, which I give you credit for having a goodly share of - ('hear, hear' from Mr. Ling and laughter). You see your strength here. Now, it is quite clear that it is lawful to make a church-rate; and this factious opposition can be of no use. The rate is the most moderate I ever remember to have seen proposed.

Mr. Ling: And the most immoderate item for the provision for the theatricals, or you would not have advised them to strike it out.

Mr. Turner proposed, and there were several seconders, that the poll be open for recording of the votes of the parishioners until 4 o'clock. Mr. Ling then proposed and Mr. Hodges seconded, that the item of 15s. (75p.) for washing the minister's surplice be also struck out. Mr. Turner moved, and Mr. Carey seconded, that it stand as it appeared in the estimate. On a division there were about 30 for the amendment, and 6 for the original motion. Mr. Ling then demanded a poll on that item also, and at the same time proposed that the meeting be adjourned for a week in order to enable the churchwardens to produce an amended estimate. Mr. A. Ling seconded this motion. Mr. Turner proposed an amendment, which Mr. Fry seconded - that the estimate should stand as it was, with the exception of the £6. The amendment was carried by the same majority as the previous item.

Mr. Ling: Then I demand a poll of the whole of the parishioners on that point.

Mr. A. Ling seconded the demand. - The ratepayers then adjourned until four o'clock, that a poll might be taken, Mr. Winter being appointed poll-clerk.

"On their re-assembling, the poll-clerk stated that there were 68 votes recorded in favour of washing the minister's surplice and striking out the choir-mistress's salary: for the surplice item to be struck out, 1; for the £6 to remain, 8. Mr. Ling: And how about the other item?

Mr. Lovibond: These were the only two items that you demanded a poll upon.

Mr. Ling: I demanded a poll upon your refusal to adjourn the meeting for the purpose of allowing the churchwardens to prepare an amended estimate: and I still persist in that demand.

Mr. Lovibond said he remembered something being said about an amended estimate, but he did not hear a poll demanded upon it. If he did, where was the resolution?

Mr. Ling: I gave it to you.

Mr. Lovibond: Was it in writing?

Mr. Ling: No, there was no need.

Mr. Lovibond: I shall advise the churchwardens to abide by the resolutions that are recorded.

Mr. Turner proposed a rate of a penny-farthing in the pound, amounting to £13 7s. 9d. - Mr. Carey seconded the motion."

Things started to get even more heated!

"Mr. Ling then proceeded to argue against church-rates generally, but was interrupted by the Chairman who was about to put the resolution to the meeting.

Mr. Ling: You sit down, sir, and behave yourself.

The Chairman: Order, sir. Have you any amendment to propose?

Mr. Ling: I have.

The Chairman: Then propose it, and do not keep us here all day.

Mr. Ling, however, resumed and remarked on the anomaly of having a gentleman to defend church rates at Chedzoy who had been the means of breaking down the church rates in Bridgwater.

Mr. Lovibond: I must protest against such statements; they have nothing to do with my position here today.

Mr Ling: You have no right to protest, sir; you have no standing here as a ratepayer.

Mr. Lovibond observed that he had not spoken to Mr. Ling in such a way as this, although Mr. Ling had laid himself open to it many times. He was not here as a ratepayer, and had no opportunity of replying to any charges Mr. Ling might bring against him: therefore it was ungenerous and unfair of him to make use of his position in such a way.

Mr. Ling said Mr. Lovibond had thrown himself open to these remarks in coming there and upholding church rates.

Mr. Lovibond: Have I no right to come here in my profession as a lawyer? Have I no right to come here and advise the churchwardens in their duty? Who has a right to say that I shall not come here? Not Mr. Ling, nor anybody else - (cheers).

The Chairman: None of your fine talking, Mr. Ling, will alter our opinion.

After Mr. Ling had proceeded a little more on the subject of church-rates, he concluded by proposing 'that this vestry requests the churchwardens to apply to the parishioners for subscriptions to meet the expenses of the year and adjourn for three months to enable them to do so.' Mr. A. Ling seconded the amendment. The original motion for the making of a rate was carried by a majority of 31 against 6. Mr. Ling then requested that his protestation against these proceedings might be entered in the minutes, in consequence of the refusal to insert his resolution; but, on the advice of Mr. Lovibond, the Chairman refused to enter either.

Mr. Ling: That is all I want - a refusal.

The meeting then separated."

It seems that one of Mr. Ling's relations delayed paying the church rate until the eleventh hour. A footnote to the Bridgwater County Police Court column in the Bridgwater Mercury in February 1864 noted,

"There were a few other cases but they were devoid of public interest. The Chedzoy church rate case which was likely to come on this morning, was settled by Mr. Marmaduke Ling paying the amount due for which he had been summoned."

The Weights and Measures Inspector for Bridgwater continued to keep an eye on traders from Chedzoy. In February 1864,

"John Rainey, carpenter and farmer, of Chedzoy (48 years old and born in Chedzoy), was summoned by Mr. James Boulting, Inspector of Weights and Measures, for exposing for sale in the market a quantity of butter deficient in weight. The Inspector stated that he found twenty half-pounds of butter in the defendant's basket, which were all one quarter of an ounce or more deficient in weight. The defendant was fined 20s. (£1) and costs."

The same edition of the paper included a report on proceedings in Bridgwater County Court. The plaintiff was not fully identified, but was probably William Lovibond, 32 years old and born in Chedzoy.

"LOVIBOND v. JEANES. This was an action to recover the sum of £3 2s. 6d. damages sustained through the alleged breach of warranty of a pig. Mr. P.O.H. Reed appeared for the defendant. The plaintiff, a labourer, who lives at Chedzoy, stated that on the 16th of September last he bought of the defendant, a farmer, of North Petherton, in Bridgwater market, a pig which was warranted as 'hearty and sound.' He paid £2 1s. 6d. for it, and drove it home, a distance of three and a half miles. A day or two afterwards, he found that it would not eat heartily, that it 'ground its teeth, and was rather hushy.' He afterwards found that the pig was not sound and hearty, and had a letter sent to the defendant to tell him of it, but he took no notice of it. The pig did not thrive, and though it was still alive, had not recovered from the unsoundness. Plaintiff did not return the pig. Susan Woodland and Mr. Fry, farmer, of Chedzoy, and master of plaintiff, confirmed the warranty and the unsoundness. The latter said he saw defendant a week after the deal, and told them that the pig was not worth a penny-piece and that he ought not take in a poor man. To this the defendant replied, 'I won't allow him a —- farthing (a quarter of a penny).' - Mr. Winter, another farmer, of Chedzoy, saw the pig the morning after it was bought, and it was then unsound. Witness said it was not worth a farthing now. - For the defence it was contended that the pig was sound, but it had been 'doctored' by the plaintiff. Evidence to this effect was called. - His Honour said the only question was the amount of damages. There was no doubt as to the warranty or the unsoundness, but the plaintiff ought not to have kept the pig after he discovered that it was not sound. The pig must be returned, and defendant must pay plaintiff the sum of £2 5s. 6d."

As has always been the case, children were being born out of wedlock. In April 1864 the Bridgwater Mercury County Police Court column reported the case of an employee in Chedzoy as follows.

"AFFILIATION. Henry Luff, the eldest son of a farmer living at Mark, was summoned at the instance of Sarah Warner, to show cause why he should not maintain her bastard child. Mr. Paul Reed appeared for the complainant, and Mr. Greata, of Axbridge, for the defendant, who did not appear personally. - The complainant stated that she was a single woman living in the service of Mr. Derrick, farmer, of Chedzoy. On the 5th July last she was delivered of a male child born in Bridgwater union-house, and the defendant was its father. At Lady-day, 1859, she entered the service of the defendant's father, and continued in his service until Lady-day, 1862. Defendant was about 20 years of age, and had six brothers and one sister, all at home. Complainant recollected Woolavington fair, in October, 1862, and defendant's leaving home to go there. After the family had gone to bed he returned home, about midnight, and the first impropriety then took place, which was afterwards repeated. About five weeks after this time defendant left home for three months, and about two months afterwards she found herself in the family-way. When he returned she told her mistress of the state she (complainant) was in, and that Henry was the child's father. He was present, but made no answer. The mother, however, said she knew it was going to be put on her son by people's talking, but rather than he should pay he should go to New Zealand. Complainant left the service the next day, at her mistress's request. Complainant afterwards went ... to Mark, and saw defendant, who did not deny paternity. ... The Bench, after consulting about ten minutes, said they did not consider the charge made out, and they must dismiss the complaint. - This decision surprised everyone in court, and none more so than Mr. Reed, who observed that he had refrained from cross-examining the defendant's mother, and had not thought it necessary to sum up, so convinced was he that the case was satisfactorily made out."

Some of the prosecutions reported in the local paper would probably not even warrant a caution in modern times. In June 1864,

"Joseph Potter, charged with stealing two pennyworth (less than 1p.) of clover hay, the property of Benjamin Turner of Chedzoy, was fined 10s."

However, while some residents were appearing in court as defendants, others were trying to avoid appearing as jurors.

"A Petty Session was held for the revision of jury lists, when Henry Hodges and Samuel Hodges of Chedzoy, objected to their names being inserted on the grounds that they were not householders. It appeared on enquiry that they were partners with their father in a farm at Chedzoy and their names were therefore included."

Disorderly conduct featured in two cases which came before the Bridgwater County Police Court in late 1864 and early 1865.

"John Raing was charged by Mary Stone with an assault committed on her at Chedzoy."

This may have been a misprint for John Rainey, aged 20, a carpenter. Mary Stone was 50 years old and the wife of a butcher. Both were born in Chedzoy.

"The defendant and some other young men were drunk on the night of 5th inst. and complainant went out and requested them to go away. They refused and a tussle ensued, in which the complainant received the blows complained of. The defendant was fined 10s. and costs."

In the second case

"Thomas Wilkins of Chedzoy was charged by Edwin Fry with an assault. There was a cross-summons in which Fry was similarly charged by Henry Hodges. ... It appears that Fry had hired a threshing-machine, which was afterwards engaged by Hodges, who sent his servant, Wilkins, to fetch it. Wilkins complained that the machine was in an awkward place to get out, and used some rough language, in consequence of which a quarrel arose, and blows were exchanged. The magistrates, after a patient hearing, dismissed both cases."

Failure to keep livestock under proper control resulted in various prosecutions over the years. The earliest recorded in the Bridgwater Mercury was in June 1865 when

"Elizabeth and Samuel Hodges were fined 5s. and costs for allowing a cow to stray on the public highway at Chedzoy."

At one time there was a toll gate on Bath Road, somewhere near the point where the motorway bridge now stands. In 1865 and 1866 two cases in relation to this were reported in the

Bridgwater Mercury's County Police Court columns.

"James Pitman, a carter, was charged with defrauding the toll collector at Chedzoy turnpike-gate. - On the particular day which was named in the information, defendant passed through the gateway, which is kept by one William Atwood, with a horse. Shortly afterwards a waggon upon which was some harness passed through, and suspecting that it was intended to attach the horse that had previously passed to the waggon, which would have increased the toll, he sent a person to watch it and it was found that after the waggon had passed some distance the other horse was attached to it. The defendant admitted that the horse was put to the waggon but denied it was done by him. The collector said that parties had claimed to pass through the gate this way, and his wish was to show that it could not be done. - The defendant was ordered to pay the toll and expenses."

"James Reeves was charged with unlawfully claiming exemption from toll, at the Attwood turnpike gate in Chedzoy."

Note the different spelling of his surname.

"Reeves was defended by Mr. Reed. It appeared that on Sunday night ... the defendant was returning to Bridgwater in a gig with one or two friends, when he went laughingly past the gate without paying, his reason being that the toll-man owed him 6d. on another occasion.
The Bench fined him the mitigated penalty of 5s. and costs."

Each year the scrapings from the roads, gutters, ditches and watercourses within the parish were sold. In March 1866 the parish records noted,

"Lot 1: Mr. Gillett - from end of Chedzoy Lane to Slape Cross - 10s. Lot 2: Mr. Hodges - Slape Cross to Cross Tree, Pig Lane, etc. - £1 8s. Lot 3: Mr. Fry - church gate to Parchey Bridge - 15s. Lot 4: Mr. Hodges - from Mr. Derrick's to New Cut - 13s. The road earth from the church to Mr. Derrick's and Parsonage Lane was reserved for the purposes of the Parish."

Other minor offences continued to take place. In May 1866

"Elisha Day and John Stone were summoned for having at Chedzoy ... wilfully committed certain damage to certain beans and vetches growing on enclosed land, the property of John Dawbin. Mr. Robert Dawbin, a farmer of Chilton Polden, and a brother of the complainant, proved that he saw defendants trespassing on the land, and said the amount of damage was fixed at 2s. 6d. He spoke to the defendants at the time and they told him they were going to the woods to look for some weed called 'Senegal.' Fined 1s. each and costs."

Two months later

"Thomas Broomfield was summoned by George Giles for allowing a horse to stray on the highway in the parish of Chedzoy. ... Superintendent Jeffs stated that in consequence of the horse in question laying on the highway for some time, several accidents had occurred. - The defendant was fined 5s. and the expenses."

Later in 1866

"James Parsons (a 59 year old cordwainer, i.e. shoe maker) was summoned by the overseers for Chedzoy for the non-payment of 2s. 3d. poor-rate. He pleaded poverty, but Mr. Samuel Hodges, one of the overseers, asserted that he was able to pay, and that he spent a great deal of money on drink. Payment was ordered."

Presumably, he didn't pay his rent either as in January 1868,

"James Parsons was summoned, but did not appear, to show cause why he should not quit possession of a cottage and garden belonging to Robert Boon, situate at Chedzoy. The notices having been proved, the usual order for ejectment was made."

In June 1867 a disturbance took place on licensed premises in the village, but whereabouts is unclear.

"Elika Day (presumably an error for Elisha Day, aged 21), a labourer, was summoned for assaulting John Stone at Chedzoy on 4th May. The defendant was also charged with having assaulted Percival Bell and done wilful damage to a door to the extent of 2s. 6d. Stone said that after leaving work he went to Mr. Bell's public house to have some cider when the defendant came into the room and took up his cup to drink. He (complainant) said, 'That is mine,' and tried to take it from him, when defendant 'up with his fist and knocked him down.' Mr. Bell deposed that after the above occurrence he told defendant that he should have no nonsense in his house, and the defendant then knocked him backwards, and also split open a panel of a door. - Defendant denied the above statements, and said they fell out about the reckoning of some money, and he was badly served, being beaten with a poker and tongs. The Bench considered the charges proved and fined the defendant £1 and the costs in each case, in addition to the damage done to the door; in default, defendant went to prison for a month."

It seems that people were frequently prepared to sue their neighbours in relation to disputes: numerous cases heard by the County Court in Bridgwater were reported, sometimes with a note as to how many cases were listed on a particular day. This could be as high as 300, but most were settled out of court or uncontested. Only a few cases were reported in detail, and occasionally Chedzoy cases were featured.

"Elias Potter v. George Conduit."

Elias Potter would have been 88 at this time; George Conduit was 26.

"The plaintiff, a farmer, living at Chedzoy, claimed of the defendant, a labourer, in the employ of the Rev. W. Mullins (sic), vicar of that parish, the sum of £5 for damage sustained by the plaintiff in consequence of the alleged poisoning of his sheep-dog by the defendant. Mrs. Potter, wife of the plaintiff, said on 2nd December last the defendant came to her house shortly after two o'clock in the afternoon, and asked for some peas that had been ordered. ... He then went away and soon afterwards witness heard the dog growl. On looking out of the back door ... she saw the defendant giving the dog something to eat out of his hand. ... She went to the dog and saw that it was licking its mouth. She tried to open its mouth, but it desisted, fearing it would bite her. ... She went to the dairy to work and afterwards hearing a 'rattle' in the back kitchen, she called out to the dog, 'Come out, you.' - His Honour: What you said to the dog is not evidence. (Laughter.) Witness said on going into the kitchen, she saw the dog with its head on the fire. It was all but dead then, and only breathed once or twice afterwards. Mr. Joseph Reeves, veterinary surgeon, said he made a post-mortem examination of the dog, and found inflammatory action of the coats of the stomach. The only contents of the stomach was a little meal, and from its condition witness concluded that the dog was poisoned. ...He was of the opinion that the poison was strychnine or something of the sort used for the destruction of vermin. ...His Honour said the case was nothing more than one of suspicion. It might be that the dog had taken poison before the defendant's visit to the house, for it had not been shown where the dog had previously been. Moreover, there was no ground for supposing the defendant had any provocation. Judgement was given for the defendant."

Premature death was a frequent occurrence. In March 1868 the Bridgwater Mercury reported the following case.

"An inquest was held in [Chedzoy] on Thursday last before Mr. W.W. Munckton, Esq., on the body of an illegitimate male child of Jane Stone, a girl of only about 16 years of age, formerly in the service of Mr. Derrick. The girl was confined in Bridgwater Union-house about three months ago, since which she had been living in this village with her father and stepmother. According to the evidence, on the previous Friday the child was suddenly taken ill, but soon recovered and until Monday morning appeared in its usual health. On that day the mother of the child sent for Mrs. Rainey, a neighbour, stating that it was ill or dying. On the arrival of Mrs. Rainey it was found dead in its mother's arms. A post-mortem examination, by direction of the coroner, was made by Mr. Richard Axford, of Bridgwater, who deposed that he found the stomach and intestines entirely empty, the child being also in an emaciated condition. From certain appearances, which he described in detail, he was of the opinion that the child suffered from chronic disease of the brain, which resulted in its death. Verdict accordingly."

Some village residents were guilty of what, today, would be regarded as sharp practice, as this Bridgwater County Court case from April 1868 demonstrates.

"Jane Derrick v. William Potter. The plaintiff, represented by Mr. Reed, is a widow, living at Chedzoy, and she sued as executrix of her husband, the defendant, late of Chedzoy, but now residing at 8 St. Anne's-road, Notting-hill, London (sic), for the sum of £10 7s., the value of some sheep sold to the defendant in June 1862. Mr. James Trevor, for the defendant, set up a plea of infancy (i.e., that he was under 21 years of age), and called Mr. James Potter, father of the defendant, who swore that the latter was born on February 3rd 1842. He showed an entry to that effect in a book, which, he said, he made a few days afterwards, and likewise produced a certificate of baptism in May 1842. - Mr. Reed explained as the reason why the summons had not been taken out before, that the defendant, having again sold the sheep soon afterwards, had absconded. - His Honour said there was no doubt about the plea of infancy being proved; but it was a scandalous thing that the defendant's father should allow his son to trade at his house, and then run away, and afterwards set up such a plea. Judgement for the defendant. His Honour refused to allow the costs."

A Friendly Society had been established in the village and in June 1868 this report appeared in the Bridgwater Mercury.

"On Thursday morning members of the Chedzoy Friendly Society celebrated their sixth anniversary. ... The members and stewards met at ten o'clock and, headed by the Westonzoyland band, paraded the village; but there was no service at the church [as the Rector was ill]. They were, therefore, able to extend their walk to East Bower, where they found a supply of cider, &c., which by this time was needed. They returned via Fowlers Plot, calling at different farm houses, and ultimately reached the Crown Inn, where a capital lunch awaited them." Various toasts were drunk. "Mr. Winter returned thanks on behalf of the treasurer and himself and availed himself of the opportunity to give the members some good advice. He persuaded them to be merry and wise, and resume their daily occupations the next morning, so letting it be known that the club day was a day of rejoicing and not drunkenness. ... The utmost good feeling and harmony prevailed throughout the day. In the evening various outdoor amusements were indulged in." Speaking in 1955 Mr. B.T. Jeanes recalled that his father, Thomas Jeanes (1861-1932), always carried a wooden staff surmounted with the 'Sick Club brass' of a lion surmounted by a crown, the brass still being in the family's possession.

Two amusing reports appeared in the court columns of the local paper in the summer of 1868.

"Henry Green was summoned for assaulting Charles Bell at Chedzoy on 6th June. The complainant and defendant are both young boys. - The former said he was on Mr. Potter's ground where he saw the defendant who called him a 'mackerel.' He retorted by calling the defendant 'spring bottom' (laughter); whereupon the latter struck him heavily on the shoulder and other places, which were much bruised, with the stock of a gun. - Defendant said that complainant flung stones at him, and called him a 'ring-tailed monkey.'

(Laughter.) The Bench fined the defendant 1s. and costs."

"Henry Hayes, of Huntspill, was summoned for having at Chedzoy caused to be erected a steam engine within the distance of 25 yards from the highway. Defendant pleaded ignorance of the law, which was explained to him. He was told that if his threshing-machine had been screened from the road he would not be liable. - Superintendent Jeffs explained that Sir Alfred Slade was driving along at that time, that his horse took fright, and that Sir Alfred was nearly upset. - The chairman said it was necessary to inflict a fine in this case, in order to show defendant, and through him the public, that this could not be done with impunity. They ordered defendant to pay 10s. and costs."

One can't help but wonder if a prosecution would have followed had the owner of the horse been some lesser mortal than Sir Alfred Slade (1834-1890) who was Receiver General for the Inland Revenue in the Bridgwater area.

Also in the summer of 1868, notices were published in the Bridgwater Mercury to the effect that it was intended to carry out improvements to King's Sedgemoor Drain at a cost of over £1,000. The river was to be deepened from Greylake Fosse Bridge to Bawdrip Bridge and various sections, including one at Parchey Bridge, were to be widened.

In November 1868 a disturbance of a different kind probably took place in the village: at least, the disturbance was felt over a wide area and was reported in the Bridgwater Mercury.

"On Friday night, between half past ten and quarter to eleven o'clock, a shock of an earthquake was experienced in [Bridgwater] and the neighbourhood, which caused considerable alarm. All those who felt the shock concur in stating that there was a slight but perceptible trembling of the earth; windows were rattled, as also was crockery, &c., and bells were set ringing. The shock was preceded or accompanied by a low rumbling sound resembling distant thunder, or the passage of a heavily loaded waggon along the street. At Wembdon, Chilton, North Petherton, Stowey, Catcott, &c. the shock was felt in a like manner. ... Throughout the whole of the West of England, the shock was distinctly felt."

In 1846 "Your Inquirer" had complained about the sale of underweight loaves of bread. It seems that the problem still persisted in 1869. In November that year the Bridgwater Mercury reported

"Frank Morris, baker, was charged with delivering bread and neglecting to provide a beam and scales with proper weights at Chedzoy. - Superintendent Jeffs, inspector of weights and measures, said he found the boy in charge of a bread cart, which had no scales. - In answer to the Bench, he added there had been complaints at Chedzoy for a considerable time of short weight. - Defendant said he always gave his servants instructions to take out scales and weights. He was fined 20s., including costs."

Different food was the subject of a case reported the following month.

"Benjamin Yarde was charged with stealing apples, the property of Robert Boon. The prosecutor, a farmer, in Chedzoy Lane, said that whilst in his field he saw a person standing at the gate. On going towards him he ran away. Witness then went to a part of the field where he had a heap of apples, and saw the prisoner picking up some of them. His pockets, a handkerchief and a small bag were full of apples, the value of them being 1s. 6d. He took the defendant to his house, where he told him if he had only just put a few apples in his pocket he would have let him take them, but he was too covetous. Defendant pleaded guilty and was sentenced to 14 days' hard labour."

The Fracas in Chedzoy Church

It was not only villagers' livestock which caused problems, but also that belonging to travellers. In July 1870 the Bridgwater Mercury reported

"Jane Joles and Henry and Joseph Joles, gipsies, were severally charged with permitting horses, their respective property, to stray on the highway at Chedzoy, and were fined 1s. each and costs."

The social life of the village featured in the local paper in August.

"On Thursday last the most esteemed rector (Rev. G.O. Mullins) (sic) gave the members of the Chedzoy church choir their annual 'outing.' They were conveyed in a brake, supplied by Mr. Ricks of Bridgwater, to Weston-Super-Mare where they did ample justice to an excellent dinner. They then dispersed and after enjoying themselves in a variety of ways partook of tea."

Some disagreements over work were still being dealt with by the magistrates' court.

"BREACH OF CONTRACT. George Lee and Joseph Stone were summoned for unlawfully leaving the service of Mr. Robert Boon at Chedzoy [Lane]. It was proved that defendants left before the completion of certain work they undertook to perform, and complainant alleged he had been damaged to the extent of £5 in consequence. It appeared that Stone had done about half of the work, but that Lee had not done any. The case against Stone was dismissed; Lee was fined £1 and costs."

The Elementary Education Act was passed in 1870. On 20th October that year

"At a vestry meeting duly convened and held in the

School Room for the purposes of 'taking into consideration how far it may be possible to adapt the existing Parish School to the requirements of the Elementary Education Act or whether the Parish would be prepared to establish a rate aided school.' After a lengthened conversation upon the subject it was unanimously resolved to await the Government Inspector's visit or until some further information as to the working of the Act and its requirements was obtained."

Tradesmen in the village continued to fall foul of regulations. In February 1871 it was reported that

"James Gilbert, grocer, of Chedzoy, was summoned by Superintendent Jeffs, Inspector of Weights and Measures, for having in his possession three weights, two of which were unstamped, and the other light. Defendant said he bought the weights about three years ago when they were new. He was fined £1 and costs."

A diary kept by Francis Lovibond (born 1825) offers and insight into the hard times in which he lived. He made several entries in relation to illness and death.

"June 13th 1871, Henry Stone died and buried the 17th aged 33 years of Small Pox. He died at Chedzoy Lane and was brought to be buried in Chedzoy churchyard. He was not carried in the church. July 1st 1871, Rose Stone, daughter of the above Henry Stone, died and buried July 4th aged 4 years of the same disease. She was not carried in church. June 15th, John Day died from an injury he inflicted on himself on the 30th May 1872. An inquest was held at the Crown Inn, Chedzoy by Mr. P. Munckton, Esq., when a verdict of temporary insanity was returned June 18th. He was buried June 22nd aged 70 years at Chedzoy".

Hard times, indeed, but Francis Lovibond also recorded other events.

"July 4th 1871, Joseph Jeanes' house known as Tuttons in Ward Lane, Chedzoy was sold by Mr. Lilly at the Crown Inn, Chedzoy kept by John Palfrey for the sum of £148 0s. 0d. Edwin Fry bought it."

Another villager was before the court in April 1872 when

"George Stone, farm labourer, of Chedzoy, was summoned for refusing to maintain his two children, who are chargeable to the Bridgwater Union. ... It appears that one of the daughters was 22 years of age, and that the defendant was not, therefore, liable for her maintenance. - Defendant agreed to pay 1s. per week for the other; an order was made for payment of that sum."

In June 1872 it was reported in the Bridgwater Mercury that

"The members of the Chedzoy Friendly Society, between 50 and 60 in number, celebrated its [10th] anniversary on Tuesday. In the morning a procession, headed by the band of the 26th S.R.C., paraded the streets of the village. After attending Divine service at the parish church ... the members partook of a substantial dinner at the Crown Inn. ... After the loyal toasts ... Mr. John Cary said he did not think the society would have lasted so long if the treasurer had not stuck to it as he had. ... The chairman said ... it was the worst year he had known; but if they looked at it carefully it was not so unsatisfactory as one might imagine considering the amount received to put to the club. When the club was established it was not to put money in their pockets, but to provide against sickness and to make some provision for the survivors of those who died. They gladly welcomed that festive day in their quiet village as the anniversary of the club formed to help each other, and there was no prouder moment than for a labouring man to be able to say, after recovering from sickness, that he had been able to maintain his family without parish relief."

The accounts were then detailed.

"Receipts in hand from last year, £7 7s. 5d.; members quarterly payments, £50 15s.; subscriptions, £4 7s. 6d.; total £62 9s. 11d. Expenditure: surgeon, £8 2s.; band £4; clerk's dinner, 2s. 6d.; printing 4s.; paid sick members and funeral expenses, £20 14s.; to balance £29 7s. 5d.; total £62 9s. 11d. The funds were invested as follows: in savings bank, £90 13s. 6d.; cash in hand, £6 7s. 5d., total £97 0s. 11d."

Controversy struck the village in March 1873. Below the village name the Bridgwater Mercury reported

"A correspondent informs us that on Sunday rather discreditable proceedings took place in the parish church, both morning and evening. It appears that one of the pews formerly occupied by Mr. Richard Denning has lately, in the absence of the latter, been used occasionally by another parishioner - Mr. Parfitt. On Sunday morning Mr. Charles Denning (son of Mr. R. Denning) accompanied his sister to church and seated themselves in what they regarded as their father's pew, whereupon, Mr. W.G. Winter, one of the churchwardens, ordered them to leave, and Denning declining to do so was, it is asserted, dragged out by force, his sister voluntarily moving into Mr. Carey's pew. At the evening service, young Denning and his two sisters again took possession of the pew in question, and just as the service was about to commence, Mr. Winter again ordered them to leave. Denning refused, and Mr. Winter again caught hold of him, and a violent struggle ensued, in the course of which a portion of the seat was broken, and Denning's clothes torn. After being dragged out of the pew, Denning left the church, accompanied by several members of the congregation, his sisters remaining behind. The affair is reported to have caused some excitement in the parish."

This clearly was a matter which was going to rumble on for some time. The following week a letter from Mr. Winter was published in the correspondence column of the Mercury under the heading THE FRACAS IN CHEDZOY CHURCH.

"Sir, Herewith I beg to forward a copy of a letter addressed to the Churchwardens of Chedzoy, from the venerable the Archdeacon at Taunton. Will you kindly favour me by inserting the same in your next publication? - and oblige by so doing.
Your obedient servant, George Winter, Churchwarden.
Chedzoy, 8th March 1873."

Following which:
East Brent, Highbridge, March 5th 1873.
Gentlemen,
Your Rector, the Rev. G. Mullens, had been with me this morning and has given me the particulars of a case of resistance to your lawful authority on Sunday last, 2nd inst., in the church at Chedzoy. It appears that you directed, as your office requires, a resident parishioner, Mr. Parfitt, to be placed with his family in certain vacant sittings in the nave. It appears further that notice was duly given, signed by both Churchwardens, to a certain other parishioner, that the sittings in question were to be occupied by Mr. Parfitt and his family.

"That after such notice given the parishioner upon whom it was served did, nevertheless, both at morning and evening service, occupy by two members of his family in the morning, and by three in the evening, the sittings in question. That in the morning the parish Churchwardens removed the persons so occupying. That in the evening the persons so occupying, again being desired by the parish Churchwardens to remove, one of them refused with violent words and actions. There is no room to doubt that all that has been done on the part of the Churchwardens has been properly and legally done, and without any force but such as was made necessary by resistance to the law. It appears that the matter is about to come before the magistrates. I beg that this letter may be produced in court.
I am, Gentlemen, your faithful servant,
George A. Denison, Archdeacon."

As was mentioned in the Archdeacon's letter, the matter came before the County Magistrates' Court the following week, occupying $2^1/_2$ full columns of the Mercury under the headline DISPUTED POSSESSION OF A PEW IN CHEDZOY CHURCH. Although somewhat lengthy, the report deserves repetition almost in its entirely as several villagers are mentioned.

"Charles Denning, son of Mr. Richard Denning, farmer, of Chedzoy, was summoned for riotous and violent behaviour in the parish church of Chedzoy on Sunday, the 2nd March; and in a cross-summons Mr. George Winter, churchwarden, was charged with assaulting Charles Denning and Rhoda Denning, his sister, at the same time and place. Mr. Gabriel Poole appeared for Mr. Winter, the churchwarden, and Mr. Cook represented Mr. Denning. The case excited considerable interest, and the court was crowded. After some conversation between the advocates on either side and the magistrates, it was agreed that all three cases should be heard at the same time.

"Mr. Poole said that the case involved the right of sitting in a certain pew in Chedzoy Church. Mr. Winter, the churchwarden, alleging that Charles Denning (20) was guilty of riotous and violent conduct on the 2nd March, in taking possession of a pew which had been assigned to another person, and resisting his removal therefrom when Mr. Winter, in the exercise of this duty as churchwarden, bound thereby to maintain order, endeavoured to remove him without unnecessary violence. Mr. Winter was charged with assaulting the defendant, and also Rhoda Denning, his sister (whom he believed Mr. Winter did not touch at all), and the whole question would depend on this, viz., whether Mr. Winter acted in the exercise of his authority, and with due discretion - whether, in fact, he was justified in removing Mr. Denning from the seat; and if so, whether he used any unnecessary violence.

"Mr. Poole then stated the facts of the case as detailed in the evidence, after which he said there could be no doubt that the power of assigning seats in the church was vested in the Bishop, and that the churchwardens were his officers, and that they, acting under the advice of the minister, had the power, and it was their duty, to assign pews for the accommodation of the several inhabitants of the parish, at their discretion. The object of taking out this summons was not to inflict a fine or punishment of any kind whatever, but to elicit an expression of opinion from the Bench as to the conduct of the defendant, and to correct a notion which seemed to exist in the parish that when a sitting was once assigned to the occupier of a farm any subsequent occupier of the same farm had a right to that seat without the sanction of the churchwardens. After hearing the evidence, he hoped the magistrates would say it was perfectly clear that, unless there was a faculty - and he conceived there was no such claim in this case - the churchwardens had a right to assign the seats in any way they pleased.

"Mr. Poole proceeded to support his argument by reading quotations from 'Prideaux on the Duties of Churchwardens' and 'Blant's Church Law,' revised by Dr.Phillimore, to prove, first that all pews in a church were prima facie at the disposal of the churchwardens as the parochial officers of the ordinary; next, that it was the duty of the churchwardens to make all the seats available as they could, for the accommodation of the parishioners, having regard, in the arrangement, to their respective stations and conditions; and that in order to accomplish this the churchwardens might 'place or displace at pleasure' taking care not to exercise such authority indiscreetly or capriciously. Mr. Poole also pointed out that 'if anyone felt aggrieved by the conduct of the churchwardens he might cite them to show, in the ecclesiastical court, why they had so seated him or omitted to seat him.' With regard to the alleged assaults, his contentions were that Mr. Winter did not, in ejecting Mr. Denning from the pew, as was his duty, use unnecessary violence; and, in the next place, he laid it down, as a general principle, from 'Stone's Justice Manual,' that if a man committed an assault in the exercise of a right or supposed right, and the magistrates were satisfied that he did so act, their summary jurisdiction was outsted.

"Mr. Poole then called Mr. George Winter (50), who deposed that he lived in the parish of Chedzoy, and was the parochial churchwarden. He was present in the church on the 2nd March, both at the morning and evening service, and knew the seat in front of the reading-desk . It was formerly assigned to Mr. [Thomas] Hurford, who left the parish about two years ago. Mr. Richard Denning (41) came to live in the parish in 1869, and a seat in the church was assigned to him when he came - the third seat in the south transept. His family were not frequent attendants; they were Dissenters (Non-conformists). - [Mr. Cook remarked that he did not see the relevancy of this point.] When Mr. Parfitt came to the parish at Michaelmas he and his family were put into the seat in front of the reading-desk by the witness as churchwarden. Understanding that members of Mr. Denning's family occupied this seat on the Sunday previous to the 28th of February, a notice was addressed to Mr. Denning, of which the following was a copy:

Chedzoy, 28th Feb., 1873

Sir, In consequence of a report having reached us that your family attended Divine Service at Chedzoy church on Sunday, evening last, and sat in the front seat of the nave opposite the reading-desk, which seat has been regularly occupied by Mr. and Mrs. Parfitt since September last, we feel it is our duty to inform you that the one intended for you and your family is the third seat in the south transept, which the sexton will be glad to point out to any of your household if they will kindly apply to him when next they attend the church; and in order to prevent any unpleasant occurrence for the future we must beg you to accept this intimation, and remain, Sir, yours, &c.,
GEORGE WINTER and WILLIAM CARY, churchwardens.

"On the following day witness saw Mr. Denning, who asked him why he had sent him such an insulting letter, and who signed Mr. Cary's name to it. Witness said he saw Mr. Cary sign his own name. On Sunday morning, the 2nd of March, witness was standing in the church porch, and, seeing Charles Denning, the defendant, and his sister enter the church, he said to him that he would place him in his seat. Witness then walked to the third seat in the south transept and, placing his hand on it, said, 'Here is your seat.' Charles Denning, however, walked to the seat in front of the reading-desk, and seated himself there with his sister. Witness went to him and said, 'You must leave this place,' and defendant replies that he should not. Witness said, 'Then you will excuse me if I eject you.' and taking hold of him by the coat he removed him from the seat, but without using more violence than was necessary. Defendant resisted, but not violently. Addressing Miss Rhoda Denning (18), sister of the defendant, witness said, 'I must trouble you to move also.' He put his hand under her arm, and she at once rose and left, going into Mr. Cary's pew. He used no violence at all towards her. - By Mr. Evered (one of the magistrates): The cushions in the seat belonged to Mr. Parfitt. He (witness) adjusted the cushions, and afterwards Mr. Parfitt and members of his family came, and occupied the pew.

"In the evening witness stood in the porch until the service commenced, and he then went into his own seat. Just afterwards he saw Charles Denning coming up the aisle, preceded by a young friend of his and his two sisters. Witness stepped out from his seat with the intention of preventing their taking the seat in front of the reading-desk, but Mr. [Thomas] Barnstable (34) stood in the way. Denning then made a quick step into the disputed seat (which was, by implication, unoccupied) and, shaking his hat at the witness said, 'Remove me if your dare,' or 'Turn me out if you dare,' witness could not say which. The rector (Mr. Mullens) was then going through the Exhortation. Witness asked Mr. Denning several times to move, and he said he would not. Mr. Mullens then called upon the churchwardens to maintain order.

"Witness spoke to Denning two or three times, in an undertone, but he still refused to leave, and witness then took him by the coat to pull him out. Defendant placed his hands on the seat and resisted. His sisters moved out at the other end. Witness then stepped into the pew, caught hold of the defendant and carried him out. Defendant resisted, and witness used no more violence than was necessary to eject him. Denning then left the church, and his sisters went into Mr. Cary's pew. Mr. and Mrs. Parfitt came up the aisle at the time of the occurrence and went into another seat.

"Cross-examined: Witness had lived at Chedzoy ever since 1859. Fowler's Plot, occupied by Mr. Denning, comprised two farms, to the occupiers of each of which a seat was allotted. When there was an alteration of pews, nine or ten years ago, he believed the third seat in the south transept was assigned to one of the farms, and the disputed pew to the farm now in the occupation of Mr. Denning, the defendant's father. Mr. Hurford, who previously occupied that farm, was accustomed to use the disputed pew. When the alteration of the pews took place Mr. Denning was not resident in the parish. Up to the moment of writing the letter on the 28th February last no notices, verbal or otherwise, had been given to Mr. Denning that the disputed pew was to be dealt with in any particular way; and that was consequently the first notice to him that it had been assigned to Mr. Parfitt. He saw Mr. Denning the next day, 1st March, and he accused him (witness) of being on his farm trespassing in pursuit of rabbits, and asked him if he had a gun licence. It was after that that Mr. Denning told him he considered the letter was insulting. He (witness) was not aware that he had torn out any buttons, either from young Denning's waistcoat or his shirt collar. A good many people went out of the church with Denning. Mr. Cary, his brother churchwarden, had somewhat disagreed with him in the course he had taken.

Mr. Cook: Has he not told you that it ought not to have been done?

Witness: I dare say he did, I don't remember his words. -

Mr. Cook: Was that the effect of it?

Witness: He wished it had not been done.

Mr. Cook: Did he also tell you that he considered Mr. Denning was entitled to the pew?

Witness: I don't remember his telling me that.

Mr. Cook: Did you go up to the Archdeacon?

Witness: No.

Mr. Cook: But you had the honour of receiving a letter from him?

Witness: Mr. Cary had the letter; it was addressed to the churchwardens, and delivered to him by the postman.

Mr. Cook: Is this your letter addressed to the Bridgwater Mercury?

Witness: Yes, sir.

Mr. Cook: Your own composition?

Witness: Yes.

Mr. Cook characterised it as a most improper proceeding for a churchwarden, under such circumstances, on receiving a letter from Archdeacon Denison on the subject, rushing into print with it for no other apparent reason than that of prejudicing the public mind.

Mr. Poole: It was merely a reply to a note he had addressed to his superior officer asking if he had done right.

"In re-examination by Mr. Poole the witness added that the assignment of the pews when they were altered was made by the two churchwardens - himself and Mr. Benjamin Tazewell - and the seats were assigned, not to the farms, but to the occupiers. He had never intimated to Mr. Denning that he might use the disputed pew.

By the Chairman: Since October last Mr. Parfitt had occupied the disputed pew, and had sat in it almost every Sunday, and his possession of it was never disturbed until the Sunday preceding the 28th February.

"Rev. G.O. Mullens (43) deposed that he was the rector of Chedzoy. He was not present in the church at the time of the occurrence spoken of in the morning. At the evening service, when he had just commenced the Exhortation, he saw the defendant, Mr. Charles Denning, coming up the south aisle, and his sisters up the centre aisle. The defendant rushed into the seat immediately in front of the reading-desk and shook his hat, or 'wide-awake.' at Mr. Winter, and witness heard the words, 'Dare you,' or 'I dare you.' He (witness) at once stopped the service, and called on the churchwardens to keep order. Mr. Winter stepped out of his seat, and some conversation took place between him and the defendant. Witness heard Mr. Winter say, 'You must come out' once or twice. There was a scuffle, resulting in the ejection of Mr. Denning by the churchwarden.

"Some thirty or forty people left the church, and the service proceeded without further interruption. Mr. Winter did not use more violence than was necessary. A few years back a portion of the church was reseated, and a re-appropriation of the seats took place, each occupier being allotted one by the churchwardens. That was nine years ago. Mr. Denning had only been there four years, and when he came he was allotted the third seat in the south transept. The members of his family had only come to the church three or four times since, and with one exception they had always occupied the seat assigned to them. That exception was about a year since, when Mr. Charles Denning sat in the disputed seat. It was then, in fact, a vacant seat. Mr. Parfitt had had undisturbed possession of it since the 29th October until the 23rd February last. No violence was used towards the Misses Denning. Cross-examined: Mr. Denning was not the first to leave the church, by a score or more. He had been in the parish seventeen years. When Mr. Hurford was in the occupation of the same farm as Mr. Denning now held he occupied the disputed pew. - By Mr. Broadmead (another magistrate): In consequence of the disturbance he had to stop the service for two minutes in the evening.

"Mr. Edward Parfitt said he went to reside at Chedzoy, in October last, and was first shown into the disputed pew by the sexton. He afterwards sent some cushions and books to the church, and they were placed in that pew for him. He had been to church every Sunday since, and was not disturbed in the occupation of it until the evening of the 23rd February. He saw young Denning ejected from the seat on the evening in question by Mr. Winter, who did not use more violence than was necessary. Denning resisted violently.

"Edward Nooks, carpenter (this should be Edward Noakes, aged 43), deposed that on the evening in question he saw the defendant after entering the disputed pew wave his hat to Mr. Winter. He shook his hat defiantly. Mr. Winter did not use more force than was necessary to eject him.

"Mr. Cook addressing the Bench said the defendant considered that he had a perfect defence to the charge. In cross-examination two or three facts had been elicited which he (Mr. Cook) thought must influence the magistrates in their determination, because, according to the authorities, if it could be shown that from time immemorial a particular pew had been allotted to a tenant, for the time being, of a particular house, that was sufficient to establish a prescriptive right to use that pew. He was prepared to admit, however, that it was not part of their duty to determine the legal question as to the prescriptive right, which, if thought necessary must be determined in a superior court. He submitted that in this case there had been, on the part of the defendant, only a fair and reasonable exercise of what he believed to be a right to go into the disputed pew, which, it had been admitted, was assigned to the occupier of a particular farm which his father occupied. The former occupier (Mr. Hurford) constantly used this pew, and since Mr. Denning had changed his residence and had lived in this farm he or members of his family had used that seat, and that seat only; and it was, he contended, a matter of perfect indifference whether a man, or any member of his family, went to church once on a Sunday or only once a year for the maintenance of that right.

"With regard to the duties of churchwardens, he laid it down as a proposition of law that churchwardens had no right whatever at their caprice and will to remove persons from one pew on one day and from another pew on another day, and that they could not interfere with rights which were prescriptive, such as was claimed in this instance. Proceeding to deal with the charge preferred against the defendant of 'riotous and violent' behaviour in the church, Mr. Cook contended that these words implied some voluntary or wilful and intentional conduct on the part of the person accused; and he asked, if that was the proper definition of those words, whether, according to the evidence, Mr. Denning had been guilty in such a sense of the offence with which he was charged. He was prepared to show that the defendant neither by word or deed was guilty of anything which he could be found fault with until he was molested by the churchwardens; that he did not, as alleged, shake his hat or utter the words, 'I dare,' or any words whatever, and therefore, that the witnesses on the other side must be mistaken with regard to this. He should show, moreover, that Mr. Winter was guilty of unnecessary violence. In the 'Solicitors' Journal and Weekly Reporter' he found a case reported of an action before Mr. Serjeant Wheeler in the county court, in which the plaintiff claimed £50 as damages for being disturbed in the enjoyment of his alleged right to a pew in his parish church, and his Honour, in giving judgement, remarked that it was distinctly stated in 'Addison on Torts' that 'churchwardens are not justified in dispossessing anyone without giving notice of their intention, and offering an opportunity and explanation' - an opportunity which Mr. Cook submitted had not in this case been afforded.

"Mr. Poole submitted that this was not a case in point, inasmuch as the plaintiff in the action had a seat assigned to him, which the defendant in the present case had not. Mr. Cook contended that his client had a prescriptive right, and that the disputed pew was assigned to the occupier of the farm which he rented and was in occupation of. He submitted, therefore, that the quotation was applicable. Another authority he would quote was 'Heales on Church Seats,' in which it was stated that churchwardens, in exercising their duty, must act with discretion, and with due regard to any legal or equitable title. In conclusion Mr. Cook said he admitted, most fully, that Mr. Denning was a Dissenter, although he did not think the fact of his being so (which Mr. Poole seems to make so much of) had anything whatever to do with the case, and it ought not, therefore, to have been mentioned. Mr. Poole: I only mentioned it in order to show why he was not in the habit of attending the church.

"Mr. Cook again alluded to the conduct of Mr. Winter in sending the letter and enclosure for publication in the Bridgwater Mercury, which, he said, circulated to the extent of thousands in that neighbourhood, and remarked that such conduct on the part of a suitor in one of the superior courts would probably be followed by a fine or imprisonment. He hoped, however, that the letter of Archdeacon Denison would not have any influence. Mr. Poole observed that it was a very harmless letter.

"Mr. Cook having made some remarks in reference to the charges of assault, called the following witnesses:

Rhoda Denning said she accompanied her brother (the defendant in the last case) to church on the morning of the 2nd March. They went into the seat in front of the reading-desk. Mr. Winter asked him to come out, and her brother said he had a right there. Mr. Winter said he would take him out by force, and then caught hold of him and pulled him out. In the evening she and her sister accompanied her brother to the church. He did not shake his hat at Mr. Winter or say 'I dare you' or anything to that effect. He did not, in fact, say a word until Mr. Winter went up to him and said he must come out. Her brother then said he had a right there. Mr. Winter said he would take him out by force, and her brother said he would come out by and bye. Mr. Winter then caught him by the collar, and used considerable violence.

Mr. Poole: Your brother resisted?

Witness: Yes.

Mr. Poole: And Mr. Winter used enough violence to overcome that resistance?

Witness: Yes.

Mr. Cook: Did he use more than enough?

Witness: Yes. (Laughter.)

The Chairman: How long have you sat in this pew? - Witness: Occasionally ever since we have lived in the house.

The Chairman: How many times do you think you've been there?

I don't know.

Mr. Broadmead: Half a dozen times?

I don't know.

The Chairman: Have you ever been there before the 23rd February last?

I can't tell.

"Harriet Denning (17), sister of the last witness, gave almost precisely similar evidence. - In cross-examination she said before going to the church she had seen the notice addressed to her father by the churchwardens and knew that her brother and sister were forbidden the pew in the morning. She did not go in the evening on purpose to defy Mr. Winter, or 'out of spite,' but to 'hear Mr. Mullens.' (Laughter.)

"John Cary (23), son of Mr. Cary, deposed that on the evening in question he saw Mr. Winter go to young Denning just as he sat down, and afterwards pull him out as hard as he could, and very violently. The effect of what Mr. Winter did was to disturb Divine service, and many persons at once left the church. He did not see Mr. Denning wave or shake his hat. He supposed he carried in his hat with him as people usually did; for they all walked into church in style - (laughter) - and then, when he got into his seat, he deposited the hat there. Did not hear him say 'I dare' or any words to that effect.

"Frederick Barnstable (19), a farmer's son, gave corroborative evidence, adding that Mr. Winter spoke first, and used great violence.

"Mr. William Cary (51), in answer to Mr. Cook, said he had the honour to hold the distinguished position of churchwarden at Chedzoy. (Laughter.) Mr. Winter brought to him the notice which had been produced, and he had signed it without a thought, and had since thought he ought not to have done it. He always understood that when the pews were altered and re-allotted 'No. 3 south transept' was assigned to the tenant of the farm formerly occupied by Mr. Denning, and the disputed pew to the occupier of the farm which Mr. Denning now tenanted. Mr. Denning having told him that he intended, as did also part of his family, to go to church, witness told him to take the seat which had always belonged to the farm. He had also offered Mr. Denning his own pew. After the morning service on the day in question, witness said to Mr. Winter, 'George, I don't like this going on in the church.' He had told Mr. Mullens the same, and that he would not pull anyone out of a seat during Divine service for £500.

"Henry Fry (26), of Chedzoy, said he saw Mr. Winter first catch hold of young Denning by the sleeve, and afterwards by the collar, and used great violence. Denning said, 'Don't break my clothes,' or words to that effect, and 'I've got a right to the sitting.'

"Mr. William Rainey said he had lived at Chedzoy for 58 years (all his life). He remembered the tenants of the two farms which had been spoken of occupying the pews in question, and had seen Mr. Hurford, who was the former tenant of the farm now in the occupation of Mr. Denning, in the disputed pew.

"Mr. Richard Denning next gave evidence respecting his occupation of the two farms, to the occupiers of which he said were assigned the pews 'No. 3 south transept' and the disputed one. When he took these farms he was told by the churchwardens that he must contribute something, which he promised to do. - In reply to Mr. Poole he said he had never sat in the disputed pew in his life. When his son and daughters went there he told them that if nobody was sitting in the disputed pew they were to occupy it, but not to cause any disturbance.

"This was the whole of the evidence, and after a short consultation, the Chairman said the facts of the case were very clear. The magistrates believed - at any rate it was his own belief - that both Mr. Winter and Mr. Denning thought they were doing that which was right: but, at the same time, they (the magistrates) thought Mr. Denning had no pretence for claiming the pew in question. He seemed to be under the impression that because it was some years ago allotted to the tenant of the farm he now occupied he was entitled to sit there now, whether it had been appropriated to anybody else in the meantime or not. In this he was clearly wrong. Moreover, according to his own admission, Mr. Denning had never been an attendant at the church, and his daughters could not say that they had been, consequently it could not be pleaded that they had been accustomed to go there. The seat, being left void for some time, appeared to have been allotted to a newcomer to the parish - Mr. Parfitt - and therefore, especially after receiving a notice of this, and being told by the churchwarden not to go there, Mr. Denning was wrong in occupying it. As had been pointed out, if he wished to assert any right to it, he had another remedy. He (the chairman) was sorry to say that but little discretion and good temper had been shown, and had Mr. Cary's good nature been displayed throughout instead, the probability was that no such proceedings as these would have been instituted. He was very sorry, indeed, that the transaction had taken place. Mr. Poole did not wish to ask for a fine, and the Bench did not intend to impose any, but would be content with an expression of opinion that Mr. Denning had clearly acted in a wrong way, and that Mr. Winter had not used more violence than was necessary.

"Mr. Broadmead said that to suppose because a tenant of a particular house had occupied a certain pew for a great many years, whoever might hereafter live in that house had a right to the pew was a great mistake. There was no such right without a faculty or prescription. Capt. Hickley remarked that the person who made it necessary for violence to be used was guilty of it all."

Unfortunately a precise location is not given in this Mercury report of May 1873.

"Bridgwater Highway District Board. A meeting of this body was held on Wednesday. The Surveyor (Mr. Hicks) produced a notice which he had received from Mr. Ling, sanitary inspector, to abate certain nuisances at Chedzoy, which he (Mr. Hicks) pointed out could only be removed by the construction of a sewer at a cost of £20 to £25, an expense which he did not feel justified in incurring without consulting them. He also pointed out that there was no compulsion on the surveyor of highways to clean out ditches on the sides of the roads, the law only stating that he 'may' do so, and, moreover, that in the case referred to by Mr. Ling, though cleansed out one day, the drain might be fouled again the next day by the cottages close by. After a discussion it was agreed, on the suggestion of the Clerk, that Mr. Ling should serve notices of abatement on the owners of the cottage property."

Six months after the controversy in the church, Edward Parfitt appeared in Bridgwater County Court as a defendant. In September 1873 the following report was published.

"THOMAS STOCKHAM v. PARFITT. Plaintiff, a builder, residing at Bridgwater, claimed of the defendant, a gentleman residing at Chedzoy, £ 1 1s. for services rendered. According to the evidence on the part of the plaintiff, the defendant on 25th September last (1872) called upon him and told him he was about to remove from Middlezoy to Chedzoy and wanted a greenhouse pulled down and rebuilt. At the request of the defendant the plaintiff went to Middlezoy to advise as to what should be done. Upon that occasion Mr. Parfitt asked plaintiff to give him an estimate for the work. Plaintiff replied that he could not very well do that until the greenhouse was pulled down and he saw the condition it was in. Defendant said he should like for the plaintiff to go to Chedzoy and advise him as to the best situation for erecting the greenhouse, and subsequently plaintiff made a journey to Chedzoy for that purpose. Plaintiff heard nothing more for a month: at the expiration of that time the defendant told him he had employed someone else to do the work. Plaintiff did not like this treatment, and defendant requested him to send in the bill, and he would pay. - Defendant said he did not recollect saying this, adding that he could not remember what he did say, or whether he said anything. He asserted the plaintiff refused to give any estimate. - His Honour said he had the positive oath of the plaintiff that the defendant had agreed to pay his expenses, and requested him to send his bill. The defendant did not contradict this, and therefore he must give judgement for the plaintiff.

As is still the case, problems occurred at Bridgwater Fair in 1873.

"George Ferris of Bridgwater and Isaac Day of Chedzoy (whose eyes were much blackened) were charged on the information of Sergeant Cheriton with creating a public annoyance on 26th September. - Defendants pleaded guilty. - Superintendent Lear said defendants had a fight in St. Matthew's Field [Bridgwater], and the marks on their faces were the effects of the blows. - The Magistrates' Clerk: It appears to have been 'six of one and half a dozen of the other.' Superintendent Lear: They are penitent now, I believe. (Laughter.) - Day said he was forced to fight. The evening before he went into a boxing-booth at the fair, put on gloves with Ferris and 'bested' him. The next morning Ferris, who always wanted to fight him, called him 'a great fat-head,' and struck him, and he then, of course, took his part. - The Magistrates' Clerk: Did you best him again? - Day: I done the best I could till all of them falled on me. I was forced to fight with seven or eight men, and he had a big dog with him that tore the leg out of my trousers. - Ferris said Day had gone about telling 'a lot of lies' about him, and he asked what he meant. - In reply to the Bench, Superintendent Lear said the men fought for about twenty minutes. As soon as he heard of it he sent two policemen to the spot to stop it. - The Mayor said the magistrates were of the opinion that Ferris was the aggressor, and they fined him 20s. (£1), including costs; in default fourteen days imprisonment. Day had told them that Ferris always wanted to fight with him, and if that was so he should not throw himself in his way. He (Day) had broken the law, and must be fined 10s., in default seven days."

Another assault was reported in the same edition of the Mercury.

"Thomas Wills was brought up in custody by P.C. Larcombe, charged with assaulting Elizabeth Ann Cox, a widow, living at Chedzoy Lane. Complainant said that on the previous afternoon, between three and four o'clock, the defendant came to the house where she lived and asked for some water. She gave some to him. He was drunk and wanted to come into the house. She told him to go away. He pushed the door against her three times, and afterwards opened it and threatened to kill her. He seized her by the hair of her head, dragged her out of the house into the garden, and struck her with his fist. She had a black eye from the effects of the blow, and was covered with blood. Her dress was torn. Mary Dowden came and asked if he was going to kill her. He then let her go, and she went into the house. He came and tried the door again, but it was locked. He tried to open the door and window, and swore he would kill her that night. She had known him a little time, and went in fear of him. Cross-examined by the defendant: You have been at the place before, but not into the house. You gave me some 'fairing' on Thursday night, but I did not ask you for money to pay my rent nor say I wanted money for the purpose. Mary Dowden said the complainant lodged with her. About four o'clock the previous afternoon defendant came to the house and asked for the complainant. She told him he had better go home. He then came in, and pulled her by the hair out into the garden, where he 'hammered' her on the head with his fists for some time. She ran into the house, and the door was locked. Defendant pulled a stick from the hedge, and threatened to break the window in. Defendant and two other men came the same evening, and witness's sons had to remain at home to protect them. Defendant was remanded in custody."

The following week a further report appeared.

"Thomas Wills was charged on remand with assaulting Elizabeth Ann Cox. The evidence already published having been read, the following witnesses were examined: Ephraim Dowden said that on Sunday afternoon defendant came and asked him for water, and he called complainant out. She said to him, 'You are drunk.' Defendant then burst open the door and tried to come in. Witness told him to go out. Defendant caught hold of complainant by the hair of her head, struck her in the face with his fist and threatened to kill her. Defendant wanted to break in the window. Cross-examined by the defendant: You pulled her out from the door by her hair. She was standing near the stairs. - Albert Dowden said he heard complainant tell defendant he was drunk. Defendant then caught hold of complainant by the hair, and struck her in the face until she was covered in blood. Complainant was not abusive to him, and only told him to go away. She did not 'blackguard' him at all. - Defendant was sentenced to be imprisoned at Taunton gaol for twenty-one days with hard labour."

Another local case was heard by Bridgwater County Court in October 1873.

"GEORGE BELL v. MARY RAINEY (50 years of the Post Office - now Cadbury House). The plaintiff, a labourer of Chedzoy, claimed 9s. (45p.) for balance of work done. Plaintiff said defendant had agreed to pay him 1s. per rope for throwing a ditch. He did 15 feet and had only been paid 6s. Defendant said plaintiff agreed to do the whole for 12s. and nothing was said about so much per rope. Having worked three days, and done half the work, she paid him 6s., and had paid the remaining 6s. into court. - Florence Rainey, daughter of the defendant, gave corroborative evidence and judgement was given for 6s."

In October 1873 almost a full page of the Bridgwater Mercury was devoted to "The Floods in Somersetshire," a small portion of which related to Chedzoy.

"Mr. Grantham next describes the Lower Parrett Valley, with especial reference to the districts formed under the 'Land Drainage Act, 1861' in Chedzoy, Aller Moor, North Moor, Stanmoor, Curry Moor and Othery, Middlezoy and Westonzoyland; the extent to which they have been flooded; the effect produced by the pumping-engines employed; the cost of their working, &c. In reference to Chedzoy district he says:- 'A pumping-engine of 30-horse power has been erected since the district had been formed, but its full power cannot be developed in consequence of the main drains leading to it not having been made of sufficient dimensions or proper form to allow the water to flow freely to it. ... The total expenditure up to the present time has been about £5,000, which is to be paid off in fifteen years from 1867, at the rate of £482 16s. 3d. per annum, and the average annual working expenses have been for five years £323, the whole being at the average rate of 8s. 2d. (41p.) per acre for the present. ... During the winter,' he adds, 'the whole of this district (Chedzoy) has been flooded, owing to the waters on King's Sedgemoor having risen above the parting bank and overflowed it. Had it not been for this circumstance the area could have been kept perfectly free from floods by means of the engine and clyces."

In February 1874 Edward Parfitt returned to the County Court, this time as the plaintiff.

"EDWARD PARFITT v. JOHN QUICK. The plaintiff, residing at Chedzoy, claimed of the defendant, a fishmonger and general dealer of Taunton, the sum of £10 13s. balance of account for apples sold. In August last the defendant sent the town-crier around Bridgwater with a notice to the effect that he was prepared to buy any number of apples known as 'Morgan Sweets' at 10s. per bag. Defendant (sic), on hearing this, went to the place indicated, St. John-street, and there entered into an agreement for the purchase on these terms of all the 'Morgan Sweets' he had at Chedzoy, he (Mr. Parfitt) agreeing to pick the apples and deliver them. In accordance with that agreement, Mr. Parfitt picked up and sent in twenty bags of apples. Defendant received them, and paid for them. Some little time passed, and at length Mr. Parfitt got impatient at the remainder of the apples not being sent for, and sent two more waggon loads. Defendant's men would not take in the apples, and they were in consequence carried back to Mr. Parfitt again. Mr. Parfitt thereupon put the matter in the hands of Messrs. Babbage and Boys, auctioneers and accountants, and they wrote to the defendant giving him notice that, on the following market-day, they should proceed to sell the remainder of the apples, and that he (Mr. Quick) would be held liable for all loss, damage and expenses which Mr. Parfitt might sustain. On Wednesday morning (market-day) four waggon loads were sent into Bridgwater. Defendant then went and saw Messrs. Babbage and Boys, taking with him a letter from Messrs. Reed and Cook, his solicitors, which contained an offer to attend on another day with empty barrels to receive the apples. Mr. Boys, who had an engagement out of town, had written out a statement, which it was mutually agreed should be received as his evidence. This was read and in it Mr. Boys said he informed Mr. Quick that certain expenses, amounting altogether to £3 4s. 6d. (the particulars of which he gave) had been incurred, which he (Mr. Quick) would have to pay, and Mr. Quick replied, 'You know me very well, and the expenses will be all right.' He also said he was much pressed for empties, but would take the apples on the Friday, which he did.

"On the 3rd September, Mr. Quick paid £10 on account, and on the 10th September he paid a further sum of £18 on account, leaving due the amount claimed. Mr. Boys further stated that when Mr. Quick paid the £18 he said his lawyer was out of town, and that he would be advised by him, before paying the balance. He (Mr. Quick) also said he should be able to prove that they were shaken down apples. Mr. Barham (for Mr. Parfitt) added that he was rather surprised, under the circumstances, that he should be called upon to make any statement, and that he was curious to know what defence there could be.

"Mr. Reed (for Mr. Quick), in reply to his Honour, said his instructions were that all the apples were to be hand-picked and marketable. The first lot answered very well, but when the last supply came defendant was away from Bridgwater, and his foreman received them. They were taken in waggons, and he was instructed that, although the apples on top were of the quality described as hand-picked and marketable, when they were removed the residue were found to consist of those that had been shaken off the trees. They were considerably bruised and damaged, and were not worth half the price offered. The defendant in consequence suffered a considerable loss on the re-sale, and alleged that the money already paid represented the full and complete value of the apples delivered. - His Honour: Why did your client take them in and receive them? - Mr. Reed said that was the difficulty he felt in the case, and he had told his client so; but his explanation was that he was away at the time, and that his men took them in. He (Mr. Reed) did not impute to Mr. Parfitt that he had been privy in any way to the inferiority of the apples, and their alleged concealment under the top. - Mr. Barham said he might mention that the apples were weighed basket by basket at the defendant's stores, and he was in a position to prove that those which were in any way injured were thrown aside and rejected. - His Honour said if there was any evidence to show that there was a deliberately concocted fraud practised and imposed on Mr. Quick with the concurrence of Mr. Parfitt he should have difficulty in dealing with it; but there was none, and they had only to deal with the specific bargain, and the acceptance of the apples. - Mr. Quick said he had a witness to prove that Mr. Parfitt said all the best apples were to be put on top. - Mr. Reed said he was only anxious to impress on his Honour that Mr. Quick came there in good faith, being a heavy loser by the transaction. - His Honour, after remarking that a specific price was here agreed upon, and that it was not in the power of the defendant, after accepting the apples, to turn round and say he should not pay the price agreed upon, gave judgement for the plaintiff."

In February 1874

"At a vestry meeting duly convened to consider the best means of providing and managing a school in this Parish, it was unanimously determined that the members be empowered and requested to consult a Solicitor forthwith with a view to the formation of a School Board. At the same time the Rector stated he was willing to lease the school buildings to the School Board when formed at a nominal rental under certain restrictions." On 20th August 1874 "At a vestry meeting duly convened and held in the School Room for the purpose of taking into consideration communications from Her Majesty's Inspector of School (sic), it was unanimously resolved to immediately appoint a School Board to carry out the government requirements."

In May 1874

"The members of the Chedzoy Friendly Society, about forty in number, on the occasion of its [12th] anniversary, discourse was delivered to them by the Rev. G.O. Mullens. Afterwards, preceded by the band of the 26th S.R.C., they paraded the village, and then repaired to the Crown Inn, kept by Mr. Haynes, who provided a capital dinner, which was presided over by Mr. John Tazewell. ... Mr. John Cary, the honorary secretary, reported that the funds were in a flourishing condition. The receipts were, in hand from last year, £5 9s.; members quarterly subscriptions, £31 8s. 6d., total £36 17s. 6d. The sum of £6 was paid to Mr. Hurman, surgeon, the cash in hand amounted to £9 9s.; and £21 8s. 6d. was invested in the Savings Bank."

Francis Lovibond was still making entries in his diary.

"April 17th, Ernest Fred Banfield Lovibond died and buried April 23rd 1874, aged 2 years, 11 months and 23 days. He died in Hope Cottage, Chedzoy, the same house in which he was born. He was taken ill with the measles the 2nd and daily grew worse. His mother carried him to bed on Tuesday the 7th, he was blind from that time till the following Sunday, then he opened his dear eyes, for which we thank God, but they was so very weak the dear Lamb could not bear the light, then he seemed to rally a little and our hopes grew brighter. We prayed he might be spared to remain with us a little longer but our brightest hopes soon faded for we could see plainly that he would soon be in that happy land up there."

He also noted that on

"March 23rd 1874, George Wilkins Bennett's house, garden and workshop was sold at the Crown Inn, Chedzoy by Mr. J. White for £285 0s. 0d., two hundred & eighty-five pounds, to George Conduit for Caroline Jewill and L.W. Barnstable."

In September the following brief report was published in the Bridgwater Mercury.

"About one hundred men are now daily employed in throwing that portion of the Sedgemoor river, the liability to cleanse which has been so long disputed, but which question was recently settled by the resort to legal proceedings, in favour of the occupiers, &c., against the Sedgemoor Commissioners."

Also in September, Edward Parfitt was again in the County Court: this time he had reverted to being the defendant.

"FREDERICK DAVIS v. EDWARD PARFITT. The plaintiff, a mason and plasterer of Middlezoy, for whom Mr. Cook appeared, claimed of the defendant, a farmer, of Chedzoy, £3 balance of account for work done. - Plaintiff said in July last, the defendant came to him and told him that he wanted some cottages plastered and that Mr. Turner, his landlord, wanted it done as fast as possible. He told the defendant that he never did that sort of work by the day. Defendant asked what he got by the yard, and he replied, 'Sixpence or sixpence-halfpenny' (2.5p. - 2.7p.). Defendant asked if he could do it for sixpence, and he said that he could, whereupon defendant promised to pay that, also finding the material. Plaintiff recommended two coats of plaster, but Mr. Parfitt asked whether one coat of plaster and two coats of whitewash would not be cheaper, and plaintiff replied it would be about 30s. (£1.50) less. It was then agreed he should do this work. During the progress defendant had paid £2 on account, and before it was finished £1 more. He asked defendant to measure it, but Mr. Parfitt said he had no time. He asked, however, how many yards it was and he (plaintiff) replied 'Three hundred.' Defendant said, 'D—- you, then you earned good wages while you were at it.' Witness replied that he ought to earn a little extra, having to go five miles to work, and pay the boy who assisted him, as well as for his lodgings. Defendant subsequently asked him to bring his bill, to be shown to the landlord. He thereupon sent in his bill, claiming for the three hundred yards. At another interview the defendant told him he would only pay him by the day, adding that if the landlord liked to do so he might. Witness replied that the landlord had nothing to do with it, and that he expected payment by him (defendant). The sum of £1 10s. had been paid into the court, leaving a balance of £3. - In cross-examination by the defendant, witness admitted that he made up an account with him of the time he was engaged in the work which was twelve days and twelve quarters; he also gave information about the cost of his lodgings. He did so at the defendant's request, who said, 'We had better get it by the day.' - Defendant was examined and stated that the plaintiff ultimately agreed to do the work by the day, also that it was plaintiff's suggestion that one coat of plaster and two coats of whitewash were used instead of two coats of plaster. - His Honour said his impression was that neither of the parties thoroughly understood what the bargain was, and as £3 was the balance claimed, he should give judgement for half that amount, namely 30s."

The same month Edward Parfitt also appeared in the Magistrates' Court.

"Messrs. Parfitt and Carey, overseers of Chedzoy, were charged by Mr. Reed on behalf of the Bridgwater Rural Sanitary Authority with non-payment of the sum of £80, amount of rate. - Mr. Reed said that on the 13th May the Sanitary Authority issued a precept on the overseers of Chedzoy for the payment of £80 by the 17th June. It seemed the overseers - Messrs. Parfitt and Carey - could not 'pull together,' Mr. Carey having signed the rate while Mr. Parfitt declined to do so. The money was required for the construction of sewers, and the work was at a standstill in consequence of its not having been paid. It had been applied for over and over again. - Mr. Parfitt said he was not aware a rate had been made. - Mr. Reed answered that he had not only written to the overseers, but his Clerk had been to Chedzoy for the purpose of urging the matter. - Mr. Crocker, Clerk to Mr. Reed, proved an order being made for the rate, and posting a precept to the overseers, and that the money had remained unpaid. - Mr. Parfitt said if the rate had to be made and collected he supposed it must be. He did not, however, think the proposed sewer would be very advantageous. - The Bench made an order for payment of the rate and the expenses within a fortnight. - Mr. Parfitt: There is no fall in the drain. - Mr. Reed: Give us the money and we'll make it fall. (Laughter.)"

As a result of the vestry meeting's decision in August, the first meeting of the School Board for Chedzoy was convened in the village Church of England School on 5th November 1874. Three months later the minutes recorded,

"As to plan for altering said premises so as to meet requirements of Education Department. Resolved by being supported by all present that Messrs. Chedzoy and Son be instructed to prepare a plan for altering premises in question so as to carry out the requirements of the Education Department as set out in their notice under date the eighteenth June 1873".

Edward Parfitt was becoming a familiar figure in the County Court: he was back again in July 1875.

"Edward Parfitt, farmer, Chedzoy v. William J. Coleman, farmer, West Newton, Near Bridgwater. Sum claimed £12 for a double-furrow plough. £9 was paid into court. Mr. Swain of Glastonbury, for the plaintiff, and Mr. Cook for the defendant. - The plaintiff said that in the spring of 1874 he met the defendant in Bridgwater market, when the latter asked him his opinion respecting double-furrow ploughs. He told him the had recently bought one, and would let him try it. Mr. Coleman accepted the offer, and took the plough. He (plaintiff) saw the defendant some time afterwards, and, on asking to have the plough sent back, the latter said he would buy it. He (plaintiff) then showed Mr. Coleman the original invoice, from which he had deducted the odd shillings, as he had used the plough on half and acre of ground, leaving £12 as the amount which he asked for it. No distinct bargain was come to, but at a subsequent meeting he (plaintiff) offered to take the price of the plough in beans. To this the defendant at first agreed, but he did not stand to the bargain, which was that he should allow thirty bushels of beans or pay him £12. He (plaintiff) wrote on the 10th and 17th November asking the defendant to send him a cheque. - Cross-examined: At the conversation on the 9th November the defendant did not say the price of the beans was 6s. per bushel (8 gallons). - Eliza Rainey (16), servant in the employ of Mr. Parfitt, said that she heard her master say that he would take £12 for the plough or thirty bushels of beans. To this Mr. Coleman said he would either send or write to Mr. Mogg, telling him to let Mr. Parfitt have the beans. - The defendant said that, on being on Mr. Parfitt's farm one day, his attention was drawn to the plough, which Mr. Parfitt said his men could not manage, and he (defendant) said he would like to take it and try it. He did so, but although he subsequently met Mr. Parfitt many times there was no mention made as to price. On the 9th November, after some discussion, it was agreed that he (witness) should have the plough, and that Mr. Parfitt should have thirty bushels of beans. On the Tuesday following the plaintiff told him that Mr. Mogg would not let him have the beans, and that he had supplied himself with beans elsewhere. At further meetings he (defendant) offered to return the plough, to pay the market price or thirty bushels of beans, or to leave the matter to arbitration. - Judgement for plaintiff in the amount claimed."

In October 1875

"William Andrews and George Hunt were charged with stealing some pears, value 1s., the property of Mr. John Hooper (80), farmer, of Chedzoy. Ann Smith, servant of Mr. Hooper, said she saw a man dressed in dark clothes getting out of a tree in the orchard, and also saw Hunt running away therefrom. ... Dismissed."

Two men from the village both appeared before the court in January 1876 in connection with their families. Firstly,

"James Stone (65) of Chedzoy, was summoned by Mr. Reed, clerk to the guardians of Bridgwater Union, for non-maintenance of his mother. Mr. Reed said the defendant owned a property at Chedzoy and elsewhere, and the guardians were of the opinion that he was in a position to maintain his mother. - Mr. Cozens, relieving officer, proved the chargeability, and stated the defendant was a small farmer, living at Chedzoy, and had three or four cows, and some other stock. The defendant's father was also chargeable, and he believed the defendant allowed them something. - The Bench made an order for payment of 2s. per week."

Next,

"John Gilbert (31), of Chedzoy, was called on by Lucy Ellen Gully (26), to show cause, &c. (sic). An order for 1s. 6d. per week was made until the child should attain the age of 14 years."

It seems that Lucy found happiness as the 1881 Census records Thomas Stokes, Mrs. Lucy Ellen Stokes and

Tillie Gilbert Gully (step-daughter) as living in Front Street near the chapel.

Another family affair was reported on 1st March 1876.

> "George Stone, a little boy, aged 11 years, was charged under the Vagrancy Act, with sleeping out and having no visible means of subsistence. Defendant, on being questioned, stated that he was living at Chedzoy with his grandparents, and that his mother lived at Burnham. The Rev. G.O. Mullens said he had come before the magistrates to ask their advice respecting this boy. He was an illegitimate child, and his mother lived at Burnham, but he had for some time been living with his grandmother. His mother had been in the habit of paying the grandmother something per week for his maintenance, but she had recently got married, and since then the pay had been discontinued. The grandmother was in poor circumstances, and unable to maintain the boy without assistance, and he had been allowed therefore to wander about. He had asked the boy several times to go to his mother, and had on one or two occasions sent him to her, but he had always returned to Chedzoy, saying his mother would not let him remain with her. For the last fortnight or three weeks he had been sleeping in a pig-sty, in the most inclement weather; and on one occasion he was found in the morning in a pig-stye (sic) buried in snow. He (Mr. Mullens) had communicated with the mother, and she now stated that she was willing to keep him if he would live with her. - The magistrates decided that the boy should be detained until his mother could be communicated with by the police."

Five months later another person was dealt with under the same Act.

> "George Jeanes, labourer, brought up in custody by P.C. Hawkins charged with sleeping in an outhouse at Chedzoy on the previous night, was discharged with a caution."

Although the subject matter of the meeting was unimportant, the opening line of these minutes for 25th March 1876 are well worth repeating:

> "At a vestry meeting duly convened in the church porch and on the proposition of Mr. Winter and seconded by Mr. Cary adjourned to the Crown Inn...." I'm sure most readers will agree that this was an excellent example of practical committee work!

Plans for the school were prepared and tenders accepted which resulted in the improvement of the old building and the construction of the school house, both of which were taken into use in 1876. The School Board met again on 8th March that year at their Clerk's office in King Square, Bridgwater. The Bye-Laws for the School Board for the Parish of Chedzoy required that

> "The parents of every Child not less than five years nor more than thirteen years residing within the Parish shall cause such child to attend School unless there be some reasonable excuse for non-attendance"

such as receiving an education in some other manner, illness or there being no school within three miles by road. Children between ten and thirteen years old who had reached the fifth standard were exempt from this requirement and those who had reached the fourth standard need not attend for more than ten hours per week.

There were two headmistresses between the opening of the school in 1876 and before the appointment of Joseph Brooks (1857-1930) in 1879. The first was dismissed after a year for "immoral conduct" and the second simply because the School Board felt that a man would be more suitable.

In March 1876 the Bridgwater Mercury announced under the heading SOMERSETSHIRE LANDOWNERS that it intended to publish a new Doomsday Book and began printing an alphabetical list of every landowner in the county. However, in late May it noted that

> "Having received many complaints of incorrectness in the new Doomsday Book, we deem it advisable to discontinue the insertion of the list from the present time." By this time five Chedzoy entries had been recorded:

Name	**Acres/Roods/Perches**	**Estimated Rental**
Mrs. Barnstable	122 - 1 - 2	£287 5s.
William Carey	19 - 3 - 7	£54
John Coney	282 - 1 - 34	£630 5s.
E.U. Derrick	11 - 0 - 4	£30
William Derrick	147 - 1 - 16	£376 4s.

In April 1876 a short report of interest was published in the Bridgwater Mercury.

> "It was decided a short time since by the parishioners to appoint an assistant-overseer for Chedzoy at a salary of £12 per annum. Mr. George Winter and Mr. Henry Fry were the only candidates and a poll was taken when 49 votes were recorded in favour of Mr. Winter and 47 for Mr. Fry. Mr. Winter was therefore declared elected, but Mr. Fry has given notice of his intention to dispute the poll."

No further item on this subject was published.

Public money was one of the issues when the Rural Sanitary Authority met in November 1876.

> "Mr. Tazewell again brought under attention the part of the balance of £25 remaining in the hands of the treasurer over and above the amount expended in connection with sewage works at Chedzoy. In accordance with the estimates made for the proposed works, a much larger sum, the ratepayers were called upon to pay the above amount in excess of that actually required, and he now asked how it

was proposed to appropriate the balance, or whether it could not be returned to the ratepayers. The Clerk said the matter had been brought before the auditor from time to time, and he stated that inasmuch as it was raised for a special purpose it could not be applied to ordinary purposes and must remain invested for any other purposes that might from time to time arise in connection with the parish. Mr. Tazewell complained that this would be a great hardship to the ratepayers, inasmuch as no special purpose might arise for a great number of years, and after some conversation it was agreed that the clerk write to the Local Government Board and apply for permission to appropriate the sum in question for payment of the ordinary purposes of the parish."

Some lovely examples of Victorian English were included in a court report which was published in December 1876.

"Mr. James Lovibond, farmer, of Chedzoy, was charged with assaulting Mr. William Slocombe Carter, another farmer of the same place. Complainant said that on the afternoon in question, when coming out of a field with two horses and a putt (a two-wheeled cart), he met the defendant who also had two horses and a putt. Defendant shouted to him, and witness asked him what he wanted. Defendant came to him, wrung up his fist in his face and said he would hit his —- head off, but did not strike him. Witness said he should summons him. - Defendant said that on 6th November, two days before, the complainant insulted him by making some reference to his (defendant's) wife and another man. On this occasion he (defendant) accosted Mr. Carter and asked, 'What have you got to say about me and my wife?' Mr. Carter replied, 'Nothing my man; you can go about your business,' adding, 'If you don't go on I shall put this whip-stick about you.' Defendant said, 'I don't want to use such a thing as that; I can use my fists.' Mr. Carter denied that he said anything to Mr. Lovibond about his wife. After hearing the evidence the magistrates dismissed the case."

Flooding in the winter of 1876/77 was extensive and caused serious disruption throughout the area. Lengthy accounts were published but only a few relate directly to Chedzoy. On 10th January 1877 it was reported that

"During the past week the inundation of West Sedgemoor, in the parishes of Westonzoyland and Chedzoy, has been greatly increased by an influx of water through the gap in the South Lake Bank of Aller Moor. No doubt is entertained that this bank was cut wilfully for the purpose of relieving the banks behind it in the direction of Langport, and a reward of £10 has been offered for the detection of the offenders."

A week later,

"At a meeting of the Chedzoy Drainage Commissioners ... a report was presented to the effect that it will be impossible to repair Aller Moor gap, or even to approach it, before the arrival of the next high tides. The consequence of this no person can now foretell; but that a disaster of great magnitude is imminent seems no longer to admit of doubt."

The following week a near disaster was reported, although not of the sort envisaged by the Commissioners.

"On Sunday afternoon a party of workmen in the employ of Mr. Edwin Fry (of Cranes Farm, now Frys Farm), farmer, and one or two others, had a narrow escape of being drowned. The party, ten in number, consisted of Mr. [Alfred] Salmon (31), landlord of the Crown Inn; Henry Haines, Thomas Stokes (25), Richard Giles (26), Henry Millard, William Weller (Wheeler? 21), Levi Rainey (24), Robert Fry (19), Thomas Fry and a lad named William Fry (8). With their master's permission they started in a boat belonging to Mr. Fry, and named the 'Star,' for Westonzoyland to witness the gap at Lakewall. They left Chedzoy about three o'clock, and neared their destination about an hour and a half afterwards. Rather suddenly and unexpectedly a strong breeze sprang up, and this caused the water to dash against and over the sides of the boat in such a manner as to excite the alarm not only of the occupants, but of some boatmen not far distant, and who feared the Star would almost every moment be swamped. With some difficulty the boat was rowed ashore, but not before she contained a large quantity of water. The spectators had no difficulty in persuading its former occupants, after they had landed, that it would be madness to think of returning home the same night, so long as the water remained in its then turbulent condition; and they were all, therefore, compelled to stay at Westonzoyland until the next morning, when they were rowed home in safety, their return being heartily welcomed by their relatives and friends."

Although there was extensive flooding across the levels, the worst was not in the village area and the Chedzoy Commissioners fears proved unfounded. On 7th February it was reported that

"The Aller Moor gap was stopped on Wednesday night, the men to the number of 40 or 50 working all night afterwards to make it secure. The water running through the gap on Wednesday was 40 feet wide by 10 feet deep and by Thursday morning it had decreased on the Aller side to about two feet."

In March 1877 the Bridgwater Mercury reported two cases involving brothers and sisters who had appeared before the court on the same day.

"Frederick Stone was charged by his brother, John Stone with an assault at Chedzoy. Defendant said they fell out on the night of 21st February and upon seeing complainant on the following morning he asked to fight. Complainant refused, and defendant then struck him. - Complainant denied having drawn a knife, and alleged that defendant struck him without provocation. - Fined 10s. and costs."

In the next case,

> "Lucy Bird and Sarah Bird, little girls, sisters, were charged with assaulting Mary Ann Dowden. Complainant said she lived at Chedzoy and went to school in Bridgwater, and on returned from school on the day in question the defendants struck her several times because she would not speak to them. - Sarah Turner, wife of a labourer, and Walter Dowden, cousin of the complainant, gave partially corroborative evidence. - Peter Bird, brother of the defendants, stated that the complainant struck his sisters and that they struck her. - Case dismissed on payment of costs."

It would seem that both Rev. Mullens and his wife had suffered from poor health as this report was published in the Bridgwater Mercury in April 1878.

> "The Rev. G.O. Mullens, rector of Chedzoy, who has for the past year been obliged to leave Chedzoy in consequence of the ill health of Mrs. Mullens and himself, returned home on 28th March and found placed on their dining-room table a piece of silver plate (silver salver), with an address as under, signed by the inhabitants, every house being represented. 'We beg your acceptance of this token of our appreciation of your long ministrations in this parish, and sincerely trust that the change which you and Mrs. Mullens were compelled to take for your health has been beneficial, and that you may be both many years enabled to perform the duties of this parish incumbent on you, which you have so long and ably fulfilled.' The salver bore the inscription, 'Presented to the Rev. G.O. Mullens, M.A., having been rector of the parish of Chedzoy for 22 years, upon his return home after a year's absence, by the parishioners. March 28th, 1878."

The Problem with Pupils

1880 opened with a villager losing an action in the County Court. The Bridgwater Mercury for 14th January reported,

> "JAMES REED v. THEODORE BOWERS. The plaintiff, a carpenter, of Chedzoy, sued the defendant, a gentleman (or was he?) of Dunwear, for £4 for work done. Plaintiff said defendant ordered him to make and supply two recesses. When he finished them defendant declined to have them, saying he wanted a wardrobe instead. He (plaintiff) still had them in his possession. Defendant said he never gave any order for the recesses in question in any shape or form. He merely asked plaintiff to give him an estimate of the cost of making them. Plaintiff did not bring him an estimate but three months afterwards brought him the recesses. Plaintiff said his instructions were, 'Do it as cheaply as you can.' His Honour said the plaintiff had failed to make out his case and he was consequently non-suited."

The winter of 1880/81 saw widespread flooding. As part of a much longer report in February 1881:

> "During the past week the water has been gradually rising over the lands included in Chedzoy drainage district consequent on the dilapidated state of the bank of the main Sedgemoor drain, forming the boundary of the district. In the Chedzoy district the water is now almost level with that on the King Sedgemoor side of the drain, having during the week increased in height from a foot to eighteen inches."

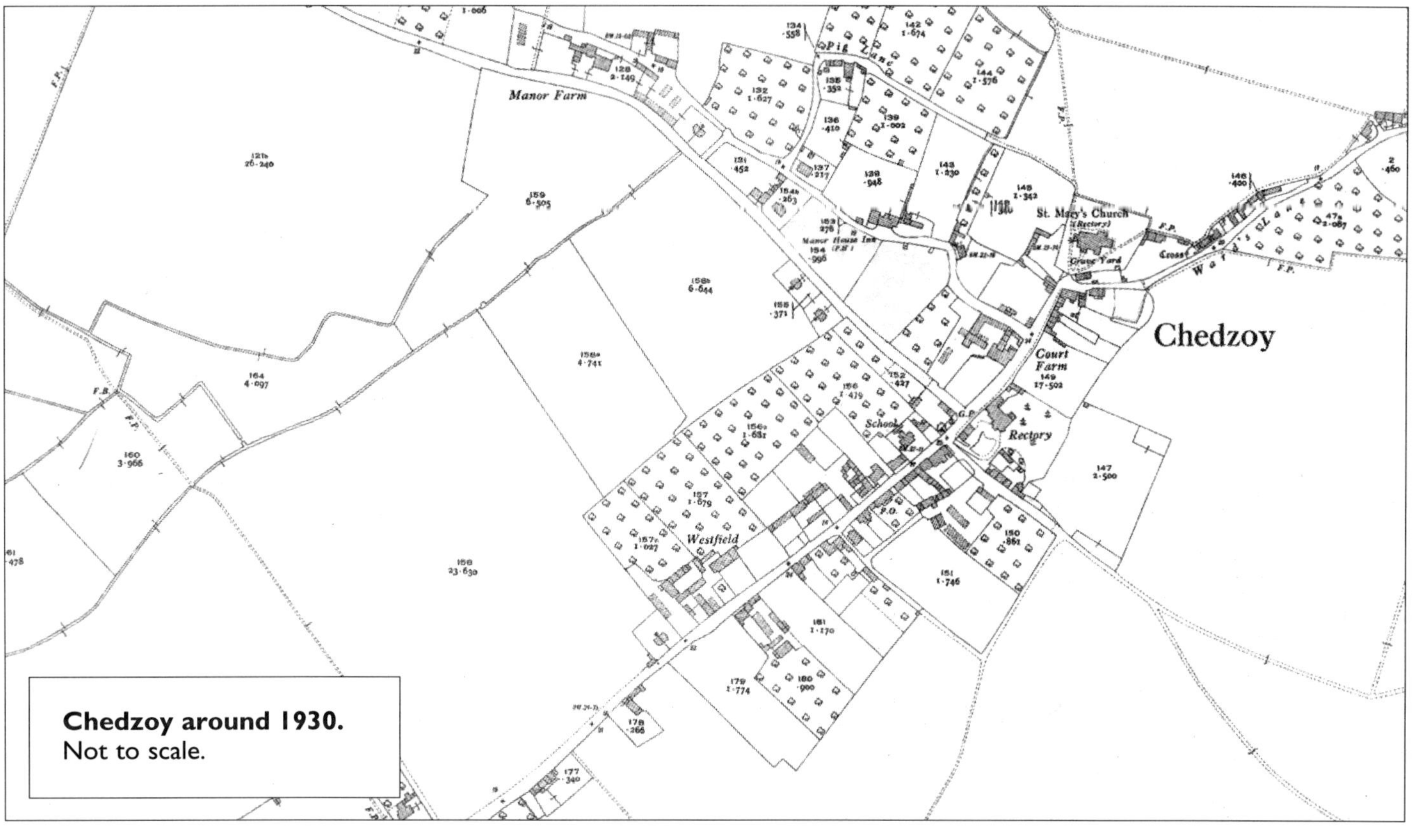

Chedzoy around 1930.
Not to scale.

In 1881, just two years after becoming Head Teacher, Joseph Brooks was very concerned at the level of absenteeism at the school: his salary was in part governed by the number of pupils and their success in the annual examinations. The School Board minutes record some interesting correspondence in relation to this matter. Mr. Brooks wrote,

"Dear Sir,

I send you a list of Scholars who have been most irregular in their attendance at school during the current year. The attendance, so far, had been very unsatisfactory, and especially has this been the case since the summer holidays. Many children have not been to school at all since the re-opening after the holidays, or in other words have not been to school in more than eleven weeks. I think this very bad and trust that the School Board will at once find some means of enforcing a more regular attendance, or the school must become less and less efficient. I do not like to complain but really the absence of some of the scholars has now become so prolonged that if they come at once and attend regularly for the future, it will be difficult to prepare them for the Inspector's next visit. I therefore venture to hope that the Board will give this subject immediate attention." This list of names then followed:

Name	Age	Name of Parent	Out of 123 attendances	Present	Absent
James Hook	11	James Hook, Chedzoy	"	50	73
Oliver Bennett	10	William Bennett, Chedzoy	"	60	63
Albert Stone	10	John Stone, Chedzoy	"	48	95
Wm. Chapple	9	Wm. Chapple, Chedzoy	"	34	89
Fred Jeanes	9	Jas. Jeanes,Chedzoy	"	50	73
James Fry	10	Chas. Fry, Chedzoy	"	41	82
Richd. House	11	Wm. House, Chedzoy	"	24	99
Thos. Phillips	11	Wm. Phillips, Chedzoy	"	23	100
Wal. Phillips	9	Wm. Phillips, Chedzoy	"	41	82
John Andrews	10	Jesse Andrews, Chedzoy	"	46	77
Chas. Andrews	12	Jesse Andrews, Chedzoy	"	40	83
Fred. Fry	8	Wm. Fry, Chedzoy	"	20	103
Francis Toogood	10	John Toogood, Chedzoy	"	52	71
Sarah Giles	12	Mrs. Giles, Chedzoy	"	23	100
Caro. Rainey	10	Edmd. Rainey, Chedzoy	"	41	82
Emily Stone	11	Chas. Stone, Chedzoy	"	35	88
Eva Bryant	12	Mrs. Bryant, Chedzoy	"	15	108
Theresa Hunt	11	Geo. Hunt, Chedzoy	"	57	66
Albt. Phillips	8	Wm. Phillips, Chedzoy	"	48	75
Simon Stone	8	John Stone,Chedzoy	"	44	79
Mary Stone	7	Chas. Stone, Chedzoy	"	44	79
Flora Stone	9	Thos. Stone, Chedzoy	"	45	78
Geo. Rainey	7	Edmd. Rainey, Chedzoy	"	47	76
S. Stone	7	Thos. Stone, Chedzoy	"	24	99
Amelia Stone	6	John Stone, Chedzoy	"	33	90
Alice Bennett	5	H. Bennett, Chedzoy	"	45	78

List of children who have not attended school since holidays

Name	Parent	Possible Number of Attendances	Present	Absent
Wallace Lovibond	Jas. Lovibond, Chedzoy	123	0	123
Sarah Giles	Jemina Giles, Chedzoy	123	23	100
Edwin Chapple	Wm. Chapple, Chedzoy	123	0	123
Thos. Phillips	Wm. Phillips, Chedzoy	123	23	100
Richd. House	Wm. House, Chedzoy	123	24	99
Emily Stone	Chas. Stone, Chedzoy	123	35	88
Charlotte Andrews	Jesse Andrews, Chedzoy	123	40	83
Jane Stone	Thos. Stone, Chedzoy	123	24	99

The Board took proceedings against the parents of some of the worst offenders and some of these cases were reported in the Bridgwater Mercury in January 1882.

"Wm. Phillips, of Chedzoy, was summoned for neglecting to send his child to school. Defendant's wife said she had eleven children, five of whom were sent to school. Defendant was not fined and the costs were remitted. Thomas Stone, of Chedzoy, for a similar offence was ordered to pay 3s. including costs; Charles Stone and William Fry, also of Chedzoy, were ordered to pay 1s. each, including costs."

Freak weather struck the village in May 1882. In the Bridgwater Mercury

"A correspondent states that early on the evening of Whit Sunday, a whirlwind visited the village and played some curious freaks especially in the neighbourhood of Mr. Edmund Derrick's farm, where it blew a trap from under a shed, turned round a heavy putt, carried away as far as Parchay bridge (sic), nearly a mile distant, the greater part of a stump of hay and straw, and twisted off two withy trees and an apple tree. The whirlwind was experienced within a very limited area."

The School Board proceedings in January went some way towards resolving the problem of absenteeism, but Mr. Brooks was not satisfied and in November 1882 again wrote to the Board, apparently after further proceedings had been taken.

"Dear Sir,

In placing before you a report of the effect which in my opinion the proceedings taken against the parents of defaulting children have had upon the attendance it will, of course, be necessary to review the attendance for a few weeks past and compare with that of this week. This may or may not be a fair criterion of the effect but at least it will serve to guide in some degree when judging whether it was good policy or not to take the proceedings. At the beginning of this week I did not think that what had been done would be of little or no use. Since then however my opinion has been slightly modified, and I now think (if I may presume to judge) that the course taken by the Board has not been wholly ineffectual. I may here quote a few particulars from my register. Average attendance for whole of last quarter was 62. Average attendance for the 3 weeks ending November 11th 1882 was 71. Average attendance for present week 73, and this 73 would probably have been 74 or 75 but this week I have had 3 scholars who are as a rule very regular away the whole week through sickness.

"With one or two exceptions, those families directly concerned in the proceedings have not been much, if any, better in their attendance. The proceedings have had a general rather than a particular effect. But I think that if the Board are firm in their determination to secure a regular attendance they may attain their object by judicious exercise of the compulsory powers which they possess. Even the seemingly defiant I think would in time learn obedience to the law from a repetition of last week's unpleasant though necessary proceedings.

"The following shows the number of attendances made this week by the children whose parents were proceeded against, and their several brothers and sister:

William	Chapple	7 out of a possible		10
Clara	do	0	"	10 (sick)
Richard	do	10	"	10
William	Phillips	6	"	10
Albert	do	2	"	10
Charlotte	do	10	"	10
Fanny	do	8	"	10
Albert	Stone	8	"	10
Simon	do	7	"	10
Amelia	do	7	"	10
James	Fry	8	"	10
Lilly	Gully	9	"	10
Theresa (half time)	Hunt	5	"	10
Arthur	do	8	"	10
Frank	do	9	"	10
Sydney	do	8	"	10
		113 total		160 total or 70 per cent."

Joseph Brooks.
Headmaster of Chedzoy School from 1879 to 1920.
Photograph courtesy of Margaret Alsford.

Three months later Mr. Brooks again wrote to the Board.

"Dear Sir, I have to report a decrease in three in the average attendance for the four weeks ending this day as compared with that of last month. I attribute this mainly to the rather unfavourable weather we have experienced for the last ten days. This reason satisfactorily accounts for the falling off in the Infants department, but I also noticed a greater amount of irregularity in the upper classes than there ought to be.

"I have submitted the name of one defaulting child, Amelia Stone, for the consideration of the Board. It is a bad case. This week she has been away from school 5 out of 10 times, and a brother of hers 4 out of 10 without any reason whatsoever. At the examination in July last, owing partly to a naturally very dull intellect but principally to her irregular attendance, she failed in every subject. This year out of a possible 202 attendances she has made only 126. Absent 76 times or *seven and a half weeks* already and not quite half the year gone. Such children do themselves no good and their school great harm. I therefore trust that the Board will take proceedings in this case.

"The following figures will enable you to see how the attendance stands at present. Average for 4 weeks ending 16th Dec., No. on books 94, per cent 74. For corresponding week last year, No. on books 93, per cent 76. Attendance for this year (July 1st to present time) 66 or 69 per cent. A.P. Graves, H.M. Inspector of Schools for this district, states, I believe, in the Educational Blue Book of 1882, that the attendance in his late (Huddersfield) district was 89 per cent of the names on the books, or 20 per cent higher than ours. Mr. Graves strongly recommends a prize scheme for the encouragement of regular and punctual attendance."

The winter of 1882 was unusually wet with extensive flooding throughout the area, although contemporary reports contain no references to Chedzoy. On 13th December 1882 the Bridgwater Mercury reported,

"Some of the customary Christmas donations have already been distributed in the village; amongst others two hundred bags of coal had been given by the University of Oxford, to which the greater part of the parish belongs. This was an especially welcome and seasonable gift after the long-continued floods and rain and was fully appreciated by the recipients."

A special meeting of the School Board was called in February 1883.

"The Clerk reports having called meeting in consequence of a letter from the Vice Chairman with reference to a letter as underneath set out from the Chairman of the Board (Rev. G.O. Mullens) resigning office as a member as also to a complaint made by one John Stone as to Mr. Brooks, the Master, having severely beaten his son who at the time was a scholar in attendance at the school.

"The Vice Chairman now placed before the Board the several facts hereinbefore referred to and states that the Chairman's resignation arose from his considering that the Schoolmaster had not treated him with proper respect or attention on his recently visiting the School, the particulars whereof the Vice Chairman now places before the Board.

"Mr. Brooks comes before the Board and states with reference to complaint made as to having severely beaten Stone's son that lad was very dull and on day in question during a spelling lesson he exhibited more than an ordinary amount of stupidity and which he alleges was not natural stupidity but of wilful and persistent inattention, and that in consequence in raising his cane to strike the lad over one of the shoulders the latter suddenly moved aside and so caused the cane lightly to touch one of his ears and which he much regretted, and the Schoolmaster now produced the cane so then used.

"That as to the want of paying proper courtesy and attention towards the Chairman he had never intended lacking paying due and proper respect and that if his actions had been misconstrued, he much regretted it and would most willingly and fully so write the Chairman and apologize for any apparent lack of attention on his part.

"The Board consider the several complaints and come to the conclusion that Stone's parents had no cause to complain and accept the Schoolmaster's explanation as to apparent want of respect and attention towards the Chairman but the former is to write the latter and fully set out such explanation with an expression of sincere regret at his conduct having been misunderstood."

Rev. Mullens subsequently withdrew his resignation as Chairman of the School Board.

The problem of defaulting pupils continued to concern Joseph Brooks and in April 1883 the subject again came before the Board.

"Clerk read letter from Mr. Brooks as hereunder set out and reports having on receipt thereof given warning to the parents and Mr. Brooks now stated that such warnings had had no effect. Board considered subject matter and directed Clerk to give further warnings and if parents continued in arrears after Tuesday next to issue summonses against such as were then in default.

"Also to call upon Mr. John Tazewell who employed William Chapple, Joseph Ashford who employed Frank Toogood, Elias Potter who employed John Andrews and Walter Barnstable who employed Wallace and Albert Phillips to desist doing so or proceedings would be taken."

"Dear Sir,

Will you please be good enough to send special warnings to the parents of the following defaulting children:

Child	Father	Times absent for week ending		
		31st Mar	7th April	14th April
Wm. Chapple	Wm. Chapple	10	10	10
Albert Stone	John Stone	6	4	6
Simon Stone	John Stone	6	4	6
Frank Toogood	John Toogood	10	10	10
Fred Jeanes	Joseph Jeanes	3	8	10
Wallace Phillips	Wm. Phillip	0	5	6
Albert Phillips	Wm. Phillips	0	5	6

"The attendance in the lower Standards (1 and 2) and Infants at the present time is fairly regular. Of the above mentioned Defaulters who are all in the upper part of the School (Standards 3 and upwards) William Chapple has only been to school 2 days for the last four weeks. Frank Toogood only $3^1/_2$ days for the last five weeks. This state of things is most unsatisfactory and as several members of the School Board are, I regret to say, among those who employ children illegally, it is unjust to me as part of my salary and all my professional reputation depends on the results of the examinations. As you will see, sir, it is not just for one week or so at any especially pressing time but week after week for which I think there is no good excuse."

The exasperation of Mr. Brooks with the School Board was demonstrated in a letter written to them in February 1884.

"To the Members of Chedzoy School Board.

Gentlemen, Having now for a period extending upwards of four years been in your Board's service, and never having had any increase made to my salary, I think the time has now arrived for a re-arrangement, and therefore I venture to make an application for an advance on the present rate of stipend, feeling confident that my application will meet with liberal and considerate treatment at your hands.

"I take this step for other reasons than that of long service:

1. The present salary is more than £40 below the average salary paid to Male Teachers of Elementary Schools throughout England and Wales.
2. When I accepted the post in 1879 Mr. John Tazewell, the then Chairman of the School Board, gave me to understand that should things go on satisfactorily I might depend on the Board making things better for the Teacher, with respect to emoluments than they were at that time.
3. The lowness of salary prevents my making any provision for times of sickness or old age, and consequently I look into the future with anything but feelings of serenity. With my fixed stipend I cannot pay my way as I go, with the greatest of frugality, my expenses being on the increase and so although my share of the Grant may seem rather large to receive at one time, the greater part of it is in reality expended before I touch it.

"While on the subject of 'Grant,' I should like to suggest that if a large proportion of my salary must depend upon the Grant from the Government I should greatly prefer its being paid monthly. This might be done by paying one twelfth of average grant for the last two, three or four years along with the usual monthly salary and would be practically fixed and paid monthly. Some such arrangement as this obtains under the London School Board. It would be a great convenience to me and no burden whatsoever on your Board. I often feel the inconvenience of having to wait 14 months (as I had last year) for more than one third of my salary. Placing my care in your hands with confidence as to the result of your deliberations on it,

I remain Gentlemen,
Yours respectfully,
Joseph Brooks."

The letter had the desired result as he received an increase in salary from £50 to £60 per annum, or from £4 3s. 4d. to £5 per month.

Mr. Brooks was not respected by all members of the community. In June 1884 he wrote to the Clerk thus:

"I have to report to you the fact of having had since the last meeting of the School Board the mother of one of the children attending my school up at the school and there making use of vile and abusive language. The child was kept in after school hours to complete work given to her to do. The mother made her appearance about 12.20 p.m. threatening to break down the —- door if her child did not at once leave the school. Woman left school premises about 12.30 with her child and all her way homewards used very bad language. Further one day this week as pupil teacher was passing down street same woman tried to annoy her by calling after her 'The Old Devil.' What think, Sir, under the circumstances had best be done."

Kelly's Director for 1883 notes that "recently" 36 skeletons buried 20 inches from the surface had been exhumed,

"evidently remains of persons killed in the fight (Battle of Sedgemoor) or immediately after,"

but no mention of this was published in the Bridgwater Mercury or is recorded in parish records.

Francis Lovibond was still making notes in his diary:

"William Giles died of Diphtheria and buried June 27th 1884, aged 17 years. He was not carried in church" and "Ellen Giles died July 3rd 1884 and buried the same evening between the hours of nine and ten of Diphtheria, aged 24 years. She was not carried in church."

They were brother and sister and lived with their widowed mother at Parchey.

Although not mentioned in the School Board minutes, action was still being taken in regard to absenteeism. In December 1884 a very short paragraph appeared in the Bridgwater Mercury's court column:

Wm. Fry, of Chedzoy, was charged with neglecting to send his child to school. He was fined 6d. (2.5p.) and costs." Was it the same person in trouble in February 1883? No address was given. "Wm. Fry was summoned for not sending his child to school. - Mr. T.M. Reed prosecuted, and said that the child made only 76 attendances out of 118. - The wife of the defendant appeared, and stated the child was too ill to attend school regularly. - No certificate, however, was produced to that effect, and defendant was fined 1s. and 2s. costs."

In June 1885 tragedy returned to the village and was reported in the Mercury.

"An inquest was held at the Crown Inn by the district coroner (Mr. W. Munckton) on the body of James Fry, aged 13 years, the illegitimate son of Charlotte Fry (46), of Parchay (sic), in this parish, who was accidentally killed on Saturday last. Mr. Henry Conduit, dairyman for Mr. Edwin Fry, of Chedzoy, said on Saturday afternoon, he was milking in a field called 'Eight Acres' at Parchay, and the deceased and his mother (Charlotte Fry) were assisting. The horse and the milking cart, in which the deceased rode with the witness to the field, were left close to the gate. Witness told deceased not to meddle with the horse and deceased replied, 'I shall pick some grass and give him.' Shortly afterwards, as he was milking, witness heard the horse make a bolt, and looking round he saw the boy fall in front of the near wheel, which passed over his head. Witness and others ran to help him, and lifted him up, but he only breathed a few times and then died. Henry Tambling said he was in 'Eight Acres' at the time, and saw the horse running away as described by the last witness. He ran to the spot and found the deceased in the arms of Conduit where he died soon afterwards. - Conduit, on being re-examined, added that no one was near the horse at the time of the occurrence but the deceased. His mother (Charlotte Fry) was nearest; she was about twelve yards off. Witness's opinion was that the deceased must have removed, or was in the act of removing, the blind halter at the time the horse ran away, for he saw it on the horse just previously, and when the animal was running away it was off. He found part of it by the boy's side. The jury returned a verdict of 'Accidentally Killed'."

In most years accounts of the annual choir outing were published: that for June 1885 illustrates some of the problems of transport in those days.

"The choir in this village had their annual excursion on Tuesday. This year, and for several years past, the outing has consisted of a drive to Weston-super-Mare. The choir has lately been strengthened by the addition of five boys, having which extra number necessitated the employment of a conveyance of greater capacity than has been used for these outings in past years. Hence, Mr. G. Ricks' 'four-in-hand' was brought into requisition. Amidst the joyful cheers of the occupants of the brake the start was effected at nine o'clock. Weston was reached about midday. A capital dinner was speedily placed on the table in a room which had been previously engaged by Mrs. Mullens. The afternoon was slightly wet, but not withstanding this, all thoroughly enjoyed themselves. The return journey was commenced immediately after tea. Rain fell rather heavily during the latter half of the drive home and this made it somewhat unpleasant. On reaching Chedzoy hearty cheers were accorded to the Rev. G.O. Mullens, the rector, to whose kindly generosity these annual outings are entirely due. The reverend gentleman expressed his regret that they had not been favoured with a fine day, and wished them all 'Good-night'."

"A MAN FOUND DEAD IN CHEDZOY LANE. SINGULAR AFFAIR" was the headline in the Bridgwater Mercury in December 1885.

"A good deal of excitement prevailed in Bridgwater on Saturday morning on its being rumoured that a man had been found dead, under some very suspicious circumstances, in Chedzoy-lane, near this town, and that a woman, supposed to be his wife, had been apprehended on suspicion of having caused his death. It soon afterwards transpired, however, as is so frequently the case in connection with events of this description, that the facts had been greatly exaggerated, and although the circumstances are of an extraordinary character, the police appear to have no suspicion of foul play. It appears that about six o'clock in the morning, it being quite dark at the time, some men whilst on their way to work, and when passing through Chedzoy-lane, were startled on being accosted by some one on the roadside, the voice, a very hoarse one, being apparently that of a female. Some matches were ignited, and the men then perceived a woman, who was in a half-stupified condition, crouched down on the brink of the ditch. By her side was the body of a man lying face downwards and covered with mud. The woman said the body was that of her husband, who had died that morning about three hours previously, and that she had remained by his side ever since. She added that he had fallen into a ditch, from which she had dragged him. ... P.C. Gould hastened to the spot and found the woman still there. He caused the body to be removed to the Hunter's Lodge public-house, and brought the woman in custody to Bridgwater where she was lodged at the county police station. ...

"The identity of the deceased was soon afterwards discovered, and proved to be Andrew Colman, the holder of a pedlar's certificate, granted some time ago by Superintendent Lear, and a man who is well known in the neighbourhood. The woman, who has recently been cohabiting with him, and is not his wife, proved to be Elizabeth Wilson, also well known in Bridgwater where she has been living in a lodging house at the Mount. ... On Saturday afternoon Elizabeth Wilson (but who at the inquest on Monday said her name was Elizabeth Perington) was brought up in custody before Mr. R.E. Price on suspicion of causing the death of Andrew Colman." She was remanded in custody.

"THE INQUEST was held at the Hunter's Lodge, Chedzoy-lane on Monday, before the district coroner (Mr. W.W. Munckton)." Medical evidence was that "the deceased died from exposure to the inclemency of the weather, probably whilst in a drunken state, causing exhaustion." After hearing from Elizabeth Perington, "Arthur Clement Ashford said: I live at Horsey. On Friday evening, about twenty past eleven, as I was walking home I saw a man lying on the side of the turnpike on the grass and a woman sitting down by his side, about fifty to one hundred yards from Merritt's house, on the eastern side. The following morning, about twenty minutes to seven, I passed the place and saw them by Chedzoy-lane, the man lying downwards and the woman by his side. ... They were moved back 200 or 300 yards towards Knowle. ... After some observations by the coroner, and by his advice, the jury returned a verdict according to the medical testimony, namely, that the deceased died from exhaustion and exposure to the weather whilst in a state of drunkenness. On Monday afternoon the prisoner was brought up on remand from Saturday, and Superintendent Vowles having stated what had transpired at the inquest, she was discharged."

In August 1886 a short report was published in the Bridgwater Mercury which tends to indicate that the members of the School Board may have been somewhat economical with the truth in regard to finance.

"[Chedzoy Board] School was recently examined by Mr. A.P. Graves, her Majesty's Inspector, assisted by Mr. A.H. Lacey, and the managers have now received the following report:- 'Mixed School: This school is under very good discipline, and is extremely well taught by Mr. Brooks. He has, in fact, raised it from the discreditable condition into which it had fallen by the employment of two inferior mistresses by the Board, on the grounds of economy, into a very high state of efficiency. I am surprised to learn on inquiry into the condition of the school staff that it is proposed to impair it by again reverting to a policy of what I cannot but characterise as parsimony. Infant's class: The infants are decidedly well taught." As the first mistress had an annual salary of £70, but her successor and Joseph Brooks were taken on at £50 per annum, it is difficult to comprehend the Inspector's comments in regard to economy!

In September 1886 Harvest Home festivities in the village received considerable coverage in the Bridgwater Mercury. Various decorative arches were erected around the village.

"The first arch on entering the village was very prettily trimmed with flowers, corn and hops, with the motto on one side, 'Welcome to the Harvest Home' and on the other 'May success crown our efforts,' the work being done by Mr. and Mrs. Wheeler and family, and Mr. and Mrs. E. Rainey. Over the gate leading to Mr. Derrick's field was another arch inscribed with the words, 'A welcome to all friends,' and on the other side 'Success to agriculture'." 250 people took tea at Fishers Farm and this was followed by a dance.

Uriah Martin died on 5th January 1887 at the age of 78 years. Francis Lovibond's diary records that he had been the village blacksmith and for fifty years served as clerk to the parish of Chedzoy, resigning only two years before his death. As a mark of respect a muffled peal of bells was rung at the church on the evening of his burial. Although well respected in the community, it would seem that his wife did not hold him in the same high regard.

"An inquest was held at the Crown Inn, [Chedzoy], by the district coroner (Mr. W.W. Munckton), on the body of Uriah Martin, labourer, who had been sexton of the parish church for about fifty years. The wife of the deceased said that on Sunday morning he was in his usual health, and went to church, after which he returned and partook of dinner with her and her two grandchildren. Shortly after she noticed he was in a strange position, and his mouth down on one side, and he was sliding off the stool upon which he was sitting. Witness admitted some altercation had taken place between them, but the only thing she had asked him was, 'Where did you get that shilling that I found in your trousers pocket one day?' and he replied, 'Farmer Winter gave it to me.' Jane Bryant said she lived in the adjoining house ... The last witness called her and her husband into the house. ... She attended the deceased up to the time of his death. ... She had frequently heard disturbances between the deceased and his wife, but on the day in question no noise or disturbance at all." Dr. Kemmis gave medical evidence. "The coroner explained to the jury that there had been a report in the neighbourhood that the deceased had received foul treatment from the hands of his wife. The only evidence that could be called to prove this was that of the two grand-children, one aged four and the other six. Superintendent Vowles remarked that if necessary the children could give evidence, as they were present, but the jury thought this unnecessary, and returned a verdict that 'The deceased died from an attack of paralysis'."

Later that year the Bridgwater Mercury reported that

"The tombstone which Miss Winter, of Fowler's Plot, has been collecting for, to erect in our beautiful churchyard to the memory of our late clerk (Mr. Uriah Martin) was erected on Tuesday. The deceased was for fifty years a faithful servant of the church and during those many years in office he was a witness of 664 baptisms, 106 marriages and 603 burials. It may be truly said of him he never made an enemy and never forgot a friend."

His grave and the headstone may be found near the north door of the church.

In 1887 the country celebrated the Golden Jubilee of Queen Victoria: residents of Chedzoy also took part.

"On Monday afternoon, June 20th, the aged poor and widows were invited to tea at Fowler's Plot, the residence of Mr. G. Winter, where a first class tea was provided. The room had been prettily decorated for the occasion with mottoes, flags, &c. After tea the aged were delighted at seeing over the poultry houses, and inspecting the alterations and improvements of the farm buildings. ... The evening was spent in music, &c. ... Many of the aged were too infirm to walk so they were driven for and taken home by Messrs. J. Hook and Rainey, all being delighted with the arrangement. - On Tuesday the festivities were resumed. A procession of schoolchildren at twelve o'clock met at Mrs. J. Gilbert's, each carrying flags, flowers, &c., and headed by a large banner of her Majesty. ...Cheers were given by the children at each house they visited." Prizes and medals were later presented at Westfield Farm. "The thoughtful present ... of tobacco and long clay pipes was highly appreciated by those who enjoy a smoke, and also the barrel of cider." Later there was dancing and Mr. Winter said, "He was more than glad to say he thought all the men deserved the highest congratulations from their masters, for although they had been the greater part of the day in the hay field, not one of them had taken more intoxicating liquor than had done him good. ...

It should be added that the bells rang merry peals during the day."

In September 1887 the village had some unusual entertainment.

"On Tuesday the little village was en fete on the occasion of the harvest home celebrations. The weather was extremely propitious and a large number of persons from Bridgwater visited the place during the afternoon and evening. ... The day's proceedings commenced with a procession starting from Chedzoy-lane and marching through the village." A meat tea was provided and a presentation made to Miss Elizabeth Winter. "An adjournment was made to the field to witness a pig chase by women. The pig was greased and painted in different colours. There were only two competitors who were attired in rather light costumes. The pig having been let loose, was pursued for a short time by both women, when the animal made a rush for the top of a heap of straw, which it mounted, and there it was caught by one of the women named Ellen Bell."

This was probably Ellen Bell, 34, who lived in Chedzoy Lane near Hunter's Lodge.

"The remainder of the evening was spent in dancing to the strains of the band, which kept up until eleven o'clock with much spirit. ... On Friday a tea was given in the tent to all the children attending the day and Sunday schools."

It seems that success with the annual Harvest Home prompted a more ambitious event. In September 1888 the Bridgwater Mercury reported,

"The little village of Chedzoy was en fete on the occasion of a local Dairy Show and Harvest Home, promoted chiefly by Miss Winter of Fowler's Plot, who has for some time past taken considerable interest in making known the improved methods of butter-making, &c., and the success attending Thursday's proceedings must have proved very gratifying to herself and every member of the committee. Shortly after two o'clock, several members of the committee on horseback assembled at the entrance to Chedzoy-lane from Bath-road, where a pretty arch had been erected inscribed on one side, 'Success to the Chedzoy Dairy Show,' and on the other, 'May Agriculture Flourish.' ... A procession was then formed [and] passed through the centre of the village. ... The procession arrived at West Field Farm, the residence of Mr. and Mrs. W. Brake." Amongst other exhibits there was a demonstration of butter making and this was followed by a dinner at which the Member of Parliament, Mr. Stanley, said the show was "the first of what all persons interested in farming must hope would be a series of such shows in other parishes throughout Somersetshire had been held in Chedzoy, and that they had therefore set a very good example." Later dancing was "Indulged in to a late hour."

Absenteeism at the school seems to have continued.

In October 1888

"William Chappell, farm labourer, Chedzoy, was summoned for not sending his child to school. - Mr. T.M. Reed prosecuted and stated that the child had only made 43 attendances out of a possible 83. Fined 6d. and 4s. 6d. costs. - Charles Hunt, also of Chedzoy, was summoned for a like offence. Fifty attendances were only made out of a possible 83. - Fined 6d. and 4s. 6d. costs."

Although no address was given for either defendant, this report from December 1888 probably relates to villagers.

"Wm. Ware, labourer, and Henry Hill, labourer, of the same place, were charged with being drunk and disorderly at Chedzoy. P.C. Gill proved the case. He stated that the defendant Hill challenged to fight a man named Stone. The defendant Ware also interfered, and both the defendants, in fact, were excited with drink. They also went fighting. He had considerable difficulty in parting them. The defendant Ware stated that the disturbance took place through Hill, who was fighting with another man, but he (Ware) said, 'Don't knock he, 'cause he's drunk.' Defendant added, 'As I was going up to the bobby, Hill knocked me down alongside the bobby.' (Laughter.) The defendant Ware was fined 5s. and costs, and Hill 7s. and costs."

The Bridgwater Mercury reported in March 1889 that

"A confirmation service was held in Chedzoy church by the Right Reverend Bishop Hobhouse. ... The candidates number as follows: Chedzoy, 10 males and 19 females, ... Before the right of Confirmation the candidates were addressed by the Bishop, but unfortunately in so low a tone of voice from the chancel that only a few comparatively of those present were able to hear him."

In May 1889 a Chedzoy resident appeared before the Borough Magistrates.

"Henry Whitfield of [Front Street], Chedzoy, was summoned for furious driving in Fore-Street, [Bridgwater]. P.C. Bailey stated that he saw the defendant driving a horse and cart in High-street. He drove very recklessly, and beat the animal severely. Witness had received a number of complaints respecting the defendant's driving, especially by persons in Eastover and Monmouth-street. - Mr. Frank Rose, High-street, also gave evidence. He added that a serious accident was prevented by one of the cab-men taking hold of the head of the horse driven by the defendant, or it would have certainly dashed into the vehicles on the cab-stand. Defendant was fined 40s. (£2) and costs."

That same month a fire occurred in a cottage which was located in Front Street somewhere in the vicinity of Westfield Farm. It was reported that

"Shortly before midnight on Wednesday the West of England Fire Brigade were called to a fire which had broken out on the premises of Mr. James Potter of Chedzoy. The brigade, under the superintendence of Mr. T.H. Willis of Bridgwater, at once proceeded to the scene of the conflagration, but it was discovered that the house had been completely burnt down. With difficulty, however, the whole of the furniture was saved, none of the inhabitants sustaining any injury."

The quality of food was an issue in December 1889:

"Mr. William Coles, Inspector of the Rural Sanitary Authority, appeared in court and stated from the information he received on the previous day he went to the premises of one John Potter of Chedzoy, and found there a portion of the carcase of a sheep. He enquired for the remaining portion, and the wife of Potter acquainted him that it had been sent to Bridgwater for sale. Witness examined the portion on the premises, and subsequently seized it as being unfit for food. - In answer to the Chairman, the Inspector added that he found the meat in question hung up on Potter's premises where other meat was usually hung for sale. - By Mr. Strangeways: The meat was not actually exposed in the shop for sale as the defendant had no place to expose it other than to drive it round the village in a butcher's cart. - Mr. F.J.C. Parsons, medical officer for the district, stated that he had carefully examined the meat in question which was, in his opinion, unsound, diseased, and unfit for food for man. - In reply to the Clerk, the Inspector stated that his application was for an order condemning it unfit for food, and the magistrates thereupon granted the order."

Later that month,

"John Potter, general dealer, Chedzoy, was summoned for unlawfully being in possession of meat dressed for sale, certified by the medical officer of health to be unfit for human food. Defendant in reply to the Clerk pleaded guilty and said he gave 25s. for the carcase of lamb without the skin, and he was under the impression the meat was in a proper condition. - Mr. Barham stated that the facts of the case had already appeared before the court, but he would ask the Bench to deal with the case as a serious one to prevent impossible further practice of such an offence. - Defendant was fined £3 and costs, the Chairman remarking that he was liable to be fined as much as £20 or be sent to prison for three months." John Potter should have listened to the Chairman.

The End of the 19th Century

The start of a new decade did not mean that the School Board were going to spend money unnecessarily. In January 1890 the Bridgwater Mercury published a short report in relation to a School Board meeting.

"... Mr. Derrick reported ... a globe and map were needed, but although a globe may be purchased at a high price, one costing less than £1 would meet their need. - A letter was read from Mr. Brooks, the schoolmaster, saying that Mrs. Brooks would oblige the Board by arranging for the pupil teachers to receive their lessons at the school-house instead of the school-room, and that Mrs. Brooks would thus be enabled to sign the necessary papers. - Miss Winter proposed that the Board thank Mrs. Brooks for her kindness in arranging her household duties to oblige at the early morning hour, which would save the ratepayers the expense of engaging a person to be present in the school-room to comply with the Act."

Having failed to heed the warning of the court, John Potter appeared again in April 1890 when he

"was summoned for being in possession of the carcase of a sheep, seized by Inspector Coles on behalf of the Rural Sanitary Authority, and condemned as unfit for food of man. Mr. William Coles, Inspector, stated that on the day in question he had occasion to pass through Chedzoy, and he called at the defendant's house. Witness went down the garden there and looked into the defendant's shop, and saw the carcase of the sheep in question. It was properly dressed, as for human food, and witness having examined it, seized it as unfit for food. Potter then came into the shop and said, 'Don't take it away,' and after witness had put it in his trap, defendant added, 'I didn't intend to sell it, we intended to boil it up.' Mr. F.J.C. Parsons, medical officer of health, proved having certified the carcase of the sheep in question as unfit for human food. Mr. Edwin Ware, veterinary surgeon, also proved seeing the carcase of the sheep in question and gave evidence to the effect that he considered the meat totally unfit for human consumption; in fact it was watery and flabby, and scarcely fit for animals to eat. The meat was properly dressed. Mr. Dyke, butcher, Eastover, [Bridgwater], also gave corroborative evidence; and Superintendent Vowles having stated the defendant had already been fined £3 for a similar offence on the 28th December last, the Bench inflicted the full penalty, viz., three months' imprisonment without the option of a fine, to pay the costs, in default distress or a further imprisonment."

Disease returned to the village in November 1890 and was referred to in a letter from Joseph Brooks to the School Board.

"I have to report that since the last sitting of the School Board, this parish has been visited by an outbreak of Diphtheria. This has had a most injurious effect on the attendance, and worse still it has unfortunately resulted in the deaths of several persons, two of whom were scholars in my school - a little boy in Standard 1 and a sister of his is the fourth standard. The little boy was at school on Friday, Oct. 17th, and died on the following Friday, Oct. 24th. His death was followed by the death of the little girl on Tuesday, Oct. 28th." Parish records reveal that the two children who died were Sidney William Bennett, aged 6 and Agnes Mary Bennett, aged 9. "Under these circumstances parents of scholars became alarmed and many kept their children from school. I saw Mr. H. Fry and Mr. Derrick on Wednesday, Oct. 29th and as a result of talk with them the school was closed until the end of the week commencing Nov. 3rd. The same morning I sent to inform Miss Winter what was contemplated being done, and on the evening of that day I met Mr. J. Ashford and told him. School resumed on Nov. 10th with many children still absent, especially among the infants.

"This week I am pleased to notice a marked improvement in the attendance. Up to this Tuesday afternoon we have had present this week 48 in the standards and 17 infants. Now that all seems safe I trust that, should I be spared until next month, I shall be able to report a considerable improvement even on this."

At their next meeting the Board approved the action taken by their Head Teacher.

In 1851 there were 576 residents in the parish (including Chedzoy Lane and Horsey); subsequent Censuses were for "the whole of the Parish of Chedzoy, including that part of Chedzoy Lane in the Parish of Chedzoy." In 1861 there were 442 residents; 384 in 1871 and just 356 in 1881. The Census for 1891 (see Appendix 1) shows a drop in the population of the parish to 315. There does not appear to be any reason for this noted in the records, but it would seem likely that this was brought about through a general drift towards towns caused by the decline in agriculture and, possibly, mass emigration as North America welcomed thousands of immigrants from Europe.

Children were very hardy in those days, or was it just that the School Board were reluctant to spend money? In December 1890 the Bridgwater Mercury reported a meeting of the Board.

"The only requirement for the school was 50 cwt. of coal. Miss Winter brought before the notice of the Board the temperatures of the large school-room, which she feared was too low for the children's comfort. In order to ascertain the heat of the room she had taken a tested thermometer and found the temperature to be as follows: November 28th, 42° Fahr. (5°C.); December 8th, 42° Fahr.; December 15th, 38° Fahr. (3°C.); December 17th, 38° Fahr., although there was a capital fire burning in the grate at the top of the room, and on each occasion when she had visited the school she had seen the children warming themselves by the fire, they having been allowed to do so by the master (Mr. Brooks). - Mr. Fry said he had visited the school some days previous, and found the temperature of the room to be 46° Fahr. (8°C.). The Clerk read art. 73 in the New Code on the subject, and then the matter was left for a month that the other members present may have an opportunity of visiting the school for the purpose of seeing for themselves the temperatures which at present they felt was sufficient to meet the requirements of the Act."

Miss Winter did not wait for that next meeting and on 7th January 1891 a further report was published in the Bridgwater Mercury saying that she had written to the Education Department on the matter.

"She has been favoured with a reply from Whitehall, London.

'Education Department, 2nd January 1891.
Chedzoy School Board, West Somerset.

Madam,

Adverting to your letter ... I am to state that their lordships have received the following report from H.M. Inspector:- My assistant, Mr. Lacey, visited the school on 22nd December, the ground being covered with frost and snow, and found the temperature of the school at 36° (2°C.). There was a good fire in the room, but there were no children present owing to the deep snow. Mr. Lacey saw the chairman of the Board and he has undertaken to put a stove in the room.

I have the honour to be, Madam,
your obedient servant, G.W. Kekewich'."

The School Board minutes for January 1891, under the heading "Heating of the School," record that

"The Board further discussed the above question and Mr. Fry stated that he had since the last sitting visited the school three times when he found the temperature to be as follows: on 1st instant 40°, 6th instant 44° and on 16th instant 46°. Mr. Ashford also stated that he had visited the school on four occasions when he found the heat to be 46°. After a long discussion it was resolved that a stove was not necessary at present as no complaint had been made by anyone whatever and the Board object to one being placed in the school. Miss Winter voted against the motion."

Well, 40°, 44° and 46° Fahrenheit converts to 4°, 6° and 8° Celsius, so there was no point in making children soft!

The School Board minutes do not reveal the full story, but further details were published in the Bridgwater Mercury. The New Code required the temperature in the classroom to be between 56° and 60° Fahrenheit (13° and 15° Celsius) and the Chairman insisted he had not said they would provide a stove, but only that a stove would be provided if the other members of the Board agreed.

"The chairman raised an objection to have a stove to raise the temperature to 60° Fahr., as that was the heat to grow cucumbers. - Mr. Brake said he should oppose the stove, as such a heat as the Code mentioned would suffocate the children. Mr. Fry ... said he felt assured the school-room was warmer than the labourer's cottages and somewhat different to school-rooms when he was a boy (as often he had picked sticks from the roadside to heat the school-room)."

The subject was raised again in March when reference was made to the report which had been published in the Bridgwater Mercury.

"Some of the [Board] members, and especially the fathers of children, had raised an objection to a stove which was for the health and comfort of every child attending the school. Mr. Reed then read them a letter in which the Lords of the Council on Education ordered that the temperature of the school must not fall below 58° Fah., and unless the order was complied with the grant would not be given at the next examination".

However, Her Majesty's Inspector of Schools did not think the Board was doing enough and in March reported,

"The temperatures as tested by my assistant on the 19th with a brisk fire and at the end of the afternoon meeting was only 50° (10°C.). I am to direct the attention of your Board to their Lordships' letter of 16th February last, and to enquire why no effective means have been taken for securing greater warmth in the school-room and whether measures will at once be adopted so that in future the temperature will not be allowed to fall below 58° (14°C.)."

This issue was causing quite a bit of animosity between the Board members. In May the Bridgwater Mercury reported

"A somewhat long list of defaulters was gone through, and there being several defaulting 'half-timers' the Clerk was directed to write 'That as to any child exempt from attending school, but attending as a volunteer, such child be required to attend regularly, so as to prevent the school grant from suffering from irregular attendance of such children.' - In the case of William Fry, whose child George has been a repeated defaulter, various warnings have been sent and there being no improvement in attendance, it was decided to issue a summons."

And so back to heating!

"Mr. Ashford proposed ...that a letter be sent to a company of 'Refrigerators' asking their lowest price for supplying two refrigerators for the school in order that they may lower the present temperature. - Miss Winter said she perfectly understood Mr. Ashford's allusion, but in trying to get a stove during the cold weather it had been as much for his own children's comfort and health as for the other little ones attending the school. ... Mr. Ashford said Miss Winter quite misunderstood him in taking it as an insult, but he thought the temperature should be considered as much during the summer as in the winter. - Miss Winter said the stove had not yet been placed in the school and to lower the temperature when the warm weather came could be easily done - by opening doors and windows."

The government resorted to threats in August that year:

"The difficulty which has arisen as to the heating of the school will be sufficiently met by the undertaking on the part of the Board to provide a stove to be lit when occasion demands. ... I am to warn the Board that if H.M. Inspector at any future time reports that the school is insufficiently warmed the grant may be withheld......."

In response to these threats the School Board (reluctantly?) purchased a stove at a cost of £1 6s. 7d. but they were soon complaining about the costs involved. In December cheques had to be written for 2 tons 17 cwt. of coal (£3 4s. 9d.) and one ton of coke (13s. 4d.) for the stove.

"Mr. Fry declined to sign the cheque for £1 6s. 7d. for the stove pipe and fixing ... saying he still much objected to the stove being placed in the school."

Twelve months later the Board's minutes recorded,

"Resolved that the Clerk call the attention of the Head Teacher to the larger consumption of coal which appears for the past year to have cost twice as much as for the years prior to the introduction of the stove and request his in future being as careful as possible in the use of the fire."

So a second fire was installed and twice as much fuel used? Amazing!

On 31st December 1890 the Bridgwater Mercury reported a remand hearing under the headline SHOOTING AFFRAY AT CHEDZOY.

"At the county magistrates' clerk's office on Monday, before Sir Francis Hartwell, Bart., George Wheeler (26), labourer, of [Batch], Chedzoy, was charged with having maliciously and feloniously, with a certain gun, loaded with gunpowder and shot, shot at one Vincent Mountstevens and others with intent to do them grievous bodily harm, at Chedzoy, on the 27th inst.

"Vincent Mountstevens deposed that he was a labourer and lived at Westonzoyland. On Saturday last he went to Chedzoy with Richard Hucker, Alfred Snow and Oliver Pitman They got there about six o'clock in the evening and went to the Crown Inn, and remained there about a quarter of an hour. They left and subsequently returned again, and remained until closing time. They then went down the road, and heard a man playing an accordion below the prisoner's house. They presently saw Js. Wheeler, the prisoner's brother, and William Fry. Words passed between them, and shortly afterwards the prisoner joined his brother, both of whom came out of the house with their coats and waistcoats off. A fight ensued, and the two Wheelers got knocked down. The prisoner then ran back into his house, and witness and the others with him ran up the road towards the Crown Inn. When they had got about fifty yards away they heard the report of a gun, and the discharge came up behind them. Witness felt himself struck in the back of the head and neck with shots, and there were shot holes and marks of blood in his hat (produced). Those with him were also more or less wounded in the head, and they went together to the Bridgwater Infirmary. They did not go back to see who fired and could not say who fired off the gun. At the Infirmary they had the shots taken out of their heads, and the wounds dressed. Mr. Reed (for the defence) here intimated that he should reserve his cross-examination of the witnesses.

"P.C. Cooksley was the next witness. He stated that from the information he received on Sunday, the 28th inst., he went to Chedzoy, and made enquiries at [Miss] Emma Bennett's" - she was 56 years old and lived in a cottage which is now the site of The Gables, Front Street - "who was struck by a shot. He found four panes of glass downstairs broken, and one pane in the upstairs window. They appeared to have been smashed by shot. There were also shot holes in the wood work of the window. Witness went to the prisoner's house to make enquiries respecting the discharge of the gun, and he found the prisoner sat by the fire with his brother. Witness asked, 'What about this row down here last night?' Prisoner replied, 'They were pitching into my brother, and I went to his assistance. I took the gun up and it was cocked, but I didn't know it, and it went off accidentally.' In further reply to witness, prisoner said, 'There's the gun in the corner.' It was a double-barrelled gun and a breechloader. After witness had seen the shot wounds he apprehended the prisoner and charged him with discharging the gun with intent to do bodily harm to the complainants. Prisoner said, 'I did it, and what's the best to do; plead guilty or not guilty?' Witness informed him that he was not to advise him, but what he said he should take and give in evidence at the hearing of the case.

"Supt. Vowles here applied for a remand, remarking that there were witnesses to be summoned, and the application was granted. Mr. Reed applied for bail on behalf of the prisoner, but the application was refused, and prisoner was thereupon removed in custody to the county police cells."

The following week there was much fuller coverage of events.

"George Wheeler, labourer, of Chedzoy, was charged on remand with maliciously and feloniously firing a gun at Vincent Mountstevens, Richard Hucker, Samuel Alfred Snow and Oliver Pitman, labourers, with intent to do them grievous bodily harm at Chedzoy, on the 27th inst.. Mr. T.M. Reed again appeared on behalf of the prisoner. The evidence of Vincent Mountstevens (as appearing in our last issue) was read over, and in reply to the Magistrates' Clerk (Mr. E. Trevor) he added that the reason of their running away when the prisoner went in the house was in consequence of something a woman had said.

"Cross-examined by Mr. Reed: He (witness) and the other men arrived in Chedzoy on the day in question at six p.m., and called at the Crown Inn on two occasions. They left there at closing time. They did not see the prisoner at the Crown Inn, but at the Manor House Inn. No words passed between them.

Mr. Reed: Now, when you left, you say you went down towards the prisoner's house?

Witness: Yes, sir.

And that was in the opposite direction to your own home?

Yes

What made you go that way?

We heard a man playing an accordion.

That, you say, was your sole reason - the love of music?

Yes

Now is it a fact that you four men were concealed and waiting for the prisoner or the prisoner's brother?

No, sir.

"You say that words passed between you and James Wheeler. What were these words?

I can't remember the words, sir.

You must, please.

He asked us to have a drink and we refused.

Is there any ill-feeling between you and the Wheelers?

Oh, no.

What followed the refusal to drink?

He asked us to come into the garden to fight, but we told him we did not want to fight.

Now, are you not known in the neighbourhood as a fighting man?

Oh no, sir.

Tell the Bench what followed.

James Wheeler ran into his house.

Now, is it not a fact that you four men hid in the hedge and molested James Wheeler?

No.

Did you not kick him on the ground?

No.

What reason do you give for James Wheeler calling his brother to the spot?

I don't know.

When James went into the house both the brothers came out, and a fight took place.- Then you waited until they came out?

Yes.

Now, what I want to know is this - is it not a fact that you attacked James Wheeler first, and got him on the ground and kicked him severely, and do you remember saying 'Let us do for the —-?'

No, I do not remember having made use of such words.

"Did you say, then, 'Let us do for them both, kick them and murder them?'

No, I made use of no such words.

Did you hear James Wheeler shout out to his brother, 'George, come down and help me, they are killing me?'

No, I did not.

Do you not know that James Wheeler was kicked and severely bruised, and received two black eyes and a swollen nose?

I noticed that he had a swollen nose, but I did not see the black eye.

Now, have you not told the constable Cooksley that you had a bad feeling against these two men?

No, not to my knowledge; and I have no bad feeling against them.

Then which of the men said, 'We'll murder them both?'

Neither of us, to my knowledge.

"The evidence of P.C. Cooksley was next read over, and in reply to the Magistrates' Clerk he added that when he (witness) apprehended him the prisoner said, 'We'll go down the field, so no one shan't see us,' and when going through the field he said, 'It's all Jim's fault; I was having my supper and he came in for me, and we both went down to the gate together, and as soon as I got there I was knocked down. I got up and ran in after the gun and came to the gate and fired after them.' Witness had since measured the distance from the road to the prisoner's house and found it was 35 yards 2 feet, and from the gate in question leading from the prisoner's house to Mrs. Bennett's house (Miss Bennett according to the 1891 Census), where the glass was broken, he had found it 96 yards.

"By Mr. Reed: To his knowledge, the Wheelers were quiet men. Neither of the four men had told him that they had any ill-feeling against the prisoner or his brother, but they knew the prisoner was causing a disturbance at one of the public houses some four months ago. The words made use of by the prisoner - 'I did it, and what's the best to do, plead guilty or not guilty' - were not said until after the witness had arrested him.

Mr. Reed: And after he had said that you advised him that what he did say you should take down and give in evidence against him at the hearing of the case. Why did you not caution him before? It appears you cautioned him after he had opened his mouth.

Sir Francis Hartwell: Yes, if he kept his mouth closed there would be no evidence against him, no doubt.

Mr. Reed: It's unfair on the part of the constable. He ought to have previously cautioned the man. The question has been strongly spoken upon by judges in superior court.

Sir Francis Hartwell: And they might refer to it at the assizes, if they like.

"Samuel Arthur Snow deposed that he was a brickyard worker and lived at Dunwear. He was at Chedzoy with the other men referred to on the day in question. He corroborated the evidence of the last witness, and added that when near the prisoner's house, the prisoner struck him (witness), and he struck him in return, and followed him into the garden gate. Witness, when prisoner went into the house, heard a woman scream, and in consequence of what they heard he and the other men ran away. He heard the report of a gun when about fifty yards from the prisoner's house, and was shot in the head, side of the eye and the arm. He did not know who fired the gun.

The Magistrates' Clerk: What made you run away when prisoner went into his house?

Witness: I thought he had gone for a stick.

"Cross-examined by Mr. Reed: Why did you think he had gone for a stick?

Well, I didn't think he had gone for a gun.

You say you knocked this man down?

Yes.

And then the prisoner ran into his house?

Yes.

What words passed between you and the others with you and the prisoner and his brother?

Wheeler tumbled against the gate, and Mountstevens said, 'Mind you don't knock your teeth out.'

And you say nothing else passed?

No.

Were those the first words?

Oh, no. I can't remember all. He gave a challenge to fight.

Did Wheeler ask you in to have a cider?

No, but he asked me to have a drink.

You were four against two in the fight, and you say you put them on the ground?

Yes, but it was four against three.

"The Chairman here intimated that the Bench considered a prima facie case had been made out, and suggested that a lengthy cross-examination of the various witnesses in that court would be useless.

Mr. Reed: After what has fallen from the Bench I shall curtail my cross-examination of the witness.

"Richard Hucker, labourer, Dunwear, in corroborating the evidence of the previous witnesses, stated that he was also shot in the head.

By Mr. Reed: The row lasted only a few minutes. When the Wheelers were on the ground they did not kick them, but ran away.

By the Magistrates' Clerk: He did not know who had fired the gun.

"Oliver Pitman, labourer, Huntworth, also gave corroborative evidence. Directly he heard the report of the gun he felt he was shot in the arm. He did not know who fired the gun. He did not go to the Infirmary, but picked the shot out of his arm himself on his way home.

By Mr. Reed: They got the best of the fight, which only lasted a few minutes. They ran away when they heard a woman scream out about the gun.

"Walter Tucker (20), labourer, Chedzoy stated that he lived [in Batch] near the prisoner's house. On the night in question witness was in his mother's garden and saw James Wheeler and another man in the road. He went in the house, but about a quarter of an hour afterwards he heard the prisoner's wife scream. He then heard the report of a gun and went outside the door. He then saw the prisoner coming from the direction of the road with the gun in his hand. James Wheeler and William Fry were with him.

By Mr. Reed: He was sure it was the prisoner's wife who screamed.

Mr. Reed: How could you tell that?

Oh, I know her screams. (Laughter.)

What do you mean: can you touch the key-note now?

No, not likely, sir. (Renewed laughter.)

"Emma Bennett, an elderly woman, of Chedzoy, said she was going to bed on the night in question, and was upstairs. She heard the report of a gun. Her window was broken and she was struck in the face with a shot. Upon looking out of the window she saw four men running, but she did not know who they were. By Mr. Reed: She heard someone call out, 'George, come out,' and the man who called out appeared to be in distress.

"P.C. Carter stated that on Sunday last he went to the prisoner's house with P.C. Cooksley. Prisoner was then in bed. Cooksley said, 'George, we want you to go with us,' and prisoner then washed, and when charged and cautioned by Cooksley said, 'Yes, I done it, and what's the best to do - plead guilty or not guilty?' Nothing else was then said, but on the way to Bridgwater prisoner said, 'It was my brother Jim's fault, I was in the house having supper when he came after me, and I went with him to the road, and as soon as I was there I was knocked down. I then went into the house after the gun, and went down to the gate, and shot after them.'

"Mr. Thomas Edward Spencer, house surgeon at the Bridgwater Infirmary, stated that four men came to the institution about 12.20 a.m. on Sunday morning. He examined them, and found Snow to be suffering from a shot mark over the right eye, one on the back of his head, and one in the right shoulder. He was faint from the wound in the shoulder. He next examined Mountstevens and found two shots, one behind either ear, one at the top of the head in the skull, and one mark on his right arm, but there the shot had not penetrated. He extracted the shots behind the ear. Hucker was shot behind the left ear, and on the top of the head. Witness extracted the shot behind the ear. Witness did not examine Pitman inasmuch as he did not complain. Witness had further examained the men that morning, but saw no signs of danger. The shots behind the ears in the case of Mountstevens had travelled about an inch under the skin, but he did not apprehend danger in either case. By Mr. Reed: The wounds sustained by the men are neither permanent or dangerous.

"This was the whole of the evidence for the prosecution, and prisoner, in reply to the charge said, 'I'm not guilty; I was brutally assaulted.'

"Mr. Reed then called James Wheeler, the prisoner's brother, who deposed that he went out shooting on the day in question, and afterwards remained at the Crown Inn, and waited there until shortly before closing time. On leaving the inn he took the gun under his left arm and went in the direction of his brother's house. When he got to the gate he put his hand on it, and Mountstevens (who was amongst the other men - Hucker, Snow and Pitman) said, 'Look out, old man; don't knock your teeth out.' Witness turned round and asked 'What's the matter?' Mountstevens then deliberately came up and knocked him down, and the gun fell out of his hand. Hucker then came up and kicked him, and then the was continually kicked and knocked about for some time. He then shouted for his brother, George Wheeler, and said, 'Come down, George, they'll kill me.' Whilst on the ground Mountstevens said, 'Kick him; do for the —-.' Some one then kicked him from behind again, and he was rendered insensible. After he recovered himself he went in the direction of his brother's house, and found him with his coat and hat off, and having his supper. Witness asked him to come down and help him, as they were waiting for him at the gate. His brother George went down with him, and on going from the gate to the road they were both knocked down, and whilst on the ground Mountstevens said, 'Do for the both; do for the —-,' and repeated this twice. Witness's gun was inside the gate, and his brother did not take it from the house. It was left near the garden gate by witness. He remembered hearing the report of the gun, but at the time he (witness) was left on the ground, and did not see who fired it. He was left lying on the snow, and when he called to his brother he felt he was in danger of his life from the threats he heard Mountstevens use. Threats were made towards him and his brother. He was left lying on the ground for nearly ten minutes. On Monday last witness showed the bruises on his face to Supt. Vowles, and told him of the assault committed on him.

"This was the whole of the evidence offered on behalf of the defence, and the Bench then committed the prisoner for trail at the assizes to be held at Taunton. Mr. Reed applied for bail, and the application was granted, prisoner being released in his own recognisance of £100, and two sureties of £50 each."

George Wheeler appeared before the Assize Court in February when he pleaded not guilty to feloniously shooting Mountstevens and the other men, but guilty to unlawful wounding, a charge which was accepted by the court. The judge deferred sentence and he was released on bail. Unfortunately, the result of the case does not appear to have been published, so the outcome is unknown: since bail was granted one would assume that his sentence would have been minimal.

In July 1891 Rev. George Oakman Mullens (1830-1895) retired as Rector of Chedzoy. His nephew, George Richard Mullens, who was born in Chedzoy on 26th April 1864, was inducted as Rector of Chedzoy on 4th November 1891. The new rector was to remain in the post until his retirement in 1940 and was a great benefactor to the village.

Reverend Mullens.
George Richard Mullens (1864-1947), Rector of Chedzoy from 1891 to 1940.
Source unknown, courtesy of Audrey Fry.

Christmas 1891 was special for the village children as it was the first time there had been a Christmas tree in the school. The Bridgwater Mercury reported

> "Tuesday evening last week will for many years be remembered by the children. ... Miss Winter ... arranged for a Christmas tree and a present for every child. ... A splendid tree, 16 feet in height, was very kindly contributed by Mr. E.J. Stanley, M.P. The branches were laden with oranges, apples, Christmas prize packets, bon-bons, coloured muslin bags containing nuts, &c., and each child received separate parcels of fancy sweets, selected from the large assortment of Mr. Cave's confectionery establishment in Bridgwater. ... Mr. G. Winter acted as 'Father Christmas' to perfection. His coat and hat were made and designed by Mr. and Mrs. T. Butler, being dotted with white wool which was a good representation of snow-flakes, and gave the impression that 'Father Christmas' had experienced much difficulty in coming through a heavy snowstorm, while he carried in his hand a long pipe and a big walking stick."

Books were presented to those pupils with good attendance records, the first prize going to Augusta Brooks, daughter of the headmaster, who had missed just one session out of 452 in the previous year.

In 1894 young men were creating a disturbance in the village. In June that year the Bridgwater Mercury reported that

> "John Pierce, a young man of Bridgwater, was summoned for being guilty of disorderly behaviour at Chedzoy, on 6th May. He pleaded guilty. P.C. Golledge said he saw the defendant in Chedzoy in company with three other young fellows from Bridgwater. He was in the road in a fighting attitude, but his companions tried to get him away. When they saw the witness coming, two of them ran away, but the other remained with the defendant. He managed to get away from them, and after that took off his coat and went into a garden, telling the man in the house that if he would come out in the road he would fight him. Defendant used bad language, and people were passing. When witness spoke to defendant he replied that he was not doing anything. Defendant refused to give his name and address for some time.
>
> Supt. Vowles (to witness): Why were you at this place on the afternoon in question?
>
> Witness: I was sent there especially on account of the disorderly conduct in the village on Sunday afternoons by young men from Bridgwater and Dunwear, numerous complaints having been received.
>
> The Rev. G.R. Mullens, rector of Chedzoy, stated that half past two on Sundays was his hour for service. About twenty-five minutes past two on the afternoon in question he came out and found four men parleying in the road. He beckoned to the policeman, and when they saw him two men left and the defendant pulled off his coat, went into the garden of a man named Stokes, used bad language and wanted him to come out and fight. When the Sunday School were passing to church with several ladies, defendant used very bad language indeed. The reason he (the rector) was connected with this case was because all last summer they had men coming out from Bridgwater causing a nuisance in the parish, which otherwise on a Sunday would be quiet and orderly. Young fellows came out and plucked the flowers, took off the gates in front of gardens, got drunk and generally upset the whole place. He was glad to have an opportunity of mentioning the matter to Their Worships to make an example of somebody. - The Chairman said it was a most insulting thing, and he should not have thought there were young men in Bridgwater who would have acted in so disgraceful a manner. In the interests of morality the Bench were exceedingly obliged to Mr. Mullens for bringing the matter forward. Defendant would be fined £1 and costs, or 14 days' imprisonment."

The Local Government Act, 1894 established Parish Councils which were to come into effect on 13th December 1894. These were to be preceded by a Parish Meeting on 4th of that month at which councillors would be elected. Chedzoy's Parish Meeting was held in the school room on the appointed day with between 30 and 40 electors present. The first councillors for the year 1895/96, elected on a show of hands, were John Baker, Joseph Ashford, William Bennett, Tom Butler and Theodore Henry Hook. The first meeting of Chedzoy Parish Council was held at the same venue on 20th December 1894 when John Baker was elected Chairman, although he was to resign 18 months later on leaving the neighbourhood and was replaced by Joseph Ashford. Joseph Brooks was appointed Parish Clerk "at a sum of one guinea (£1.05) per year, the first year to end in April 1896." The following year his pay was increased to £2, but he was also required "to find lights for the Council's meetings." The Wilts and Dorset Bank, Bridgwater were appointed as Treasurers and it was decided that the Council would meet four times per year. Bridgwater Without Parish was also formed on 13th December 1894 and consisted at that time of Dunwear, East Bower, Chedzoy Lane and Haygrove.

Parishioners continued to fall foul of the magistrates. In June 1895 the Bridgwater Mercury court column reported that

> "Joseph Potter, of Chedzoy, who did not appear, was, on the evidence of Mr. D.K. O'Sullivan, Excise Officer, fined 10s and costs for keeping a dog without a licence. William Brake of Chedzoy, for having no licence for a carriage, his property, was fined 10s. and costs. It appeared that defendant had no name on his cart, which was a market cart, and thus rendered it taxable. He would not have required a licence if the cart had borne his name."

At the Chedzoy annual Parish Meeting on 1st April 1895, 22 parishioners petitioned for allotments in the village, requiring 40 acres of pasture and 16 acres of arable land. It was felt that the Council should make application to the University of Oxford but

> "no resolution was submitted, and the matter was left with sundry hints of 'Councillors Beware' for the consideration of the Parish Council at their Annual Meeting."

Following that meeting the Council applied to the University for the necessary land, but this was refused. However, in February 1896 William Brake offered to give up 15 acres of land at Westfield for the purpose, if the University agreed.

Consent having been obtained a Parish Council meeting was held the following month at which

> "some five and twenty would-be allotments holders were likewise present" and "the whole 15 acres were speedily applied for."

The rent was to be sixty shillings (£3) per acre per annum, and the allotments were allocated in quarter acre lots. Mr. Brake was paid nine guineas (£9.45) in order to plough the land before the allotment holders took over their plots. However, establishing these allotments was not without some dispute as later the same year the Parish Council minutes note

> "Remeasurement of the allotment ground on account of its being alleged by the late occupier that the plot enclosed within the Council's boundary pegs contains one rood and twenty-odd perches in excess of fifteen acres, to which the Council is entitled."

This was indeed the case, so the boundary had to be changed slightly.

In October 1895 the School Board resolved to appoint Bessie Stokes as a pupil teacher at the school

> "for a four year period from 1st July last at a salary at the rate of two shillings and sixpence (12.5p.) per week for the first year, three shillings (15p.) per week in the second, four shillings (20p.) per week in the third and five shillings (25p.) per week in the fourth and last year of the engagement."

In June 1896 a whirlwind struck Chedzoy and East Bower. Although of a very local nature this storm blew down about thirty elm trees, half the trees in an orchard and blew in the windows of a cottage. Three elms were felled at William Cary's and part of a shed damaged. Trees were uprooted in Mr. Ashford's orchard and ten elms uprooted in Joseph Potter's field. A large number of trees were also destroyed in Robert Clarke's orchard. The Bridgwater Mercury reported that the storm abated before reaching the town and that damage was limited to an area about half a mile long.

In 1896 officials from the parish fell foul of the magistrates. Under the headline AN OVERSEER FINED FOR NEGLECT the Mercury reported that

> "John Baker and Robert Fry, overseers of Chedzoy, were charged with on 29th September, they then being overseers for the parish of Chedzoy, did unlawfully neglect to show the jury lists given at the special sessions on the church doors. Fry pleaded not guilty, as he said he was not responsible, as Baker and himself took a half a year each for the work, and Baker was now doing his half year. The Bench considered Fry not responsible and dismissed the charge, Baker admitting it was his fault, and that he had forgotten to place the list on the doors. He stated they had placed him in that office, and he did not understand the work. The Chairman said that as it was the first offence they had the power to reduce the fine, the maximum being £10, and they fined him 5s. and 10s. 6d. costs."

The following year new overseers were in place and they too got it wrong! In October 1897 the Mercury reported that

> "Sidney Denning and Benjamin Winter, overseers for the Parish of Chedzoy, were summoned for neglecting the jury list for the parish at the special sessions held for such a purpose. Denning said he did produce a list, but the Assistant Clerk pointed out it was not signed properly. Mr. Winter said when Denning and himself were appointed overseers for Chedzoy they had an understanding that each should act one half year, and it was now Mr. Denning's turn, and he had nothing to do in the matter. The Assistant Clerk pointed out that the parish of Chedzoy was in default last year, and that this neglect caused great inconvenience to both Magistrates and the police. The Bench let the defendants off on payment of costs (6s.) (30p.)."

The minutes of the Parish Council meeting of 11th December 1896 contains the first reference to an ongoing problem in the village: footpaths.

> "The Clerk be instructed to write to the following, namely Messrs. John Baker, Sidney Denning and Robert Fry calling on them to restore to their original state any paths or roadways they may have disturbed and for the future to leave all such paths and roadways in their original and proper width."

Similar motions have been passed ever since!

Constance Brooks (born 1884), one of Joseph Brooks' daughters, used to relate a story which would have taken place about this era. It seems that as a young girl she had to walk across fields to Bridgwater in order to attend French lessons. In one of the fields was a bull. The owner had fixed a board across the bull's horns so that in order to see it had to raise its head very high. The bull couldn't run like that so, hopefully, it was supposed to lose its sense of direction when lowering its head to charge any intended victim!

In 1897 the village celebrated the Diamond Jubilee of Queen Victoria. According to Parish Council minutes,

> "The Festivities consisted of a Free Dinner to the whole adult population on the 'Diamond Jubilee Day' at 1 o'clock on Mr. Cary's premises. The afternoon was given up to sports, held in Mr. Cary's home field, at which suitable prizes were awarded to the winners of the several events. The sports were followed by 'Tea.' The weather was glorious and the festivities passed off splendidly. It may be mentioned that the children of the Parish were given a Tea and Treat on the Rectory lawn by The Revd. G.R. Mullens."

Queen Victoria's Diamond Jubilee. Villagers gather at Manor Farm in 1897. Courtesy of Duncan Bouchier.

The report in the Bridgwater Mercury also mentioned that for making the arrangements William Cary "to his surprise" was presented with a silver pencil case and Mrs. Cary was given a tea pot. The evening concluded with the singing of the national anthem.

The Early 20th Century

In May 1900 the Parish Council discussed "The water supply of the Parish for dietetic purposes" as the County Analyst had offered to analyse a number of samples of water at half a guinea (52.5p.) per sample. Of the twelve samples submitted it was reported

> "With respect to five samples the Analyst says of each 'A good water' and with reference to seven of the twelve the Analyst says of each 'An impure water; dangerous for dietetic purposes'."

The Council unanimously resolved to let the matter rest at that time. However, at their next meeting they were informed that the Clerk of the Bridgwater Rural District Council had written

> "Stating that that body had on 10th instant resolved 'That your (Chedzoy) Parish (amongst others) be provided with a proper and wholesome supply of water for the use of the inhabitants." The estimated cost to the parish was £1,700.

The Parish Council countered by proposing its own scheme and an engineer was engaged to explore the possibilities, but in due course the Council was informed by the Local Government Board that

> "It has no power to withdrawn the Parish from the Bridgwater R.D's Council's (sic) scheme for providing this and other parishes with a water supply nor to carry out a scheme of its own."

Strange events have taken place in Chedzoy. The Bridgwater Mercury for 20th June 1900 contained the following short report.

"On Saturday night last a mare, the property of Mr. Joseph Ashford, gave birth to a colt having five feet, two separate legs below the knee. The colt is a strong one and doing well."

The colt's fate was not recorded.

More mundane things were also reported in the Mercury in July 1900.

"ORGAN FUND - this fund amounts to £105 at present, and a sum of £95 is required before the order for the organ can be given. Towards obtaining this sum a jumble sale will be held in the schoolroom on Friday, July 27th. Contributions of all kinds, including fruit, flowers and refreshments will be most acceptable." In a subsequent report Mrs. Mullens said that the event had raised 14 guineas (£14.70). Sedgemoor weather was suitable capricious for the event: "The tent kindly lent and erected by Mr. B. Winter was quite invaluable, affording a pleasant shade during the heat of the afternoon and a protection from the violent thunder-storm which burst over the village towards the close of the proceedings."

In recent years there has been much concern at the suicide of farmers, but this is not new. SHOCKING SUICIDE OF A FARMER AT CHEDZOY was the headline to a Mercury report in 1900 about an inquest held at the Crown Inn into the death of Levi Bampfield Rainey, a bachelor, aged 46 years. His exact address was not given, but the 1891 Census records him as living in Front Street with his father and sister. The detailed report included transcripts of evidence given by three witnesses, including his sister, Sarah.

"I did not hear anything during the night. I went downstairs in the morning ... Afterwards I found him in my father's workshop hanging from a beam." Robert Fry, of Frys Farm, said Sarah Rainey had come to him and said, "Do run into the carpenter's shop and see Levi." He had gone there and found him hanging four feet from the ground. "There was a razor in his right hand and it was covered with blood. The throat was cut halfway across and there was a lot of blood on the floor. I felt the body and it was nearly cold."

Dr. J.R. Rygate of Westonzoyland was asked by the Coroner, "Did you consider his mind unhinged?" to which the witness replied, "Yes, temporarily. - Were you surprised to find that he had committed suicide? - No, I was not." The report concluded, "The Coroner, in summing up, observed that the jurymen, he was sure, all very much regretted this sad occurrence in their midst. The evidence pointed very conclusively to the fact that the deceased for some time past had not been in his usual state of mind, and the doctor very properly advised he should be watched. His sister seemed to have done all she possibly could, and her fears were, to a certain extent, lulled by the fact that recently he appeared to have got better. The foreman of the jury asked a very pertinent question with regard to the deceased working during the excessive heat, which was very likely, under the circumstances, to have a prejudicial effect, and Miss Rainey had told them that the deceased complained of heat on the night in question. The deceased had undoubtedly committed a very deliberate act of self-destruction, but judging from the evidence of all three witnesses who had been examined, there could not be the slightest doubt at the time of committing it he was not responsible for his actions. The jury at once unanimously returned a verdict that the deceased committed suicide whilst in a state of temporary insanity."

On 1st February 1901 a special meeting of the Parish Council was called:

"On the proposition of Mr. Bennett, seconded by Mr. Brake, and supported by Mr. Hook, the Clerk was instructed to convey to His Majesty the King and to the Royal Family a message of loyal and dutiful condolence in the great grief which has fallen on them and the whole Empire by the death on 22nd ultimo of our dearly beloved Queen." Subsequently, "The Chairman reported having received from the 'Home Office' a communication conveying His Majesty's thanks for the Loyal and Dutiful Message of the Chedzoy Parish Council, expressing sympathy on the occasion of the lamented death of Her late Majesty Queen Victoria, and congratulations on His Majesty's accession to the throne."

In order to commemorate the Coronation in 1902, two oak trees were planted at Fowlers Plot. These were placed near similar trees which had commemorated Queen Victoria's Diamond Jubilee in 1897 and also the relief of Kimberley, Ladysmith and Mafeking during the Boar War.

Following the Coronation, Parish Council minutes record that

"It was mentioned that a sum of some £3 odd remains from the moneys raised by voluntary subscriptions, at the time of His Majesty's proposed Coronation, for local festivities, and on the motion of Mr. Tom Butler, seconded by Mr. Wm. Bennett, it was unanimously agreed to expend such sum in coal for distribution among parishioners - exclusive of farmers and some few others - generally. It was further resolved on Tuesday evening next to proceed to distribute sundry lots of Calico used in the recent festivities as tablecloths, to such persons as the Council may deem would be most benefited.

However, three days later

"Three members, namely Messrs. Wm. Bennett, Tom Butler and T.H. Hook attended a meeting arranged for this evening with reference to disposal of properties belonging to the Council as 'Coronation Festivities Committee', but in as much as the Chairman failed to put in an appearance absolutely nothing was done in the matter!"

The early years of the 20th Century were recalled by Cecil Cary (1900-1990) who was born at Manor Farm. He had two elder brothers, Harold (1892-1918) and Hubert (1896-1951), two elder sisters, Mabel and Hilda, and a younger sister and brother, Dorothy and Clifford (1905-1960).

Cecil Cary.
Pictured outside Manor Farm about 1905.
Courtesy of Muriel Brown.

Their parents, William and Clara Cary, employed two maids. Emmie Newton was responsible for the upkeep of the house and Lily Clapp took care of the children. Mr. Cary recalled that his father had a bad temper and, on one occasion, knocked Harold from his mother's arms in a fit of rage. Perhaps this was something to do with their courtship: Cecil's father said that his wife would not allow him to kiss her until after they were married! Life was not easy for the Cary boys: they all slept in one room and, if they were naughty, their mother would go up to their room and beat them with a stick. One time, in order to escape from his mother, young Cecil jumped from the bedroom window, his fall being broken by a pile of faggots (sticks) below. He was so frightened that he didn't re-enter the house for a week! One of the two maids took pity on him and fed him at the window sill.

William Cary owed nine horses. One was used to draw his buggy, another for the trap, and the rest were working horses on the farm. When Cecil was about five years old his father saddled a pony for him, but the saddle slipped and Cecil was dragged around a field. The family attended the village church and, as seats were allocated by the churchwardens, always sat in the second pew on the left behind the door. Both of Cecil's parents are at rest in the churchyard.

Young Cecil attended the village school. The headmaster was Joseph Brooks who was assisted by Mrs. Heal who walked from Peasey Farm, Bradney each day. There was no school uniform, just ordinary clothes with leather boots. The regime was strict: no talking in class and having to put your hand up and say, "Please may I leave the room?" when necessary. For talking in class the culprit would be placed across Mr. Brooks' lap and firmly beaten with a stick.

The family were always in the forefront in making use of new technology, indeed Mr. Cary had the first potato digger in the area and used to make its services available to other farms in the district. By the time he was 15, Cecil was the proud owner of a plate camera - quite a rarity in those days. He was always keen on photography and some of his pictures appear in this book. From about 1930/40 Cecil was generating his own electricity by means of an old car engine; long before an electricity supply was brought to the village. When they were old enough, the young Carys owned motorcycles: Cecil had a Royal Enfield twin with a sidecar, Clifford owned a Levis whilst Harold had a Sunbeam. Even Dorothy owned a Douglas motorcycle, which got her into trouble. In August 1924 under the headline A YOUNG LADY'S MISUNDERSTANDING, the following report appeared in the Bridgwater Mercury.

> "At Weston-Super-Mare Police Court Dorothy Cary, who was summoned for disregarding the signal of a constable engaged in the direction of traffic, was alleged to have ignored P.C. Lamb's shouts and hand signals both on proceeding to and returning from the Old Pier on a motorcycle. A letter was now read from her in which she explained that she had not been riding long and did not understand signals. Fined £1."

It seems that Cecil's mother and father did not get on well and she refused to ride in his horse drawn buggy, preferring to travel in the sidecar of Cecil's motorcycle. On one occasion Cecil was giving his sister, Hilda, a ride into Bridgwater in the sidecar. During the course of the journey she saw a young man named Arthur Brown of Street, in whom she was interested - indeed, they were subsequently married - but Cecil refused to stop the motorcycle so that she could get out. Not to be beaten she jumped from the sidecar whilst it was still moving!

Perhaps Cecil's actions were influenced by his own romantic experiences. As a young man he was engaged to be married to Hilda Day who lived in the North Newton area. Although the exact reason can only be known to the couple, the marriage was called off, allegedly following a dispute because Cecil refused to spend money to purchase a new three piece suite for their home. Cecil was sued for Breach of Promise and, like fisher men's "one that got away" stories, each time he told the tale the amount which the action cost him increased. Sadly, it seems that no report was published in the local papers, so the figure remains a mystery. Perhaps it was as a result of this experience that Cecil remained a bachelor.

He continued driving vehicles well into his old age and was a familiar figure in his immaculate old Rover 90 car driving slowly along Chedzoy Lane oblivious to following vehicles and usually in the middle of the road, much to the consternation of oncoming drivers!

But back to the early days of the 20th Century and other Chedzoy residents. Two local boys were in trouble in November 1902.

> "George Day (15) and Lewis Fry (15), lads of Chedzoy, pleaded guilty to discharging fireworks at Chedzoy within 50

feet of the highway. Reginald Bennett said he saw the defendants letting off a squib and a cracker. They were putting the squibs under people's doors in the night. Superintendent Vowles said the two defendants were very well behaved as a rule. The vicar of Chedzoy said he thought the Bench should remember that the boys saw a lot of this kind of thing in Bridgwater at this time of the year. (Laughter.)" Both were Bound Over for six months.

Since its formation the Parish Council had dealt annually with the letting of Moor Drove but they were obviously unsure as to their legal position and the Clerk reported that he had written to the Local Government Board in the following terms:

"Chedzoy, Near Bridgwater, Augt. 11th 1,903 (sic).
Sir,

My Council would be extremely obliged if you would kindly inform them whether or not they are within their rights in dealing with certain moneys in a precisely similar way to that which was followed for many years by their predecessors, the Vestry in this parish.

"The money accrues from the annual letting of a 'drove' or grass roadway. The amount produced annually during the last 15 years has averaged nearly nine pounds. Before the advent of 'Parish Councils' when parochial matters were dealt with by a Vestry, that body, from the proceeds of the annual letting first made provision for such repairs to the Drove and Gates as were necessary, and any balance remaining after these expenses were provided for, was regularly handed to the Churchwardens towards the Church Expenses; and was not applied to the relief of Rates. Such was the old usage and up to now the Parish Council have adopted a similar course, believing it to be the right method of dealing with the fund, the plan being in consequence with the feeling very generally prevalent amongst parishioners. But inas-much as there is a small minority of parishioners who suggest that the whole of the proceeds should go to the relief of the Rates:- and as the Council are desirous of doing that which is absolutely right in the matter they would esteem it a favour to be told, which, in the opinion of the Local Government Board, is the correct course to follow - to pursue their present plan? - or are they compelled to apply the proceeds from the annual letting of the grass roadway in question to the relief of Rates?"

In reply the Local Government Board wrote that

"the matter is not one in regard to which the Board can undertake to advise the Parish Council." In the light of this advice, the proceeds from the letting continued to be passed to the Churchwardens.

In February 1904 the Parish Council finally got around to distributing items left over from the Coronation Festivities. It was

"Resolved that the goods, consisting of knives and forks, calico, trestles, etc. which were acquired on the above occasion and which since then have been stored at Mr. Cary's shall be removed and disposed of in such manner as the majority of the councillors shall determine." In the event, six dozen knives and forks were retained, Rev. Mullens agreed to store the trestles, 40 ounces of tea were distributed "among widows and others (8 equal shares of 5 oz. each)" and "Calico to be given in lots of about 5 yards each to mothers with long families of small children."

Although no reference appears in Parish Council minutes, mains water was brought to the village and at a meeting of the School Managers in April 1904 a

"letter [was] read from the Head Teacher as to the Mangers applying for sanction to the necessary expenditure as will be necessary to provide for laying on a water supply from the Rural District Council's mains to the School premises and Teacher's house. The Managers, being of the opinion that the present supply from the well was good, decided not to entertain the application at present."

In the first month of 1904 a special meeting of the Parish Council was called

"To consider communication from T.M. Reed, Esq., Clerk to the Bridgwater Rural District Council with reference to 'Water Supply - Extension to Parchey.' ... Mr. Reed's letter, the Engineer's report and plan were carefully considered and it was the unanimous feeling that Parchey cottages must be supplied even if the extra outlay estimated to amount to £116 10s. should necessitate a further application to the L.G. Board for powers to effect further loan."

The Clerk was instructed to write to Mr. Reed

"Expressing Council's surprise at learning that somehow or other Parchey had got overlooked; and further to state the reasons why under any circumstances Parchey must, in the opinion of the Parish Council, certainly have the water laid on to the cottages situated in that portion of the parish."

On 4th May 1904 the following report appeared in the Bridgwater Mercury.

"THE WATER SCHEME. The Clerk reported that the Local Government Board Inspector held an inquiry on April 19th into the application by the Council to borrow sums for the extension of the scheme to the Chedzoy and North Petherton districts. During the inquiry the Inspector drew attention to what he described as the imperfect condition of the drainage in the parish of Chedzoy. Had the parish not been so heavily rated, and not been in a position to stand a drainage scheme, the Inspector would probably have reported to the Local Government Board that they would have directed the Council to provide a proper drainage scheme for the village. The Rev. G.R. Mullens was present and pointed out to the Inspector that greater attention had been given to the drainage of the village by Mr. Popham and it was now in a much better condition than formerly. The Inspector, however, made certain recommendations and directed him (the Clerk) to bring the matter before the District Council. The sanction of the Local Government

Board would probably be received to the borrowing of the money in a few weeks."

In June it was reported that the estimated cost of the water scheme was £25,500 and this would supply an anticipated 20 gallons a day per person. The Mercury reported,

> "It is hardly necessary to remark that 20 gallons a head is a very copious supply for a rural population, even when large quantities are consumed in agricultural operations and it is quite clear from what has been said that the quantity of water at the command of the council is ample".

Further, in October 1904:

> "The Water Committee recommended that the attention of the Parish Council of Chedzoy should be drawn to the fact that very few houses had as yet taken the water, and suggested that steps be taken under the Public Health Act 1875".

Another major issue to occupy the Parish Council was the risk of fire. In 1904

> "It was unanimously agreed to deposit five pounds in the post office or other bank to form the nucleus of a fund it is proposed to raise to provide the parish with suitable length of fire-hose."

This same subject was considered in conjunction with problems over the supply of water.

> "A communication from the Clerk to Bridgwater R.D.C. directing the attention of the parish council to the fact that comparatively few owners and occupiers had as yet applied for a supply of water to their premises in this parish, and recommending that steps be taken under the 'Public Health Act 1875' was considered."

It was agreed

> "To make a further canvass of the parish first and then if thought well, take steps under the 'Act' referred above."

At the same time the Council recommended the fixing of four additional fire hydrants:

> "One about midway between Fowlers Plot and Three Oaks Farm. One near Miss Jewell's garden hedge. One near Mr. Ashford's premises and one still further down Chedzoy Lane."

Social events were not to be ignored in the village and received suitable coverage in the Bridgwater Mercury. The heady social life is best summarised by two 1904 reports which concerned the Chedzoy Cricket Club concert in January which raised £4 14s. 3d. on the door for donations to church funds and, later the same month,

> "A well attended lecture took place on the husbandry of poultry."

How many modern residents keep chickens? Probably the village telephone kiosk would now be a suitable venue for any lecture on the subject!

In 1905, under the heading, "Appliances for extinguishing fire," the Parish Clerk had been instructed

> "To wait on Thompson Bros., Bridgwater and obtain from them price lists and particulars with view to the Council providing these necessary appliances for the Parish."

'Fire Hose and Fire Extinguishing Equipment' consisting of six 75 foot lengths of hose, couplings and fittings were purchased for £20 11s. and in 1908 the Parish Council minutes note

> "That the Custodian (Mr. Butler) of the above appliances be paid the sum of one pound annually from moneys at the Council's disposal, for their safe keeping and proper care; and a further sum of five shillings (25p.) on each occasion the appliances are requisitioned for the extinction of an outbreak of fire."

In June 1905 the village was shocked to learn of the murder of a former resident. Miss Henrietta Caroline Cary had been born at Manor Farm in 1865, the daughter of William and Elizabeth Cary. After training as a nurse she had worked in India and then moved to France where she obtained a position as a governess at Nanterre, near Paris. Her body had been discovered in a rural area and the cause of death was strangulation. Auguste Gaillard, aged 29, was soon arrested and confessed to the crime: his clothing was muddy and this, combined with an English coin and part of Miss Cary's jewellery found in his possession, was sufficient evidence. In October that year he appeared before the Seine Assise when he pleaded guilty to the murder and was sentenced to penal servitude for life.

Although the motor car was becoming more common, animal horsepower was still the main means of transport. The old power was not without its problems. In June 1904 the Bridgwater Mercury reported that

> "Sidney Bryant of Chedzoy was fined 1s. and costs for riding without reins at Bawdrip, and his father, James Bryant of Chedzoy, for a like offence was fined 2s. 6d. and costs."

However, technology was not without its problems: in December 1907 a further report noted,

> "Henry Fry pleaded guilty to riding a bicycle without a light at Chedzoy. Defendant stated that his lamp was blown out, and as he was not far from home and it was raining hard, he did not light it again. Fined 2s. 6d. and costs."

Respect for authority existed across society and is illustrated by a report in the Mercury in April 1906.

> "Louisa Wood, gipsy, was summoned for having allowed

a horse to stray at Chedzoy. Defendant did not appear, but sent a letter enclosing a postal order for 2s. 6d. hoping it would be sufficient to meet the fine. If not, she would pay the balance when next in Bridgwater. Fined 2s. 6d. and costs."

It is difficult to imagine today's travellers behaving in such a manner. I wonder if Louisa Wood paid the costs?

In 1906 it was proposed that a miniature rifle range should be established for youths of the village but, after visiting the Borough of Taunton Miniature Rifle Club the Parish Council "considered [it] to be absolutely beyond our means." But not to be defeated "Catalogues of Air Rifles and other appliances were examined" and it was unanimously decided by the Council to purchase one Britannia air rifle, one covered target, paint, brush and pellets and the Clerk was instructed to despatch an order for these. There is no mention in Parish accounts as to these items being paid for, so it is not clear if they were obtained by the Council, but the Bridgwater Mercury regularly reported miniature rifle shooting competitions which took place between teams from Chedzoy and other villages.

In 1908 the Parish Council received a letter from the Postmaster in Bridgwater as a result of which it was resolved

> "That this Council entirely approves the proposal for affording a weekly half holiday at Chedzoy Post Office, each half holiday being arranged - if possible - for Saturday afternoons."

In October 1913 another resolution was

> "That this Council do support the petition now being made to the Postal Authority asking that arrangements be made for a Sunday Postal Service for this parish."

In June 1911 the village celebrated the Coronation of King George V and Queen Mary.

> "The Coronation was loyally celebrated in this parish on Thursday, the festivities being of a highly successful character. Many of the parishioners were awakened at an early hour in the morning by the discharge of small cannon and the pealing of the church bells, the latter being continued at intervals throughout the eventful day. The village hall (probably a error for 'school') had been gaily decorated for the occasion, and, in addition to the display of flags, etc. on private buildings, three decorated arches had been erected."

200 people attended a free luncheon at the Rectory.

> "It had been found impossible to engage a band for the day, and selections on a gramophone were given instead at intervals."

Eighty children and their mothers attended tea and this was followed by sports.

CHEDZOY.

Arrangements for Celebrating the

Coronation

OF

KING GEORGE V. & QUEEN MARY

ON THURSDAY, 22ND JUNE.

12 noon. DIVINE SERVICE in the Parish Church.

1 p.m. A DINNER for every person in the Parish above School age, including non-parishioners who work regularly in the Parish, or who have subscribed to the funds.

N.B.—Each person must bring his or her own knife and fork.

4 p.m. A TEA for all the children attending Chedzoy Council School.

N.B.—Children must bring their own mugs.

4.30 p.m. A Programme of Sports (as under) will commence.

If fine, the Dinner, Tea and Sports will be held in the "Rectory Lawn"; if wet, the Dinner and Tea will be held in Mr. R. Fry's Buildings.

A MEAT TEA will be provided at 4 p.m. for any persons who cannot attend the dinner.

PROGRAMME OF SPORTS.

	1st Prize	2nd Prize	3rd Prize
1. 220 yards Flat Race (open)	5/-	2/6	1/-
2. 100 yards Flat Race (Boys under 16 years)	2/6	1/6	1/-
3. 100 yards Single Women's Race	2/6	1/6	1/-
4. 50 yards Sack Race (open)	4/-	2/-	1/-
5. 1 mile Bicycle Race (open)	5/-	2/6	1/-
6. High Jump	4/-	2/-	1/-
7. Hurdle Race (5 flights)	4/-	2/-	1/-
8. Apple and Bucket Race on Bicycles	4/-	2/-	1/-
9. 100 yards Flat Race (Boys under 14 years)	2/-	1/-	6d.
10. 100 yards Flat Race (Girls under 16 years)	2/-	1/-	6d.
11. Long Jump	4/-	2/	1/-
12. Bun and Treacle Race	3/-	2/-	1/-
13. High Jump (Boys under 16 years)	2/6	1/6	1/-
14. Egg and Spoon Race (for Women)	3/-	2/-	1/-
15. 100 yards Flat Race (Girls under 14 years)	2/-	1/-	6d.
16. Wheelbarrow Race	4/-	3/-	2/-
17. Putting the Weight	3/-	2/-	1/-
18. Potato Race (for Women)	3/-	2/-	1/-
19. Obstacle Race	4/-	2/-	1/-
20. 100 yards Married Womens' Race for Bread or Calico.			

N.B.—No Competitor will be allowed to win more than two Prizes.

(Signed) for the Committee, GEORGE R. MULLENS.

WALTER BELCHER, PRINTER, FORE STREET, BRIDGWATER.

Courtesy of David and Jeannette Butt.

Some well known village names were amongst the winners: Cecil Cary won the sack race, Bill Collard the obstacle race and 220 yards, and Albert Fry the long jump.

The population of the village appeared to be remaining fairly stable. The Census of 1911 recorded 323 inhabitants, just one lower than ten years earlier. This in itself would not seem remarkable until taking into consideration mass emigration: in 1907 235,000 people had emigrated from the country and during the first nine months of 1911 another 249,000 had left. Throughout the first decade of the 20th Century the Bridgwater Mercury carried glowing reports of life in the colonies, particularly Canada, where land was readily available for settlement. In 1912 the headmaster was required to conduct a census of the parish and this revealed that on 30th June the population was 297 - 26 down on the previous year's figure. Although not directly involving the village, the School Management Committee's minutes for July 1913 indicate that the County Council had decided to construct and maintain a school at Bawdrip.

Winter flooding on the levels around the village continued to be a feature of village life, and two reports in the Bridgwater Mercury illustrate some of the problems. In January 1912 John Coles of Stawell had a nasty experience.

Flooding near Parchey Bridge in 1919 or 1920.
Note the marker posts showing the edge of the road.
Photograph courtesy of Helen Hunt."

"The road between Chedzoy and Stawell is submerged for a long portion to a depth of several feet and several of the inhabitants have had alarming and terrifying experiences in attempting to pass along the flooded road, the location of which is difficult to determine owing to the absence of rhine trees."

A cart driven by Mr. Coles overturned into a deep ditch.

"He struggled to his feet, but could not free himself from the trap and horse. The water was well above his waist."

Fortunately the horse did not panic and both were rescued by Tom Irish. The following January it was reported that there were

"Serious floods around Bridgwater. Many thousands of acres are under water east of Chedzoy, and the damage would have been worse if the bank on the western side of the main drain had not given way, and so letting an enormous quantity of water out over the land. The flooding of King's Sedgemoor takes place nine years out of ten, but this year the water has been over now for some weeks, and likely to remain so for some time longer."

As has probably always been the case, from time to time disputes between neighbours arose in the village. In April 1913 one resident found himself before the Magistrates.

"George Martin, a carter, of Chedzoy, was charged with having assaulted Edith Jones, a married woman, of the same village. Defendant pleaded not guilty. Complainant, wife of Frederick Jones, a farm labourer, said on the day in question she was in the garden putting in some potatoes. The defendant was also there. As soon as her husband's back was turned defendant commenced to insult her and jeer at her. She said she would not stand for it any longer, and would fetch her husband from Mr. Ashford's farm. She returned with her husband, and on the way back they met the defendant in the road. Defendant gave her a violent blow in the eye. She could not see out of her eye for three or four days. She was knocked down by the blow, and defendant kicked her on the ground and used bad language. She could give no reason for the defendant's conduct. She had known defendant for twelve months. There had been unpleasantness between the families over the children. Her husband closed with the defendant and knocked him down. Mr. Chapman, for the defence, said Mrs. Jones had been very unpleasant towards the defendant's family ever since her boy fell into a ditch a few Sundays ago. Mrs. Jones called the defendant a thief and rogue. Nobody was more sorry than the defendant that the woman should have been struck, but he was acting in self defence. The Bench fined defendant 5s. and costs - one guinea (£1.05) in all."

Like their predecessors in the 1820s, young men were still fathering children outside wedlock. In April 1914 it was reported that

"James Webb, a butcher, of Bristol, and formerly of Wembdon, was summoned by Fanny Woolley, single woman of Chedzoy, to show cause, &c. (sic). Mr. H.W. Chapman, representing the complainant said, 'The defendant had promised marriage, but had not fulfilled his promise.' Evidence was given by the complainant and her mother, Sarah Woolley, wife of Samuel Woolley, labourer, of Chedzoy. The Bench made an order upon the defendant to contribute 2s. 6d. a week towards the support of the child until it reached the age of 14 years and to pay the usual costs."

Although some residents may have fallen foul of human authorities, others obviously had a higher authority on their side. In June 1914 it was reported in the Bridgwater Independent that

"The Rev. G.R. Mullens had a narrow escape from a serious accident when returning from Burnham. His horse appeared to have shied at a piece of paper in the road and becoming unmanageable backed into a rhine which adjoined the thoroughfare. Mrs. Mullens jumped from the trap and escaped with a shaking, but the rector held to the reins and he and the trap were precipitated into the ditch. The reverend gentleman was pinned underneath the vehicle and was in a serious position when fortunately Mr. Toogood and P.C. Thorne arrived and quickly extricated Mr. Mullens from his perilous position."

The following week in the Bridgwater Mercury:

"The Rector (Rev. G.R. Mullens) experienced a very narrow escape on Saturday morning last. He was standing close to a large tree opposite the Rectory when the tree, without a moment's warning, fell, and the reverend gentleman had a really extraordinary escape. He had only a second or two to spare in getting out of the way. The tree, which had become rotten at the base, fell across the road."

Manor House Inn, around 1912. Source unknown, photograph courtesy of Helen Hunt.

The First World War

The First World War dealt harshly with the village. By January 1915 twenty residents or natives were serving with the colours. The initial optimism of an early victory was soon tempered with reality as the casualty figures increased. The first local casualty came in November 1914 when the death of Sergeant Ernest Fry was reported in the Bridgwater Mercury. His parents were William and Jane Fry of Ward Lane, but he had left the village to join the Metropolitan Police from where, as a reservist, he had been recalled to the colours on 26th September and was killed in October. Subsequently a letter sent to his brother was published:

> "In the field, 22nd December 1914. Dear Mr. Fry, Your brother, Sergeant Fry, was killed in action at Ypres, on 29th October last whilst commanding his section in a counter attack with the bayonet on the Germans. He was his own jolly self right up to his death; and during the long and tiresome marches which preceded the fighting, although somewhat handicapped by his size, he kept up with the best of us. We were sorry to lose a good sergeant and a real pal. Hoping you will accept my condolences,
> I remain, yours very sincerely, —- —-,
> Sergeant Major, 1st Battalion, Grenadier Guards."

Like many local families, Joseph and Jane Ashford of West End Farm were affected by the war. Their son, Leonard Joseph Ashford, had emigrated to Australia in 1913 and, on the outbreak of war, had enlisted as a private in the 3rd Infantry Brigade of the Australian Imperial Forces. In June 1915 the Bridgwater Mercury reported that he had died as a result of injuries received at Gallipoli and reproduced a letter which had been sent to Mr. Ashford by the Rev. A. Lee Warren, the chaplain on H.M. Hospital Ship Gascon. The letter, with what would now be considered unnecessary detail, indicates the horrors of that campaign.

> "Dear Mr. Ashford, I'm sorry to have to tell you that your boy, Leonard Joseph Ashford, died on board ship on Monday May 10th at 12.30 mid-day. He had been badly wounded by a bomb in the right arm and left leg, and it was found necessary to take off his arm. He lost, however, too much blood, and never recovered. He was buried at sea next day three miles off Cape Gaba Tepe, Gallipoli, between that and Sausthrace, by the chaplain of the London. He has left some articles which will be forwarded on to you. The Australians have fought magnificently everyone agrees. They had to capture and hold a cliff from the ships, and they had done this and had been entrenched for a fortnight when your boy was hit. I send you my deepest sympathy, and pray that God may give you His strength to bear your sorrow.

At the same time I know you will be proud of your son. His Lieutenant tells me that he was a very good soldier, obedient, always doing his duty without a murmur. I thought you would like to know this."

Post war reports indicate that fifty men who were natives or residents of Chedzoy joined the forces. In all, ten local men never returned from serving their country, a tremendous number when you consider the population at that time. Their names are recorded on the memorial plaque in the village church, see Appendix 3 for details. 584 men from the Bridgwater area were killed during the war: 326 from Bridgwater itself and the remainder from the surrounding villages.

One report which conjures up a wonderful image of a policeman standing outside a cottage appeared in the Bridgwater Mercury in July 1915.

"William Stone, farmer, was summoned for using bad language in his dwelling house. P.C. Williams said that at 11.30 p.m. he heard defendant cursing his wife for five minutes, and he'd never heard language like it. Fined £1."

No address was given, but it seems likely that William Stone lived in one of the cottages which stood on the site of what is now Kalina, Front Street.

Severe weather struck the village in early 1916. Joseph Brooks recorded in the school log book in February that

"The weather during the past week has been exceptionally severe - an almost continuous succession of blizzards - and as a consequence the attendance has been very low."

A month later he noted,

"[The] weather this morning was very tempestuous; there was a violent wind accompanied with rain, hail and snow, indeed a perfect blizzard. We had but four infants present out of a total of fifteen."

The Military Service Act was passed in 1916 and under this Local Tribunals were established to hear from those who wished to defer or avoid military service: by this time so many men were being killed or injured that one can hardly blame those who tried to avoid becoming casualties. The Bridgwater Mercury carried many reports of local men who appeared before the Tribunals, and some of these were from Chedzoy. On 17th May it was reported that

"Walter James Tucker (19), blacksmith, of Chedzoy, appealed for conditional exemption. He was in partnership with his brother, Frederick E. Tucker, and they were the only blacksmiths for at least four villages. The appeal was supported by two farmers of the district, who wrote that the young man was badly needed in the district, being blacksmith for six parishes. Appellant said that his brother had been exempted as being engaged in a reserved occupation, but had recently received notice that he was now under the age for such exemption, the age having to be over 35. His brother was single and aged 21. The Chairman pointed out that appellant was not of legal age to be a partner in a business. In reply to a member of the Tribunal as to whether he and his brother had been doing any government work, appellant said they did some and never got paid for it, so would not do any more. Appeal dismissed."

The following month

"William Cary applied for exemption on behalf of his son Hubert (20), described as a stockman. He said his son milked twice daily and assisted in general management of 30 cattle and managed 150 sheep. The farm was 240 acres, 80 being arable. His eldest boy was in the Navy. He had two men join the army and had had no one to take their places. There were three men and himself on the farm, and casual labour was also employed. A member: Have you told your son not to join the army? Mr. Cary: No, what do you ask that for? The application was disallowed and Mr. Cary remarked, 'Well, I shall have to sell my stock'."

Also in June,

"The Rev. G.R. Mullens applied for a total exemption for George Sloman (36) and explained that he had about 12 acres of land. He had six head of cattle and two horses. Sloman milked the cows and did the work in the kitchen garden. Sloman was a married man with two children. Sloman was not the Sexton but he (Mr. Mullens) was responsible for keeping the churchyard in order, he mowed the churchyard himself and Sloman worked there when he could be spared from the kitchen garden. A churchyard should be kept as well as, if not better than, the parson's garden. A member remarked that there was no churchyard kept like Chedzoy churchyard. Three months' exemption."

Those who were unsuccessful in their applications to the Local Tribunals had a right of appeal. In July 1916

"John William Clapp (40), a market gardener of Chedzoy, in making an appeal, explained that he had two acres of allotment and worked it all himself. He traded to Burnham twice a week with vegetables and also poultry. He had a wife and five children. His wife was a higgler. Conditional exemption."

Later that same month,

"An agricultural appeal was that of Mr. William Cary for his son, Hubert Hardy Cary, 20, milkman and stockman, who was described as being 'absolutely indispensable to the cultivation of the land.' In answer to Mr. Bishop, appellant said he farmed 240 acres, and was mowing 60 acres of grass. His eldest son had joined the Navy. The local tribunal said that appellant was 'very shifty' in his answers before them. By Mr. Bishop: Five or six members of the local tribunal all asked him questions at the same time and they puzzled him.

He had done his best to get labour and had applied to the Labour Exchange offering £1 a week, cottage free, and potato ground, but he did not receive a single application. Appellant was questioned as to whether a daughter, aged 16, could not assist in milking the cows. He replied, 'She would not milk a cow if you gave it to her for doing so. She is afraid of them, and you can not expect a girl to get up on wet and frosty mornings. It would be the death of her.' The Chairman: The case will be adjourned for a month then dismissed. Appellant: I shall leave the country, that's what I shall do."

The Local Tribunals were still hearing cases in January 1917.

"Mr. J.V. Baker, farmer, asked for exemption on behalf of his son, John Ruscombe Baker, 20, single, cowman and general worker on the farm. Mr. Baker said the farm was one of 126 acres, and the services of his son were quite indispensable. He had been passed for general service. A medical certificate was handed in from Dr. Coates stating that the father was unable to do anything but very light work. His son was the only one on the farm to do the work of cowman. Four sons were with him before the war and the present labour consisted of the son he was applying for, one man over military age, and one boy. The advisory committee recommended substitution. Three months' temporary exemption, a re-examination of the man being recommended."

Two weeks later,

"There were two applications by Mr. Joseph Ashford of Chedzoy in respect of his son, Walter John Ashford, 19, single, and Samuel Henry Gigg, 19, single. The application stated that Walter John Ashford was the driver of an oil engine and also shepherd and milker. He was the only son left at home. Mr. Ashford, Snr., occupied two farms, the acreage being 350. His son was indispensable on the farm. Three of his men had joined up since the outbreak of war and could not be replaced. One son was on active service, and another had been killed at the Dardanelles whilst serving with the Australians. Gigg was the only man he had left who was capable of looking after eight working horses, and was indispensable for the cultivation of his arable land. Six months exemption was granted to Mr. Ashford, Jnr., and the case of Gigg was adjourned sine die for substitution."

In March 1917,

"The Tribunal reviewed the conditional exemption which had been granted to Frederick Tucker, 21, single, blacksmith, of Chedzoy, who has been passed for general service. Tucker stated that he had been in business for three years and did shoeing and general smithing for farmers in the villages of Bawdrip, Bower, Sutton Mallet and Chedzoy. A brother who was in business with him had joined the army, and there was no one to help him. He shoed an average 30 to 40 horses a week. A conditional exemption was withdrawn and four months temporary exemption substituted."

In July the Tribunal allowed a further six months exemption on condition that he worked at Westonzoyland for two days a week. In December that year a further six months exemption was granted with similar conditions.

In October 1917 William Cary of Manor Farm appeared before Bridgwater Borough Police Court on serious charges which warranted two whole columns in the Bridgwater Mercury. The report said,

"The Bench had before them for hearing 20 summonses against William Cary, farmer, of Chedzoy, of having sold milk at an excess price to a Bridgwater dairyman. The first summons was that defendant had sold wholesale a quantity of milk - 154 gallons - at the price of 1s. 2d. (5.75p.) a gallon, such a price being in excess of the rate prescribed by the Milk Order of 1917 made under the Defence of the Realm Act. He was only entitled to charge $11^1/_2$ d. - a profit of $2^1/_2$ d. a gallon. The 20 summonses amounted to an excess profit of £32 19s. 7d. The Mayor said the Bench considered the evidence put before them was very clear and distinct, and that there was no doubt whatever that an overcharge had been made. In order to emphasise the view they had decided to inflict a fine of £50 and to allow £5 5s. in costs. Mr. Clark (for the defence): I take it that is to cover all the cases? The Mayor: The Bench would like to hear further what is said about the other cases. Mr. Reed (for the prosecution), after consulting the Chief Constable, said as the fine was a substantial one, and would have undoubtedly a big deterrent effect in the whole district, the police did not wish to press the other charges and asked for them to be dismissed on payment of ordinary court fees. The Mayor said they were reluctant to consent to the other cases being withdrawn but they had decided to assent to the withdrawal on the payment of £5 5s. additional costs." One week was allowed for payment with three months' imprisonment in default.

In December William Cary returned to the court to give notice of appeal. He was required to pay a recognisance of £100 plus two sureties of £50 each.

"Would the Bench accept Mr. Cary in his own recognisance of £150? The Mayor said that if Mr. Cary would pay into the Court £150 as security, a surety would not be required. Mr. E.J. Pope asked whether the Bench would accept as security some boat shares Mr. Cary was prepared to deposit. The Mayor: No, the Bench would accept a cash deposit of £150." The appeal was heard at Bridgwater Quarter Sessions in January 1918 when "The Recorder did not think the fine of £50, considering Mr. Cary had made a considerable profit in the way he should not have done, was at all excessive." The appeal was dismissed with costs.

Even during the war the thoughts of the Rural District Council were turning to the future, although residents of Chedzoy were more pragmatic. The minutes note that in October 1917 a Parish Meeting was called

"to consider the question of the provision of housing for

the working classes at the conclusion of the war. The opinion of the Parish was sought by the Bridgwater R.D.C. on two points:

a) will the present available accommodation then be sufficient?, and if not -

b) what deficiency will then arise?

There was practically no interest whatever taken by the parishioners in the two questions, the members (three) of the Parish Council being the only parishioners present at the consideration of the two points; and they felt that it is quite impossible to forecast with any degree of accuracy the probable needs which will arise under the, what will be, vastly changed conditions. The Chairman undertook to reply to Mr. Reed's letter in consonance with these views."

The views of the Rural District Council were mentioned in a report of their meeting in March 1918.

"The style of house built a hundred years ago was not suitable at the present time. Women would not be content to live in houses with damp floors, and wooden floors must be provided, whilst there would have to be better sanitation and baths provided."

The cost of such improvements would be between £10,000 and £20,000 for the district.

In May 1918 William Cary appeared before the magistrates again.

"There were three charges against William Cary, farmer, Chedzoy, for having unlawfully sold cheese at the price of 1s. 8d. per pound (about 18p. per kilo), being in excess of the maximum price of 142s. per cwt. (about £7.10 per 50 kg.). The summonses were brought under the Defence of the Realm Regulations. Mr. Cary had a certain quantity of cheese on his premises which he did not want to sell. The cheese was, apparently, of excellent quality, and three other defendants begged him to let them have a little. Mr. Cary was tempted for a moment and allowed them to have the cheese at 1s. 8d. per pound as he was quite unaware there was an Order restricting the price. At the price of 1s. 8d. per pound he would have had £1 13s. 4d. for the cheese sold, whereas at the price of 1s. 3d. per pound, which he was entitled to charge, the amount received would have been £1 5s. The excess profit thus amounted in all to 8s. 4d., or 5d. a pound (about 5p. per kilo). Cary would be fined £1 in respect of each case (£3 in all)."

During the war children were frequently absent from school with permission to help with the various harvests, and holidays were arranged to accommodate these. Children were also set to collect wild herbs, presumably for medicines, for the war effort. Apparently with a view to ascertaining future educational requirements, the Head Teacher was required, but paid ten shillings for his trouble, to carry out a house to house survey and prepare a census of the population of Chedzoy: there were 297 resident (the same as in 1912) on 30th June 1918. On 11th November 1918 the school log book records,

"News reached the village about half past eleven this morning that an armistice has been signed. In honour of this first step towards a victorious peace the flag was hoisted and the children were arranged near the base of the flagstaff where they sang the National Anthem; and were then dismissed about 12 o'clock for the remainder of the day."

On 19th July 1919, following the signing of the Peace Treaty on 28th June, a celebration was held. The Headmaster wrote in his log book that it was a

"Day of rejoicing to celebrate the re-establishment of Peace after nearly five years of horrid war. The whole body of Parishioners - children and grown-ups - were entertained to tea in the croft at Fisher's Farm. Unfortunately it was too wet to carry out the programme of games and sports which had been arranged."

The sports were eventually held on 22nd July, again at Fishers Farm, when "the children were regaled with cake and lemonade, which they greatly appreciated." Joseph Ashford (1856-1943), Chairman of the Managers, kindly announced a holiday for the following day and in September the autumn holiday was extended by one week in honour of 'Peace Year.'

In October 1919 a supper was held in the village hall to welcome home the ex-servicemen of the parish. About thirty men sat down to a hot supper which was served by the ladies and gentlemen of the parish. Toasts were drunk to the King, Fallen Heroes and Absent Comrades.

Something which the author has been asked about, but can find no reference to, is when the roads of the village were first surfaced. No reference appears in Parish Council minutes or any other papers which have been read. When asked in 1999 Norman Fry recalled that shortly after the First World War gangs of men with a steamroller began to spread chippings onto the dirt roads of the village, but this was done piecemeal and he was unable to be more specific as to any date. He recalled that the workmen would make regular visits to Sibleys Farm in order to quench their thirsts with cider!

What would seem to have been two cases of indecency occurred in the village in June 1919, but in coyness typical of the era, and totally the reverse of modern reporting, the details were not given, although the newspaper report included the full details of the victims.

"Albert Stoyles (41), farm labourer of Chedzoy, was brought up in custody on two serious charges. Prisoner was first charged with unlawful conduct towards [a named girl], aged 12. On the Sunday afternoon prisoner asked her to go for a walk to see some birds nests. Jane Fry, wife of William Fry, said she saw them go into the field and when they came back the girl looked frightened. Prisoner pleaded guilty and was sentenced to six months' imprisonment with hard labour. The second charge related to a [named] five year old Parchey girl. The little girl went to the prisoner's house for some firewood. As she did not return quickly her parents went to look for her. They saw prisoner peeping through the bedroom window and on going upstairs found the girl in the room with the prisoner. The father of the girl said he made a charge against the prisoner, and told him if he did not tell the truth he would kill him. Prisoner made an admission, and witness gave the prisoner a thrashing, blacking his eye. Sentenced to six months hard labour, the sentences to run consecutively (12 months in all)."

A county-wide collection was started with the aim of building a Somerset County War Memorial and Chedzoy Parish Council contributed the sum of £1 1s. to this. In the event, only £8,410 13s. 5d. was raised, an insufficient sum, so £3,192 was spent on a memorial chapel at Wells Cathedral, £500 on a memorial book and the remainder went to the Educational Aid Scheme for the children of those killed or disabled whilst serving their country. In May that same year an artillery shell was mounted on a plinth: it was reported that

> "A large shell has been placed in front of the Parish Hall to commemorate the local war savings efforts during 'Guns Week.' A brass tablet on the shell bears the following inscription: PRESENTED BY THE NATIONAL WAR SAVINGS COMMITTEE TO THE PEOPLE OF CHEDZOY TO COMMEMORATE THEIR NOTABLE SUBSCRIPTION TO WAR SECURITIES DURING GUNS WEEK 1918'."

The shell appears to have been removed during the Second World War.

Communication Problems

A stained glass memorial window for the village church was constructed by Messrs. Powell and Sons of London at a cost of £150. It was dedicated in April 1920, but there was still a deficit of £24 to be met. The Parish Council resolved

> "To realise sundry War Savings Certificates and give the proceeds to the Fund being raised to render the Memorial Window free of debt."

For many years the affairs of the church had been decided at Vestry Meetings, but the last of these took place in April 1920. Later the same month the Parochial Church Council (PCC) was formed: it consisted of nine members and remains at that figure.

In September 1920 Joseph Brooks retired as Head Teacher of the village school, having served in that position for 40 years. He moved to Ashleigh Avenue, Bridgwater and was replaced by Miss Ellen Nichols. To commemorate his many years of service he was presented with a solid silver teapot inscribed PRESENTED TO MR. J. BROOKS BY HIS MANY FRIENDS IN CHEDZOY ON HIS RETIREMENT AFTER 40 YEARS SERVICE AS HEAD TEACHER IN THE VILLAGE SCHOOL. SEPTEMBER 1920. Mr. Brooks died in July 1930, aged 72, and was buried in Quantock Road Cemetery, Bridgwater.

On 27th November 1920, after 26 years of meeting in the schoolroom, the Parish Council met for the first time in the Parish Hall. The following March they met to consider the rent for allotments. It was agreed that the rent for the acre nearest to the entrance gate should be £4 10s. 8d. (£4.53) per annum, with the rental for all the other plots descending by 4d. (about 1.5p.) per plot down to the furthest from the gate which would cost £4 6s. (£4.30) each year.

The question of the fire hose and appliances re-appeared in 1922 when the Parish Council were informed that a thorough test and examination had been carried out, and two lengths of hose were found to be defective. The quotation for repairs to one length were between 18s. (90p.) and 75s. (£3.75), but the other length was beyond repair and replacement would cost £6 or more. The Council decided to have one length repaired, the eventual cost being £1 5s. 6d., "Leaving the question of replacing the badly damaged and decayed length in abeyance."

In 1923 the village was visited by an epidemic of whooping cough. In June the school was closed for four weeks on the authority of the County Medical Officer of Health. The closure was extended for a further week as

> "the scholars affected with whooping cough did not seem sufficiently recovered to return to school."

Later that year it seems that weather conditions were ideal for spontaneous combustion - or an arsonist was at work in the area. In August it was reported that on one day there were fires at Three Oaks Farm, Manor Farm and Bradney Farm, with more haystack fires in nearby villages over the following days.

> "Three ricks containing over 100 tons of new hay were destroyed. There were many willing helpers after the alarm had been given , and the district fire hose was called into service. The flames were prevented from spreading to the farm buildings."

In 1925 five 60 foot lengths of fire hose together with the fittings were purchased for the sum of £22 5s., although some money was recouped by the sale of the damaged length for £3 15s. The Parish Council minutes noted that the fire hoses and appliances were now "in an efficient and satisfactory condition." The use of the equipment was formalised and a scale of charges printed. To use the equipment

> "The Form of acceptance of the terms of loan of Fire Hose, etc. must be signed by the person requisitioning for use, the appliances, or by some responsible person on his behalf."

How applicants were supposed to sign whilst their homes burned is not recorded! The charge was £1 on each occasion it was used, £2 if used outside the parish, in addition to which a minimum of 10s. (50p.) was to be paid to the custodian of the hose for his time and services up to five hours and thereafter at the rate of 2s. (10p.) per hour. Users were also required to make good any damage caused to the equipment.

In 1924 attempts had been made to obtain "an up-to-date Fire Engine and appliance for the Bridgwater District." After due consideration it was agreed

> "That this [Parish] Council supports the efforts now being made by the Bridgwater Branch of the National Farmers Union to impress on the Bridgwater Rural District Council the very great desirability of themselves - or if it can be arranged, in conjunction with the Bridgwater Town Council - taking such steps as shall be considered best to secure for the Bridgwater District adequate means of combating any fires whenever and wherever, in the district, they unfortunately may occur."

In January 1925 the Rural District Council considered a request for improvements to two dangerous corners in Chedzoy: unfortunately contemporary reports do not indicate which corners these were, but as they had high hedges it seems likely that they may have been in Ward Lane. Later that month the Council agreed to the work being carried out at an estimated cost of £75 to £100. However, the following month the local newspaper reported that "when a sub-committee went to Chedzoy to inspect the road there, they saw that some of the district roads were in a very bad state. When the Council's men were working on improving corners, they could not be working on the roads," so the planned improvements were abandoned.

However, it seems that the Council still did nothing about the state of the roads. At a meeting of the Rural District Council in February 1926

> "Rev. G.R. Mullens said he had been asked by constituents in the parish of Chedzoy to call attention to the conditions of Chedzoy Lane. There were enormous holes in the road, and it was hardly safe to drive along it now. The Surveyor promised to give the matter his attention,"

but the outcome was not reported.

The airfield at Westonzoyland could so easily have been at Chedzoy. In the spring of 1925 representatives of the Air Ministry interviewed land owners and farmers regarding the purchase of part of

> "a huge field known as Chedzoy Field, in connection with a similar one in West Somerset and which this summer will be used for the purpose of manoeuvres. Only about one sixth of the 300 acres would be required and, as there were no hedges or ditches, the site was described as ideal."

In April 1925 it was reported that

> "The Air Ministry have been recently making investigations at Westonzoyland and interviewing tenants of land with a view to securing a suitable site for air manoeuvres during the coming summer, the Chedzoy project having been abandoned."

The site of the manoeuvres, scheduled to take place from 1st June to 30th September, was eventually to become a permanent airfield and aircraft flying over Chedzoy were a familiar sight.

Indeed, in June 1927 Mollie Mullens, the youngest daughter of Rev. Mullens, married Flight Lieutenant Aleth de Lacroix and during the service aircraft circled overhead "at a very low altitude, round and round the church, the roar of the engines at times drowning the voices of the officiating clergy."

Village children were also enjoying the benefits of modern life. In August 1925 the Bridgwater Mercury reported,

> "The first outing of scholars of the Council School to the sea took place on Saturday. The children, accompanied by teachers, friends and mothers, travelled by bus and motor cars through Huntspill and Highbridge to Burnham. On arrival the children made for the sands, where they keenly enjoyed themselves. At 4 o'clock the party reassembled at Marchant's Tea Gardens and did ample justice to the good tea provided. They left for home at 7.45. The outing was successfully arranged and thoroughly enjoyed."

In 1924 and 1925 Chedzoy was at the cutting edge of technology. Experiments in trans-Atlantic radio communication were conducted at Three Oaks Farm, Fowlers Plot. Although shrouded in secrecy, it was inevitable that the locals would become aware of the experiments and in April 1925 the following appeared in the Bridgwater Mercury under the headline LATEST WIRELESS WONDER. TELEPHONY WITH AMERICA. CHEDZOY RESIDENT 'PICKS UP' AMERICA. The report reads as follows:

> "One of the outstanding news items last week was the fact that wireless telephony with America has been successfully accomplished - accomplished, too, by means of a wireless station established almost at our doors; no further off than at Chedzoy, within easy reach, as everyone knows, of Bridgwater. Profound secrecy has surrounded the experiments, which have been going on for some time, the operations being carried on by the British General Post Office authorities in conjunction with the Western Electric Company of America. In spite of the secrecy, gossip has been busy, with the knowledge that experiments of a wireless nature have been going on; now the reserve has been penetrated, and it is known that telephonic communication has passed through the Chedzoy station with mid-America.
>
> "A representative of the 'Mercury,' who visited Chedzoy, found two wireless stations, both situated adjoining the road on Mr. Edwin John Fry's farm. One belongs to the British General Post Office, having been converted from a garage; the other - on the opposite side of the road - belongs to the Western Electric Company, America, and consists of a wooden hut, protected by wooden fencing, the interior containing elaborate apparatus used in connection with the experiments. A double length of wire, suspended on ordinary telephone poles, is connected with the stations, and stretches a distance of about seven miles, over Sedgemoor to Henley, near High Ham.

"Great reserve is still being maintained by the officials and all concerned, but our representative learned that a married daughter of Mr. Fry - Mrs. Wilkins, of Bridgwater - who formerly resided with her father at Chedzoy, has actually spoken to someone in America by wireless. One evening she was asked by a Post Office engineer at the station if she would like to hear a message from across the Atlantic. Instantly accepting, she hastened to the garage, and she received a message from 'the other side'."

Speaking shortly before his death in 1998, Wyndham Fry recalled that experiments took place over two or three years and he remembered hearing "Cardiff calling" from the eight-valve radio which was powered by a generator. His sister maintained that she didn't actually hear someone speaking from the United States, but only some noises.

The Mercury report concluded,

"An announcement in the Press on Friday morning, issued by the Postmaster-General, says: 'Statements have recently appeared in the Press on the subject of transatlantic wireless telephony to the effect that two-way telephonic communications have already been established between England and America by means of a new and secret system. The Postmaster-General desires it to be understood that this is not the case."

Perhaps Mrs. Wilkins' assurances to her brother were correct. Many years later it was reported that the equipment used for the experiments cost £2,000.

More established modern technology was not to be allowed to pass by the village, and in March 1926 the Parish Council resolved

"That it is desirable, if possible, that public telephone facilities be provided for the village,"

and the Clerk was instructed to investigate the possible cost. He subsequently reported that the Post Office required that the Council

"Become guarantors for the receipts up to annual costs - £21 if pattern be telephone without an enclosing cabinet or £25 with cabinet provided,"

the equivalent to £630 or £750 in 1999 terms. The matter was discussed again the following year when the Council decided against committing the parish to this expense.

In June 1928 the Parish Council was approached by the Rural District Council in order to suggest suitable sites for the erection of two houses. Agreement was reached, although the location was not noted in the minutes, and the information sent back. In October that year the local paper reported that the Rural District Council had agreed to purchase sites for council houses in various villages, including Chedzoy. It seems likely that the Chedzoy site was that where Nos. 1 and 2 Higher Road now stand.

By 1929 the matter of the Fire Engine had still not been resolved. Councillor Tarr moved,

"'That this Council gives its approval to the scheme'; and spoke strongly in favour of his fellow members giving the scheme their hearty support, begging them to take a broader view from a merely parochial aspect. The members, however, were not impressed: and while whole-heartedly sympathising with Mr. Tarr in his endeavours to do what he can to benefit the district generally, the members could not forget that this Parish has spent a very considerable sum of money, within the last three and twenty years in doing their best to render every individual in the parish as safe as human forethought can avail to provide against dangerous and extensive outbreaks of fire. The argument appeared to be 'we have spent and are spending considerable amounts in pursuit of this object and in the light of these facts do not feel that we should be justified in shouldering what may turn out to be further burdens.' There being no seconder to Mr. Tarr's motion, the matter fell through."

The same year, and perhaps influencing their lack of support for Mr. Tarr, the Council had agreed to purchase additional hydrants and two extra 75 foot lengths of hose with fittings

"and also a piece of metal tubing, shaped with an 'elbow,' capable of being fitted to the hydrant to convey water from below ground level to hose fittings at an above ground level."

Footpaths, and complaints of their obstruction, were still regularly discussed by the Parish Council. In 1929 the minutes refer to

"Alleged trespass on, and consequent serious damage to 'Church Path' in Chedzoy Eastfield. Consideration was given to this matter; and it was very generally felt and strongly held among the Councillors that grave damage had been done here; and serious inconvenience caused to the users of this useful and much-treasured path by Mr. Arthur Baker and/or his agents unlawfully using this 'church path' - which from time immemorial had been used exclusively by travellers a-foot - as a wheel track, and thus rendering it unclean, uncomfortable, unsafe and unsuited for the purpose for which it was originally designated: and which, until this recent trespass it had so admirable fulfilled. The Clerk was instructed to write to Mr. Baker directing his attention to his probably illegal and, without one jot of doubt, his very selfish, utterly unwarranted, and most unneighbourly conduct."

By way of explanation, it should be remembered that East Field is the area to the south of Front Street. Church path ran from Myrtle Cottage on Ward Lane almost directly to Fowlers Plot, so was the most direct route for Fowlers Plot residents wishing to reach the church.

It was not only footpaths which were causing problems. At a meeting of the Bridgwater Rural District Council in October 1929

"The Surveyor presented his report with regard to Parchey Bridge and said its approaches had now become in such a condition and shape as to be dangerous and unsuitable for traffic. The Drainage Board had hitherto accepted responsibility for the maintenance. Mr. White remarked that the bridge was almost impassable and was very dangerous at the present time. During the dry weather the road at the side of the bridge had dropped down. The Council agreed to do temporary repairs to the road where they were urgently required."

The Thirties

In February 1930, because of ill-health, Joseph Brooks resigned as Clerk to the Parish Council and he was replaced by Harold Wilkins of Bridgwater at an annual salary of £5. In August that year the annual Bawdrip and Chedzoy Flower Show was held at Fishers Farm. The importance of this event can be illustrated by the fact that five special buses, one leaving Bridgwater every hour from 3.00 p.m. onwards, provided a shuttle service to the show for a return fare of 6d. (2.5p.). Admission to the show was the same price and entertainment was provided by the Bridgwater Imperial Silver Band. Attendance was down on the previous year as high winds caused some concerns about the safety of the marquee.

By 1931 the population of the parish had reached an all-time low of 277, but visiting motorists were finding their way to the village as

"Mr. Ashford made a request [to the Parish Council] that a finger post was necessary opposite his residence denoting the way to Westonzoyland and Bridgwater pointing out that motorists and others often at night got lost when they came as far as Fishers Farm."

The Council agreed to bring the matter to the attention of the Rural District Council and at their meeting in June

"Rev. G.R. Mullens stated that he had been asked by the Parish Council to request that a further signpost should be put up at Chedzoy by the turning near Fishers Farm, as at present many motorists went down that way and found themselves going across the fields."

Whether or not a signpost was ever erected does not appear to have been recorded.

An inquest took place in May 1932 into what would probably now be regarded as sudden infant death syndrome.

"An inquest was held at Chedzoy on the body of an unnamed infant daughter of 'A' and 'B'." The names and address of the parents were given. "The mother gave evidence and said she took the baby, aged 19 days, upstairs at 8.30 p.m. and placed her in a cot. The baby slept till 5 a.m. when the witness fed her and put her in bed with her. At 6.30 a.m. witness and her husband got up. The baby was still sleeping. At 7.45 witness looked into the room to see if the baby was alright. She noticed the baby was pale, and that its mouth was open. On examination witness came to the conclusion that the child was dead. Dr. Martin said the cause of death was asphyxia.
The Coroner returned a verdict of 'Death by Misadventure'."

It would seem that Flight Lieutenant de Lacroix, Rev. Mullen's son-in-law, and his wife must have lived at the Rectory. In September 1932 it was reported that

"Mrs. Mollie Constance Laquen de Lacroix of Chedzoy was summoned for driving a motor car in Eastover, [Bridgwater] without having a licence. P.C. Miners said he had occasion to take particulars of an accident in which the defendant was involved. He asked her to produce her licence and on examining it found it had expired. The fine was 10s."

It should be pointed out that in those days a driving licence required renewal every three years.

For 15th April 1933 council minutes note that

"The Annual Meeting of the Parish Council called for this evening at 7 p.m. was postponed as the Chairman and Mr. A.H. Tarr being the only members present and the Clerk was instructed to call another meeting."

An indication as to agricultural wages at this time appeared in a report which was published in the Bridgwater Mercury in March 1933: the names have been omitted here to avoid any embarrassment.

"'A', a single woman of [a given address] Chedzoy, applied for a paternity order against 'B', a farm labourer of Chedzoy. Applicant said the child was born in January and that 'B' was the father. Defendant admitted the paternity of the child and said he was a farm labourer and his weekly wage was 30s. 6d. (£1.52). The most he had ever got was 35s. (£1.75) and he could not afford to pay more than 5s. a week. He was married in November last. The Bench made an order for the defendant to pay 5s. (25p.) a week until the child reached the age of 14 and allowed an advocate's fee of £1 1s."

Problems with Parchey Bridge had still not been resolved by April 1933. It was reported that Bridgwater Rural District Councillors were informed that

"A Stawell annual parish meeting decided to call attention to the condition of Parchey Bridge. The meeting considered that the bridge in its present condition was a source of danger to present day traffic, which included the local 'bus service, and they requested the District Council to take action to bring about an improvement to the bridge and the approaches thereto. The Surveyor said there was a notice on this bridge and that it was the property of the drainage authorities. Several members pointed out that the bridge was in a very unsafe condition and that someone should be called upon to put it in repair, and the Surveyor was instructed to inspect it and report."

A month later at the next District Council meeting

"In reference to the complaint as to the unsafe condition of Parchy Bridge, Stawell (sic), the Surveyor stated that the Drainage Commissioners had previously accepted liability for this bridge, and had in fact paid for repairs thereto. As, however, the bridge was now called upon to carry extraordinary traffic, he thought the matter might well be considered by the County Council."

Fire prevention continued to be a concern in the parish and in 1933

"It was decided to proceed with the complaint of Mr. Fred Tucker who had been invited to attend before the Council. Mr. Tucker referred to the unsatisfactory state of the fire hydrants being examined periodically. After discussion it was agreed that the Fire Hydrants, Hose and Appliances be examined in May and November in each year and should the necessity arise he would be able to report at the Audit Meeting of any defects. Mr. Tucker pointed out that he could not make two inspections at the present amount allowed and it was agreed that a further sum of 7s. 6d. be granted, making £ 1 17s. 6d. annually."

Twelve months after Stawell residents complained about Parchey Bridge, it seems that nothing had been done, so Moorlinch had a go. In April 1934 a meeting of Bridgwater Rural District Council was told

"The Rev. J.R. Hearn, Chairman of the parish meeting of Moorlinch, forwarded a resolution in regard to Parchey Bridge, stating that its present state was a real danger to the travelling public, and that a better, wider, straight bridge should be built. The Surveyor said he understood the County Council were considering this matter, and he thought before long a new bridge would be provided. Mr. Wilson (one of the Councillors) remarked that this matter would affect the Catchment Board, as there was a scheme going forward for widening all these bridges in order to get a better flow of water right through the Brue. Parchey Bridge at present was only 11 or 12 feet wide through the archway."

One can't help wondering about Councillor Wilson's knowledge of the area. How was water from Parchey Bridge going to negotiate the Polden Hills to reach the River Brue?

Drainage in Hollow Road, also known as Hollow Lane, between Fishers Farm and Fowlers Plot has long been a bone of contention. In June 1934 at a meeting of the Rural District Council

"The Sanitary Inspector reported that he'd now investigated the complaint made by the Chedzoy Parish Council as to the ditch in Hollow Road and recommended that the uncovered portion (approximately 150 yards) be piped in in 9-inch pipes, complete with three manholes, and the existing length in 6-inch drainage across the orchard (approximately 50 yards) be taken up and laid in 9-inch piping, the estimated cost of the work being £40. The matter was referred to the Parish Council for their views thereon."

The village may have had a mains water supply, but proper sewage disposal was a long way in the future.

In September 1934 the Parish Council considered a complaint by Mr. H. Pearce relative to the sewer at Manor Farm emptying into an open ditch near his residence. The Clerk was instructed to communicate with the Rural District Council

"pointing out this was a matter that should receive immediate attention and requesting it may be possible for the Sanitary Inspector to meet the members of the Council on the spot to inspect drain recently laid."

Two months later at a meeting of the B.R.D.C.

"The Surveyor reported that he had inspected the drain at the back of Manor Lane (sic), Chedzoy with the Parish Council, and the only possible course appeared to be to pipe the ditch and provide two manholes for cleansing regularly. The Council gave their sanction."

A tragic death occurred in the village in February 1935 and lengthy report of the inquest was published in the Bridgwater Mercury under the heading CHEDZOY INFANT'S DEATH. THREE WEEKS AFTER BIRTH. EXTREME DEGREE OF WASTING.

"The West Somerset Coroner, sitting with a jury, held an inquest in the Parish Hall, Chedzoy on Friday afternoon on the body of an infant child of Mr. and Mrs. 'X' of Chedzoy" - their names and address were given - "who died on Sunday, February 10th. The child, a female, was born on Friday, January 18th and appeared to be perfectly normal and healthy, and progressed favourably until Monday, February 4th, when it began to get thin. On the following Friday it developed a slight cold, and died two days later.

"Mr. E.J. Fry was foreman of the jury. The County Police were represented by Supt. S.C. Edwards, P.S. Field and P.C. Greed. At the outset the Coroner explained to the jury that a post-mortem examination showed the cause of death to be asphyxia, double pneumonia and malnutrition. The main point was that the examination revealed an extreme degree of wasting, and Dr. Carter would tell them that the child was practically a skeleton. It was therefore their duty to decide whether the child was properly looked after, and whether a doctor or nurse might have been summoned earlier.

'X', wife of 'X' of Chedzoy, the mother, gave evidence of identification, and after being cautioned said the child was born at 3 a.m. on Friday, January 18th, in the presence of Nurse Newton and weighed $6^1/_4$ lbs. at birth. The child appeared to be progressing favourable until Monday February 4th when she started getting thin and going back although still taking her food regularly. The condition of the child appeared about the same on the Tuesday, Wednesday and Thursday, but on the Friday she developed a slight cold. She did not send for Nurse Newton until the next day, when the child was tight on the chest. Nurse Newton arrived at the house at 3.30 p.m. and told her to rub the child well with olive oil, which she did. She put the child in the pram where she left her until 6.30 in the evening, when she took her out and fed her, and put her back in the pram again. Witness went to bed about 10.30 p.m. but before going she fed the baby again, and placed her in a big easy chair in front of the fire in the bedroom. About 3 o'clock in the morning she heard the child crying, but did not take much notice of it, and after feeding her, she went back to bed again. She and her husband got up about 6.30 a.m. and she went to the child.

The Coroner: What did you find when you went there?

The child was cold, and I thought she was dead.

"Continuing, witness said she had told her husband and then went on her bicycle to tell Nurse Newton and Mrs. Fry (no further identification) telephoned for the doctor. Nurse Newton and Dr. Cromie came to the house in the afternoon. She told the nurse the child was dead when she went to tell her in the morning.

The Coroner: Did Nurse Newton say she would call again the next morning (Sunday)?

Yes, she did.

Witness went on to say she used to feed the child five times a day with two teaspoonfuls of cow's milk, two of water, and one of sugar from a bottle. She did not notice the existence of a small place on the child's left heel until after she was dead, although she bathed the child every morning. She had four other children whose ages ranged from six years to nineteen months.

The Coroner: Did the nurse say to you on Saturday afternoon that the child was ill or that you should get a doctor that day?

No.

In answer to further questions by the Coroner witness said she thought the child was getting on all right, as she was taking her food in, and she saw no signs of convulsions. Answering a question by the Coroner, Dr. Carter said the child did not suffer from vomiting, and he found no sign of indigestion. Convulsions, he added, would be quite capable of causing asphyxia.

"Edith Doris Newton, private nurse, of Chedzoy, who gave her qualifications as C.M.B. (Central Midwives' Board), said the child was perfectly normal and healthy at birth. She called daily at the house for ten days, and the child was then going along all right.

The Coroner: How far away do you actually live from this house?

About ten minutes' walk.

Supposing for the sake of argument, if Mrs. 'X' sends for you, does she have to pay for you per visit?

It is left to me, but I should not charge.

Continuing, witness said she went to the house on Sunday in response to a message from Mrs. 'X', and noticed the child was wheezy on the chest, and appeared to be wasting. She did not consider the child was very seriously ill at the time, and not ill enough for a doctor to be called in. She said she would call again the next morning, and if there was no alteration in the child's condition then a doctor must be called in. She advised Mrs. 'X' to alter the child's food. Mrs. 'X' called at the house the next morning just before 7 o'clock to say the child was dead. Witness did not see her as her husband answered the door.

The Coroner: Why didn't you go round to see the child before 4 o'clock?

If the baby was dead, there was no need for me to go round.

When you and the doctor called in the afternoon was Mrs. 'X' upset?

Yes.

Was she crying?

I can't remember.

Were the other children well looked after?

Yes, they were.

"Dr. Godfrey Carter, pathologist, of Taunton, said the baby showed an extreme degree of wasting. He attributed the cause of death to asphyxia, associated with double pneumonia and malnutrition. The child was exceedingly thin when he saw it.

The Coroner: Was it in such a state that medical attention should have been called in earlier?

I am of that opinion.

Was it obvious the baby was going downhill very fast?

Yes, very fast.

Continuing, Dr. Carter said the child had suffered from congenital disease of the heart, and in its debilitated condition death might have been preceded by convulsions. In his opinion the asphyxia was consistent with having been produced by natural causes.

"P.C. Greed was called, and stated he interviewed Mrs. 'X' on February 12th and questioned her about the way she fed the baby. She told him she gave the child two teaspoonfuls of cow's milk, two of water, and one of sugar, and if it required more she gave it more. Nurse Newton said when she left calling the child was being given feeds of one tablespoonful of milk and one of water.

"Addressing the jury, the Coroner said he did not think that there was any real evidence of wilful or deliberate neglect on the part of the mother. No doubt medical aid should have been called in. They would probably return a verdict of 'Death from natural causes.' The Foreman remarked that they did not wish to add a rider, although they did not think that what the child was receiving was sufficient to maintain it."

On the national scene, a speed limit of 30 m.p.h. was introduced in built-up areas on 18th March 1935. The Chief Constable of Somerset announced that the police motor corps was being enlarged to seven men.

"A number of police cars will be employed on patrol and will from time to time be travelling at a speed of 30 miles an hour. Any car overtaking a vehicle proceeding at that speed will be infringing the law, and action will have to be taken by the police authority."

It was intended to expand the police vehicle fleet to have cars of various types and colours.

This did not mean that other road users were to be ignored as in October

"Vivian Hallett, single woman, of the Post Office (now Cadbury House), Chedzoy and Kenneth Williams, of 70 St. John's Street, Bridgwater were each fined 5s. for contravening the regulations regarding two persons being carried on a pedal cycle."

The couple subsequently married. Possibly Kenneth bought a new made-to-measure suit for the big day: in 1935 Burtons were advertising suits for 45s. (£2.25).

Although a speed limit had been imposed, there was not one in Chedzoy and in March 1935 an accident occurred. The report is somewhat ambiguous, but it appears that the location was probably Manor Road near the narrow section leading out onto Chedzoy Lane.

"John Harold Brown, salesman, of Springfield, Chedzoy was summoned for driving without due care and attention. Mr. Arthur King appeared on his behalf and pleaded not guilty. Herbert William George Palfrey, taxi driver, of Monmouth Street, Bridgwater, said at 10.50 p.m. he was in company with a young lady near the Manor House Inn, Chedzoy, and saw the lights of a car coming towards him going in the direction of Bridgwater. He took no notice of the car, and thought it would pass him. He was suddenly hit into the air, and landed between the two front lamps of the car after somersaulting twice. The accident happened about eleven paces on the Bridgwater side of Chedzoy corner. He thought the car must have touched the bank on its proper side of the road, and shot straight across the road in his direction. He sustained slight injuries to his legs and bruises to his body.

"Violet May Collard, of Yew Tree House, Chedzoy, who was with the last witness, gave evidence, and said there were three people in the car. The driver said he was in a hurry. She was home from work for two days after. P.C. Greed stated defendant called at the police station to report an accident in which he was involved. Asked if he wished to make a statement defendant said, 'I don't think I will if you don't mind.' When asked if there was anyone else in the car defendant said, 'Yes, Wm. Rogers of North Street was sat in the front seat with a young lady on his knees.' In answer to Superintendent Edwards, defendant said the other two passengers in the front seat would not impede his driving.

"Defendant was sworn, and said he was a sales manager for the Bridgwater Gas Company. On the date in question he turned into Chedzoy Lane towards Bridgwater, and as he approached the corner he went into bottom gear, as he knew it was a very narrow lane. It was a fairly long car, and he had to lock the wheels hard. As he swung round the corner the lights shot (sic) on the two people, and the car immediately hit them. The couple were standing three or four feet away from the bank. Mr. King submitted there was not sufficient evidence to convict defendant, who had been driving for seven years, and had never had a complaint against him by the police before, and had never had an accident previously. He suggested defendant took all reasonable precautions, and that the accident was inevitable. The Bench dismissed the case, the Chairman remarking that the evidence was not strong enough to record a conviction."

In 1935 King George V celebrated his Silver Jubilee. The School Managers minutes record that

"The Chairman read a letter from the County Secretary embodying the King's expressed wish that the school be granted a holiday on Monday, 6th May on the occasion of the celebration of His Majesty's Silver Jubilee: the Mangers unanimously agreed to honour his Majesty's wish, and gave the school a holiday."

Celebrations in the village were duly reported in the Bridgwater Mercury.

"The Church bellringers awoke the parish to the fact that the great day had dawned by a joyous peal at 5 a.m., and the bells were rung at intervals throughout the day. The main street of the village was gaily decorated with flags and streamers. The proceedings commenced with a thanksgiving service in the Parish Church at 12 noon, at which the special form of service was used, and an address given by the Rector, the Rev. G.R. Mullens. The church was filled to its capacity with such a numerous congregation as had not been assembled within its walls for a very long time.

"At the close of the service practically the whole adult population repaired to the large Dutch barn at Sibley's Farm, which had been placed at their disposal by the great kindness of Mr. F.C. Fry. On arrival they found that the barn had been converted into a most attractive-looking dining room, enclosed, as it was, with rick sheets, and decorated with flags and bunting, and a bright display of flowers and evergreens. Two long tables, daintily laid, stretched the whole length of the barn, and all sat down to a good old-fashioned English luncheon of bread, beef, ham and beer. At the close the Rector proposed a toast to 'The King', which was duly honoured, and a collection was made for 'The King's Jubilee Trust Fund.'

"A very pleasing incident then followed, when the Rector proposed the health of Mr. Joseph Ashford, the parish churchwarden, whose 80th birthday it was, and wished him many happy returns of the day. To this Mr. Ashford suitably replied. At 4 p.m. all the children sat down to an excellent tea, and a Jubilee mug was presented to each child. At 5 p.m. a long programme of sports was commenced in the 'Rectory Lawn' and was not concluded till 9 p.m. A thoroughly enjoyable day was spent by all in perfect weather. The great thanks of the whole parish are due to the ladies' committee who worked so untiringly in carrying out the arrangements for the luncheon and tea. The expenses of the day's celebrations were met by public subscription."

The local residents were looking to the future. In June 1935 the Rural District Council's meeting was reported under the headline DEMAND FOR CHEAPER HOUSING.

> "With regard to the erection of further houses at Chedzoy, the housing committee reported that the Rev. G.R. Mullens stated that a request had been made by the Parish Council for the erection of four of the cheaper rented cottages in the parish, and that there was a demand for these houses. The Clerk explained that houses should only be let at cheap rents with exchequer and rate assistance, and such assistance was at present only available in respect of accommodation provided for persons displaced from unfit dwellings. The committee decided to await the report on the question of building houses without subsidy."

Of greater importance was the supply of electricity to the parish. In May 1936 the minutes record,

> "Electric Light. The Chairman reported that he had enquired of the R.D.C. as to the steps to be taken to obtain an Instalment of this in the Parish and on the information received by him it was decided that the Clerk be instructed to write to the Bridgwater Electric Light Co. for terms."

At the next meeting,

> "The Clerk reported he had had an interview with Mr. King, a representative of the Electric Light Co. Ltd. and he intimated that it would be better for the Parish Council to submit a concrete scheme - e.g., the number of parishioners wishing to take advantage of the light. In his opinion if the light was laid properly to supply the whole of the village it would be a costly one. A transformer would be required each mile and as the estimated cost would be about £400 for each plus £300 for laying cable, etc. and approximately between 3 and 4 miles of low tension cable would be used, he doubted whether it would be a paying proposition as the houses are so scattered. It was agreed that as the Company would eventually benefit they themselves should interview the various persons to obtain the light and the Clerk instructed to write to the Company to this effect."

Having canvassed opinion and established that 40 householders were in favour of the scheme, the Clerk was instructed by the Parish Council in October 1937

> "to write to the Electric Light Co. informing them that the Oxford University was prepared to wire their farmhouses and cottages subject to terms with their tenants and the Council would now like to have the Company's decision on the matter,"

but it was to be some time before a reply was received.

Also in 1936 a Parish Meeting was held at the request of the Rural District Council to consider a proposed scheme for the removal of household refuse in the several parishes of the district.

> "The Chairman read a statement setting out the working and cost of the scheme, and after general discussion the following resolution was proposed... 'That we, Householders and Ratepayers of the Parish of Chedzoy, in Parish Meeting assembled, welcome the R.D. Council's proposed scheme for the removal of House Refuse and hope that it will be put into effect in this Parish.' The Chairman promises to enquire further of the R.D.C. (1) as to whether there was a likelihood of the estimated cost of 2d. (less than 1p.) rate being increased, and (2) as to whether in the light of expenses, it would be compulsory for owners and occupiers to provide a standard type of covered bin."

The number of motor vehicles in the village was increasing and causing concern for the School Managers. In the summer of 1936,

> "Mrs. Fry commented on the danger to children attending the school from motor vehicles coming round the corner from Chedzoy Lane, and asked if some warning sign could be placed at the corner."

A request was passed to the Rural District Council without success. Two years later,

> "The correspondent read a circular received from the Chief Education Officer with regard to the safeguarding of children from the dangers of road traffic: and after full consideration the correspondent was instructed to write a suitable reply stating that while the Managers were willing and anxious to do all in their power to protect the children from road dangers, they were of the opinion that the County Council might be held largely to blame in the event of an accident happening to a child by being run over by a car at the 'Cross Tree' corner, seeing that they had refused the erection of a Danger sign at that corner nearly two years ago."

By October 1941 the problem still had not been resolved and the minutes note that

> "The Headmistress asked the Managers to recommend the erection of two 'School' road signs near the school. After some discussion the Managers decided that such signs were necessary, especially on account of the greatly increased amount of military traffic passing the school and also as the door of the Parish Hall opened almost onto the road."

There is no further mention of road signs in the Managers' minutes, but signs certainly existed for a number of years before the final closure of the school.

However, although motor vehicles were much more common, older horsepower had not been forgotten. In September 1936 the Bridgwater Mercury reported

> "An excellent and enjoyable programme of riding and jumping was witnessed by a large crowd of followers and friends of the Bridgwater Harriers and the Hunt Committee's annual horse show and gymkhana. The meeting, as in former years, was held at Fishers Farm, Chedzoy by kind

permission of Mr. A.E. Ashford, to whom the committee were greatly indebted for the loan of his spacious home meadow. In all there were thirteen events, and each attracted a surprisingly large entry, with the result that there was some keen competition. Most interesting and creditable were the turnouts of farm carts and horses and the best farm horses.

"The weather held fine until just before the tea interval, when a heavy deluge sent the spectators hurrying to the farm, where they were well catered for with teas. The programme was afterwards continued without further interruption of rain, and concluded with a clever display of trick riding by the North Somerset Yeomanry. Earlier in the afternoon the hounds paraded the course, accompanied by the Master, Captain A.H. Daniel and his sons. One of the young riders, Miss. J. Eastment, met with an unfortunate accident while exercising. She was thrown from her mount and was picked up in an unconscious condition. Later it was learned that she had received a slight concussion. ... The results and music were broadcast by the Western Accumulator Service."

Following the abdication crisis, national rejoicing took place on 12th May 1937 with the Coronation of King George VI. The Bridgwater Mercury carried reports of the local celebrations.

"The parish was awakened to the fact that the great day had dawned by the sound of the church bells very early in the morning, soon after 5 o'clock. There was a celebration of Holy Communion in the parish church at 8 a.m., when a few of the faithful were present. The bells rung again during the morning, till they finally summoned the parishioners to a second service in the church at 12 o'clock which was attended by a very large congregation. Immediately after the service the whole adult population, with but very few exceptions, repaired to Sibleys Farm, where they found Mr. Fry's Dutch barn enclosed with rick sheets, and gaily decorated with evergreens, flowers and bunting. Two long tables stretched from end to end of the barn, laden with large joints of beef and ham. Full justice was done to the good fare provided, and at the close the toast of 'The King' was proposed by the Rector (the Rev. G.R. Mullens), and duly honoured, as also was the toast of 'The health and happiness of Mr. and Mrs. F.C. Fry' coupled with a very hearty vote of thanks to them for their great kindness in placing their premises at the disposal of the committee.

"A splendid tea was provided for all the children of the village at 4 p.m., and a Coronation mug was presented to each child. A long programme of sports, with events to suit all ages and both sexes, commenced in the Rectory lawn at 5 p.m., and continued till 9 p.m., and the day's proceedings were brought to a close by a dance in the parish hall. The weather was all that could be desired and the committee are to be heartily congratulated on the entire success of the arrangements which they made to provide a day of happiness and pleasure for all."

In June 1937 Miss Nichols announced her intention of resigning as Head Teacher on account of ill-health, and at the end of term she was presented with an oak gate-legged table, silk table centre and a hearth rug. Candidates for the post were interviewed in August and Mrs. Eleanor Jane Davies of Ilton was appointed to replace her.

In July 1937 a disturbance was reported in the Bridgwater Mercury as having taken place in 'Chedzoy Vale.' None of the older residents have every heard this name, so it seems the location was reported incorrectly.

"Frank Morse, labourer, of Chedzoy was summoned by Henry Hill, labourer of Pig Lane, Chedzoy, for an assault on the 8th July. He pleaded not guilty.

"Mr. Harold Scholfield appeared for the complainant, and said on the 8th July at 7.30 p.m., complainant was riding his bicycle in a field in Chedzoy Vale and defendant was in the field. As soon as complainant approached him, defendant started making allegations against complainant's wife in connection with an egg that had been missing. Complainant denied any knowledge of it, and words passed between them. The complainant left defendant, who followed him, took off his coat and waistcoat, and struck him four or five blows in the face. The assault, added Mrs. Scholfield, was entirely unprovoked, and complainant did not even strike back. He asked their Worships, in addition to inflicting punishment, to bind over the defendant to keep the peace.

"Complainant, in his evidence, stated that Morse said that his (Hill's) wife was nothing but a —- thief. He said she was not, and that he would make him prove it. As a result of the blows he had several marks on his face, and went and complained to the police. In reply to defendant, complainant denied that he first attempted to strike Morse with a hoe he was carrying.

"Herbert Philip Baker, of Chedzoy (Herbie Baker of Rose Bower) said he saw Morse strike Hill several times, and Hill had blood on his face. P.C. Greed gave evidence of seeing defendant (sic) just before ten o'clock when he made a complaint. The appearance of the man's face bore out the accusation he made against the defendant, there being blood on his chin and one side of his face.

"Defendant, giving evidence, said about seven o'clock he was walking out of the field with Baker and two wagons. Hill was coming out at the same time, and asked him about an egg which he had made his wife put back, and said it was her egg. They were having words about shutting out his fowls. Hill called him a —- liar, put his hoe up to strike him and he (defendant) hit him to defend himself. The Bench fined defendant 10s., with 7s. 6d. costs of the witness Baker, and also bound defendant over in the sum of £5 to keep the peace for twelve months."

In September 1937 Bridgwater Rural District Council discussed the erection of more houses in their area and accepted tenders from various builders for houses in several villages. R.T. Hanham & Son had their tender of £793 accepted: this was to construct two four-bedroomed houses now known as 3 and 4 Higher Road. Two months later the Council considered an associated matter.

"It was reported by the Housing Committee that a letter was read from the Clerk of the Chedzoy Parish Council suggesting that there was a need for two smaller type houses in the parish to be let at a rental within the means of an agricultural labourer. The Council pointed out that there was not at the present time any subsidy available for any houses other than those erected for the accommodation of persons displaced from overcrowded or unfit houses, and that it was not possible without additional rate charge to let houses at a rent which might be regarded as within the means of an agricultural labourer. It was decided that the Chedzoy Parish Council be informed that due consideration will be given to the needs of the parish in any future building programme."

Gradually the roads of the village were being improved for the benefit of motor traffic. The Bridgwater Mercury reported a meeting of the Rural District Council in January 1938:

"The minutes of the General Purposes Committee stated that the Surveyor reported having inspected the corner near Fishers Farm, and expressed the opinion that a good improvement could be effected by removing existing hedge and setting back on a new line a new open fence. He had interviewed Mr. Ashford, the tenant, who stated that the owner was prepared to give the necessary land. The Surveyor stated that the improvement could be carried out within the terms of delegation. The Committee recommended that the improvement be carried out subject to the observations of the County Surveyor thereon.

"The Surveyor also reported that his attention had been directed to a bend in Chedzoy Lane near Mr. Carey's (sic) farm. The road at this point was narrow and the hedge owned by Mr. Tarr badly overhung the ditch and verge and obstructed the view. The Surveyor suggested piping the ditch and cutting back the hedge. The owner would agree, subject to a post and wire fence being erected to make good his fence. The Surveyor stated that the work could be carried out within the estimate, and the Committee recommended that same be authorised. The recommendations were adopted."

In March 1938 there was an outbreak of foot-and-mouth disease and two local farmers fell foul of the regulations which were imposed as a result.

"Albert Edmund Ashford, farmer, Fishers Farm, Chedzoy pleaded not guilty to allowing two sows and seven slips to stray on the highway in an affected (sic) area of foot-and-mouth disease at Chedzoy. P.C. Greed gave the facts and said when he asked for an explanation defendant said, 'I am sorry; I don't know how the gate came to be open.' Defendant told the court he had been to considerable expense in wiring all the way through during the foot-and-mouth disease, and there was no negligence on his part. The case was dismissed on payment of 4s. costs."

"Albert Stone, farmer, of Rugs (sic) Farm, Chedzoy was similarly summoned in respect of four bullocks. Defendant, who pleaded not guilty, said the cattle could not have got on the road from his field, but must have got into the next field, where the gate must have been open. Fined 5s."

In May 1938 the Chairman of the Parish Council produced a housing questionnaire which had been received from Bridgwater Rural District Council. This was discussed by the Council and they decided to apply for four houses of the three-bedroom type. Presumably this application was overtaken by international events as the country moved closer to war. At their meeting in November 1938 the Parish Council discussed the accounts and

"the Clerk reported having attended an Audit and wished to call the attention of the Council to the extra charge of the Audit Stamp, viz.: £2 instead of £1 as hitherto. All the members agreed this was an exorbitant charge and it was proposed that the Clerk should write to Mr. Blay (Clerk to the B.R.D.C.) protesting against such an excessive charge."

Drains continued to concern both the District and Parish Councils and in January 1939 plans and estimates were produced for a new drain, tank and filter in Manor Road. At a meeting of the Rural District Council

"The Public Health and Sanitary Committee's minutes stated that the Engineer presented his plan and estimate of proposed drainage works in the Manor House-lane area of the parish of Chedzoy, providing for the laying of a new six inch drain from the rear of Mr. Hanham's house (Quantock View) to the existing manhole near Mr. Pearce's (Laburnum House) and provision of a sedimentation tank and filter in the ditch near the plough field where the existing effluent discharges. The estimated cost was £112. It was resolved that the proposal of the Engineer be provisionally accepted and submitted to the Parish Council for observations. The Engineer was instructed to approach the owners for permission to construct the tank and filter in the position indicated on the plan."

The Parish Council duly discussed the scheme and whilst agreeing that the work should be carried out, councillors suggested that a letter should be sent to the B.R.D.C. asking for a contribution towards the cost as the Council owned houses were to be connected to it

In February at the next B.R.D.C meeting,

"It was reported that the Chedzoy Parish Council agreed with the Council's proposals for drainage work in the Manor House-lane area, at an estimated cost of £112. The Council resolved to make application to the County Council for a contribution towards the costs, but could not agree with the suggestion from the Parish Council that the contribution of the cost should be made from the housing fund. The expense would be a special purpose charge upon the parish, subject to any contribution from the County Council or from the District Council."

1939 must have started with an abnormal amount of rainfall as the Bridgwater Mercury reported,

"The efforts of the committee and members of the Cadbury Cricket Club [Chedzoy] met with success at the whist drive and dance held in the parish hall on Tuesday. Many were prevented from attending owing to flooded roads from neighbouring villages."

Unlike previous reports of this annual event, the number of persons attending was not indicated.

In January 1939 the School Managers were informed of a major change in the status of the school.

"A letter from the Chief Education Officer was read stating that the County Education Authority had decided that after the Easter holidays the Chedzoy Council School would become a Junior School for children under 11 only, and that the children above that age should be sent to the West Huntspill Council School and ultimately to a new school which it was proposed to erect at Burnham-on-Sea."

The change was implemented in April and the older children had to travel by bus to West Huntspill, leaving 70 pupils at Chedzoy: 48 Juniors and 22 Infants.

A reduction in the number of pupils also meant a reduction in staff. It was reported by the Bridgwater Mercury that

"On Monday, 3rd April in the presence of the managers, teachers and pupils of Chedzoy Council School, the correspondent and chairman (the Rev. G.R. Mullens) presented Mrs. F. Rays (whose resignation is due to reorganisation) with a silver teapot, fish knives and forks, and a toast rack. The chairman ... said the presents were a token of the esteem in which Mrs. Rays was held by the whole village. She had looked after the children and 'mothered' them well for 16 years. ... Mrs. Rays said he would always remember with pleasure her stay at Chedzoy."

Travel by bus to West Huntspill was not without its problems as in 1944

"The Chairman (of the Managers) raised the matter of unruly behaviour of children whilst journeying in the bus to senior school. He considered the waving out of handkerchiefs, etc. and the shouting inside the bus were a positive danger to horses. After some discussion Mrs. Fry remarked that she had heard of further misbehaviour,"

although what this misbehaviour was is not recorded.

In April 1939, ten years after problems first being mentioned, Parchey Bridge was again brought to the attention of the Rural District Council.

"The General Purposes Committee reported a letter from Stawell parish meeting asking the Council if, in the event of nothing being done at Parchey Bridge shortly, an enquiry could be held by the proper authority to decide the responsibility for maintenance of the bridge. The Committee recommended that the County Council be asked to endeavour to arrange that priority of action be given to work at the bridge under the King's Sedgemoor Drain improvement scheme, and that the County Council be informed that in view of the present unsatisfactory condition of the bridge, and the delay in effecting improvements, the County must consider what further action can be taken by them in the matter. Approved."

The bridge was mentioned in May when

"The General Purposes Committee reported a letter from the County Surveyor stating that the County Council had agreed with the Catchment Board to rebuild this bridge and to maintain it in the future, but he could not state definitely when the work would be commenced, but until the rebuilding took place measures would be taken to safeguard users of the road. The committee resolved that the County Council be asked to indicate when the work of rebuilding the bridge was likely to be commenced."

The bridge was not further mentioned by the District Council, but in July 1939 work started on widening King's Sedgemoor Drain over an eight mile length from Greylake to Dunball to double its capacity. This involved the excavation of 960,000 cubic yards of material, plus associated bridge works. These improvements also provided an additional supply of water to that from the Huntspill River which was being constructed to provide water for the Royal Ordnance Factory at Puriton. The estimated cost of the King's Sedgemoor Drain improvements was £550,000.

The matter of the fire hose had still not been resolved by April 1939. Parish Council minutes record that

"The Chairman then spoke on the matter of the fire appliances belonging to the Parish Council, stating that as the B.R.D.C. were amalgamating with the Bridgwater Town Council to provide a fire engine, etc. for the town and district, this would mean that the Parish Council would be compelled to hand over their fire fighting appliances to this authority. The Council were unanimous in sending a strong protest to the Joint Council, stating that as these appliances belong to the Parish Council they should be allowed to keep it."

All the members of the Council then signed a letter which read,

"We, the members of the Chedzoy Parish Council, are profoundly astonished to hear that under the proposed scheme for a joint 'Fire Brigade' organisation for the Borough of Bridgwater & the Rural District, it is proposed to remove from our parish the fire fighting appliances which we now have. These appliances were originally bought by the Parish Council and maintained by them. On several occasions in the past these have proved to have been of the greatest value in coping with outbreaks of fire, and we feel that they would continue to do so in the future, especially in the early stages of a fire, before the services of the Borough Brigade could be obtained. Therefore, for that reason, we must strongly protest, and shall continue to protest, against the removal of any part of the fire fighting appliances from this parish."

The letter was delivered in person by the Chairman to the Joint Fire Brigade Council and had the desired effect as it was agreed the parish should retain their fire equipment.

In May 1939, as the country edged closer to war with Germany, more important topics were being discussed locally: could Chedzoy have a petrol pump? A very lengthy report on a meeting of the District Council shows how important this matter was.

> "The Housing and Plans Committee reported that the Clerk stated that the proposal of Mr. [Percy] Tucker to erect a petrol pump in a position almost opposite the entrance to Chedzoy church was before the Town Planning Joint Advisory Committee, and referred to the Council for observations. The pump was to be used in connection with the existing blacksmith's business carried on by Mr. Tucker. ... It was suggested that the erection of the proposed petrol pump would cause serious obstruction on the highway, particularly having regard to the proximity of a sharp and dangerous corner opposite the entrance to Chedzoy church and would seriously injure the amenities of Chedzoy village, which so far was entirely unspoilt by such erections. The committee recommended that the application be not approved.
>
> "Captain Bernard proposed that the Housing Committee be asked to refer the matter back to the Town Planning Committee. The Chairman: This has already been referred from the Town Planning Committee to us for observations. We can't refer it back to them. Captain Bernard said the petrol pump would not be a source of danger and there was proper space for cars to use the pump. He knew that corner almost as well as anybody, except members from Chedzoy, and he thought the Town Planning Committee in turning the proposal down could not have given due consideration to it. The pump would be a great use to the village of Chedzoy. The Vice Chairman (Rev. G.R. Mullens) seconded the motion, and said he agreed with what Captain Bernard had said. He did not think it would interfere with the amenities of the villagers, and there was no danger arising from the corner.
>
> "The Chairman said the motion was a very direct negative to the recommendation. The Town Planning Committee were very much against it; Chedzoy was a charming little village. There was not a petrol pump there now, and the Town Planning Committee agreed that to put a pump where proposed would be detrimental and a great obstruction to the highway. The Town Planning Committee turned it down unanimously, and agreed to ask the District Council whether it met with their approval. The Housing and Plans Committee recommended the application be not approved.
>
> "Major Browning said stress had been laid on the fact that the spot was a dangerous one and that the pump would be a serious obstruction to the highway. That had now been contradicted, and perhaps the Town Planning Committee were under a misapprehension. The Vice Chairman said he could not see any danger there at all. The Chairman: If you grant this, where are you going to stop? There are applications galore coming along. Mr. Paul said the Housing Committee were unanimous in their decision and should be supported. He proposed the adoption of the recommendation.
>
> "The Vice Chairman said the only reason he supported the proposal was because many people in the parish said the pump would be a great convenience to them to be able to get petrol for their cars. He did not care whether there was a pump or not because he did not use petrol, but certain people would like to have it there. Major Hamilton: Any other pump in the village? The Vice Chairman: No. Captain Bernard felt the Council should not turn down the application, and asked in what form he could propose a resolution to enable the people of Chedzoy to have the opportunity of having petrol near. Their nearest petrol pump was in Bridgwater.
>
> "The Clerk explained that the application in its present form would not be approved by the Town Planning Committee, but if there was a desire for some facility for obtaining petrol, then the Town Planning Committee might be invited to suggest to Mr. Tucker that he might put in a fresh application showing a better position for the pump to service through traffic. That would ensure Mr. Tucker being able to supply people in the locality. The Vice Chairman: That I think would meet the case quite well. He added that if Mr. Tucker put the pump inside his yard that would meet the case. The recommendation of the committee was then approved, with a suggestion that Mr. Tucker should indicate some more suitable spot."

A petrol pump was never installed at Crown House.

In June 1939 the Parish Council were again able to discuss the supply of electricity to the parish.

> "The Clerk read a letter from the Electric Light Company stating that they required the guaranteed sum of £216 for supplying only a small part of the parish. This the Council felt could not be guaranteed for such a short circuit and the Clerk was instructed to write to them to that effect, also stating the requirements for lighting the whole parish."

On 29th September 1939 the Clerk was able to read their reply which stated

> "that they would require the guaranteed sum of £318 to light the whole of the parish. The members of the Council present agreed that owing to the international situation, it should be allowed to lapse for the time being."

The Second World War

Within days of the outbreak of war, the first wave of evacuees arrived in Somerset. The Bridgwater Mercury reported

> "On each of the three days on which consignments of women and children were received, they were in their billets

> within four hours of the arrival of the trains in Bridgwater. Altogether 1,850 evacuees have been placed in the [Bridgwater] country area. The names of the women organisers for the various villages and the number of evacuees billeted: unaccompanied children, teachers, helpers, children with mothers, mothers and other persons... Chedzoy, Mrs. Fry, 43."

This was Dorothy Fry (1895-1960) who lived at Sibleys Farm.

Eighteen evacuees from Barking, accompanied by two teachers, arrived at the school in September 1939. All Chedzoy pupils were taught in the main schoolroom and the evacuees in the infants' room. In June the following year five more evacuees, this time from Ilford, and another teacher also had to be accommodated in the school. Evacuees from Bristol and Plymouth also arrived. Because of the overcrowding, local children and those from Bristol and Plymouth were taught in the school, whilst the London evacuees were educated in the village hall.

The school admissions book for the years 1902 to 1976 includes details of the evacuated children from 1939 to 1941 plus three more Londoners from the second evacuation in 1944, although it does appear that a page between these entries has been lost as it is known that Bristol and Plymouth children were amongst the evacuees. 36 children are on the first page, mostly with addresses in Dagenham and other areas of east London. Many of these children are noted as having returned to London in 1941 and 1942, but at least two returned in 1940.

The outbreak of war also coincided with an outbreak of swine fever in the area.

> "Wyndham Fry, Ye Olde Cross Cottage, Parchy (sic), Chedzoy, pleaded not guilty to a summons for contravening the Gloucestershire and Somerset Swine Fever Order 1939 by permitting a sow and four suckers to stray on the highway. P.C. Greed said ... he saw a sow and four suckers straying on the highway near Three Oaks Farm in a swine fever affected area. He drove them back to the entrance to the farm and they went into a field. Witness interviewed defendant and told him the circumstances and he replied, 'I don't know how they got out.' The Magistrates' Clerk pointed out to the defendant that he had laid himself open to a penalty of £50. Defendant: I was busy with the harvest and I didn't have time to attend to it. I didn't know they were out until the police reported it to me. The Bench inflicted a fine of £1."

Hostilities were not allowed to spoil the fun for local children. In January 1940 the Mercury was able to report,

> "By the kindness of the Rev. and Mrs. Mullens, the children attending the church Sunday School in this parish were given a most enjoyable treat. They were taken in a Western National double-deck bus to the Town Hall, Bridgwater to see Shirley Temple in the picture 'Just Around the Corner' and afterwards they all sat down to a sumptuous tea at the Steyning Dairy Tea Shop. The party consisted of 60 children, including all the evacuees of the parish, all of whom attend the Sunday School."

In 1940 a Home Guard unit, known as the Parchey Platoon, was formed in the village: by the time it stood down in 1944 the unit consisted of a Company Sergeant Major, three Sergeants, five Corporals, one Lance Corporal, 28 privates and two cadets, all under the command of Second Lieutenant S.W. Fowler. Like their television counterparts in the 'Dad's Army' series, the unit was not without its humorous events. On one occasion a regular army Sergeant was visiting in order to demonstrate the use of 'sticky bombs' against enemy tanks. There being no suitable target, Private Cecil Cary suggested they could use one of the trees in his orchard at Manor Farm: the demonstration was so successful that the tree was chopped off and felled!

On another occasion, members of the unit were cleaning their weapons in the village hall when 'Herbie' Baker, a private, accidentally fired his rifle. Fortunately no one was injured as the bullet went through the ceiling. The following evening Eddie Hanham returned to the building under cover of darkness to replace the damaged tiles before anyone in authority noticed. Apparently the bullet hole in the ceiling could be seen for many years by those who knew where to look.

January 1940 was very cold. A school log book entry reads,

> "Jan. 18th. Very cold: main room 28°F. (-2°C.). Did not start school till 9.45 a.m.: allowed children to run round the yard to keep themselves warm."

Later the same year village children collected blackberries at 40 lbs. a time and rose-hips for their vitamin C content.

The country was at war, but this did not mean that local problems could be overlooked: disputes between neighbours continued. In June 1940 the Bridgwater Mercury reported proceedings at Bridgwater County Police Court.

> "An alleged threat to kill was the complaint in a summons which Mrs. Annie Jennings of Chedzoy brought against Mrs. Bessie Irene Hill (1892-1986), also of Chedzoy. Mrs. Jennings, who was represented by Mr. Arthur King, was taken ill and left court, and the doctor who saw her said she was unable to give evidence. Mrs. Jennings' brother, Percy Guntripp of Chedzoy, said he went to see defendant's husband and found both Mr. and Mrs. Hill in the garden. Mr. Hill did not reply when witness asked whether he could speak to him, but defendant told witness to 'clear off.' Witness replied that he had to defend his sister, and that defendant made a remark about Mrs. Jennings, and then said, 'I shall kill that woman.'
>
> "William Lampert, farm labourer of Chedzoy, who said he was with Guntripp on his visit to the defendant's home, stated that Guntripp went to see Hill 'about a lot of dirt which had been thrown in Mrs. Jennings' house.' Defendant, who denied the alleged threat, said she had had trouble with Mrs. Jennings for a year and had had solicitors' letters sent to complainant. Mrs. Hill complained about 'dirty writing

The Home Guard, Parchey Platoon, May 1944

Back row (left to right):
Privates Bill Collard, Jack Butt, Ern Brooks, H. Overd, Ted Triggol, Fred Tucker, Cecil Cary, Len Gigg, A. Lockyer, Herbie Baker, Dennis Morse, Harry Hill, Fred Stone.

Centre row (left to right):
Privates Ern Clapp, Bill Davies, M. Sullivan, Les Pinchen, Bill Morgan, Ern Hucker, Gordon House, Lionel Butcher, Herbie Ashford, Charlie Stone, A. Baker, Graham Stone, A. Davies, Fred Prowle.

Front row (left to right):
Lance Corporal Tom Chappel, Corporal Jack Stone, Corporal Lampert, Sergeant Pomeroy, Company Sergeant Major Trimbell, 2nd Lieut S. W. Fowler, Sergeant Percy Guntripp, Sergeant Eddie Hanham, Corporal Bert Stokes, Corporal Wallace Hooper, Corporal Sam Gigg.

At front (left to right):
Cadet Roy Newton, Private Bill Collard, Cadet Cuthbert Stokes.

Photograph by S. W Palfrey, courtesy of Ray and Amanda Triggol

on the road' and said when she questioned Mrs. Jennings' son and also Lampert's son, who was with them, they abused her. Defendant alleged that Guntripp and Lampert created a disturbance during the visit to her home. The Chairman announced that defendant would be bound over in £5 to be of good behaviour for a year, and would have to pay 4s. costs."

July 1940 saw the end of an era when Rev. George R. Mullens retired. This momentous event received extensive coverage in the Bridgwater Mercury and much of that report is reproduced here as he was such an influential person in the life of the village.

"The Rev. G.R. Mullens has retired as Rector of Chedzoy after a ministry of almost half a century, and the parishioners have shown their appreciation of that ministry by presenting gifts and also an expression of the great esteem in which he is held by them all.

"Mr. Mullens, who was born at the Rectory at Chedzoy, succeeded to the living which had been held by his uncle, the Rev. G.O. Mullens, for 35 years. When he gave his farewell talk to the congregation in the Parish Church on Sunday, July 21st, Mr. Mullens made reference to various incidents in connection with his long ministry. The day previous he performed his 100th marriage ceremony, and on the Sunday his last baptism. Mr. Mullens has also christened 338 children, and officiated at 280 burials. In the beautiful churchyard of Chedzoy he has always shown much care and attention.

"In addition to his ministerial duties ... Mr. Mullens devoted himself to public affairs. He represented Chedzoy on the old Board of Guardians, Highway Board and Rural District Council for 33 years, and when he retired as a member of the Council a short while ago he had been vice-chairman for a considerable period. Mr. Mullens was also chairman of the Parish Council, and correspondent of the school. He was formerly on the governing body of the County School for Girls in Bridgwater. In all of these and other activities, Mr. Mullens has taken a keen interest.

"Mr. and Mrs. Mullens celebrated their golden wedding on the 11th of last month, when the bells were rung, the [wartime] ban on the ringing of church bells being imposed immediately after. Mr. and Mrs. Mullens had intended going to Bournemouth to reside, but shortly after their golden wedding day the parishioners heard with deep regret of the serious illness of Mrs. Mullens, with whom and the rector deep sympathy has been expressed. The new rector of Chedzoy, who is to be inducted next month, is the Rev. [Cecil] Hunt of Birmingham, a personal friend of the present Bishop of Bath and Wells.

"The presentation of the parishioners' gifts took place at a Parish Meeting held in the Parish Hall. The occasion aroused much interest and the hall was filled. Mr. A.H. Tarr presided, and having explained briefly the object of the meeting and asked those present to assist in the matter of civil defence, said the real reason why they were there was to show their respect for a gentleman who had put in fifty of the best years of his life for them in many ways. He referred to Mr. Mullens. He had known Mr. Mullens for forty years, and had always looked up to him with respect. He was sure they all had respect for him. They knew the public work Mr. Mullens had done for the parish. He had been a good chairman of the Parish Council and had represented Chedzoy on the Rural District Council. No matter what they had asked Mr. Mullens to do, he had always been willing to do it (Applause). He, Mr. Tarr, used to look upon Mr. Mullens with a certain amount of awe - (laughter) - but in later years he had respected him more and more, and he was sure they all thought a wonderful lot of him (Applause).

"Mr. A.E. Ashford, churchwarden, said several of them had thought for some time past about such an occasion as that evening, but they were very sorry indeed that owing to serious illness Mrs. Mullens was unable to be with them. Mr. Mullens had been their Rector for 49 years. Some of them had known him all those years, but all the parishioners had the greatest respect for him (Hear, hear). He found that out when going round as one of the collectors for the gifts they intended presenting that evening. There were several collectors, and each one of them had expressed the pleasure experienced when going round collecting. They all, he added, knew the good counsel and judgement of Mr. Mullens and whenever they wanted advice from anybody they had always gone to the parson. ... Mr. Ashford added that it was interesting to know that 100 per cent of the parishioners had contributed towards the gifts, and no person had given more than 10s. (50p.) which was the highest individual sum required. The gifts, therefore, did not come from a few but from the whole parish, and he was certain that fact would be appreciated by Mr. Mullens. They had, he said, tried to keep the presentation a secret until that evening and he believed they had succeeded in doing so. The presentation would be accompanied by a little book containing the names of the subscribers, and an inscription recording that the armchairs were presented to the Rev. and Mrs. Mullens by the parishioners of Chedzoy on the occasion of their leaving the parish, as a small token of appreciation of good guidance and administration of their regret at their departure after Mr. Mullens had been Rector for 49 years, and of their sincere wishes for health and happiness in their retirement.

"The Rev. G.R. Mullens, in a speech of acknowledgement, first referred to the ladies having been able to keep silence concerning the presentation and said he generally knew what was going on in the parish, but in this instance he had not the faintest idea anything was being done regarding a presentation. He was struck by the large number present when he entered the room, and thought the meeting that had been called must be a very important one. (Laughter.) Having appreciated the words spoken by the chairman and churchwardens, Mr. Mullens said when one had been in Chedzoy as long as he had and looked back over the years that had passed, memories were brought back of many one used to know, but he felt as he said on the previous Sunday, it was something to be thankful for and proud of that he did not believe there was a house in the village which he had been called upon to visit in cases of sickness and other reasons where he had always been given the most ready and kindly welcome. The welcome given to him had added largely to the great pleasure it had given him to be among them. ... He and Mrs. Mullens celebrated their golden wedding last month, but within one week of that time there was the heavy sorrow he had to bear now. Mr. Mullens referred feelingly to the illness of Mrs. Mullens and thanked the parishioners for the kind sympathy that had been shown them. ... He hinted some time ago that when they retired he hoped they would not present him with anything because they were living in troubled times and it was difficult for people to pay their way, but he had not forgotten that in years gone by when his children married, each one of them was given a beautiful present, they all valued highly. He therefore felt the parish had done so much for his children that he could not really hope to have any present himself. ... Mr. Mullens concluded by again expressing the sincere gratitude of Mrs. Mullens and himself for the kind thought that had prompted the gift of the chairs, and assured them that their kindness would never be forgotten. (Applause.)"

Sadly, Mrs. Ethel Mary Mullens did not live to share her husband's retirement, and died just twelve months later at the age of 72 at their daughter's home at Wick House, Stogursey. Her obituary noted that she was the daughter of the late Bishop Wilkinson, Bishop of Central Europe.

After his wife's death Rev. Mullens moved to Bournemouth where he passed away in April 1947 at the age of 82. It was reported that he died sitting at his desk while writing a letter. His body was brought to Chedzoy and he was laid to rest with his wife. His will was subsequently published, which showed that his estate was valued at £27,496 2s. 1d. (gross), £23,399 2s. 1d. (net) - a small fortune in those days.

Although it did not directly concern the village, on 1st October 1940 the Somerset County Constabulary and the Bridgwater Borough Police were amalgamated, so that the village now came under the Bridgwater Division rather than Glastonbury Division as had been the case previously. The Bridgwater Borough Police had been established in 1835 and was the last non-County Borough force in Somerset.

The war caused some village residents problems as they fell foul of emergency regulations. In November 1940 the Bridgwater Mercury reported

"Cecil R. Cary of [Manor Farm] Chedzoy pleaded not guilty at Burnham-on-Sea Police Court to a summons for failing to immobilise a motor car at Burnham-on-Sea. P.C. Edwards stated he was on duty in College Street at 8.30 p.m. and saw a Standard motor car left unattended. The front door adjoining the driver's seat was unlocked, and the ignition key had not been removed. Cary came to the car, and stated in answer to questions that he locked the door before leaving, but in some manner the lock could not have acted. Witness inquired if Cary had removed any part of the ignition and he replied that he had not. Cary told the magistrates that he thought the door was locked, otherwise he would not have left the car. The Clerk pointed out that after dark, in addition to locking the car, further steps had to be taken to immobilise the car. Defendant was fined 5s."

How did Cecil lock the car with the key still in the ignition?

Six months later at Bridgwater Police Court

"Albert Edward Treeby, painter, Crossway House, Chedzoy [Lane] was fined £1 for breach of the [emergency] lighting regulations with bicycles"

and in July 1941

"Wilfred James Barrow, mechanic's apprentice, Chedzoy Lane, was fined £1 for breach of the black-out regulations."

In August 1942, 27 residents from the Bridgwater area, including three from Chedzoy, were in trouble over rationing.

"Wyndham Fry, Three Oaks Farm, was alleged in two summonses to have supplied pork. A third summons alleged he obtained a quantity of pork. Mr. Pardoe said ... Wyndham Fry had killed pigs under permit and [they] supplied each other with a quantity of meat. Wyndham Fry, after saying he was in partnership with his father, Douglas Fry, said his father had part of the meat, and a small joint was given to his brother, Hubert, in exchange for a joint. Fined 10s. 6d. and an advocate's fee of a guinea for obtaining and 10s. 6d. for supplying. A third summons was dismissed on payment of 14s. 6d. costs.

"Edward Geo. French, dairyman, Chedzoy, was fined two sums of 10s. 6d. for obtaining pork valued at 9s. from E. Clifford Heal, Slape Farm, Chedzoy and supplying him with pork, and Heal was fined the same sum for supplying French with pork value 9s. and obtaining pork from him. They also had to pay an advocate's fee of two guineas. Both pleaded guilty and Mr. Scholfield explained that it was a case of two men keeping pigs in the same sty and of an exchange of pork between them. Neither party obtained any advantage from it."

Although the country was at war, Chedzoy residents were going to make the best of things. On 1st January 1941 two reports appeared in the Bridgwater Mercury.

"PARISH PARTY. A very happy evening was spent in the parish hall on Friday evening when over 100 people from the parish gathered for a family party. Games, dancing, etc. were fully enjoyed. ... The Rector said such an evening together helped to create the true family spirit in the parish and that, even in war time, it was possible to meet together and find that friendship with one another." Unwilling visitors to Chedzoy were not forgotten. "EVACUEE PARTY. A delightful Christmas party was arranged on Saturday for all the adults and children who had been evacuated to Chedzoy. This took place in the parish hall where a splendid tea was provided and enjoyable games for the children followed. The Rector told the assembly how much they owed to Mrs. F. Fry of Sibleys Farm for all the splendid work she did for the evacuees. He reminded them that when more favourable times came they would all look back with happy memories of their stay at Chedzoy. The task of billeting officer was a difficult and thankless task, but Mrs. Fry was most indefatigable in her work and had a real care and love for all her evacuees. Hearty cheers were given to her for all she had done, and for the tea she had provided."

Despite its being the darkest days of the war, villagers were determined to 'do their bit' and in March 1941 contributed £62 in savings towards War Weapons Week. In the Bridgwater district the amount of savings reached £207,150 - more than double the target figure of £100,000. The sum of £5,000 was need to purchase a Spitfire. During Warship Week in November 1941 the village raised £300 in savings towards the district total of £300,949. Throughout the war villagers rallied round to support various causes: during 1942 the Penny a Week Fund in aid of the Red Cross raised £15 9s. 5½ d. (why the odd halfpenny?); in February 1943 a dance in aid of the Prisoners of War Fund raised £5 19s. 9d. and in June 1943 another dance raised a further £16 11s. 10d. for the Red Cross Aid to Russia Fund. The British and Allies' Comforts and Victims of War Fund benefited to the sum of £14 from a collection in October 1944.

A fatal accident occurred outside Frys Cottages, Higher Road in 1941 and the inquest was reported in detail in the Bridgwater Mercury.

"The distressed widow of a Bridgwater soldier, herself in hospital with a broken leg as a result of a road accident in which her husband was killed on the night of April 6th, gave evidence from a bath-chair in which she had been brought from her ward at the inquest on Mr. Arthur Leonard Barrow, aged 23, a butcher of 47 St. John Street, Bridgwater.

The accident happened at Chedzoy Lane, near Bridgwater, and Mr. Barrow, who joined the Army recently, and was home on leave at the time, was killed almost instantly following a collision between a motorcycle he was riding with his wife on the pillion and a car driver by Mr. George Alfred Tarr (the farm bailiff) of Frys Farm, Chedzoy.

"The widow, Mrs. Bryla Jane Barrow, who was accompanied by a nurse, sobbed continuously as she told the Coroner what she knew of the accident. 'We were riding my husband's motorcycle to Bridgwater from my home at Stawell and passed Chedzoy Lane about eleven o'clock that night,' she said. 'I had my head down as it was cold, and I happened to look up and saw lights approaching in what seemed to be the middle of the road. Then there was a crash.' Mrs. Barrow said her husband was driving on his correct side at not more than 20 miles an hour, and in the accident she was pinned under the wheel of the motorcycle. Mrs. Barrow said there were regulation lights on the motorcycle and that her husband and herself visited the Toby Inn that evening, but did not stay long.

"P.C. Greed gave evidence. ... Questioned by Mr. Pardoe [he] said there was no question of either driver coming on the other suddenly as there was clear vision for considerably over 100 yards in both directions. He admitted he took the measurements by moonlight, but pointed out that he visited the scene again the next morning.

"The driver of the car, after saying he was returning from Stogursey, driving steadily on his proper side of the road at not more than 20 miles an hour, continued: 'I did not see anything and heard no warning until the motorcycle was practically on me. I didn't see any lights. The cycle, when I saw it, was eight to ten paces away, and was travelling at high speed. I braked and slipped my clutch. I saw the machine coming straight at me, and then the cycle hit the car and ran down the side.' ... He denied the suggestion he was hurrying to get home because of delay caused by a puncture. Inspector Burton asked the driver whether he had anything to drink on the evening of the accident, and Mr. Tarr replied he had only about half a glass of cider with bread and cheese. Dr. J.B. Brownlie, house surgeon at the hospital, said that Mr. Barrow, who was dead when he was admitted, sustained multiple fractures of the upper and lower jaws and facial lacerations. Death was due to shock and haemorrhage. The Coroner returned a verdict of 'Accidental Death'."

The war came close to Chedzoy on the night of 11th/12th April 1941 when bombing occurred across the county and in Bristol. A land mine exploded in a field behind Three Oaks Cottages at Fowlers Plot, fortunately causing only minor damage and no injury. Another night about the same time, a string of bombs was dropped near Slape Cross, roughly along the line of Park Wall Drove but, again, only minor damage was caused. A month later on 7th May there was great excitement in the village. Squadron Leader John Cunningham and his radar operator, Sergeant Jimmy Rawnsley were patrolling the skies above Somerset in a night fighter when they were directed to investigate a 'contact.' Sergeant Rawnsley described how they came up behind a Heinkel He111 bomber which was on its way from Rennes, France to bomb Liverpool docks. It was piloted by Oberfeldwebel (Senior Sergeant) Heinz Laschinski, a veteran of some 120 missions over England, and his crew were Feldwebel Heinz Schier, navigator, Feldwebel Otto Willrich, wireless operator and Feldwebel Fritz Klemm, air gunner. The night fighter fired at the German aircraft, causing an explosion and fire in which Schier and Klemm died instantly and were later buried in Wembdon Road Cemetery, Bridgwater. Laschinski and Willrich were able to bale out before the aircraft crashed out of control into a field adjoining Bull Horn Drove, Andersea. Both were captured and Laschinski was taken to Bridgwater Hospital for treatment to his injuries. Heinz Laschinski spent the remainder of the war as a prisoner in Canada and died just two weeks before a planned visit to Bridgwater in 1972 when he was to meet those who had befriended him during his stay in hospital.

A report of the incident, with suitably vague locations, appeared in the Bridgwater Mercury in May under the headline "BOMBER DOWN IN WEST. Two of Crew Killed. Captured Officer in Incident with Farmer." The report reads

> "An enemy bomber was brought down in a rural district near a town in the west last Wednesday night. Two members of the crew baled out and were taken prisoner. One, an officer, aged 27, was taken to hospital with burns to his face and hands. The bodies of two others were found among parts of the machine. The officer came down in a ploughfield (sic) adjoining a river. On releasing himself from his parachute he went towards a farmhouse nearby, and was met along the road by the farmer, who had been watching the descent of the burning machine. The German could speak some English, and his first words were to ask for the police. The farmer, who noticed the German's hands and face were badly burned, took him to the nearest farm from where a telephone message was sent for the police. While waiting the German made signs that his helmet strap was too tight. The second farmer, a burly man, being unable to undo it, took out a knife with which to cut it. Apparently the German thought he was going to be killed, as he held up his hands and asked for mercy. A police car arrived, and he was taken into custody. It is understood the second man who baled out was captured in a neighbouring village."

It seems the press report confused the two Germans as it was Laschinski who went to a farmhouse near Westonzoyland, whilst Willrich was confronted with Sam Gamblin, the knife carrying farmer at New House Farm, Moorland.

Douglas Fry, who was a farmer at Three Oaks Farm, saw the blazing aircraft come down as he drove his car home along the road from Westonzoyland and thought it was going to crash onto him. He returned home to awaken his brother, Wyndham, and then both went to investigate the crash site and saw the body of one of the crew in the burning wreckage, but were unable to approach too closely because of the intense heat and flames. Like many other local residents, they tried to gather pieces of the aircraft as souvenirs, but were prevented from doing so by the Police and Home Guard.

In January 1942 the Ministry of Works scheduled Chedzoy amongst churchyards from which iron railings would be removed for war salvage purposes; evidence that this was carried out can be seen by the cut off remains on a grave near the south transept of the church. In July the following year the railings were removed from the village hall, school garden and school house, but those around the school playground were left as removal would have caused danger to the children.

The effects of the war are reflected in Parish Council minutes for May 1942 when

> "Mr. Ashford brought forward the matter of meat pies which could be got through to the rural parishes as supplementary rations. It was proposed by him and seconded by Mr. W. Fry that the Clerk should write to Mr. Blay, Clerk to the B.R.D.C., as to the procedure to be taken."

At their next meeting,

> "The Council again discussed the matter of supplementary rations for rural districts, viz. 'Meat Pie' scheme, but decided to take no action in the matter at the present time."

On 15th November 1942, in common with churches throughout the land, the bells in the village were rung as the country rejoiced at the victory of the Eighth Army in Egypt: the start of a string of victories which would eventually bring hostilities to an end. From April 1943 church bells could again be rung for Sunday services. Those still working on the land received a pay rise in August 1943 when it was agreed that the minimum agricultural wage should be increased to £3 5s. a week.

An unusual case was reported in the Bridgwater Mercury in October 1943.

> "A woman traveller, who left her pony and caravan by the roadside at Chedzoy, whilst she went to Bridgwater Fair, gave evidence against two men, John Smith, 17, and Michael Holland, 20, both of no fixed address, who were committed for trial on charges of stealing a pony and caravan and the contents of the van. The owner of the property, Mrs. Elizabeth Loveridge, a widow, said that on the morning of Sunday 29th she left the mare and caravan in Chedzoy Lane, tying the pony by a chain to a thorn, and went to Bridgwater Fair. The mare and van were gone when she returned in the evening. P.C. Cook (Williton) saw [the youths] near Williton and they were taken into custody. P.C. Treeby (Puriton) said the men made statements admitting the theft and saying they had 'never done such a thing before' and it would never happen again." Both were committed to Bridgwater Borough Quarter Sessions where they appeared in November 1943. The court was told that the pony was valued at £40 and the van and contents at £51. In binding over both defendants for two years the Recorder told them, "A hundred years ago you would have been hanged for this offence."

By October 1944 victory was within sight and local people could start to look towards the future.

> "A dance held in the Village Hall under the auspices of the Home Guard (Parchey Platoon) proved to be a huge success. Proceeds from the dance and various competitions will enable the platoon to send about £3 at Christmas to each village man and woman serving in H.M. Forces."

By the following month things were looking even better.

> "Invasion Danger Over. The closing down of the Invasion Committee was celebrated with a social. A whist drive was held and refreshments were served. Mr. A.H. Tarr, chairman of the committee, in the course of his remarks, emphasised how everyone on the committee had worked harmoniously, and that the committee had been an asset in bringing the people of the village together. Mr. H.G. Blay (Clerk to the Rural Council) who, with Mrs. Blay, were the guests of the evening, gave some interesting facts of the work as it affected the Rural District,"

although these were not reported.

> "Turning to the post-war period he said there would be much to be done in the way of reconstruction and he appealed for the interest and help of everyone to further efforts of the Rural Council. Thanks to Mr. Blay were recorded on the proposition of the Rev. C.B. Hunt (rector) and seconded by Mr. R.T. Hanbar (presumably a misprint for Hanham), Chief Warden of the A.R.P. (Air Raid Precautions). Thanks were also extended to Mr. Tarr for his work as chairman and for his other services. He was presented with an 'iron cross', suitably inscribed. The evening concluded with dancing and music."

Sadly this report in the Bridgwater Mercury of proceedings of the Rural District Council in February 1945 does not include an exact location.

> "Mr. A.H. Tarr drew the Council's attention to the Gypsies encamped between Chedzoy and Westonzoyland. He said their horses wandering on the road held up motorists. The Gypsies tethered their horses one side of the road, yet the horses were able to feed on the opposite verge! It was agreed that the Clerk draw the attention of the police to the matter."

V.E. Day merited two days holiday for the schoolchildren and the last of the evacuee children left a week later. Following the end of the war in Europe, the Parish Council were again able to return to more mundane matters. For 26th May 1945 the minutes note that

> "The Council considered the matter of the usefulness of a kiosk for the parish. It was proposed that the Clerk should write to the telephone authorities with a view to erecting a kiosk in the centre of the village. Following which, "The Council also considered the advisability of writing to the Electric Company again as to supplying the Parish with Electric Light. The Clerk was instructed to write to the Company again asking them if they could now consider the matter."

School Dinners were introduced in June 1945. The Managers' minutes in July note that

> "Reference was made to the satisfactory way in which the school dinners have been appreciated. The Correspondent said he had been present on the opening date. There were at the time - 17th July - Eighteen (18) who were availing themselves of the dinners. They commenced on 15th June 1945 and the charge was 2s. 1d. per week for one child or 1s. 8d. for more than one in a family."

Press reports of V.J. Day were generally much less detailed than those for V.E. Day, although celebrations in Chedzoy had not been reported in May.

> "V.J. celebrations at Chedzoy took the form of a free social evening at the village hall, and as the result of a collection taken during the evening the sum of £16 was given to the local Welcome Home Fund."

The following month a fete and dance raised a further £72 for the same fund, but this was shared with the church for the purchase of a motor mower. An extra day's holiday was granted to the school pupils for V.J. Day but was not taken until 29th October as part of the half term holiday.

The Second World War was more merciful than the First: only two sons are recorded on the memorial plaque in the church as having given their lives in the service of their country, see Appendix 3 for details.

The Post War Period

In November 1945 the Parish Councillors were in for a disappointment.

> "Correspondence was read from the Telephone Manager in which he stated that the Council's application for providing a kiosk for the parish at the present time could not be considered, but as soon as conditions permitted, the application should receive attention." Further, "The Clerk reported that no reply had been received from the Electric Light Company re. the supplying of electricity to the parish. Mr. Ashford then stated that he had had an interview with the Manager of the Company who informed him that it would be impossible to carry out the supplying of electricity to the Parish for a very long time."

In response to this the Council instructed the Clerk to write to the B.R.D.C.

> "Asking him to do his utmost in providing the Parish with Electricity and a Telephone Kiosk."

In February 1946 the Bridgwater Rural District Council debated mains drainage and sewerage for the area and categorised parishes according to their needs. Chedzoy was included in 'Group 1' schemes:

> "those urgently necessary. Approximate estimates of consulting engineers based on 1939 prices [for Chedzoy]: £8,700."

Two months later at a further meeting of the B.R.D.C.

> "The Council agreed that application be made to the Minister of Health to borrow the sum required for the Chedzoy [and other] schemes based on the estimates of the consulting engineers. ... It was further reported that a letter had been received from the Clerk of Chedzoy Parish Council stating that his Council felt rather alarmed at the high cost of the proposed drainage scheme, but before making observations would like to see the plan. The Clerk reported having replied that the notification to the Parish Council should be regarded as a preliminary, and a copy of the detailed plan for the parish would be submitted as soon as possible."

In June 1945 a re-organisation of education in the county had envisaged the closure of up to 200 schools, including Chedzoy. In March 1946 a special meeting of the School Managers was called

> "To discuss the notification received from the Chief Education Officer with regard to the proposed closure of Chedzoy Council School. It was agreed that the Correspondent should write to Pawlett, Cossington and Woolavington and ask whether we at Chedzoy could assist in any way to prevent the closing of our schools. The Correspondent was instructed to write to the C.E.O. and inform them that the Managers could not concur with the suggestion of closing the school. They felt that with certain minor structural alterations the building could be made to fulfil the requirements."

Their efforts did not go unrewarded as the school was to continue to serve the village for another fifty years.

At the Parish Council's meeting in March 1946 it was reported that

> "The Clerk to the B.R.D.C. had forwarded their Consulting Engineer's report as to the system of drainage for the Parish. After considering the report, Mr. Ashford proposed that the Clerk should write to the B.R.D.C. asking for the plans of the new system to be forwarded, so that the Council could inspect and consider same."

It would appear that the plans were not forwarded as the minutes for April 1948 record that

> "As the Council had received no details on the scheme from the B.R.D.C., it was proposed that the Clerk write to Mr. Blay asking for details."

In May that year the Parish Clerk was able to report that a letter had been received

"From the Telephone Manager stating that the Kiosk would be available for service very shortly outside Chedzoy Post Office."

However, the councillors considered that this was not the suitable place for it and the Clerk wrote back suggesting that this would be better located opposite the Rectory. By April the following the year the kiosk had still not been established in the village and the Clerk was again instructed

"To write to the Telephone Manager asking him to expedite matters, also to fix the kiosk on waste land opposite the Rectory, this site being more central for the Parish."

There is no further mention of the kiosk in the minutes, but evidently the Parish Council's request fell on deaf ears as the kiosk was placed in Front Street and it was not until the closure of the Post Office that the kiosk was moved to its present central location, close to that originally suggested by the Parish Council.

In June 1946 the Bridgwater Rural District Council again debated drainage:

"The Clerk reported that he awaited the detailed plans and estimates for the Cannington, Chedzoy, East and West Huntspill, Nether Stowey and Puriton schemes. On receipt of these application will be made to the Minister of Health for sanction to borrow the sum required for such schemes."

The estimated cost for Chedzoy was £13,050.

The 8th June 1946 was designated as 'Victory Day' and celebrations were held throughout the country, although many local events were postponed because of torrential rain all day.

"Chedzoy residents celebrated the day in fitting style by entertaining the returned servicemen to a supper. During the evening each of the guests was presented with an engraved wallet and cheque in appreciation of his or her services. Thanks are due to the local Welcome Home Fund Committee for such an enjoyable evening."

There was a desperate shortage of housing in the immediate post-war years and in August 1946 a number of local builders attended a meeting of the Rural District Council and offered to build houses in a number of villages, including Chedzoy. Four months later

"In connection with the small builders' scheme, plans for layout of houses in Pawlett, Cossington and Chedzoy were approved for submission to the Minister of Health."

Two pairs of houses were to be built in Chedzoy.

Atrocious weather with temperatures down to -20ºF. (-29ºC.) was recorded in the early months of 1947. The school log book noted that as soon as the taps were unfrozen, they froze again and attendance, not surprisingly, was very poor in the deep snow and Arctic temperatures.

In May 1947 the Parish Council again considered the fire hose. The minutes note that

"The Council considering the matter of the Fire Appliances belong to the Parish agreed that the members of the Council form the Fire Brigade. In the event of being called to a fire, the Council's minimum charge should be Two Pounds plus 3s. (15p.) per hour per man. It was also agreed that each time the Fire Hose was used Mr. F. Tucker should be paid the sum of Two Pounds for drying same."

Despite post-war austerity, residents of Chedzoy continued to enjoy themselves as this short report shows.

"Challenged by lady supporters of the Cadbury Chedzoy Club, a comic cricket match was played and caused much amusement. The men, wearing women's attire, had to bat and bowl left-handed, while the women wore men's clothes. The women, 19 in all, batted first, enjoyed 'lives' and survived numerous appeals. They put together 75, Mrs. H. Hill going in first wicket down, making 21. The men found batting a big handicap. Hooper made 22 before being run out, but the team (batting 11) could only equal the ladies score. The feature was the wicket-keeping of the ladies' 'stumper' who conceded only two byes. Refreshments were provided, and a collection realised £3 6s., which will provide prizes for the forthcoming children's sports."

But the Cadbury Club did not only think of themselves and later that summer collected £27 which was forwarded to Whitehaven following a disaster at the William Mine.

Early in 1947 the Rural District Council's plans had suffered a setback when a shortage of materials forced the cancellation of the planned houses in the village, but in July that year it was agreed that ten Airey houses should be erected instead. These were prefabricated constructions with concrete wall panels placed over each other in the manner of a clinker-built boat. At their meeting in August

"The Council agreed to the Council Houses Committee recommendation that the tender of Messrs. Smith Brothers (Burnham-on-Sea) in the sum of £2,698 10s. 9d. per pair for the erection of 38 Airey houses for Chedzoy, Chilton Polden, West Huntspill, Pawlett and Puriton be passed to the Ministry for approval. ... Regarding layouts for construction works for roads and sewers, it was agreed that the tenders of Messrs. W.J. Channing & Sons of Burnham-on-Sea, in the sum of £2,316 8s. 11d. in respect of Chedzoy be passed to the Ministry for approval."

However, these plans also suffered a set-back as in September they were told the Ministry of Health has rejected the tenders for the road and sewer works as being too high.

> "The Ministry are not in favour of the whole of the Chedzoy site being Airey houses and the architects were especially requested to consider some modification or special treatment for the exterior of the Airey houses proposed for the site to fit in with the traditional house which could fill up the site at a later date."

Despite this request, the houses were built in their original form on part of a field between Higher Road and Manor Road which the Council purchased for the purpose. The houses are now known as 1 to 6 Manor Road and 5 to 8 Higher Road. In 1986 their exterior walls were replaced with bricks and the houses properly insulated by the provision of cavity walls.

In seems that some things never change and this short report from March 1948 could equally apply to 1999.

> "Chedzoy Parish Council has complained to the Bridgwater Rural District Council of the bad condition of the roads in the parish. The District Highways Surveyor has reported that the roads require re-surfacing, but owing to expenditure cuts this is not possible at the present time. He is doing his best by patching thoroughfares."

In April 1948 at a Parish Council meeting

> "Mr. Tucker brought forward the matter of Playing Fields, stating that such a thing was now required for the Parish. The Chairman spoke of the necessity of all lands being cropped during the present world food crisis, stating that he did not think it was an opportune time to consider the need for Playing Fields. On a vote being taken the Council decided not to entertain the matter for the time being."

Entertainment of a different type was introduced to Chedzoy in July 1948 without any advance publicity in the Bridgwater Mercury, but it was not without its difficulties:

> "The opening meeting of the greyhound venture at West End Farm, Chedzoy was attended by over 400 people, but, unfortunately, serious trouble with the hare mechanism prevented racing being held, and the promoters kindly refunded entrance money to the supporters."

The races were held in the field on the south side of Chedzoy Lane opposite the farmhouse.

Things were much better the following week:

> "There were over 400 people present at Chedzoy Lane when some enjoyable racing was witnessed. Mechanical defaults (sic) which had marred the previous week's gathering, had been rectified, and the meeting was brought to a successful conclusion with several local dogs winning, as well as some from outlying districts." The races were run over distances of 300 and 475 yards and it was reported that "efforts are also being made to provide transport for meeting supporters to the track from Bridgwater." The venture looked like being a huge success as 450 people attended the next week. "A special bus service from Cornhill [Bridgwater] to the track, picking up at the Cross Rifles and the B.C.L. factory (now UCB Cellophane Ltd.) begins at 6.15 and returns at the close of the meeting."

The greyhound racing may have been popular with the public, but just as suddenly as the racing commenced, reports of the meetings ceased to be published in the Mercury. The reason for this became clear in September when their main headline read

> "ENGINEER ACQUITTED OF THEFT CHARGE. Sequel to dog race track meeting at Chedzoy." It was reported that "Reference to greyhound race meetings near Bridgwater were made at Taunton County Magistrates' Court during a hearing against Cyril George Hack (36), engineer, Obridge Road, Taunton. Hack was accused of stealing track equipment valued at £13, but the magistrates found that there was no case to answer, and the charge was dismissed. The prosecution alleged that Hack stole 25 6 ft. posts, 100 iron stakes, 600 yards of cod wire, a roll of wire and wheel equipment, it was alleged, which were used by him at Chedzoy, Bridgwater, where a series of greyhound racing meetings were held earlier in the season. Hack pleaded 'Not Guilty.' The property alleged to have been stolen was stated to belong to Mr. David Pipe. ... Mr. Pipe stored the equipment in a field at Lyngford. ... Part of the field in which the equipment was stored was also occupied by Hack, who kept some greyhound kennels. ... In an alleged statement Hack said, 'I do not deny having taken the stuff, but I certainly did not steal it. I entirely refute the allegations that I stole the property'." The defence "submitted that the evidence of the prosecution was most unsatisfactory, and that there was no case to answer. The magistrates upheld this submission, but declined to award costs to the accused."

During the early part of 1949 the Bridgwater Mercury published a series of articles entitled "Our Village" by Ken Powell. No. 12 in the series commenced

> "An old-world village with its ancient candle-lit church surrounded by tidy cottages and trim farm houses. A treasured stop of lovers of rustic life in its true sense is CHEDZOY, a village of antiquity and of strong association with Sedgemoor days." Although parts of the article, particularly those in relation to the history of the village, have already featured there, some of the more contemporary part of the article are worthy of repetition. The author's account commences, "It was, perhaps, symbolic of Chedzoy that my entry into the village should have been halted by a herd of cows hesitantly making their way along that country lane as if time counted for nought. As I paused on the outskirts of the village waiting for the farm dog to see his charges safely inside the gate, I had the greatest difficulty in convincing myself that the hustle and bustle of Bridgwater's busy streets were less than three miles distant. The rich Somerset dialect of the villagers, the very atmosphere of Chedzoy, suggests a forgotten community miles from civilisation. The undulating countryside stretching away to the distant horizon, the unbroken views from the rear of the church, seem to sever

all connections with anything so mundane as a town."

After an interview with Rev. Hunt, in which much of the ancient history was mentioned, there followed a description of the church and the candle auction and then items on various residents.

"The tidy churchyard and the clean interior of the village church reflect great credit on the sexton and his wife, Mr. and Mrs. H. Newton (of Cadbury House), who devote many hours towards this end. Chedzoy may well be proud of its church and, from what I gathered during my tour, the villagers are as one many in their devotion to this lovely old edifice. For instance, Mr. John Baker (of Tower View) grows flowers specially for the church at his own expense, and many others contribute in no mean way towards its upkeep.

"Two young men from Chedzoy gave their lives during the last war and a tablet to their memory was unveiled some months ago by Admiral of the Fleet, Sir James Somerville ... A parish hall was built in 1914 by the Rev. G.R. Mullens, who left its upkeep in the hands of a band of trustees which must always include the existing rector. The hall is often the scene of some form of activity organised by the Social Committee of which Mr. Newton is the chairman.

"While in many villages the blacksmith has ceased to exist, Chedzoy boasts of two 'smithies.' Or rather, three, as Mr. Fred Tucker is engaged in one business and his two brothers, Messrs. J. and P. Tucker in the other. Then there is the village school where the juniors are trained by Mrs. Davies, the headmistress, with the able assistance of Miss Hopkins, who has been in the village many years.

"As for personalities in Chedzoy - they are legion. I think I am right in saying that the honour of being the oldest inhabitant goes to 88-year old Mr. F.C. Gully, who lives quite alone in a cottage adjoining the rectory. Mr. Gully was busily engaged in his workshop when the Rector introduced us, but later he appeared at his front door to pose for photographer Douglas Allen. But on one condition only - that he was 'taken' holding his cider cup! A great character is Mr. Gully.

"A drive out to Fowlers Plot [Farm] to see that well known farmer, Mr. Ben Winter - Uncle Ben to all - was worth while. Mr. Winter, well over 80, retired a few years ago on doctor's advice, and the farm has been taken over by his nephew, Mr. [Dover] May. Part of the centuries old farmhouse, including a room with a real old-fashioned chimney nook, are being prepared for Mr. May's son and his fiancée, who are to be married at Easter. Good luck to both of them in their farmhouse home!

"For some time I have known that my milk came from Chedzoy, but it was not until last week that I tracked down the source of supply, which is none other than the farm (West End Farm) of that great authority on agriculture, Mr. A.E. Ashford. In his model dairy I was shown milk passing through the most modern pasteurisation plant, and in another department I saw it being bottled and put ready for dispatch. Cleanliness is the keynote at this farm, where an accredited herd, including Guernsey cows, is always open for inspection. And from what Mr. Ashford told me, Ministry officials pay him quite a few visits.

"As for Mr. Ashford's activities - well, here are just a few: Churchwarden for 28 years; a member of the Parish Council; chairman of the N.F.U. Regional Producer Retailers; member of the N.F.U. County Executive; member of the Juvenile Employment Committee; member of the County Milk Subcommittee and chairman of the Bridgwater Dairymen's Association. There is no doubt that Mr. Ashford's advice on any matter relating to dairy farming is sought after by many organisations. Even the Ministry of Agriculture are mindful of his great experience on such matters, in spite of their many inspection visits!

"Mr. Ashford is one of those who has waged a hard and prolonged fight for the supply of electricity to be brought to Chedzoy and at present he admits temporary defeat, Like many others, he is at a loss to know why the village should have been deprived of this amenity, especially as the district is a matter of but a mile from the nearest source of supply. At his farm he has installed his own generating plant which supplies not only his own up-to-date machinery, but also lights the farmhouse, and when the main supply is eventually brought to the district he will just switch from one source to the other as all his equipment is 'A.C.'

"Milk production figures shown to me by Mr. Ashford prove that the country is now far more milk-minded today than before the war. 'I can remember the time when many families took half-a-pint for the cat while the family lived on tinned milk not fit for human consumption,' he told me. 'Now it is different and people are realising the food-value contained in milk and are taking advantage of free milk in certain cases. The medical profession has educated them and made them take advantage of these offers.'

"Church records held by Mr. Ashford date back to 1821 and for some years items of income included a church rate which varied between one penny and threepence. Recently a friend took me to task for not mentioning companology in my village articles and perhaps it would interest him, and many others, if I record an item in the church accounts for 1872 - 'To Mr. Waddon for two new bell ropes, 15s. 6½ d. (77p.)' Mr. C.C. Waddon, of Messrs. John Waddon & Son, rope manufacturers, informs me that the present day price of those two ropes for Chedzoy church would be in the region of £6!" In 1999 the price is between £60 and £150 per rope. "Another item of interest in those old records was 'funeral, 1s. 6d.' (7.5p.) which included the cost of grave digging. That was in 1832.

"Mr. Ashford took over the farm from his father and for several years father and son were church wardens together. Mr. Ashford's co-warden today is Mr. R.T. Hanham, a local builder (of Quantock View), who succeeded Mr. A.H. Tarr (of Westfield Farm), R.D.C. representative for Chedzoy and another local farmer.

"Now for a brief visit to the only inn in the village, the Manor House, kept for the past 23 years by a Chedzoy man, Mr. Oliver Bennett, a bell-ringer of long standing. No man could be better suited for this job that Mr. Bennett who, having spent 77 years in the parish, knows the village 'inside out.' Ten 'Airey' houses now occupy the site opposite the inn and eight more are planned, which is all good for trade, of course.

"A name familiar to all at Chedzoy is Henry Chappell, now in his 86th year, who was a bell-ringer for over 50 years. His son, Mr. T. Chappell, is now foreman ringer. Apart from a few years in Canada, Mr. Chappell has spent his life in the village. I sat with Mr. and Mrs. Chappell in their cottage parlour (at 1 Springfield Cottages) and heard of the changes they had seen during their lifetime in the village. They recalled the time when there were two inns at Chedzoy, and Mr. Chappell went back as far as 1867 when the village post office (now the Old Post Office) was built. He also spoke of the time when he carried 85 sacks in a day, and of the days when he drove his horse and cart to Burnham Brewery with loads of barley. Opposite his cottage is a field comprising no less than 365 acres where he worked for 3d. a day at the age of nine." Henry Chappell died in August the following year and his obituary noted that he "began work at the age of nine years, earning 3d. a day for scaring birds from the cornfields. On one occasion he and two other men scythed an eighty acre field of corn in three days, commencing at four o'clock in the morning."

"A few yards past Mr. Chappell's cottage lives 84-year old Mrs. Giles (at Parchey View) who has never left Chedzoy, and enjoys her own quiet surroundings. Mrs. Stokes, another charming old lady at the other end of the village (3 Springfield Cottages) is surprisingly active for her years. There are many others who contribute their share towards Chedzoy's happy life - Mrs. Stone at the (Old) Post Office, Mrs. Conduit at the thatched village store (Myrtle Cottage) and those honest-to-goodness country folk, Mr. and Mrs. Robert Baker (of Rose Bower), whose son, Sam, is a familiar figure in Bridgwater's streets with his market grown produce. All these good folk of Chedzoy have pride in their village, their church and their land. And surely it is a heritage of which they may be well proud!"

Drainage was again on the mind of the B.R.D.C. in March 1949.

"In regard to Chedzoy, a modified scheme has been agreed between consulting engineers of the County Council and the Rural District Council. The Somerset Council are prepared to approve (sic). It will now be possible for the R.D.C. to submit the Chedzoy scheme to the Ministry with a view to holding a local inquiry." However, a month later, "Despite modification in the new sewer scheme in the main

The Manor House Inn around 1951.
The picture was taken shortly after the council houses in Manor Drive were built.
Photograph courtesy of Helen Hunt.

area, Chedzoy, the cost involved is still in excess of the Ministry of Health's figure. The Health Committee feel that there can be no further reductions, owing to the difficulties of ground surface and of the number of farms affected. It has been resolved to submit the scheme, as it stands, to the Ministry for approval, and to apply for sanction to borrow £13,610. In accordance with the Public Health Act 1936, notice of the scheme was sent to Chedzoy Parish Council."

In June 1949 the Bridgwater Mercury reported

"Bridgwater Rural District Council is to apply to the Minister of Health for consent to borrow £13,520 for sewage disposal works for Chedzoy. The next step will be the calling of a public inquiry. ... The County Council has approved the scheme. The Chedzoy scheme is second on the priority list for sewage disposal, Cannington being the first, where a start has already been made." Representatives of the B.R.D.C. were in attendance at a meeting of the Parish Council later that month. They produced plans of the new drainage scheme proposed for the parish and explained the details. Afterwards the Council agreed to accept the scheme but were reminded that there would be an Inquiry by the Ministry of Health before the new scheme could be put into operation. However, only one month later, the B.R.D.C. were told that the Ministry had informed the Clerk that

"Tenders for Chedzoy were considered too high and would have to be revised."

But even if the sewerage scheme was in difficulty, at least housing was progressing as in August 1949 at a meeting of the B.R.D.C. it was reported that

"Eight houses at Chedzoy, the tenders of which were considered by the Ministry to be too high, have been reduced after negotiation with the contractors. Application has now been made by the Bridgwater Rural District Council Housing Committee for approval."

The 'Pet' Dispute

The village expanded considerably in the post-war period. As has already been mentioned, in 1948 Bridgwater Rural District Council constructed five pairs of prefabricated 'Airey' houses in Higher Road and Manor Road. In 1950 eight Council houses, this time of brick, were erected and a new road was constructed to service them - Manor Drive. Their construction was not specifically mentioned in Bridgwater Mercury reports.

In June 1950 a Mercury report was headlined

"CHEDZOY HAS MORE COWS THAN PEOPLE. Peculiar feature is mentioned at Inquiry. There are more cows than people at Chedzoy, according to evidence given at an inquiry by the Ministry of Health at the Village Hall on Thursday into Bridgwater Rural District Council's application to borrow £13,520 for a sewerage and sewage disposal scheme for the parish. That there was serious risk from present sewage conditions was pointed out by the Clerk to the Council (Mr. H.G. Blay) who added that development of the parish should be restricted unless conditions were improved.

"The Population was about 300: there were 11 farmhouses, 19 farm cottages, 60 other dwellings, one licensed house, a village hall and a school. The war had curtailed the previous scheme, but the problems had been taken up again and a comprehensive survey by the Council's consulting engineers was made in 1945. Mr. Blay explained that land for the sewage disposal works was part of Manor Farm, owned by Oxford University - the principal landowner in the parish - who had repeatedly called the Council's attention to sewage disposal conditions in Chedzoy.

"'It was apparent to everyone concerned that the cost based on accepted standards is high,' said Mr. Blay, 'but there are special features in regard to this scheme which justify the high cost.' Pointing out the peculiar feature of the cow population exceeding the human population, Mr. H.S. Whittaker of the consulting engineering firm of Messrs. Lemon and Blizzard, said it had influenced the design of the works to a great extent. It was a feature which had not been experienced elsewhere and the trouble at sewer outfalls arose more from farm drainage than from domestic. Mr. Whittaker added, 'I consider that if the sewerage scheme is carried out and maintained in good order, there will be a very great improvement in the condition of several rhines around Chedzoy from which cattle can drink.'

"Engineer to the Rural District Council, Mr. L.S.O. Clatworthy, explained that a septic tank received the drainage of the larger part of the village, but owing to a lack of fall the effluent was often far from satisfactory. Recommending the Council's scheme be adopted as soon as possible, the Medical Officer of Health, Dr. R.H. Watson, described the existing sewage disposal as 'thoroughly unsatisfactory.' The Chief Sanitary Inspector, Mr. F.H. Maile, referred to complaints received from farmers, who had expressed concern at the risk of cattle drinking polluted water. Complaints had also been received from the general public in regard to the Ward Lane outfall which ran in an open ditch alongside the highway for 250 yards. Existing conditions were serious nuisances and definitely prejudicial to health. At the nine farms in the parish which would be connected to the proposed sewer, there were about 300 milking cows. Mr. A.H. Tarr, Chedzoy's Rural District Councillor, and Mr. F.W. Moverley, chairman of the Public Health Committee, also spoke of the need for the proposed scheme."

In December 1950 it was reported that

"At a meeting in the village hall, Chedzoy, approximately 60 people heard a talk by the manager of the Bridgwater District of the South Western Electricity Board in which he explained the details of the new method of charging for electricity in rural districts and the reasons for making these charges. It was stated that supplies could be available in Chedzoy in the very near future, if sufficient people were prepared to join the scheme, but if only a poor response resulted it would not be possible to proceed with the work."

Only two weeks later the Mercury noted that

"There is to be an extension at Chedzoy included in the current year of the Electricity Board."

Things were progressing: in January 1951

"The Council Houses Committee, reporting on details of proposed electricity services to villages, stated they had been informed by the South Western Electricity Board that an annual revenue required was 20 per cent of the capital cost, and in the case of Chedzoy a return of £998 was needed. That sum would be apportioned among consumers on a line rental scheme, and so far as council house tenants were concerned they would be asked to pay approximately 15s. a quarter, reducible if justified by consumption."

At the next B.R.D.C. meeting

"Mr. A.H. Tarr (Chedzoy) said he thought the [Electricity] Board were out for what they could get."

The minutes of the Parochial Church Council in 1950 show that they discussed the implications of having electricity in the church and it was agreed that

"when the Electric Light is available that we should proceed with the installation of Electric Light in the church."

The meeting was also reported in the Bridgwater Mercury:

"Now that electric light is being brought to the village of Chedzoy, it has been unanimously agreed upon by the church council that immediate steps shall be taken to illuminate the parish church by the same means. To accomplish this, the sum of at least £200 will be required and a special appeal is to be made in the parish to raise this amount."

At the annual Parish Meeting in April 1951

"Mr. A.E. Ashford reported favourable progress regarding the installation of electricity in the village and, at his suggestion, it was agreed that the Clerk should make inquiries about the cost of three street lights."

Electricity finally reached the village at 7.30 p.m. on Friday, 22nd June 1951 when it was switched on by Albert Ashford at a ceremony "at a pole near the Rectory." A platform was erected at the junction of Front Street and Higher Road and the ceremony was witnessed by a crowd of villagers, including 90 year old Frank Gully, the oldest resident.

Mr. Ashford commented that for some years it had been a

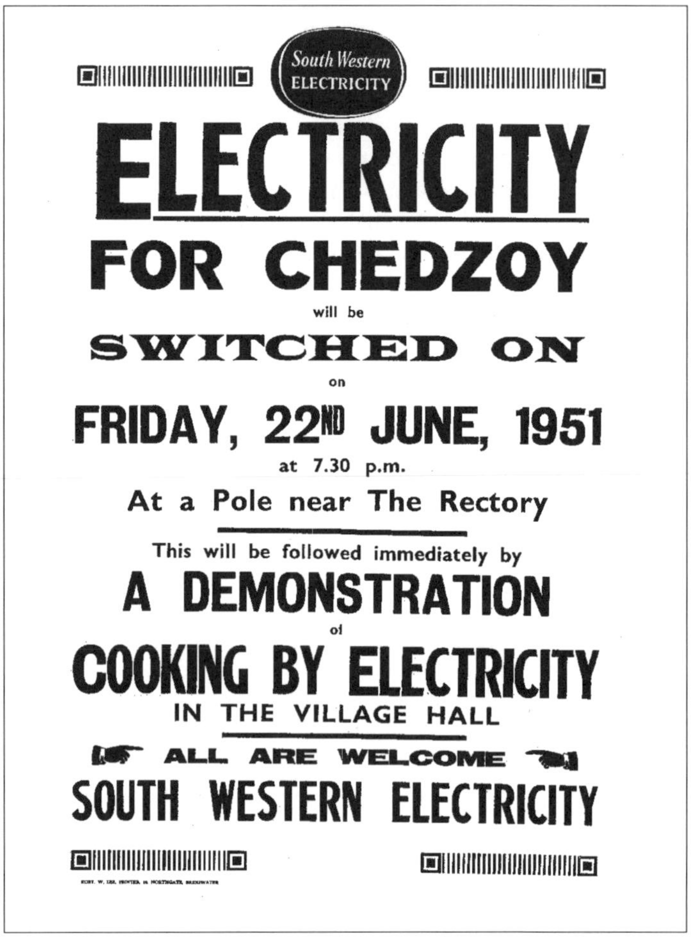

Poster courtesy of Allan and Carol Stokes.

sore point that high tension wires passed through the parish without benefiting Chedzoy.

"With a little hard work which can be attributed to some of those in the parish, we have at last managed to get a supply, and this is the great moment we have been waiting for," he added, as he threw the switch.

The ceremony was followed by a demonstration in the village hall of cooking by electricity. Now residents would be able to buy electric cookers instead of having to use solid fuel or unreliable and smelly paraffin cookers.

Fund raising took place in the village and almost enough money for the installation of electricity in the church was collected. The work was carried out by Mr. F.W. Welsh of Bridgwater at a total cost of £286 18s. 7d. Church funds then stood at £271 15s., but the Rector, Rev. Cecil Hunt, said that he would make up the difference. On 16th September 1951 a thanksgiving service was held in the church when it was lit by electricity for the first time: 250 candles would in future only be used on special occasions, usually at Christmas. Full electrification of the village seems to have taken some time as it was not until March 1954 that it was finally installed in the school. In that same month the Housing Manager of the B.R.D.C. said that he "wished to point out that many of the Council's pre-war houses were not fully wired for electricity. ... In many houses there was a light only in one bedroom, no landing light, no bathroom light, and only one plug point."

The police seem to have been far more vigilant in those days. In May 1951 the Mercury reported

"For riding a bicycle at Chedzoy without a rear light, Denis Harold Carter, Higher Road, Chedzoy was fined 15s. A similar fine was imposed on Anthony James Newton, Avalon House, Chedzoy for riding without front or rear lights."

A month later,

"A fine of £1 was imposed at Bridgwater Magistrates' Court on Rex Eric Newton (19), blacksmith, Avalon House, Chedzoy for riding a bicycle without lights at Sydenham Road, Bridgwater,"

and in October,

"A fine of 15s. was imposed by Bridgwater County Magistrates on Patrick Mathews (32), milk roundsman, Yew Tree Cottage, Higher Road, Chedzoy for riding a cycle without lights at Chedzoy."

These days cyclists seem to ride without lights with impunity, even in the centre of Bridgwater. In January 1952

"Cuthbert John Stokes (23), Ward Lane, Chedzoy, was fined 15s. by the Borough Magistrates for failing to observe a Halt sign at Wellington Road [Bridgwater] with a bicycle".

Some modern cyclists even ignore red traffic lights, seemingly without being prosecuted.

Things were dragging on slowly as far as drainage for the village was concerned. At a meeting of the Rural District Council in November 1951

"It was reported that a suggestion from the Somerset River Board to discharge sewage from Chedzoy district direct to the river had been forwarded to the Ministry for observations. The Chairman of the Public Health Committee (Mr. Moverley) stated that an alternative scheme for a sewage works in the moors would not be satisfactory. Mr. Seymour confirmed that the Committee was in entire agreement with the scheme suggested by the Board's chief engineer."

It was not only the Rural District Council who expressed concern for the area. In November 1951

"Because of a narrow bridge at Dunball, farms at Stawell, Sutton Mallet and Chedzoy districts are being seriously affected by flood water, it was stated at the annual meeting of the Bridgwater Branch of the National Farmers' Union." The comment was made that the bridge was only seven yards wide. "Unless we can get that bridge widened the river will do no good at all. If we had a bridge at Dunball 21 yards wide, the same as the river, the water would go away a lot quicker."

In June 1952 it was announced that weekly rents for Rural District Council houses were to be increased. Of particular interest in Chedzoy was an increase from 14s. 3d. (71p.) to 17s. 9d. (88p.) per week for 'Airey' houses.

An innovation occurred on 15th August 1952 when the television transmitter at Wenvoe, Cardiff began broadcasting BBC programmes in black and white to the Somerset area. However, with sets costing anything from £50 to £350 it was not for most people. Table top sets were priced at £72 10s. for a 12-inch screen and £93 for a 15-inch. Just how unaffordable these sets were for most people is indicated by the fact that a month after just 250 television licences had been taken out in the Bridgwater area. It was not until 14th January 1958 that commercial television reached the area when the St. Hilary aerial, not far from Wenvoe, began transmitting programmes for Television Wales and West Ltd., better known as TWW.

Clearly the Parochial Church Council were fired with enthusiasm for electricity as in August 1952 they decided that they should purchase "an electric blower" for the organ which had been pumped by hand since it was installed about 1902: in the years before the electric bellows were fitted, Colin Hill had been paid the sum of £1 2s. (£1.10) per year to pump the organ when required. In September a three day skittles content was held at the village hall and this raised £84 9s. 1d. towards the cost. But although the villagers were raising money for their own community, other communities were not forgotten and a collection the same month raised £27 7s. 4d. for the North Devon and West Somerset Relief Fund. Most of this went to Lynmouth following the flood disaster.

With the increase in vehicle ownership, Parish Councillors were concerned about the possibility of an accident at the junction of Front Street and Higher Road, so an approach was made to the Highway Surveyor to see if a 'Halt Major Road Ahead' sign could be erected. In due course the Rural District Council considered the matter and it was reported in March 1953 that

"The Ministry's approval is to be sought to a Halt sign at Bridgwater-Chedzoy road at its junction with Sutton Mallet road near Chedzoy School."

As part of the Coronation celebrations in June 1953 the children were granted a three day holiday and it was decided that a bus shelter, originally proposed in 1948, should be erected in the centre of the village. A total of £170 10s. 9d. was raised to be spent on Coronation celebrations in the village. The Bridgwater Mercury reported events throughout the area, including Chedzoy.

"A barn was converted into a banqueting hall at Chedzoy, where 250 sat down to a substantial luncheon in a gaily decorated building lent by Mr. F.C. Fry. Earlier in the day, at

5.30 a.m., the church bells heralded the great occasion, and special services were held by the rector (Rev. C.B. Hunt), including a well attended celebration of Holy Communion. One of the chief attractions in the afternoon was a fancy dress competition for the young people, followed by tea for the women and children, when the latter were presented with souvenir mugs. Sports were held, and, later, dancing at the Village Hall. Mr. A.H. Tarr was chairman of the general committee, Mr. B. Stone of the men's committee and Mrs. Coward of the ladies' section. The village's oldest inhabitant, 92 year old Mr. Frank Gully, participated in the celebrations, and was presented with a box of cigarettes."

The annual Parish Meeting minutes mention that

"Every lad away on service with H.M. forces to be sent a postal order for five shillings."

As an aside to the Coronation, any couple who became engaged in 1953 could visit H. Samuel's and spend between ten guineas (£10.50) and £21 on an engagement ring. Those who tied the knot found their wedding rings priced from 37s. 6d. (£1.87) to £4 4s.

Further changes were about to affect the schoolchildren in the village. At the School Managers' meeting in June 1953

"A letter was read from the Divisional Education Officer stating that it was proposed at the beginning of the Autumn term that the children at Chedzoy School who will have reached Secondary School age, and who would normally be transferred to the Huntspill West County Primary School (sic), are to be transferred instead to the Westonzoyland County Secondary School."

This arrangement lasted until the opening of Sydenham Secondary Modern School (now East Bridgwater Community School) in 1961. At the end of 1953 Mrs. Davies announced her resignation as headmistress. Interviews took place and Mrs. G. Brazier, head teacher of Norton Canon, Herefordshire was appointed to replace her.

In September 1953 a sale and competitions were organised in the village and these raised £70 8s. 11d. towards the fund for a new coal-fired boiler for the church. This was installed the following year at a cost of £112. In November 1953 the Bridgwater Mercury reported that

"An event of considerable importance in connection with the life of Chedzoy church took place when the Bishop of Bath and Wells (Dr. H.W. Bradfield) administered the sacrament of confirmation. It was 51 years ago, on November 19th 1902, when the last confirmation was held in Chedzoy church."

Eleven of those confirmed came from the village.

Coronation celebrations, 1953. Villagers gather in a barn at Sibleys Farm. Photograph courtesy of Audrey Fry.

It seems that the police had been busy once again. In January 1954 the Bridgwater Mercury reported,

> "Fines of 15s. were imposed on each of three farm workers from Chedzoy who were summoned at Bridgwater County Magistrates' Court for riding cycles without lights. They were Frederick George Harries of Leacroft, Ware Lane (sic); Gerald Arthur Fry, Palfrey House and Salvatore Zuncheddu, Noraud (3 Frys Cottages), Higher Road."

Mrs. Audrey Fry owns a press cutting taken from an unknown newspaper which would appear to relate to this case. Under the headline "Curious Case of Mr. Zuncheddu's Lights" the report, with some rather quaint grammar, reads as follows:

> "When Salvatore Zuncheddu, farm worker, of Higher Road, Chedzoy was summoned at Bridgwater yesterday, for cycling without lights, he sent this letter to the Court. 'Lights were in perfect order so far, went in the shop where I found the policeman doing his shopping. He came out five minutes before I did so the lights were alright sure of. I took the cycle and started to pedal to reach where I was going. About 20 yards away from the lights of the shop I began to notice that my cycle head light was not giving any light. About 10 yards further I heard a call say (Where is your light?). Well, it's a mystery.
>
> "'If a farmer happens to be in Court will you please ask him if he would let the fowls house doors open when they hear the foxes are near. Therefore I should say if my cycle and dynamo was out of order I should never risk to ride it.' Mr. Zuncheddu was fined 15s."

In March 1954 the village was mentioned during a meeting of the Rural District Council when it was reported that

> "Roads on housing sites [in several villages, including Chedzoy] are to be improved for acceptance by the Highway Authority. ... The Ministry's attention is to again be drawn to the inadequate sewerage arrangements at Chedzoy."

In October it was reported that it was hoped that mains electricity would be provided to the Chedzoy Lane area during the financial year ending 31st March 1955.

In March 1954 the Parish Council considered the plans for the bus shelter. Arthur Tarr reported that he had purchased a plot of land which he had donated to the village and that construction work would commence as soon as possible as sufficient funds had already been raised in the village. Once it had been built, the remainder of the plot was cleared and flowers planted. Speaking in 1998 Herbert 'Herbie' Ashford remarked that Arthur Tarr always grumbled that although the plot of land had only cost him £1 he had to pay a further £7 in legal fees!

At a Parochial Church Council meeting on 11th July 1954 Rev. Hunt announced his intention to resign as the upkeep of the Rectory and its large garden had become too much for him. It appears that about this time a decision was made to rename the Parish Hall as the Village Hall as Parish Council, Parochial Church Council and School records all started to use that name from that year.

Despite the impending departure of Rev. Hunt, the church was still very active:

> "SUNDAY SCHOOL OUTING. A party of 86 children, parents and others went by Western National motor coach to Weston for their annual summer outing. It was delightfully sunny all day and a very enjoyable time was spent. Tea was served on the beach. Bathing, games, donkey rides, etc. all formed part of the programme for the day."

By January 1955 no progress had been made on the question of drainage for the village and at a B.R.D.C. meeting

> "Mr. Blay stated the Public Health Committee had given further consideration to sewage disposal at Chedzoy and were recommending the Council to ask consulting engineers to further a scheme providing for discharge direct into the River Parrett."

Then in May,

> "A report on Chedzoy revealed that existing conditions could not be materially improved without a comprehensive sewerage scheme for the parish, and it was agreed to submit an estimate to the Ministry."

In March, the rents for Council houses were increased again, that for 'Airey' houses being raised from 17s. 9d. per week to 19s. 6d. (97.5p.).

December 1955 again saw villagers entertaining themselves.

> "An enthusiastic audience packed the Village Hall at Chedzoy for the concert held in aid of Chedzoy Cricket Club funds. The show opened with carols and festive songs by children under seven years of age. This was followed by a performance of 'Cinderella' by the older children and a dance routine by 'The Chedzoy Toppers' - five buxom lads attired in costume."

Severe weather struck the village once again in early 1956. The school log book entry for the last day of January reads,

> "The weather was bad - snowing all day"

and, ten days later,

> "Owing to severe frost the village has been completely without water for two days."

Rev. Hunt and his wife retired to Stolford Manor in February 1956 and before their departure were presented with various gifts, including an armchair and an electric heater.

Their move was not without incident: Miss Margaret Smith, aged 83, had lived with the Hunts since 1940 and on the day they left the village she fell and fractured her femur, an injury which resulted in her death five months later.

In August 1956 the Rev. Alexander Pickering was inducted into the parish, having moved from Billinghay, near Sleaford, Lincolnshire.

Proper sewerage arrangements for the village were turning into a saga. At a meeting of the B.R.D.C. in February 1956

> "The Clerk (Mr. H.G. Blay) reported that the Ministry had indicated that due to the high cost per house of the alternative scheme they were unable to recommend approval of either of the proposed sewage schemes for Chedzoy. They would be prepared to consider a simplified scheme to deal with the main outfall at Pig Lane only."

A month later,

> "The [Public Health] committee's recommendation regarding Chedzoy was that consulting engineers be instructed to proceed with the preparation of a modified scheme to deal only with the main outfall at Pig Lane."

An emergency meeting of the Parochial Church Council took place in March 1956. Bridgwater Rural District Council had proposed making a compulsory purchase order in relation to the Rectory garden as they were hoping to build council houses on the site. A letter of objection was sent to the District Council on the basis that it was hoped to build a new rectory on the land and possibly use the site as a burial ground. In June at a meeting of the B.R.D.C.

Reverend Cecil Hunt.
Rector of Chedzoy from 1940 until 1956.
Photograph by Cecil Cary, courtesy of Muriel Brown.

> "It was reported that construction of new houses to replace unfit property were to be considered at [various villages, including] Chedzoy. They had also inspected a site at Chedzoy but decided against the acquisition if it was to be used for a new parsonage house."

Subsequently the Ministry of Housing and Local Government wrote that an order would not be confirmed.

> "The way is left open for the land to be acquired by the Church Commissioners for building a parsonage house at a future date."

In 1956 Chedzoy was entered in the Somerset Best Kept Village competition and, out of 75 entries, was the winner in the Bridgwater Rural District. The village was entered again the following year and was county runner up to Williton, although still winner in the Bridgwater Rural District.

Social life in the village continued apace with regular whist drives in aid of church and village hall funds, but other events also took place. In February 1957

> "A very pleasant evening was spent at the village hall when Mr. C. [Cecil] Cary kindly gave a show of coloured films made by him during recent months. They included views of places visited on a continental tour in 1956 of Belgium, France, Switzerland and Italy, in addition to many taken in this country, both locally and further afield."

More physical entertainment took place in April:

> "Despite plenty of encouragement from the touch-line, age succumbed to youth in a couple of hilarious soccer matches at Chedzoy. In the first game, on a shortened pitch, the fair maidens of the village proved superior to the more matronly ladies, who were nevertheless accorded a great reception for the sporting way they tackled the youngsters. The local 'Teddy Boys' trounced the 'Old Crocks' in the second game in which the 'ref.' participated during the final stages of the match in the hopes of saving the honour of the 'old uns.' But all to no avail; goals were scored in such rapid succession that players and supporters almost lost count! Fears that one of the 'Old Crocks,' a well-known local milk retailer, would be so puffed that his cheery whistle would be impaired were unfounded when his familiar tune aroused the village at dawn today!"

This era was the height of the Cold War. Nuclear attack was considered a real threat, so the Civil Defence Corps was active. In May 1957 a dinner for fifty was held in the village hall for all those who had just completed eight weeks of training which culminated in an exercise followed by a demonstration of emergency feeding centre techniques at Sibleys Farm.

Civil Defence Corps, 1957.
Members practice emergency feeding techniques.
Note the mature elm trees in the background.
Photograph by Cecil Cary, courtesy of Muriel Brown.

In March 1958 the Parish Council, which had consisted of five members since its formation in 1894, was increased to seven members, a figure at which it remains to this day. Also in March, just two years after becoming Rector, Rev. Pickering announced that he would be retiring as he was suffering from severe rheumatism. He expressed his sincere regret at having to take such a step as his original intention had been to stay in the parish for a further four or five years.

In the late 1950s and early 1960s village expansion continued with the construction of three houses at the junction of Front Street and Manor Road (1958), a shop in Manor Road (1960) and then bungalows in Front Street and St. Mary's Close during the 1960s.

In August 1958 it was announced in the Bridgwater Mercury that

> "Considerable pleasure has been expressed at Chedzoy with the news that the Rev. Mervyn [Basil] Bazell, vicar of Fenton, Stoke-on-Trent, is to be the new Rector. Mr. Bazell knows the locality extremely well, for his late father, Preb. C. Bazell, was vicar at St. John's church, Bridgwater for many years."

However, that pleasure soon evaporated. Roy House had told the Parochial Church Council (PCC) that

> "He had been approached by a number of people who complained of the Rector taking his dog 'Pet' into church. He would therefore like to propose that the Rector's dog be banned from the church." In reply, Rev. Bazell pointed out that as Rector he controlled admission to the church and "He could not delegate this authority by accepting the proposition to ban the dog!"

In March 1958 the matter featured as the front page story in the Bridgwater Mercury under the headline "SHOULD RECTOR'S DOG BE TAKEN TO CHURCH? Chedzoy Parishioners Strongly Object. MAY APPEAL TO ARCHDEACON." Rev. Bazell and 'Pet' were pictured with the caption,

> "The rector had a little dog, it was a Kerry Blue, And when the Rector went to church, The doggie went there too." The matter was reported in some detail and it is clear that the local community was split on this weighty subject.
>
> Mrs. Elizabeth Baker of Rose Bower complained that "Dogs never used to be allowed in the churchyard, never mind in the church. We always used to 'shoo' them out. It is wrong of the Rector to upset people in this way."

The report continued,

> "Seated in his comfortable study, the Rector replied to this criticism. He said, 'I have held a living since 1933, and my dogs have always accompanied me to church. I have held two previous livings in the diocese. I came here to my home county from a parish of 20,000 in Staffordshire. No-one has objected before. I regard all animals as God's creatures and would never turn any animal out of the church. If other people wish to bring their dogs into my church they will be welcomed so long as the dogs are well behaved and under control.'
>
> "Reverting to the objection on the ground that Pet carried dirt into the church, the rector declared that the amount was negligible. 'I take far greater concern at the spiritual mud which is brought into the church by certain people through their venom, malice and uncharitableness'."

The following week the matter was again on the front page of the Mercury.

> "Miss Daisy Tucker, organist at Chedzoy parish church for the last 25 years, has been dismissed by the rector (the Rev. Mervyn Bazell) because - he says - he has not her 'full co-operation and loyalty.' In a letter to Miss Tucker and her sister, Miss Edna Tucker, who acts as her assistant, the rector said: 'In view of the unpleasant happenings of the past week, and the knowledge I have not your full co-operation and loyalty, I am sorry to have to tell you after Sunday next I shall no longer require your help.' Miss Daisy Tucker said, 'The rector has ordered me to hand over the keys of the organ, but I have refused. I am paid quarterly, and am therefore entitled to have three months notice. I have not missed a single week-end service for 25 years, and I am not going to give up without a fight'."

It was reported that as an appeal by some members of the PCC to the Rural Dean had failed they were considering taking the matter to the Archdeacon of Taunton. The Bridgwater Mercury reported that

> "The Bishop of Bath and Wells has confirmed the right of the Rector of Chedzoy to take his 14 year old Kerry Blue terrier 'Pet' to church. In fact, the Bishop said, legally, it would be possible for everybody in the parish to take a dog to

church, though I recognise that the result would be completely unseemly. The Bishop's attitude is revealed in a letter sent to Mr. Percy Tucker of Crown House, Chedzoy, a member of the Parochial Church Council and one of the parishioners who had objected to the Rector taking 'Pet' to weekday services and the children's service on Sunday."

In April an account of a stormy public meeting was published:

"Parishioners of Chedzoy stormed out of their village hall on Friday after the rowdiest annual Parochial Church Meeting in the history of the parish, declaring 'We shall go to chapel in future'." The Rector refused to allow the press to be present at the meeting other than for the appointment of church wardens. The report continued, "The local constable patrolled the street outside the hall throughout the meeting. Villagers were expecting to see him - his bicycle had been noticed outside the Rectory that afternoon.

"During the proceedings the Rector refused to put a resolution that his 14-year old Kerry Blue terrier should be barred from the church. He also refused another resolution calling on the reinstatement of Miss Daisy Tucker, organist for 25 years, whom he dismissed. Mr. Bazell, whose voice could be heard clearly from outside the building, said that the parishioners did not apparently know that an incumbent had an absolute right to decide on his organist. He had decided to dispense with Miss Tucker's services because he felt he did not have her co-operation.

"The Rector was asked why he had also dismissed Miss Tucker's sister, Edna, from her post as a Sunday School teacher, and he replied, 'I considered it best that as her sister was no longer organist, she should not come and teach the children.' A voice: 'I think you did that out of spite.' The Rector: 'As a spiteful person yourself, you should know.' Vociferous applause greeted shouts of 'Dictator!' and the Rector's reply was inaudible in the storm of clapping. After the meeting the village constable maintained his stolid patrol.

"Mr. Percy Tucker, a member of the Parochial Church Council and brother of the dismissed organist told [the reporter]: 'On the new Council we have a majority of people who oppose the Rector. We'll make it red-hot for him now.' The Rector refused all comment except to say: 'It was a very successful meeting for the Church.' Then the villagers - and the constable - went home."

Later in 1959 the PCC Secretary resigned on moving to Burrowbridge and, as things seemed to be going from bad to worse, no one was prepared to take his place. Consequently the Rector wrote the minutes for the remainder of his stay in the parish and, at times, these read more like a diary than minutes. The Treasurer of the Restoration Fund, Miss Daisy Tucker, was dismissed (according to the Rector) or resigned (according to Miss Tucker) as the Rector refused to allow another resolution in relation to his dog entering the church.

Problems seem to have been finally brought to a head with a dispute over replacing the clapper stiles in the rear wall of the churchyard.

In July 1959 it was minuted that parishioners had offered to provide the materials, transport and labour, but by November it seems that the person responsible for the transport and labour had submitted an account for £30.

Instead of the customary one or two pages, minutes of this PCC meeting merited ten pages!

"It was indeed a great pity to him (the Rector) to say that this year at Chedzoy was the unhappiest in the 34 years of his ministry. He had been patient during the year, but he was no longer going to tolerate the sort of things which had happened in the past." He then transcribed his letter to Miss Tucker: "I called on you this afternoon. ... I rang the bell twice and knocked on your door, but received no answer," and a reply which had been received: "You say that you rung the bell on my door twice on Tuesday afternoon. This is incorrect........."

How did Miss Tucker know, unless she was at home?

In reply to a question from a member of the PCC as to why money from collecting boxes had been taken directly to the Rector instead of the Treasurer, the Rector replied,

"The answer to your question is simply that I happen to be the Rector!" This hardly seems to have been the most tactful way a of dealing with a delicate situation.

Early in 1959 Jimmy Gough, who had been the village policeman since 1950, was replaced by a new constable who found himself in difficulties in May:

"P.C. Peter Parrish (Chedzoy) was dazed but uninjured when his motorcycle struck a grass verge at Middlezoy in the early hours of Saturday morning and he was thrown from his machine."

Speaking in 1999 Pete Parrish recalled that about 2.00 a.m. he was riding through Thorngrove when he dozed off and collided with a tree. He went to a nearby house to ask for assistance, but the lady refused to answer the door. After he had collapsed she telephoned the police to report a man acting suspiciously in her garden!

Further changes were taking place in relation to the school. In April 1959 the School Managers gathered as

"The meeting had been called to consider the plan for the proposed classroom hut. The Chairman had seen the Divisional Education Officer about the plan and after a full explanation and lengthy discussion by the Managers it was agreed that the proposed classroom hut be erected, although the Managers still preferred the enlargement of the infants room."

This building was erected in 1960 and was to last until the closure of the school some 35 years later. At the same meeting, the Managers were informed that Mrs. Brazier had resigned as she wished to return to Herefordshire for health reasons.

Mrs. Nina Fels was appointed to replace her and took up her duties in September 1959, at which time there were 33 pupils at the school.

The Sixties

In January 1960 Fred Tucker drew the attention of the Parish Council to the Fire Equipment which he had held for many years. With the establishment of a Fire Brigade in Bridgwater and telephone facilities in the village, he felt that this was of no further use to the village. After discussion, the Clerk was instructed to approach Station Officer Faulkner of the Fire Station, Bridgwater for advice as to its disposal. As a result of advertisements placed in the local paper it was sold for £10 to Mr. Butcher of Cannington, bringing 55 years of parish fire fighting to an end.

Still the question of a proper sewerage system for the village had not been resolved. At a meeting of the Rural District Council in March 1960 councillors were informed that eight sewage schemes in the Bridgwater area would cost between £350,000 and £400,000.

> "Mr. Blay commented on the fact that although the Public Health Committee would recommend to the Council [that schemes] should be placed in order of priority, it was not intended that the order be applied rigidly. The Committee recommended that proposed schemes take the following order of priority: 1, Chedzoy..."

By April 1960 relationships within the church had not improved and the Rev. Bazell recorded that

> "As all of you will know, my first full year as your Rector has not been at all easy, but I do thank God that He has given me strength and courage to go on steadily with my work."

When it came to elections Percy Tucker said that he no longer wished to stand for the PCC whilst the Rector continued his "monkey tricks."

At the same meeting the Treasurer of the Restoration Fund, Daisy Tucker, accused the Rector of having gone behind her back in the matter of the Church restoration fund. The minutes note that

> "At this meeting Miss Tucker excelled herself in remarks, calling the Priest of the Parish on two occasions, 'a wicked scamp.' She nearly got herself into serious trouble when she suggested that the Rector had taken money from the Garden Fete takings to pay for a bottle of whisky which he had. Fortunately for her, she hastily withdrew her remarks and the rector generously took no further action."

Clapper Stile.
John Weeks demonstrates the operation of one of the stiles at the rear of the church.
Photograph by Maureen Weeks.

Constable Jimmy Gough.
Seen here in the kitchen at Manor Farm. Note his medal ribbons which were typical of most police officers until the late 1960s, as they had joined the police after military service during the war.
Photograph by Cecil Cary, courtesy of Muriel Brown.

Perhaps there was some substance in Miss Tucker's accusation as, according to some residents, Rev. Bazell had a liking for strong liquor.

In 1960 the PCC were informed that the Church Commissioners had approved the building of a new Rectory in Chedzoy before September 1963 at a cost of £5,750 to £6,000 maximum. Most of the cost would be borne by the Commissioners. The Rector reported that work had started by June 1963 and he moved in before June 1964. However, that was in the future and in April the vexed question of the clapper stile was still playing on the Rector's mind as he recorded that the balance of the accounts would have been better

> "If we had not had to pay for the making of the church stiles."

The drive to modernise the village continued and in May 1960 at a Parish Council meeting

> "a letter from Mr. F.E. Dare was read relating to the ditch in Manor Road: after discussion the Clerk was instructed to write to the Clerk of the Council, Bridgwater Rural District Council, asking for the road to be piped from the corner of Manor Drive to the last house on the south side of Manor Road, with a grating to take surface water and to be connected to the main sewer."

This refers to an open ditch which ran in front of numbers 3 to 6 Manor Road. Later the same year the Parish Council again discussed yet another sewage disposal scheme which had been proposed by the R.D.C. as they were concerned that the scheme did not appear to include the area from the church to Parchey. The Clerk to the B.R.D.C., Mr. Blay, attended their next meeting and councillors were assured that the whole of the parish was to be included. The minutes record that

> "after the Chairman had reminded the Council that he had pressed for priority of action for this Parish, Mr. Blay appealed for the co-operation of the Parish Council in implementing the scheme which had been so fraught with difficulties and which, as a result, had had to be altered from its original conception."

Two improvements in communications came to the area in 1961. On 23rd March Subscriber Trunk Dialling (STD) began for the telephone system so that it was no longer necessary to go through the operator for calls to about 600 exchanges

> "and by 1970 we expect that anyone anywhere in the country will be able to dial anyone else."

On 29th April Westward Television began transmissions.

As had been the case for many years, complaints about footpaths continued to be recorded at Parish Council meetings. In March 1961 they considered a complaint that the footpath leading from the church to Pig Lane had been ploughed up. The complainant had been invited to attend the Council meeting and re-stated his complaint. The minutes record,

> "The Chairman then stated that a footpath was four feet wide from the crown of the hedge, and pointing out the hedge was overgrown to some extent and spreading out into the field of Mr. [Cecil] Cary. When they measured it there was sufficient land left for the footpath from the centre of the hedge. The members inspected the path from the church to the land and there was no evidence of encroaching upon the path, the distance being left and available. At one point there was a slight encroachment which could have been due to an error of judgement by the tractor man ploughing the field, but the amount was negligent (sic). The council unanimously agreed the footpath was not ploughed up and Mr. Cary said instructions would be given to his men in future to try and avoid encroachment or tractor marks on the path."

Villagers causing a disturbance, although not a common occurrence, was still continuing. In September 1962 it was reported that

> "For being drunk and disorderly 'X' of Chedzoy was fined £3 at Bridgwater Borough Magistrates' Court. Superintendent L.F. Hewitt told the magistrates that 'X' entered the enquiry office at the station, being abusive, crying and waving his arms about. He complained that his shirt had been torn in an incident and said to P.C. Bath, 'If you did not have that —- coat on I would drag you over the counter.' 'X' then collapsed and was placed in the cells. When he was charged he said, 'I don't think that's right. You ought to have called a doctor'."

In common with the rest of the country, Chedzoy suffered during the severe winter of 1962/63. On 1st January 1963 the Mercury reported

> "P.C. Peter Parrish (Chedzoy) escaped injury when his police motorcycle skidded at the Silver Fish but the machine was slightly damaged."

Mrs. Fels made several references to the weather in the school log book:

> "Jan. 10th, 1963: All Primary Schools opened 3 days later than scheduled because of the severely cold weather. All toilets were frozen, but two of which were freed by paraffin lamps. There was no taxi service.
> Jan. 24th: Infants told not to come to school until further notice as there were insufficient toilets unfrozen. Outside temperature 8°F. (-14°C.).
> Feb. 6th: Snow drifts prevented many children and Mrs. Smith from arriving at school. Chedzoy Lane and Westonzoyland Road were completely blocked .
> Feb. 7th: All back at school. Temperatures higher, 28°-32°F. (-2° to 0°C.)."

Although the winter may have been severe, this did not deter visitors. In August 1963 it was reported that

"Mr. Douglas Perrett, a Bridgwater naturalist, reports having seen a pair of collared doves in his garden. This is the first time they have been recorded in the town. A European bird, the collared dove has not been breeding in this country for many years."

Now they are common here.

Motor vehicles were becoming far more numerous as prosperity followed the austerity of the immediate post-war period, but motoring was not cheap: in 1964 Vehicle Excise Duty (Road Tax) was £15 per annum for a car - this at a time when most people were earning about £10 a week. This expense received indirect comment at a Parish Council meeting in August that year after they had complained to the highway authority about the state of Chedzoy Lane.

"The Clerk read a letter from the Divisional Surveyor which referred to the difficulty of drainage because of the absence of discharge points but stated that the matter would be borne in mind in the autumn when the next estimate was being prepared.

"The Council were not impressed with this reply. It was felt that very little money was expended on the village roads in comparison with the contributions made by villagers in the form of Road Fund licence, etc. and the Clerk was instructed to write to the Divisional Surveyor requesting that some immediate action be taken before the onset of winter and the consequent increased hazard and nuisance to the large number of villagers, both adult and children, who traverse the lane either by car, cycle or on foot. At the same time the Surveyor should be asked to arrange for the hedges to be trimmed."

This sounds so familiar, the complaint could almost have been made in 1999!

At the next Parish Council meeting

"The Clerk read a letter he had received from the Divisional Surveyor which stated that no further funds were available to carry out any drainage improvements in the current financial year but that in carrying out normal maintenance efforts would be made to keep as much water off the road as possible."

Definitely shades of 1999.

"The Council was not satisfied with this reply and felt that more should be done to clear existing pipes and ditches. The Chairman said that he would take up with the Rural District Council these questions of drainage and general maintenance together with the need for road improvements at Nelson Lodge, Slape Cross, Tar Barrel Corner and the provision of a central white line at the main road junction all of which had been the subject of a recent visit by the County Council Road Safety Officer; and that he would press for action to be taken not only for the sake of villagers, but also in view of the increasing through traffic to and from other villages, e.g. Stawell, Moorlinch."

Surely this refers to 1999 and not 1965? Nothing's really changed!

In late 1964 the Parish Council again considered the desirability of street lighting in the village and asked for an estimate as to the costs involved. The Clerk duly reported that if would cost £8 10s. per lamp if an existing pole could be used, or £20 per lamp if a pole had to be provided. In addition to this, the annual costs would be £10 per lamp plus £3 for each time link required. Again, nothing further was done in view of the costs involved.

Village residents were the subject of the leading article in the Bridgwater Mercury in February 1965. The full details of both men were reported.

"SEQUEL TO POLICE CHECK ON FACTORY. Three Accused of Break-in. One Man Sent to Prison. - Two Chedzoy men, both 23 years, appeared with a 15 tear old girl in the dock at Bridgwater Borough Magistrates' Court charged with breaking into the factory of Quantock Preserving Company, Ltd. at Wembdon Road, Bridgwater. One of the accused, 'X', elected to go for trial but the other man, 'Y', pleaded guilty and was sent to prison for three months. The girl was committed to the care of Somerset County Council. ... They were caught by police after P.C. Stabbins, on patrol, heard a noise and checked the premises. 'Y' was also charged with taking and driving away a motor car from Sedgemoor Filling Station."

The case against 'X' was dismissed at committal proceedings, but he was committed for trial for breaking into the offices of C.J. Harris (Bridgwater) Ltd. in Church Street, Bridgwater. He subsequently appeared before Bridgwater Borough Quarter Sessions when he was found guilty and sentenced to three months' imprisonment plus a further month, to run consecutively, for breach of a Probation Order.

An innovation in April 1965 was a weekly household refusal collection service: since its introduction shortly before the Second World War, collections had only been made fortnightly. The Bridgater Rural Disrict Council also announced that a sewerage scheme would be implemented for Chedzoy during 1967/68 at a cost of £51,000: this was to provide drains to a settlement tank in Pig Lane. In September 1965 BBC2 television came to the village, with improved picture quality using 625 instead of 405 lines which was still in use for BBC1 and the two commercial stations. The Bridgwater Mercury also noted that the cost of a return rail ticket from Bridgwater to Paddington had risen to £3 17s. 6d. with the comment that it had been 13s. 6d. (67.5p.) in 1902.

Further changes in the education of the village children came about in 1966. In April the School Managers were read a letter

"Regarding the reorganisation of Chedzoy and Bawdrip

Schools the new arrangements taking effect from September 1966, Bawdrip receiving from both villages the Infants and Standard I range and that Chedzoy would receive the Junior aged children."

Reflecting the new arrangements, the name was changed from Chedzoy County Primary School to Chedzoy County Junior School.

In the mid-1960s the bungalows adjoining Front Street were built as well as two more behind them and Parish Councillors raised no objection to the Rural District Council's proposal to name the access road to the latter two as St. Mary's Close. By early 1967 further construction was taking place in the village as three bungalows were built between the Manor House Inn and Moggs Farm. The Parish Council were seriously concerned that one of the properties was being built so close to the highway that it would impede any widening of Manor Road at that point. Planning Permission had been granted without any reference to the Parish Council who could have raised this point before permission was granted. In due course the builder of these properties was declared bankrupt and in June 1969 the Council again raised the matter with the Rural District Council before the new developer commenced work. However, the views of the Parish Council were ignored and construction of the three bungalows, now named Willow Green, was completed with them all in their originally planned locations.

In June 1968 Rev. Bazell informed the PCC that it was his intention to retire at the end of November. For a few months the church was without a Rector, but in May 1969 Rev. Ian Seward became the incumbent and promptly set about improving relationships with disillusioned parishioners, as well as establishing bell ringing lessons so that the bells could be rung on a regular basis. Heating in the church was improved by the replacement of the coal fired boiler with a new, oil-fired one, which was cheaper to run as fuel cost 1s. 2d. per gallon (1.3p. litre). In order to reduce draughts in the church, the west door was sealed, and has not been used since. Wooden paling fences which once stood either side of the church gates were removed in 1970 and the area surfaced with tarmacadam to provide parking for visitors' cars.

On 15th April 1969, following a Parish Council meeting, a report appeared in the Bridgwater Mercury under the headline MAKE DO AND MEND. This again has shades of 1999.

"A letter has been received by Bridgwater R.D.C. from Chedzoy Parish Council complaining of delay in execution of works to verges opposite the Post Office and at Higher Road; and of unsatisfactory condition of roads in the Parish, particularly Ward Lane. These matters were referred to the Divisional Surveyor who has reported that delay in execution of works had been due to shortage of labour and funds."

Some things never change!

Also in April parishioners were becoming increasingly angry at the failure of the B.R.D.C. to implement mains drainage for the village which had been first proposed 24 years earlier. The annual Parish Meeting was reported by the Bridgwater Mercury:

"The 16 year old topic of Chedzoy's sewerage scheme was once again the main point of discussion at the annual Parish meeting held in the Village Hall. The Clerk to the Parish Council, Mr. Charles Hiscox, read a letter which he had received from Bridgwater Rural District Council, saying that the sewerage scheme had been included in the Council's financial programme, but due to the financial squeeze, it might have to be postponed. In reply to the Rural District Council Mr. Hiscox claimed that industrial developments were frightened away from Chedzoy because of the lack of adequate sewerage disposal there. He added, 'Do we have to suffer an outbreak of typhoid before something is done?' The Chairman, Mr. Norman Fry, said that it seemed like a vicious circle as the village could not develop. It is known that planning permission has been refused in Chedzoy on the grounds of drainage. The health hazard is said to exist in two places - in Manor Road, where a ditch overflows onto the road and in Ward Lane where there is a cracked drainpipe. It was decided to write to the Medical Officer of Health to see if the places have been inspected by him, and ascertain his views."

The next report was in May.

"If there was a competition for 'the worst kept village in Somerset', Chedzoy should enter it,' said Mr. A.E. Ashford at last week's meeting of Bridgwater Rural District Council. Mr. Ashford, who was speaking about sewerage conditions in his parish, said that sewage had come up through the grids in the road, hit the surface water and then flowed down the highways. He added, 'The smell is awful, and on health grounds something should be done about it.' The Clerk said that twice the Ministry had looked into the situation at Chedzoy, but a scheme had been turned down because of the cost. He pointed out that there was a number of other parishes in the Council's area with conditions equally as unsatisfactory as those at Chedzoy. A report would be considered by the Health and Works Committee later in the week, so he would ask that Chedzoy be a little patient. Retorted Mr. Ashford, 'We have been very patient for twenty years and I hope we don't have to wait much longer before something is done'."

In July 1968 a severe storm, with thunder and lightning, accompanied by torrential rain following a steady downpour for the preceding two days, caused severe flooding in Chedzoy and the surrounding villages. Between 12.30 p.m. Wednesday and 9.00 a.m. the next day over four inches (100 mm) of rain were recorded at Sydenham School, Bridgwater: six people died in Somerset. Norman Fry of Sibleys Farm lost over £1,000 worth of stock and crops, a not inconsiderable sum at that time, and his losses were typical of those suffered. A child at the village school recorded that fields were a strange sight as the floods subsided, being covered with bloated worms which had risen to the surface seeking air, only to drown in the all engulfing waters. The School House and Court Farm had water running through the front door and out the back.

In a never ending quest for funds it was reported in August 1969 that

> "Chedzoy has a population of only about 350, but in only three months the villagers have succeeded in raising over £250 for the restoration and repair of their beautiful parish church. Their target is a sum of £1,500; of the £600 raised to date, £132 resulted from the fete held in the Rectory garden. ... Competition winners were: Best decorated bicycle - Brian Kidner; Under 8 painting competition - Andrew Denning; under 14 - Linda Miles."

Two months later a harvest thanksgiving service was held at the Manor House Inn,

> "This was the first time such an occurence had taken place in Chedzoy, and it was followed by a floodlit auction of produce on a farm wagon in the Manor's car park." It raised £32.

In 1969 and 1970 King's Sedgemoor Drain was widened to its present width, and this also caused some minor concerns to the Parish Council as the contractors planned to close Parchey Bridge for a length of time. The councillors were insistent that a Bailey bridge should be provided in the event of a prolonged closure, and one was erected and used in April and May 1970.

Village Expansion and the M 5 Motorway

The population had expanded to 326 and the Parish Council were still concerned to provide a playing field for the village. In November 1970 Norman Fry agreed to release part of his orchard in Pig Lane for a trial period to see how things developed.

Chedzoy was in the news again in June 1971. The Bridgwater Mercury reported,

> "A Chedzoy man who burgled the home of an elderly widow was given a six month jail sentence suspended for two years at Somerset Quarter Sessions. [He] admitted entering Hoopers Cottage, Burrowbridge and stealing a clock worth £70 ... while the occupier, Mrs. Syliva Bell (73) was in bed upstairs. ... [The defence] said his family faced eviction from his home in three weeks time unless he had his freedom."

Four months later

> "A police officer found a man lying half in a hedge and half under a bicycle and when he asked him to get up the man said, 'Leave me alone, I want to sleep. I'm drunk.' Chief Inspector David Little told the Bridgwater County Magistrates about the incident which happened in Chedzoy. Before the court was [a Bridgwater man] who pleaded guilty to being drunk in charge of a pedal cycle. He was fined £2."

Probably the most violent crime to take place in Chedzoy in living memory occurred in November 1971. Desmond 'Dezzie' and Audrey Fry lived at Inkers Farm and had been married for about six years. For about ten years Mr. Fry had employed Francis Henry Reed, aged 48, as a labourer on the farm. Francis Reed was a well known local character, having been born in the village, but he was always a loner and kept himself to himself. Despite his mother living in the village he frequently used to sleep either in an old cottage in Frys Lane or even in a milking parlour at Brentsfield Lane. In addition to working part-time for Mr. Fry he also used to keep the churchyard immaculate. Before weddings and funerals, he would arrive outside the church between midnight and 2.00 a.m. in order to sweep Front Street by lantern light as far as the junction with Manor Road so that it was spotless for the happy or solemn occasion. It seems that for some unexplained reason, Francis Reed resented Mr. Fry's marriage, feeling that his wife had come between the two men, although quite why he should have thought this is not known.

About eight o'clock on the morning of 6th November, Mr. and Mrs. Fry went to the milking parlour at Brentsfield Lane, expecting to find Francis Reed to be there and milking the cows, but there was no sign of him. The couple began milking and during the course of this Mrs. Fry went to get some cattle cake from the rear of the parlour. Francis Reed was hiding in the hedge about thirty feet away and, without any warning, he fired a 12-bore shotgun at Mrs. Fry, the pellets striking her about the head. Mrs. Fry fell to the ground. Mr. Fry ran to her assistance and, after a struggle, he disarmed Reed and knocked him to the ground. As Mr. and Mrs. Fry made their way towards the village, Reed attempted to run over them with a tractor, driving through a hedge and barbed wire fence, after which he returned to the cottage in Frys Lane and set his bed on fire, and it was there that he was arrested by the police.

Audrey Fry was in hospital from that date until Christmas, returning for further treatment in February 1972. A total of 48 pellets were removed from her face but, despite all their efforts, surgeons were unable to save Mrs. Fry's sight. Francis Reed appeared before Bridgwater Magistrates and on 1st December 1971 he was committed to Bristol Crown Court for trial. He appeared before that court in January when he pleaded 'Not Guilty' to attempted murder, but 'Guilty' to malicious wounding and arson. The defence were unable to offer any explanation for his violent behaviour. Medical opinion was that Reed had an unstable personality and that the pattern could be repeated. He was sentenced to seven years' imprisonment for malicious wounding and a further three years for arson, the sentences to run concurrently.

The 1970s brought further development in the village. In 1972 the "new" houses between Higher Road and Manor Road were built by Messrs. Harris Brothers and Collard on the paddock of Court Farm.

New Houses.
Manor Road showing the trees which stood between the council houses and the new houses which were under construction in February 1972. All the trees were felled in 1977 and 1978 after Dutch Elm disease. 7 and 8 Higher Road can be seen in the background. Photograph by John Weeks.

They originally came onto the market at a cost of £6,500, but for an extra £150 a utility could be built behind the garage. Shortly after this the houses on the opposite side of Higher Road were built by the same company and this phase of construction was completed in 1976/77 when Nos. 40 and 42 Higher Road were erected.

In December 1972 Mrs. Pauline Clapp was appointed as an Assistant Teacher at the school, commencing work the following month. Mrs. Clapp was eventually to become the Head Teacher and remain in the post until the closure of the village school.

In May 1973 a Pre-School Play Group was established by two local mothers; Mrs. Catherine (Cathy) Arden and Mrs. Maureen Weeks, a State Registered Nurse. For the first year meetings were held informally once a week, but after the annual general meeting the following May a more formal structure was adopted with a committee under the chairmanship of Mrs. Lesley Burgess. The fee per session was set at 20p. per child. From November 1974 two sessions were held each week and it was agreed that supervisors should be paid 50p. each per session. Amongst events organised was a visit to Bristol Zoo in 1976, when the cost of hiring a coach for the day was £17.50: adults paid 60p. and children 30p. for the trip! Although there have been many changes in personnel, and even more changes in the children, the play group is still active and celebrated its 25th anniversary in May 1998.

In the late 1960s there had been an active Youth Club in the village, but this had faded away. In December 1973 a new club was formed which lasted for some considerable time. Under the chairmanship of Gordon Baggs, who lived at Myrtle Cottage, other members of the management committee were John Weeks (Secretary), Christopher Fry (Treasurer), Robert 'Bob' Clark and Allan Stokes, whilst Richard May and June Carter represented the young people. An initial drive for funds raised £80 in the first month and this was used to purchase equipment. Soon some 50 youngsters were taking part in the activities and a rota of 18 adults had been arranged to act as supervisors. The club ran successfully for a number of years until, like its predecessor, support and interest amongst the youngsters waned and the club closed. In the summer of 1999 attempts were being made to re-form a youth club for a new generation of children.

As an aside, and to keep you in touch with costs, the rate for the year 1972 was 74p. in the pound (up 4p.), of which 61p. was for the County Council, 12p. for Bridgwater Rural District Council and 1p. the Chedzoy precept. The annual rate for the "new" houses in Higher Road and Manor Road was £73.98. At that time a side of pork could be purchased for under £11 but a colour film cost £1.89 and the annual Vehicles' Excise Licence had gone up to £25. Maternity allowance was a single payment of £25.

Chedzoy, in common with many areas of Somerset, was affected by the construction of the M5 Motorway. The road had first been suggested shortly after the Second World War and in March 1953 the Bridgwater Mercury reported that members of the National Farmers Union were making individual protests about the plans for the road to the Ministry of Housing and Local Government.

> "The proposed trunk road as it affects the Bridgwater area, will run west of North Petherton and Huntworth (it was eventually built to the east), cross the Bridgwater-Taunton canal, the main railway line and River Parrett and, by-passing Bridgwater, will cross the Bridgwater-Glastonbury road. Travelling through Puriton it will run parallel for a mile or so with the main line, cross the River Brue at East Huntspill, and travel through Burnham Without, Rooks Bridge and East Brent. The new route does not use any existing roads and, according to the N.F.U., crosses farm lands without any consideration for the boundaries whatever."

In February 1954 a public inquiry was held in Taunton in relation to the scheme. In the early 1960s an alternative plan was for the motorway to end at a junction to be built on the A38 at East Brent, with the A38 being upgraded across Somerset, and a start on improving sections of this road was made. Some short sections of dual carriageway were constructed. The motorway scheme eventually went ahead as originally conceived.

This mammoth engineering project commenced and, although not directly involving the village, did create some inconvenience and it was not until it was completed that the village was able to return to normal. The motorway opened in sections, not all of which were in sequence, and each had a differing effect on Chedzoy. Although sections of the motorway north of the River Avon had been opened in the 1960s, it was not until the early 1970s that work commenced on the length through Somerset and Devon.

Contracts were awarded for the sections of motorway from

Edithmead to Dunball (junctions 22 to 23) and Dunball to Huntworth (junctions 23 to 24), the latter going to Cementation Construction. Work commenced on these two sections early in 1971 and 1972. A veritable army of workmen were engaged on the project, which was probably the largest civil engineering project to be undertaken in the county since the construction of the Bristol and Exeter Railway some 140 years earlier. The Somerset Levels offered particular challenges to the engineers because of the unstable nature of the ground. In order to overcome this the entire site from the Mendip Hills to Dunwear was covered with a layer of rock six feet thick. On top of this was a further six feet of pulverised fuel ash from Aberthaw Power Station in South Wales. This was brought by train to a specially constructed siding at Highbridge from where a huge fleet of earth moving trucks conveyed it along the site to be dumped to form an embankment. The intention was that this would settle so that the motorway could be constructed a year later after the surcharge of ash had been removed.

Although there was to be a twelve month settlement period for the majority of the site, other work continued with the construction of the various bridges along the route. The present bridge carrying the A39 Bath Road over the motorway stands close to what was the location of the original junction of Chedzoy Lane with Bath Road which was directly opposite Sunny View (on the old road between Mole Valley Farmers and the motorway). During the construction phase the abutments which now stand either side of all the over-bridges on the Levels were built of pulverised fuel ash. The bridges carrying Bath Road and Westonzoyland Road over the motorway were built close to the line of the existing roads: the old Bath Road is still used as access to Mole Valley Farmers and Little Sydenham Farm, but the old Westonzoyland Road, south of the bridge, has all but vanished. As a temporary access to Chedzoy Lane, a road was built to a new junction almost opposite Horsey Lane, and the remnants of this road can still be seen outside the Morganians Rugby Club. Other than the closure of Crow Lane, between Chedzoy Lane and Bower Lane, this was the only aspect of the motorway construction which directly affected the village.

One casualty of the construction of the motorway was Sedgemoor Service Station, owned by Mr. and Mrs. Croft. The garage stood on what is now the site of Mole Valley Farmers and, as it would no longer be adjacent to the road, the owners decided that it would be prudent to relocate and built new premises on the present site closer to Bridgwater. The Crofts received no compensation.

The first section of the motorway in Somerset, opened on 25th January 1973, was the 22.6 miles from Portbury (junction 19) to Edithmead (junction 22), but traffic on this was comparatively light as it stood in splendid isolation and was not connected to the existing motorway north of the River Avon. Any motorist using the motorway had to make a detour via Bristol in order to re-join the motorway at Avonmouth or Portbury. Because of this, many local people continued to use the A38 between Bridgwater and Bristol.

On 5th July 1973 the motorway between the Edithmead and Dunball junctions, built at a cost of £7.5 million, was opened. On the face of it, this should not have caused any difficulties for Chedzoy residents, but now, particularly as it was during the summer, thousands of tourists were pouring south on the M5 and rejoining the existing road network at Dunball. The result was inevitable. All roads in the area became choked with traffic: the A38 from Dunball into Bridgwater; the route over Puriton Hill to the A39 and thence along Bath Road into town, and even a longer diversion which took traffic out on the A39 to Ashcott and then joined the A361 at Pedwell to continue towards Taunton. Any attempt to travel into Bridgwater by car, particularly on a Saturday, was a nightmare as it meant joining queuing traffic from the junction with Chedzoy Lane: the alternative route along Westonzoyland Road was almost as bad. It was a summer best forgotten!

The sheer enormity of this engineering project can be demonstrated by a few facts and figures in relation to the Bridgwater section of the motorway, which cost £5.25 million. A total of 46,000 cubic yards of topsoil were removed, together with 192,000 cubic yards of marl and alluvial deposits. 35,000 cubic yards of peat were replaced with rock infill. After twelve months of settlement, 514,000 cubic yards of surcharge were removed before construction commenced in earnest. The biggest single construction was the viaduct over the River Parrett, Bridgwater and Taunton canal, the railway and two roads at Huntworth, which consumed £2.25 million of the contracted sum. This 810 metre long structure took 22 months to build. It has 17 spans, each 51 metres in length, and contains about 4,600 tons of steel and 6,000 cubic metres of concrete, each weighing two tons per cubic metre. This was just the actual viaduct: even more steel and concrete were used for the foundations. Most of the work did not cause much disruption but on a Sunday in October 1972 railway services were suspended for the day whilst the huge girders above the track were edged into position. The problems caused by the unstable ground meant that even the 'small' bridges at Bath Road and Westonzoyland Road required steel piles to be driven 90 feet into the Somerset peat.

Traffic problems caused by the termination of the motorway at Dunball were short lived. On 20th November 1973 the Bath Road bridge and a new junction for Chedzoy Lane were opened to traffic. A month later, at 11.30 a.m. on Tuesday, 18th December 1973, John Peyton, Minister of Transport, cut a ribbon at Huntworth and declared the piece of motorway from Dunball to Huntworth open to traffic. One would have thought that this would solve the local traffic problems, but it was not to be. Because of delays in building the bridge over the River Tone, the Huntworth to Blackbrook section of the motorway (junctions 24 to 25) became a 'missing link' after the Blackbrook to Chelston section (junctions 25 to 26), built at a cost of £6.5 million, was opened on 11th April 1974. Traffic now thundered south all the way from Portbury and came to a grinding halt at Huntworth. It was not uncommon on a Saturday morning to see three lanes of queuing traffic on the southbound carriageway back to well north of Dunball - even at six o'clock in the morning.

The congestion on the motorway meant that drivers would turn off at Dunball and try to find an alternative route, usually meaning that they used the old roads around Bridgwater, adding to the congestion. On one occasion a particularly impatient motorist cut the wire fence so that he was able to turn off the motorway onto the old Bath Road by Mole Valley Farmers. His example was promptly emulated by many other drivers. The summer of 1974 saw even heavier traffic as the Avonmouth Bridge over the River Avon was at last opened to traffic on 23rd May 1974, meaning that drivers had an uninterrupted motorway from Birmingham to Huntworth. It does not take much imagination to visualise the effect that this had on North Petherton in the middle of the 'missing link.'

News reports on Saturday, 24th May 1974 spoke of queues of traffic stretching back twenty miles from Huntworth to St. George's (junction 21 for Weston-Super-Mare). As an interim measure, a temporary junction at Moon Lane, south of North Petherton, was opened on 2nd July 1975 and this then became the southernmost end of the motorway. In early November that year the southbound carriageway was fully opened from Huntworth to Blackbrook, with a slight delay on the northbound carriageway as the temporary junction at Moon Lane was removed, the motorway opening fully on 25th November 1975. This last section was built at a cost of £6 million. At last, local traffic could return to normal and through traffic could use the motorway right across Somerset, although it would be some time before the project was completed and the road opened to beyond Exeter.

Finally, it is worth mentioning that the sheer enormity of the motorway site meant that theft of plant and materials was a major problem. In an effort to combat this the police used to patrol the site regularly, their Land Rovers being dwarfed by the huge construction machinery. One night a patrol was driving just north of what is now Taunton Deane Services when, inadvertently, they drove onto a section of freshly laid concrete. The driver reversed and made good his escape, but for many years a double "Y" shaped patch could be seen on the northbound carriageway where damage was caused by the front wheels. The Constable concerned eventually became a Superintendent and has now retired.

In April 1974 Bridgwater Rural District Council ceased to exist with the formation of Sedgemoor District Council. This change made very little difference to the village except in the initial months when the telephone directory still contained details of the former Councils, so finding who was responsible for dealing with matters could be a problem.

Between 1975 and 1978 the landscape of the village was changed dramatically through the effects of Dutch Elm Disease. All of the mature elms in the area succumbed to the ravages of the beetles. The most significant losses were a line of trees adjacent to the road near West End Farm, a line between Higher Road and Manor Road alongside the "new" houses, a line along the hedgerow behind Croftside and another line in the field behind the church. Not a single mature elm remained afterwards. Twenty years later those elm trees which have grown since are again being killed by the same disease.

The autumn of 1975 and early months of 1976 saw the arrival of mains drainage to the village. Previously sewage had been piped to a settlement tank situated alongside the orchard in Pig Lane - an area best avoided, especially in warm weather! During the later months of that year much disruption was caused as all the roads had to be dug up in order that new sewers could be constructed. Officially, diversion routes were via existing roads, but two unofficial routes were used extensively by villagers. Whilst Ward Lane was closed, local drivers used

Front Street, October 1975.
The children are running home after the arrival of the school bus from Bawdrip. In the foreground are Gabriel Coombs and Lynda Weeks. Note the Old Coach House on the left, before its conversion to a house.
Photograph by Ken Coombs, courtesy of Beryl Coombs.

May 1976.
Mrs. Nina Fels, head teacher, and John Cox, one of the school governors, pictured during the school centenary celebrations in 1976.
Courtesy of Margaret Cox.

Frys Lane and Moor Drove in order to get from the centre of the village to Parchey: good advance observation was essential on this single track route! When Front Street was being excavated the unofficial alternative route was through the field behind Sibleys Farm.

The amount of sub-surface water meant that pumps had to run day and night in order to keep the excavations from flooding, and this caused not a little annoyance to those unfortunate enough to have a pump immediately outside their home for several weeks. Access to private driveways was also difficult and temporary ramps of sand were constructed over drainage pipes for some residents, not always with the greatest success. One Sunday morning John Weeks was unable to leave for work after his car "grounded" with wheels either side of two pipes, but neighbours were on hand and helped to lift the car from its suspended position. The contractors reinforced that ramp with aggregate!

In May 1976 the village school celebrated its centenary. On Friday, 22nd May the children and staff, under the watchful eye of Mrs. Fels, dressed in Victorian clothes to re-enact a typical day's education from 100 years earlier. Many people attended to view the proceedings on this special day.

On Friday evening and Saturday afternoon the children gave a performance of "Alice in Wonderland" for parents and distinguished guests, who included the Rev. Ian Seward and Tom King, Member of Parliament for Bridgwater. Afterwards there was a demonstration by the Chalice Morris Dancers and Albert 'Bert' Ashford, Chairman of the Managers, planted a commemorative tree. A supper party was held at Sibleys Farm and on Sunday a special service held at the church.

In December 1976 Rev. Seward left the village and the living at Chedzoy was suspended, initially for a period of five years. The following month it was proposed that the parish should be merged with St. John's, Bridgwater with the Rev. Clifford Jones taking over pastoral care. It was also proposed that the Rectory be sold. These proposals were adopted by the Church Commissioners and on 1st November 1978 the new parish of "Bridgwater St. John Baptist and Chedzoy" was formed and the Rectory handed over to the diocese for disposal.

Early in 1977 a stormy meeting was held in the village hall between representatives of the Somerset County Council and local parents. It had been decided that children living in the centre of the village would have to pay £8 per term to use the school bus to travel to and from Sydenham Comprehensive School (East Bridgwater Community School). Many parents objected to having to pay for a service which had previous been provided free of charge and a representative of the Surveyor's Department was greeted with howls of derision when he said that children could safely walk along the verge in Chedzoy Lane - over twenty years have passed and still there is no suitable verge for pedestrians!

In common with the rest of the country, Chedzoy celebrated Queen Elizabeth's Silver Jubilee. On Sunday, 5th June 1977 a service was held at the church followed by tea and cakes. The following day 154 people attended a supper at Sibleys Farm at which the Loyal Toast was proposed by the Chairman of the Parish Council, Bernard 'Bern' Stone (1902-1984). On Tuesday, a sports day was held for the village children and each of them was presented with a commemorative mug. Many of the houses were decorated and the prize for the best decorations was won by Mr. and Mrs. Fred Tucker. Three commemorative trees were planted on the verge in Front Street near the telephone kiosk.

Christmas Eve 1977 saw tremendous gales sweep across the village. Many residents lost roof tiles and two large trees behind the church were brought crashing down, causing damage to some gravestones. February 1978 brought the most severe weather since 1947. On the night of Thursday, 16th, several inches of snow fell on the region, continuing in earnest on Saturday evening. People returning to the village about 10.30 p.m. were confronted with blizzard conditions with snow drifts creeping across Chedzoy Lane from every gateway. By Sunday morning every road in the area was filled with snow to the tops of the hedgerows. Around the centre of the village wind sculptured drifts had built up several feet high around the houses. Chedzoy Lane was impassable to traffic for 24 hours until cleared by local farmers and Ward Lane was closed for three days. Even the nearby motorway was reduced to a single lane in each direction with drivers having to exercise great caution and make use of all three lanes in order to find a route through the huge drifts. Mrs. Fels recorded in the school log book that

> "the school was unable to open as roads and buildings were blocked by snow from a violent blizzard on Saturday night."

After the overnight snow the community was out clearing paths. Donald Anning, aged 71, who lived at Parchey, collapsed and died as a result of his exertions.

6th January 1979.
Hollow Lane with Three Oaks Farm in the background. Photograph by Ken Coombs, courtesy of Beryl Coombs.

With Ward Lane being completely impassable it was Wednesday before an undertaker was able to attend.

In the summer of 1979 thieves struck twice in the village. On the night of 29th June an attempt was made to steal lead from the roof of the north transept of the church, but it was only damaged and not removed. Temporary repairs had been effected by the time the same thieves returned on 11th August, this time removing the lead from the same roof and taking it away in a vehicle which had been driven into the field behind the church. The cost of replacement lead was so expensive that roofing felt was used instead. Later that month one of the offenders appeared before Sedgemoor Magistrates' Court when he was sentenced to six months' imprisonment, suspended for two years, and ordered to pay £269 in compensation. He was subsequently imprisoned for failing to pay the compensation.

Ten days after the theft, as dusk was falling, an explosion reverberated around the centre of the village: the electricity pole in the front garden of 14 Manor Road had shorted, plunging the centre of the village into darkness. For some strange reason No. 14 and two nearby houses still had power! Whilst waiting for Electricty Board engineers to attend an impromptu neighbourhood party was held. When the engineers arrived about 10.15 p.m. and said they would have to switch off power to the whole village, they took little persuasion to go the Manor House Inn until closing time so that those still with electricity could get to bed before it was switched off!

The Last Twenty Years

On 26th March 1980 the Chancellor of the Exchequer announced increases in indirect taxation: road tax was raised by £10 to £60 per year and 10p. added to the price of a gallon of petrol, taking it to £1.35 gallon (30p. litre). Twelve months later another 20p. was added to a gallon.

In June 1980 the Parochial Church Council decided that the oil-fired central heating boiler in the church had reached the point of being beyond economical repair. Gas heaters were purchased for use in the church and the oil tank drained and sold. However, the gas heaters do not appear to have been the wisest of purchases as six years later they were declared unsafe and the present electric heaters were installed. Also in June that year, Rev. Jones announced that he had been asked by the Bishop to move to Timsbury and he left the parish shortly afterwards. In May 1981 Rev. Barrie Newton became the new Rector, but he was only to remain for three years.

The playing field in Pig Lane was acquired in 1981. This is held on a 25 year lease from the University of Oxford, and although the District and Parish Councils make contributions, most of the running expenses are raised by the hard working Playing Field Committee, now under the Chairmanship of Stephen 'Steve' Hill with Mrs. Amanda Triggol as Secretary. Several times it has been planned to improve the facilities but, almost every time sufficient funds have been raised, vandalism has meant that money intended for improvements has had to be used for repairs to equipment.

Almost ten years to the day after the shooting of Mrs. Fry, violence returned to the village on 1st November 1981.

About 8.50 that evening, Cecil Cary, then aged 81, and his housekeeper, Miss Eileen Webber, aged 78, were at home at Manor Farm when two masked men kicked open the door and burst in. They struck Mr. Cary on the head with an iron bar, rendering him unconscious. He was then tied up and gagged with adhesive tape. Despite her arthritis, Miss Webber was pushed to the floor and similarly bound and gagged, after which their two assailants searched the house and stole £2,430 in cash from a bureau. Before leaving the house they ripped the telephone from the wall. When Mr. Cary recovered consciousness, he released himself and Miss Webber and then, with blood streaming from his head, staggered to the home of Derek and Eileen Growtage to raise the alarm. Mr. Cary and Miss Webber were conveyed to hospital where they recovered from their ordeal, but Miss Webber was so traumatised by the attack that she never returned to live in Chedzoy. An account of the attack appeared in the Western Daily Press after two men from the Sydenham area of Bridgwater appeared before Bristol Crown Court in April 1982 and were jailed for five years and three years respectively for robbery and causing grievous bodily harm.

December 1981 saw the coldest December day for 90 years. Shrewsbury recorded -23°C. and in Chedzoy it was -10°C. On 13th December as many families were looking forward to their Sunday lunch, the power failed at 1.08 p.m. It had not been restored later in the day when it began to snow heavily, so villagers had to hunt for candles and alternative forms of heating. In the centre of the village power was eventually restored at 2.25 p.m. the following day, but some houses were without electricity for three days and had to rely on their more fortunate neighbours with extension cables criss-crossing garden fences. On Sunday night gales added to the misery, causing some damage: Chedzoy Lane was blocked by fallen trees and Fowlers Plot by fallen electricity cables, so the only way out of the village was via Parchey. The same gales brought serious flooding at Burnham-on-Sea and large areas of the levels around Stolford were inundated.

Minus 10° temperatures and heavy snow returned to the village in the first week of 1982 with a foot (30 cm.) of snow; some houses had icicles up to six feet long hanging from the eaves. Fortunately this time there was very little wind, so the drifting which had caused so much trouble the previous month did not reoccur and electricity supplies were not interrupted.

However, temperatures remained below freezing for over a week, so it was some time before all the snow had melted. The school log book records,

> "Jan. 11th.: Bitter cold, snow frozen in playground. 16 children came. No dinners as so few children and schools at

work. All cold water pipes frozen. Plumbers unfroze the mains but they immediately refroze.

Jan. 12th.: The majority of children back today despite still deep snow. Children requested to bring sandwiches and hot drinks as the water system was completely frozen in the main school.

Jan. 13th.: School dinners served on paper plates as we have no water turned on. Freezing temperatures all day. Maximum temperature in schoolroom, 56° (13°C.)" - sub-tropical temperatures for the members of the School Board in 1890!

"Jan. 15th.: Temperature outside 20° (-7°C.). Roads and yard all gritted but no salt, terribly icy and slippery. The gas froze in the pipes so we had only lukewarm dinners. Mrs. Clapp's car skidded and crashed on the way to school. Dinner again eaten off paper plates as all waste pipes are frozen. County fears for the safety of the hut roof which has sunk 9 inches. Children evacuated to school room - again very cold - only 56°.

Jan. 18th.: School reopened after a slow thaw during the weekend. Messrs. Pollard began work on the roof of the hut. The floor was found to have moved also."

In November 1982 Mrs. Joyce Collard retired after eight years as a dining room supervisory assistant - a "dinner lady" - at the school. She was presented with a sandwich toaster and flowers and the children at the school gave a "This is Your Life" presentation in which one of the pupils, Angela Derry, described Mrs. Collard as having

> "White curly hair and blue eyes. She always wears smart clothes. She is understanding and kind but she had to be strict as well."

Many former pupils recall her with great affection.

In May 1984 the Rev. Roger Fry was appointed Rector and this heralded the start of yet another troubled period for the ministry in Chedzoy. Although he could be charming, Rev. Fry could also be abrasive and was soon upsetting his parishioners. The tone was set at his first Parochial Church Council (PCC) meeting on 29th May 1984. The minutes record that

> "Before the minutes were read, the Rector gave details of his proposals for the conduct of PCC meetings. They were as follows:
> (a) Meetings should begin promptly;
> (b) They should be reasonably short (not more than 2 hours):
> (c) All contributions should be made via the chair."

A reorganisation of parishes took place with effect from 1st March 1985 when the Church Commissioners established the new parish of "Westonzoyland with Chedzoy." This remains the present ecclesiastical parish (which should not be confused with the civil parish).

The tercentenary celebrations in 1985 for the Battle of Sedgemoor involved the village in a commemorative exhibition staged in the village hall by the school children and a flower festival in the church depicting the history of the village mounted by all the village organisations: the Parish Council, church, school, women's group, playing field association, youth club and drama group; cream teas were provided and there was a souvenir shop. The celebrations in Chedzoy culminated with the annual Flower Show.

The Sealed Knot staged a re-enactment of the battle on 6th July - 300 years to the day after the actual battle - but not on the original battlefield but in fields at Burdenham Farm on the far side of Westonzoyland airfield. Roderick Dixon drew a pictorial map of the village and this was placed in the churchyard: although only intended to last for one year, it was not until 1997 that it was removed as it had become badly discoloured through dampness and bright sunlight.

Another highlight of 1985 was the filming in June at Parchey Bridge of part of the BBC Television series, "The Monocled Mutineer," which involved several villagers as extras and many were interested spectators. For a few days the area became unrecognisable as it was transformed into a part of northern France. The railings of the modern bridge became "stone" to match the older bridge and the car park area became a British army barracks with the stern military warning ALL PASSES TO BE SHOWN. The "barracks" was complete with several stone and wooden buildings. Opposite the barracks entrance were various French advertisements as well as road signs for Etaples, 2 km. (towards Chedzoy) and Boulogne, 35 km. (towards Stawell).

On the other side of King's Sedgemoor Drain were two cottages which were complete with two rowing boats, a landing stage, dovecote, old fashioned mangle, washing out to dry and even a cobbled yard. Painting on the wall proclaimed that this belonged to M. CHERAMY. Of course, as soon as anyone walked behind any of these buildings, the illusion crumbled as they were simply facades: within days of the completion of filming there was no trace at all of this French village.

The 1980s saw major changes taking place in the village. Ten years earlier Court Farm had ceased to be a working farm, but during the 1980s both Frys Farm and Westfield Farm ceased operation: no longer would the cows cross Front Street twice a day in order to be milked. The farm buildings were converted into dwellings. Not too long afterwards Moggs Farm ceased operation and this was followed by Manor Farm and Sibleys Farm. During the last 25 years the number of working farms in the village has been reduced from eleven to five: the importance of milk to the village can be seen by the number of milk churn stands which still exist. The most prominent is at the junction of Manor Road and Front Street, but there are others at Meads Farm and Slape Farm on Chedzoy Lane, in Pig Lane behind Moggs Farm and a larger platform by the old milking parlour behind Sibleys Farm.

On Saturday, 28th September 1985 there was a major fire at Doltons Farm. In the inferno two hay sheds were destroyed as well as a tractor and trailer, the damage being estimated at £50,000. Despite investigations the cause was never established, but there were no suspicious circumstances. This event was recorded in the school log book.

> "A disastrous fire, which raged all night and necessitated the attendance of 6 fire engines, one from as far away as Yeovil, began in Mr. Les Heal's hay barn at Dolton's Farm at approx. 2.30 p.m. Two barns of hay, 1 cattle shed and fertiliser were destroyed. No person or livestock were injured, fortunately."

January 1987 again saw severe weather affecting Chedzoy and the details were recorded by Mrs. Clapp.

> "Jan. 12th.: Bawdrip Infants' bus from Chedzoy was very late - delayed by the exceptionally cold weather which caused waxing of the diesel fuel. Jan. 14th.: It snowed heavily nearly all day. Mrs. Robertson collected the bus children at 1.45 p.m. as the road conditions were hazardous. Jan. 15th.: It has stopped snowing - we have had about 6 inches. This has drifted in the night from the fields - roads tightly packed with snow in the morning, but passable with care. Parchey River is completely frozen over."

In June 1987 the whole community was shocked at the sudden death of one of its more popular young men: the accident was the leading story in the Bridgwater Mercury.

> "Bridegroom to be David Clapp, aged 21, was killed last week in an horrific farm accident at Chedzoy shortly before he was due to be married. David, a farm worker, of Ruggs Drove Farm, was crushed to death between a tractor and a hydraulic fertiliser tipper he was operating at Three Oaks Farm. He was to have been married at St. Andrew's church, Burnham-on-Sea to 21 year old Alison Skinner ... of Highbridge Road, Burnham-on-Sea. The accident happened when David was detaching a fertiliser spreader from a tractor inside a barn at Three Oaks Farm. It appears that he was operating the hydraulic release mechanism when the trailer trapped him against the back of the tractor."

An inquest was held in August and a verdict of "Accidental Death" was recorded.

Disaffection with the church, mainly caused through antagonism towards Rev. Fry, can be demonstrated by the drop in the number of persons recorded on the church electoral roll, again, not to be confused with the civil electoral roll. In 1920 it had stood at 180 persons, dropping to 159 by 1970. In 1979 it had been reduced to 41 but after the appointment of Rev. Fry it dropped to 26. Because of his insistence on becoming "Tower Captain," the bell ringers all resigned and the church bells were no longer rung. Apparently Rev. Fry would remain in the vestry until services started, and then leave during the closing hymn so that he did not have to speak personally to his congregation.

Matters came to a head at a PCC meeting held on 9th June 1987 at which Rev. Fry and eleven parishioners were present. The minutes record that

> "At the conclusion of the business on the Agenda, the Rector expressed his reluctance to allow matters to be raised under Any Other Business. He pointed out that Church Law stated that such matters must be notified to the Chairman or Secretary prior to the meeting."

One person present

> "Was however allowed to ask a question concerning the bellringing. Following protests from some members of the PCC, a very heated exchange took place between the Rector and the Churchwardens, after which the Rector left the meeting."

There is no mention of the meeting closing with the usual blessing.

For the remainder of the year other priests were found to conduct services in Chedzoy and two further PCC meetings were chaired by the Archdeacon. At a meeting held in November 1987 future pastoral arrangements were discussed.

> "The Archdeacon reported on the meeting held between himself, the Rural Dean and Deanery Lay Chairman and the Churchwardens, at which the Churchwardens had said that reconciliation between the Rector and PCC was unlikely. He said that he now wished to hear the views of the PCC and made the following points. (a) There would be no further cash available to pay temporary priests from the Diocesan Funds after 31st December 1987; (b) The Diocesan Pastoral Committee had decided that the parish of Chedzoy would remain part of the United Benefice of Westonzoyland with Chedzoy; (c) The Revd. Roger Fry would resume Pastoral Care of the Parish on 1st January 1988.
>
> "When invited to comment, the whole PCC, with the exception of the Secretary, declared their intention to resign when the Rector resumed pastoral care of the parish. Following a heated exchange between the Secretary and some member of the PCC the Archdeacon expressed his disappointment at the outcome of the consultation and closed the meeting with prayer."

True to their word, both churchwardens resigned on the last day of the year and at the next PCC meeting just four parishioners were present. By 1990 the number on the church electoral roll was at an all time low of just twelve persons. It seems that Rev. Fry had learned nothing from his experiences in Chedzoy as at one of the earliest PCC meetings in 1988 "The rector quoted from the booklet, Church Representation Rules, and said that all future meetings of the PCC would be conducted strictly by the rules set out in the booklet. He emphasised that all Questions, Statements and Comments were to be addressed to the Chair." This seems to have been rather pointless as at most of the PCC meetings only the Rector and his two new churchwardens, who also doubled as Secretary and Treasurer, were present!

The infamous "hurricane" which crossed southern England in

October 1987 caused great devastation generally, but only relatively minor damage in Chedzoy. Although they did not achieve the same notoriety, far greater local damage was caused by gales in December 1988 and during the winter of 1989/90. The school log book for 1988 records,

> "Dec. 19th.: After a severe gale last night, continuing this morning, the conical metal cover of the main ventilator of the schoolroom roof was found to have blown into the playground. Pollard's men came as soon as the wind abated to seal the vent against any rain. Mr. Burt called in the afternoon to inspect the work, and decided the best course would be to remove both vents, which no longer served any purpose and were badly rusted. Ridge tiles would be replaced at the same time."

On 24th December 1989 gales brought down tiles from many roofs in the village, completely wrecking that of Three Oaks Cottages at Fowlers Plot. Most of the damage had been repaired by the time gales returned in greater strength on 25th January 1990: gusts up to 104 m.p.h. were recorded on Dartmoor! This time the motorway was completely closed from Bristol to Taunton as so many commercial vehicles had been blown over. In the village many people lost tiles for a second time or suffered other minor damage. A huge poplar tree which stood in Manor Road was blown down and demolished most of the garage at the Manor House Inn: a second one was cut down the following day as it had been loosened on its roots and become unsafe. A branch fell through the roof at Manor Farm.

In 1990, following the death of Cecil Cary, Manor Farm was sold by the University of Oxford. However, in a generous act before the sale, the church was offered a strip of land 77 yards long and ten yards wide beside the north boundary of the churchyard. This land is to be used as an extension of the churchyard for future burials. For complex legal reasons the offer was declined and the land instead donated to the Parish Council and will be held by them until such time as any extension may be required. The footpath from the churchyard along the rear of the houses in Ward Lane was diverted to its present position about the same time: previously it had passed directly behind the houses until the residents purchased land from the University in order to provide gardens.

In January 1995, following the decision of the Somerset County Council Education Committee to close Chedzoy school, a reunion of former pupils governors, staff, parents and friends was held on the premises. Well over 300 people attended, including Mrs. Joan Morgan, nee Fry, who had been a pupil between 1920 and 1929 and Wilf Hutchings who had attended from 1921 to 1924, leaving at the age of 14 years. Friday, 10th February was the last day on which pupils attended the school, and it was with sadness that they left the premises at 3.30 p.m. However, there were still some tasks for the staff and the last few poignant entries made in the log book by Pauline Clapp sum up the general feeling of sadness.

> "Feb. 13th.: A week of packing, removing and cleaning the school site began for the staff. Feb. 15th.: The staff's final day with Mrs. Clapp as from now on they are needed at Bawdrip to help Mr. Bird prepare the new school for the children. It was a very sad moment as keys were handed in and final farewells were said.
> Feb. 17th.: Electricity, water turned off and the school finally closed up.
> Sunday, 26th Feb. 1995: The last day of Half-Term and the last official day in the existence of the school."

Thus over 150 years of education at the village school came to an end. The building and adjoining school house were sold and younger village children are now transported by coach to the new Kingsmoor School at Bawdrip.

In September 1995 the Rev. Peter Richmond became incumbent of the parish and set about re-establishing the status of the church in the village after the difficulties caused by some of his predecessors.

In February 1998 a public meeting was held in the village hall to discuss the manner in which the new millennium should be commemorated in the village. The general consensus was that a fitting memorial would be the refurbishment of and improvements to the village hall. A group called "Chedzoy 2000" was established to co-ordinate the necessary fund raising and other activities. Andrew Denning was elected as Chairman and Mrs. Maureen Weeks as Secretary. Plans which had previously been drawn up by Geoff Dickens in 1995 were re-drawn by him to take into account changes in Regulations and in April 1999 planning permission was granted by Sedgemoor District Council and applications have been submitted for grants towards the work. Continuing their long assocaition with the village, the University of Oxford has made a donation towards the building fund. All proceeds from this book will go towards the improvement fund.

For many years there have been reports of "panthers" having been sighted throughout the Southwest of England. Chedzoy has not been immune to such reports. In July 1998 Roger and Mandy Sutton of West End Farm discovered four clear paw prints in damp soil on their land. They measured 5 inches (125 mm.) across and were made by a cat-like animal with a stride of at least 30 inches (750 mm.): so far there have been no actual sightings of the creature itself.

As the 20th Century draws to an end the population of the parish has grown to 473, with a further 74 people living in the "greater village" area. Modern residents were born in many parts of the country, indeed in several different countries, and their jobs are far more varied than could have been envisaged at the time of the 1891 Census. Details of the current residents are recorded in Appendix 2.

Chedzoy, in 1999, looks forward to the 21st Century, but wears its past with pride. Look around you and enjoy the stories about individual properties which follow in the village guide.

Chedzoy - A Somerset Village

Village Guide - Chedzoy Lane

A complete walk around the village will take between three and four hours. As the majority of visitors arrive in the village by car from the A39, this seems to be a suitable starting point.

Turn into **Chedzoy Lane** from **Bath Road**. The original junction is now buried under the abutments of the motorway bridge but at one time appears to have been quite dangerous. In August 1931 it was reported in the Bridgwater Mercury that at a meeting of Bridgwater Rural District Council

> "Rev. G.R. Mullens stated that he had been asked by several people to bring to the notice of the Council the bend at the end of Chedzoy Lane where it came out on the main Bath Road. With the fast traffic passing on the main road one had to crawl out from the lane at a snail's pace, and there had been one or two cases of accidents there. The fault was through the hedges being too high. What was wanted was to improve the visibility, and the best thing would be to cut the hedges down altogether and put up a wire fence, but that, perhaps, would be a large order, and he suggested that something might be done if only by cutting down the hedges to make the view better."

As is so often the case, a serious accident had to occur before any improvements were made. In July 1932, just under a year after Rev. Mullens' request, it was reported that

> "A collision between a governess car and a motor car occurred in Bath Rod, and resulted in serious injury to Mr. William Cary, of Chedzoy, well known as an agriculturist. Mr. Cary, who was driving the governess car, came out of Chedzoy Lane with the object of proceeding towards Bawdrip. At the same time a motor car came along from the direction of Bawdrip. A collision occurred. Mr. Cary was thrown out of the trap, and received a compound fracture of the leg. The Bridgwater motor ambulance was sent for and Mr. Cary was conveyed to Bridgwater Hospital. The horse drawing the governess car was uninjured, and the vehicle little damaged, but some damage was done to the motor car, neither of the occupants receiving injury."

Speaking in 1999 Norman Fry recalled the accident and that throughout his stay in hospital Bill Cary insisted on wearing his bowler hat - even when he was in bed!

At a meeting of Bridgwater Rural District Council the following month it was reported that in relation to that corner

> "The Surveyor recommended that an open fence be erected on both corners for a distance of thirty yards each way and he estimated the cost to be £24 if any help could be forthcoming from local people in hauling away any surplus soil. The Council agreed that the work should be carried out as suggested."

The work was completed at the estimated cost and Rev. Mullens told the Council that the task

> "had been carried out very satisfactorily and was a vast improvement."

What would Rev. Mullens have thought of the junction in its present form?

Having descended the motorway abutments, visitors will notice that the first part of the lane is unusually wide. The 1904 Ordnance Survey map shows several properties here: at least five on the left and groups of four and five on the right just before the former Hunter's Lodge Inn. There were two more properties adjoining the former inn and yet another stood in what is now the road, roughly outside the farm buildings on the left. The map does not indicate what type of buildings they were.

Properties around this location were the subject of a sale which took place in April 1881 at the Crown Inn, Chedzoy. Described as being located in Chedzoy Lane they were offered as

> "All those substantially built cottages with the gardens, cart house, stable and other outbuildings now in the respective occupations of George Bell, William Parsons, Joseph Stone, James Andrews and Fanny Bell. The above property is in good repair and well tenanted, and will be sold for the residue of a long absolute term of 5,000 years created in the year 1812."

The original builder certainly had faith in their construction! What would appear to be the adjoining cottages were auctioned, this time at the Hunter's Lodge Inn, in March 1885, when they were described as

> "two tenements occupied as four dwellings on the south side of Chedzoy-lane occupied by James Andrews, James Andrews, jun., Charles Sparks and George Bell."

Another sale took place at the Crossed Rifles Inn, Bridgwater in February 1892 of

"All those two substantially built cottages situated adjoining Chedzoy-lane together with the large gardens, stables, potato house, cart shed, furnace house and premises and belonging to one now in occupation of John Andrews and the other void. The premises are in an excellent state of repair. There is a capital well of water, and the annual rental amounts to £8 10s. The property will be sold for the remainder of a term of 5,000 years commencing on the 1st July 1836 at a pepper corn rent."

No reports of any of these sales were publishted.

At one time some residents of these cottages were regularly in trouble. In 1878 William Dowden was 40 years old and living in one of them. This amusing report was published in the Bridgwater Mercury in July that year.

"William Dowden, mason, of Chedzoy, was summoned for being drunk and disorderly in the Bath-road [Bridgwater]. - P.C. Porter said he saw the defendant at the top of Union-street about quarter past eleven at night. He was drunk, and made use of a lot of abusive language. Several persons looked out of their windows and complained of his conduct. Witness threatened to lock him up, but some friends promised to take him home. - Defendant said the policemen (two of them) were in private clothes. He (defendant) was talking to his wife and some other relations when P.C. Porter came up to him and said, 'If you don't got home I'll beat your ----- brains out,' at the same time catching him hold roughly by the collar. Defendant added: I have been a teetotaller for more than a month.

The Clerk: Do you mean seriously to say that you had drank nothing that day?

Defendant: Well, I had something then.

The Clerk: It is the old story, I see.

P.C. Wilkins gave corroborative evidence, denying the allegation of the defendant, and adding that the latter exclaimed, 'Go home and put on your —- buttons.'

Defendant: He said he would give me a black eye. I am innocent as a baby just come from his mother - (laughter) - and the policemen were both 'tight.'

Defendant called Thomas Maddocks, bootmaker, living in Wellington-road, who said the defendant was neither drunk nor disorderly, and did not make use of any foul expressions.

Superintendent Lear: The fact is that the witness was himself too far gone to know what took place.

The Clerk: Then he ought to have been up, too.

Superintendent Lear: He was very quiet, and I was not aware of it until this morning.

The Clerk (to defendant): If your statement is untrue it very much aggravates the case, and you ought to have four times the punishment. ... The Bench would mark their displeasure of the defendant's conduct by fining him 10s. and costs, in all £1 3s. 3d."

There were also problems amongst the residents. In June 1880 it was reported that

"George Bell (27) of Chedzoy-lane, Bridgwater was charged with assaulting his wife, Ellen Bell (27) at Chedzoy-lane. - Complainant stated that she locked her house up and took the children to a neighbour's while she came into Bridgwater. The defendant was not able to get into the house, and as soon as she came home and went into it her husband, without the least provocation or saying a word, knocked her down and beat her severely. She ran out into the road, and he knocked her down again. - She called a young man named Walter Dowden, who stated that he saw defendant come out into the road with his wife quarrelling and because she would not come into the house, he knocked her under the ear, and she fell into a dry ditch near. Defendant picked her up again, and she ran in the house. - The defendant stated that he did not strike his wife, but simply pushed her indoors. He had repeatedly spoken to her with regard to going away and leaving the children in the care of a neighbour named Bird, as he did not think it was a fit place. When he told his wife about this she became abusive, threatened him, and took up a poker for him. - Amelia Dowden (13), called as a witness by the complainant, said she saw Bell and his wife quarrelling, but did not see Bell strike her. She had never heard Bell tell his wife she was not to let the children go to Bird's. - The case was dismissed."

This case was clearly not forgotten by the Dowdens as only two months later this report was published.

"A TRUMPERY (i.e. worthless) CASE. Ellen Bell, a married woman, was charged with using threats towards William Jasper Dowden, a stone-mason, in Chedzoy-lane. - Complainant stated that on the day in question he was passing the defendant's house, when she came out, and, making use of bad language, said she would put some poison in the pump and poison his whole family. He had had no quarrel with defendant, although his wife had, and he went in fear of the defendant who he was afraid would carry out the threat she had made. - In cross-examination witness added that the pump was used by both parties. The water was not good, and neither of them used it much. The reason witness had allowed nearly a month to elapse before taking out this summons was that he was afraid his wife and family were in danger as he was out of town to work, and only came home on Saturdays after the office shut. He took out the summons against the defendant after a quarrel between defendant and his daughter. - The Bench would not hear any further evidence as they thought the case was a trumpery one, and it was therefore dismissed."

Another resident was in the news in November 1881.

"Joseph Stone (40), labourer, of Chedzoy, was charged on remand with unlawfully and maliciously wounding Herbert Hann, wheelwright. Herbert Hann, the complainant, living at Knowle, stated that he was in Mr. Clothier's cider-house at Coxpit Farm. He was sitting down after dinner talking to a man named Lee, about the wages they were paid, and defendant struck him twice from behind with his dinner-basket. He had not said anything to defendant, who was standing behind him, and knocked him over the left ear. The basket was an ordinary rush basket. The blow paralysed him and he could not speak. ... John Lee, labourer, in the employ of Mr. Clothier stated ... Stone threw his dinner-basket, which he had fastened round his hand with a piece of string, at Hann, and struck him on the head. ... P.C. Hawkins stated that he apprehended the defendant at his house in Chedzoy-lane and locked him up. After the defendant had been remanded, and whilst witness was taking him to the police court, he said, 'I shall tell the truth. After I knocked Hann I opened the bag, and there was a big nail in it, but I did not think of it at the time.' ... The Chairman said that believing it was a thoughtless act on the part of the defendant, and that the injury inflicted was unintentional, they had suggested that the defendant should make the injured man some compensation and defendant agreed to pay him £1 now and £1 more in a month."

A few months later in May 1882 a familiar face appeared before the court.

"George Bell, of Chedzoy-lane, was charged with assaulting William Towler. - Defendant pleaded guilty. - The complainant said the assault complained of was a very dastardly and unprovoked one and was committed by the defendant entirely through trade jealousy. Some years ago Mr. Towler carried on the business of a coal merchant, but through unforeseen circumstances had to give up for a time. During the interval Bell started a similar business. By-and-by Mr. Towler resumed his business and it seemed that this provoked Bell's jealousy. On the day in question Bell asked Towler what business he had to lower his coal, and Towler replied that Bell lowered the price of it first. Bell then used some filthy expressions, and afterwards knocked Towler down, and bruised and battered his face very badly. Towler knew nothing of 'the noble art' and could not therefore defend himself. The fact was that Bell, not being able to compete in the regular way of business, wanted to punish Towler physically. - Defendant was fined £1 and costs, 12s."

Two weeks later another neighbour was in court!

"John Andrews (28) was charged with assaulting Amelia Bird (46) in Chedzoy-lane. Complainant, wife of Jeremiah Bird, said she fetched her husband home from a public house. She and her husband quarrelled and fought after returning home, and defendant ran into the house and interfered with them, and struck her, saying if she wanted to hit anyone, she must hit him. Her daughter took up a poker to defend her with, and defendant took it away. - Lucy Bird, daughter of the complainant, gave corroborative evidence. - Defendant said he saw Mrs. Bird holding the tongs over her husband who was on the floor bleeding and crying 'murder,' and he simply ran in and took the tongs from her. - Mary Ann Merrett (35 years [1847-1939], who lived in the cottage now known as Glencairn) and Joseph Stone (41), neighbours, gave partially corroborative evidence, and the case was dismissed.

"Sarah Bird (17), daughter of the complainant in the last case, was summoned for assaulting Elizabeth Parsons (29) at the same time and place. - Complainant, a married woman, said she was attracted to Mrs. Bird's house by cries of 'murder' and on getting there defendant ran out and struck her without receiving any provocation. She only called upon a neighbour to come out of the house. - Mary Ann Merritt (sic) and Harriet Andrews corroborated. - Defendant denied alleged assault, and called Lucy Bird, her sister, who also asserted that complainant was not assaulted. - Defendant was fined 1s. (5p.) and costs."

John Andrews was in court again next month

"John Andrews, jun., of Chedzoy-lane, near Bridgwater, was summoned for carrying a gun without a licence. Mr. Cottier of Excise called P.C. Hawkins who said that on the day named he saw the defendant fire off a gun in a field near Chedzoy-lane. When defendant saw witness he ran away. - Witness asked for his licence and defendant said he had none. - By the Bench: He fired at rook. Defendant was a notorious poacher. The Bench imposed a penalty of £1 and costs."

The Bird family was back in the news in July 1885.

"Lucy Bird (Moorlinch) and Sarah Bird (Chedzoy-lane), sisters, were charged with being drunk and disorderly in Monmouth-street, [Bridgwater]. P.C. Bailey said between seven and eight o'clock he saw the defendants in Monmouth-street very drunk. They were cursing each other and caused a great disturbance. Sarah Bird refused to give her name. Sarah Bird was fined 5s. (25p.) and costs and Lucy Bird 2s. 6d. and costs, in default, seven days."

The subject of this report from November 1885 was Thomas Merrett (1838-1921) who was then 47 years old and living at Glencairn.

"Thomas Meriott, labourer, Chedzoy-lane, was charged with being drunk. - P.C. Fish said about half past one on Thursday morning he was on duty on the riverside [Bridgwater] and saw the defendant 'stuck in the slime.' He went to the defendant's assistance and pulled him on top of the embankment as well as he was able. Defendant had evidently been in the water and was 'shaking tremendously.' - The Mayor: Had he fallen over the quay? - Witness: I don't know how he got in, but it was a miracle he was not drowned. - Defendant said he was drunk on the occasion, but he was not 'given to it.' He was very sorry. - Superintendent Lear, in reply to the Bench, said the defendant, who had a wife and ten children, had received £10 on the previous day and the money was found upon him. - Defendant was fined 2s. 6d. and costs, or seven days, the Mayor remarking that he must consider himself very fortunate that the policeman came to his assistance at the time he did, or he would in all probability have been drowned."

Other members of the Bird and Merrett families appeared before the magistrates in May 1886.

"Fredk. Andrews (14), George Bird (16), James Stone (14), Arthur Merriot (sic) (15) and John Andrews (15), all of Chedzoy-lane, were charged with maliciously breaking a fence belonging to Mr. Wm. King, farmer, and doing damage to the amount of 1s. 3d. (6p.). - Mr. King said he had brought forward the case as an example and warning to others. His fence had been continually broken, and damage was done to the land. The defendants were fined 6d. each and costs; in default seven days."

Another dispute between these troublesome neighbours took place in July 1886.

"Harriet Andrews (35), of Chedzoy-lane, was charged with assaulting Elizabeth Parsons (33), also of Chedzoy-lane. Elizabeth Parsons said on the day in question, whilst she went to draw a couple of buckets of water, the defendant had been to her house beating her children, and saying they had beaten hers. When she came in and said, 'It is a pity people can not keep their children in their own house,' she (defendant) at once challenged her to fight, and because witness would not do so, defendant threw a knife at her, and it struck her. She (complainant) said she would bring her 'before her betters,' and defendant said she would give her the money to do so. - William Parsons (12), son of the complainant, gave corroborative evidence. - Jane Dowden (42), wife of William Dowden, mason of Chedzoy-lane, said Mrs. Parsons was abusing the children, and said she would twist their necks because they had beaten hers. - The case was dismissed."

In August 1882 another resident from somewhere in this area appeared before the Magistrates.

"Benjamin Reddick, of Chedzoy-lane, was summoned to show cause why he should not contribute towards the maintenance of his mother, Anna Reddick. Mr. Roberts, relieving officer, said the defendant's mother was 75 years of age and unable to do anything. She was chargeable to the Union (Poor House) to the extent of 2s. 6d. weekly. - An order was made for the defendant to pay 1s. weekly and half the costs." However, it seems he did not pay as two months later, "Benjamin Reddick, carter, in the employ of Mr. R. Harden of Bower, was summoned for non-payment of arrears due from him in respect of his mother's maintenance. Mr. Roberts, relieving officer, said the defendant was in receipt of 12s. (60p.) per week. - Defendant pleaded inability and said his wife was subject to fits. - The Bench made no order."

One of Mary Merrett's sons appeared before the court in May 1890.

"Henry Mettiott (22), labourer, Chedzoy, was charged with assaulting Henry Wilkins of the same place. ... Complainant stated that on the day in question he was in Bridgwater when the defendant came up and said, 'Stand a quart of beer.' Complainant said he was not going to stand any more that night, whereupon defendant up with his fist and knocked him in the mouth. The blow caused his nose to bleed. - Mr. Chapman, for the defendant, stated that his client was the worse for drink on the day in question, and whilst in the company of the complainant, with whom he was on very good terms, it appeared to take the upper hand of him. He knew the complainant did not wish to press the case, and the defendant, through him, expressed his regret at having committed the offence. - P.C. Hutchings stated that the complainant was not as sharp as some men, and was consequently taken advantage of. - Defendant was fined 5s. and costs."

Another resident from this vicinity appeared before Bridgwater County Court three times in March and April 1883.

"HENRY HOOK v. THOMAS PARSONS. Plaintiff, a confectioner, of Eastover, Bridgwater claimed of the defendant, a haulier of Chedzoy, 8s. 6d. for damages sustained through the end of a timber-waggon, belonging to the defendant, being pushed against his shop window. - Defendant's wife appeared and denied that her husband had a timber-waggon, saying that it belonged to her son. - The case was adjourned to enable the plaintiff to prove that the driver of the waggon was in the defendant's employ." At the next court, "... Mr. Chapman said the only question left open for consideration was that of ownership, the defence set up at the last court being that the dray was the property of the defendant's son. He called Mr. Wm. Brewer in the employ of Mr. G.B. Sully, who stated that the defendant had often been employed to haul timber with the waggon in question and that Mrs. Parsons, defendant's wife, had been paid for it. - Mrs. Parsons now said that her husband was not near the place at the time of the occurrence and that it was purely accidental. - Judgement given for the plaintiff."

A second case was heard against him in April:

"JAMES REED v. THOMAS PARSONS. Plaintiff, a joiner, of Chedzoy-lane, claimed £2 10s. balance of purchase money on the sale of apples and grass. - Plaintiff alleged that in October last he saw the defendant who, after going through his (plaintiff's) orchard in company with his wife, agreed to give £4 10s. for the apples there and after his grass. Two instalments of £1 cash were afterwards paid on account, but he (plaintiff) had been unable to get the remainder, though payment had been promised from time to time. In cross-examination plaintiff denied that he told defendant there were five or six bags of apples in the orchard. He valued the grass at £2 and the apples at £2 10s. - Reginald Reed, son of the plaintiff, proved receiving one of the instalments and a promise being given to pay the balance. - For the defence it was alleged that the plaintiff said he would warrant there were six bags of apples at least in the orchard, and that the plaintiff was relying on such warrant, whereas it turned out that only a bag and a half of apples could be gathered there. Defendant had paid £2 into Court for the grass, and £1 for the apples, considering that to be their full value. It was admitted that the defendant and his wife went to the orchard before the bargain was entered into, and plaintiff denied having given the alleged warranty. - His Honour thought the defendant had been negligent in his own interest in this matter, having an opportunity to judge for himself what quantity of apples were in the orchard and gave judgement for the amount claimed."

It was not only residents, but also people passing along the lane, who found themselves in trouble with the magistrates.

"EXTRAORDINARY ASSAULT CASE" was the headline in the Bridgwater Mercury in July 1884. "William Stone, labourer, of Chedzoy was charged with assaulting Henry Gant, described as a turf-merchant, of Ashcott, at Chedzoy. John Stone, labourer, of Chedzoy, and father of the last defendant, was charged with aiding and abetting his son in assaulting Henry Gant at the same time and place." William and John Stone lived in Front Street, somewhere near the church. "Mr. Gooding appeared for the complainant and Mr. P.O.H. Reed for the defendants. - Mr. Gooding, having opened the case for the prosecution, called the complainant who said on the day in question he and a hawker named Albert Gillingham, of Bridport, Dorset, were riding in a waggon belonging to and driven by Mr. Thomas Chapman, a carrier, from Taunton to Ashcott. In the morning he left Taunton ... and [in the evening] when near Bath-bridge the two defendants and some others in a trap passed them. They passed the defendants again a little way from Bath-bridge. When near Chedzoy-lane the defendants called out to them and challenged to fight them. There were five persons altogether (including the defendants) in the defendant's trap. ... Witness jumped out of the waggon before Mr. Chapman pulled up, and asked defendants, 'What do you mean, which of you?' At the same time the defendant, William Stone, struck him across the head with a stick, and he fell to the ground. He had a cut on his head now. He jumped up and ran, got over some railings, and into a garden followed by the defendants, who again assaulted him in a most savage manner. They struck him with their fists and sticks, and the defendant, William Stone, said, 'I will kill the —-, and throw him down the well.' ... He said to the defendant, William Stone, 'Don't kill me or throw me down the well.' He afterwards managed to get up again and ran back to the waggon, followed by the defendants, and while he was getting up into the waggon they took hold of his coat, and in trying to pull him down they tore his coat (produced) right off. ... Mr. Chapman chose to go through Chedzoy as it was a more level road. Cross-examined by Mr. Reed: He did not say, 'I will fight any of the Chedzoy men,' or words to that effect.

"Thomas Chapman, carrier, of Ashcott, partially corroborated the complainant's evidence, and added that when the defendants challenged to fight them he heard the defendant, William Stone, say, 'I'll fight the —- best man in the cart.' Gant at that time was going to jump out, but he said to him, 'Stay a minute, Gant, I know they people before today.' Gant afterwards got out. When Gant was in the garden lying down, and the defendant attacking him, he was crying out 'murder.'

"Albert Gillingham, hawker, of Bridport, gave corroborative evidence, and added that whilst Gant was lying on the ground he heard the defendant, William Stone, say, 'I will kill the —-.' After imploring the defendants not to murder him they came back, and William Stone attacked him and threw him into a ditch, where he remained for three-quarters of an hour up to his waist in mud. Some neighbours came along and helped him out. Amelia Bird, living in Chedzoy-lane, said on the night in question some one got over the stile and into her garden. She got out of bed with her husband, and saw a man knocking Gant, who cried to him not to throw him into the well, and not to murder him. Another man came up and knocked Gant three times, and made the blood flow. The garden the next morning was blood all over. ...

"For the defence, William Bennett, labourer, of Chedzoy, said on the day in question he had been sheep-shearing with the defendants and another man. They were returning home about half past ten, when a cart passed them, and one of the inmates said, 'Come on you —- monkeys.' They drove on to the lane, and the other cart followed them. Gant then got out, and came up with his coat off and sleeves turned up, and said, 'Now you're on your own ground, and I'll fight the best man in the cart, or the best man in Chedzoy.' ... Cross-examined by Mr. Gooding: He might have drank a gallon of cider that day, but he did not have too much. ... George Bell, living in Chedzoy-lane, said on the night in question he saw the two horses and carts referred to. The parties were all talking together, and Gant had his coat off and sleeves turned up. He saw no fighting, as it was all over. - The Chairman said the defendants would be fined 10s. each and costs, making £1 4s. each, or a month's imprisonment, with hard labour."

This certainly was an area which kept the Justices busy. In June 1885,

"George Bell (32), living in Chedzoy-lane, Bridgwater was charged with assaulting Eliza Dowden, wife of John Dowden, mason. Complainant, an elderly woman, said on Tueday morning she went to the defendant's house in company with Mrs. Andrews, and asked him why he had given her such an infamous character. Defendant replied that the could prove she was one of the guilty parties in trying to prove an abortion, referring to his (defendant's) wife. The wife was present, and she (complainant) addressing her, asked, 'Did you ever tell your husband that I gave you a bottle of medicine?' and Mrs. Bell replied, 'Never.' Defendant turned to the wife and exclaimed, 'You —-, will you say that?' and Mrs. Bell replied,. 'Yes, I never said it.' Defendant struck his wife with his fist, and then turned round on her (complainant) and, after exclaiming, 'Go, you old —-,' took her by the shoulders and slung her round towards the path. There was a cart outside, and to prevent her being thrown against that she caught hold of the wall, and so injured her right arm that it had since been rendered useless, and Dr. Kimmis had told her that the cords of the arm were very badly sprained.

She was a tailoress by trade and could not now do her work. She was 69 years of age.

"Mr. Reed, for the defence, alleged that the complainant had come to the defendant's house at half past six in the morning, and after some conversation with the wife, said to the defendant, 'Now I know who is the liar, you are the one, you dirty beastly fellow.' - Mr. Bell denied having struck her, but he said he simply used sufficient force, by gently placing his hands on her shoulders, to put her outside. She returned a second time and was very abusive and the defendant was obliged a second time to put her out. - Mr. Reed called Hannah Ruddock (sic), who said she heard the complainant call the defendant more than once a dirty scamp, adding, 'I see who is the liar now.' - She saw complainant fall against the cart. - Mrs. Parsons, wife of William Parsons, labourer, called by Mr. Chapman, said she heard the last witness say she didn't see what took place, as she was not looking. - The Bench fined defendant 15s. and costs, the Chairman remarking that no honest woman would be otherwise than very indignant at such a charge being preferred against her. - Defendant: I had grounds for making it. - Mr. Chapman said the police had made inquiries and there was no foundation for the charge, except in the defendant's own mind. - Mr. Reed replied that the subsequent investigation would show that the husband was perfectly justified in the course he took. - When told he had to pay £1 6s., defendant said he would rather go to gaol, adding, 'I should like to have twelve months there very well: I shouldn't be worse off than I am now.' - The money was subsequently paid."

In September 1890 George Keirle, a 61 year old labourer, who lived somewhere in this vicinity

"was charged with stealing a hammer, value 5s., the property of Messrs. Cuthill, Son and de Lunge, contractors for the Bridgwater railway. ... P.C. Carter, stationed at Bawdrip, stated that he found the hammer produced at the prisoner's house. Prisoner was there when he found it. ... The Bridgwater railway had recently been constructed across the Bath-road. ... In reply to the charge prisoner pleaded not guilty, and, in defence, stated that he picked the hammer up between Merry's house and Chedzoy-lane in the evening when he was coming from Bridgwater. - After a short deliberation the Bench sentenced prisoner to three weeks' hard labour in Shepton Mallett gaol."

The house on your left which juts into the road about 200 yards from the junction with Bath Road was once an inn known as **HUNTER'S LODGE**. The 1891 Census and press reports show the name as **Hunter's Inn**, which seems to have been an alternative name. Although the property is not specifically identified, it may be that the following County Police Court case, reported in the Bridgwater Mercury in April 1860, took place at the property.

"Mary Giles, of Chedzoy-lane, summoned her brother-in-law, Frederick Giles, for assaulting her. The complainant deposed that the defendant keeps a cider-shop, and to that shop she went on the night of Saturday last to fetch her husband away, in order that he might not spend in drink what he should bring home for his family. As soon as she asked her husband to come away, the defendant ordered her out of the house, and struck her on the mouth. She protested that she would not go without her husband, and the defendant then took her by the hair and pushed her outside the door, knocking her down. Elizabeth Bell stated that she lived near the defendant, and on the evening of Saturday ran out of doors because she heard cries of 'murder.' She saw complainant's husband lifting her from the ground. Mrs. Giles hair was all down her back and her clothes were torn. Mr. R. Smith, who appeared for the defence, urged that the woman behaved violently and uproariously in the house and was put out without unnecessary violence. If the house of the defendant was used as a cider-shop, the sooner it was put down the better, for such places were pests, wherever they were. He called John Stone to state that the complainant made a great disturbance, and was pushed out by her husband and the defendant. She was not struck. - The magistrates considered that the complainant was justified in going to the defendant's house to induce her husband to go home. Defendant had acted in an unmanly way, and must be fined 5s. and 7s. costs, or 14 days hard labour in default of payment."

In 1871 the licensee was James Reed, and his widow was still resident in 1891. Being the only "large" building in the locality it was used for important events and featured in May 1876 under the heading SINGULAR DEATH.

"An inquest was held at Hunter's Inn, Chedzoy-lane, before Mr. W.W. Munckton, coroner, on the body of Baniah Sparks, one month, the child of Albion Sparks, a labourer. - Lucy Bird said: I am 14 years of age, the daughter of Jeremiah Bird, a labourer, and I live in Chedzoy-lane. On Monday, the 24th April, Mary Sparks, mother of the deceased, came to our house and asked me to look after the child as she was going washing for Mr. Harding. She left it with me about half past twelve o'clock in the day. I was going to Mr. Dowden's for some bread and took the child in a perambulator. When I was near the Hunter's Inn I stopped to speak to Mr. Reed's child, and as I was about to move on the perambulator turned over and the child fell out on his head. I picked him up, put him into the perambulator, and went for the bread. The child did not seem much hurt. I wheeled him home, and left him in the perambulator by the fire. I thought he was asleep. My mother was not at home. About twenty minutes to one o'clock my mother came home and took the child from the perambulator. It was then dead. - Mr. H.B. Hurman deposed: I am a surgeon, and reside in Bridgwater. On Monday afternoon I was sent for and went to Jeremiah Bird's house. I found the deceased child in a perambulator quite dead. I examined it carefully, and came to the conclusion that it had died from concussion and compression of the brain. Having heard the evidence of Lucy Bird I am of the opinion that the injuries were caused by the child falling from the perambulator. - The jury returned a verdict in accordance with the evidence."

An inquest report mentioning all three licensed premises in Chedzoy was published in February 1883.

"An inquest was held at the Crown Inn by the district coroner (Mr. W.W. Munckton) on the body of Charles Giles, a farm labourer, who died suddenly in the road on the previous Monday. It appeared that on that day the deceased went into the Hunter's Inn in Chedzoy-lane, and had a pint of ale. Shortly after leaving the house and whilst walking along the lane, he was observed to stagger and fall. A man named Joseph Stone, a labourer working for Mr. Clothier, assisted him to rise and afterwards placed him against the hedge whilst he went to fetch some water. Mrs. [Eliza] Butler (25), wife of Thomas Butler of the Manor House Inn, Chedzoy, also went to the assistance of the deceased, but he died almost immediately. The body was afterwards seen by Dr. Kemmis of Bridgwater who, at the inquest, expressed the opinion that death resulted from heart disease, and a verdict to that effect was returned."

By 1894 Frederick Jesse Parsons (1858-1943) was living at the inn. The Bridgwater Mercury in August that year reported another inquest.

"On Tuesday last Mr. T. Barham, District Coroner, held an inquest at the Hunter's Lodge Inn, Chedzoy-lane on the body of Lucy Maud Rudick (sic), aged 1 year, 9 months, daughter of a labourer, who was found drowned in a ditch in Chedzoy-lane." Her parents were Benjamin and Lucy Reddick. "Emily Andrews (31), widow of Chedzoy-lane, deposed that the body viewed by the jury was that of her niece. On Sunday last she took the deceased out for a walk, returning about six o'clock. The child went out to play with her own children in the road. In about ten minutes she heard her children asking for deceased as they could not find her. Witness went out and asked her sister, Mrs. Parsons, if she had seen her. Her husband came out and they all went to look for the deceased and found her in a ditch opposite witness's house. Mr. Parsons took her out, and they found that she was quite dead. The children said they had not seen her fall in the ditch and did not know where she was. Jesse Parsons, landlord of the Hunter's Lodge, proved finding the body in the ditch at 6.45 p.m. on Sunday. She was head downwards. He took her out and found that she was quite dead. Witness thought that deceased, whilst playing, must have fallen head first into the water and have been strangled. He held her up but very little water came from her mouth. She was tied up in a shawl so that her arms were not free. The water was about four feet six inches deep at the place he found her. The Coroner having summed up, the jury returned a verdict of 'Accidentally drowned'."

In August 1907 Theodore Dowden of Bailey Street, Bridgwater appeared before the County Magistrates' Court

"charged with having been drunk and disorderly at the Hunter's Lodge Inn and refusing to quit. He was also charged with breaking the glass of a window. Dowden asked for one pint of beer and tendered $2^1/_2$ d (1p.). Frederick Fry, the landlord, told him the price was three pence and the defendant, after giving him the halfpenny, used disgusting language to Fry, threatening him and put himself in a fighting attitude. Dowden was ejected and ten minutes later he smashed the window. Fined 10s. and costs on each charge."

This seems to suggest that Frederick Fry was a temporary licensee, or had Jesse Parsons moved by January 1914 when the Bridgwater Mercury published this report?

"THEFT OF NAILS IN CHEDZOY LANE. William Caple of Taunton was charged with having stolen a pound of nails, value two pence, the property of Frederick Jesse Parsons, dairyman, of Chedzoy Lane. He was erecting some fencing on his premises and adjoining the road. He went indoors and remained about five minutes. Whilst in the house the prisoner came to the door, selling boot laces and oranges. Witness declined to buy, and on going back to the fencing he missed a packet of nails, which had been left near the fence. P.C. Williams saw the prisoner just over Bath Bridge. Witness said to him, 'I want those nails you have stolen out in Chedzoy Lane.' Prisoner handed the packet of nails to witness, remarking, 'I picked them up in the road. I was just going to hand them over to the police in here.' Superintendent Williams said there were only two previous convictions against prisoner. The Bench decided to bind the prisoner over under the Probation of Offenders Act for a period of six months."

Later in 1914 Frederick Porter was the licensee, indeed for a while, the property was known as Porter's Lodge. Mr. Porter died in May 1930 and two months later the licence was transferred to his wife, Eliza. The skittle alley wall can still be seen shielding the garden from view. Apparently this was an excellent alley, but patrons were not permitted to use it on a Sunday. The premises were last used as a public house in February 1952 as the licence was not renewed at the annual licensing session.

A tragic case was reported in the Bridgwater Mercury in December 1877, and although the actual location was not given, it would appear to have been between the inn and Church Acre.

"Ann Cousins, wife of William Cousins, a labourer living in Chedzoy-lane, near Bridgwater, was brought up in custody, charged with having assaulted Mary Cousins, her step-daughter, a young woman 28 years of age, and an imbecile. P.C. Charles Hawkins deposed as follows: I was on duty in Chedzoy-lane on Saturday night between nine and ten o'clock. I had my attention called to the defendant beating her daughter-in law (sic) by Mr. Robert Boon and Mrs. Ann Clarke. Mr. Boon and me went down in front of the prisoner's house. We both heard distinctly several blows, and then I went and tried the door. The husband, who was drunk inside, unlocked the door. I walked in, and went upstairs, where I heard the blows proceeding from. I saw the young woman on the bed uncovered. The prisoner had hold of her by the head; I can't say by the hair, and she was thumping her daughter-in-law on the head with her other hand as hard as she could drive. She exclaimed, 'If you make a noise I'll have a knife to you and rip your —- guts out.' I then arrested prisoner and took her to Bridgwater for the safety of the step-daughter. I searched the prisoner and found two knives on her. The young woman is 28 years of age, and I have several previous complaints of her ill-usage. Cross-examined by the prisoner: You were beating her when I came upstairs. - The prisoner was remanded, and the magistrates refused the application of her husband and son to admit her to bail."

The case received more detailed coverage the following week.

"Ann Cousins, wife of a labourer living in Chedzoy-lane, near Bridgwater, was charged on remand with assaulting Mary Cousins, her step-daughter, aged 28, and an imbecile. P.C. Hawkins having repeated the evidence already given, and which has been published, was briefly cross-examined. He added that Mr. Boon, a farmer, was close by him at the time and he heard the blows inflicted, and before entering the house. He saw the prisoner inflict several blows when he was at the top of the stairs. He had found two clasp knives in the prisoner's dress pocket. He never heard that the step-daughter was sometimes violent. Prisoner walked about twenty yards from the house with her boots off, but he had previously asked her several times to put them on. He did not examine the step-daughter to see if she had any bruises or other marks upon her, but thought from the nature of the blows inflicted she must have suffered a good deal.

Mr. Robert Boon (60), farmer, of Chedzoy, said he first saw the step-daughter outside the prisoner's house on the night in question. She was crying and she had hardly any clothes on. He told P.C. Hawkins that if she was in the yard much longer she would be 'scrammed' with the cold. He afterwards accompanied Hawkins to the premises, and stood in the road with him underneath the window of the room, wherein they could distinctly hear every blow that was struck. It was impossible to hear all that was said because the prisoner was cursing and hammering away at the girl. The prisoner's husband opened the door at the request of P.C. Hawkins, who then went upstairs, and in a few minutes brought the prisoner down. He knew that the girl, who was an imbecile, had been served horribly on several occasions. The girl had been let into the house before he and the policeman arrived there. - By Mr. Chapman: He had in the meantime told the parents that the girl was waiting outside. They were then down at the public house. - Prisoner: We had been to market. - In reply to further questions, Mr. Boon added that his wife occasionally gave the step-daughter something to do in his house out of charity; that she had been there on the day in question, and that she left that night a little earlier than usual. - By the magistrates: She was dressed when in the road in the same clothes she had been to work in, but they were only rags.

"Ann Clarke (33), wife of Mr. George Clarke, farmer, of Chedzoy, said she lived about thirty yards from the prisoner. She saw Mary Cousins in the road crying, and had heard before of her being locked out of doors. She saw her father come and let her in, and presently her step-mother (the prisoner) also arrived, coming from the direction of the public-house. She was very tipsy, and rambled from one side to the other. Almost directly after she entered she heard such exclamations as 'You —. I'll kill you,' and 'Go to bed, you ---.' The father said, 'Put away that knife,' and subsequently the prisoner exclaimed, 'Now I'll kill thee. I don't care for old Boon or the bobby, or anybody else. If you make the least bit of noise I'll rip thy —- out.' Witness dared not interfere and soon afterwards the policeman arrived, and demanded that the door should be opened. After the policeman came down with the prisoner witness heard the former say, 'Put your boots on; you will go with me.' The prisoner called the policeman very disgusting names. Cross-examined: She only heard the threats, but no blows, being too far distant. She believed the step-daughter to be quite harmless and inoffensive. The girl never spoke in the least.

"Mr. Chapman, for the defence, said Mr. Boon occasionally employed the step-daughter, and did so on the day in question. The parents had been to the Bridgwater market, locking the door and returning home before the time they thought the step-daughter would return. The latter, however, came home earlier than usual. Directly they heard the girl had returned they at once went to the house and let the girl in. She was then, as he was instructed, saucy to the prisoner, who might have smacked her once or twice, but who denied that she inflicted any severe blows, and if she did so he (Mr. Chapman) submitted there would still remain some evidence of them. He had caused the step-daughter to come before them to be asked any questions the magistrates thought proper to put to her, and she had no marks of violence upon her, and stated, moreover, that she was not assaulted on the night in question. He admitted that being an imbecile, she deserved pity, and ought to be more kindly treated in consequence, but he was instructed that she was very annoying, and that her step-mother only administered a little correction, and that her conduct was certainly not such as was represented, and as some neighbours appeared to suspect her guilty of."

The final part of the article is incomplete as the original paper had been damaged and not fully straightened before microfilming. However, most can be deciphered.

"He [Mr. Chapman] reminded the Bench that the prisoner had been incarcerated since Monday and submitted that that was sufficient punishment for such an offence as she might have committed. - Mr. Boon said he believed the girl would be killed if the prisoner was not bound over, and Mrs. Clarke added that she had not interfered until she had been compelled to for the poor girl's protection. Mr. Broadmead said the case had been very clearly proved. The prisoner had come home in a drunken state and committed this assault upon her step-daughter and the magistrates felt they must do something to protect the poor creature in the future. The prisoner would be —- hard labour in Taunton gaol, and —- peace for six months."

Unfortunately the period of imprisonment is completely

missing as is any sum in which she was bound over to keep the peace.

The last bungalow on the right is known as **SOUTHSIDE**. This was the venue for a case which was reported in the Bridgwater Mercury in July 1949 under the headline

> "SEQUEL TO POULTRY THEFTS AT CHEDZOY. Bridgwater Police Officer Tells of Visit to Bungalow." The report read, "How a police officer had a door slammed in his face and then saw smoke belching from the chimney as if something was being destroyed, was described at a special sitting of Bridgwater County Magistrates' Court when a Chedzoy man and his landlady appeared to answer charges concerning poultry. Ernest Henry Brooks (48), single, of Southside, Chedzoy admitted stealing two hens, valued at £2, the property of Miss Vida Ruby Fry, Meads Farm, Chedzoy, and asked the Magistrates to take into consideration four previous thefts, involving three cockerels, valued £4 10s., the property of Mrs. E.M. Heal; six hens and two pullets, together valued £8, the property of Mrs. B.M. Baker.
>
> "P.C. Anning said Brooks made a statement that he got up at 3 a.m., stole the hens belonging to Miss Fry, and left them in the hall of the bungalow. Brooks, who had no previous convictions, said he did not know what made him do it. His landlady, Mrs. May Elizabeth Betty Banfield (44), a native of Langport, admitted receiving the two hens and asked the Bench to take into consideration the receiving of the other poultry. Det.-Constable Brooks stated that on calling at the bungalow Mrs. Banwell agreed to him having a look round the premises and started to accompany him. Suddenly she turned, ran indoors and slammed the door. Within a few seconds he saw smoke pouring from the chimney and could smell that feathers were burning. He returned later and found Mrs. Banwell standing on the doorstep on the verge of collapsing." After detailing further evidence the report concluded, "Because of their good characters formerly the Magistrates dismissed the charges under the Probation Act but ordered them to pay £7 10s. each as recompense to the owners of the poultry and 15s. costs. They were allowed 14 days in which to pay."

Sadly, Ernest Brooks was found hanged at East Bower in June 1954.

Church Acre to Field Barn

Immediately after the bungalows on your right, and just before a sharp bend, lies a field known as **Church Acre**. The field actually measures 3 rood and 19 perches (4 roods = 1 acre) or 0.871 acre. It has been auctioned every 21 years in the famous Candle Auction for about five centuries. The most popular story says that the land was left to Chedzoy church by Sir Richard Sydenham whose will was proved in 1500. His ancestral home now forms part of the UCB Cellophane complex. Another suggestion is that the land was left by a different member of the Sydenham family in 1490. Yet a third version is that it was left, again in 1490, by an old solider named Yeo, who wished to be buried at Chedzoy. Both the Sydenham and Yeo families were large landowners with property in the district.

The document which started the sale has never been found, although an inventory four centuries old refers to the original being stored in the church. This later document, dated 1599, refers to a feoffment (a lord's act of granting property to a vassal in return for service), dated 14th February 1529 of

> "one acre of arable land in Martins Field within the tithing of Dunwear to the use of Chedzoy church for ever."

The same inventory also records two leases on the land, one undated and the other in 1589. Using 21 years as the basis, neither 1529 nor 1589 fits in with the 1490 or 1500 theory nor does working backwards from the sale in 1673!

This earliest record of a sale of the lease in 1673 was when it was sold to Thomas Edwards for £6 in addition to which an annual rent of 1s. 6d. was to be paid. The rent remained at this sum until decimalisation in 1971, at which time it was changed to 8p. per year. At each sale the auctioneer accepts the last bid before half an inch of candle flame gutters and dies, a neat way to keep pace with inflation.

Records show the various sums which have been paid for the lease over the years since 1673. In 1694 the sum fell to £4 but in 1715 rose to £7 1s. In 1736 it fell again to £6 8s. 6d. Parish records show that in 1757 John Newman purchased Church Acre from the churchwardens, Richard Stradling and Thomas Hurman, for £8 11s. and at the next sale in 1778 it fetched £13 2s. In February 1821 an indenture was made between William Stradling and Joel Crane, churchwardens, and William Bennett, a blacksmith, of Chedzoy which required the latter to pay £32 10s. for the 21 year period. In 1841 the winning bid of £53 was made by William Stone. The indenture, dated 24th December 1841 was also signed by the churchwardens, William Crane and John Sibley. In 1862 the sale, conducted by Christopher Babbage, raised £72: the churchwardens were John Lawrie and John Tazewell.

Parish records note that in July 1865,

> "Mr. J. Cass, the occupier of Church Acre, having expended £8 or £10 upon repairs had requested the Churchwardens to make him a present of the stick of timber blown down, to which the parishioners in the vestry meeting assembled consented."

By the mid-1870s the cottage on Church Acre was occupied by Robert Boon. In June 1878 he took action in Bridgwater County Court and the details were duly reported in the Bridgwater Mercury.

> "ROBERT BOON v. GEORGE PUDDY. The plaintiff, a farmer, of Chedzoy, sued the defendant, a dealer, of Blackford for the sum of £3 10s. damage sustained from the trespass of

defendant's cattle. - Plaintiff deposed that on the 17th April he had a six-acre field of grass laid up for mowing. On the following morning, from information he received, he went to the field, and found that, the night having been a wet one, the grass had been 'pounded all to pieces' by cattle. A quantity of hay was also lying about the field. He afterwards saw Mr. Puddy, and said to him, 'Mr. Puddy, you did stock my field very bad last night.' Defendant asked, 'What do you mean?' He said, 'I am informed that you put thirty beasts or more in my field,' and defendant replied, 'Our people put sixteen beasts there, and no more.' Plaintiff asked, 'Who gave you authority to put them there?' and defendant first said, 'Your son,' and afterwards, 'If it was not your son, it must have been you.' He (plaintiff) said decidedly he never did, and it would have been most absurd for him to have done anything of the kind. He also told defendant he should make him pay for it, and the defendant made use of some vulgar expressions and went away. He (plaintiff) estimated the damage at £4. - Cross-examined: Mr. Puddy had a field adjoining, and the fields were divided by a so-called hedge or ditch, but it was now nearly level in consequence of continual trespassing.

"Mr. John Potter stated that the damage at a low estimate was £3 10s.; and Mr. James Brake, farmer, having confirmed the evidence of the plaintiff as to the conversation he had with the defendant, Mr. Good (for the defence) said he was instructed that the cattle which did the damage in question trespassed from an adjoining field, and that although defendant admitted there were sixteen beasts there, he did not say they belonged to him, or that he had put them there. - He called Mr. Puddy, who said that on the plaintiff telling him he had put thirty or forty beasts into the field he replied, 'I should not think it was quite so many; say half of them.' Plaintiff said he should make him pay for it, and he (defendant) told him to 'go on with his bother and not trouble him about what he knew nothing about.' - His Honour (to Mr. Good): What did you put the defendant in the witness box for? He has confirmed almost every word of the plaintiff and his witness have said. - Mr. Good: He states that cattle were there, but that they were not his. - Defendant: I mean to say that it was not my cattle, and I know nothing of it. My cattle were somewhere else, and I have got a receipt for the keep the same day. - His Honour: I don't remember any instance in which an admission was so clear and so unequivocal. - Defendant: I can prove whose cattle it was. - His Honour: All I can say is that upon this evidence my judgement must be for the plaintiff."

Robert Boon appeared in the County Court again in July 1879, but this time as the defendant.

"ARTHUR GEORGE PAIN v. ROBERT BOON. - Plaintiff, a solicitor, of Bridgwater, sued the defendant, a yeoman of Chedzoy, for whom Mr. Chapman appeared, for £3 0s. 1d.; £2 deposit paid in respect of a purchase of some land, and £1 0s. 1d. for professional attendance and letters consequent thereupon. Plaintiff said defendant called at his office and instructed him to write a letter to Mr. Elias Porter, of Chedzoy, to ascertain from him whether he would sell a certain close of land for £400, and if he was willing to do so he (Mr. Pain) was then to purchase it for the defendant for that sum. Mr. Potter called on him (plaintiff) the following day, and a contract was signed, he (plaintiff) buying the land for the sum named. He informed the defendant of the purchase, and the defendant then thought fit to repudiate the transaction, stating that he (plaintiff) was only to have made an enquiry." A letter from Mr. Boon was read which ended, "However, you appear to have bought it without my knowledge or consent in any way, and therefore, of course, you will have to make the best of your bargain."

"In reply to his Honour, Mr Pain said: I did not take a memorandum in writing of the instructions he gave me. He (defendant) certainly instructed me to buy the land, which I did. He told me verbally that I was to close for £400, and I wrote the letter to Mr. Potter in his presence. ... The land is of no use to me, and I did not buy it for myself. As for the defendant not knowing the land, he rents a close of land close by, and was anxious to buy this close some years ago. ... I have already sworn that I parted with the cheque in good faith for his benefit. - His Honour: I should be happy, if I could, to assist you; but you have not made out your case. Mr. Pain (excitedly): But surely I am entitled to charge for attendance and instructions: so there must be a decision in my favour.

"Mr. Chapman said that he was instructed that the plaintiff offered to write the letter in question without charging for it. - Mr. Pain: It's a tissue of lies. ... His Honour repeated that the plaintiff had not made out his case by satisfying him that he had instructions to purchase. - Mr. Pain (excitedly): You would surely believe me, as a professional man, before a yeoman! I am certainly to be believed in reference to this matter." Obviously not: "His Honour gave judgement for the defendant."

In August 1881 Robert Boon was the plaintiff.

"ROBERT BOON v. JOHN DOWDEN. The plaintiff, farmer, of Chedzoy, claimed of the defendant, a mason, 15s. (75p.) for rent of a garden. - The defence was that the plaintiff's horse had been allowed to trespass in the garden and that it did considerable damage there. Defendant had paid 5s. 3d. into the court. - A witness having been called by the defendant's wife to prove the trespass which plaintiff said had not been complained of before, his Honour said he should allow 5s. for the damage and gave judgement for the remainder."

The next sale of Church Acre took place on 7th August 1883 at the Crown Inn, Chedzoy. Notices of the sale indicated that the land had been "Lately occupied by Mr. Boon." The auction was reported in the Bridgwater Mercury:

"A sale of a most uncommon nature was held in Chedzoy on Tuesday last by Mr. F. Babbage. It appears that in 1490 an old soldier particularly wished to be buried in the parish churchyard and left - if his wish was carried out - a piece of land called 'Church Acre' and a cottage which was to be sold by an inch of candle every 21 years towards defraying the expenses of the church. On Tuesday there were about 150 present to witness the sale, and the biddings were very brisk. Directly the conditions of the sale were read over the inch of composite candle was lit and the bidding became very spirited indeed. After the candle had been burning for 35 minutes it fell over, but as it continued burning the bidding was carried on amidst the wildest excitement, some getting upon the table and others upon the mantelshelf in order to catch a glimpse of the now fast expiring flame. Forty minutes after it was lit the candle burned out, the last bid being £71 5s. by Mr. [William] Ashill. The late Mr. C. Babbage conducted the last sale - 21 years ago - when the property realised £71." William Ashill in turn rented the land to the Banwell family. At the time of this sale the churchwardens were Edmund Derrick and John Cary and parish records indicate that the money was used to buy a dial for the church clock, replacement gates for the churchyard and new surplices.

The Crown Inn closed in 1901 and all subsequent sales have taken place at the Manor House Inn.

The Bridgwater Mercury reported that on 29th August 1904 the candle was lit to applause and cheering.

"The enthusiasm having subsided an old villager exclaimed, 'That's the third 'un I've seen started!'" The bidding opened at £50 and the final bid of £68 came from

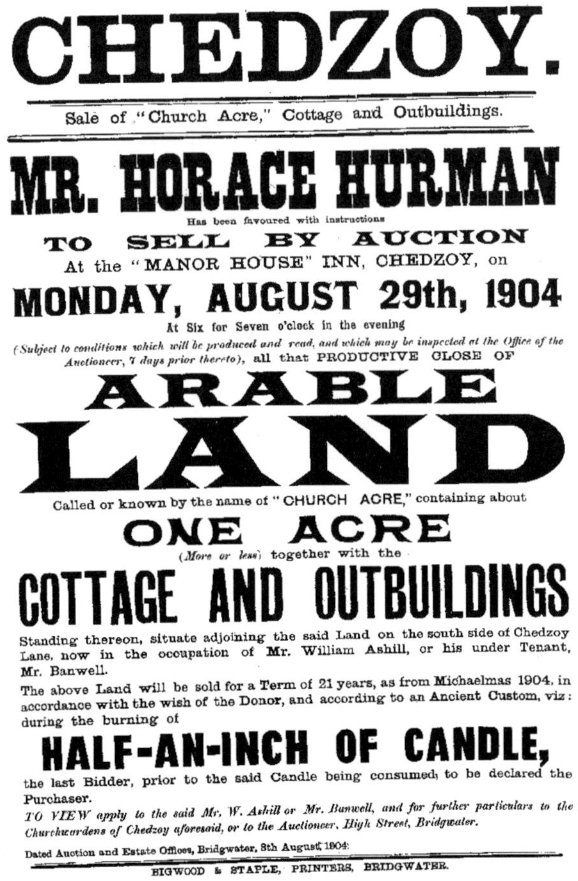

Poster courtesy of Helen Hunt

Edwin Cox. The Rev. Dr. Powell of Bridgwater spoke during the proceedings and said, "Let them just think what a splendid book it would make if someone could write a history of the whole neighbourhood for the last 400 years - the enormous changes in the history of the old place and the places around, the enormous changes for the better in happiness and welfare of man with what they were, in their food, their clothing and recreation, in all the things that went to make life happy."

95 years later this book goes some way towards Dr. Powell's suggestion.

The Banwells continued to live on the property and one of them was in trouble in December 1922.

"Sidney Banwell pleaded guilty to having four nets in his possession, having come from land where he had been in search of game. P.C. Hill saw the defendant come from land in Westonzoyland Road. He noticed the defendant's pockets were bulky, and asked him what he had there. He replied, 'String.' He searched defendant, and found upon him four nets, a ferret, and a moorhen. He asked him how he became in possession of the moorhen, and he said his dog had caught it. Witness seized the nets and moorhen, and when he served defendant with the summons the moorhen was handed back to him. Fined 10s."

On 26th August 1925 Church Acre was sold for the sum of £80 to Mrs. Rose Leake of East Bower who assigned it to Mrs. Elizabeth Banwell and her two sons. On this occasion, as normal, those present at the auction were local people, mostly farmers, who sat around a table on which the candle burned for 23 minutes.

In 1931 Bridgwater Rural District Council (B.R.D.C.) deemed the cottage on Church Acre to be no longer fit for human habitation and made a demolition order. At a B.R.D.C. meeting in October 1934

"The Rev. G.R. Mullens referred to a demolition order which had been made in regard to a house at Chedzoy and which was sold every 21 years by the light of a candle. The person who acquired the property gave an undertaking to leave it in the same condition as when he took it, but if the Council enforced the demolition order the man would be unable to do that, and there were twelve more years of the 21 to run. Furthermore, this man kept a number of pigs, and was doing his best to assist the government pig marketing scheme. The Council offered him as alternative accommodation a Council House at Woolavington Corner but if he went there he would have to give up the keeping of pigs. It was pointed out that the demolition order would not be enforced by the Council and the house need not be pulled down if the man gave an undertaking that it should cease to be occupied and went to live in the house which the Council had offered him."

Elizabeth Banwell died in February 1935, having lived in the cottage on Church Acre for 45 years. The property was still standing that November when mention of it was made in the Magistrates' Court.

"Mr. L.C. Brown, on behalf of the Bridgwater Rural District Council, made an application under a notice served by Mr. V.C.G. Callen (Sanitary Inspector), for an order of ejectment against Arthur Sidney Banwell, in respect of a dwelling house at Chedzoy Lane, Bridgwater Without, occupied by him. Defendant said he had nowhere to go at present. Mr. Brown explained that a demolition order in respect of the house was made by the Council, and became operative on 2nd December 1931. In accordance with the Act, notice was served on the defendant to give up possession but he failed to do so. The Council felt the time had now come when the order must be complied with. Negotiation between the Council and the defendant had failed. An order for possession was made within 28 days."

No further mention of the property appears in the local paper which, as far as can be ascertained, was demolished shortly afterwards.

However, the family continued to live in the area as this Bridgwater Mercury report from December 1936 shows.

"Ernest Banwell, tile maker, and Edwin Banwell, labourer, both of Chedzoy Lane, were both charged with being suspected of coming from land where they had been in search of game and conies (rabbits), and there being found upon them game, guns, and nets. They pleaded not guilty.

P.C. Greed said he was in Chedzoy Lane and saw two men come from Chad Lane (Shoe Lane?) into Chedzoy Lane. Each man was carrying a gun under his arm. He saw their boots were wet and muddy, as also were the bottoms of their trousers. He asked them if they had gun licences and they replied, 'Yes.' He asked if they had permission to take game and they replied, 'No.' He told them he suspected them of coming from land where they had been in search of game. On Ernest Banwell he found one rabbit and seven nets. On Edwin Banwell he found one rabbit and one ferret. He took possession of the rabbits and nets. They retained their guns. Ernest Banwell said they got the rabbits up the drove. He had never been stopped before from coming through the drove and did not think anyone would say anything to him. Edwin Banwell said it was only a case of suspicion as the constable did not see them coming from any ground. The Bench fined each of the men £1 and ordered the nets to be forfeited."

The 1946 Candle Auction took place in July at the Manor House Inn in the presence of the Bishop of Bath and Wells, Dr. H. Bradfield. The candle was lit by the rector, Rev. Hunt, and the opening bid was made by the Bishop: £21, or £1 for each year of the lease.

Further bids came from different parts of the room, and during one lengthy pause between bids the Bishop remarked, 'This is worse than a sermon with an hour glass!' The rector jocularly remarked, 'There are no free loaves with this'."

Candle Auction, 1967.
This took place in the grounds of the Manor House Inn. The candle can be seen burning at the front of the table.
Photograph by Cecil Cary, courtesy of Muriel Brown.

After 41 minutes, thought to be a record, the candle died, the winning bid of £125 having been made by Theodore Henry Newton, the village sexton. The candle used on this occasion was made by Stanley Stone of Kendale Road, Bridgwater, an employee of Messrs. Jarman Brothers who had supplied candles for every auction during the preceding 300 years.

In 1967 the lease on Church Acre was sold for £204 to Reginald 'Reggie' Rex of Bridgwater, a former professional boxer who fought as "Jack Marino." On this occasion the auction was comparatively brief, the candle guttering after just 19 minutes. The occasion was presided over by the Bishop of Bath and Wells, Dr. Edward Henderson, who commented that the auction was unequalled in the whole history of the church throughout the country.

The auction is still held at the Manor House Inn in the presence of the Bishop. In the 1988 auction, held on 19th July, the candle burned for 20 minutes, 26 seconds and had also been made by Stanley Stone who made the 1946 candle. The bidding opened at £2 but quickly reached £100 and then increased by £100, £50 and £25 increments to a final bid of £1,600. In addition to this the buyers, Timothy Howes, a plumber, and Phil McLarnon, a driving instructor, both of Bridgwater, were required to pay £20 plus 17.5% V.A.T. to both the auctioneer and the solicitor, although these gentlemen then donated their fees to the church. Two signed posters of the sale were auctioned and raised a further £18 for church funds. The next candle auction will take place in 2009.

Behind Church Acre is another field which was known as **CHEDZOY CAUSEWAY**, although quite how it got this name is not known. The land was purchased in 1928 by Edward Merrett and during the Second Word War he marked it out in small plots which he rented to local people as part of the "Dig for Victory" campaign. After the war Mr. Merrett purchased fruit trees with a view to establishing an orchard, but ill health intervened and this project was never completed.

Immediately opposite Church Acre is a drove known as **SHOE LANE**. Although no report of the sale was published, an advertisement in the Bridgwater Mercury in March 1885 noted that an auction was to take place at Hunter's Lodge Inn of meadowland known as "Shoe Lane Two Acres" which, at the time, was occupied by George Bell. A brief report in the same paper in August 1932 noted that just over three acres of pasture "approached over Shoe Lane" had been sold for £205.

In 1898 Chedzoy Lane was the scene of two fatalities, the first one probably taking place near Church Acre since the waggon concerned was moved by "a young lad named Banwell." On 9th February the Bridgwater Mercury reported,

> "A little boy named Frederick Collard, aged 6½, son of James Collard, farm labourer, met with a shocking death on Wednesday afternoon, when the wheels of a waggon, laden with coal, passed over him. He was taken home at once, and although everything was done for him, he expired in the arms of his mother, who was at work and had to be sent for. The district coroner held an inquest on Friday afternoon. The jury returned a verdict of 'Accidental Death'."

In June that same year a further report appeared under the headlines

> "SAD FATALITY IN CHEDZOY LANE. A LAD TRAMPLED UPON BY A HORSE. On Monday morning at about 9.30 an accident, unfortunately attended by fatal results, befell a lad named Joseph Parsons, aged 15, who lived at Chedzoy. It appears that the deceased was driving a horse and cart on the morning in question through Chedzoy Lane, when by some means, he fell beneath the horse's feet. A man named West (not further identified) at once went to his assistance, but the horse bolted and the poor boy was severely trampled upon, and killed instantly. The jury returned a verdict of 'Misadventure'."

Beyond Church Acre you pass through a double bend known to older residents as **REED'S CORNER**, apparently named after the family who once lived in one of two or three cottages which stood at this location. The area was also the scene of tragedy. In May 1910 under the headline "CHEDZOY FARMER'S GHASTLY SUICIDE," the Bridgwater Mercury gave details of an inquest which had taken place in the cottage into the death of James Reed. Mrs. Sarah Ann Reed, a widow, told the coroner that her son was a 36 year old bachelor and that he had been ill with influenza. About 11.00 p.m. the family retired for the night but about 12.30 a.m. Mrs. Reed and her daughter had been awoken by a gunshot. They dressed and, finding James missing, commenced a search. At the back door they heard a second shot in the home field.

> "The night was very dark and as the frightened women looked across the meadow they were horrified to see a blaze in the far end of the field. At first the women conjectured that the deceased, in a moment of insane mischief, had set fire to a rick of hay ... and that he had fired the gun to attract their attention. Still gazing at the lurid flare they were dumbfounded to note that the uncanny blaze flittered hither and thither about the meadow. The movement of this will o' the wisp fire was accompanied by maniacal yelling and groaning, and they then saw that the fire came from the clothing of the deceased, who rushed about gun in hand."

The women called upon neighbours for assistance and then approached James and found that he was dead. Dr. Hartnell and P.C. Giblett, of Bawdrip, arrived on the scene.

> "In the light of the rising moon the doctor examined the body, but when pulling away a portion of the deceased's partly burnt clothing a cartridge, which was apparently in his pocket, exploded narrowly missing doing injury to those around." The doctor gave the cause of death as a gunshot wound to the heart. "The coroner, in summing up, said he remembered holding an inquest in that very house on the deceased's father, who had taken his own life." The verdict was "Suicide whilst temporary insane."

At the end of the same month some of James' livestock was auctioned and, six months later, the remaining livestock as well as furniture and effects were sold by Mrs. Reed as she had decided to go out of business. Perhaps the suicide of her husband and son at the same address made her decide to seek pastures new.

At a meeting of Bridgwater Rural District Council in August 1930,

> "Rev. G.R. Mullens stated that he had been asked to bring to the notice of the Council a dangerous corner in Chedzoy Lane. It was the spot where the old tumble-down houses were, and he then asked that the road might be widened. The Committee viewed it and turned it down, because of the great value the owner put on the property. Recently at this point there was a near shave of an accident which might have proved fatal. He was not asking now that the corner should be improved, but that a white line be put there as the next best thing. The Chairman said that the point was whether the road at the bend was wide enough for two vehicles to pass, as, if it were not, the white line would make the spot more dangerous. The Rev. G.R. Mullens thought there was room for two vehicles to pass, and the matter was referred to the Surveyor."

Two weeks later,

> "The Rev. G.R. Mullens again brought forward the question of the dangerous corner in Chedzoy Lane, and said

although the white line had been put there, he thought they should put it forward, with a strong recommendation to the County Council, that the road should be widened by getting rid of the old cottages. It was agreed to take this course."

In October that year Bridgwater Rural District Council were informed that the County Council were prepared to make a grant of £150 towards the cost of improvements at this spot.

In the 1950s the double bend was also known as **Tar Barrel Corner** after a collision between a car driven by Albert 'Bert' Ashford and a barrel which had been left there. Over the years numerous vehicles have been driven into the ditch on this sharp bend, so in the summer of 1998, at the request of Bridgwater Without Parish Council, supported by Chedzoy Parish Council, reflector posts were erected as a warning. However, these had little effect and within twelve months at least six more cars ended up in the deep ditch. Reflective chevrons were erected in October 1999 and the road marked with lines.

CROW LANE, the no through road on the right, used to lead through to **Bower Lane** before the construction of the motorway. This minor road made the Bridgwater Mercury in February 1961:

"Two roads in Chedzoy were blocked within an hour when two lorries were involved in separate accidents. The first, driven by Mr. Alec Pickering of Taunton, left the road in Chedzoy Lane, ran into a ditch, and blocked the road for an hour. Shortly after a second lorry, driven by Mr. Arthur Howes of Bridgwater, left the road in Crow Lane, Chedzoy and blocked this route also for about an hour."

Bridgwater Without Parish Council asked that a footbridge be provided when the motorway was being constructed, but their request fell on deaf ears.

On the left stands **MEADS FARM**. In the early 1960s the property found itself mentioned in the Bridgwater Mercury on several occasions. In May 1963,

"For using a scooter without insurance cover, Victor Alfred Gardener, plasterer, of Meads Farm, Chedzoy Lane was fined £15 with licence endorsed."

Not too much later further minor motoring offences were reported and then in July 1964,

"A 22 year old married Chedzoy man, said to be building his own 'special' sports car, was found guilty of receiving an engine he wanted for the vehicle, knowing it to have been stolen, at Somerset Quarter Sessions at Taunton. Victor Alfred Gardener, a plasterer, of Meads Farm, Chedzoy was fined £15. ... When interviewed by police accused said, 'I know it looks bad, but I didn't pinch it'."

Like their neighbours near Hunter's Lodge, some residents of Chedzoy Lane had difficulty in keeping out of trouble. In January 1896,

"James Stone, labourer of Chedzoy Lane, was summoned for assaulting his step-mother, Mercy Stone, on 25th December 1895 and also for doing damage to a door. The defendant, who was the worse for drink, knocked the complainant down and she fell against a stone step. Defendant afterwards went to her house and broke the panel of a door. She asked the Bench to bind him over as she went in fear of him when he was in drink. Fined 10s. and bound over." In December 1897 it was reported that, "William Stokes, labourer (a cider maker), of Chedzoy Lane, was charged with assaulting Mr. William May of East Bower Farm at East Bower. There was a cross summons. Mr. Hagon said it the case was one of a workman assaulting his master. They were in these days used to hearing of workmen striking, but they didn't generally strike in the way the defendant had done, he hoped." He was fined £1 and costs, "the Chairman remarking that masters must be protected from such conduct. They dismissed the case against Mr. May."

Residents were also the victims of crime. In February 1906 the Bridgwater Mercury carried a report of committal proceedings against Henry Holland 16, a labourer of Westonzoyland Road. He was charged

"With having broken and entered the dwelling house of John Henson and stolen one pair of boots, value 3s. (15p.), a padlock and key, value 6d. (2.5p) and one penny in money." Mary Henson told the court that her husband had gone out at six o'clock on Sunday morning and an hour later she heard noises downstairs and then saw a man leaving the house. Holland was also charged that he "Stole a pair of boots, value 5s., and a pair of leggings, value 1s. 6d., the property of George Davis of Chedzoy Lane."

On this occasion he had visited the house and, when the owner went out, took the property.

"Superintendent Pitman said there was a previous conviction against the prisoner for larceny at Somerton where he was sentenced to a month's hard labour. Prisoner bore a very bad character. Farmers would not employ him, he being lazy, untruthful and dishonest."

He was remanded in custody to the Quarter Sessions but no further report of this case was published.

A graphic description of other events appeared in the Bridgwater Mercury in June 1910 under the headline "EXCITING INCIDENT NEAR CHEDZOY. BULL ATTACKS BOY AND PONY." It was reported that,

"An exciting incident, and one attended with considerable danger to a lad, who was the chief participant in it, occurred in Chedzoy Lane on Friday morning. It appears that a boy, named Frank Hale, aged 14 years, son of Mr. Geo. Hale, of Chedzoy, was returning through the lane, driving a pony, attached to a spring cart, containing two churns of milk, when he was met by an infuriated bull, the property of Mr. (Robert?) Fry, farmer, of Chedzoy, and which had escaped from a field. The bull, on meeting the pony, at once made a dash for it. The result was that the pony and cart were overturned into a deep ditch which runs parallel with the road. The lad was thrown into the water, but was pinned against the bank by the vehicle. His head was just above the water, then one of Mr. Fry's employees raced up, the bull having been missed from the field. The man hastily beat the animal off, and released young Hale from his perilous position. One of the shafts of the cart was broken off, and the pony was cut about the body. The lad, beyond a bruising and shaking, was little the worse for his alarming experience."

SLAPE FARM, which was demolished in October 1999, used to stand on the right hand side of the road . This farm featured in a Bridgwater Mercury report in October 1948.

"Two boys appeared before Bridgwater County Juvenile Court summoned for stealing four sheaves of wheat valued at 10s., the property of Ewart Heal, Slate Farm (sic), Chedzoy Lane, Bridgwater Without. Mr. Heal told the justices that he discovered that in all 25 sheaves had gone from his field. Two complete stacks had been taken, whilst several stacks had one or two sheaves missing. Since the wheat had been cut he had received considerable trouble. Witness identified the six (why not four?) sheaves as his property. The boys, aged 12 and 15 years, were placed on probation for twelve months and ordered to pay 25s. (£1.25) costs between them."

Slape Farm, 1928.
Ewart Heal and his daughter Audrey (now Mrs. French).
Courtesy of Duncan Bouchier.

In March 1952 advertisements were published in the Bridgwater Mercury to the effect that the 10 acre Slape Farm was to be sold by auction. At that time it was occupied by Ewart Heal at a rent of £45 per annum. No report of the sale was published.

A report in September 1875 concerned an unspecified part of the lane.

"Joseph Bacon was charged with being the driver of a waggon drawn by three horses, and with riding on the same without reins and without having any control over the horses. P.C. Southerwood said he met the defendant and another man in Chedzoy-lane riding on the shafts. He cautioned them, and they got off, but as soon as they considered they were out of sight they again got up and rode off. Defendant, who denied the latter allegation, was fined 2s. 6d. and costs."

Next on the right stands **CROSSWAY HOUSE** which was previously a farm. In July 1924 the farmer appeared before the magistrates. The Bridgwater Mercury reported,

"Tom Hawkins of Crossway Farm, Chedzoy Lane, was summoned for having sold milk which was deficient in milk fat to the extent of 10.5%. P.S. Sealey purchased a pint of milk from the defendant at the price of 2d. and when a sample of it was submitted for analysis it was found to contain only 2.68% of fat. When seen, defendant said, 'I am innocent of it. It was put in the churn. I milked it from the cows. The quantity is more this time of the year, but the quality is poorer.' A second sample of milk was taken from the cows and the fat content was 3.4%. When told of the second analysis he said, 'I will defy any man to prove I have tampered with the milk, and they can't find me guilty'." They could, and they did! "The Bench imposed a fine of £2 and £3 3s. costs."

In August 1928 notices appeared in the local paper that Crossway House, as a result of the death of George Clark, would be sold by auction on 11th September unless sold by private treaty before that date. As sale notices were discontinued prior to that date, it seems likely that an auction was not held. No report of the sale was published.

The next time the property was mentioned in the Bridgwater Mercury was in December 1953: "The Local Valuation Court reduced the proposed assessments of £20 and £12 on Crossway House, Chedzoy Lane to £16 and £10, the chairman stating the Court would direct that the property should be recognised as an agricultural dwelling house."

The Parish of Chedzoy begins at **SLAPE CROSS** where a drove crosses the lane. The site of the two new houses on the right (built in the 1990s) was formerly the location of Frankcom Dairies, later Cricket Malherbie Dairies, and older residents still refer to this area as Dairy Bend or Dairy Corner. Interestingly, one of Monmouth's officers was one Richard Slape, Captain in charge of Musketeers and Scythemen. It is said that the name came about after his body, or part of it, was hung at the cross-roads after the Monmouth rebellion, but this seems unlikely as it is known that Richard Slape was pardoned on 2nd October 1686.

A dairy employee appeared before the court in November 1951. The Bridgwater Mercury reported that,

> "A former milk roundsman, Patrick Joseph Matthews (34) of Yew Tree Cottage, Chedzoy, was sent to prison for one month by [Bridgwater] Borough Magistrates yesterday for embezzlement and falsification of accounts." Only a month earlier his age had been given as 32 and his surname as Mathews when he was convicted of cycling without lights. "Matthews admitted embezzling seven sums totalling £8 7s. 0d. and falsifying the round book while employed by Frankcom Dairies Ltd., Chedzoy." He had received money from customers and, while acknowledging receipt on the customers cards, had failed to enter the money in his own book. "Dealing with the case of falsification, Mr. R. Ash, for the prosecution, stated that a sum of £6 6s. 5d. shown as due had ... been altered to £1 6s. 5d. Matthews had made a full statement admitting all the offences and had given a list of some fifty customers from whom he had said he had received sums totalling £81 5s. 10d. ... He did not know what he had done with the money, although he admitted he had been drinking and smoking."

In the turning on the right, just behind the new houses, stands **SLAPE CROSS COTTAGE**, much modernised and extended from its original form. The cottage featured in a case brought in June 1952.

> "'This is the fourth time proceedings have been brought against me,' said Frederick Charles Dibble at Bridgwater County Court when an application for possession of Slape Cross Cottage, Chedzoy, was brought by Albert Edmund Ashford, farmer, of 'Croftside,' Chedzoy. Mr. J.C. Perks appeared for the plaintiff [and] said there was a certificate from the Agricultural Executive Committee and a contract of service had been signed by a farm worker, conditional on accommodation being provided. 'This is a case that has been beset with ill fortune from the plaintiff's point of view, everything imaginable having gone wrong on previous occasions,' he stated. Mr. Ashford said he owned Fishers Farm and was a tenant of West End Farm, the two farms comprising 310 acres with about 200 head of cattle. He purchased Slape Cross Cottage in 1940, which was occupied at that time by the defendant, who paid £3 a quarter for rent. The cottage was required for an agricultural tenant. [When] questioned he agreed that Mr. Dibble was a satisfactory tenant. Proceedings had been instituted in 1949, but had been dismissed by Judge Wethered.
>
> "Defendant told his Honour, Judge W. Paton, that he had been a tenant of the cottage since 1928 and for 30 years until the premises were acquired by Mr. Ashford they had not been owned by a farmer. He had made repeated applications for alternative accommodation, but had been unsuccessful. 'I am 69 and should not like to leave there at my time of life,' he added. As he was a retired railway worker he was in receipt of a small pension and could not afford a high rent. ... After a long hearing his Honour made an order for possession in two months."

Further along Chedzoy Lane the large farmhouse on the left, **TEMPLE FARM**, now modernised with new windows, is probably over 150 years old and retains many old features in the interior. In February 1890 the farm was sold by auction at the Royal Clarence Hotel, Bridgwater at which time it was described as being a

> "freehold farm, farm-house, cottages and outbuildings and lands;" just over eight acres in all. "The farm-house, cottages and outbuildings are well arranged and substantially built with bricks and tiled."

No report of the sale was published. The farm was brought by the present family at an auction held in 1903.

NELSON LODGE, a little further along the road on the left, has an interesting history. It was built in 1910 for the Cary family of Manor Farm and William Cary lived here in his retirement from about 1923 until his death in May 1935. The Carys were related to the Hardy family. It was in Captain Hardy's arms that Nelson died at Trafalgar, uttering the famous words, "Kiss me (or 'Kismet'), Hardy." Hence the association of this house with Nelson's name. The present house was built by a builder named Davis of Middlezoy.

Wheeler's House.
Nelson Lodge is built on the site of this earlier house, which was demolished in 1909.
Courtesy of Duncan Bouchier.

The original cob farmhouse, owned by James Wheeler until he sold it to the Cary family, was a typical Somerset long house which was pulled down in 1909 because it was considered to be in a dangerous state. Silver coins, retained by the Cary family, were found there and dated from the reign of George I. After re-building, the first occupiers were Christopher 'Chris' and Beatrice Denning, parents of Philip 'Phil' Denning, now living at Ponsfield.

Still further along the road on the left stands **WEST END FARM**, a beautiful Georgian farmhouse. Its buildings were tastefully converted into a group of dwellings in the early 1980s.

In 1880 Joseph Ashford (1856-1943) moved from Knowle Park Farm, Wincanton, to become the tenant at West End Farm.

About 1927 he purchased an Austin tourer from the Bridgwater Motor Company on condition that he received six driving lessons - there was no driving test in those days. After three lessons the salesman, Mr. Richards, said that no further lessons were necessary, so the remaining lessons were to be taken up by Mrs. Ashford. On her first lesson she drove the car into a deep ditch on the sharp corner outside what is now Penwood Farm, Parchey. Mr. Ashford was not amused and asked, "Why did you let her do that?" The hapless salesman replied, "It's no good blaming me! She drove the thing and got hold of the steering wheel like she's got hold of a horse! I can't steer it." Mrs. Ashford never drove again.

In October 1929 a member of the family appeared before the County Magistrates' Court.

"Walter John Ashford, farmer, of Chedzoy, was summoned for using indecent language on the Pawlett Road and also for assaulting Cyril Fisher on the same occasion. Defendant pleaded guilty in the first case but not guilty in the second. Mr. A. King, who prosecuted, said in view of the defendant's plea in the first case the summons for assault would be withdrawn as it was not a serious matter. Mr. King said the complainant was returning on his motorcycle from Brent Knoll Harvest Home in the early hours of the morning, and was accompanied by a young lady, to whom he was engaged. He was taking her to her home at Bawdrip, and she was riding on the pillion. When on the road between Pawlett and Puriton they approached a stationary car, in which was the defendant and two other men. As the motorcycle passed a very objectionable word was shouted by defendant. Fisher went back and remonstrated with the three men and subsequently very indecent expressions were used.

"Mr. Tyrrell expressed defendant's regret for the use of one word which in law was indecent. The explanation given was that as the complainant and the young lady were going home something was said to which the defendant took offence, and he shouted the expression. He had never previously been before the Court, and Mr. Tyrrell asked the Bench to dismiss the case on payment of costs. The Bench agreed to this course, and ordered defendant to pay the costs and advocate's fee, totalling £2 11s."

Joseph Ashford (left) and Walter Tucker, 1910.
Courtesy of Duncan Bouchier.

An amusing case was reported in the Bridgwater Mercury in March 1935 following an accident on the bend outside the farm.

"John William Coombes, fishmonger, of 8 Elmwood Avenue, Taunton Road, Bridgwater, was summoned for driving a motor van without due care and attention at Chedzoy on the 14th February, and also for being involved in an accident whereby injury was caused to a sheep, and failing to report the accident to the police within 24 hours of the occurrence. He pleaded not guilty on both summonses.

"Harry Chiswick, farm labourer, employed by Mr. Cecil Carey, farmer, of Chedzoy, and residing at Pig's Lane (sic), Chedzoy, said at 11.30 a.m. on Thursday, the 14th February, he was driving 44 ewes and 55 lambs from Chedzoy to Horsey. As he got by Mr. Ashford's farm in Chedzoy Lane, a motor van came round the corner, 'all at once' from the direction of Bridgwater. It came round the bend at a 'tidy' speed, and no horn was sounded. The wing of the van touched the wall, and the van then came out, and a ewe was jammed under the axle. The ewe was crippled for three weeks. Defendant had to jack up the front of the van in order to get the ewe out. Witness asked him, 'Couldn't you see what you were about?' Defendant replied that it was a blind corner. In reply to defendant, witness admitted that he did not ask defendant for his name and address, as he was more concerned with looking after the sheep.

"Joseph Ashford, of West End Farm, Chedzoy, said he saw the van come round the corner at a tremendous speed, and he heard no horn sounded. He helped to get the sheep out. Douglas George Tucker, farm labourer, an employee of the previous witness, corroborated. P.C. Greed said he interviewed defendant at his home in regard to the occurrence, and he admitted that he was the driver of the van.

Witness asked him why he had not reported the accident, and in a statement which he made, defendant said he was driving the van along Chedzoy Lane at about 20 miles an hour, and on reaching the bend in the road he came suddenly on a flock of sheep coming in the opposite direction with a dog chasing them on. There were so many sheep that it was impossible to get out of the way of them, but he pulled up, and one of the sheep was caught by the front axle. He did not report the accident, as the man in front said it was quite all right. The man in charge of the sheep was gone before he (defendant) had time to speak to him about it.

"Addressing the magistrates, defendant said he had absolutely stopped, and one of the sheep ran into the van, and not the van into the sheep. As the man in front with the sheep told him everything was all right, he went on, and before he had time to speak to the other man he was gone with the injured sheep. Mr. Ashford was 200 or 300 yards up the road at the time, and came up and asked what was the matter. The bench fined the defendant £1 for driving a motor van without due care and attention and 10s. for not reporting the accident, with costs of witnesses a total of £2 5s. They did not endorse the licence."

Joseph Ashford appeared in Bridgwater County Court in October 1936, the details being reported in the Bridgwater Mercury.

"John Archibald Tambling, of Cannington, claimed of Joseph Ashford, of Chedzoy, £10 3s. 6d. for board and lodging. There was a counter claim of £3 2s. 6d., one week's wages for leaving without notice and goods sold. Mr. Clarke (representing Tambling) explained that the claim was for board and lodging while plaintiff was engaged by the defendant to go round with an entire (i.e. uncastrated) horse, 'Causeman's Forest King,' He went from April to July last year and the claim was for board and lodgings for 14 weeks at 15s. 6d. (77p.) a week. The agreement was made about a fortnight before April 1935, by which plaintiff was employed at £2 a week plus groom's fees and plus board and lodging. ... At the end of 14 weeks plaintiff went on to work for Mr. Ashford on the farm. ... Plaintiff on several occasions mentioned about the lodging money to Mr. Ashford, and on 21st December he received 10s. on account. Ultimately his employment ceased. He asked defendant to pay the £10 8s. The defendant said he would have nothing to do with him. On one occasion he offered him 8 guineas.

"Defendant, giving evidence, said he owned an entire horse for five years. The terms on which he engaged plaintiff were £2 a week, plaintiff to have groom fees and pay his own lodging. He denied giving plaintiff 10s. on account of lodging money. He had never paid lodging money for any man, and he did not tell plaintiff he would give him 8 guineas for lodging money after he had collected the service fees. His Honour, in giving judgement, said he was fully conscious he must decide the case upon one point - whom did he believe? He must be careful not to attempt to guess. He found it very difficult to say whether plaintiff had been deceiving him or whether defendant had been deceiving him. He did not feel inclined to jump to a conclusion on it. He must follow the old rule of law. Had the party making the claim made it out? The burden of proof lay upon the plaintiff. He did not say plaintiff had not told him what was not true, or that defendant had told him what was not true, but he was not satisfied plaintiff had made out his case, and there would be judgement for defendant on the claim and judgement for Tambling on the counter-claim."

In December 1951 a Chedzoy front page story was published in the Mercury.

"A Chedzoy Special Constable and member of the village church choir, whose rector told the court, 'I would always trust him,' was cleared of theft charges at Bridgwater County Magistrates' Court. Defendant was Albert Victor Coward (48), farm worker, 8 Higher Road, Chedzoy, who pleaded not guilty to the larceny of two wooden posts and one fir post to the value of 18s., the property of his former employer, Herbert John Ashford. Inspector C.W. Halse said that two months ago Mr. Ashford missed two hockey goalposts which had been placed in a waggon shed at the farm in the spring of 1950. ... Coward told the magistrates he found the two posts in long grass and it was obvious they had been there a long time. He put them in a shed to dry, and later took them home for firewood. 'I had no intention of stealing,' he added, 'I thought they were abandoned as they were of no use. With my experience in the police force I should not have taken them with any intention of stealing.' - Defendant was a former member of the Monmouth Constabulary."

Two members of the Ashford family were in trouble in October 1957:

"Albert Edmund Ashford and Herbert John Ashford, of West End Farm, Chedzoy, were fined £1 on each of four summonses at Bridgwater County Magistrates' Court for keeping bulls without licences at Chedzoy," that is, animals which had not been certified as fit for breeding.

Two fields along the road on the left beyond West End farm are some old barns which, during 1998 and 1999, were converted into a dwelling now known as **FIELD BARN**. The area was formerly known as White House Field and, as implied by the name, there was once a building at this location which was known as White House Farm. In 1832 the farmer was Joseph Crane but by 1840 he had been replaced by David Brake. Cecil Cary, the last tenant of the land, thought that in much earlier times, the road to Bridgwater ran from behind Manor Farm, the next building, behind White House barns, West End Farm and Temple Farm to join the present route at Slape Cross. The 1836 Tithe map confirms that this was indeed the case, but by the first edition of the Ordnance Survey map in 1887 only the present road was shown, not even footpaths marking the second route

Manor Farm to Parchey Bridge

Manor Farm, modernised in the mid-1990s, is possibly over 200 years old: parts of the building are of very ancient cob. The farm buildings, beautifully built of stone, may well be older than the present house and, in Cecil Cary's time, presented a veritable time capsule of farming in the olden days when horses were used and the toil of many labourers was not eased by mechanisation.

There had been Carys at Manor Farm since at least 1861, but James Cary, buried in the churchyard, was born in Chedzoy in 1796, so the Cary association with the village is very old. Cecil Cary (1900-1990) was the last tenant of the University of Oxford, who owned the farm, and had traced his family tree of Carys and Hardys back to 1719. There were several old wells on the property, one at the front and back of the present farmhouse, now known as **Banfield Barn**, which was once the garden of Banfields, a thatched cottage long since pulled down.

In December 1866 the farm featured in a case before Bridgwater County Petty Session and was reported in the Bridgwater Mercury. Readers will no doubt notice that quite a few of the press reports quoted in this book have the family surname as Carey, a common mistake.

William and Clara Cary, 1902.
Pictured with their children Hilda, Harold, Cecil and Hubert.
Courtesy of Muriel Brown.

> "John Rainey and John James were charged with having at Chedzoy unlawfully trespassed on a certain close of land in the possession and occupation of Mr. Wm. Carey (1822-1875). Rainey pleaded guilty; James pleaded not guilty. Mr. Lovibond appeared for the prosecution. It appeared from the evidence of the prosecutor and his son, Mr. John Carey (16), that on the afternoon of the day in question about three o'clock they went to a field called North-splat to look for some sheep, when they perceived the two defendants in a ditch, and close by the spot where they were seen then directly afterwards saw a ferret emerge from a hole, which they took possession of, and which was afterwards claimed by Rainey. There were a good many rabbits to be seen generally in that field. - The defendant James denied that he was ferreting, and asserted he was going across the field in the direction of Mr. Bennett's at Bawdrip to seek for a job. - It was proved, however, that the field in question was not a path field, and that neither of the defendants had any right to be there. It was stated that about a year ago they were both fined for a similar offence. They were both now fined 10s. (50p.) each and costs; in default 14 days' imprisonment."

William 'Bill' Cary (1856-1935) sued in Bridgwater County Court in July 1877 and the case was duly reported in the Bridgwater Mercury.

> "CAREY v. SHEPHERD. Plaintiff, a farmer, of Chedzoy, claimed of the defendant, of Highbridge, 6s. 7d. (33p.) for alleged breach of contract. The plaintiff alleged that he took 79 lbs. of butter to Bridgwater market, and after some negotiation with the defendant, he sold the latter the whole of the butter for 13d. (5.5p.) per pound. The defendant proceeded to put it in his own hamper, but soon afterwards unpacked it again, and left it on the stall where he (plaintiff) had been standing with the intimation that the butter was bad, and that he should keep it. He (plaintiff) afterwards sold the butter again to Mr. Alway, grocer, in Bridgwater, for 1s. (5p.) per pound, the market price having gone down a little towards the close. - In cross-examination the plaintiff stated all the butter was made on one day. - Mr. John Webber deposed that he tasted the butter, and found it to be as good as any he bought on the day in question: a Mr. Boon of Sydenham House, said he tasted the top row of the butter in the basket, and also found it good. He heard the defendant say he should not unpack any more butter because it was bad. - Defendant said there were several layers of butter in plaintiff's basket, each being covered with a cloth. He tasted it on the top, and finding it was good asked the price. Plaintiff replied 16d. (6.5p.) per pound and he (defendant) walked away. Plaintiff came to him afterwards and ultimately agreed to sell it for 13d. per pound, assuring him at the same time that the quality of the butter was the same all the way through. After unpacking the top row he smelt the

butter was 'rank' and told the plaintiff she should not keep it. Plaintiff said he had bought it, and that he would sell it by auction and sue him for the difference. Mr. Charles Parsons of Bridgwater, Mr. Charles Hobbs of Brent, and Mr. James Perry deposed tasting the butter and they all stated that whereas that on the top was good butter, underneath was of inferior quality. - Mr. Chapman stated that Mr. Alway, who repurchased the butter, had been subpoenaed, but had gone to Bristol market. - His Honour non-suited the plaintiff, but without costs."

In April 1880 Manor Farm was the scene of a serious crime.

"Frederick Giles (67), labourer, was charged with having stolen a quantity of rhubarb, the property of Elizabeth Carey (1823-1898), at Chedzoy. - P.C. Hawkins proved the service of the summons as the defendant did not appear and a warrant was issued for his apprehension." It was not until the end of August that the case was heard. "Frederick Giles, a very old and dirty-looking man, was brought up in custody charged with stealing a quantity of rhubarb, value 1s. (5p.), the property of Mrs. Elizabeth Carey at Chedzoy. Mrs. Carey, widow (of William, senior), living at Chedzoy proved that the rhubarb was her property and that a large quantity had been stolen. - John Andrews, labourer, in the employ of Mrs. Carey, stated that he saw defendant pulling the rhubarb about half past four in the morning and on speaking to him he begged him not to say anything about it. He (defendant) pulled the rhubarb and put it in a bag, afterwards getting over the rails and leaving. - Defendant said he made a 'chop' with Mrs. Carey's son, giving him a potato-mill in exchange for the rhubarb. He was fined 20s. (£1) and costs, in default 14 days' hard labour. - A further charge was made against the defendant for breaking up his quilt in the police-cell, but this case was withdrawn. Superintendent Jeffs said the defendant had a very bad character and Superintendent Lear stated that his behaviour in gaol was disgraceful."

It seems that his appearance was no better in November.

"Frederick Giles, a very old and dirty-looking man, was brought up in custody charged with stealing a drake and sixty pounds of apples, the property of Mrs. Elizabeth Carey at Chedzoy. - P.C. Hawkins stated that on Sunday morning, about eleven o'clock, he saw the prisoner in Chedzoy-lane. He went into a house there, occupied by a man named Dowden. Witness went in after prisoner, who had a bundle with him, and asked if it was his bundle. The prisoner replied, 'Yes, it is.' On opening the bundle, witness found the drake produced, the neck of which had been wrung. Prisoner said it had been given to him, but he refused to say by whom. He was taken into custody, and witness found afterwards that the duck had been stolen from Mrs. Carey. On searching an out-house at the prisoner's place of abode, witness found there sixty pounds of apples, which had also been stolen from Mrs. Carey. He afterwards took some of the apples to Mrs. Carey's orchard, and they corresponded with a heap there, some of which had been stolen during the night. Prisoner's boots correspond with footmarks near the heap of apples in the orchard. He had since charged the prisoner with both offences and he admitted that they were Mrs. Carey's things. - Caroline Phillips, married woman of [Ward Lane], Chedzoy, stated that she saw the prisoner in Mrs. Carey's orchard between ten and eleven at night. He had a bucket in his hand. - Mrs. Elizabeth Carey, widow, of Chedzoy, stated that the drake produced corresponded exactly with the one she had missed. She had 46 ducks, and missed the drake produced on Sunday morning. They were all right up to Friday night. - James Carey, son of the last witness, stated that the duck produced was exactly similar (!) to the one he had missed the previous Sunday. He had also missed a number of apples from the heap in his mother's orchard, and those produced correspond with those in the heap. - Prisoner denied that the things produced were the property of Mrs. Carey, but he said that he took them from 'Farmer Fry's' and they were his things, remarking, 'Let he transport me if he like.' - The prisoner refused to be tried by the Bench, remarking, 'I will have it different from this,' and adding that they were all wrong and he would swear the apples and drake produced were not Mrs. Carey's. He was committed for trial at the quarter sessions in January next. - Prisoner: I wish the policeman to take the drake back to Farmer Fry and also the apples. (Laughter.)"

The case was reported again in January 1881 when it was heard at the Somerset Quarter Sessions.

"THEFT OF POULTRY AND APPLES AT CHEDZOY. Frederick Giles (67), labourer, was charged with stealing a tame drake and sixty pounds of apples, the property of Mrs. Elizabeth Carey at Chedzoy. Elizabeth Carey, the prosecutrix, stated that she was a widow, and carried on the business of a farmer at Chedzoy, where she had also got an orchard. On Saturday, the 30th October she had a heap of apples in her orchard, and had some ducks in her possession. She missed them on the same day that the apples disappeared. The duck produced was similar to the one she missed. - William Carey, son of the prosecutrix, stated that apples which had been found in the possession of the prisoner were similar to the ones which had been missed from the orchard. He generally corroborated the evidence of the previous witness. - Other witnesses were called. - P.C. Hawkins stated that he had known the prisoner for five years and on Sunday morning he saw him in Chedzoy-lane about eleven o'clock. He had a bundle in his hand, and he followed him into a cottage. He asked the prisoner if the bundle was his, and he said it was, and on opening it he found it to contain a drake. - He was found guilty and sentenced to one month's imprisonment with hard labour."

Just three months later the same persons appeared before the Somerset Quarter Sessions: on this occasion proceedings in the Magistrates' Court had not been reported.

"Frederick Giles, 67, labourer, was charged with having stolen seven tame fowls, value 21s., the property of Elizabeth Carey, at Chedzoy on 12th February. He pleaded not guilty. Charles Gully stated that he knew the prosecutrix and was walking along the lane near her home on the day in question. He went with the prosecutrix's son to where the fowls were kept and saw the prisoner there and found seven of them dead. - The prisoner interrupted the proceedings by stating that he though he would go to gaol for something this time; the last time he was sent to prison for five months for nothing. He would have killed the whole of them, and all the sheep too, if they had not stopped him. - William Carey, the son of the prosecutrix, corroborated the statement of the last witness. - The prisoner said in excuse that his 'head was not right' and that he was frequently not responsible for what he did. - He was found guilty and as a previous conviction was recorded against him, he was sentenced to six months' imprisonment with hard labour."

Elizabeth Ann Cary, this time referred to as Ann Carey, was involved in a case in September 1889:

"John Wilkins, labourer, was charged with committing a trespass on land in the occupation of Mrs. Ann Carey in search of game and conies. Mr. Wm. Carey, son of the complainant, stated that on the day in question he saw the defendant in some potato ground in the occupation of his mother. He had a gun with him, and when he got down the end of the ground he rose a covey of partridges, but they were out of shot and defendant did not fire. Witness said to defendant, 'I've got you at last,' and defendant replied to the effect that he should like to 'make it up,' and that he would not trespass again. After defendant had been served with the summons he came down and abused and swore at witness. - Superintendent Vowles stated that the defendant had been previously convicted of a similar offence, and had also been convicted under the Game Act. - Defendant was fined 10s. and costs."

Bill Cary fell foul of the law on a number of occasions. The Bridgwater Mercury report of proceedings at Bridgwater County Petty Sessions in July 1893 stated that

"Francis Mills, labourer, was summoned for carrying a gun without a licence. Mr. O'Sullivan, Revenue Officer, said defendant was employed by Mr. William Carey, and on the day in question he used the gun for the purpose of scaring birds. Mr. Carey had refused to take out a licence. Defendant was fined 2s. 6d. and costs; in default 7 days' imprisonment."

In December 1896 the Mercury carried an amusing report under the headline

"WERE THE PIGS PROPERLY MARKED? William Carey was charged with having caused three pigs to be removed along Chedzoy-lane, they not having been marked" as they were being taken for slaughter. "P.C. Carter said ... he saw a cart ... being driven along Chedzoy-lane. There were three pigs in the cart, and they were not properly marked in red as required. A lad named Temblett in charge of the cart, told witness that he had asked Mr. Carey to mark the pigs, but Mr. Carey would not do so. Witness saw Mr. Carey and asked him why he had not marked the pigs, and defendant said he had done so, but added that it was rot that he had to mark them in red. There was a mark on the pigs, but it was very faint, and had not been done in red. Defendant stated that the policeman had been into the public house just before he saw the pigs, and therefore could not see what colour the mark was." Another witness said the mark was rather dark and was not a good red colour. "The Bench decided that it was a case in which they could not convict."

Bill Cary returned to court in December 1899. On this occasion,

"William Carey, farmer, was summoned by Charles Stone, labourer, for an assault. There was a cross summons for assault. Complainant stated he was working for Mr. Carey cider making. Defendant came home about three o'clock in the afternoon, he (complainant) told him the ropes had broken and he ought to have new ones. Defendant said, 'What —- odds is that to you?' Witness said, 'Suppose I had been killed then?' Defendant replied, 'What —- odds if thee hast been killed? If thee disn't like to do it come up for thee money.' Defendant then hit him with his hand ... and defendant hit his hat off. Defendant caught him by the neck and got him down, and he told Carey not to serve him like he served Tom Giles. Defendant said, 'I'll serve you a —- sight worse than I did Tom Giles.' Defendant also called George Hunt and said, 'Let us put him in the —-.' Defendant caught him hold, but Giles came up and said, 'You are making a mistake, sir; you had better come on milking.' Defendant had since paid complainant his wages and offered him plenty of cider not to say any more about it." Case dismissed!

In February 1901,

"William Carey, farmer, of Chedzoy, did not appear to answer a charge of allowing ten pigs to stray on the highway. P.C. Fry proved the case, remarking that defendant said he would give him a pig to keep his mouth shut. (Laughter.) Fined 22s. 6d. and costs."

In October 1910 Bill pleaded guilty to a similar charge concerning nine pigs and was fined 30 shillings and costs.

He appeared again in May 1901 after his violent temper got the better of him.

"William Cary was charged with cruelly ill-treating a cow by beating it. Inspector Johnstone, R.S.P.C.A., said he was passing through Mr. Ashford's farm when he heard the sound of blows. He saw the defendant holding onto a heifer by a rope tied round the horns and was beating the heifer about the head, legs and nose at least 40 times with the butt end of a stick. On one occasion the heifer fell to the ground and the defendant hit her on the head and nose with all his might till she got up again. Witness shouted out to him, 'Hold on, Mr. Cary, that's enough of that. That is what I call cruelty.' Defendant answered, 'What can I do? I can't get her in to milk her. I will give you sixpence to get her in.'

Considering the defendant's position the Bench could not fine him less than £2 and costs."

Three months later he was in court yet again:

"William Cary, farmer, was summoned for driving without lights. He pleaded guilty. Defendant said he had been working hard all day and he thought the Bench ought to excuse him (laughter). He had been working so hard that he thought they ought to let him off (renewed laughter). Fined 5s. and costs. Joseph Lovibond, in the employ of Mr. Cary, was summoned for a similar offence and fined 2s. 6d. and costs. Cary paid the money, but made an uncalled for remark respecting the Magistrates' Clerk and was ordered to be removed from court. The defendant made a struggle in the gangway but was promptly ejected."

1902 seems to have been fairly uneventful at Manor Farm -

"William Cary was summoned for allowing six steers to stray at Bawdrip. Fined 15s. and costs," -

but in August 1903 he was in court again, this time with George Hunt, one of his employees. George was accused of cruelly ill-treating a mare by working the animal in an unfit state in Fore Street, Bridgwater. Bill was summoned for causing the animal to be worked. Both of them denied the charges. An R.S.P.C.A. Inspector told the court how, after seeing the animal being worked in town, he went to Manor Farm with a constable in order to carry out a further examination.

"They searched the field and could not find the horse, and after scouting about the country for an hour they found the animal in (sic) a common three miles from Cary's home. On the shoulder was a sore the size of half a crown."

George Hunt was fined five shillings and Bill Cary twenty shillings and costs.

But a far more serious charge was just around the corner. Although not reported in the local paper, Bill appeared before Bristol Magistrates' Court charged with supplying watered down milk. Things clearly did not go as planned at that time as in December 1903 he found himself before Bristol Assizes indicted

"for unlawfully committing wilful and corrupt perjury in the testimony he gave upon oath in his examination before the Court of Summary Jurisdiction at Bristol."

He gave evidence under oath in a case where he had been charged with supplying milk which had in it more than the quantity of water allowed by law. It seems that Bill Cary supplied milk which was sent by train to Montpelier station for a local dairy. At the station a sample of milk was taken by officials and divided into three, one of the samples being sent to Manor Farm. He substituted the milk from the sample with fresh milk and sent this to an analyst in a bottle without a numbered seal. The Mercury reported that

"On the following day Dr. Alford received a letter from prisoner who enclosed fee for analysis and added, 'If you have any enquiry about the milk, will you please say you received it in a plain bottle, number 147, which you omitted to put on the certificate'.... It was felt by the city authorities to be so grave an attempt to interfere with the course of justice that a prosecution for perjury was imperative. At the Magistrates' Court he stated on oath that all the milk in the churn in question was put in by him just as it came from the cow and he never interfered with the sample. He now admitted he had substituted the milk and pleaded guilty to the charge."

He was sentenced to six months' imprisonment.

In November 1908

"William Cary was charged with having allowed 28 beasts to stray on the highway at Bradney and was fined 30s. including costs." The following June, "William Cary did not appear to answer a summons for allowing two steers to stray at Bawdrip was fined 6s. and costs."

It seems that, except for stray animals, Bill kept out of trouble for twelve years, but in May 1915 he was back in court and again arguing with officials.

"William Cary was summoned for leaving his horse and cart unattended in St. Mary's Street, [Bridgwater]. He pleaded guilty. P.S. Criddle said at 12 midday he saw a horse attached to a cart near the churchyard railings. At 12.18 he saw defendant coming from the direction of Penel Orlieu. Defendant said the horse was a quiet one, and did not move an inch. The Deputy Magistrates' Clerk: It might have done. Defendant: It might not. The Chief Constable said defendant had appeared sixteen times previously before the court. Defendant was fined 10s. and 2s. 3d. as costs of the summons at Chedzoy."

In July 1915 Bill Cary was involved in two cases in the County Court.

"William Cary was sued by William Parkhouse of Bawdrip for trespass by stock and for pound breach. Defendant said the plaintiff's fence must have been bad to enable his (defendant's) cattle to get into the field. Defendant: 'It was not cows or heifers but little yearlings. You can't make mountains out of molehills. I don't reckon they did much damage.' 10s. damages awarded."

He was the plaintiff in the next case:

"William Cary sued William Wills of Westonzoyland Road in respect of 22 empty sacks at 3d. each."

It was reported that Wills had kept the potato sacks for three or four months. The judge ordered the sacks to be returned and that the defendant should pay one shilling for their detention.

Problems with milk reappeared in June 1918, this time at Bridgwater Police Court.

"William Cary, farmer, Chedzoy, was charged with having unlawfully sold milk which was not of a nature, substance and quality demanded, viz., a mixture containing 8.1% of added water. Defendant said as a practical farmer he knew that there was often a considerable difference in the quality of milk, which varied with the weather. In cold weather cows did not give such good milk. He would swear that the milk was taken into the town in the same condition in which it came from the cows. The Chairman said the Bench were quite satisfied that the offence had been committed and defendant would be fined £10."

It sometimes seems that Bill just couldn't keep out of trouble. In February 1921 it was reported that

"William Cary, farmer, of Chedzoy was summoned by Olive Thompson of Bradney for assaulting her. She and her husband had purchased a basket of potatoes in Chedzoy and he went home by the footpath having strapped the basket of potatoes on his bicycle. The strap broke while crossing one of the defendant's fields and the potatoes fell on the ground and he went on without them because it was so dark. The following day they went to look for the potatoes but could not find them. Mrs. Thompson asked defendant's son if the basket had been found, and he said it was at their house. Mrs. Thompson went to the house and defendant accused her husband of having stolen the potatoes, shook his fist in her face, and pushed her from the door, and also refused to give up the basket. Defendant said, 'He did not touch complainant enough to kill a flea.' He told her if she paid for the potatoes, she could have the basket. Defendant was fined 10s."

Continuing problems with livestock resulted in Bill appearing before Bridgwater County Court in November 1923.

"Joseph Ashford claimed of William Cary £10 10s. as damages for the conversion of a ram, or, alternatively, the return of the animal. There was a counter claim for damages through a ram belonging to the defendant being killed by plaintiff's ram. Plaintiff's ram trespassed upon land belonging to defendant, who gave notice to plaintiff that the ram had been fighting with his ram and had killed it. Plaintiff went to defendant and tendered £5 5s. under protest, but defendant refused to give up plaintiff's ram. His Honour thought plaintiff's ram did seriously injure defendant's ram and that it died of that injury. He thought the ram was worth more than £5 5s. but considered plaintiff was entitled to damages for the way his ram had been kept, and he assessed those damages at £3 3s. On the counter claim he gave judgement for £7 7s. to defendant to let plaintiff have the ram when he called for it."

His next appearance in court seems to have been in February 1930:

"A BAD CASE OF CRUELTY. CHEDZOY FARMER HEAVILY FINED" was the headline in the Bridgwater Mercury. "William Cary, farmer, of Chedzoy, was summoned for cruelly ill-treating a horse by working it in an unfit state. Inspector Meara of the R.S.P.C.A. stated he saw the defendant in High Street, [Bridgwater] driving a chestnut horse attached to a trap in the direction of Penel Orlieu. He noticed pus on the forelock and mane. There was a sore underneath the bridle; it was a very bad case of poll-evil. 'It smelt horribly,' added the Inspector, 'and nearly made me ill.' He went to get a witness, but saw Cary drive away at a trot as fast as he could down the town. P.S. Edwards stopped defendant by the town bridge. He said it was a very bad case indeed, one of the worst he had ever seen. The stench could be detected from four yards away. Defendant told the Court, 'They have come here to make mountains out of molehills, to swindle me out of my money. I think they ought to act like Englishmen and bark before they bite.' The Chief Constable informed the Court that since 1893 there had been four convictions against the defendant for cruelty to animals. The Mayor said this was a very bad case, and defendant would be fined £10 with £1 1s. special costs or, in default, one month's imprisonment. The fine was paid."

The sound of bangers set by Cecil Cary, and used to frighten the many foxes which roam the area, echoed around the orchard. He was sure there were no foxes here until they were introduced by Richard 'Dick' Hern, a keen huntsman, who married Rev. Mullens' daughter.

Cecil Cary, 1900 - 1990.
Courtesy of Muriel Brown.

(Above) Manor Farm, 1954.
Left to right; George Heard, George Clapp, Bob Heard, Herbie Baker, G. Heard, Harold Carter, Len Kidner, Percy Guntripp (with sack truck), Bert Kidner, George Palmer.
Photograph by Cecil Cary, courtesy of Muriel Brown.

(Below) Manor Farm.
Eileen Webber cleaning eggs.
Photograph by Cecil Cary, courtesy of Muriel Brown.

However, if an 1894 report in the Bridgwater Mercury is to be believed, the problem had existed long before Cecil's birth:

> "On Sunday last Mr. Wm. Carey of the Manor Farm found that a number of his geese had been killed during the night by a dog. The brute also visited another farm, where he was equally destructive." It seems that dogs were another problem. In November 1971, "Two sheep were killed by an Alsatian dog at Manor Farm, Chedzoy. The owner of the sheep, Mr. C.R. Cary fired a gun in the direction of the dog, but the animal ran off."

(Above) Manor Farm.
Cecil Cary, Charlie Stone and Steve Clapp take a break from their labours.
Source unknown, courtesy of Muriel Brown.

(Below) Manor Farm, 1961.
Charlie Stone, Les Collard, Kevin Collard and Harry Collard take a rest during harvesting.
Photograph by Cecil Cary, courtesy of Muriel Brown.

During the First World War, when William Cary was still the tenant at Manor Farm, prisoners-of-war were set to work there. Obviously farm life was not too arduous since three, all from the Vienna area, maintained contact for many years. This friendship is best demonstrated by a letter which Robert Nasskau wrote to Cecil Cary in February 1946:

> "I take the first oportunity to send you a few lines hoping you'll get them soon and will find you in as good a position as possible after this most terrible war. Please Cecil, do try to write me a few lines to let me know how you have passed

those years. Thinking very often on the time when I had the pleasure to stay with your family who all became so dear to me that I wish I could be with you again at the present time. ... Don't forget to remember me to everybody who know me in dear old Chedzoy."

In 1946 eastern Austria was still occupied by the Soviet army and the letter bears the censor's stamp.

But not all memories were so happy. Philip Dance, a 26 year old native of Stow-on-the-Wold, was a private in 449 Agricultural Company stationed at Taunton. In 1916 he was ordered to work on Manor Farm and lived with his wife at Yew Tree Cottages. In July 1917 he was kicked in the stomach by one of the farm horses and died four days later as a result of peritonitis.

As on West End Farm, technological progress was not without its problems. Cecil Cary purchased a tractor for use on the farm and insisted that one of his labourers, Percy Guntripp, could drive it - despite his protestations to the contrary. Percy set off driving across a field without any problems but then disappeared through the far hedge shouting, "Whoa! Whoa! Whoa!"

In the Second World War Manor Farm played host to three evacuees and several German and Italian prisoners-of-war worked there, helping with the potato crop and other labouring duties. Cecil Cary recalled the numerous buckets of sand which had to be placed around the buildings in accordance with Regulations in case of fire. He himself was a private in the village Home Guard and still had his uniform at the time of his death in 1990. Home Guard duties also brought about role-reversal as Percy Guntripp held the rank of Sergeant!

Originally Chedzoy Lane became Higher Road from the junction with Manor Road but modern usage places all the properties from Front Street to Manor Farm and Banfield Barn in Higher Road, and in 1998 this was extended further from the centre of the village to include Field Barn.

Neighbouring Manor Farm are two red brick cottages, originally known as **YEW TREE COTTAGES**: in the late 1980s one was extended and re-named **Valentine Cottage**. These were erected in 1873 by the University of Oxford after they had taken over the estates belonging to Henry Porter. One of their residents was in trouble in March 1888:

"Joseph Lovibond (38), of Chedzoy, was charged with riding on a waggon without being provided with reins. - Defendant said: I hope you magistrates will put it on as light as you can; 'tis the first offence. Fined 1s. 6d. (7.5p.) and costs."

MANOR ROAD, the small lane which turns left beside Yew Tree Cottages, leads the visitor past the mellow red brick **MOGGS FARM**. One of the former residents of the farm was in trouble in March 1957:

"Pleading not guilty at Bridgwater Borough Magistrates' Court to leaving his car without lights at Mount Street, Bridgwater, Wyndham Wallace Stone, farmer, of Moggs Farm, Chedzoy, said the lights were on when he left the vehicle and when he returned. He also expressed resentment at the police removing the ignition key. P.S. Peters said he switched on the lights as the car was a potential danger to other traffic. Defendant was fined 10s."

Please take care at this point, Manor Road is narrow and **Pig Lane**, beside Moggs Farm, leads to the village playing field, so watch for children. In Pig Lane, opposite the playing field, are two cottages. In December 1928 the Bridgwater Mercury reported

"On Wednesday evening at the Manor House Inn, Messrs. Tamlyn and Son sold by auction two freehold dwelling houses in Pigs Lane (sic), Chedzoy to Mr. W. Carey at £207 10s. and Mr. George Bennett at £30. The solicitors for the vendors were Messrs. Barham and Watson."

Manor Road, 1981.
Laburnum House and its garden (now the site of "Pennard". The Silver Birch is now one of the larger trees in the village.
Photograph by John Weeks.

One of the cottages, now known as **KOZ-E-KOT**, was sold by auction by Mr. Bennett in May 1956, at which time it was purchased for £875 by Mrs. Freda Stokes, mother of the present owner. The other cottage was replaced by the bungalow known as **KNOWLE VIEW**, and was the home of Oliver Bennett who died the following year. His widow, Matilda, continued to live there and tend the large garden until her death in 1966 at the age of 84 years.

Continue along Manor Road from Pig Lane and pass Willow Green to the **MANOR HOUSE INN** where, at opening time, visitors will find refreshment. When the Manor of Chedzoy was sold in 1860 the sale particulars included,

"Near the church is a newly built comfortable residence called 'The Manor House' which is occupied by the Steward, and contains accommodation available for a proprietor on his visits to view the estate or to enjoy some good partridge shooting."

Shortly after the sale of the Manor of Chedzoy the former Manor House became a beer house. The 1866 Kelly's Directory listed George Parish as being a beer retailer. On October 1869 it seems that he lost his licence for a while as it was reported that at the annual licensing of beer houses,

"in consequence of insufficient notice, the licence applied for by George Parish of Chedzoy was refused."

Like the Hunter's Lodge Inn, the Manor House has had problems at times. In November 1878 the Bridgwater Mercury reported that

"John Stone (44 years of Front Street) was summoned for being disorderly at the Manor House Inn, Chedzoy and refusing to quit when requested to do so by the landlord. Defendant pleaded guilty. - Superintendent Jeffs said defendant was the worse for liquor and an altercation having taken place on the premises the landlord ordered the defendant out, but he refused to go for some time. - Defendant was fined 5s. and costs."

By December 1875 the licensee was Tom Butler who was described on the 1881 Census as being a blacksmith and beer house keeper. This report, from that date, contains language very different from that which would be used in a similar situation today:

"William James was summoned for threatening Tom Butler (26), blacksmith, at Chedzoy. Complainant said defendant came for a pick at his shop, and began using abusive language. He went towards the defendant, who left the shop and said, 'Come out, I'll take your life, or you shall mine.' - John Butler, brother of complainant, corroborated. - Tom Butler, in another summons, was charged with making threats towards William James at the same time. Complainant said he went to Butler's shop and he (Butler) tried to strike him with a red hot iron and asked to fight. He (James) also asked the defendant to fight. - The cases were dismissed, each party having to pay their own costs."

Francis Lovibond's diary records that on 30th July 1879 the house and garden were sold to Holt Brothers Ltd., brewers, of Burnham-on-Sea for the sum of £720. As far as is known it had previously been owned by Churchill's Brewery. Francis Lovibond noted that on the same date George Hunt paid £355 for the paddock and James Gilbert paid £110 for "ground near his house" and a further £140 for the orchard. The total sale price was £1,325. In the early years of the 20th Century the western (left) end of the building was a separate dwelling, only the eastern end being used as a public house.

During the General Election campaign of November 1885 the inn was the scene of a political meeting. Edward Trevillian, the Liberal candidate, visited the village and what happened was reported in the Bridgwater Mercury.

"MR. TREVILLIAN AT CHEDZOY. ANOTHER NOISY MEETING. On Wednesday evening a meeting was held in a room at the Manor House at Chedzoy, an application for the use of the school-room having been refused, in support of Mr. Trevillian's candidature. Mr. Trevillian and friends who accompanied him were met at the entrance to the village by a body of men, most of whom were said to be electors, who released the horses from the brake and dragged it to the place of meeting. The room was a small one, and shortly after the commencement of the proceedings it became crowded. It soon became evident that a large proportion of those present, and a much larger proportion of those who filled the passage outside, were not in sympathy with the Liberal cause. The most conspicuous of the disturbers was Mr. Albert Fry, of Sutton Farm, [Sutton Mallet], who continually interrupted Mr. Trevillian with exclamations of his own, which excited the merriment and applause of his numerous backers and resulted in the break-up of the meeting at the conclusion of which the bells in the parish church were rung. Superintendent Vowles said several police-constables were in attendance, and it is believed that their presence prevented any resort to actual violence."

A detailed report of the proceedings then followed. At one stage a handful of grain was thrown at the platform. The lengthy report concludes:

"A voice: You might as well try to convert a monkey as Mr. Fry,' and another voice, 'I should think Mr. Fry never went in the oven, for he's only half-baked' - (laughter and uproar). Subsequently an attempt was made by the disturbers to storm the platform, but they were prevented by Mr. Trevillian's supporters from doing so."

Those entitled to vote had to attend Eastover School, Bridgwater. There were 9,820 registered electors in the Bridgwater area, of whom 7,820 cast a vote. Edward Stanley, the Conservative candidate, beat Mr. Trevillian by 3,935 to 3,835 votes, a Conservative majority of 100.

In February 1886 it was reported that,

"Mr. W.H. Tamlyn, auctioneer, applied for the transfer of the licence of the Manor House Inn, Chedzoy from Tom Butler, to Wm. Phillips (44), labourer. - Wm. Phillips proved he had served copies of the notices upon Mr. Edmund Derrick, one of the overseers of the parish of Chedzoy, and on Superintendent Vowles. - Superintendent Vowles said he objected to the transfer of the licence on the last occasion when an application was made. Now, however, Phillips had obtained letters from clergymen and others supporting the application and he would therefore make no objection. The transfer was granted."

Twelve months later the new licensee was in trouble, but not because of the inn.

"Wm. Phillips, beerhouse keeper, of Chedzoy was summoned for keeping a dog without a licence. P.C. Gould stated that it was a sort of spaniel dog. Witness had cautioned defendant about taking out a licence. Defendant's wife appeared in court and stated that her husband had twice given the dog away, but it came back again. Fined 10s. and costs." He appeared again in July 1889, this time as a witness: "John Wilkins, Chedzoy, was summoned for assaulting William Phillips of the above place. - Defendant pleaded not guilty. - Complainant stated that he kept the Manor House Inn. Defendant came to his house about quarter past nine and had a pint of beer. He came into the kitchen where the witness was and asked him to shake his hand, but as he (complainant) declined to do so defendant struck him on the shoulder. - The case was dismissed."

As a result of the Christmas spirit the licensee appeared before the magistrates in January 1890. The Bridgwater Mercury reported that,

"William Phillips, innkeeper, Chedzoy was charged with keeping open his licensed house after permitted hours, to wit, at one o'clock on the morning of 25th December. - P.C. Cooksley stated that on the morning in question, in consequence of numerous complaints that had been laid respecting the house, he went there and watched. Some time after he heard the landlord and a man named Whitfield come up the road, and he also heard a conversation between them."

This was Henry Whitfield, aged 38 of Front Street.

"Whitfield said to Phillips (sic), 'Well, you can have a pint of beer, a gallon for forty.' Whitfield then entered the house, soon after which witness followed and in the kitchen he saw Whitfield sat down and smoking a pipe, whilst the landlord was stood up in front of the fire. He did not see any liquor there, but in reply to witness Whitfield admitted the offence, stating, 'There is no use for me to deny it. I went in there to have a pint to drink.' - Supt. Vowles stated that he had, in consequence of complaints, placed the witness to watch the premises on the evening in question. - The bench considered the case proved, and defendant was fined £1 and costs and the licence was ordered to be endorsed."

A month later,

"Henry Whitfield, Chedzoy, was charged with being found on the licensed premises of William Phillips during prohibited hours. - P.C. Cooksley proved the case and defendant, who pleaded guilty, was fined £1 including costs."

The inn, like many others, has from time to time been the scene of confused disturbances. In September 1895 Oliver Bennett (24), George Stone (18) and Caroline Phillips (54) were summoned for assaulting John Stokes. Cross summonses had also been issued. The Bridgwater Mercury reported that

"Stokes was walking past the Manor House Inn ... and was attacked from behind which knocked him to the ground." John Stokes alleged he was punched and kicked and attacked with a belt buckle. "Allegedly Stokes was three parts drunk and offered to fight Bennett. Eliza Jane Stokes, daughter of John Stokes, said her father was brought into the Manor House that night and he was not sensible and blood all over. Her mother washed his face, and he then became sensible again. Witness added that she had seen her father in a more drunken state than on this occasion."

The case against Caroline Phillips was dismissed and the other three defendants were each fined five shillings.

In September 1901 the licence for the Crown Inn was not renewed, leaving the Manor House as the only beer-house in the village. As a result in January 1903 Caroline Phillips applied to the magistrates for a full licence so that wine and spirits could also be sold. The court refused the application at that time and adjourned consideration of the matter until the annual brewster session the following year. The next mention of the premises was in April that year when the licence was transferred from Mrs. Phillips to her son, Albert Phillips, a former member of the Cardiff City Police.

Manor House Inn.
This shows the field which existed opposite the Inn, before the council houses in Manor Road and Manor Drive were constructed. Laburnum House can be seen on the right.
Source unknown, courtesy of Helen Hunt.

Having a former policeman as licensee was no guarantee of a trouble-free pub. In May 1905 the Bridgwater Mercury reported that

"William Fry was summoned for having been found drunk on licensed premises." P.C. Fry testified that "The defendant was in a beastly condition of drunkenness" earlier in the evening in Chedzoy Lane shouting, "I don't care for the —- policeman or anyone else."

He was fined ten shillings and costs.

Two weeks later Albert Phillips appeared for having permitted drunkenness to take place on his licensed premises.

He said that William Fry had only been on the premises for ten minutes and had not been served.

> "The Magistrates retired to consider their decision and they decided there must be a conviction: they fined defendant 10s. and costs, also allowing a solicitor's fee, the total amount of fine and costs being £2 3s. 6d."

In February 1907 a full licence was granted to Albert Phillips. The Bridgwater Mercury reported that the magistrates were told,

> "The application principally was on the ground that the licence was for the benefit of the public. Mr. Phillips continually had application made to him for brandy and port wine in cases of sickness. People now went to the vicarage, and the vicar occasionally gave away a little, and it came rather hard on him that his should be the only place to which people could run."

The premises have had a full licence since that time.

Albert Phillips, together with Henry Jeanes, found himself in trouble in 1908. Both appeared in court

> "charged with having on 1st January carried a gun without a licence authorising them to do so. They were seen shooting sparrows in a field near the Manor House Inn. They did not think they were doing harm and it was not a case of carrying a gun for, as a matter of fact, there were a few people present in the field who had gun licences. Wallace Bennett, who held a gun licence, let the defendants have a couple of shots at sparrows. Fined 10s. each and costs."

The inn was the scene of another lively political meeting during the General Election campaign of January 1910. The Bridgwater Mercury devoted over a column to a report of the meeting which was organised by the Liberal Party. The Liberals were defending the seat which they had won in 1906 with a majority of just 17 votes. The candidate, Harold C. Hicks, was due to speak but things got out of hand even before his arrival.

> "Soon after the Chairman commenced his speech a large number of opponents put in an appearance. The proceedings then became quite uproarious and a severe heckling which the Chairman received rendered it almost impossible for that gentleman to make himself heard." Later he said, "'I hope Mr. Hicks will be on top. You must remember that Chedzoy is not everywhere going to be blue (applause).' 'It has done itself no good by being blue,' replied Mr. Foster.' (A voice: Anyway, we're going to elect Mr. Sanders by a thousand majority.) Disorder broke out again and the audience left en masse under the impression that Mr. Hicks would not visit the village that evening. Mr. and Mrs. Hicks then drove up in a motor car. Mr. Hicks alighted outside the inn and addressed a fairly large crowd in the open air. He received a good deal of heckling and good natured chaff and a number of questions were put to him on various political topics before he left for Bridgwater."

The seat was won by Robert A. Sanders for the Conservative and Unionist Party with 5,575 votes against Mr. Hicks 3,896 votes, a Conservative majority of 1,679.

Both licensee and customers at the Manor House were in trouble in 1915. In March the Bridgwater Mercury reported,

> "Robert Fry, Herbert Baker and Clifford Heal, farmers, were charged with having been found unlawfully on licensed premises during prohibited hours, viz. at 11.35 p.m. P.C. Gard said it was a very rough night and peeping through a shuttered window he was able to see Heal and Fry and heard the rattle of a mineral water bottle. He knocked at the door three times and he waited nearly 15 minutes before the landlord, Slade, answered the door."

Each was fined thirty shillings (£1.50) and costs. Two weeks later Francis John Drake Knight, the licensee, was fined £2 and costs for permitting persons to be on his premises during prohibited hours.

In April 1918 the licence was transferred to Uriah Ashman, but less than a year later it was transferred again, this time to William Gunningham. The first harvest after that brought some discomfort to the new licensee. In September 1919,

> "On Tuesday evening last whilst Mr. W. Gunningham, the esteemed landlord of the Manor House Inn, was engaged in gathering plums in his garden, a branch of the tree snapped, and Mr. Gunningham fell to the ground. Assistance was soon at hand, and a brother-in-law conveyed the injured man in his brougham to the Bridgwater Hospital where his injuries were attended to by the house surgeon. It was found that Mr. Gunningham had sustained a broken left arm and also dislocated his wrist, but he was able to proceed home the same evening and is now progressing favourably."

William Gunningham moved on in April 1922 and the licence was transferred to James Chapple. In March 1924, following the death of Mr. Chapple in January, the new licensee was David Henry Robinson who came from Outwood, Yorkshire.

From 1926 until 1953 the licensee of the Manor House was Oliver Bennett (1871-1954). In 1947 a very welcome visitor arrived at the premises. Charley R. Hartnell had emigrated to the United States in 1906 and, after 41 years, made his first visit back to this country in order to stay with his sister, Mrs. Matilda Bennett, at the Manor House. Today we take air travel so much for granted that it is difficult to comprehend the difficulties of such a journey in those days. He had left Border, Minnesota on 8th November, travelled 1,800 miles overland for six days, presumably to New York, then boarded the R.M.S. Queen Mary. He arrived in Southampton four days later on 18th November: ten days of travel for a trip which now takes little over ten hours. Mr. Hartnell stayed in Chedzoy until starting his return journey on 19th December.

Manor House Inn, 1926
Note the door into the bar immediately behind the man.
Source unknown, courtesy of Helen Hunt.

A short report was published in the Mercury in December 1951:

> "Licensee for 25 years of the Manor House, Chedzoy, Mr. Oliver Charles Bennett made successful application for extension of hours on December 21st from 10 to 11 p.m. for a skittle club supper. This was the first such application of its kind that he has made." In June 1953 the same paper noted, "A Protection Order was granted at Bridgwater County Sessions to Mr. George Oliver Bennett (born 1905) in respect of the Manor House Inn, Chedzoy, the outgoing tenant being his father, Mr. Oliver Charles Bennett."

In May 1954,

> "Charles William Chedgey, County Court Bailiff, Manor House, Chedzoy was fined £2 by Bridgwater Borough Magistrates for using a 1932 van with inefficient brakes. Pleading not guilty, defendant said he was not asked by the police to make an emergency stop when a test was carried out of his vehicle. He said he had been driving for over 30 years without an accident."

About 1951 the premises were sold by Holt Brothers to Messrs. Starkey, Knight and Ford and about 1960 it became the property of Whitbreads.

In August 1963 George Bennett retired and

> "Bridgwater County Magistrates approved a Protection Order being granted in respect of the Manor House, Chedzoy to Mr. Frederick Cyril White who will be succeeding Mr. George Bennett,"

with the full licence being transferred a month later. Cyril and Elaine White remained as tenants until February 1999 when they purchased the property from the brewery.
Sadly, Cyril died suddenly just three months later, at which time he was the longest serving licensee at any public house in Somerset.

The Manor House Inn may also be approached by continuing along Higher Road and turning left into Manor Drive. Using this route, after the bungalow on the left known as '**Byways**,' an old cottage, **QUANTOCK VIEW**, nestles between a newer bungalow and the Council houses. The garden at one time extended for nearly one acre, including the ground on which the bungalows now stand. This included a pig sty and, after the annual pig killing, the carcass was hung to drip onto the flagstone floor in what is now the front doorway of the cottage. By 1881 it was the home of Mrs. Caroline Jewell, a native of Chedzoy, but it not clear when she and her husband purchased the cottage.

In September 1909 Mrs. Jewell

> "sued William Arthur of Catcott to recover the sum of £5 3s. for alleged breach of warrant on a pony."

Arthur sold her an old pony but made it known that the animal was sound and would last for ten or eleven years.

> "That turned out not to be so for on the first occasion Mrs. Jewell and her sister drove it into town they had to leave by the back streets to keep out of the hands of the inspector."

A veterinary surgeon saw the pony and said it was very old and only fit to be slaughtered. The pony was sent back to Arthur.

> "Mr. Harden said his client had entered a counter claim for keep of the pony. His Honour: It is a pony about 99 years old, as far as I can gather (laughter). Mr. Harden: He said the pony was quiet. You found it quiet? I found it to be too quiet (laughter). His Honour: You wanted a quiet one? Yes, but not so quiet you couldn't get it on (laughter)."

Mr. Harry Potts, veterinary surgeon was present on behalf of the plaintiff and said the pony was thirty years old.

> "In giving his decision, his Honour said the suggestion was that defendant had tried to take in 'two dear old ladies.' It was ludicrous. Plaintiff wanted a very quiet pony and she certainly got one. It was a thirty year old pony and to suggest a man would warrant it was absolute nonsense. There would be judgement for the defendant. Defendant: What am I to do with the pony? His Honour: I don't care what you do with it!"

In 1912 the cottage was purchased from Mrs. Jewell by Robert Thomas Hanham: the conveyance of the sale records the price as £250. For over 40 years Mr. Hanham was a builder, decorator and undertaker as well as being Clerk to the Parish Council and a churchwarden. He died in March 1953 at the age of 73: his wife, Ellen, died in August 1961, aged 86. Both were laid to rest in the village churchyard.

Beyond Quantock View are three pairs of houses, originally

built for Bridgwater Rural District Council.

In April 1948 the Bridgwater Mercury reported,

"Kenneth John Hill of 2 Higher Road, Chedzoy, who attained his fifteenth birthday yesterday, has not missed a single day's attendance since he began school at the age of five years. Kenneth first attended Chedzoy School and later proceeded to Huntspill School where he will remain a pupil until the present term ends in July."

Further details were reported when Kenneth left school and was presented with a ten shilling note (50p.) in recognition of his continuous attendance. It was also reported that his elder brother, Colin, aged 18, had only missed 14 days through illness during his education; younger brother, Norman, 10, had not missed a day in five years, and sister Patricia, not quite six, had not missed a single day during her first year at school. What a record!

FRYS COTTAGES are further along on the right opposite Manor Drive. These were also built by the University of Oxford and are similar in style and age to Yew Tree Cottages. No. 3 was the home for 43 years of Annie Phillips. In September 1938 this house was at the centre of a case which was heard in Bridgwater County Police Court and reported in the Bridgwater Mercury.

"Mr. Geoffrey P. Clarke made an application on behalf of Mrs. Annie Baker of Frys Farm, Chedzoy for possession of a cottage in the occupation of Mrs. Annie Phillips at Higher Road, Chedzoy for whom Mr. C.B. Pardoe appeared to oppose the application. In explaining the facts, Mr. Clarke said the notice to quit was given on 3rd May, a month's notice, but for various reasons, Mrs. Baker had not been able to bring the case before, although in the meantime an effort had been made to get possession and also an agricultural certificate. Mrs. Phillips had known that proceedings would be taken, and that she would be required to find another house. This application was being made under the 1933 Act, and the County Agricultural Committee had certified that the person for whom the cottage was required by Mrs. Baker was an agricultural worker who was required for the proper working of the farm. Mr. Pardoe would no doubt tell the Bench that Mrs. Phillips had lived in this house for 43 years. That was so, and it was with great regret that Mrs. Baker had to apply for the order. Her husband, however, was an invalid, and a son had got married and left to go to a farm of his own, and she found that with only another son, a carter, and a boy, it was impossible for her to carry on; in fact, if she could not get another man to come to the cottage, she would have to give up the farm. The man, William Shattock, who would come to this house was a married man with four children. In her evidence, Mrs. Baker said she could not carry on any longer as she had been doing for some time in the past. It had been a very worrying time for her, and the work was always behind. She had nothing against Mrs. Phillips, who had always paid her rent regularly, and she was a widow.

"Mr. Pardoe called his client, who said she had been in possession of this cottage for 43 years, and had been a tenant since her husband's death in 1905. In March last, Mrs. Baker gave her notice to quit, but the son came to see her later, cancelling the notice saying they would not want the house until September, and that she could put in her garden, which she had done. Mrs. Baker afterwards came down and said she had bad news to tell her, as she (Mrs. Baker) would be wanting the cottage on account of someone leaving. Mrs. Phillips added that she had tried her best to get another house, and since she had received notice she had been to the Rural District Council's offices, to the Town Hall in Bridgwater, and every house agent in town to try and get a house. She would be prepared to go anywhere, although she would prefer to live in Chedzoy, but she could not afford to pay a big rent. ... The Bench made an order for possession within two months."

Opposite the Manor House Inn is **MANOR DRIVE** which leads back to Higher Road. For many years the field which was here was the site of the village football pitch. The houses in Manor Drive, plus some of those adjoining in Manor Road and Higher Road, were built by Bridgwater Rural District Council in 1948 and 1950. No. 4 (nearest to the Manor House Inn) was initially rented by the Somerset Constabulary and occupied by the village Constable, Jimmy Gough. In March 1959 he was succeeded by Constable Peter Parrish, who was the last resident policeman. P.C. Parrish moved to a new police house at Bawdrip in July 1965 but still retained responsibility for Chedzoy. Since the late 1970s the village has been policed from Bridgwater, the present community Constable being Andy Barron, but with responsibility for eleven villages he can never hope to have the same knowledge of the local community as an officer resident in Chedzoy. Older residents still speak of Constables Gough and Parrish, but in forty years will anyone recall the names of later Constables?

After the police gave up the house it reverted to normal Council occupancy and, until his death, it was the home of Frederick Charles 'Charlie' Stone (1905-1993) who was born in the village. Mr. Stone recalled that,

"I left school at 12 and was paid eight pence (3p.) a day by a farmer to work seven days a week. There were six of us in the family and mother used to sit up until the early hours making and mending our clothing. Except for his own name, Dad couldn't read or write, but there was no one to beat him with handling money. My grandfather, Frank Lovibond (Francis Lovibond, born 1825), was a cobbler here for many years. He was an educated man and used to write all the love letters for the young men of the village, and his daughters would listen outside the door as they were dictated."

From the time it was built, 3 Manor Road was home to Joyce Collard and her late husband, Les (1918-1996). Les was a great countryman who enjoyed shooting, and loved nothing more than to be out in the fields around the village.

Charlie Stone, 1905-1993.
Source unknown, courtesy of Muriel Brown.

This love seems to have run in his family as in 1910 his uncle found himself in trouble:

> "Ernest Collard, farm labourer, of Chedzoy pleaded guilty to having taken, killed and pursued a partridge without having a licence. He stated that he was out in search of hares, and a partridge flying up, he could not resist the temptation to shoot it. Fined £2 and costs."

Where exactly was not reported, but the straight piece of road now fronted by the "new" houses in seems a likely venue for this report in the Bridgwater Mercury in March 1964.

> "A collision with a car in dense fog resulted in a £5 fine with licence endorsed at Bridgwater County Magistrates' Court for motorcyclist Leonard Leslie Pinchen (18) of 7 Manor Drive, Chedzoy. Mrs. Doris Warren told the magistrates she was driving her car along Higher Road, Chedzoy at 20-25 m.p.h. It was impossible to drive faster because of the fog and she had her sidelights on. She saw a man on an autocycle approaching from the opposite direction and suddenly the motorcycle with two boys on it overtook the autocycle and banged into her car. P.C. Peter Parrish (Chedzoy) said that after the collision Pinchen said to him, 'I started to overtake. I had not seen this car and I went into it."

From the Manor House Inn continue along Manor Road. **LABURNUM HOUSE**, on the left, once had a very large garden which extended to Front Street. In April 1946 it was reported that

> "At their auction Messrs. Hamlin and Bryant disposed of a smallholding with dwelling house and 4 acres of land known as Laburnum House at £1,625."

The land was gradually sold off as building plots. The most recent house, Pennard, was completed in 1983. **MANOR VILLA**, the large white house beyond Pennard, was the village shop during the 1960s and 1970s. It was built in 1960 and the original owners were George and Stella Harris. It was then taken over by a Mr. C. Cooke and, in 1967, bought from a Mr. Griffin by Derek and Eileen Growtage. It was the centre of village activities as, about this time, the older shop in Front Street was closed. In 1973 Mr. and Mrs. Growtage sold the premises to a Mr. and Mrs. Ellis who ran it for a few months before selling it again, this time to Mr. and Mrs. Lancaster. Unfortunately, they reduced the shop hours to such an extent that custom dropped away and it was no longer a viable business, closing shortly afterwards and the shop area was then converted into living accommodation.

Opposite Manor Villa are the "new" houses. These four, and the four behind them in Higher Road, were built in 1972 and originally sold for £6,500 each: for an extra £150 a utility room could be added at the back. Rampant inflation meant that these houses were changing hands for £29,500 just eight years later in 1980. The houses on the far side of Higher Road were built three years later.

At the end of Manor Road turn left into **Front Street**. Drive past the church and continue along **Ward Lane** to **PARCHEY BRIDGE** and leave your car at the car park. Admire the peace and tranquillity of a typical Sedgemoor vista - the Polden Hills forming a backdrop to the rhynes and willows reflected in the still waters of King's Sedgemoor Drain. Watch for otters, kingfishers, swans, coots, wild duck, heron and buzzards. If you are very lucky, you may even see deer. Look north to Bawdrip and south to Westonzoyland. Nothing disturbs the tranquillity of the fisherman and the ubiquitous gaze of grazing Friesian cows, except an occasional low-flying military aircraft. On summer evenings, the beauty of the sunset dips from the sky to tinge the river with its colours and silhouette every shape above the lush green grass. Early in the morning, wraiths of mist rise from every waterway and the peat of the moor itself, like a pure, white, silken shroud.

Parchey, Fowlers Plot and Fishers Farm

From Parchey Bridge retrace your steps towards Chedzoy, passing **WEST MOOR HOUSE**, previously known at Parchey Farm, a Georgian building on the right. In September 1958 an item appeared in "Late News" in the Mercury, but a fuller report was not published.

> "Miss Margaret Clapp (17) of Parcheys Farm (sic), is detained in Bridgwater Hospital with head injuries sustained when, while walking, she was in collision with a motorcycle ridden by her 18 year old brother, Peter. He sustained an ankle injury."

Speaking in 1999 Pete Clapp recalled the accident which took place on Chedzoy Lane near West End Farm and that his sister was detained in hospital for several days.

Two more cottages once stood where the drive of West Moor House and the adjacent bungalow, built in 1968, now stand. **PARCHEY HOUSE**, beyond the bungalow is much older than West Moor House. It is built of cob and at one time had its thatched roof under the tiles: the original timbers still form part of the roof. **PARCHEY COTTAGE** had fallen into dereliction and was purchased for £175 in 1962 and then restored. The present owners have carried out considerable improvements. Opposite the cottage, turn left as Monmouth did, and follow **MOOR DROVE** onto Sedgemoor. At the third gate on your right, a footpath and drove, known as Frys Lane, offers a direct route back to the centre of the village.

Those who wish to follow Monmouth's footsteps will continue along the drove to the T-junction where Moor Drove turns right towards Brentsfield Bridge, passing a rise known as Mill Batch or Mount Close Batch, on the right. The circular route continues, with the **BATTLEFIELD** where Monmouth and Godfrey searched so desperately for the crossing of the Langmoor rhyne, on your left. Today it is peaceful with flocks of birds; plover, snow geese and greylag geese feed here in winter, as do swans for whose sake orange balls warn of the power lines which cross the moor.

It is not hard to imagine, however, on a wild and windy day, the clang of weapons and the boom of guns as men fought desperately. On a sunny, warm day, the hum of insects is all the disturbs the peace of those who lie here forever on the moor. The **MEMORIAL** may be seen on the site of the Royalist encampment by crossing the Brentsfield footbridge, over which Monmouth is said to have fled the battlefield, riding through Chedzoy in his haste to reach the Poldens on the way to safety. Brentsfield Bridge and Brentsfield Drove bring the visitor finally to Fowlers Plot at the western edge of Chedzoy. The name appears to have changed several times over the years: a deed dated 1795 refers to Brinsel Rhine while an 1860 sale notice give the name as Brinsalls. The minutes of a Vestry Meeting in April 1888 refer to it at Burnsel Bridge and various sale notices in the 1890s refer to it as Brinsfield Bridge. Where tithe map numbers were given, all of these refer to fields close to what is now known as Brentsfield Bridge.

The entrance to Brentsfield footbridge across Chedzoy New Cut to Westonzoyland lies through a field gate crossing the moor in the lee of a hawthorn hedge. This is the second hawthorn hedge on your left as you follow the drove. On the other side the footpath turns left along Chedzoy New Cut, passing through two gates. After the second gate, turn right and follow the hedge around two sides of the field. The gate in front of you opens onto a drove. Follow this drove a short way to its junction with another, and turn left to the memorial which is on the left hand side, clearly marked by two large lime trees.

For those wishing to visit the memorial, but not on foot from Chedzoy, it can be reached by car by driving to Westonzoyland and taking the first turning left into Kings Drive. Follow Kings Drive into Monmouth Road and continue to Bussex Farm (about $^{3}/_{4}$ mile in all). Leave your car and follow the signposts along the drove on your left to the memorial.

After your visit to the memorial, those who have walked from Chedzoy should retrace their steps to Brentsfield Drove. Turn left and follow the drove to its junction with the road from Chedzoy to Westonzoyland. On the right stands a pair of houses known as **THREE OAKS COTTAGES** which were built about 1928 by Messrs. R.T. Hanham and Son of Quantock View, Chedzoy.

Before the widening of King's Sedgemoor Drain, **RUGGS DROVE,** which leads towards the Westonzoyland Road, was invariably impassable for most of the winter because of flooding. Herbert Ashford recalled that when he was a boy people would hide in a hay rick on a piece of higher ground so that they could shoot ducks on the surrounding lake. The flooding was so extensive that Chedzoy was virtually an island. Water lapped either side of Chedzoy Lane at Slape Cross and it was possible to get into a small boat and row from Slape Cross via Ruggs Drove and Parchey all the way back to Slape Cross, but on the opposite side of the lane, which was the only route into the village in winter.

On the opposite side of the road from Three Oaks Cottages is a group of cottages and a red brick Victorian farmhouse known as **FOWLERS PLOT FARM**. The origin of the name is not known, but may be a reference to the days when wild fowling was a practice on the moors. The farm cottages are similar in style to those belonging to Manor Farm, known as Yew Tree Cottages, and were erected around 1873 after the University of Oxford took over the estates in the village.

In October 1863 the farm was the scene of a fire. The Bridgwater Mercury reported the affair in one long paragraph.

> "A boy aged 14 years, names James Coombes, was on Monday taken into custody by the police, on a charge of wilfully setting fire to a hay-rick on the previous Saturday, the property of George Winter. The prisoner was the same day taken before John Browne, Esq., at the county magistrates' clerk's office. Mr. B. Lovibond appeared to prosecute on the part of the Westminster Insurance Company, and Mr. Smith defended the prisoner. - Mr. Winter, farmer, stated that the

prisoner was his servant, working for him and living in the house. He had a barton (farmyard) close to his dwelling house, and in that barton he had two ricks of hay and a rick of straw, which were all right at eight o'clock on Saturday morning. At five o'clock in the afternoon of that day he was sent for from Bridgwater, and reached home at quarter past six, when he found that one of the hay-ricks had been on fire, but the flames had been put out. From the information he received he asked the prisoner if he had been smoking, and he replied that he had not. Prosecutor then sent for a policeman and gave prisoner in charge. He should estimate that 10 cwt. of hay was burnt, and a ton more injured. Prosecutor had cautioned prisoner not to smoke. He had three fires in the same place within the previous eight days - one on the 9th, one on the 16th, and the present one. That on the 9th was a straw rick, that on the 16th the manger &c., and the third the hay rick. On the 9th prosecutor and the prisoner left the barton together, about nine o'clock in the morning, but prisoner returned about eleven o'clock, and in doing his duty had to pass close to this straw rick. About an hour afterwards prosecutor met him retiring to the barton, and on going in there they saw the stack of straw on fire. Prosecutor said, 'This must have been done by a pipe or some matches; have you been smoking, Jim?' Prisoner answered, 'No, sir, I have not had a pipe for this ever so long; nearly a month.' Prosecutor asked him if he had met any one as he was coming down the road, and prisoner answered that he had met the salt-man. Prosecutor's wife was present, and prosecutor asked her if anybody had been in the barton that morning, and she answered that no one had. Prisoner helped to put out the fire. Prosecutor further asked if the salt-man was smoking, and the prisoner replied that he didn't know, and that he did not see him come out of the yard. The damage done on the 9th was only a trifle. On 16th the manger in the stable was discovered to be on fire by the servant girl, but the prosecutor was not at home. Prosecutor only employed prisoner and a man named Wm. Phillips, and the latter had to go in the barton as well as the prisoner. - Cross-examined by Mr. Smith: When the prisoner was taken into custody he was searched in my presence, and only a knife found on him; I have never seen a pipe, matches or tobacco on him in my life. Prisoner must have been gone half-an-hour from the barton to have fetched a putt, and the fire had not been burning when he returned more than five minutes. - James Lee, a little boy living with his father, said he worked for Henry Hodges, whose farm nearby adjoined that of prosecutor. On Saturday last witness saw prisoner, between one and two o'clock in the afternoon, in prosecutor's barton. Prisoner was standing near the hay-rick, and was smoking, holding his hand over the bowl of a pipe. Witness was standing about forty yards off. About a quarter of an hour after witness saw prisoner smoking he saw smoke coming from the barton, and on going down he saw the hay-rick on fire. About ten minutes after he was seen smoking, witness saw prisoner run to the orchard with a donkey and cart as fast as the donkey could go. Witness told his master (Mr. Hodges) what he had seen on the same day. - Cross-examined by Mr. Smith: Prisoner did all he could to put out the fire. I saw the smoke coming from his mouth, but his back was towards me. Between the prisoner and the rick there were some railings, and he was twelve feet from the rick. - Mr. Henry Hodges gave some evidence, but it was unimportant, as he did not see the boy smoking, and was only present after the fire had broken out. He estimated the damage at £5. - Mr. Browne did not consider the evidence sufficient, and dismissed the case."

Quite when he took over the farm is not known, but in December 1875 sale notices published in the Bridgwater Mercury noted that

> "Mr. Richard Denning is quitting." Amongst items which were offered for sale were "60 acres of grass, 25 tons of mangold wurtzel, 46 ton of swedes, 90 tons of wheat and barley, straw and pea haulm, 80 tons of meadow hay, 20 bags of keeping apples, agricultural implements, &c."

As was invariably the case, no sale report was published subsequently.

One of the best known residents of Fowlers Plot Farm was Miss Elizabeth Winter (1857-1948) who became famous as a lecturer and demonstrator in the art of cheese and butter making. Between 1894 and 1910 she ran a private dairy school at Fowlers Plot for the sons and daughters of farmers. In 1890 she visited the Royal dairy at Frogmore and in 1891 published a book about Cheddar cheese making which was patronised by H.R.H. the Prince of Wales (later King Edward VII). In May 1894 the Bridgwater Mercury wrote that

> "Readers will hear with pleasure that Miss Winter's demonstration of working Messrs. Bradford and Co. patent 'Fishback' churn at the Somerset County Show at Messrs. Thompson's stand at Bridgwater last week, was so successful that she has been engaged by the same firm to churn and make butter in the 'Fishback' during the Devon County Show to be held at Exeter this week. The week following she will visit Honiton to also demonstrate the art of making butter with the same speed churn. During the show week at Bridgwater, Miss Winter made over 40 pounds of butter in the show yard, the time of churning being from 3 to 5 minutes only. The butter was remarkable for its perfect grain and colour. The cream for the Devon County Show at Messrs. Bradford stand will be supplied from the dairy of Mr. G. Winter, Fowlers Plot."

Subsequent reports showed her travels to demonstrate her prowess with the 'Fishback' at the Royal Cornwall Agricultural Association at Falmouth in June 1894. In July at the Cork Agricultural Show

> "Miss Winter was highly successful in churning and making her butter to such perfection that the sale price was obliged to be raised to 2s. (10p.) per pound. Miss Winter was especially noted at the show as having charge in the working dairy department of 'an English dairy of cleanliness.' Her attractive way of dealing with butter making was so pleasing that she was offered the situation of head

manageress at a high salary at Lady O'Neill's dairy, which she was unable to accept, being engaged by Messrs. Bradford and Co. to attend the agricultural shows in the west of England where the Fishback is to be shown."

Later in July,

"Miss Winter attended Northampton County Show, Leicester and Bolton. Her visit in Ireland was so successful that she had been asked to write an article for the 'Irish Farming World' on improved arrangements for working dairies in that country, and a wish has been expressed that she will be able to attend the Dublin Show in April 1895."

In September 1894 she won the silver medal at the Staffordshire County Show, her sixth that year. She also appeared at the Cardiff Show as well as the British and Colonial Industrial Exhibition in Manchester. Elizabeth Winter was also a philanthropist and through her wealthy and influential contacts was able to assist her less fortunate neighbours. In May 1895 following disastrous floods at Burtle, Edington and Catcott the Bridgwater Mercury reported,

"With the generous help thus offered her, Miss Winter was enabled to extend considerably the area of her benevolent operations. For some of the distressed she bought potatoes, cheques were sent to bakers in settlement of overdue bread bills, and others were the recipients of sums of money. It is gratifying to learn that no case was brought under Miss Winter's notice without relief of some kind being afforded, and that there has been no cause for jealousy and discontent."

Following the death of Queen Victoria in 1901, Miss Winter made a collection in the village for a wreath which had a card inscribed, "A last tribute of true loyalty and affection from the villagers of Chedzoy, Somerset." She then took the wreath to Windsor and, such were her influential contacts, she was present inside the castle at the time of the state funeral as the representative of the village. Elizabeth Winter subsequently left the village and died at Bay Tree Farm, Highbridge in February 1948 at the age of 91. She was buried at Puriton.

In common with most farms, there were problems with livestock. In July 1909 the Bridgwater Mercury reported,

"Benjamin George Winter, farmer, of Chedzoy, was summoned for allowing thirteen cows and two calves to stray at Chedzoy. P.C. Gard stated the facts and defendant said, 'The animals got out because an old cow could open any gate.' (Laughter.) Fined 15s. and costs."

Smaller animals occasionally caused problems. In December 1926 the Mercury carried the headline "A DOG'S LONG TRAMP." It was reported,

"Mr. B. Winter, of Fowlers Plot, Chedzoy, lost on Friday, the 10th inst., a valuable sheepdog. On Thursday last the animal was found wandering on the Mendips by Miss Vonberg of 'Rozelle,' Wells, who at once kindly communicated with Mr. Winter, and he proceeded to Wells and recovered the dog. It is remarkable that the animal, which was wearing its owner's collar, should have evaded capture for practically a week and wandered such a long distance."

As you continue toward Chedzoy on your right are the ruins of **LOWER FARM**. It is not entirely clear, but appears that Henry Hodges lived at this farm in the mid-1860s. His name does not appear on the 1861 or 1871 Census returns, but as George Winter is mentioned in an 1863 press report which refers to his neighbour, Mr. Hodges, this venue seems probable.

Mr. Hodges probably had a temper, as suggested by two consecutive reports from the Bridgwater County Police Court column in the Mercury.

"ASSAULTING A SERVANT. Mr. Henry Hodges, farmer, was summoned for assaulting Mary Ann Day (17), a servant in his employ on the 4th of March. Defendant pleaded guilty. Complainant, in reply to the Bench, said she had forgotten to heat two pans of milk, and had told the defendant so, when the latter said to her, 'God d—- your eyes, what right have you got to think about it?' He also told her to go about her business, and threatened to kick her. Complainant said he had better do it, whereupon defendant struck her a blow in the face, which was afterwards greatly swollen. - Defendant was fined 5s. and costs."

"CHARGE OF ABSCONDING. Mary Ann Day, the complainant in the last case, was charged with unlawfully leaving the service of her master, Mr. Henry Hodges, without his consent or without just cause on 3rd March. Complainant said that on the 18th February the defendant entered his employ as a servant in husbandry. On Sunday, the 3rd inst., she left the house in his absence and locked the door, leaving the key at his mother's house, so that when he returned home he found himself locked out. - Defendant said she only left the house for a short time, returning again in the evening. - That appeared to be the fact, and the Bench dismissed the case."

At the start of the 20th Century, Lower Farm was occupied by Joseph Heal (1843-1907), grandfather of Les Heal. In March 1906 Joseph appeared before the Bridgwater Magistrates.

"Joseph Heal, farmer, pleaded guilty to being drunk in charge of a horse and cart in Church Street, [Bridgwater]. P.C. Ballamm saw defendant staggering drunk and get into a cart to drive home. Defendant said he had lately been unwell and when he went to get into the cart he stumbled. What he had took effect on him, but it was weakness more than drink. Fined 2s. 6d. and costs or seven days."

As Joseph died ten months later perhaps there was some truth in his defence.

In August 1915 George Heal (1873-1931) appeared before Bridgwater County Magistrates' Court.

"George Heal, farmer, was summoned for allowing ten cows to stray. He pleaded not guilty. P.C. Gard gave evidence and said he saw the cows straying at Rudds's Grove (presumably Ruggs Drove). Defendant said he sent his boys to take the cows five miles and told them not to hurry the animals. They took an hour and half, and he did not consider that this was an unreasonable time. The case was dismissed."

George appeared twice in 1916. In October,

"George Heal pleaded guilty to two summonses for not having front and rear lights on a pony cart. Fined 5s. in each case."

In December,

"George Heal had two summonses for being in charge of a cart in Market Street, [Bridgwater], without front and rear lights. P.C. Sugg said he saw defendant driving a horse attached to a cart which had no lamps. He asked defendant why he had not got lights, and he replied, 'I didn't think it was lighting up time. I was going to the Mason's Arms to borrow a lamp.' Fined 5s. in respect of each summons."

In March 1922 he was in court again. It was reported that

"George Fear Heal and Ewart Heal (1900-1963) were charged with assaulting Ernest Banwell. Complainant, a labourer, Chedzoy Lane, said he went to the residence of the defendants and asked for his money for $2^1/2$ day's work. George Heal paid him and as he was leaving Ewart Heal then struck him in the face." A scuffle then took place. "Complainant called him 'A —- liar' and used very bad language in front of his (defendant's) children. Mr. Tyrell, for the defence, submitted that George Heal was entitled to be discharged and suggested that if complainant used bad language in the presence of children and was clouted by Ewart Heal, he got what he deserved. The Bench dismissed the case against both defendants."

Beyond the ruins of Lower Farm a mellow Georgian farmhouse known as **THREE OAKS FARM**, lies on your right. A footpath passes through this farmyard for a short, traffic free route to the centre of the village.

In the late 1800s the farm was the home of the Baker family, a member of which found himself appearing before court in December 1889.

"Richard Baker, farmer, Chedzoy was charged with cruelty to a mare by working it in an unfit state. - Mr. Allen, Inspector R.S.P.C.A., stated that on the day in question he visited Chedzoy and found the defendant in a field there with two horses attached to a plough. He had occasion to examine one of the horses particularly and he found it in a low condition and on the off shoulder there was an old wound of at least a week's standing. The collar was cutting into the wound, and it was very inflamed. Witness called the defendant's attention to it and the latter replied that he was not aware that the mare was so bad. Defendant, acting under his advice, discontinued working the animal and he (the Inspector) consequently had no desire to press the case. - The Chairman remarked that although the case was not a serious one, animals should be protected and defendant would be fined 5s. and costs."

In the early 20th Century the farm was the home of a branch of the Fry family. In May 1917 Edwin Fry (1881-1945) found himself before the magistrates:

"THE FARMER AND THE CONSTABLE" was the headline to this report. "Edwin Fry, farmer, of Chedzoy, was summoned for allowing 18 cows to stray at Chedzoy. He pleaded not guilty. P.C. Gard gave evidence, and said there was no one in charge of the cows, defendant's daughter being half-a-mile away from the cattle. When he went to defendant and told him about the cattle straying, defendant was abusive to him and told him he ought to be in the army. Defendant alleged that his daughter was only 200 yards away from the cattle, and added that when the constable came to him he told the constable that if he had not got something better to report he had better be in the army. 'I say so now, and that is the place for him,' added the defendant. He (defendant), like other farmers, was doing a national duty, and was very short of labour. The police should assist rather than hinder. The constable had been impudent to him since a previous case of straying. P.C. Gard said he had warned defendant before about his cattle. Defendant observed that the constable had never warned him. The case was dismissed."

In March the following year Edwin was before Bridgwater Police Court.

"Edwin John Fry, farmer, Chedzoy, was charged with having exposed for sale in the Bridgwater Cattle Market six sheep which were unhealthy and subject to such physical defects as would cause the flesh of the animals after slaughter to be unfit for human consumption. The veterinary inspector examined the six sheep. One was off its legs, and died during the morning. The sheep were unhealthy, and they were all very emaciated. There was nothing infectious about them. P.S. Fowler saw defendant shortly afterwards and said, 'You brought six sheep to the market this morning and one of them is dead.' He replied, 'They are 'coathe.' I've lost about fifty the same way.' The Mayor said the Bench considered the case proved, but as it was the first of the kind brought to their notice they would deal with it more leniently than they intended to do in any subsequent case brought before them. Defendant would be fined £1."

Speaking in 1998, Norman Fry recalled family tales of sheep being "code," meaning they were suffering from liver fluke. At one time so many "code" sheep had died that a disused well was supposed to have been used as a means of disposing of them!

Animal health and welfare caused a return to court in July 1920.

"Edwin John Fry was charged with having sent to the Bridgwater market for slaughter, an in-calf cow, contrary to the provisions of the Livestock Sales Order 1919. Defendant gave evidence and said he had not the faintest suspicion the animal was in-calf. He reckoned he lost £10 by sending it in. Defendant was fined £1 1s. and £1 1s. towards the cost of the prosecution."

Edwin Fry was before the magistrates again in May 1931 when it was reported that he

"Was charged with having sold to the prejudice of Independent Milk Supplies Ltd., milk not of a nature, substance, and quality the article demanded by the purchaser, but deficient of milk fat by 22.5%. P.S. Sealey attended the farm, and there saw Mr. Fry assisting to load two churns of milk into a lorry. After the milk was duly stirred, P.S. Sealey took a pint from each of the churns, dividing the milk in the usual way, and told Mr. Fry he intended to have the milk analysed by the public analyst. Mr. Fry's observation was, 'You could not have taken it at a worse time as the cows are milked earlier on a Sunday.' The Bench knew that the question of unequal milking, to whatever extent the inequality might exist, must affect the quality of the milk." There then followed a very lengthy legal argument about milk fat according to the season, etc. "The Bench, after deliberation, dismissed the case."

The farm was back in the court columns again in December 1936, but for different reasons.

"William Charles Crocker, labourer, of Bradney, was summoned for contravening the Ground Game Act by employing a spring trap other than in rabbit holes in Chedzoy. He pleaded guilty. P.C. Greed said he had received a complaint from Mr. Winter of [Fowlers Plot Farm] Chedzoy that his dog had been caught in a trap. He interviewed defendant in the fields of Mr. Fry's farm. Defendant pointed out to him a rat gin trap set on open ground 18 inches from a rabbit hole. Witness pointed out to the defendant that he ought not to have set it on the open ground, and defendant made a statement, in which he said he was unemployed, and that he and another man had agreed with Mr. Fry of Three Oaks Farm to get rid of rabbits on his farm, and while in another part of the field with his ferret he left the trap set on open ground near a rabbit hole. He was always under the impression that spring traps could be set in the open unless there was hunting going on. Defendant told the Bench that he acted quite innocently in what he did and the case was dismissed on payment of costs."

The Bridgwater Mercury in March 1940 included this short report:

"Mr. E.J. Fry, Three Oaks Farm, Chedzoy, has a cow which has given birth to triplets and all are alive. She has in the last five seasons given birth to ten calves - three sets of twins and one single."

Although the country was at war, minor infringements of the law were still attended to by the authorities and in June 1942,

"Wyndham Fry, farmer, Three Oaks Farm, was fined £1 for not having the unladen weight marked on a trailer."

Serious indeed!

There was a problem at the farm in August 1949.

"Hay to the value of several hundred pounds was lost at Three Oaks Farm, Fowlers Plot, Chedzoy when fire broke out in a 35-ton rick belonging to Mr. Wyndham Fry. Bridgwater Fire Brigade was summoned and took with them a water tender. A strong wind and a shortage of water handicapped the fire fighters' efforts and the rick had to be left to burn itself out. The fire recalled a more serious outbreak on the same farm in 1923 when the late Mr. E.J. Fry was the occupier. On that occasion several ricks were destroyed in the farmyard."

A different problem was pictured on the front page of the Bridgwater Mercury in June 1967 when a cow somehow managed to get itself trapped inside a muck-spreader: it was released by the Fire Brigade after suffering no more than bruising!

Although by no means certain, it would seem that the **POOR HOUSE** once stood almost opposite Three Oaks Farm. In 1767 William Alexander purchased a cottage for £37 then on 29th July 1774 it was leased to Edward Stradling and John England for a period of 99 years for use as a Poor House: unfortunately the deed does not include the location for the property, but it would appear it was at Fowlers Plot. The 1836 Tithe map shows a cottage opposite the site of Three Oaks Farm which was owned by the "Parish Officers." The Census of 1851 lists three elderly, unrelated paupers living in one house and the 1861 Census has five such persons, so both may have well been the Poor House, but neither Census has any indication as to addresses.

The road from Three Oaks Farm toward the village used to be known as **HOLLOW LANE** or Hollow Road. It was very low and flooded even more frequently than now before the surface was raised by about three feet during the 1980s. Along the lane beyond the bends and on the left is the site of a cottage which was known as **STOLES**. It was marked on the 1887 Ordnance Survey map as standing in an orchard. The cottage was destroyed in August 1928, the Bridgwater Mercury reporting,

"Chedzoy was the scene of an alarming fire on Saturday morning, a thatched cottage on the farm of Mr. Albert Edward Ashford being completely destroyed. The cottage, situated in Hollow Lane, was occupied by Richard Cornall, his wife and six children, the former having been in the employ of Mr. Ashford, but now working at Cannington, where he was on the night of the fire. Mrs. Cornall and the children went to bed at 9.30 on Friday night. She slept with her young daughter in one of the rooms.

About 5.00 on Saturday morning the daughter aroused her, and Mrs. Cornall then found the room full of smoke and fire at the bedroom window. She at once awakened the other children and got them out of the cottage as quickly as possible, throwing their clothes out to them.

"Mr. Ashford was called about 5.30 by one of his workmen, and on proceeding to the cottage found the thatched roof well alight. Mrs. Cornall and her children were standing in the garden watching the disappearance of their home. The fire hose of the parish was brought to the scene in the charge of Mr. Tucker. It was affixed to a stand pipe, and began playing on the blazing cottage. Mr. Tarr, farmer, also appeared on the scene and, with Mr. Ashford, rendered whatever assistance was possible. Others to help were Mr. Jennings and Mr. Gigg. A few articles of furniture were saved, but the bulk of the household goods were destroyed. Efforts to subdue the outbreak failed, and the cottage was practically gutted. The county police were communicated with, and P.S. Sealey went out from Bridgwater to find the fire had done its work."

The cottage was not rebuilt.

As you continue along the road, **FISHERS FARM** is on the sharp bend at the start of **Front Street**. Although this name sounds evocative of former times on the moor, when the fisheries in the wetlands played an important role, it seems more likely that it is named after the Fisher family who lived in the village in the 1850s and 1860s. On the 1861 Census, which does not include addresses, Samuel Fisher was described as a 55 year old "landed proprietor" who was born in Congresbury.

He appeared before the County Police Court in May 1860. According to a report in the Bridgwater Mercury,

"Samuel Fisher, of Chedzoy, was brought up under a warrant charging him with assaulting his wife, Mary Lawrence Fisher. - The complainant stated that her husband quarrelled with her, took up a knife, and threatened to stab her. He afterwards struck her, and she was afraid he would carry out his threats towards her. - The defendant was fined 5s. and 5s. 6d. costs for the assault, and was bound over in the sum of £5 to keep the peace towards his wife for twelve months."

The Fisher family does not appear on the 1871 Census, by which time William Derrick (1844-1883) and his family were living on the 149 acre farm. No location is given for an accident reported in April 1859 before the above assault, so quite where both families lived at the time is a matter for conjecture.

"On Sunday last as a young girl, daughter of Mr. Derrick, farmer, Chedzoy, was playing in her father's barton, the body of a cart fell upon her, and fractured her thigh. Dr. Sewell's aid was obtained as promptly as possible, and under his care she is favourably progressing."

William Derrick died in 1883 and in January 1884 an auction of dairy utensils and furniture was held at the farm. Edmund Derrick (1837-1893) then ran the farm. Just months before her husband's death Mrs. Derrick (1831-1918) appeared before the Bridgwater County Magistrates in May 1893.

"Mrs. Elizabeth Ann Derrick was summoned for ill treating a horse by causing it to be worked whilst in an unfit condition. P.C. May said he was on duty on the day in question when he saw a lad named Charles Stone (14) working two horses in a field of Mrs. Derrick's. Witness noticed one horse seemed to be in pain. When examined he found an old sore from which blood was running freely. The Chairman said the Bench were of the opinion that the horse had been ill treated and they believed that Mrs. Derrick knew the horse was being used, though she might have meant it to be lightly used. They would inflict a fine of 10s. and costs."

Following the death of Edmund Derrick, the farm was sold by auction on 27th June 1894 at the Royal Clarence Hotel, Bridgwater. The winning bid of £7,950 came from Joseph Moger.

Joseph Moger sold the 150 acre farm in August 1922, at which time the annual rent was stated to be £410. It was purchased by Mr. W.C. Ashford for £7,000 and later it was passed on to Albert 'Bert' Ashford (1895-1978). An unusual case was reported in the Bridgwater Mercury in November 1929:

"Albert Edmund Ashford, farmer, of Fishers Farm, was summoned for unlawfully and knowingly and without reasonable excuse permitting the carcase of a calf to remain unburied, and in a place where dogs could gain access. P.C. Masters gave the facts, and defendant, who pleaded guilty, was fined 10s."

As at Manor Farm, prisoners-of-war worked here during the Second World War and lived in one of the farm cottages. There were four of them and each had a bicycle so that he could reach his work. They were so trusted that on one occasion one was taken to Taunton in order that he could catch a train to visit a relative who had lived in this country for many years, and he was collected from the railway station upon his return after the visit!

The lane leading from Fishers farm towards Bridgwater is known as **PORT WALL DROVE**. The route was known as Port Wall in the late 14th Century but by the middle of the 19th Century had become a drove. Partway along on the left is the junction with **LONG ACRE DROVE** where, many years ago, there were two cottages. Further on towards the junction with **PARK WALL DROVE** (which runs from Temple Farm on Chedzoy Lane to the Halfway Inn on Westonzoyland Road) there was at one time, so Herbie Ashford was told, a public house of some sort. A brief mention in the local paper noted that in April 1946

"a close of meadow land in Park Wall Drove, 2$^1/_2$ acres (let at £6 10s. a year) [was sold] for £200."

Fishers Farm to Avalon House

Beyond Fishers Farm towards the village on the left hand side of the road stands an imposing house known as **CROFTSIDE**. It was built in 1928 for Joseph Moger. The house has an unusual number of windows: the original metal fixtures were replaced with modern windows by the present owners in 1995/96. The house had changed hands by March 1933 as the Bridgwater Mercury reported,

> "Dr. George William Mackay of Croftside, Chedzoy, was summoned for driving a motor car without a front light in the parish of Huntspill. P.C. Burfitt said he saw defendant driving a motor car in the Bristol Road without an offside front light. When stopped, defendant said, 'It was alright when I left Bristol.' Witness told him he could have put it right at a garage further up the road, but witness called at the garage later and found defendant had not stopped there. Defendant, who did not put in an appearance, was fined £1."

Somehow I don't think a modern policeman would make enquiries at a garage just to confirm that a motorist had not visited them for a bulb! Dr. Mackay left Chedzoy shortly after this incident.

FISHERS COTTAGES are next on the right. In the early years of the 20th Century the Chiswick family lived at No. 1. It was a regular event for the family to boil Christmas puddings in the wash house, some of which were destined for the Rectory table. Of course, the smell announced to anyone passing that cooking was taking place. Herbie Ashford tells the story that one Christmas Bert Stokes and some friends visited the wash house under cover of darkness and removed some of the roof tiles so that he could get in. He then replaced one of the puddings with a turnip, refitted the tiles and made good his escape. His prank was not discovered until the "pudding" was unwrapped on Christmas Day to cries of, "Bert, do you know anything about this?" Another one of the village pranks regularly indulged in by Bert Stokes, was to tie a broom to the chimney of a house when a man's wife was away for the night: even Rev. Mullens was not immune to such treatment! Sometimes, a light plough would be hauled up and fixed to the chimney instead of a broom.

All three of the cottages featured in a case which came before the magistrates in May 1943.

> "'A pathetic case' was the description which a defending solicitor ... applied to a charge in which the defendant was a young married woman, Gertrude Mary Francis, aged 18, of Fishers Cottages, Chedzoy was alleged to have broken into a house occupied by William Collard, also of Fishers Cottages, and stolen a tablecloth, a pair of shoes and a bottle of perfume. Alternatively, she was charged with stealing the property. Mrs. Margaret May Collard gave evidence of missing the articles and P.C. Treeby ... said the girl, when questioned, first denied the theft, but later made a statement that she 'went to the house to borrow a tablecloth. I knocked, but there was no one at home. I tried the latch and found the door unlocked and went in, thinking Mrs. Collard did not hear my knock.' She then admitted taking the articles and expressed regret. Mr. H. Scholfield, for the girl, said defendant on April 3rd gave birth to a child which had since died. 'I ask you to say,' said Mr. Scholfield, 'that because of her condition at the time of the offence, she was not responsible for what she was doing.' He added that the girl had no necessity to take the property and had a good testimonial from the rectory where she worked until the middle of January. The girl asked the magistrates to take into consideration a charge of stealing a washbowl, value 2s., belonging to Mrs. Vera May Carter of Fishers Cottages. The magistrates dismissed the allegation of breaking and entering and on the charge of theft, taking into consideration the second charge also, the Bench bound over defendant for a year under the care of the probation officer, Miss Savage. Defendant was ordered to pay £1 costs."

Immediately on your right beyond Fishers Cottages, the former farmhouse known as **INKERS** belonged until his death in 1861 to Henry Porter, the Victorian Squire of Chedzoy, who lived in what is now the Manor House Inn. Built of blue lias stone with some brick, it was modernised by Mr. Tottle who had a joinery business in Bridgwater. Ben Hooper (born 1906) recalled that when he was a child James 'Jim' Hook lived at the property. He was the owner of a home-made donkey cart with solid wooden wheels which he used for selling milk and home grown vegetables around the village.

The house was the scene of bloody events in December 1922, at which time it had been home for about two years to Robert Percy Stockdale Craven, aged 45, his young wife (whose first name does not appear in any of the reports) and their baby. They were being visited by Robert Craven's sister. The Bridgwater Mercury reported,

> "The husband and wife occupied a room adjoining that of Craven's sister. The latter, it seems, was awakened about 6.30 on Monday morning by hearing a cry for help, and on entering the adjoining bedroom [using a candle for light] found the husband and wife struggling. The five month old baby girl was in the same room and Craven's sister at once took the child to a place of safety. What afterwards transpired can at present only be assumed, but it is evident that after a desperate struggle the husband inflicted injuries on his wife with a razor and afterwards cut his throat. Dr. Coates was summoned and on arrival found both husband and wife suffering from wounds to the throat, evidently inflicted by a razor which was found close by. The husband succumbed to his injuries the same afternoon, but it is hoped that Mrs. Craven will recover."

The following week is was reported that Mrs. Craven had been too ill to attend the inquest and, in the absence of any further reports, it would appear that she survived the attack. The jury returned a verdict of suicide in the case of Robert Craven.

The farmhouse on the left, known as **WESTFIELD FARM**, is

Westfield Farm as it appeared in the late 1970s. Photograph by Ken Coombs, courtesy of Beryl Coombs.

an 18th Century building, still retaining its exposed beams, wattle and daub walls, stone floor and inglenook fireplace.

The name was in use by 1891, but previously the premises had been known as Englands Farm. In 1901 the London Gazette announced that William Brake (born c.1859), a yeoman, had been adjudged bankrupt. At that time he had been paying an annual rent of £302 15s. for Westfield Farm. That September an auction of household and farm effects was announced in the Bridgwater Mercury.

In July 1933 an interesting report appeared in that same paper.

> "The British Friesian Cattle Society has issued particulars in reference to new 2,000 galloners, including that well known Somersetshire Friesian enthusiast, Mr. A.H. Tarr of Bridgwater [who] has developed his second 2,000 gallon cow. She is Westfield Zena, that in her third lactation period gave 2,014 gallons in 259 days, when she was still producing six gallons daily. As a heifer she yielded 1,215 gallons and after he second calving she produced 1,490 gallons, so that she should reach a total production of 5,000 gallons by the time she is six years old next September."

An account of the Somerset and North Dorset Milk Recording Association's annual report in March 1934 noted,

> "Mr. A.H. Tarr, of Westfield Farm, Chedzoy, is second, his British Friesian herd averaging 11,060 lb. with an average percentage of butterfat of 3.5... The maximum yield given by a full year cow was 24,104¾ lb., this being given by Westfield Zena, a British Friesian owned by Mr. A.H. Tarr in 344 days."

It was reported in October 1936 that Arthur Tarr was about to sell his herd of sixty Friesians but it would appear that he changed his mind since a further sale notice was published in the Mercury in August 1950 which noted that the sixty strong herd was to be sold by auction,

> "being the whole of the milking portion of the famous Westfield herd [which] has long been one of the most famous herds in the western counties, and has been in continuous existence for some 30 years. It has, for many years, been the leading herd in milk records, and is famous for its good deep cows with great milking capacity."

At the Bridgwater Agricultural Show the following year Mr. L.N. Stokes was presented with the Royal Agricultural Society's long service medal for 40 years continuous service with Mr. Tarr.

Perhaps Arthur Tarr still didn't sell his herd as it was advertised again in September 1955, but this time it was reported that,

> "The dispersal of the Westfield herd of pedigree British Friesians at Westfield Farm, Chedzoy aroused much interest. The herd was founded in 1914 by Mr. A.H. Tarr and was dispersed with the exception of the 1955 crop of heifer calves, owing to Mr. Tarr's retirement." The 39 pedigree cows and heifers in milk averaged £92 14s. each and the overall price for the 82 strong herd was £79 6s. each. When Arthur Tarr and his wife left the village the following month they were presented with a walnut bureau inscribed, "Presented to Mr. and Mrs. A.H. Tarr by the parishioners of Chedzoy in grateful appreciation of their long service in the village."

Five years later the farm was in the news again. In August 1960,

> "Using a tractor with a power take-off unshielded attached to a silorator with the take-off shaft unguarded, cost a Chedzoy farmer £15 7s. in fines and costs at Bridgwater County Magistrates' Court. Roy House, of Westfield Farm, Chedzoy was fined £5 for using a tractor without the power take-off being guarded and £3 for having no guard on the take-off shaft from the tractor to the silorator. An Inspector of the Ministry [of Agriculture] said he saw in a field at Chedzoy a tractor drawing a silorator which was cutting grass for silage. The power-take off shaft was not guarded in accordance with regulations and the take-off shaft on the tractor was unguarded."

Westfield ceased to be a working farm in 1984 with its neighbour and the outbuildings were either demolished or converted into dwelling houses in 1989.

The red brick farmhouse, **DALTON'S FARM**, built about 1910, still serves its original purpose as a working farm. Leslie 'Les' Heal, who was born on the farm in 1918, remembers that when he was a boy the church played a great part in village life: "Every Sunday we went to Sunday School in the morning, then we lined up in pairs to go to church from 11 to 12. We went to the afternoon service and the 6.30 service, rain or shine. No one tried to get out of going, because you couldn't."

Before the present property was built another house stood on this site: in November 1879 John and Jane Hooper were living there.

"Jesse Conduit, labourer, of Chedzoy, was charged with killing a goose, value 5s., the property of Mr. John Hooper of Chedzoy. - Ellen Payne, a servant girl, stated she saw the defendant in Mr. Hooper's orchard about six in the morning. On seeing witness, defendant ran away from her. Soon after witness missed a goose. When she first saw defendant in the orchard he was trying to catch a goose. There was a flock of geese there. About half an hour after defendant ran away she found a dead goose under the hedge. - Cross-examined: The goose was killed in the same way as hagglers kill their poultry. Her mistress had lost a purse, and witness was the first to find the money it contained. Three turkeys had recently been killed in the same way. Witness found one and her master and mistress found the other two. She did not try to kill a duck, and George Lock did not see her try to drown one. The people of Chedzoy were unkind enough to say she burnt down a linhay. She did not know anything about her mistress going away and on coming back finding any honey or jam gone, and the pot turned upside down. She and her mistress did not go to a fortune-teller to know about these things. The reason why she went to the orchard so early that morning was because her mistress heard the geese making a noise and told her to go and see what was the matter. - Mrs. Hooper gave corroborative evidence, adding that she had lost some turkeys, but they were killed by fighting. People tried to put these things off on the girl, but she did not do it. Witness had not been to a fortune-teller to know anything about these things, nor had she ever seen one, or a clairvoyant either. - Mr. Chapman, for the defence, contended that it was a case of mistaken identity and that if the thing was done by anyone it was the servant girl. He could clearly prove a satisfactory alibi. He then called Henry Conduit, defendant's brother, who stated that defendant had slept with him, and on the morning in question he went part of the way with defendant. - The other witnesses were Frederick Bryant (15, of Ward Lane), Thomas Stone and Geo. Leaker (55, also of Ward Lane), who proved that they had accompanied him on other stages of the journey to his work. - The Chairman stated that the Bench were of the opinion that this was a case of mistaken identity, and would be dismissed. - Mr. Chapman applied that in this case the costs should be borne by the complainant, as the defendant had hitherto borne an irreproachable character, and it was very hard for him to bring a number of witnesses. It was an exceptional case. - The Bench allowed the defendant's witnesses 1s. 6d. each."

John Hooper was in trouble himself in April 1884.

"John Hooper, poultry-dealer of Chedzoy, was charged with cruelty to an old brown gelding, his property, by working it whilst in an unfit state, in Eastover, Bridgwater. Inspector Osborne said on the day in question he saw the defendant in Eastover with an old brown gelding attached to an empty spring cart. The gelding was broken-winded, and its sides were heaving up and down. It was quite unfit to work. Defendant pleaded guilty and was fined 5s. and costs; in all 16s. 3d."

In March 1889 the Bridgwater Mercury reported,

"Messrs. Palmer and Stiling offered for sale by auction at the Crown Inn a dwelling house with land adjoining, containing 2a., 2r., 39p. The same was started at £300; the biddings were brisk and realised £470, at which sum it was knocked down to Mr. Hook, tailor, of Bridgwater."

The sale notice indicated that

"The dwelling house is convenient and well arranged, and there are numerous outbuildings. The orchard is fully planted with fruit trees, and the garden and pasture are extremely rich and very productive. The property was late in the possession of Mr. John Hooper, the owner."

A case of theft was heard by the County Magistrates in April 1934. It was reported under the headline,

"THEFT OF SWEDE GREENS. William James Hobbs of 111 Bath Road, Bridgwater was summoned for stealing a quantity of swede greens of the value of 1s., the property of Edward Heal at Chedzoy. P.C. Haycraft stated he was on duty in Chedzoy Lane when he saw defendant walking across a field. He watched him, and saw defendant come out of a gate and put something down by it. Defendant went across the road to fetch a bicycle. Witness said to him, 'Well, Hobbs, what have you been up to?' He replied, 'Nothing.' Witness looked in over the gate and saw a sack. On examination of it he found it contained swede greens. He asked Hobbs where he had got them from, and he said, 'It was from a few fields away.' He interviewed Mr. Heal, and found defendant had taken the greens from a field about three or four fields away from where he saw defendant. Defendant admitted that he stole the greens, and said he could not remember the field where he took them from.

"Mr. Heal said he did not wish to press the summons, he only wanted it as a warning to other people. He had difficulty in growing the greens, and he did not want to see them stolen. Defendant said some farm labourers told him to take the greens. If he had known they belonged to Mr. Heal he would not have taken them. The sight of him was enough. He was fined 5s. (25p.) and allowed two weeks in which to pay."

Like just about every other farm, from time to time poaching was a problem. In March 1950 the following report was published in the Bridgwater Mercury.

"Conflicting views over an alleged shooting of a partridge were expressed during a hearing of a case before Bridgwater County Magistrates on Friday involving four summons against a farm worker. Ernest John Clapp (41), of Penwood View, Parchey, Chedzoy was fined £1 for trespassing in search of game; 10s. for shooting on a Sunday; and £1 for having no game licence. A summons for being without a gun licence was discharged on payment of costs. He pleaded not guilty to the first summons and to being without a game licence, but guilty to the other two offences.

"William Charles Crocker, Laburnum House, Chedzoy, explained that he held the shooting rights at Dalton Farm (sic) and on the day in question saw Clapp, his son and another man with two guns and three dogs. He appeared to be looking for game. A shot was fired at a partridge and when questioned Clapp used abusive language. P.C. Anning stated that Clapp informed him he had shot a pigeon and not a partridge. Crocker was half-a-mile away at the time. Clapp said there had always been rows about rabbiting and alleged that Crocker trapped rabbits on his ground. He had permission from a Mr. Heal to cross the land and was not aware that Crocker had the shooting rights. He denied shooting a partridge, but said it was a pigeon. His son, 13-year-old Ernest Clapp, corroborated his father's evidence.

"Douglas Nash (24), farm worker, Broadenham Cottage, Winsham, Chard, who was alleged to have been with Clapp at the time, was fined £1 for trespassing in search of game; 10s. for shooting on a Sunday; and £1 for having no game licence. A summons of using a gun without a licence was discharged on payment of 4s. costs. He did not appear in court but wrote pleading guilty."

THE OLD POST OFFICE, adjoining Dalton's Farm, was until 1976 a shop and the village post office. The village's one petrol pump stood outside as did the telephone kiosk. Speaking in 1949 Henry Chappell said he remembered the property being built in 1867.

Post Office Stores, around 1951.
The village's only petrol pump, with the telephone kiosk next to it. Photograph by F. Frith & Company. Courtesy of Beryl Coombs.

The adjoining cob built cottage - **EASTCOTTE** - is one of the oldest buildings in the village, probably at least 300 years old and possibly older. The field behind Eastcotte was used as a cricket pitch towards the end of the 19th Century and for the first few years of the 20th Century. The Cricket Club was formed in 1892 and the following season Mr. C. Harden was their top performer, scoring more runs and taking more wickets than the rest of the team put together!

In April 1894 the Bridgwater Mercury reported that,

"The villagers intend their cricket side to be prominent this season. At a meeting held a few days ago Mr. J. Baker was elected Captain, Mr. B.G. Winter secretary and treasurer and the Rev. G.R. Mullens has accepted the Presidency. The opening match takes place on May 5th against Bridgwater Alliance and other fixtures are being arranged."

Later the cricket pitch was moved to a field opposite West End Farm.

Frederick Tucker bought Eastcotte for £500 in July 1919. He always claimed that during the First World War he served for just one day in the army, his explanation being that when it was discovered that he was a blacksmith he was sent home and ordered to make shoes for mules, but it seems more likely that he never joined the forces as he was granted an exemption by the local Military Tribunal. In June 1955 Mr. Tucker was interviewed for an article in the Bridgwater Mercury. He recalled that he had left school at the age of 12 to serve as an apprentice at Tom Butler's forge in Chedzoy. When he was 16 he moved to Westonzoyland for four years before returning to the village to set up his own business. Between 1920 and 1939 he used over two tons of horseshoes each year and even in 1955 was shoeing 40 horses most weeks.

Another member of the family was in trouble in 1944.

"Grace Tucker of East Cott (sic), Chedzoy, who was fined 10s. for having neither front nor rear light on her cycle when stopped at 7.40 p.m. on December 18th, told the court that she had that day been to Bristol, and returned by train later than she anticipated. P.W.R. [Police War Reserve] Cooksley, stating the facts, said there were no lamps attached to the defendant's cycle."

Between Eastcotte and the Old Chapel House the road meets up with one of the footpaths from Three Oaks Farm. This drove is known as **WATERY LANE**.

The **OLD CHAPEL HOUSE**, known as Brierton until about 1990, Brierton House in the early 1960s, and before that as Chapel House, was once a Methodist chapel. It dates from 1864 and has similar decorations on the roof beams to those in the old school room. Perhaps they were carved by the same village craftsmen. In 1820 permission was sought from the Bishop to use a house in Chedzoy for Protestant worship, although this was not for the present building. A document dated November 1821 states that,

"I, Joseph Copp, of Bridgwater, do certify that a certain building in the occupancy of William Bennett (Smithy), is intended forthwith to be used as a place of worship by an assembly or congregation of Protestants."

This was probably William Bennett (1800-1858), a blacksmith, some of whose descendants still live in Chedzoy.

According to Methodist records, in 1840 Rev. Joseph Earnshaw of Taunton registered the house of James Gully for Weslyan Methodist worship and in December 1861 Rev. Robert Govier requested registration of a room in the house of Daniel Newton opposite the school for Weslyan Methodist worship. Earlier, in June 1861, Rev. Henry Porter and Cecil Henry Russell sold a house, garden and outbuildings tenanted by Edward Rainey for £50 at an auction held in the Royal Clarence Hotel, Bridgwater. The new owner again sold the premises in May 1862 for £140 to four trustees of the Methodist church. In May 1866 the trustees sold the property to ten persons who were acting as trustees for the Bridgwater Weslyan Circuit. The new owners demolished some of the existing buildings and erected a chapel seating 150 persons. It was about 24 feet wide and 30 feet long with a tall, hipped roof. Access from Front Street was through a central doorway into a porch about six feet side and four feet deep.

It would appear that some of the dates given in Methodist records are inaccurate, as in April 1864 the following report was published in the Bridgwater Mercury.

> "Until recently the village of Chedzoy ... was without any public religious service except that celebrated in the Established Church and, in consequence, some time ago some members of the Weslyan connection obtained a large cottage at one end of the village, where services were held on week-days, and Sundays in the evening only, so that they should not clash with services at the parish church. Soon, however, it was found necessary to hold the meetings oftener, and their having been so successful that the cottage has lately proved too small for the purpose. The necessity of erecting a suitable building therefore became manifest, and the Weslyans of Chedzoy, aided by their brethren in Bridgwater, having set about the work, soon succeeded in raising £140 towards the project. With this fund in hand it was determined to commence operations, and a plan was drawn out of an unpretending but commodious building, the erection of which was entrusted to Mr. Kitch, of Bridgwater. The chapel will stand on the right-hand side of the road on entering from Chedzoy drove. It is to be built in the Gothic style, of blue lias, with Bath-stone dressing. It will be pewed, and when completed seat 120 persons. The services have been conducted by ministers of this circuit and their efforts have been ably seconded by itinerant preachers. ... The ceremony of laying the foundation stone took place and a number of persons from Bridgwater were present. The day was beautifully fine, and there were about one hundred persons present, villagers and townspeople. ... Mr. T. Collins read the document it was intended to put under the foundation stone. ... 'The foundation stone of this Weslyan Methodist Chapel was laid by Mr. Robert Slocombe of Westonzoyland on the 12th of April 1864 and in the first jubilee year of the Weslyan Missionary Society'."

This document was placed in a bottle and sealed in a pipe under the stone: presumably it is there to this day.

In September 1867 the Bridgwater Mercury reported,

> "CHEDZOY. On Thursday was celebrated the anniversary of the Weslyan Chapel in this place, a small but very pretty building, which was erected about four years ago." They had obviously lost track of time already! "A service was held in the chapel in the afternoon, when it was crowded with people, many having come from Bridgwater, Westonzoyland, Highbridge, &c. ... On the conclusion of the service a tea meeting was held. ... Mr. Davies of Bridgwater then greatly interested the meeting by reading extracts from the journals of the Revds. John Wesley, Charles Wesley and John Nelson concerning the introduction of Methodism into this neighbourhood."

A similar service was held the following year:

> "The anniversary services in connection with the Weslyan chapel in [Chedzoy] were held on Friday. Service was performed in the afternoon and evening, the sermon being preached on each occasion by the Rev. J. Walters of Gosport. Between the two services about 80 persons partook of tea in the chapel."

Methodist records note that in 1882 the Weslyan Methodists had debts of £184 so they sold the chapel for £120 to the Bible Christian Methodists and the adjoining cottage for £80 to William Carter Slocombe. The Bible Christian Methodists fared no better and were soon in debt so the Weslyans began raising money to buy back the building. In the event they rented it for £5 per year and in 1902 were holding two services every Sunday. A Sunday School was organised as well as a Mission Band. In June 1903 the Weslyans re-purchased the chapel for £155.

Eventually support for Methodism waned in Chedzoy and the chapel closed in 1922. In August 1924 an application to sell was made to Methodist Head Office and the building was sold in 1926 to Mr. R.S. Jones and it was converted into a private house. It now has two floors plus a loft space which still features the original carved roof timbers.

Even places of worship were almost the setting for minor breaches of the law. In April 1906

> "George Day (18) pleaded guilty to having fired off a gun within 50 feet of the centre of a public carriageway to the danger and interruption of persons travelling thereon. P.C. Catley was outside the Weslyan chapel when he heard two reports of a firearm. When defendant was near witness he turned into a lane and threw something into the chapel yard. A pistol was recovered. Mr. Chapman, on behalf of defendant, said it was a toy pistol and defendant had given it back to the person to whom it belonged. He (Mr. Chapman) had explained to defendant how dangerous it was for him to fool with such a weapon and defendant expressed his regret for what he did. Fined 2s. 6d. and costs."

The cottages which were formerly a part of the property are known today as **TOWER VIEW** and **PALFREY HOUSE**, the latter probably named after the Palfrey family, formerly of the Crown Inn. The 1871 Census records John Palfrey, 60, as an innkeeper, and his wife, Charity, was aged 59.

All that remains of **FRYS FARM** is the original house (**THE OLD FARMHOUSE**). In the 1800s it was known as Cranes Farm although farmed by a branch of the Fry family.

Frys Farm, in the late 1970s.
Photograph by Ken Coombs, courtesy of Beryl Coombs.

Two cases were listed at Bridgwater County Court in October 1866 and duly reported in the Bridgwater Mercury.

"Edwin Fry v. Henry and Elizabeth Hodges. The plaintiff, a farmer, of Chedzoy, claimed of the defendants the sum of 10s. for damages done by trespass of cattle. It appeared that the plaintiff is the owner of ten acres of land in Chedzoy, and that some time since he rented of the defendants another acre and a half of land adjoining. The defendants own other land which adjoins the property in question, and on this they were in the habit of keeping cattle, which the plaintiff alleged had strayed, and eaten the grass in not only that portion of land which he had rented of the defendants, but also a portion of land he himself owned. Judgement was given for the amount of rent to be paid, and his Honour suggested that Fry should summons the defendants for the trespass which he then set up as a set-off against the rent. Fry now deposed that in the months of September and October he had frequently seen so many as five horses belonging to the defendants trespassing on his land and eating the grass. He told the defendants of it, and they promised to drive them away, but had never done so. In reply to his Honour, plaintiff said the reason he had not sent the horses to the pound was because he did not like the pounding system. The cattle did not leave his land until they were 'drowned out.' The amount claimed, 10s., had nothing to do with the value, which he estimated altogether to be not less than £3. The defendants did not appear, and the amount was ordered to be paid in a month."

This report was followed by a second.

"Henry Hodges v. Edwin Fry. The plaintiff claimed 10s. as damages sustained by reason of the defendant's cattle straying into a field and damaging a quantity of barley. The parties are farmers at Chedzoy, and occupy adjoining land. The plaintiff admitted that he was induced to take out a summons against the defendant in consequence of the latter having summoned him for trespass of his (plaintiff's) cattle. The trespass now complained of took place about twelve months ago, and it was stated that about that time on one Saturday night about thirty cows, belonging to the defendant, broke into the plaintiff's barley field, of 26 acres, and remained there until about six o'clock next morning, having in the meantime done a great deal of damage to the barley. - The defendant said he did not know anything about it, and this was the first time he had heard of it. He denied the statement of the plaintiff, that the latter had given him notice of it at the time. - Judgement for the amount claimed."

In September 1868 Edwin was required to give evidence in the County Magistrates' Court.

"John Rainey was charged with committing a game trespass at Chedzoy on land in the occupation of Mr. Edwin Fry ... who said he rented land at Parchey, belonging to Mr. William King. On the day named he saw the defendant in a field about half past two o'clock with a gun in his hand, and a dog with him. Defendant went along kicking the hedge. Witness called to him, and defendant then ran into another field. Witness, on overtaking him, said, 'I shall summons you and there won't be any making up.' Defendant replied, 'I hope you won't.' There was no path in the field. Witness had seen game there. - George Hunt, labourer, said he heard some talking between the last witness and the defendant, whom he did not see. Mr. Fry said, 'I have been waiting for 'ee some time, and now I have got 'ee.' - Defendant denied being on Mr. Fry's ground, but said he was on Mr. Hooper's plot adjoining. - The Bench considered the case proved, and fined him £1 including costs; in default 14 days' imprisonment."

In January 1870 Edwin Fry found himself back in the County Court. Although somewhat lengthy, the report in the Bridgwater Mercury provides an interesting insight into village life at that time.

"ACTION FOR ASSAULT - John Brely v. Edwin Fry. - This was a jury case. The plaintiff, a thatcher, of Chedzoy (for whom Mr. Reed appeared), claimed of the defendant, a yeoman, of the same parish (represented by Mr. Barham), the sum of £50, damages alleged to have been sustained by the plaintiff in consequence of an assault committed upon him by the defendant in August last. The plaintiff said: I am a thatcher and live at Chedzoy. I am about sixty years of age, and my general health has been good. The defendant is a farmer in the same parish, occupying an estate of about 170 acres, and other land. On the 16th August last I was thatching for Mr. Benjamin Tazewell, assisted by my son. Between eight and nine that evening, while on the rick, Mr. Fry came up, and I heard him say to my son, 'I wonder whether John (meaning me) can come and thatch my mow to-morrow.' I heard Mr. Fry say to my son that we were both to go to his house in the evening. We had supper at Mr. Tazewell's before leaving.

"We afterwards went to Mr. Fry's, and were invited inside, where Mr. Fry was sitting on the settle smoking. Robert Clarke and Alfred Gully were on the opposite settle. They were also smoking. Mr. Fry said to me, 'John, come in, and have a pipe of tobacco and some cider.' There were some cups on the table. I replied to his invitation, 'No, thank you, Sir, I have had some ale at Mr. Tazewell's.' Mr. Fry then said, 'Well, John, how about thatching the mow to-morrow?' I replied, 'I don't think I shall be able to do it to-morrow, as I must serve others as well as you.' He said, 'For why?' I said, 'You have been rather indifferent to me lately; I don't know what it is for - whether it is because I asked Mrs. Fry for a few eggs and a little cream, or no. If she had let me have it, I should have paid for it as usual.

"Fry then said, 'The quicker thee art gone out of my house the better.' In reply I said, 'That I can do, Sir,' and I rose up and passed him. I heard a noise, and found that he had thrown down his pipe on the ground and smashed it. I went about two steps further, and Mr. Fry said, 'You b—- old hag,' and used other bad language. One of the other men thereupon said, 'Stop, Mr. Fry, what are you going about?' I turned round, and I saw that one of the men had his arm in front of Mr. Fry, apparently keeping him back. With the same a heavy blow came on my left eye, and felled me to the ground. I don't know anything that occurred afterwards until I found myself in bed, and being attended to by Dr. Farmer in my own house, about a quarter of a mile from Mr. Fry's. My shirt front was covered with blood and there was a bunch on my head nearly as large as a hen's egg. There was also a mark in my right side, and I was in pain there.

"I got up the following day, and stayed up three or four hours. On the succeeding day I came into Bridgwater to see the surgeon. Up to that time I was not aware of the serious injury I had received, and I that day took out a summons against Fry for the assault. Between that and the day of the return of the summons I became unconscious, and off and on I remained like that for a whole week. I was confined to my bedroom seven weeks. During that time I was under the care of Dr. Farmer and Mr. Axford, and attended by my wife and other people, two by night and one by day.

"Afterwards I began to walk about a little, but suffered from weakness. I tried to turn up a little ground for myself with a spade, but was too weak to do it. For the last few days I have been engaged two or three hours a day in mole-catching, but I can't stand a day's work. I am too weak, and have too much pain in my side. I have only received 3s. 6d. (17.5p.) for work ever since this occurrence. Sometimes I can't sleep more than two or three hours at night. I never had such pain before, and am in great pain now. I understand the medical charges are £14 or £15, and my wife has incurred a cost of £2 to £3 a week in providing wines and spirits, and other nourishment. During the thatching season I could earn £2 a week, and after that about 15s. per week as a gardener, &c.

"Cross-examined: With the exception of my jaw, my health had been good up to the 16th. I never suffered from giddiness. I am certain it was Mr. Fry who struck me. I did ask my son-in-law (Hunt) afterwards if he knew how the row began, and he replied that he did not, as he was out in the barn drawing cider.

"Albert Brely, son of the plaintiff, corroborated the main points of his father's statement, and added that when the defendant threw down his pipe he heard one of the men say, 'Stop, stop, master; what are you going to do?' Defendant struck witness's father, who at once fell down. Witness then got up and said, 'Stop, master; do you know what you are doing?' Fry also kicked the plaintiff when on the ground. On going towards the defendant to protect his father, witness was struck by Clarke, who knocked him down, and Fry then knelt on him, and tried to choke him. Plaintiff was pulled out of the room as a dead body would be, and witness afterwards found him outside the dairy door, lying on his back insensible. There was blood on the floor where he fell. Mrs. [Ann] Fry came outside and saw the plaintiff, and she told her husband she believed he was dead. Witness believed so too, and he met a man named Stone, and made a communication to him. He then went for medical assistance and Dr. Farmer attended the same night. He (witness) did not live with his father. His father was confined to his bedroom seven or eight weeks, and was unconscious during the greater part of that time. Cross-examined: I did not rise from my seat until my father was knocked down.

"Mrs. [Mary] Brely, wife of the plaintiff, was next examined as to the condition of her husband when he came home, his subsequent illness, and the expense which she had been put to, about £25, besides medical charges, £15; altogether £40. Some time ago Messrs. Smith and Boyle were employed to write to the defendant and claimed £30 as damages. The plaintiff was not then aware that medical charges were so high, or how serious his injuries were.

"Dr. Farmer described the nature of the injuries the plaintiff had sustained. He found the plaintiff in bed moaning, and that he had a blow just under the left eye, on the cheek-bone. He had also a lump on the top of his head, and a slight abrasion of the skin. There was some blood on his shirt-front. When he next saw plaintiff in Bridgwater on the 18th, he complained a great deal of his head. On the 24th he had become much worse. He was restless and sleepless, and again complained of his head. He was insensible for a considerable time, and nothing would rouse him. He at length became so ill that himself (witness) and his partner, Mr. Axford, saw him in consultation together, and had to use very active treatment. For seven weeks he was in great danger, and his sufferings were in proportion.

In cross-examination, witness said he believed the blow on the back of the head was caused by his coming into collision with some hard substance. - Mr. Richard Axford, surgeon, gave corroborative evidence.

"Mr. Barham then addressed the jury for the defence. He said his instructions were that the injuries the plaintiff had sustained, and which the defendant sincerely regretted, were occasioned by the fall in the defendant's kitchen, and that the row began by the son of the plaintiff attacking Mr. Fry. The defendant alleged also that both the plaintiff and his son were drunk when they entered into defendant's house. Mr. Trenchard then called Robert Clarke, who said that when the occurrence took place at Mr. Fry's house there were present the defendant and his wife, plaintiff and his son, himself, and a person named Gully. Defendant said to the plaintiff that he had tapped the first cask of cider, and asked if he would have some. Plaintiff said he should not drink any, as he 'considered himself not an ox, but a man, and ought to be treated as one.' Plaintiff also said he had been ill, and had sent for some eggs and cream, but had been denied. Mr. Fry said, 'We don't want to have no noise in my house; and if you don't like to do my work, you can leave it alone.' Mr. Fry also said, 'I want you to leave my house. If you don't, I shall put you out.' Plaintiff got up, and Fry also got up. When the latter rose, the plaintiff's son went to him, and caught hold of him by the collar, and they both fell down on the floor. Witness did not see the defendant hit the plaintiff at all, but saw the latter on the floor.

"This witness gave a very confused account of what took place, and evidently was under the influence of drink. - Mr. Reed (to witness): Have you dined today? - Witness: Yes, Sir. - Mr. Reed: May I ask where? - Witness: What do you mean by dining? (Laughter.) - Mr. Reed: Have you been drinking today? - Witness: Have you been drinking? (Laughter.) - Mr. Barham said, after the evidence of the last witness, the only independent witness he had, he should not feel justified in carrying the case any further, or in putting his client into the box. He then addressed the jury in mitigation of damages, urging that they ought not to award the plaintiff more than Messrs. Smith and Boyle had been asked for, viz. £30. - His Honour having summed up, the jury returned a verdict for the plaintiff, damages £40."

In June 1874 another case was heard in Bridgwater County Court and was reported in the Bridgwater Mercury.

"HENRY FRY v. ALFRED COZENS. - The plaintiff, a farmer, of Chedzoy, claimed of the defendant, a general dealer, carrying on business in Eastover, Bridgwater, the sum of £1 12s. 6d. for an alleged breach of contract. ... Plaintiff said that in February last he agreed to sell defendant a heap of potatoes at £5 10s. per ton, to be delivered within one month. He told the defendant they were rock potatoes, and from the same ground he had had some before, but he gave no kind of warranty. On the 28th of the month he delivered 2 tons 14 cwt., but defendant did not send for the remainder, and on the 26th of the following month defendant came to his house and said, 'I have come out to see you respecting these potatoes; the ones I have are very bad and strong.' He (plaintiff) replied that they were the same sort as he had had before. Defendant offered to take the remainder if he (plaintiff) made an allowance of 50s. (£2.50), which he refused to do, but subsequently offered to allow 10s. (50p.) per ton on the remainder if they did not meet with his approbation. About a week afterwards defendant refused to have the remainder, and plaintiff sold them elsewhere - 5 cwt. to Mr. Pitman, at the same price he now sued for them, and 3 tons 5 cwt. to three other persons, at a loss of 10s. per ton, the best price he could get. Mr. Joseph Lovibond was with him when the deal took place.

"Cross-examined: He realised by the sale of the remainder precisely the same sum he would have had if the defendant had taken them at a reduction of 10s. per ton as offered by him (plaintiff). He made that offer so as to avoid dispute. Defendant did not ask anything about their quality when the deal took place. He (plaintiff) knew they were intended to be sold by Mr. Cozens for the table. The price originally offered for them, 5s. 6d. (27p.) per bag, was above the market-price at the time, and Mr. Cozens remarked that they were dear, but that he expected prices would go up. The remainder were sold to Mr. Pitman, Betsy Reed and Samuel Brewer.

"Joseph Lovibond (25), of Chedzoy, was called, but admitted that he was not present when the bargain took place. He knew the potatoes, however, and had examined them. They were white rocks and a very fair sample of eating potatoes. - Mr. Reed (for the plaintiff): You live in potatoe (sic) country? Witness: Yes. - Mr. Reed: And have been mixed up with potatoes all your life? (Laughter.)

"John Atwood, potatoe-dealer, of Bridgwater, saw the potatoes in question when in the heap, and he tried some by boiling them. It was a very fair potatoe for eating. - Cross-examined: He had said he would not give more than £4 10s. per ton for them, because he wanted to buy them cheap. He was at that time giving £5 per ton. Mrs. Stone said that in April last she bought some of the potatoes, and they turned out very well. - Cross-examined: Had not told Mr. Cozens that they would not do for her.

"Mr. Chapman (for the defendant) contended that such a warranty was given; and that it was not probable defendant would agree to buy potatoes at such a figure if they had not been warranted, and without asking about their quality as represented by the plaintiff. He should prove that they were unfit for sale, and he submitted that even if no warranty was proved, the plaintiff knew they were intended for sale by retail as eating potatoes, and that they were not fit to be eaten, the defendant was entitled to a verdict. He called Mr. Cozens, who said that in March last he purchased of plaintiff a cave of potatoes at £5 10s. per ton. He went to look at them, but did not eat any, thinking he could take plaintiff's word. He asked if they were good and plaintiff said he would warrant them 'good eating rock potatoes.'

Fifty-five bags - 3 tons 16 cwt. - were delivered, for which he paid £15, but after selling some his customers brought them back, saying they were not fit for a pig to eat, and that if he did not take them back they would carry them to Mr. Vinton, the Inspector of Nuisances. He tried them himself, and finding their complaints to be well founded, he hired a trap of Mr. Aplin, and drove out to the plaintiff, about eight or nine days after the delivery of the potatoes, and told him that they were not according to his word, and that his customers were bringing them back in all directions. Plaintiff said he was to make the best he could of them, and that he would make an allowance. He (defendant) said he should have to use those he had for planting, as he could not sell them for eating. That he did, and lost sixpence per bag on them. Plaintiff said he would allow him 50s. if he would take the remainder, but he declined. - By Mr. Reed: Plaintiff did not tell me that if I did not take away the rest of the potatoes he would sell them, and sue me for the loss.

"Joseph Pitman, farmer and potatoe-dealer, living at Woolavington, said that about Lady-day last he purchased some potatoes of the plaintiff, at 11s. per sack. His wife dressed some of them, and she said - Mr. Reed (interrupting) objected to anything said by the wife of witness before giving evidence. - Witness (indignantly): Can't I take my wife's word? (Laughter.) The potatoes are as strong as mustard. (Renewed laughter.) Betsy Reed said she was a 'tatty' dealer, and lived at Westonzoyland. She also had bought some potatoes of Mr. Fry to sell again, and people complained of them so much that she lost some of her customers in consequence.

"Samuel Brewer, potatoe-dealer, bought a ton of potatoes from Mr. Fry. He took a load of them down to Highbridge and Burnham, and on going there two days afterwards all his customers were 'down' on him for selling such bad potatoes, which they put back into his cart again. He sold some of them afterwards at Cannington and Combwich, and another lot went to Taunton. - Mr. Chapman: Where they were not known? (Laughter.) Witness: Yes, and that is how I got rid of 'thio' (sic) lot. (Renewed laughter.) - By Mr. Reed: He went three times to Mr. Fry's to haul the potatoes, and never made any complaint to him, not having tried them.

"Charles Tozer deposed that he bought some potatoes of Mr. Cozens. Before being cooked they were very good in appearance, but afterwards they were very strong, and a large portion had to be cut off. The defendant, on being recalled, said he would not dispute the delivery of the potatoes on the 28th February. He could not say for certain how long it was after receiving the complaints that he went to the plaintiff's, but he was sure it was before Lady-day. - His Honour said if any warranty was given there ought to be a prompt repudiation of the contract if the alleged warranty was discovered to be untrue; but in this case he was satisfied that there was an acceptance of the potatoes long after their defective character and condition became known to the defendant. His judgement would therefore be for the plaintiff, but as he was not satisfied that the full amount of damages claimed had been proved he should make no order as to costs."

Robert Fry (1855-1927), who was to become the next tenant of the farm, found himself before the court twice in 1877. Although the charges were similar, the results were not. In March the Bridgwater Mercury reported that,

"Robert Fry, farmer, was charged with trespassing in pursuit of game at Chedzoy on land in the occupation of Mr. John Baker. Complainant stated that he was the occupier of a farm at Chedzoy, called 'Fowlers Plot,' and about six o'clock in the evening of the day in question he saw three men walking over Chedzoy field, a portion of his farm. On going near them they 'spread abroad,' and he saw the defendant stooped down under the hedge. Afterwards he came out and witness asked him what he did there, and defendant replied that they were shooting wild fowl. Defendant had a double-barrelled gun, and witness reminded him that he had previously cautioned him against going there. There was a path in the field, but defendant was two hundred yards from the path. Cross-examined: He spoke to one of the other men, who also told him they were fowling. Would not swear it was not after half past six o'clock. Mr. Chapman (for the defendant) said the defendant had been charged with trespassing 'in the daytime' and that it was laid down in the Act as not later than half an hour after sunset. They would find that the sun set on that day before half past five and as the complainant would not swear that it was before half past six the magistrates could not convict. - The Bench dismissed the case. - A similar charge against a man named Levi Rainey (23), at the same time, was thereupon withdrawn."

Then in October,

"Robert Fry, farmer, was summoned for trespassing in pursuit of game and conies on land in the occupation of Elias Potter at Chedzoy. George Bell, labourer, stated that he saw defendant enter the field at six o'clock in the morning with a double-barrelled gun. Saw him shoot a partridge and pick it up and put it in his pocket. Cross-examined: He was about one hundred yards distant from the defendant at the time, but he was sure it was a partridge. William Bennett, gamekeeper, in the employ of Mr. B.C.D. Greenhill, proved that his master had the right of shooting game over the land in question. - Mr. Chapman, for the defence, stated that his instruction were that the defendant shot a wood-pigeon, and that he had liberty from Mr. Potter to shoot pigeons. He called Robert Broomfield, farmer, who stated that he was with defendant on the morning in question and saw him enter the field with a gun. When about one hundred or one hundred and fifty yards distant he heard the defendant shoot, but could not see any birds. When the defendant came back he took a wood-pigeon from his pocket and put it in the cart. - Elias Potter, farmer's son, stated that his father had seen defendant in this field, and had never denied him the liberty of shooting there. - Bennett then said he wished to call another witness, but Mr. Chapman objected that the case for the prosecution was closed. - The Bench, however, ruled that further evidence was admissible, and P.C. Hawkins then stated that he afterwards asked the defendant whether he had a game licence, and he said he had not. Defendant also admitted that the bird he shot was a partridge. - The Bench inflicted a fine of 10s. and costs."

But it was not only Robert Fry who was in trouble with the magistrates.

"Mr. Edwin Fry, farmer, of Chedzoy, was summoned by the district supervisor of Excise (Mr. Brosnaham) for keeping a dog without a licence. P.C. Hawkins stated that the defendant had two dogs and no licence, but Mr. Brosnaham said the licence had since been taken out by the defendant who had given them a good deal of trouble. Defendant was fined 25s. (£1.25), one fourth of the full penalty."

Quite where the following incident took place in June 1890 is not clear, but it would appear to have been somewhere near Frys Farm.

"A BIT OF A LOVE QUARREL AT CHEDZOY. Thomas Phillips, labourer (who was probably the 21 year old son of William Phillips of the Manor House Inn) in the employ of Mr. Robt. Fry, was charged with assaulting Sarah Ann Tucker of the same place. - Complainant stated that on the day in question two horses belonging to Mr. Robert Fry were trespassing on her premises. When defendant came to fetch them she told him to let them remain until he went for his master. He refused to go to fetch his master, and told her if she did not let him take the horses through the gate he would soon upset her and her brother too. He then proceeded to open the gate and when she (complainant) went up to him he struck her in the mouth and used very indecent language. The defendant's master was milking in an adjoining ground, about two hundred yards away. - By Mr. Chapman: She did not lose her temper and strike the defendant with the butt end of a whip. She was sure he struck her. - Mr. Robert Fry stated that he saw the altercation that took place between the defendant and the complainant. He distinctly saw the complainant hit the defendant with the butt end of the whip, and what the defendant did was to put up his hands to prevent the effects of the blow. The grievance was not in consequence of the horses but 'a bit of a love quarrel' between the parties that existed. (Laughter.) - The Bench inflicted a fine of 1s. and costs."

After Christmas 1905 Robert Fry found himself appearing in the Bridgwater Police Court when he pleaded guilty to being drunk and disorderly outside the White Hart Hotel in Eastover.

"Defendant said there was not very much the matter with him. It was Christmas time and he fell in with a friend or two." The Mayor fined him ten shillings and costs, or seven days' imprisonment in default, and warned him, "Don't let this happen again at Christmas or any other time!"

Both father and son appeared before the magistrates in February 1910.

"Robert Fry, farmer, of Chedzoy, and Thomas Fry (15), his son, were charged with having unlawfully stolen a sheep-dog, value £1 2s. 6d. The Magistrates' Clerk said the offence of stealing a dog was an offence especially under the Larceny Act [1861] but was not a felony. Walter Coate lost a dog which was handed to the police. It was alleged that Robert Fry examined the dog at the Police Station and left without giving his name. Later Thomas Fry went to report losing a dog and paid 2s. 6d. after identifying the animal as his father's. The Mayor said the Bench had given very careful consideration to the case but whilst they felt it was a very suspicious one they all felt that the evidence was not sufficient for them to convict. Case dismissed."

In March 1911 the father was in trouble again.

"Robert Fry pleaded guilty to having kept a carriage without having a licence in force authorising him to do so. He explained he had previously had a licence for the carriage and he admitted quite frankly to the police and to the taxation officer he had used the vehicle once after the licence had expired. Defendant was arranging to have the vehicle done up for the Coronation, and he was under the impression it would not be necessary to take out a licence until he had the vehicle done up. The Magistrates' Clerk: Perhaps he thought that as the vehicle was to be required for the Coronation he did not need a licence. (Laughter.) The taxation officer said notices had been sent to the effect that the licence should be renewed. Magistrates' Clerk (to defendant): You had better get rid of the old cart. Fined 15s. and costs."

An incident which took place in June 1910 in Chedzoy Lane involving a bull belonging to "Mr. Fry" has already been recounted. The same bull could have been involved in another incident in May 1912. The Bridgwater Mercury reported,

"A pleasant meadow in Chedzoy was on Thursday last the scene of a grim tragedy of the animal world, a horse, the property of Mr. R. Fry, being gored to death by a maddened bull. It seems that soon after the bull was turned into the field, which contained the horse and other stock, the former animal became infuriated at the presence of the horse. Catching the horse unawares, it caught it in the side with such force that the horse was quickly incapacitated. Although there were human witnesses to the tragedy, they were powerless to intervene, so swift and fatal was the attack of the bull. The latter forced its horns into the side of the horse and inflicted a series of terrible gashes in the stomach of the poor steed. The horse soon sank to the ground, and died shortly after the bull had been driven away."

In March 1913,

"Robert Fry, farmer, pleaded guilty to having allowed his dog to be at large at night. Defendant said the dog followed him out to the sheep, and it being dark and being an old dog, it failed to find its way back with him. Fined 2s. 6d. and costs."

Robert Fry was in further trouble in April 1918.

> "Robert Fry, farmer, Chedzoy, was charged with having sold to John Genge Laver twelve sheep for slaughter, which sheep were not in a market. Laver was charged with buying the sheep. All of the sheep were killed and most of them were dispatched to the metropolitan market and sold for food. Four of the sheep disappeared mysteriously, and the prosecutor understood they were given to dogs, but Laver would have to have a large number of dogs to eat four sheep in several days. The sheep were what was termed 'coathe' and fit for food to a certain point. Fry stated, 'I have had bad luck with my sheep this year through them lying about on the low, wet land and I think they must have been chilled. I have had more than twenty die, and the others I've sold in Bridgwater market.' He had 52 ewes and many of them died. He had lost £450 worth of cattle this year. The Bench fined Fry £2 and an advocate's fee of £1 1s."

The farm was sold in June 1927 after the death of Robert Fry. It was then worked by the Baker family for some years and then the Triggol family. In February 1947 the Bridgwater Mercury reported that,

> "Percy Triggol, farmer, of Frys Farm, Chedzoy was summoned at Bridgwater Borough Court yesterday for using a motor trailer with inefficient brakes and for not having the unladen weight marked. Defendant was fined £2 10s."

Edwin 'Ted' and Rita Triggol were the last couple to work Frys Farm and in their day cows continued to be herded across Front Street twice daily. At milking time it was impossible to pass the farm without one's progress being watched by a group of curious cows all looking over the front wall as they waited their turn to be milked. The farm outbuildings were either demolished or converted into houses in 1985. The old farmhouse was on the market in 1999 for £130,000.

The **VILLAGE HALL**, on the left side of the road, was built in 1914 by Alfred Stacey and his son, Charlie, of Westonzoyland for Rev George R Mullens, at that time Rector of Chedzoy. Previously the site had been occupied by the cottage and forge of Tom Butler. In the first few years of the 20th Century Alfred Hooper (born 1886) was an apprentice blacksmith there. At a meeting of the Parochial Church Council on 26th April 1937 Rev. Mullens outlined his proposals as to the best way for providing for the care and management of the "Parish Hall" property when the time came either by his death or resignation from the Benefice to sever his connection with the parish. He said that it was his intention to give the Parish Hall, front garden and paddock to the parish, about half an acre in all, and to place the whole in the hands of a body of Trustees who should be responsible for the general maintenance of the building and payment of any expenses such as rates, insurance and repairs and also for the uses and purposes for which the property should be put for the greatest benefit of all sections of the community in the Parish of Chedzoy. Mr. Mullens went on to say that as soon as possible he would have a deed to this effect drawn up and executed. A Conveyance dated 26th May 1937 was drawn up and parish minutes for 1938 record that this deed was deposited in the Parish chest. The Village Hall was registered as a charity on 23rd March 1972.

When the hall was originally built the wing at the rear, which now houses the toilets, was the kitchen. Initially there were no toilet facilities, but later the shed to the left of the front porch (now used as storage), was provided for the gentlemen. Once indoor toilet facilities had been provided, one end of the main hall was partitioned off and adapted for use as a kitchen.

Although many events have taken place over the years, the hall was more crowded than usual in January 1933 on the occasion of a whist drive and dance held by Chedzoy Cricket Club. The Bridgwater Mercury reported that after the whist drive,

> "A good number arrived at 10.30 for the dance, bringing the total to about 180, the hall being full to overflowing. The Misses Howells' Band, which had played so excellently throughout the dance, and had won much admiration, brought a happy evening to a close at 2 a.m. with 'God Save the King'."

With 180 people, a band and, most likely, a blazing fire, the hall must have been packed.

But there was still room for more! Twelve months later the Mercury carried a report of the Cricket Club's annual event. After details of the whist drive the report continued:

> "A very large number arrived for the dance, swelling the number to about 220, the hall being full to overflowing. The spot waltz prizes were won by Mrs. Phillips of Bridgwater and Mr. Whitcombe of Meare. Time passed all too quickly, and when it was announced that the Misses Howells' dance band had decided to play on for an extra half hour, loud cheers rang through the hall. A happy evening was therefore brought to a close at 2.30 a.m. with 'God Save the King'."

During the Second World War the hall was used as a classroom for evacuated children, but it was also used by local organisations: for the Home Guard it was a Headquarters; for the Air Raid Precautions it was a Depot and for the Civil Defence Committee, a meeting place.

The Village Hall has a link to the fine equestrian monument in the churchyard which was erected in 1950 to Sydney Mason Collins (1879-1946) who died in Bournemouth. He was formerly a Fellow of Corpus Christi College, Oxford and a Barrister at Law at the Inner Temple. On his death he left an estate of £26,502 10s. 11d. (gross), £24,569 16s. (net) and having made six specific bequests stated,

> "I have in mind to cause as little untoward disturbance as possible to those next to me by my going. I am the last of my name and line, leaving none of my blood to follow; having safeguarded the life interests of the aforesaid, I feel it then incumbent upon myself to ensure as I can the ultimate issue of what I have to control. I deem that this is best done

by recurring to the soil from which my stock has sprung, that of Chedzoy, Somerset."

He therefore left the ultimate residue of his property,

"To the parson and good people of Chedzoy for a village hall, requesting that his name, a Chedzoy name recorded in the parish since Queen Elizabeth's day, be kept in remembrance." Quite why he should have made such a bequest remains something of a mystery. He had never lived in the village and his final visit had been in 1938. The Bridgwater Mercury reported, "The first record in the register for his family is the marriage of Thomas Collins in the year 1579. Mr. Collins' great-grandfather, who is buried in the village, appears to be the last of the line to have lived in Chedzoy and all connection with the village came to an end with his death."

Opposite the Village Hall stands one of the oldest houses in Chedzoy, **CADBURY HOUSE**. The age of the house is not known, but the deeds date back as far as 1791 and, curiously, include details about the construction of King's Sedgemoor Drain and ownership of the Manor of Chedzoy. It has twice served as the Post Office for the village.

Sydney Mason Collins Memorial.
The statue was designed by Cecil Thomas, R.A.
Photograph by John Weeks.

By 1859 Edmund Rainey was the "Receiver of Letters." In September 1871 his wife found herself before the Bridgwater Police Court.

"Mary Rainey (48), wife of the postmaster at Chedzoy, was charged with stealing a peck of apples, value 1s., the property of Mr. Edwin Fry, a farmer, on the 5th inst. ... William Wheeler (15), a lad in the employ of Mr. Fry, said at six o'clock on the morning in question, he saw the defendant in his master's garden pick apples from a tree, put them into her apron, and carry them into her house, which adjoined the garden. He told Mr. Fry what he had seen the same night. When he saw the defendant in the garden he was about 20 yards distant. He did not speak to her but whistled. - By Mr. Cook (for the defence): She was in the garden about ten minutes. The next day he heard the husband of the defendant tell Mr. Fry that he got up about twenty minutes past six o'clock and left his wife in bed, and that she was ill and did not go out of the house that day. - Mr. Cook said he did not know whether this was a trumped up story or not, but he should be able to satisfy the Bench that the lad Wheeler was mistaken as to the identity of the defendant, and should call evidence to prove an alibi. Mrs. Ann Gully (24), daughter of the defendant, said that on the evening of the 4th her mother was very poorly, having the 'shivers' - symptoms of the ague. On the following morning, about twenty minutes to seven o'clock, she again saw her mother, at her house, and she then appeared to be very ill. - Eliza Rainey, aged 13, another daughter of the defendant, said that on the morning of 5th she heard her father get up about six o'clock, go downstairs, and about twenty minutes afterwards unlock the door. About twenty minutes after that her mother (the defendant) also went down. She did not go out of the house until after dinner on that day. - The chairman said the Bench had come to the conclusion that they must dismiss the case. They believed Wheeler had seen a woman under the tree, but that he was mistaken as to identity."

Between 1875 and 1883 the Post Office moved across the road to Avalon House where it remained until about 1908. Cadbury House was the Post Office throughout the early years of the 20th Century and, from time to time, an indentation used to appear in the pavement where once the letter box stood. The other part of the house was a tailor's shop. In July 1913 the house was occupied by James Hook who paid an annual rent of £16 and it, together with two cottages owned by Jesse Conduit and Charles Woolley and an acre of land, was sold by Sidney Denning. The house and land were purchased by John Seaman for £250. Later owners were Mr. and Mrs. Hooper who bought the house in the early 1920s for the sum of £130, having been advised by Rev. Mullens that the asking price of £200 was too much. After buying the property they were left with just £7 in the bank. The couple raised ten children and lived in the house until their deaths in 1979 and 1994.

AVALON HOUSE, next to the former school, had a thatched roof until the early years of the 20th Century, and is much older than its present external appearance suggests.

Indeed, one source says it was an ale house known as the Three Horseshoes and is at least 400 years old.

Perhaps this was the inn owned by the Bond family between 1657 and 1690 and which was still in business in 1738 or later.

(Above) Avalon House.
Edward Noakes in his working clothes.
Photograph courtesy of Margaret Alsford (nee Brooks).

(Below) Front Street before 1914.
Note the absence of the Village Hall. A turnstile can be seen in the school wall.
Source unknown, courtesy of Eileen Growtage.

About 1861 Edward (1830-1908) and Louisa Noakes (1830-1909) and their family moved to the house from Sussex. He worked as a carpenter at the premises whilst, from about 1880, Mrs. Noakes ran the Post Office in one of the front rooms. Subsequently, one of their children, Mary 'Minnie' Noakes, married Joseph Brooks, the schoolmaster. Joseph's sister, Elizabeth, married Arthur Noakes, who was Minnie's brother. When Edward Noakes lived there the lean-to on the right side of the building was his carpentry workshop where he made gates, stiles, coffins and, for those families who could not afford headstones, headboards to mark graves in the churchyard. Perhaps the ancient wooden cross still marking one of the graves was his handiwork. One of his daily duties was the delivery of mail around the village.

The cottage was sold by auction in June 1941 when it was described as

> "stone and brick built with a thatched roof, sitting room, kitchen, scullery, workshop and three bedrooms approached by two staircases. The cottage is held by Mrs. Jeanes on a weekly tenancy at an annual rent of £5."

It was reported that the property was bought by Mr. E.J. Fry of Three Oaks Farm for the sum of £180. He sold it shortly afterwards for £200 to Mr. and Mrs. Newton.

The original thatched roof of the house was removed and the upper storey raised during the 1940s. From 1941 it was the home of Mrs. Lily Newton (1904-1994). Mrs. Newton, a triplet, was one of seven children and, speaking in 1991, reminisced,

> "Dad, who was also born in Chedzoy, was a farm worker and very good with horses, winning many prizes at local shows. He didn't earn much money, but we were always well fed and turned out. In the summer we were able to make a few extra coppers by collecting blackberries and selling them at a penny a pound to a man who used to go round the villages collecting them. There was a tailor in Chedzoy called Mr. Hook and he used to give me sixpence every year as a birthday present, because I had been born one of triplets."

For forty years Mrs. Newton was a dinner lady at the school and when a young woman had been the cleaner there:

> "I was paid less than a pound a week and had to find my own brush."

The School Management Committee minutes for 1917 noted that

> "The average payment worked out at 2s. 9d. (13p.) per week out of which she had to find all working utensils. The Managers recommended an increase of 1s. 3d. (6p.) per week."

At their next meeting they were told that the Education Committee

> "had decided to increase the salary of the cleaner of the Chedzoy Council School from £7 3s. to £7 10s. per annum as from first November 1917 and in the future the cleaning materials and utensils should be provided by the County Education Committee and not by the Cleaner as at present."

The pay for cleaning was gradually increased to £10 10s. per annum, but in view of the extra work necessitated by the arrival of evacuees during the Second World War this was raised in £12 in 1941 and, on the instructions of the County Education Authority, further increased to £18 the following year.

The present owners set about modernising Avalon House in 1996 and during the course of this found two old bread ovens, one large and one small, either side of the chimney in the wall nearest to the village hall.

The School and School House

A school was recorded in the village in 1612 and in 1662 a man was licensed to teach writing, reading, accounts, ciphering (numbering) and grammar. The Overseers maintained a school between 1694 and 1777. In 1819 there was a Sunday School which taught 64 children, although numbers had fallen to 42 by 1825. Two day schools began in 1818 and 1830, but both had closed by 1843.

The former village school, closed in 1995, was housed in a fine old Victorian schoolroom, with the original panelled walls and shelves in the interior. The original ceiling rose to over twenty feet with fine carved oak beams, still carrying the hooks on which hung the old oil lamps. Francis Lovibond recorded in his diary that the foundation stone for the schoolroom was laid by Rev. R. Luscombe on 11th July 1842. The original schoolroom was incorporated into a larger building which was erected in 1876 at a total cost to the Chedzoy School Board of £645 5s. for the schoolroom, outbuildings, school house and boundary walls with all internal fittings. The builders were Messrs. Henry Chedzoy and Son. In order to cover the costs the Public Works Loan Commissioners advanced the sum of £650 to be repaid with interest of 3% per annum "by 50 equal annual payments secured by mortgage of the rates of the parish." The mortgage deed is dated 3rd November 1875.

On 23rd June 1875 Rev. G.O. Mullens, as Manager of Chedzoy Church of England School, leased the schoolroom to the School Board for the Parish of Chedzoy for a period of 99 years at an annual rate of 5s. (25p.), payable on Christmas Day, for

> "providing instruction in the doctrines of Christianity as parcel of the daily routine of instruction but only for so many hours of each day (not including Sundays) as shall suffice to enable the Board to carry on a Public Elementary School."

The Board were to be responsible for the maintenance and insurance of the property "in the sum of three hundred pounds at least" and "at their own expense gravel and re-gravel the playground every alternate year." The legal documents were drawn up by Paul Reed, the well known Bridgwater Solicitor, Clerk to the Board. The cost of running the school was estimated at £109 10s. 6d. per annum, to include a salary of £70 for the teacher. A rate of 6d. (about 2p.) in the pound was to be levied to recoup this. The school was formally adopted by the County Education Committee in 1876.

The first teacher was Mrs. Mary Latham who came from Leicester. She was made responsible for obtaining the necessary equipment before the school opened on 22nd May 1876. The charge for each pupil was one penny per week and the hours were to be

> "from 9 to half past 12 and from 2 to half past 4 daily with the exception of Saturday and that the first half hour each day was given to religious instruction."

Mary Palmer was employed

> "at the rate of 2s. (10p.) per week to brush out and clean the school daily and wash the same once a week, she finding brushes, dusters and other appliances."

Mrs. Latham's tenure as teacher was not without controversy.

In October 1876 the School Board minutes recorded,

"The attention of the Board was drawn to statements made as to Mrs. Latham, the school mistress, having been absent during school hours & as to a night school kept at her house at which, upon the young people leaving, rough and improper language and conduct which it was alleged took place & Clerk was directed to call Mrs. Latham's attention thereto & that such night school was to cease after the end of the present week." That was not the end of the matter.

At their next meeting,

"A long discussion took place as to rumours & statements made reflecting upon Mrs. Latham's conduct & character which, if correct, unfitted her to hold her present office. Mrs. Latham denied the truthfulness of such rumours and statements except as to being on friendly terms with certain parishioners of whose character the Board disapproved & there being no direct proof of such rumours and statements being well founded the Chairman, with approval of members present, cautioned Mrs. Latham as to the urgent necessity of her being most careful as to her conduct in future and also with whom she associated, and which Mrs. Latham promised to do."

It seems she did not keep her promise as the matter was discussed two months later.

"Mrs. Latham. A report having been spread in the village and directly brought under the notice of the Board by Mr. John Potter, butcher, imputing Mrs. Latham having recently been guilty of immoral conduct, the Board gave Mrs. Latham notice thereof to attend before them with reference thereto & she now attending the Board placed such statement before her, with name of person so making such statement, accompanied with further statements from Mr. Potter that he was prepared, if it became necessary, to confirm charges so made. Mrs. Latham denied the truth of such allegations, but the Board having reference to the fact that Mr. Potter being prepared to justify his statement, suspended Mrs. Latham's appointment, informing Mrs. Latham that unless she forthwith cleared herself from such grave accusation they would feel compelled to discharge her."

The Board went on to dismiss Mrs. Latham, but she countered by taking action in Bridgwater County Court and the case received extensive coverage in the Bridgwater Mercury in June 1877 under the headline

"ACTION AGAINST A SCHOOL BOARD - EXTRAORDINARY CASE. Mary Jane Latham v. Chedzoy School Board. The plaintiff, wife of Sergeant W.J. Latham, of the barracks, Norwich, and late head-mistress of the Board school at Chedzoy, sued the defendants, members of the Chedzoy School Board, for £20 10s.; three months' salary in lieu of notice, from the 28th April 1877 to 27th July 1877, and value of house accommodation and coal for the same period.

"Mr. Chapman appeared for the plaintiff, and Mr. Poole, barrister (instructed by Messrs. Reed and Cook) for the defendants. This case, the hearing of which occupied about six hours, excited a great amount of interest, and all witnesses and females were ordered out of court.

"Mr. Chapman, in opening the case, said in April, 1876 the Chedzoy School Board advertised for a head school-mistress. His client replied to the advertisement, and sent her testimonials to the Board, and subsequently received a letter from Mr. Reed, the Clerk, stating that she had been appointed at a salary of £70 per annum, with an unfurnished house and coal found, such engagement to be put an end to by either party giving three months' notice. The plaintiff entered upon her duties, which she continued to fulfil until the 20th April last, when, in consequence of a report that had reached the School Board, a special meeting of the Board was called and attended by Mrs. Latham. A resolution was passed at that meeting as follows:- 'A report having been spread in the village and directly brought under the notice of the Board by Mr. John Potter, butcher, imputing that Mrs. Latham had recently been guilty of immoral conduct, the Board give Mrs. Latham notice thereof, and to attend before them with reference thereto.' Mrs. Latham attending, the Board placed such statement before her, with name of person making such statement accompanied with further statements from Mr. Potter that he was prepared, if it became necessary, to confirm the charges so made. Mrs. Latham denied the truth of such allegations, but the Board, having reference to the fact of Mr. Potter being prepared to justify his statements, suspended Mrs. Latham's appointment, informing her that unless she forthwith cleared herself from such grave accusation, they would feel compelled to discharge her. Immediately upon that Mrs. Latham consulted him (Mr. Chapman), and he saw Mr. Reed, Clerk to the Board, and asked if the Board would allow her to retain her situation if she brought an action for slander against her accuser. That was declined, and in consequence he wrote a letter to Mr. Reed on the 25th April, as follows:-

King-square, Bridgwater, 25th April 1877
Dear Sir,

Mrs. Latham, the Board schoolmistress at Chedzoy, has consulted me with reference to her suspension by the Board in consequence of a report which reached them through Mr. John Potter of Chedzoy. Mr. Preston, my client's father, who is the chief School Board officer of Leicester, has been down and seen the persons mentioned by Mr. Potter, and he has satisfied himself that this is not the slightest foundation for the report circulated by Mr. Potter. It was at their suggestion that Mrs. Latham ceased to be intimate with Mrs. Potter, and now this scandal emanates from her. Under the circumstances Mrs. Latham feels that it would be inconsistent with her innocence to resign her position, and she therefore leaves the matter to the discretion of the Board.
Trusting you will let me know their determination at the earliest opportunity.
I remain, dear Sir, yours faithfully,
SAMUEL CHAPMAN

"On the following day (26th April) the Board met again and passed another resolution as follows:- 'The Board met to-day further to consider the matter, and were informed of Mrs. Latham having, through her solicitor (Mr. Chapman) called upon Mr. Potter to withdraw the statement he had made, but which he declined doing, stating his being prepared to prove same; and Mrs. Latham having taken no further steps with the view of disproving Mr. Potter's statement, and the Board having had a further interview with Mrs. Latham, who was accompanied by her father, resolved, on the proposition of the Chairman, seconded by Mr. Carey, and supported by Mr. Winter, forthwith to dismiss Mrs. Latham, and the Clerk was directed so to inform Mrs. Latham and her solicitor. For the cause so leading to Mrs. Latham's dismissal any salary that was now accruing became forfeited, but the Board directed their Clerk to pay same as an act of grace, having reference to Mrs. Latham's limited means, provided she at once rendered an account of school pence received since the last account was rendered, and deliver up all books and other school appliances.' In accordance with that resolution Mrs. Latham was dismissed; she made up the school accounts, and Mr. Reed paid her salary up to the time of her leaving without prejudice. On the 22nd May he wrote to Mr. Reed applying for payment of £20 10s.; one quarter's salary, &c., due to her in consequence of improper dismissal. In reply he received a letter stating that the Board would be prepared to defend any proceedings that might be instituted for its recovery.

"His Honour remarked that the question appeared to be whether the notice of dismissal was inconsistent with the terms of the contract. Mr. Chapman replied that was so, and that in another letter he wrote to Mr. Reed he admitted that the salary paid up to the time of dismissal was paid without prejudice, and therefore would not affect the question at issue, which was simply the legality of such dismissal. It would be for the defendants, if they could, to justify such dismissal, and he would first call Mrs. Latham to establish a prima facie case.

"Mr. Chapman then called the plaintiff, who is a person of rather prepossessing appearance, and who said she was a certified schoolmistress, and the wife of a sergeant in the army. After referring to the terms, &c., of her engagement, she stated that she continued to perform the duties of mistress to the Board school at Chedzoy until the 20th April, 1877, when she attended a meeting of the Board, and was informed there of a report of immoral conduct on her part that had reached them. She was informed that if she could not clear herself she was to be dismissed. She was not confronted by her accusers. She asked to be so, and Mr. Winter, a member of the Board, said the report had been made to him by Mr. John Potter, butcher, of Chedzoy.

"Mr. Winter was called upon by Mr. Reed, Clerk to the Board, to give the statement which Mr. Potter had made to him. Mr. Winter then said it was to the effect that she had been seen on the night of 10th April, 1877, in Horsey-lane, having improper intercourse with a man of Bridgwater. She then asked for the man's name, and they declined to give it to her, saying that his name had not been mentioned to them 'legally.' She turned round to the whole of them and said, 'Surely, gentlemen, you don't believe this cruel accusation?' She was told that the Board would stand by her if she could clear herself, but they offered her no alternative but that of being suspended until she could clear herself, or being dismissed on the spot. The Board declined to investigate the matter, and left it entirely in her hands to put it into the hands of a solicitor. She was told that she was suspended. She was not told at that meeting that Mr. Winter or Mr. Tazewell, chairman of the Board, had already visited her accusers, and they gave her no chance of having her accusers there to clear herself in any possible way. She told the Board that on the evening in question she had been over to Bower to a friend of hers, a Mrs. Clarke, whom she had constantly visited when that person was residing at Chedzoy; that she stayed with Mrs. Clarke longer than she had intended; that Mrs. Clarke and her daughter accompanied her to the end of Bower-lane, to put her in the right road, as it was the first time she had been there; that she then proceeded on towards Bridgwater, where she had some business to transact; that on reaching Bath Bridge, finding it to be very dark, and knowing it was getting late, she felt timid and determined to proceed no further and to return home; that she at once turned back, and did not meet any one until she got to the end of Chedzoy-lane, where she saw some men, who wished her 'Goodnight' and that she said 'Goodnight' to them, and passed on.

"The plaintiff added that she told the members of the Board all this and denied emphatically having been in Horsey-lane that night. She had never been in Horsey-lane in her life until she went there to see one of her accusers. At the meeting, when accused, she asked Mr. Reed where Horsey-lane was as she did not know. - In cross-examination by Mr. Poole, plaintiff said she wanted to go to Bridgwater that evening to pay a bill at Mr. Fisher's, the stationer. It was nearly nine o'clock, she supposed, when she reached Bath Bridge and turned back again. It was too dark for her to recognise any of the men at the end of Chedzoy-lane. After passing that place she saw George Potter at his father's gate, and asked him to accompany her home the remainder of the way, which he did. He was one of those who was mentioned to her at the Board meeting as her accusers, the others being Thomas Boon, Elias Potter and Henry Bryant. It was not true that she walked through Horsey-lane that night on a man's arm, or that she went round from there towards Bridgwater, and out into the turnpike-road again. She was quite unacquainted with the country.

"Mr. Poole: Then you entirely deny that this charge against you is a true one?

Plaintiff: Certainly.

Mr. Poole: Did you take any steps to have it investigated afterwards?

Plaintiff: Yes, I sent for my father, and in his company, and with another witness, I went to all four of these that I have named.

Mr. Poole: This is not the first time the Board had complained of your conduct?

Plaintiff: No.

Did they complain of your drinking?

Plaintiff: Yes.

Mr. Poole: Did you deny that?

Plaintiff: I denied that I was ever drunk.

His Honour remarked that if anything of that kind had happened it appeared to have been condoned.

Plaintiff: I may mention that the School Board at Leicester, who had previously employed me, took me back again as soon as I returned there.

"The cross-examination of the plaintiff was then proceeded with as follows:

Q: Did the Board complain of your purchasing and drinking spirits during school hours?

A: No. They complained to me of having slept at Mrs. Potter's house, and warned me as to her character.

Q: Did they say anything to you about your drinking?

A: Yes, they said a report had been made to them of my drinking at Mrs. Potter's, and that I was the worse for drink then.

Q: Did they complain of your sending out for gin and spirits during school hours?

A: No.

Q: Did you ever do so?

A: No, I never drank during school hours.

Q: Did you send out a little girl named Rainey, in your employ, to an inn for bottles of gin?

A: I have done so when I was ill. I was under Dr. Hurman's treatment for palpitation of the heart, and he recommended me to take a little stimulant when I felt the palpitation coming on.

"Q: Can you tell me how many bottles of gin you have purchased in a week?

A: Not many, and when I have sent for any I have not drunk it all myself, but have had company.

Q: Did you ever drink gin in the lobby of the school, and some rum as well?

A: No, and I have never tasted any rum since I have been in this neighbourhood.

Q: Did Mrs. Rainey sit up with you one night until four in the morning when you were insensible through drink?

A: No, but she slept at the house one night when I was ill, and because I was very nervous.

Q: Did you promise her that you would become a teetotaller?

A: I may have promised her and another that, and also that I would become a Good Templar as well.

Q: Were you very sick that morning?

A: I might have been from a bilious attack I had. (Laughter.)

"Q: Do you know John Potter, who keeps a butcher's stall in the market-place at Bridgwater?

A: Yes.

Q: Have you ever been there with him?

A: Yes, with Mrs. Potter, his wife.

Q: Do you know what I am going to ask you?

A: Yes, I think I do, from what I have heard from the villagers.

Q: Did you ever kiss John Potter in the open market place?

A: No, I never did. Mr. Potter is a very jocular sort of man, especially when he has had a drink, and he may have kissed me. (Laughter.)

Q: In the open Bridgwater market-place?

A: Yes, in his wife's presence. He is an old man, nearly old enough to be my grandfather - (laughter) - and he put his arm round my shoulder. He is in the habit, I have heard, of doing that with other women. (Laughter.)

Mr. Poole: I hope not. (Renewed laughter.)

Plaintiff: I don't see much harm in that, and I took but very little notice of what he did.

Q: I ask you again whether you did not kiss John Potter?

A: No, I should want to kiss him very badly if I kissed an old man like that. (Laughter.)

Q: Your health was not affected by John Potter's kiss?

A: No, certainly not. (Laughter.)

Q: Did you refresh yourself after the exertion?

A: I had a drop of gin with Mrs. Potter and him.

Q: Had you got a jar of gin of your own?

A: Yes, it was sent there for Mr. Potter to convey it home in his cart.

Q: Then you could not get enough at home or not good enough?

A: That is my business.

Q: Was the kiss the payment for taking it home for you?

A: No. (Laughter.)

Q: You kissed somebody else in the market that day, didn't you?

A: No. By his Honour: I may say that this is not the first scandal that has been brought against me at Chedzoy. Before this they alleged that I was not married at all. That was mentioned to me by a member of the Board.

"Mr. P.O.H. Reed, Clerk to the Chedzoy School Board produced the notice convening the meeting held on the 20th April 'to consider certain statements made reflecting upon the character of the schoolmistress.' The notices were posted on the 18th, and would have been delivered on the 19th, the day before the meeting. There was no other circular convening the second meeting the following week, at which the plaintiff was dismissed, but that was an adjourned meeting. The suspension took place at the meeting on the 20th. The minutes of neither of the meetings were signed, but they were read over at the subsequent meetings. He was not present at the adjourned meeting on the 27th.

"Mr. Chapman said he would at once take the objection that the dismissal was ultra vires (beyond the powers of the Board), because the third schedule of the Act of Parliament, 36th and 37th Vict., provided that notice should be sent to every member of the Board four days at least before any meeting held for the transaction of any business involving the appointment or dismissal, &c., of the teachers. In this case only two days' notice was given, and he contended, therefore, that the dismissal was illegal. His Honour (to Mr.

Poole): Have you any answer to that? Mr. Poole said his answer was that the dismissal did not take place until the adjourned meeting was held, a week after the former one. The plaintiff was only suspended in the meantime. Mr. Chapman pointed out that no fresh circular was issued of the adjourned meeting.

"After a good deal of conversation upon this point his Honour observed that his opinion was that there had not been a proper compliance with the provision of the Act referred to, and that, therefore, there had been a wrongful dismissal. In reply to his Honour, Mr. Chapman said the plaintiff's father, who had already made an investigation, had perfectly satisfied himself that there was no truth in these imputations. His Honour said it seemed then that all he could do would be to say that the defendants were precluded from going on with the case. After further discussion, his Honour said he would allow the case to proceed, reserving the point raised by Mr. Chapman.

"Mr. Reed was then cross-examined by Mr. Poole. He said he was present when the charge was mentioned to Mrs. Latham at the Board, and the names of the accusers were given to her. She was urged to clear herself by putting Mr. Potter to the test, Mr. Potter being a local man and possessed of ample means. She was suspended on that day, and paid up to the time of her dismissal. The plaintiff was present when the meeting was adjourned to the 26th April, and she afterwards came to his office and received her salary.

"The plaintiff was re-called by his Honour, who asked: At the time you were dismissed were you told by any member of the Board what specific charges were brought against you?

A: No.

His Honour: You were told that there were allegations of misconduct, and that you were called upon to answer that general allegations?

A: Yes.

"Mr. Poole then, at some length, opened the case for the defence, pointing out that the defendants were a body of gentlemen elected by the ratepayers, and responsible for the good conduct and management of the Board school at Chedzoy; and submitted that having heard charges preferred against the plaintiff, which they had investigated, and which he believed should be in a position to prove, of gross immorality, and of her being a drunken woman, it was their duty, and they were morally bound, to adopt the course they had. They had acted with perfect bona fides in the matter, and believed that the dismissal was a rightful one.

"Thomas Boon, farmer and dealer, of Chedzoy, said he knew the plaintiff. On Tuesday, 10th April, he was in Horsey-lane with Elias Potter, Geo. Potter and Henry Bryant. He saw a man and a woman pass up the lane about nine o'clock at night. It was light enough for him to see very plainly. He saw the face of the woman, but could not recognise her. A name was mentioned as she went by, by one of his companions. She was leaning on the gentleman's arm. Having heard a name mentioned he followed them. They saw through the hedge the improper familiarity which was alleged, and spoke to the parties, but received no answer. About half an hour afterwards he saw Mrs. Latham, the plaintiff, come up through Chedzoy-lane from the direction of Bridgwater. It was not light enough for him to see whether it was the same person as he saw in the lane. There was a way from the top of Horsey-lane, leading across some path fields, in the direction of Bridgwater, by which a person could come out into the turnpike-road, and return thence to Chedzoy, and it would take a person to go round that way about the same time that had elapsed between the time he saw the persons in the lane and when he met Mrs. Latham.

"His Honour: Then you saw this man?

Yes.

His Honour: Was he young or old?

I can't say.

His Honour: Was he a gentleman or what?

I cannot say.

His Honour: You say you saw him plainly, and yet you cannot say whether he had the appearance of being a gentleman or a working man?

Well, he appeared to be a gentleman by his dress.

His Honour: You can't give me any opinion as to his age?

No.

His Honour: Was he dark or fair?

I could not see his complexion; it was not light enough for that.

His Honour: That is what I thought, and why I asked the question. You can go down.

"Elias Potter, another young man, gave similar evidence, adding that when the persons were proceeding through the lane George Potter, his cousin, said it was Mrs. Latham. - In reply to his Honour, witness said he saw the man plainly. He was 'rather tall, of middle height, and a rather big man' about 40 years of age. Witness did not think he should know the man again, and he knew nothing of the lady except hearing a name mentioned by one of his companions.

"Henry Bryant, a lad, gave corroborative evidence, adding that he recognised Mrs. Latham in the lane. When there the gentleman said 'Goodnight' but Mrs. Latham did not speak. The gentleman was on the further side, the lady being nearest. Mr. Chapman: The two other witnesses have sworn the gentleman was nearest. Which is true? Witness: He was not; I knew better than that. (Laughter.) He (witness) could not say how this lady was dressed, but he recognised the features. The man was a 'biggish' man, and had on dark clothes. He had seen 'Bridgwater couples' in the lane many times at night. (Laughter.) Mr. Preston, the plaintiff's father, and Mrs. Latham had since called upon him, but he did not tell them he could not say who the lady was. He was not bound to tell every 'hobbledehoy' what or whom he had seen. They 'asked' him whether it was Mrs. Latham, and he replied if it was not her it was one about the same height.

"George Potter, a young man, son of Mr. John Potter,

butcher, of Chedzoy swore that he recognised Mrs. Latham, the plaintiff, in the lane. He saw her face, and as she was passing he told his companions it was the mistress of Chedzoy Board school. - In cross-examination witness said that after seeing Mrs. Latham returning on the turnpike-road from Bridgwater and bidding her 'goodnight' she saw him at his father's gate, and asked him to go the rest of the way home with her. She said he had seen some men at the corner of Chedzoy-lane, and felt rather frightened. He did not tell her that he was one of them, or say a word about his having seen her in Horsey-lane. Mr. John Potter, who had made the communication with the School Board, was his father. When Mr. Preston came to him he (witness) said he heard an action was going to be brought against his father, and if so he should tell the truth, which was that Mrs. Latham was in Horsey-lane.

"Mr. John Potter (60), butcher and farmer, of Chedzoy, said he kept a stall in the market at Bridgwater. He remembered the plaintiff coming to him there one evening when lots of people were about.

Mr. Poole: What did she do?

Witness: Well, she came and kissed me, if I must tell you the truth about it. (Laughter.)

Q: Did she kiss you or you kiss her?

A: Oh, her kissed me. (Laughter.)

Q: In the public market, before all the people?

A: Yes.

Q: What then?

A: Well, next she produced a jar of gin and said, 'We'll have a drink.' (Laughter.)

Q: What then?

A: Oh, then we 'drawed' the cork - (laughter) - and sent over to Mr. Stuckey's, the confectioner, after a glass. I can't tell whether it was a pint and half or a quart of gin, but 'howsomever' we finished it - (laughter) - I and Mrs. Latham and four or five others; and I should think there were about twenty of them, more or less, looking at us.

Q: What state was she in?

A: Well, both of us had had enough. (Laughter.)

Q: Did she do anything with another young man?

A: Yes, I saw her kiss another young man with a blue slop (a type of smock) on. - Mr. Water's young man, I think it was, who is now with the Yeomanry at Taunton. Witness added that he drove the plaintiff home the same night at her request. He had three children at the Board school at Chedzoy, and after hearing what he did from his son he felt it his duty to make the communication he did to the 'stewards' of the Board.

"Mr. Chapman (in cross-examination): It is not an uncommon occurrence, I think, to have a carouse at your stall on the market?

Witness: A 'crouse,' (sic) what do 'ee call a 'crouse?' - (Roars of laughter.)

His Honour: Are you often very jolly then, that is the question. (Renewed laughter.)

Witness: Why, every Saturday night I am sure to be jolly, but I don't mean to say I be 'tight' mind. (Laughter.)

Mr. Chapman: You were pretty jolly that night?

Witness: I be always jolly. (Laughter.) In further cross-examination witness said his wife was not in the habit of drinking at his stall in the market place. The plaintiff used to visit his wife, but had not done so lately. He was not aware that the School Board had intimated to the plaintiff that his wife was not a proper person for the plaintiff to visit.

"Mary Louisa Nooks (Noakes), assistant mistress at the Chedzoy Board school, deposed that on Monday, 9th April last, the plaintiff came to the school in a very excited state. She could scarcely articulate her words and her impression was that she was under the influence of drink. Witness told Mr. Winter of it. - Cross-examined: The plaintiff conducted the school throughout the day, but left the room several times in the morning. She had told witness that she suffered from heart disease.

"Mary Parkin, wife of the landlord of the Dolphin Inn, Binford Place, Bridgwater, said on Saturday evening four or five months ago, the plaintiff came to her house intoxicated. - Cross-examined: She came there with Mrs. Potter. She was very excited, and went in her private room and sang a song. (Laughter.) Re-examined: She did not believe anyone asked the plaintiff to sing. Mrs. Potter, the plaintiff, witness and her servant were present. Plaintiff could not talk plainly or walk straight.

"Lillie Rainey, aged eleven years, said she was in the service of the plaintiff for about eight months. Plaintiff used to send her to the village inn for gin, beer and brandy. She had been two or three times a week for a bottle of gin, but sometimes the plaintiff had company, and then they helped to drink it. She once saw the plaintiff intoxicated in the schoolroom on a Monday morning. She was obliged to guide herself along. Witness had taken a noggin of gin to her in the school lobby. She remembered her one night helping herself upstairs by the banisters.

"Mary Rainey (54), wife of the postmaster at Chedzoy, and mother of the last witness, said on one occasion, when her daughter was away for a holiday, she went to the plaintiff's house and found her in bed. Plaintiff said she was suffering from a bilious attack. She had then some company there, Mrs. Potter being one of those present. At nine o'clock at night plaintiff sent her for a bottle of gin. At ten o'clock plaintiff was singing in bed. (Laughter.) At twelve o'clock the same night the bottle was on the washstand empty, and the plaintiff was quite unconscious. They lifted her up in bed, but she remained insensible until four o'clock in the morning. Witness then gave her a cup of tea, and the plaintiff vomited.

"Subsequently witness said to her, 'Mrs. Latham, do guide yourself. If you get into this state again, I shall not come here.' Plaintiff said she had not been in the habit of drinking before, adding that it was trouble that had driven her to it. She also said, 'Don't leave me; if I live to get about again, I'll become a teetotaller. My dear father was a teetotaller.' - In cross-examination witness said she took her daughter from the plaintiff's house. The daughter was punished for alleged insolence, but she was not insolent. When she took the child away witness did not say she would be revenged. At the time she was no more violent or excited than at that moment. [This remark caused a good deal of merriment, the witness whilst under cross-examination betraying much excitement and speaking very loudly.]

"Mr. Winter, a member of the School Board, said Mr. Potter made a communication with him on the 16th April of what had taken place in Horsey-lane, and he and the Chairman of the Board saw Boon and Elias Potter, two of the witnesses. In consequence a meeting was called. The plaintiff was made acquainted with the charge, and she was suspended to give her the opportunity of clearing herself. He also gave her the names of the witnesses. During the week's adjournment he made enquires respecting the drinking habits of the plaintiff, and at the adjourned meeting the Board decided to dismiss her. He had gone over the ground leading from Horsey-lane round by the Bridgwater way, and the plaintiff had plenty of time to get round in the time spoken of by the witnesses.

"This was all the evidence, and Mr. Poole, in briefly addressing his Honour, submitted that he had placed before him very cogent evidence of the acts complained of, and had clearly proved that the plaintiff's behaviour was such as clearly to justify the Board in dismissing her. Mr. Chapman replied at some length.

"His Honour remarked that this was an extremely painful case, and one the importance of which could not be exaggerated. On the one hand the issue of it might possibly affect the future career and destiny of the plaintiff throughout her life; on the other hand, it was, of course, of some importance to the School Board. There was another party who was not, however, strictly before them - [His Honour was here understood to allude either to the plaintiff's father, a man of evident respectability, who was in court, or to her husband] - whose feelings and interests were deeply concerned. Although he had formed an impression at an early stage of the enquiry he now thought it was right and just to all parties concerned that he should postpone his judgement, and in the meantime he would go carefully through the whole of the evidence to see whether the opinion he had earlier formed was a just one or not. He would take an early opportunity of transmitting his judgement to the Registrar."

True to his word, the Judge dealt with the matter promptly and a further report was published two weeks later under the headline

"THE CHEDZOY SCANDAL. The County Court Judge (Mr. Serjeant Petersdorff) has forwarded to the Registrar his written judgement in the action brought by Mrs. Latham (schoolmistress), against the Chedzoy School Board at the last court. ... The judgement is as follows:- This was an action brought to recover £45 (sic), three months' salary, and £5 10s. for the value of house accommodation and coal for the same period, by Mrs. Latham, under an engagement made with her as the head mistress of the Chedzoy Board School. She was engaged upon the terms of £70 per annum, with an unfurnished house and coal, terminable by either party on giving three months' notice. She commenced her duties in April, 1876 and continued to perform them until 20th April, 1877. She produced high testimonials, and, I understand, she has returned to a school in Leicester, and resumed her employment there, where she has been a mistress for a considerable period.

"The inquiry is an extremely painful one, as it involves the investigation of charges that imperil the future career of Mrs. Latham, and which may be fatal to her domestic life. No doubt the Board have very anxious and responsible duties to fulfil, requiring the union of firmness with consideration and forbearance. In the early stages of the case I had an impression that the plaintiff had been treated harshly and too peremptorily, and that sufficient opportunities for investigation and explanation had not been afforded. But as the case progressed my unfavourable impression was weakened, and almost dispelled, by the testimony of Mr. Reed and Mr. Winter. The Board justified their dismissal of the plaintiff without giving the stipulated notice of three months, on two grounds - first, unchaste and immoral conduct; and secondly, inebriety. On dismissal she was paid and received the salary then due to her, and duly rendered and closed her accounts.

"Four lads were called to prove her incontinence - her commission of a shameless act of adultery in a place accessible to the public. The evidence of Thomas Boon is a fairly illustrative specimen of the testimony of the other three. I asked the witness if the man he saw with the plaintiff was young or old. He could not say. I asked whether he was a gentleman or a working man. He could not tell. He was asked if he could give an opinion as to the age of the party. He said, 'No.' He was asked if tall or short, no information could be elicited. I enquired if fair or dark. He said it was too dark to see, though he swore positively to identify the plaintiff.

"The others failed to satisfy me that they were not mistaken. Two swore that they had witnessed the act of sexual intercourse, but in every essential portion of their evidence there was irreconcilable discrepancy; no two described the man alike with whom the alleged adultery was committed. Every detail and particular, more or less, varied. Their demeanour and flippancy in the witness box disentitled them to my confidence. Besides, there is something infinitely degrading in persons volunteering to come into court to assert without a sense of shame that they had the pruriency and depravity of mind to seek to minutely watch the progress of a vicious indulgence they seem to deem it meritorious to describe. I am satisfied that no jury would have accepted this statement as reliable, but would unhesitatingly adopt the view I take - that they must be in error as to the identity of the woman if any such act occurred, and this is rendered almost a certainty by their inability to describe the man without numerous discrepancies and direct contradictions.

"The inebriety which constitutes the second ground of defence appears at intervals to have been brought under the cognisance of the Board for a considerable period, and dismissal was not, avowedly, based upon any contemporaneous special or particular occasion, but founded upon an amalgamation of statements that had been made at different times. Many alleged acts of misconduct were passed over or condoned. Still, it is impossible to doubt that they had shown reasonable forbearance in not dismissing her on satisfactory proof of some of the incidents brought before them. They forbore, I presume, because they heard that she had, unhappily, sought refuge from painful thought and troubles in the treacherous and dangerous temporary relief alcohol affords. They thought, I dare say, as I think, that much of the evidence of misconduct was exaggerated. Some of it was absurd and ridiculous, and not wholly exempt from ill feeling. Fulfilling my functions as a jury I award £5 damages, but as I judge, looking at all the circumstances, and the embarrassing and perplexing duty the Board had to perform, I decline to give costs against them. Each must pay their own. As I find for the plaintiff the point of law raised by Mr. Chapman does not arise."

The School Board's minutes simply recorded that

"His Honour reserved judgement & he had subsequently sent a written one to the Registrar at the County Court awarding the plaintiff £5 but under the circumstances directed each party to pay his own costs."

The school accounts show that six witnesses were paid their expenses in connection with their attendance at court.

In May 1877 Mrs. Latham's replacement was Mrs. Caroline Hobbs who was appointed at a salary of £50 per annum plus house and coal. It seems that she was not the best of teachers: the Inspector's report for 1879 read:

"The results of the examination are rather disappointing, the children not having done as well as I had hoped. The reading of the Second Standard is weak and the Upper Standard somewhat broke down in Arithmetic. The Infant Department is the best, the Geography is not well learned, the Needlework only fairly well done, the Music good."

This adverse report was considered and,

"Having reference to the unsatisfactory nature of the report lately received as to the annual examination, the Board discussed the advisability of giving notice to Mrs. Hobbs & appointing a Master to fill up vacancy so arising." As a result of an advertisement, several candidates were considered in October 1879, and the post was offered to Joseph Brooks of Oxford: "Salary £50 - house rent free - coal - half the Government grant & £10 in addition to the £50 in consideration of Mr. Brooks' sister teaching sewing in the school." Mr. Brooks took up his post and the 1880 annual report stated, "This School has improved since I last examined it. Most of the work is neatly and carefully done, especially that of the younger children. Some of the elder broke down in arithmetic. The singing is good."

By 1880 it was compulsory for all children to attend school. At first the cost was anything from 1d., the charge in Chedzoy, to 9d. (0.5p. to 3.75p.) per week. In 1881 the Chedzoy charge was increased to 2d. per week per child or, if there were more than three children, 2d. for the eldest and 1d. for the others. Teachers were paid by results and schools given 8s. (40p.) per year for each child, but the government carried out annual examinations and deducted the sum of 2s. 8d. (12.5p.) for each child who failed to meet the standard.

Two reports in the Bridgwater Mercury in August 1881 concerned the school.

"On Thursday last the school children in this parish (Chedzoy) were given their annual tea in the schoolroom, after which they engaged in a variety of out-door sports, in a field placed at their disposal by Mr. Edwin Fry."

The following week:

"This school has been recently examined by Mr. Boyle, Government Inspector, who expressed himself pleased with progress made. The Clerk of the Board (Mr. P. Reed) has received the following report: 'This school is decidedly improving, and has passed a sufficiently good examination. Most of the failures are in arithmetic.' The grant earned for the passed (sic) year is upwards of £60."

In August 1887 the results of another inspection were published in the Bridgwater Mercury.

"This school was recently examined by Mr. A.P. Graves and the following report has been received by the managers:- 'In spite of an epidemic of measles which threatened to seriously influence the result of the examination, the scholars have done well in the elementary subjects, and in English and geography. Of course there is a proportion of shaky passes arising from the physical condition of the children, only just convalescent. The infants have done well in the first class and fairly well below.' The average attendance during the past year was 67.7 and the amount of grant earned £65 17s. 8d. It may be mentioned that the epidemic of measles referred to above unfortunately broke out among the scholars about ten days before the day fixed for Her Majesty's Inspector for his visit. The school had to be closed and the inspection and examination were postponed for three weeks."

In August 1891,

"Mr. Derrick proposed and Mr. Ashford seconded, that free education be adopted ... on September 1st." This proposition was adopted by the School Board.

The minutes of the School Board record that the school was closed between 1st December 1896 and 11th January 1897 "on account of prevalence of measles." The cause of some of the health problems at the school were not too difficult to discern. At a meeting of the Board in October 1898

"Clerk read notice from the Sanitary Inspector as to a nuisance on the school premises arising from impure water in the well through contamination with sewage and organic matter and which was quite unfit for human consumption. The Sanitary Officer attended and after a discussion was instructed to have the well opened and cleaned out, and thereupon report to the Clerk."

The next paragraph reads:

"Clerk reported the school having been closed since 3rd instant (3rd October 1898) on account of the prevalence of diphtheria and the Sanitary Officer undertook to see the Medical Officer of Health with the view to his giving permission for school being reopened."

At their next meeting,

"Clerk reported school reopened on 24th ultimo. (24th October 1898). Having regard to diphtheria having again broken out in the parish, Miss Winter proposed and the Vice Chairman seconded resolution which was unanimously passed that the school be closed until the Medical Officer of Health certifies that school could safely be opened."

The school reopened on 8th November.

The minutes of a meeting of the School Board in September 1899 record an amusing incident.

"It was stated that Bertram Hook, a son of Mr. Henry Hook the Attendance Officer, had been firing off a gun in the school playground and Clerks were directed to communicate with the Father of the lad thereon and, if the act was repeated, proceedings would be taken against him." At their meeting the following month a letter was read from Joseph Brooks, the headmaster.

"Dear Sir,

Mr. Hook, the father of the boy who was alleged to have fired off a gun in the school yard came to me this afternoon with your letter. I believe the offending gun was a tiny brass cannon belonging to my little boy who, although Bertram Hook supplied the powder, is therefore partly to blame. I have forbidden its being fired again either in the school yard or elsewhere unless I am present."

A letter sent by the Clerk to the Chairman of the School Board in November 1899 would appear to refer to the cost of gravel for the school yard.

Chedzoy School. Joseph Brooks and some of his pupils at the school, around 1902. Courtesy of Duncan Bouchier.

"Dear Sir, From enquiries we have made we find that the material used by the District Surveyor on the Bath Road was obtained by him from Gloucester, he arranging with the Captain of a vessel to bring back a quantity as ballast. It costs about 4s. (20p.) per ton delivered to Bridgwater. Gravel from Shepton Mallett costs about 5s. 6d. (27.5p.) per ton delivered to Bridgwater and Westleigh chippings about 6s. (30p.) per ton to which would have to be added haulage to Chedzoy. Perhaps the Board will decide as to material to be used at the meeting on Wednesday next."

The Education Act 1902 created a County Education Committee to take over responsibility from local School Boards from 1st July 1903. Chedzoy became Somerset School No. 83. Attached to the minutes of the final meeting of the School Board is a letter from the headmaster to the School Board Clerk.

"Dear Sir, I am conscious, as I send you this the last set of monthly accounts which will be rendered to you as Clerk to the local School Board, of a certain sense of parting. And I wish first to thank the Board for every kindness and sign of good will they have shown towards myself; and secondly I desire to place on record my appreciation of your late father's never failing kindly interest for so many years, in the welfare of both children and teachers connected with our village school. My present managers I shall soon cease to know under their present appellation but shall, in the future, I trust be associated in educational work with them under another name, that is, as Members of the local managing body under the new 'Authority.' I am, Sir, Yours faithfully, J. Brooks." At one of their first meeting the new Board of Managers for Chedzoy, the report of Her Majesty's Inspector of Schools (H.M.I.) was read: "The discipline shows considerable improvement and the work, as a whole, is now fairly satisfactory. The infants are very well cared for."

Following the installation of a mains water supply to the village, the headmaster requested that the supply be connected to the school and school house. The minutes for June 1904 record,

"The Mangers being of the opinion that the present supply from the well was good, decided not to entertain the application at present."

However, the H.M.I. did not share that opinion as his report the following year stated,

"Neither the main room not the class room is well ventilated. As a water main passes along the front of the school, provision should be made for proper flushing of the offices (toilets)."

In 1906 it was resolved that school holidays should be fixed until further notice: there were to be three weeks from about 29th June, two or three weeks from about 28th September, two weeks at Christmas and one week at Easter. Two years after this the headmaster requested a bathroom be provided in the school house, and improvements to the school building:

"Correspondent reported having written County Secretary that Managers considered present lighting (windows) ample and read letter from County Secretary under date 18 October asking for total area of glass as distinct from framing in 5 windows & referred to, reported having replied thereto & also read letter from County Secretary under date 3 Novr. 1910 pointing out that the window area was exactly 1/8th of floor area, whilst the general rule was that the area of clear glass, even when on South side, should not be less than 1/6th of the floor area & that therefore there were very substantial grounds for complaint that the schoolroom was not sufficiently lighted & that it was desirable that the Managers should reconsider the matter & that to secure adequate lighting the window area should be increased by not less than 20 square feet. Managers fully considered the matter when it transpired that the top panes of the glass in the windows were colored (sic) and Correspondent was directed to write to the County Secretary suggesting that these top panels should be removed and clear glass substituted in their place or, in the alternative, that a skylight should be placed in the roof which would probably meet the requirements of the Inspector."

The H.M.I. again expressed concern over sanitation in 1913:

"Correspondent was also directed to write County Secretary stating in the opinion of the Managers there was absolutely no necessity to provide steps to the [water] closets for the infants as such closets were far better than those found in general in the homes of the children and what they would be accustomed to after their schooldays and that the Managers therefore did not recommend any steps being taken in the matter." At their next meeting, "Correspondent reported having written Mr. Brooks, County Secretary, as directed at last meeting & read letter from Mr. Bothamley dated 3rd July stating the Board of Education's recommendations about the steps to the closets for Infants does not imply that the closets themselves are not satisfactory, but the seats are too high & that the provision of steps is a comparatively inexpensive matter. Correspondent was directed to write County Secretary pointing out that if steps were provided, it would entail the doors of the closets being made to open outwards, thereby exposing same to the weather & that the Managers were still of the opinion that the steps were quite unnecessary."

The school log book, in which important events were recorded by the Head Teacher, dates from 1910 and provides an interesting insight into the life of the school. One of the earliest entries notes that the headmaster, Joseph Brooks,

"Received notes from several parents this morning, complaining of their being very much annoyed and insulted by the School Nurse intimating to them that the state of their children's heads needs attention."

Two years later he noted that,

"The School Nurse called at the school this morning and

examined some of the children's heads. Several cases of children in a verminous condition were discovered,"

and in 1913,

"My attention was drawn to a child with a very verminous head. Child was sent home with a note to its mother asking her to cleanse its head of filth and then send it on back to school."

At the end of the 20th Century, outbreaks of head lice still cause occasional problems for schools.

Some things never change in school. In July 1914 Mr. Brooks recorded that he had just completed the end of term tests and he commented that,

"Some [children] however, instead of relying entirely on their own, endeavour, whenever opportunity offers, to make use of their neighbour's intelligence."

Two months later he wrote,

"These holidays have been full of disquiet, war being declared by England on August 4th and August 12th against Germany and Austria-Hungary respectively."

Disruptive pupils occasionally caused problems. In October 1918 Mr. Brooks wrote,

"This child, who is old enough and big enough to know better, caused me much annoyance first by her own stubborn and wilful disobedience and later by instigating a smaller child to commit acts of insubordination and disobedience. A bad feature of the affair was that the bigger girl exercised her evil influence on the sly; and when set apart from the rest of the class evinced petulance and nastiness of temper by giving loud expression of threats of ominous kinds."

What happened to the girl is not recorded. The following month he wrote,

"During the morning I was annoyed and the school work upset by the persistent idleness, stubbornness and rudeness" of one of the boys. In 1927 the school had a new bully: "Rev. G.R. Mullens visited. Head Teacher complained to him (Chairman of School Committee) of the behaviour of a big boy, 13 years of age, recently admitted from Bridgwater. He is continually setting small boys to fight outside the school yard, and knocks down girls going to and from the school. He is unruly, but not in the schoolroom. The Chairman promised to speak to his father."

Having had to make do with a gravel surface in the playground, the area was at last to be properly surfaced but, demonstrating a wonderful lack of forethought, the work commenced on the first day of term in August 1921. The following day Mr. Brooks noted,

"Floors, doormats, lobbies, etc. covered with tar which children have brought in on their boots. As the playground is completely covered this cannot be avoided." A year later the number of children attending the school was dramatically increased: "Attendance Officer visited and stated that some Stawell children will have to attend this school. The school and schoolhouse were burnt down about a month ago. Nothing is left but the walls."

The school was regularly closed following outbreaks of mumps and whooping cough and in 1930 it was closed for three weeks:

"March 3rd. School re-opened after the closure for Scarletina. 32 pupils present. There are no fresh cases. The school and premises have been thoroughly fumigated and disinfected."

The disease was also mentioned twice at meetings of Bridgwater Rural District Council:

"Rev. G.R. Mullens referred to a case of scarlet fever at Chedzoy, and asked for an assurance from the Sanitary Inspector that everything that is necessary to be done in regard to disinfecting and fumigating the house had been carried out. The Inspector stated that everything necessary had been done." And, "The Medical Officer of Health reported three cases of scarlet fever at Chedzoy. These were of a very mild type, and he thought it was very probable that some of the other schoolchildren had had it, but were not ill enough to keep away from school, and so the cases had not come under his notice."

In 1934 pupils were able to take part in a gardening competition, but some parents seem to have been determined that their sons should win. The school log book records,

"This week the Senior Boys have held a competition for the best tray of vegetables grown in their home garden plots. The seeds were given to them in March last. There were ten competitors and the results were fairly good. Three were disqualified because their seeds were not used but others substituted as shown by the results. The other seven were awarded small prizes."

After being appointed as head teacher in 1938, Mrs. Davies repeated the request first made by Joseph Brooks in 1908: please could a bathroom be provided at the school house? Her request met with no more success than that of her illustrious predecessor. The question of a bathroom re-emerged in 1948 when the headmistress again requested one be installed. On this occasion the Managers supported her request. Nine months later the minutes notes,

"In reference to the proposed bathroom to be erected in the scullery of the Head Teacher's house, this was not considered satisfactory by the Head Teacher. It was proposed that a letter be sent to the County School Surveyor in these terms: viz. 'that the Managers unanimously agree with the

Head Teacher's disapproval of the proposed arrangement of placing a bath in the scullery, they consider this will be most unsatisfactory and they request the Surveyor to make alternative plans."

The school log book continued to record minor as well as national events, such as the Coronation in 1953. At the end of 1953 Mrs. Davies retired as headmistress and was replaced by Mrs. G.C. Brazier in April 1954. The supply teacher noted that in March that year electricity was being installed in the school. In August 1954 a short report was published in the Bridgwater Mercury:

"At the end of last term Miss E.A. Hopkins retired from the teaching staff of Chedzoy County School. She had been assistant teacher for 21 years and the loss to the parish has been keenly felt. ... She spoke of her happy time at Chedzoy and the kindness she had received from the several head teachers under whom she had served."

In February 1956 it was noted in the log book that,

"Owing to severe frost the village has been completely without water for two days."

The Suez Crisis of January 1956 also affected the school:

"School re-opens one week late owing to petrol rationing, as declared by the Somerset Education Authority."

Although somewhat lengthy, the report made by Her Majesty's Inspector on 17th February 1958 is worth repeating in full as it describes the running of the school at that time.

"Since the last report on this two-class primary school was issued after a full inspection in Dec. 1942, the nature and scope of the school have remained the same, & will in all probability remain unchanged for some years to come. It serves a small village three miles to the north-east of Bridgwater in an area which is mainly agricultural, though various light industries have developed in the neighbourhood within recent years. The present number of 46 children on the roll has remained fairly constant since the school lost its senior pupils in 1939; at present there are 28 children of junior school age and 18 infants, each class containing exactly equal numbers of boys and girls. While no substantial increase in numbers is envisaged beyond the admission of four more infants next term, it seems fairly certain there will be no fall in numbers for some time. For this reason of impending increase in the number of infants it must be recorded that the very insufficient accommodation for this class - which was mentioned in the full inspection reports dated 1937 and 1942 - still persists as acutely as ever, & while it is realised that the school was scheduled for closure in the Development Plan for the area in 1944, it must be regarded as very unsatisfactory that a class of 18-22 infants is still housed in a room with a floor area of only 192 sq. ft. This in itself entirely prevents any freedom of movement outside the limits of the desks and tables, and also renders the use of apparatus for learning difficult, if not actually impossible. There is only one window, which is high on the wall & facing due east, so that no sunlight ever enters the room during teaching hours, and artificial light has to be used frequently in Winter.

"The larger room houses the junior class and is of good size with satisfactory conditions of lighting, heating and ventilation. The artificial lighting is generous and the heating has been supplemented in both rooms by electric heaters fixed high on the walls & directed downwards. The furniture in the large room is mainly satisfactory and modern, as is that in the infants room, but there the larger tables and dual desks contribute substantially to the effect of overcrowding. Further inconvenience is caused through the fact that for medical inspections or for the taking of the Authority's selection tests, the infants room is the only one which can be used, and wholesale movement of furniture out of and into the room on each occasion is unavoidable. This has taken place no less than four times during the present term, one of these migrations being observed at the end of the inspection.

"Sufficient washing and sanitary facilities are provided for the number of children in attendance. The general structural conditions of the building, and its decoration, are good, but there is urgent need for the replacement of a totally rotten beam in the infants cloakroom. It is understood that the playground will shortly be re-surfaced.

"In addition to the usual furniture and equipment the board possesses a piano which is in good condition, also a radio receiving set which was provided by and remains the property of the managers. Every effort has been made to brighten both rooms by means of flowers and growing plants. It is understood that the bookshelves containing the books of the local branch of the County Library, which are at present in the large classroom, are to be removed; this will afford necessary space for books belonging to the school and those supplied on extended loan by the County Library. Each of the two classes has its own portable book corner which contains suitable books for individual reading.

"The head mistress was appointed in April 1954 after having served in the same capacity under two other Local Authorities. She has thus had good experience and her teaching is notable for patience and clarity. Her schemes of work are well thought-out so as to secure the utmost co-operation from her colleague in the infants room. The infants teacher likewise has had good previous experience and brings with her a sound knowledge of the needs of children in the infant stage. She is, however, greatly handicapped in her work by the conditions mentioned earlier.

"Despite all the difficulties, however, the children proceed to the junior class with a sound knowledge of the basic skills, which they have acquired by their own individual experience. At this later stage the other English-based subjects of the curriculum enter more into their own, and the written and illustrative work done by the children gives evidence of careful and interesting teaching, especially in history and geography. Religious instruction is given daily in a short period, principally in the form of stories suitable to the age and understanding of the children, who though they are not outstanding in the academic sense still provide a slender but steady flow of entrants to the local grammar school.

"A simple and reverent assembly begins each day's work, and the singing is bright and energetic. In spite of the cold weather not a single child was absent from school on the day of the inspection. Only about fifteen take the daily school meal, which is conveyed from a central kitchen in Bridgwater and served on desks in the larger room. It is a pity that at present no tablecloths are used; there are some, but they are too large for use with the present desks. The school as a whole offers a pleasant picture of a closely-knit little community working cheerfully and as well as some difficult circumstances permit."

At the end of the summer term in 1959 Mrs. Brazier retired and was replaced in September by Mrs. Nina Fels, who recorded that there were 33 pupils on the roll. During the Christmas holiday work commenced on the construction of a base for a prefabricated building which was to provide additional classroom space. The infants moved in "The Hut" at the end of January 1960.

Still things were delayed in relation to a bathroom for the school house. It was not until 1961 that the School Managers were read a letter from the Divisional Education Officer,

"Saying that Messrs. R.T. Hanham & Sons had had a tender accepted for the provision of a bathroom and food cupboard in the School House. Mrs. Fels reported that several schemes had been suggested for the alteration and the worst possible one had been selected, causing a bedroom to be divided in order to make the alternative as cheap as possible. In her opinion it was useless to comment on the letter of the D.E.O."

And so in 1962, 54 years after Joseph Brooks' first request, a bathroom was at last provided in the school house.

The school log book records that, following the decision that Chedzoy would become a Junior School from September 1966, there were 24 pupils on the roll. They were divided into two classes: one taught by Mrs. Fels and the other by Mrs. Smith. The headmistress noted that the cost of school meals was increased to 12p. in September 1971 and there were now 37 pupils. By January 1972 Mrs. Smith had left and her position as Assistant Teacher was filled by Mrs. Pauline Clapp.

With the expiry of the original lease for the building, a new one was signed on 19th August 1974 between the Bath and Wells Diocesan Board of Finance and the Somerset County Council. Under the terms of this lease, for a period of 21 years, the annual rent was increased to £140 which could be reviewed every seven years.

A week's celebration of the school's centenary was held in 1976, when a cherry tree was planted near the main gate as a part of the celebrations.

In January 1977 the school was finally connected to mains drainage. It had also been decided that the division of children between Chedzoy and Bawdrip schools should continue with a bus service being provided between the two. However, those children living under two miles from the school were required to pay 25p. per week towards the cost of transport.

Centenary Celebrations, 1976.
Mrs. Nina Fels (head teacher) gives instruction, whilst Mrs. Jay Jenkins cleans the blackboard. Andrew Fry concentrates on his work.
Source unknown, courtesy of Pauline Clapp.

There was a change of staff in September 1979. Following the retirement of Mrs. Fels, Mrs. Clapp was promoted to head teacher, whilst Mrs. Clapp was replaced by Miss Helen Gaylard. As Mrs. Clapp lived at Parchey she did not require the use of the school house so this was rented out by the Education Authority. On her first day as headmistress, Mrs. Clapp noted in the log book that there were 34 pupils, 14 being new entrants from Bawdrip. School meals now cost 30p., and the bus fare had been increased to 35p. The following April the price was school means was increased again, this time to 40p. Mrs. Clapp recorded that "As a result, only 10 children are eating school dinners, 4 go home and the rest bring sandwiches."

A problem occurred with the school house in May 1982. The log book records,

"A swarm of bees was discovered in the wall of the school house. As they were coming up through the floorboards, the family were advised to evacuate the house for the night. Mr. [Roger] Coleman (who lived at Byways, Higher Road), a local beekeeper, was contacted and promised to help as soon as the bees had stopped working."

On Friday, 13th January 1984 part of the original plaster ceiling in the classroom collapsed. Mrs. Clapp reported the event in the log book:

"A large portion of plaster fell from the ceiling in the schoolroom. Pollards had replaced the loft entrance in the morning before school. A strong gale was blowing all day. Mrs. Clapp and Miss Duthie were both struck by falling plaster, but appeared unhurt."

The resulting damage to the rest of the ceiling necessitated the erection of a false ceiling, covering the vault.

In 1988 there had been concern about water bills which had been received for the school. Mrs. Clapp recorded a visit by an employee of the Water Board.

"They found the mysterious leaking pipe which has been causing such large water bills. It is located under the cloakroom floor, which accounts for the dry rot recurrence in the walls and the very wet floor. The pipe is to be cut off to avoid taking up the floor and a brand new pipe put around the exterior of the cloakroom to a tap and drinking fountain."

In 1987 it had been proposed that Chedzoy and Bawdrip schools should be combined on the Bawdrip site. Chedzoy residents were strongly opposed to this course of action, preferring to retain the existing system or, if that were not possible, the construction of a new school on a new site. The proposal reappeared in January 1990 and was discussed at a consultative meeting held at the school in June. Mrs. Clapp recorded,

"Staff expressed forcibly their feeling that the opinion expressed in the Consultation on the School 3 years ago should still stand. They were opposed to the County proposal for amalgamation on the Bawdrip site. The Governors' and Public Meetings, the latter attended by 80+ villagers and parents, expressed these views most forcibly." A similar meeting took place at Bawdrip the following day: "Mrs. Clapp and several staff and governors attended. The feeling was the same as that expressed at Chedzoy - that the schools should remain as they are."

A fateful meeting of the Education Committee took place on 19th September 1990 at County Hall at which the proposal to build a new school at Bawdrip was agreed. The Statutory Notice of Closure was received at the school on 23rd October and an appeal lodged with the Secretary of State, but on 2nd September 1991 Mrs. Clapp recorded in the log book,

"We have heard that the Secretary of State has agreed to the proposal to amalgamate Chedzoy and Bawdrip Schools on the Bawdrip site. The scheme will be proceeded with when capital funds become available. There seems to be no appeal."

The fate of the school was sealed and it closed in 1995, but not before the services of a bee-keeper were required again:

"May 9th 1991: The weather was very warm and we were plagued by bees in the hut. Mr. Coleman, local bee-keeper called in the late afternoon."

The school and school house were bought by a local Estate Agent who carried out some improvements to the house and erected a garage. The house and unimproved school were then sold to the present owners. The new owners began converting the school into a dwelling in 1997 and moved in a year later. The 1842 foundation stone mentioned by Francis Lovibond in his diary was not found during the conversion, so is either still in place or, possibly, was removed when the building was improved in 1875/76.

Sibleys Farm to Rose Bower

Opposite the former school stands **SIBLEYS FARM**. The farm and farmhouse are built of stone and are between two and three hundred years old. The walls in the lounge are three feet thick and some of the floors retain their old flagstones. Norman Fry, the present owner, but formerly the tenant while the property was owned by the University of Oxford, belongs to the third generation of his family to farm the land. Henry Fry, Norman's grandfather, lived there in the 1880s. He died in 1894 at the age of 45, and his wife ran the farm until one of their sons was old enough to take over: this was Frederick Fry (1888-1976), the father of the present owner. He was born in Sibleys Farm and lived and worked there until 1961 when, at the age of 73, he retired to Inkers Farm. Norman Fry was also born at the farm in 1919 and farmed it following his father's retirement.

John Cary, born about 1850, the brother of William Cary of Manor Farm, farmed here in his father's footsteps before the Fry family, and before them John Sibley (born c.1790), after whom the place is named. The 1841 Census records John and Sarah Sibley, their five children and two labourers as living at the address. From time to time American descendants of Mr. Sibley call at the farm searching for their family roots. By the 1851 Census the Cary family was living there. Sibleys was a dairy farm but cider has been made here for many generations, and still is today. The cow sheds, byres and ancient buildings arranged around a central courtyard were the scene of feasts to celebrate George V's Silver Jubilee, George VI's Coronation and the present Queen's Coronation and Silver Jubilee, as well as the school centenary in 1976. In the late 1990s parts of the buildings around the courtyard were converted into dwellings.

As on other farms, and reflecting the general poverty at that era, thefts occurred from time to time. In November 1859 the following report was published in the Bridgwater Mercury.

"Isaac Stokes, labourer, of Chedzoy pleaded guilty to a charge of stealing 70 lbs. of swedes, the property of Mr. John Cary, his master, at Chedzoy and was fined 5s. (25p.) together with the costs and value of the swedes."

On 23rd July 1885 the "crops, potatoes, orchards and implements" of Sibleys Farm were sold by auction at the Manor House Inn as John Cary "is quitting." Unfortunately, the next edition of the Bridgwater Mercury is missing from the archives, so it is not known if a sale report was published. The Fry family then took over the tenancy of the farm.

In October 1886,

> "Benjamin Meaker, of Woolavington, was charged with assaulting Henry Fry, at Chedzoy. - The complainant said he saw the defendant driving a horse very furiously. When the horse was passing he spoke, and the animal shortly afterwards stopped. Defendant came out of the cart cursing and swearing, and followed him up and struck him a severe blow on the shoulder. On the Tuesday following defendant came to him and asked him to settle it, and because witness refused to attempted again to strike him. He (complainant) did not wish, however, to press the case. - Defendant was fined 10s. and costs."

In June 1889 Henry Fry went to Bridgwater County Court. Under the headline "SHEEP IN A FIELD OF WHEAT" it was reported that,

> "Henry Fry, farmer, of Chedzoy, brought an action against Walter H. Bell, farmer, of Woolavington for the recovery of £2, money alleged to be due to the plaintiff in respect of damage done by the defendant's sheep to a field of wheat belonging to the plaintiff. ... The plaintiff and the defendant met together and agreed to render the matter to the arbitration of two gentlemen ... who gave an award against the defendant of £2, but the latter refused to pay the amount." Details of the damage to the crop and the arbitration were reported. "His Honour gave judgement for the plaintiff in the amount claimed."

In 1983 during re-wiring, there were found under the floorboards of one of the bedrooms several tickets for Chedzoy Harvest Home Tea on October 2nd 1877.

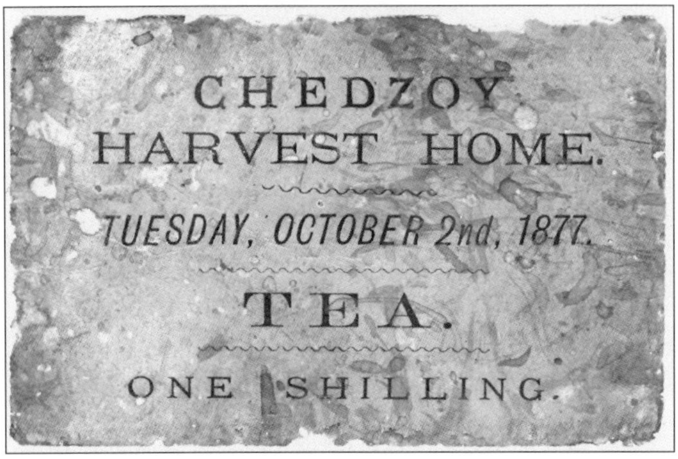

Courtesy of Norman and Valerie Fry.

The cost was one shilling (5p.), which seems expensive, considering the average agricultural weekly wage at that time was probably less than ten shillings (50p.).

Indeed, in March 1905 Mrs. Emily Jane Fry sued William Thomas in Bridgwater County Court

> "To recover fifteen shillings in damages through defendant leaving his employment without giving notice. His Honour gave judgement for plaintiff for the amount of one week's wages (13s.) and pointed out that there was a mutual obligation on the part of persons to respect notice when it was given."

A dispute lead to local farmers appearing before Bridgwater County Court in February 1916. Below the headline "A CHEDZOY DISPUTE - ACTIONS BETWEEN FARMERS" the Bridgwater Mercury reported that

> "Frederick Charles Fry and Albert Leonard Fry, farmers, claimed of William Cary, £4 10s. damages caused by the trespass of cattle and sheep on their land. Defendant brought a counter-claim for £4 damages for wrongfully cutting a hedge in 1914 and 1915 and £1 10s. for cows trespassing in January 1916. Defendant's cattle trespassed in a field of growing swedes belonging to the plaintiffs. The cattle trespassed on a great many occasions and did considerable damage to the swedes. The trespassing sheep numbered from 60 to 100. Plaintiffs had not been anxious to rush into litigation because there must be a certain amount of give and take between farmers who were neighbours, but the trespass of the defendant's cattle and sheep had been so continuous that plaintiffs were obliged to take notice of it.
>
> "Robert Fry, uncle of the plaintiffs, said during November he saw the defendant's cattle in plaintiff's field on three occasions. He turned them out twice. There were 50 to 60 sheep and several beasts. Defendant: 'I only had 41 sheep. Your eyes magnify.' Several other questions were put by defendant and His Honour then asked him if he had any more questions for the witness. Defendant: 'No, that's enough for 'ee.'
>
> "Frederick Charles Fry, one of the plaintiffs, said he saw defendant's cattle and sheep in the field eight or ten times and on more than one occasion he reported the matter to defendant who replied he wanted to keep sheep at Parchey to eat the rough grass in his fields. Witness spoke as to damage done to swedes and mangolds, and said the sheep he saw in the field numbered about 50. Defendant: 'All the same tale. Will 'ee bet a sovereign I had 50 there?' His Honour: 'That is not the question. We don't bet in this court'." Evidence was then heard about the hedge, it being stated that the Frys had broken down a wire costing 15s. and that swedes had been eaten. "Defendant added, 'If they make I pay, I'll catch 'em before next Christmas, I'll bet a sovereign I do.' His Honour: 'I dare say there will be trouble if you go on like this.' Defendant: 'No, they have made war against me, and I shall against them'." Judgement of £4 10s. was given for the Frys and the counter-claim dismissed.

Frederick 'Freddie' Fry appeared before the magistrates in April 1932. It was reported that he

> "was summoned for being the owner of a dog not under

proper control at night in Monmouth Street, [Bridgwater]. P.C. Harvey found the dog straying at 2.5 a.m. and he conveyed it to the Police Station where it was claimed next morning. The Bench fined defendant 5s."

After Sibleys Farm, a drove known as **FRYS LANE**, but in earlier times called **Dippet Path**, leads onto the moor, back towards Moor Drove and Parchey Bridge. About fifty yards along the lane, opposite Mr. Fry's main farm entrance, stands a red brick building which belonged to his brother, Desmond Fry (1928-1997), and was used for cider making. This building was once the village tithe barn, and still has vents for winnowing the grain.

The far end of the barn was once used as dwelling. Speaking in 1998 Ben Hooper (born 1906) recalled that about the time of the First World War the cottage was occupied by Jockie Conduit. Each day he would walk a mile to Godbury's (a field near Mount Close Batch) to milk his two Jersey cows and he would then return with the bucket balanced on his head in order to deliver the contents to the Rectory, where some would be used for making butter. About 1930 Ben and his late wife, Mabel, lived here when they were first married: the rent was 2s. 6d. (12.5p.) per week which was paid once a month to the Rector.

In April 1951 the cottage was featured in a Bridgwater Mercury article entitled,

"Grand Old Man of Chedzoy. Mr. Frank Gully's Ninetieth Birthday. - Frank [Clifford] Gully, of Chedzoy, tidied up his cottage, put on his best suit, pinned a blue rosette in his cap, and strung his numerous birthday cards over the mantelpiece. It was a special occasion and there were many visitors - for Frank was 90 on Sunday. Few nonagenarians can claim the independence of Mr. Gully, who for many years 'has done' for himself in his trim little cottage tucked away at the back of the Rectory. Villagers have helped him with his shopping since he had bronchitis and influenza earlier in the year, but Frank still does his own cooking and cleaning.

"Most of the villagers paid their respects to the G.O.M. of Chedzoy on Sunday, including the Rector (Rev. C.B. Hunt), who rarely lets a day pass without a call on his old friend. 'Visitors, sir? I've had more today than in a whole year,' said Frank to a Mercury reporter who called to offer greetings on Sunday evening. Comfortably seated in his favourite chair by a glowing fire, his pipe well alight and his cider mug handy, he recalled life in his native village when parents paid a penny a week to send their children to school. 'That, of course, was the old village school, not the present building,' he said. 'About one day a week at school was all I had, and I was at work at the age of 10 for 3d. a day.'

"His father and grandfather were the village carpenters, and Frank used to walk to Bower to assist with sawing timber. Sixty years of his life were spent in Devon, but in 1935 he returned to his native village, and later occupied the cottage, which is church property. Looking back on the village of his boyhood days he recaptured the Chedzoy of 80 years ago, when wages were small but happiness prevailed - when young couples married on little more than 10s. a week and when the horse pulled the plough. 'The country for me any day,' he said. 'Give me the country, and let those who like the towns live in them.' And judging by the visitors who were still calling on Frank on Sunday when our reporter left, little wonder that he prefers village life."

Frank Gully died in October 1954, aged 94 and was laid to rest in the village churchyard.

Beyond the barn is **OLD RECTORY FARM** which, despite its name, was built in 1995 and 1996.

A little further along the lane, the second gate on the left affords a glimpse of a sheltered garden. In the opposite corner of this, the entrance to an underground store may be seen; formerly the Rector's potato store. Between 1980 and 1983 this small garden was used by the children from the village school. The garden and the adjoining field, which contains a fine copper beech, once belonged to the incumbent of the Rectory.

At the junction of Front Street and Higher Road is the **BUS SHELTER** which was erected in 1954 to commemorate the Coronation of Queen Elizabeth II the previous year. Long the gathering place for the youngsters of the village it was frequently the target for graffiti. In order to combat this, in June 1996 the Walt Disney designs were drawn up by Nick Mawson and Robert Matthews and then painted by youngsters from the village, including Sam Edmonds, Brodie Jasinski, Chris Mawson, Tom Morris, Paul Smith, Chris Peppin, Jodi Peppin and Lincoln Pether. Thanks to their efforts, graffiti has almost been eliminated.

Front Street, around 1955.
Note the Coach House on the left, before its conversion into a dwelling.
Photograph by Cecil Cary, courtesy of Muriel Brown.

The junction would seem to be the location of an incident which was reported in the Bridgwater Mercury in June 1916.

"Frederick Newton (26), Frederick Tucker (21), William Phillips (18) and Walter Brooks (21) of Chedzoy were charged with disorderly behaviour at Chedzoy. P.C. Gard said that at 10.30 p.m. he was proceeding to Chedzoy Rectory and when he got within a quarter of a mile he heard shouting, singing and the playing of a mouth organ. He had listened for ten minutes when P.C. Williams approached from the opposite direction. The defendants then wished one another goodnight and parted. Witness stopped Brooks and Newton and said he had received a complaint about their behaviour, and that he should report them. He had had complaints about similar behaviour, and he had previously cautioned Tucker and Phillips. The defendants were each fined 2s. 6d."

Twelve months later,

"Walter Brooks, a respectably dressed young man, was summoned for having been disorderly at Chedzoy. Defendant: 'I only said one wicked word.' P.C. Gard said the offence was at night, and he heard it 200 yards away. When spoken to defendant said he was sorry; he had been keeping up his birthday. He was convicted a year ago for a similar offence. Mr. E. Trevor (Magistrates' Clerk) to defendant: 'This seems an annual amusement of yours on your birthday. How old are you?' Defendant: 21. Mr. Trevor: You ought to be in the army. Defendant: I have been up twice but they won't pass me. Mr. Trevor: I think you should try again. It would be better for you. Fined 5s."

The junction was also the scene of an incident at the time of the Silver Jubilee in May 1935 which was to return to haunt one of those involved. Doubtless it was caused by an excess of beer or cider at the village celebrations. "CHEDZOY JUBILEE CELEBRATION. WHAT FOLLOWED THE LUNCHEON. A JOY RIDE LEADS TO TROUBLE" were the headlines to a court report in the Bridgwater Mercury.

"Hubert Fry, farmer's assistant, of 13, Melbourne Square, Bridgwater; was summoned for on the 6th May, at Chedzoy, unlawfully driving away a motor vehicle without having either the consent of the owner thereof or other lawful authority. Henry ('Harry') Moore, Ernest Clapp and William Henry Collard, all of Chedzoy, were summoned for aiding and abetting Fry. They all pleaded guilty except Moore.

"P.C. Greed said on Monday, 6th May, he received a complaint from Mr. Ben Winter that his car had been driven away without his permission. He interviewed Fry, and told him of the complaint. He cautioned him, and asked him if he wished to make a statement. Fry said, 'I work for my father. At 3 p.m. on Monday, I was with Clapp, Collard, Moore and Frank Stone, near the Rectory at Chedzoy. They all said to me, 'Going to give us a ride?' I went to Cecil Cary's car, also near the Rectory. Ernest Clapp and I got in it. I said, 'I can't drive this thing: I don't understand it.' We then got out, and we all got in Ben Winter's car and I drove it down Chedzoy-lane, round by Yew Tree House, and past the Manor back to the Rectory. Then I turned it round and left it where I found it. I only did it for the fun of the thing. I have no driving licence, and I am not insured to drive a motor vehicle.' Witness interviewed Moore at his residence, and Moore said, 'There is no statement to make: I don't know that it is needed.' Clapp, when interviewed, said, 'I don't want to say anything about it.' Collard was also interviewed, and said, 'About 2.30 on Monday, May 6th, I was standing in the roadway near Chedzoy Rectory with Fry, Clapp and Moore. We all four got into Ben Winter's car, which was stationary there. Hubert Fry drove the car, and I sat beside him. Clapp and Moore sat in the seat behind. We went for a ride and a few minutes later we brought the car back to where we found it.'

"Benjamin George Winter, farmer, Fowler's Plot, Chedzoy, said on May 6th his car was taken away. He gave no permission to Fry to do so. He was annoyed at the time the car was taken. He would not have given the men any authority to take the car.

"Fry told the Court they had all been to a dinner and had a good time. They walked down the lane and were enjoying themselves and they thought they would go for a ride. He was sorry it happened. Moore said he was returning to work after the luncheon. The engine of the car was running. Someone said, 'Jump in, Henry' and he innocently did so, he did not know to whom the car belonged. 'We are all as bad as one another,' said Clapp. 'We all jumped in together. We came along together, and we all jumped in and thought we would have a Jubilee ride.' Collard also said, 'We were all as bad as one another.'

"The Chairman said the defendants did a very wrong thing in taking somebody else's car, and riding about in it, but seeing it was Jubilee Day and the bench did not think defendants meant any harm, the case would be dismissed on payment of costs. 'It was only because it was Jubilee Day when people were very happy and enjoying themselves,' said the Chairman, 'that we take this course.' The Chairman pointed out to Fry that no doubt there were a good many people about that day, and he might have had an accident, and it would have been a very serious thing. Fry was summoned for driving without a licence, and also for not being insured, and he was fined 10s. for each of these offences. He had to pay £1 7s. 9d. and the other defendants 7s. 9d. each."

Speaking in 1998 Herbie Ashford recalled the incident with Ben Winter's Morris car and said that Ben had called the police before knowing who had taken it. By the time he discovered who it was, it was too late to do anything about it. Some years later a theft took place at West End Farm and, as a result of interviewing all employees, the police discovered that Harry Moore had been fined for taking a car, so he became their prime suspect. The police had to be assured that he was a trusted employee and had only been involved in a stupid prank on Jubilee Day!

THE OLD RECTORY, part of which is now a separate residence and known as **Crosstree House**, was sold by auction by the Church in June 1964 for the sum of £2,700 with part of the walled garden sold separately for £700 as a building plot. It is typical of buildings of Queen Anne's reign, and is thought to date from the very early 1700s.

Part was possibly built when Walter Rawleigh was Rector between 1620 and 1622. This man was closely related to the family of the famous Sir Walter Raleigh of Sherborne Castle.

A previous owner came across documents in Northern Ireland, where the Raleigh family had possessions, relating to the house.

The main house would appear to date from 1848 after plans were drawn up for Rev. George Nutting as an extension to the original rectory, and is entered through an octagonal porch which leads to the main hall, where the beamed ceiling is of particular note, being some 30 feet above the floor. A fine, wide curving staircase leads to the upper storey. The dining room is, perhaps, the most imposing of the rooms and retains the original wood panelling. The carvings around the top of the wall are of a pattern found in many Somerset rectories and are repeated around the top of the front porch.

Upstairs all the original fireplaces have been boarded up. The most interesting room on this floor is that which was used by the Bishop of Bath and Wells when touring his diocese. It has a curved ceiling, possibly reminiscent of a bishop's mitre. The loft contains all the original servant bell pulls, from the days when the rector was a wealthy man in his own right. An interesting feature to note on the outside, is that there are three false windows on the front of the house. This was presumably done to give a better visual balance. The original coach house and stables, now converted to a dwelling - the Old Coach House - could have taken a coach and four with ease.

Previous owners of the house were told that the Duke of Monmouth dined here or in the Rectory existing at that time. This fact is felt to be implausible, as the Rector of the time was an ardent Royalist, and thus hardly likely to invite the Duke to dinner (although it would have made a good and topical story). It is much more likely that King James II called there on his progress through the West Country in 1686 when he is known to have visited Chedzoy.

In mid-1998 the Old Rectory was sold for about £175,000 and later that year some of the rooms were photographed for Crown Paints for use in one of their catalogues. In the autumn of 1998 the Old Coach House was placed on the market for £89,750, although this figure had been reduced by the time it was sold early in 1999.

The adjoining **CROSSTREE HOUSE** formed the servants' quarters and was part of the older, original Rectory. There is a huge inglenook fireplace; the kitchen is formed from the original butler's pantry and still contains the lead lined sink, now boarded up. This wing originally extended much further onto ground now occupied by the adjoining bungalows in St. Mary's Close and contained a bake house with a bread oven where the lounge fireplace now stands, and beyond that a dairy. The bedroom window above the entrance gate looking onto the street, was a projecting lantern window until modernisation in the early 1960s. From the window, occupants had a view of the church and approaches to the house. The room was used in the 1950s and early 1960s by the ladies of the church sewing circle.

Under this part of the Rectory is a cellar still containing the Rector's wine bins. There is a story that a secret passage leads from the cellar to the church but, despite many searches, none has ever been found, not even when deep excavations were necessary for the provision of mains drainage throughout the village in 1975 and 1976. In mid-1999 the house was on the market for £180,000.

Two very reverend occupants of the Rectory were the two Rev. Mullens, uncle and nephew, who occupied the house in succession from 1855 to 1940. The Rev. George R. Mullens had six daughters: the school children were given an afternoon's holiday for the marriage of one of them. Some of the oldest Chedzoy residents still remember with nostalgia the tennis parties and great occasions at the Rectory in the old days.

A conveyance dated 19th December 1957 records the sale of a plot of land of some 3 roods and 30 perches known as Woodward's Garden: a map shows this plot of land comprised the area now occupied by Glebe House, St. Mary's Close and the three adjoining bungalows in Front Street. A wall along Front Street from the Rectory to West View screened this former garden from view. The land was sold by Rev. Cecil Hunt for the sum of £500.

Opposite the bungalows stands **COURT FARM**, one of the oldest farms in the village. In the 1840s and 1850s this was the home of James and Elizabeth Hardy.

One of their sons emigrated to Australia in April 1850, and in July 1881 the Bridgwater Mercury published a short report under the heading,

"A SUCCESSFUL EMIGRANT. The 'Evening Journal,' published in Adelaide, contains a long and interesting account of the annual 'vintage festival' given by Mr. Hardy at his 'Bankside Vineyard.' The Mr. Hardy referred to is the son of the late Mr. James Hardy of this parish, and he emigrated to Australia more than twenty years ago. The 'Journal' says; 'The total quantity of wine made by Mr. Hardy this year shows, not withstanding a much larger acreage, a falling off of 20,000 gallons from that of last year, the respective figures being 55,000 and 75,000. There are now in stock 200,000 gallons, the greater part, of course, in bulk. ... Mr. Hardy has now 230 acres of vines, and intends increasing the number to a quarter thousand by next season."

Still owned by the family, this is the renowned wine company, Thomas Hardy and Sons Pty. Ltd., of Reynella, near Adelaide, South Australia, which was founded by Thomas Hardy (1830 - 1912) of Chedzoy.

In the 1860s and 1870s the tenants of Court Farm were Mrs. Betsy Barnstable and her son, Thomas. In 1869 a serious offence was committed against her granddaughter:

"George Stone, aged 17, labourer, was charged with indecently assaulting a little child, daughter of Mr. W.S. Carter, farmer, at Chedzoy. The girl assaulted is only four years of age. For a few weeks she had been staying at Chedzoy with Betsy Barnstable her [63 year old] grandmother who keeps a farm there. Defendant was in her employ, and on the afternoon in question he enticed the little girl from the house, and whilst in a linhay (open fronted building) committed the assault complained of. The grandmother missed the little girl, and went in search of her, finding her in the company of the defendant. From what the girl told her she discharged the defendant from her employ on the following morning, and on assigning the reason for doing this, defendant said, 'Please forgive me, missus, this once.' After hearing the evidence of Dr. Farmer, who had examined the child, the charge against the defendant was reduced to one of aggravated assault. To this he pleaded guilty and was sentenced to two months' hard labour."

In January 1870 Thomas Barnstable appeared in court as a defendant:

"Thomas Barnstable, farmer, of Chedzoy, was charged by P.C. Foster with creating a public annoyance in High Street, [Bridgwater]. ... P.C. Foster deposed he was fetched from the Gaol ... to go to the back of the Golden Ball Inn. On arriving in the butcher's market he saw defendant with his coat off, surrounded by a crowd of people. Complaints were made of the defendant's conduct. Defendant said he had been turned out of the Golden Ball, but it was not his fault. He was removed to the Gaol, but afterwards bailed and summoned. Mr. Harden, landlord of the Golden Ball complained ... of broken windows." A fight had then taken place. "The Mayor said the Bench were of the opinion there were some palliating circumstances in the case, but the charge of public annoyance was proved beyond doubt, and defendant must pay 5s. and costs; in default seven days' imprisonment."

In September 1871 a sale of livestock and implements took place at Court Farm as Thomas Barnstable was about to quit the premises. As was invariably the case, no report of the sale was published subsequently, but the sale notice provides another interesting inventory of a small farm at that time.

"LIVESTOCK: 15 first class dairy cows in full milk and in calf; iron grey cart mare, 16 hands high, 3 years old, very good and staunch in harness, warranted sound and free from vice; brown cart horse, 15 hands high, 12 years old, very good in harness and free from vice; 5 small fat pigs. IMPLEMENTS: 2 strong waggons, one quite new; spring cart, 2 sets of trace harness and 2 sets of breeching harness; bridle and saddle, nearly new; reaping machine; horse gear and chaff cutters; double action root cutter, corn blower, iron cultivator, set of zigzag drags and bodkin, Howard's double action wheel plough, set of Howard's spike harrows, potato mill, 26 round ladder, bullock's crib, sheep troughs, iron pigs ditto (sic), lot of deal plank, lot of poles, 12 gate hurdles, picks, rakes, large winnowing sheet, staddle stones, stock and covers, 1,000 long spars, hay knife, &c. DAIRY UTENSILS &c.: Double action cheese press, near new; large copper cheese tub, 3 milk pails, milk trunk, pans, tubs, buckets, and the usual dairy utensils. 10 hogsheads prime cider, about 5 acres of mangolds, swedes, and potatoes in lots, large heap of manure."

In October 1872 Betsy Barnstable was still in business at the farm. The County Court column of the Bridgwater Mercury gave details of a case.

"REED v. BETSY BARNSTABLE. The plaintiff said on 8th September he entered into a contract with the defendant, of Chedzoy, for the purchase of two tons of potatoes at £10 17s. 6d., which were to be delivered, at her expense, at the Bridgwater Station. Plaintiff was proceeding to draw a comparison between the sample and the bulk of the potatoes, with a view to showing non-fulfilment of contract, when his Honour asked whether the contract was in writing. Plaintiff replied in the negative, whereupon his Honour said an old Act of Parliament was still in force, whereby a contract of the value of more than £10 was not legally binding unless there was a written memorandum, or there had been part payment, in reference to it. He was bound to administer the law as he found it, and under the circumstances must non-suit the plaintiff."

A major fire at the premises was reported in the Christmas Day 1878 edition of the Bridgwater Mercury:

"Early on Friday morning, between one and two o'clock, some persons in a neighbouring house, who were remaining up picking poultry, discovered that one of a row of straw ricks on the farm premises in the occupation of Mrs. Barnstable, a widow, and situate near the parish church, was on fire. An alarm was raised and assistance soon procured, a messenger being dispatched to Bridgwater for the engine kept there by the West of England Insurance Company, of which Mr. Baker is the local agent. Before the arrival of the engine and brigade, not withstanding the strenuous efforts of the villagers, the fire had extended to two other ricks close by, all three being then in flames. Some other ricks, and also the farm premises, were in close proximity, and one of the former was in considerable danger of being ignited, and would undoubtedly, in the opinion of most of the spectators, have been destroyed but for the exertion of the fire brigade in pouring over it a large quantity of water, obtained with some difficulty, from three or four pumps in the neighbourhood, and brought to the engine in buckets. The three ricks, which were the property of Mr. Carter of Westonzoyland, were wholly destroyed, but the loss is fortunately covered by insurance. It is generally believed that the fire was the work of an incendiary."

Contemporary reports made no reference to an arsonist appearing before the court.

In the summer of 1881 an advertisement in the Bridgwater Mercury noted that Court Farm was available to be let by tender and consisted of

"104 acres, 2 roods, 14 perches (more or less) of first class arable pasture, meadow and orchard as now rented by Mr. William House."

The term of the lease was to be for 3, 5 or 7 years. The following January a further advertisement appeared for an auction of

"Dairy cows, cart, hack horse, agricultural implements, 10 tons of hay and straw (to go off), 30 hogsheads new cider, 16 tons potatoes, casks, etc.," the property of William House, who was quitting the premises.

In the late 19th Century and early years of the 20th Century, Court Farm was the home of John Baker who, like all farmers, suffered at the hands of thieves from time to time. In January 1898 it was reported in the Bridgwater Mercury that

"George Hunt (52 and living at Batch) was charged with stealing 15 lbs. of hay, value 8d. (3p.). John Baker, farmer, of Chedzoy, said he had been missing hay for some time from his ricks. About quarter past five in the morning witness, with P.C. White, was watching the ricks. Hunt was seen taking the hay away in his arms, P.C. White remarking, that he saw the prisoner take away about 15 lbs. of hay. Prisoner said, 'If you will let me go, I will take it back.' Defendant threw himself on the mercy of the court and he hoped the Bench would deal leniently with him and impose a small fine. The Chairman said the Bench must mark the offence and they sentenced him to three weeks' hard labour."

In September 1900 another fire occurred at the premises:

"SERIOUS FARM FIRE. On Sunday morning a fire broke out on the premises of Mr. John Baker, Court Farm, Chedzoy, in the barn and waggon house, and would have soon assumed large proportions had not a number of willing helpers set to work to keep the fire under control. A number of ricks of corn and hay were only a few feet away from the blazing buildings, but these were saved. The loss is covered by insurance with Hickman and Son, Phoenix Fire Office."

In October 1917 the farmhouse, together with 105 acres, was sold by auction. It was then owned by a branch of the Fry family. One of the family was in trouble in December 1952:

"Two Chedzoy farm workers, Samuel Robert Baker (28) of Rose Bower Cottage and Roy Fry (18) of Court Farm, were each fined £2 with £3 12s. costs at Bridgwater County Magistrates' Court for trespassing in pursuit of game and conies. Mr. Coles, an employee of Mr. Reginald Roe, saw the defendants in one of Mr. Roe's fields accompanied by a boy and a dog. Fry was carrying a rifle and was being followed by Baker and the boy who was holding a ferret. Asked who had given them permission to be in the field Baker replied, 'Who gave you permission? I thought this was Mr. Ashford's ground'."

The paddock of Court Farm was sold for £11,100 in 1971 and the eight houses now fronting Higher Road and Manor Road were built on the site.

In April 1979 the farmhouse and outbuildings were sold by auction for the sum of £35,500. They were purchased by Ken and Joyce Palmer who lovingly set about modernising the farmhouse whilst retaining all the important historical features. During excavation of the fireplace in the room adjoining Front Street a horde of clay churchwarden pipes were found, presumably thrown away by previous owners. The removal of a Victorian fireplace revealed an old bread oven and its chimney and can be seen in the inglenook: Mr. Palmer thoughtfully placed a spotlight in this chimney so that visitors may examine the construction. Between the hall and living room three panels of daub and wattle were found; unfortunately two crumbled, but the third was protected and remains a feature of the premises.

After Mr. and Mrs. Palmer had sold the property to Arthur Miller he sold part of the garden as a building plot, and Birch House was built on it in 1989. The out-buildings were converted into the four separate dwellings which now stand on the site. Mr. Miller sold the farmhouse for about £178,000 and left the village in the summer of 1999.

Almost opposite stands **GLEBE HOUSE**. From 1964 until 1978 this was the Rectory.

Ben Hooper was born in 1906 in **WEST VIEW** and was the youngest son of Edward and Sophia Hooper. Ben had at least five brothers and one sister, there having been eight or nine children in all. At that time **HOPE COTTAGE** stood opposite (now the site of Crayston and Kalina, built in 1959) which was the home of Mrs. Edith Lovibond. Ben's daily job for Mrs. Lovibond was to draw one bucket of water from a standpipe which stood outside the house, or two buckets on Saturday as

Front Street in the 1930s.
The Gables can be seen immediately to the left of the church. On the right, West View and Crown House appear much the same as they do today.
Courtesy of Duncan Bouchier.

Rose Bower, February 1999.
The house stands neglected after the death of Herbie Baker nine months earlier.
Photograph by John Weeks.

none was allowed to be drawn on Sunday as this interfered with attendance at church. For this task he was rewarded with sixpence (2.5p.) each week. Ben would spend this money on biscuits and a bottle of pop at Tom Conduit's shop (now known as Myrtle Cottage) in Ward Lane.

At Church Corner stood a small red brick house on the left hand side, sideways on to the road. This was incorporated into **THE GABLES** in the early 1990s. The original house replaced a much older cob cottage which was burnt down in the early years of the 20th Century.

Beside the churchyard, tucked away in a corner, stands a very old dwelling, **ROSE BOWER**, which is reminiscent of the typical worker's cottage of a century or so ago. Until his death at the age of 81 in May 1998, this was the lifetime home of Herbert 'Herbie' Baker, one of the village's characters. He was known to everyone and, until suffering a stroke, could be regularly seen driving his Reliant Robin three-wheeler around the village. In earlier years he used to ride a motorcycle and in November 1965 it was reported that,

> "Injured at Chedzoy was a motorcyclist, Herbert Baker of Rose Bower, Chedzoy, whose machine ran into a hedge on a bend. He was taken to Bridgwater Hospital."

Even after his stroke, Herbie continued to ride around the village on a bicycle. A lifelong bachelor, he was found dead in bed when the police forced an entry to the house after a neighbour had been unable to get a reply to his repeated knocking on the door. In September 1999 an application was made for the demolition of the cottage and the construction of two houses on the site.

The 1836 Tithe Map shows several buildings on the site of Rose Bower, including the village pound. The 1881 Census lists three families as living in Church Hatch (from the Old English meaning "gate") which may have been this same area: a further three families lived at "Batch." Ten years later the 1891 Census does not mention Church Hatch but does record six families at Batch. Quite where this address was is a matter for conjecture, but would appear to be the area immediately outside the church.

Which property the following refers to is not known, but the 1881 Census shows James Stone as a 72 year old yeoman, living at Batch.

A sale was to take place on 14th March 1883 at the Bath Bridge Inn, Bridgwater of

> "A cottage and dwelling house with garden, building and premises adjoining thereto, close to the church and in the occupation of Mr. James Stone, the owner."

No report of the sale was published.

One of the residents of Batch was George Wheeler, 34, who was summoned to appear before Bridgwater County Magistrates' Court in February 1899. The Bridgwater Mercury reported that he

> "was summoned for assaulting Mary Giles, wife of Thomas Giles, labourer." This couple were both 37 and lived in Pig Lane. "Mary Giles went to the house of the defendant to assist his wife. Whilst there defendant came in under the influence of drink, and not only threatened to kick her out of the house if she did not go, but he carried out his threat and threw water over her. The disturbance took place close to the church, and the service had to be stopped in consequence. Defendant served everybody the same way as he served her. Fined 5s. and costs or 14 days."

It seems George Wheeler got off lightly: Chedzoy was back in the news two weeks later.

"Henry Merriott was summoned for being drunk and disorderly. P.C. Fry said the disturbance caused by the defendant lasted an hour.

Defendant was ordered to be imprisoned for 14 days, the Chairman pointing out that his was the second case of the kind from Chedzoy within a fortnight, and in future any other similar disturbances of the peace would be punished double to that inflicted that morning."

It seems probable that the subject of this report was Henry Merrett, aged 29, of Chedzoy Lane.

Another resident of Batch, aged 16 in 1888, was

"Walter Tucker, of Chedzoy, [who] was charged with riding on a waggon without being provided with reins.

P.C. Gould stated the defendant was stood up on the shafts. - Fined 5s. and costs."

St Marys Church, between 1884 and 1905.
The clock face can be seen in the tower, and the old lead roof is in place. Note the wooden fencing either side of the gate.
Photograph by A. Squibbs, courtesy of Audrey Fry.

Chedzoy Church

At this point visit the beautiful church of St. Mary the Virgin. The church was at one time the property of the Order of St. John of Jerusalem at Mynchin Buckland, Somerset. One of its rectors, Richard Nikke, became Bishop of Norwich in 1501. One was deprived by Queen Mary in 1554 when she restored the Medieval rite. A more famous Rector, Dr. Rawley, nephew of Sir Walter Raleigh, was deprived during the Commonwealth on account of his Royalism, and was driven from gaol to gaol until he was barbarously killed by the gaol keeper at Wells.

St. Mary's Church.
This is the oldest known photograph of the church.
It was taken before the clock face was added (1884).
Source unknown, courtesy of Norman Fry.

In an address at the dedication service for a processional cross in memory of Mrs. Ethel Mullens in May 1942, the Bishop of Bath and Wells, Dr. Francis Underhill said,

> "In Chedzoy they had one of the few churches of the thirteenth century and the church today was very much as it stood when it was built about 1230 or 1240, or even a little earlier."

Fortunately the church has suffered little at the hands of thieves and vandals and is unlocked during daylight hours, so visitors may explore at their leisure. In 1937 Miss Elizabeth Winter wrote a guide to the building and this is used to this day. Her explanation still holds good over sixty years later and is repeated here with some additional information to that contained on leaflets available in the church.

Your exploration of the church should start with the exterior. The walls are of blue lias random coursed stone with Ham stone dressings to the copings, door and window openings and buttresses. The tower is a good example of the famous Somerset church towers and was built in the 15th Century. It is of the Quantock class, having double light belfry windows as distinguished from Mendip towers which have triple lights. The pierced parapet at the top of the tower is of great interest.

The tower is not normally open to the public. It holds six bells, the heaviest being the tenor which weighs 14 hundredweight - about 710 kg. The bells are supported by an unusual octagonal frame, one of the beams having the date 1760 carved into it. At one time there were only five bells, but the sixth was added at the time of Queen Victoria's Golden Jubilee. In June 1887 the Bridgwater Mercury reported that,

> "The peal of bells in [Chedzoy] church has always been five, but when the tower was built space was left in the loft for the sixth bell. This year, Mr. Derrick, who was born in 1837 ... wished to commemorate her Gracious Majesty's Jubilee, and also his own Jubilee 50th birth-year, by making a gift of the sixth bell. On Saturday, May 28th, it was successfully lifted into position in the church tower amidst cheers from the ringers and villagers who had assembled at the church gates. ... The bell, which weighs 5 cwt., 1 qr., 10 lbs., bears the following inscription: 'Given, 1887, by Edmund Derrick and Elizabeth, his wife. A thank offering to God for his blessings in their family for many years. Casted by Llewellyn and James, Bristol."

Church records note that new bell ropes were fitted in 1957 and that the present ropes date from 1979. An undated printed notice, signed by the Rev. George R. Mullens, details the belfry rules. In brief, the leader was to be elected by the other ringers at an annual meeting to be held, if possible, on New Year's Day. The names of the ringers were to be approved by the Rector. ***At least*** one night's practice a week was required and the bells were to be rung every Sunday, Christmas Day and New Year's Day. The fine for swearing or quarrelling in the belfry was 3d. (1.5p.) and for entering the belfry in a state of intoxication, 2s. 6d. (12.5p.). The rules were to be agreed to and signed by every ringer in a book kept specially for that purpose.

Another notice in the belfry records that on 10th December 1927 in 2 hours 50 minutes a peal of Grandsire Doubles was rung: 5,040 changes. The bell ringers were Ernest Heal (treble), Bertram T. Jeanes (No. 2), Oliver Bennett (No. 3), Leonard F. Gigg (No. 4), William G. Gigg (No. 5 and conductor) and Henry Chapple (tenor), all of whom had learned their craft in the tower at Chedzoy. A change is when a bell is rotated once about its axis as opposed to chiming when it swings from side to side or the clapper is swung to strike the bell. Grandsire Doubles is a method by which the treble bell is rung in relation to the other five bells.

The mechanism for the clock by Thomas Bayley is dated 1762. Housed in the belfry it requires winding every three days, and this task has been undertaken since 1986 by Peter 'Pete' Dodge. On average it requires 36 turns of the mechanism to wind the clock and a further 48 turns for the chime. In order to advance the clock to Summer Time, it must be stopped, the adjustment made with a spanner, and then re-started. Although this procedure could also be used in the autumn, it is simpler to stop the clock for one hour and then re-start it since the hour hand can not be moved backwards.

Originally the clock only had a chime, but in 1884 it was restored by Dell and Company of Bristol and a dial fitted with money raised by the 1883 Candle Auction.

A vestry meeting in August 1883 resolved,

> "With a view to improving the church clock and affixing a dial, the church wardens were requested to invite an estimate from Messrs. Dell and Co., Bristol and it was determined that should their estimate be within the amount of money in the hands of the church wardens or any sum that can be raised to meet the costs, that instructions be forthwith given for the completion of such work: any surplus to be expended upon church yard walls."

Parish records for 19th November 1929 showed that Mr. T. Jeanes (probably Thomas Jeanes, aged 71) resigned after winding and generally attending to the church clock for 44 years and that Mr. H. Newton had been appointed as his successor. In January 1939 the clock face required repainting and Messrs. R.T. Hanham & Son undertook to do this in the spring. That was probably the last time it was painted until about 1990 when the face was refurbished with the money being raised by sponsorship of the various elements: £1 for a minute marker up to £25 for a hand. The colour of the clock face was suggested by Mrs. Pat Lennard, Secretary of the Parochial Church Council, her inspiration being her wristwatch, which has the same colour scheme. On tower open days, usually held annually towards the end of June, it is well worth climbing the 99 spiral steps to the top of the tower for a panoramic view of the village and the surrounding countryside. The bells and clock may also be inspected during such visits.

But to continue our exploration of the rest of the building. At the west door at the foot of the tower, notice the deep undercutting of the stonework in the sporadrels under the large square head.

The wall on the south side of the building probably dates from as early as the 13th Century, about the time of the signing of the Magna Carta by King John, but the north wall is 200 years newer. The clerestory, which has the smaller windows below the main roof, was built in the Perpendicular, or 15th Century period.

The south porch should be noted on account of the sundial and the very curious panel, with the date 1579, above the doorway. On the right are the initials RB in beautiful Gothic lettering: Richard Beere was one of the most famous, and last but one, Abbots of Glastonbury. RF is for Richard Fox, Bishop of Winchester and Lord of the Manor of Taunton. The most curious part of the panel is the bird standing over an object: the bird is a wyvern with knotted tail and the object below is thought to be a weaver's comb, with leather hoops on the shafts through which hands could be passed. A wyvern was the badge of the Pembroke family and the HP on the badge possibly stands for a steward of this family, or perhaps for the Reverend Hugo Pole who was the Rector in 1523.

St Mary's Church, before 1884.
Note there is no clock face, and the old lead-covered roof was still in place. The gentleman in the stove-pipe hat would appear to be a policeman.
Source unknown, courtesy of Helen Hunt.

Most of the windows in the nave are in the 15th Century Perpendicular style, with characteristic tracery, but the smaller one is earlier. All of the windows on the north side of the nave are square headed and of the late 15th Century. The church has five consecration crosses, two on the south side and three on the north. It was, and is, the custom of the church that the Bishop who consecrates a church should walk right round it and touch the walls, and wherever he touches a small, circular cross is cut into the stone of the wall. The deep indentations in the buttresses outside the south transept are popularly supposed to have been made by the sharpening of scythes or other weapons by the Monmouth rebels before the Battle of Sedgemoor. However, as no Chedzoy man enlisted in the rebel army, the story is probably a myth. The Rev. Andrew Paschall, Rector of Chedzoy at that time, persuaded his flock to keep clear of the rebellion. Without doubt, the buttresses have been used for sharpening something, but most probably workmen's tools.

The chancel was demolished and rebuilt in 1884 and 1885 at a cost of £2,000, all of which was paid by the Rev. G.O. Mullens. The architect, Mr. Slingsby Stall, had reported that

> "the walls were on an average eleven or twelve inches (28 to 30 cm.) out of upright and very loose and shaky, and the roof timbers are quite decayed, it would be absolutely necessary to pull down and reconstruct."

As far as possible the original stone wall was incorporated into the new building and, at the same time, a vestry was built. The stained glass was provided by Messrs. Gibbs and Howard. Restoration work was carried out at the same time in the nave and this cost a further £700, although there was "a handsome donation from Oxford University." The church was formally reopened on 2nd June 1885 in a service attended by the Bishop of Bath and Wells, Lord Arthur Harvey. On the south side of the exterior of the chancel may be seen the remains of a chapel in the early English or 13th Century style. The north door should also be noticed: the ancient bands and hinges of hammered iron are good examples of 15th Century metalwork.

The roof of the nave was restored early in the 20th Century. A long report appeared in the Bridgwater Mercury in June 1904 under the headline "PROPOSED RESTORATION OF ROOFS."

It seems that some artistic licence was allowed to creep into the report in order to further the quest for funds.

"The roofs of the nave in this ancient and historically interesting church have long been falling into decay, and the rector and churchwardens are about to undertake their complete restoration at an estimated cost of £700. With a view to obtaining this sum, the following appeal is being issued, signed by the rector (the Rev. George R. Mullens) and Messrs. Joseph Brooks and Joseph Ashford (churchwardens):-

"The parish of Chedzoy played an important part in connection with the last battle fought on English soil, the battle of Sedgemoor having been actually fought within its boundaries. It is said that while Monmouth was halted at Bridgwater the first information of the position of the Royalist troops was brought to him by a Chedzoy man, who had spied them out with the aid of a telescope from the top of the tower of Chedzoy church; while on one of the buttresses in the south wall of the church are still to be seen the marks made by Monmouth's men when sharpening their rough weapons in preparation for the battle of 5th July 1685, which resulted so disastrously for their leader and caused many of them to find themselves prisoners within the walls of Chedzoy church. The church, so interesting for the above reasons to all lovers of history, is one of the most beautiful in the county of Somerset. Some twenty years ago the chancel was re-built and beautified by the late rector and his relatives at a cost of £3,000, and at the same time a sum of some £800 was raised by the churchwardens and expended upon the nave; lack of funds however, prohibited a complete restoration at that time, and the work of restoring the roofs, which even then were acknowledged to be in a very bad state, was postponed till some future date. We, the undersigned, rector and churchwardens, now feel that that work can be delayed no longer. For many years past, whenever we have experienced heavy falls of rain during the time of Divine service, worshippers have frequently been unpleasantly reminded that there are serious leakages in the ancient leads of the roof, and - what is more significant to those who have the custody of the building - damp patches and decaying ends of rafters point unmistakably to the fact that water is, and has been for years, finding its way into the walls, with the certain result that, if allowed to continue, this ancient and valuable building must fall into ruins. Even so recently as last year £10 was spent by the churchwardens in soldering the cracks in the lead, with little, if any, result; and we have come to the conclusion that the present roof is absolutely beyond repair, and that nothing short of complete restoration can save the church from ruin. We are confirmed in our opinion by the diocesan surveyor, who reports adversely on all the roofs of the nave and tower, and even goes so far as to pronounce some parts to be actually dangerous. To place all in a satisfactory state of repair the surveyor considers that it is absolutely necessary to undertake the work, which he estimates to cost £700. The parish, which does not contain a single wealthy resident, is ready and willing to do its utmost to raise as much as possible, but obviously so large an expenditure cannot be met without application being made to the outside public. We, therefore, earnestly appeal to you to come to our aid in the difficult task we have before us, by kindly giving us a generous subscription towards our Restoration Fund. Subscriptions will be most thankfully received and acknowledged by either of the undersigned, or may be paid to the account of 'Chedzoy Church Restoration Fund,' Messrs. Stuckley's Banking Company, Bridgwater."

Yes, all one paragraph!

"The scheme has the hearty approval of the Lord Bishop of the Diocese, who writes as follows:-

'I heartily endorse the appeal made by the rector and churchwardens in the very interesting letter which they have written asking for worthy contributions towards the quite necessary work of placing a new roof on the nave of this beautiful church. Many people interested in English history, to whom Macaulay has made the story of the Monmouth Rebellion and the battle of Sedgemoor vivid and fascinating, will be glad to do what they can to preserve a church which bears so many evident and curious marks of the preparations made by simple villagers to meet their better-armed opponents. But I am able to speak of other reasons which will appear more strongly to Church-people. I can bear my testimony to the reverent worship, to the regular Church-going habits, and to the earnestness of candidates for confirmation. The church and churchyard are well cared for. It seems to me to be a parish worth helping, and I hope that liberal subscriptions will be given by those who can afford them.'

"The following subscriptions have already been promised:- The Lords of the Manor, the University of Oxford, on condition that a like sum is raised from other sources, £300; the Rev. R.H. Mullens, Abbey Wells, Newbury (on certain conditions), £100; Mrs. G.O. Mullens, £15; the Rev. J.B. Anstice, £10; the Rev. G.R. Mullens, £10."

The necessary £1,131 was raised and a new pitched roof, with Broseley tiles, replaced the older, flatter, lead covered roof. In November 1905 the church was re-dedicated in a service conducted by Dr. G.W. Kennion, Lord Bishop of the Diocese after which a public luncheon took place in the schoolroom. In the evening,

"Supper over, the men lit their pipes and listened to a concert, composed chiefly of the popular songs of the day, in the choruses of which the audience joined with a will. A most happy social evening was spent, closing at 9.30 with the singing by the whole company of the National Anthem."

There was sufficient food left over for a children's dinner on the Saturday. Speaking in 1955, Mr. B.T. Jeanes recalled the dedication service and meal but also said that the organ was installed at the same time.

To the west of the church is a magnificent equestrian figure, designed by Cecil Thomas, R.A., which is a monument to

Sydney Mason Collins (1879-1946) who was a student at Corpus Christi College, Oxford between 1898 and 1902. He became a Fellow of the Society of Antiquities. Between 1914 and 1918 he served with the Signals in France and was mentioned in dispatches. Later he was a Barrister. The intriguing inscriptions on the plinth are thought to be in Norman French and read "May God in his compassion have mercy" and "Collins make a clear mark" - apparently a pun as a notary was also known as a marker.

The beech tree behind the church is estimated by experts to be between 150 and 200 years old and described as one of the best specimens in the area. Before leaving the churchyard, be sure to visit the two unusual clapper stiles in the rear boundary wall. The originals were made by Edward Noakes in 1912 when the wall was built, but the present stiles, identical in design, date from 1959. They are said to be two of only three in the county and are also known as Sussex fall-stiles: more than one young visitor has fallen over these, caught out by their unusual operation. In 1911 the University of Oxford donated a 35 feet wide strip of land running parallel to the wall which existed at that time in order to provide an extension to the burial ground. It would appear that the old wall ran along the line of the two large trees behind the church. As a condition of the gift, the University required that the land be enclosed. Church minutes record that in July 1912 an agreement was drawn up between the churchwardens and James Shepherd of Cannington and Henry James Squire of Bridgwater for the construction of the present wall which cost £173 10s. The stone used was transported by horse and cart from Puriton by George Guntripp. This churchyard extension was consecrated by the Bishop on 17th June 1913.

The tranquillity of the churchyard was disturbed in July 1884, according to a report in the Bridgwater Mercury.

> "William Mills, farm labourer, was summoned [to appear before Bridgwater County Magistrates] for unlawfully disturbing a burial-service in the parish churchyard at Chedzoy. - Defendant pleaded guilty. - The Rev. G.O. Mullens, rector, said he did not appear there with any vindictive feelings towards the defendant, but merely to warn him and others that they could not with impunity interfere with the clergy in the discharge of their duties in the manner the defendant did on the occasion referred to under very painful circumstances. Just as the coffin had been lowered into the grave, the defendant rushed forward with some earth in his hand, exclaiming, 'Let's give the poor fellow a bit of sand.' He (the rector) was obliged to stop the service, and to tell the defendant that if he did not behave properly he must leave the churchyard, or a policeman would be sent for to take him into custody. Defendant's answer was, 'I suppose I must go off at once.' The mourners were naturally greatly affronted. His only motive in summoning the defendant was to teach him and others that conduct of this kind could not be permitted, and that the churchyard was as holy and sacred at the church itself. - Defendant said the boy had been working on the farm with him, and he didn't mean any harm to the deceased or the minister by throwing a piece of dirt into the grave. - Defendant was fined 2s. 6d. and costs, and was informed he was liable to a penalty of £5 or to be sent to prison for two months."

Although the name of the deceased was not reported, parish records indicate that he was William Giles, aged 17, who was buried on 27th June 1884.

Now go into the church. The south door is from the 17th Century and of oak with lozenge ornaments in the panels. Inside the church visitors will immediately notice the massive circular pillars of the nave which are as old as any part of the building. They are in the Early English style of Gothic architecture as is the font which dates from the same period. At one time the only illumination in the church was by means of candles around the pillars. When Edward Noakes came to the village in the 1860s, one of his tasks after evening service was to extinguish all the candles which he did with the aid of a long blowpipe. Since the installation of electricity the candles are only lit at Christmas and on other special occasions.

The rails beneath the tower are from the 17th Century and were, presumably, once before the altar. The brass on the floor near the south door shows a Knight in armour of the late 15th or early 16th Century: the dog at his feet is taken to mean that he had been to the wars and had returned safely. The man was Sir Richard Sydenham of Chedzoy whose will, dated 13th November 1499, stated, "I bequeath my body to be buried in the chancel of the Parish church of Chedsey." His will was proved on 20th February 1499, i.e. 1500 as the year commenced in April under the old Julian calendar. Sir Richard is supposed to be one of those who left Church Acre to the church. As has been previously described, the land is sold every 21 years whilst half an inch of candle burns and the tradition continues to this day, the next auction being in 2009.

A holy water stoup is to the right of the main door. It was originally used by those entering as they crossed themselves, but in 1937 it was used as a visitors box. It has now been returned to its original use. Above the stoup is a board showing all the Rectors of Chedzoy: this was donated by Rev. George R. Mullens in January 1938. It starts from 1317 when there were two Rectors: Michael de Drokensford and Michael fil (son of) Michael de Drokensford. Long serving Rectors were Walter Raleigh (1620-1662), John Coney (1698-1750) and, more recently, George R. Mullens (1891-1940).

The ancient oak chest dates from the 15th Century and was formerly used to store Parish Registers. The pews are reputed to be the oldest complete set in the country. In Somerset churches there are many hundreds of fine bench ends and those in Chedzoy are no exception, but they are cut much more deeply than is usual. Notice St. John with the lamb; a serpent surrounding the letter W; the letter M surrounded by a crown (possibly for Queen Mary); the Tudor double rose; a garter enclosing a bird; the wyvern, similar to the wyvern on the panel above the south porch. The lectern is dated 1618 and is in the Jacobean style. The oak screen surrounding the organ seat is of the same period as the lectern and was formerly the front of the old reading desk. The pulpit dates from the 15th Century and the carving is notable, being in "Linen Work" style with a curious appearance like folded linen.

There is a late 15th Century arch surmounted by a defaced Calvary in the north aisle. This was probably the entrance to a chantry destroyed during the Reformation. Chantries were common in Medieval churches and were usually cut off from the body of the church by a wooden screen. They were endowed by private owners for the purpose of having daily Mass said for the repose of their souls by the Chantry Priest.

A small door in the north transept close to the screen is known as a rood door; behind it is a stairway within the wall leading to the rood screen. The screen is partly old and partly modern, in the style of the 15th Century. "Rood" means that the screen was surmounted by a rood or cross. Such screens were probably used by those who played music during services in the church in Medieval times.

On the south side of the chancel there is a wide and deep squint cut through the wall. It was probably cut to allow the congregation in the south transept to come forward at the appropriate moment to behold the Elevation of the Host during Mass. The squint is connected with the small blocked window which can be seen outside the church in the wall of the south transept. This shows the method by which persons not permitted to enter the church on account of disease or wrong doing, were enabled to stand in the churchyard so that they could look through this window and the squint to behold the Host as it was raised by the priest above his head in the Elevation at the consecration in the Mass. The position of the window, as connected with the squint, would seem to make this process rather difficult and one can see that standing outside at the window it would have been easier to see through the archway, the outline of which is still visible, to the side altar in the Lady Chapel.

The altar frontals are of elaborate ancient embroidery, English or possible Flemish of the 15th Century. The needlework is technically known as "Opus Plumarium" and includes pomegranate flowers with diversified centres, formed by chevrons curiously raised by cords underneath them. Conspicuously shown are figures of the Cherubim and scrolls with the words, "Sanctus, Sanctus." This embroidery originally formed part of a cope found hidden in a box beneath the pulpit and was adapted into three altar frontals by the Sisters of St. Mary's Home, Wrantage.

The majority of the stained glass windows speak for themselves in regard to the subjects they are intended to depict. St. Oswald of Northumbria is the central figure in the war memorial window which was installed in 1948 at a cost of £44 14s. 6d. St. Oswald was born in 605 A.D. and was the son of Ethelfrith. When his father was killed by Redwald, and himself and his brother driven north, they took refuge with the Scots at Iona where he was converted. Caedwalla, the Christian Welsh King, out of hatred for the race of Ethelfrith, made an alliance with the ferocious pagan king of Mercia, Penda. Against them the joint forces of Oswald led a small host, and before going into battle at Heawenfield, a few miles north of Hexham, he set a large cross as a standard and bade his men to fall on their knees and pray in the words which the visitor will see at the foot of the window: "Let us all kneel and beseech the Living God to defend us from the haughty and fierce enemy for He knows that we have undertaken a just war for the safety of our nation." Oswald was victorious, the enemy utterly defeated and the Welsh king slain. In 642 war broke out again between him and Penda. Near Oswestry, Oswald was defeated and killed.

Before leaving the church, please remember that the maintenance of the fabric of the church is expensive and a generous donation towards the restoration fund would be much appreciated. As you leave please close the screen in the porch which is there to prevent house martens from nesting in the porch and making a mess with their droppings.

Crown House

On the corner opposite the church is **Crown House** which was, until the mid-1990s, a blacksmith's and formerly the **Crown Inn**. The first mention of the property as a beer house appears to have been in 1857. The Bridgwater Mercury in September that year reported that at the County Magistrates' Court,

> "Mr. Smith applied for a new licence on behalf of Mr. John Gully, keeper of the Crown beerhouse, Chedzoy. He informed the court that the parish of Chedzoy was almost exclusively the property of Mr. Porter who was represented by the steward, the rector of the parish, the guardians, the churchwardens, the overseers and the respectable yeomen of the locality - a memorial signed by whom was presented. The establishment of an on licensed inn would be a great accommodation to the inhabitants of Chedzoy as there was no other place. The application was granted."

John Gully was living at the premises in 1857 and may have been born there. He appears on the 1841, 1851 and 1861 Census returns which show he was a carpenter born in Chedzoy about 1823. He was the only son of John Gully, also a carpenter, who was born in Chedzoy in 1790.

It was not long after the granting of a full licence that disorder was reported at the premises. In June 1858,

> "Thomas Broomfield, a morose-looking fellow, was summoned for assaulting Aquila, the wife of Mr. John Gully, jun., innkeeper of Chedzoy. Mr. Smith appeared to support the complainant. On the evening of the 14th of June, defendant and some others were drinking at Mr. Gully's, and a dispute arose as to the quality of cider which had been supplied to them. Broomfield used bad language to Mrs. Gully, who endeavoured to turn him out of the bar, upon which he struck her a violent blow in the side. Another complaint was also made against the defendant for assaulting Mr. Gully, and

in this case a man named George Giles also figured as a defendant. The offence was clearly proved. Broomfield was fined 10s. and costs, and Giles was ordered to pay 5s. and costs."

The Crown was the scene of a crime on New Year's Eve 1859. In May 1860 the Bridgwater Mercury reported,

"Henry Reed, an ex-policeman, was charged with stealing six loaves of bread, of the value of 1s. 6d., the property of Frank Morris, baker, of Westonzoyland. Mr. Morris stated that on the evening of 31st December he left his cart containing bread in the barton of Mr. Gulley (sic), innkeeper, of Chedzoy. Half and hour after he had seen the bread all right, six loaves had disappeared. The day subsequently, the prisoner came to him, and said he knew who stole the bread, declaring it was a man named Giles; but in a few minutes afterwards, he said it was himself who had committed the theft, and asked for forgiveness. Witness refused to forgive, and told the prisoner he would have a warrant for him the next day. The next day the accused left the place, and witness had not seem him again till last week, when Superintendent Dowde gave him notice that he had been apprehended. Mr. Jno. Gully (sic) said that his son heard some one at the cart on the night of the 31st, and on going to the spot they met the prisoner coming from the direction of a hayrick. In the hayrick the loaves were found concealed the same night. - The prisoner denied the charge at first, but pleaded guilty rather than have the case committed to sessions. - Superintendent Dowde informed the magistrates that the prisoner's character was bad. Some time ago he was wanted to give evidence in some cases of cider selling without a licence, but decamped on the parties charged giving him £5 or £6 to go. He had a warrant out against him in consequence. - The prisoner said this was untrue, and that he had never been before a magistrate previously in his life. The Bench sentenced the accused to six weeks' imprisonment. [The lightness of this sentence, as compared with that of three months passed a few minutes before upon the boy Kerle, caused some surprise amongst the people assembled in the court.]"

This latter case was that of James Kerle, aged 10, of Othery, who had been sentenced to three months' imprisonment with hard labour for stealing 13 eggs.

A disturbance took place in November 1867 which may have involved George Jeanes, a 19 year old labourer - there was no James family in Chedzoy.

"George James, a labourer, was charged with being drunk and disorderly and refusing to quit a public house at Chedzoy, when requested to do so, also with unlawfully damaging a coat the property of Mr. Jno. (sic) Palfrey, the landlord, and injuring it to the extent of 2s. 6d. When asked if he had done this defendant replied, 'Dash'd if I know whether I did it or no - I was so tipsy.' This was an admission of drunkenness, and Mr. Palfrey said his coat was torn by the defendant when he was assisting to remove him from the house. - Defendant: He caught hold of my waistcoat and broke it, and then I caught hold of him. - Defendant was fined 10s. and costs for the first offence, in default 14 days, and 6d. and costs, besides the amount of the damages, in default seven days, for the second offence."

John Palfrey found himself a defendant in November 1869 when he

"was charged with having in his possession six imperfect measures. - He pleaded guilty, but said he was entirely ignorant of the fact. Fined 10s. and costs."

Long one of the places for social gatherings in the village, it was also the venue for more serious events. In March 1871 the Bridgwater Mercury reported an incident of a type which, sadly, still occurs to this day.

"An Inquest was held in the Crown Inn on Tuesday by Mr. Munckton, the district coroner, on the body of George Fry, four years of age, the son of a labourer (who was not further identified) who died on the previous Friday. On Thursday afternoon the deceased and other children were left at home for a few minutes by themselves, and in the temporary absence of their mother, a brother of the deceased lighted some paper, and with it caught the clothes of the deceased on fire. He ran out of doors screaming, and Mrs. Conduit, a neighbour, seeing his clothes in flames, ran to this assistance. She quickly extinguished the fire, but not before the poor child had been seriously burnt in various parts of his body. He was taken into the house, and Mr. H.B. Hurman, surgeon, of Bridgwater, was sent for. The deceased expired on the following morning, and Mr. Hurman said death was caused by a shock to the nervous system. The jury returned a verdict of 'Accidental Death'."

In June 1872 a short report was published in the Bridgwater Mercury:

"Last week a labourer named Day, who was ill in bed, asked his daughter to get his razor for him to look at. She did so, and he then desired her to go downstairs for a cup of tea. On her return she perceived blood on his fingers and afterwards discovered that he had cut his throat. He has since been greatly prostrated."

Two weeks later a further report appeared.

"An inquest was held at the Crown Inn before Mr. W.W. Munckton, Esq., coroner, on the body of John Day labourer, 70 years of age, who died as a result of self-inflicted injuries. Fanny Day (Francis Day, 62, according to the Census), wife of the deceased, deposed that on Thursday, 30th May, she left him at seven o'clock in bed. He had been suffering from coughs and rheumatism, and had seemed lost at times. Just before leaving the house, the deceased asked her to bring his razor to him. He said, 'I want to give it to my son-in-law.' She went out and about ten o'clock was told by Mary Ann Conduit (58) that something had happened at home. On seeing her husband he said, 'I wish the razor had cut as it ought to; I should have stretched out before this time.'

He continued very wild until his death on Saturday last. Charles Conduit (63) said on being sent for on the 30th ultimo., he went to the deceased and found him lying on his back in bed with his throat cut. The razor was lying by his side, open and bloody. Witness said, 'For God's sake, what have you been about?' Deceased replied, 'What odds is that, go out of the room.' Rev. George Mullins (sic), rector of Chedzoy, deposed that on hearing of the occurrence he went to the deceased who refused to have the wound dressed. Witness sent for Mr. H.B. Hurman of Bridgwater. On speaking to the deceased, the latter told him to mind his own business and not to speak so fast. He appeared very irritable, but rational. - Mr. H.B. Hurman, surgeon, of Bridgwater said the wound was about an inch in length. He continued to attend the deceased, and saw him three days before his death, when he was in a very collapsed and bloodless state. Witness thought his mind was weakened, more or less, by old age. - The jury, after some deliberation, returned a verdict of suicide whilst in a state of temporary insanity."

John Palfrey was still the licensee in July 1871 but had left by June 1873 when the new licensee was in trouble.

"Henry Haines, landlord of a public house in Chedzoy, pleaded guilty to a charge of keeping open his house during prohibited hours on 22nd June, his excuse being that it was the morning succeeding a club anniversary, and that he could not keep his people out. Fined 14s. (70p.) and costs, the licence not being endorsed.

Presumably this was a reference to the 11th anniversary of the Chedzoy Friendly Society.

Three weeks later,

"Joseph Lovibond (24), Frederick Stone (22), William Bennett (35), George Day (41) and Charles Pounsford (58) were charged with being found on certain licensed premises at an hour when they should have been closed. Stone was stated to be at Dartmoor with the militia, 'serving the Queen,' but all the other defendants pleaded guilty. P.C. Salmon said that about half past ten o'clock on Sunday morning, the 22nd June, he visited the 'Crown Inn' at Chedzoy, and saw the defendants go out the back door and into a stable. On the table he saw part of a pint of porter. The defendants were not in the least drunk. The landlord was summoned and fined for keeping open his house at the last petty session. - The defendants were told that they each incurred a penalty not exceeding 40s. (£2), but as this was the first offence of the kind they were only fined 1s. (5p.) each and costs, together 6s."

Another case featuring the premises occurred in March 1874:

"John Rainey (23, a carpenter) was charged with refusing to quit the Crown Inn at Chedzoy when requested to do so by the landlord. Complainant said that the defendant had several times come into his house, and behaved in a disorderly manner. On one occasion he had insisted on playing a concertina, although he (witness) objected; and on another occasion he and three others went into the passage, and one of them, at least, if not the whole, was guilty of beastly conduct. On the Thursday in question the defendant did not behave improperly, but he refused to go out of the house when ordered to do so. Witness ordered him out on that occasion for his previous conduct. The case was dismissed, the complainant being told that he was only justified in ordering a man to leave for misconduct at the time. - Defendant, who denied the complainant's allegations, was cautioned as to his future conduct and advised not to enter the house again."

No location is given for this September 1874 report, but in view of previous accounts, the Crown Inn seems likely.

"On Thursday an inquest was held at this place (Chedzoy) by Mr. Munckton, coroner, on the body of Samuel Palmer, labourer, aged 38 years, who died on the previous Tuesday. - Lewis Durston, labourer, said about half past eleven o'clock on Tuesday morning he saw the deceased in the stable at Mr. Parfitt's farm, and near his house. They drank some cider together, and deceased then appeared to be well. He left deceased there cleaning harness. About ten minutes past two o'clock witness again went to the stable, and found the deceased lying on the face on the ground in one of the stalls. He was quite dead. His feet were towards the manger, and his head in the drain. He (witness) went to Mr. Parfitt, who came and saw deceased, after which the body was removed to his house. - Henry Bailey, working for Mr. Parfitt, said he last saw the deceased alive about five minutes to one o'clock on Tuesday, when he was cleaning some harness. He then appeared well. About ten minutes past two o'clock the last witness came to him and said Bown (sic) was lying dead in the stable. - Mary Stone (67), who laid out the body, said there were no marks of violence about it. He had some old marks on the left side of his face. - This was all the evidence, and the jury returned a verdict of 'Death from natural causes'."

By January 1877 Alfred Salmon was the licensee of the Crown Inn and at the time of the 1881 Census he was described as a butcher and inn keeper, so a sale which took place there in February 1877 does not appear to have been of his property. The items indicate the typical contents of a small dairy at that time.

"Mr. Boys will sell by auction at Salmon's Crown Inn the undermentioned superior and valuable DAIRY UTENSILS, valuable bay hack mare, spring and other carts, harness, sheep dog and other effects, removed to the above named premises for convenience of absolute sale. viz., two capital single iron screw presses, almost equal to new, by Woodland and Day respectively, 70-gallon cheese tub, 3 milk pails, 13 milk pans, 2 truckle tin vats, 2 screw wood vats, 2 other ditto followers, butter churn, cheese turner, curd grinder, curd range and breaker, 2 tub horses, vat hoops, whey shute, lot cheese boards, forms, rail back seat, 4-prong fork, stove, wheelbarrow, pair trucks, ladders, calves' stage, pigs' troughs, pigs' bed, set light cart harness, set breeching ditto, capital spring cart, in excellent condition; also a very useful bay hack mare, about 15 hands 2 inches, fast, good in saddle and harness, a good sheep dog, &c."

Alfred Salmon found himself in Bridgwater County Court in April 1878.

"JEFFERY DENHAM v. SALMON. The plaintiff, landlord of the White Lion, and a general dealer, in Bridgwater, sued the defendant, landlord of the Crown Inn, Chedzoy, for £3 damages alleged to have been sustained in consequence of a breach of contract to deliver a certain quantity of apples which plaintiff alleged he had purchased. The case for the plaintiff was that he met the defendant and Mr. C. Babbage, the auctioneer, on the Westonzoyland-road; that plaintiff was then informed that the defendant had purchased at a sale by auction Mr. Tazewell's orchard of apples, consisting of about forty bags of Morgan sweets, and a like quantity of Hermon pippins; that plaintiff agreed to buy the whole at 6s. 6d. per bag, the former to be delivered forthwith and the latter as soon as ripe; and that the 'pippins' were not delivered at all. In consequence the plaintiff purchased elsewhere, at an advanced market price, resulting in the loss of the sum claimed. - The defence was that there was no bargain to deliver the 'pippins' at all, and that there were, in fact, only 19 bags of that description in the orchard. - Several witnesses were examined on both sides and the evidence was very contradictory. - His Honour remarked that he had no doubt of the intention of all the witnesses to speak the truth, but as the statements made were so much at variance he should like to look over his notes at leisure, and he should therefore defer judgement until the next court."

Unfortunately, subsequent County Court reports made no further reference to the case so the outcome is unknown.

In May 1879 the premises were again mentioned in the court columns of the Bridgwater Mercury.

"Joseph Porter (31, a groom, living in Front Street) was summoned for refusing to quit the Crown Inn, Chedzoy. - Mr. A. Salmon, landlord of the Crown Inn said the defendant was 'chaffing' some of the other persons in the house and making a row. - He refused to go, and had to be put out. - Defendant said that he was not making any noise. The landlord began the 'chaff' over a pig's head he had for sale. The landlord bet him sixpence the head was not of a certain weight. Witness accepted the bet and lost. - The magistrates dismissed the case."

Alfred Salmon was still at the premises when the 1881 Census was taken but had left by February 1890.

"John Wilkins, labourer, Chedzoy, was summoned for being drunk and refusing to quit the licensed premises of the Crown Inn, Chedzoy. - Mr. Thomas Pent, landlord of the Crown Inn, stated the defendant came to his house about half past seven on the day in question and asked for a glass of beer, but he refused to supply him with it as he was drunk. Defendant then became very disorderly and witness requested him to leave, but he remained in the house until ten o'clock. - Defendant, against whom there were several previous convictions, was fined 15s. and costs, or one month's imprisonment with hard labour."

John Wilkins would have even more convictions later.

When the 1891 Census was taken, Thomas Spence was the licensee of the Crown. A short report published in the Bridgwater Mercury noted that a meeting was held at the Crown Inn to form a branch of the Bridgwater Equalization Order of Druids - a Friendly Society.

"The meeting was fairly well attended." It was agreed to form a Lodge at a later date, but no further mention appeared in the paper. The licensee didn't spend all his time behind the bar: in September 1892 it was reported that "Thomas Spence, of this village, recently dug a stalk of potatoes which weighed 11 lbs. (5 kg.)."

He was in the news again two months later.

"Edward England Wilkins, labourer, was summoned for being drunk on the premises of Thomas Spence at Chedzoy. Defendant on being charged with the offence said, 'Gentlemen, I beg to be excused.' (Laughter.)

The Magistrates' Clerk: You are drunk now as it is.

Defendant (who had been described as 'James' Wilkins): Begging your pardon, gentlemen, there is no such man.

The Magistrates' Clerk: No such man as who?

Defendant: No such man as James Wilkins. My name is Edward England Wilkins.

The Magistrates' Clerk: Well then, Edward England Wilkins, you are charged with this offence.

The defendant, whose manner was very strange, again muttered something about being 'excused.'

Thomas Spence deposed that the defendant came to his house in the evening and ordered some 'half and half.' He (witness) refused to serve him afterwards until he had paid for it, and defendant then became very abusive, and refused to leave the premises. - The Magistrates inflicted a penalty of £1 and costs."

The inn also featured in breaches of public health. In January 1893 the Bridgwater Mercury reported that

"Walter Palmer and Henry Chick, brickyard labourers, were summoned for having exposed for sale certain herrings which were unfit for human food. Defendants pleaded not guilty. Mr. W. Coles, Inspector of Nuisances for the Rural Sanitary Authority deposed the defendants came into the Crown Inn with the herrings. Witness asked the price of the herrings and was told 3d. (1.5p.) per dozen. He examined them and it was his opinion they were unfit for human food. The defendants stated they had bought them the previous day and hawked them all that day as well. The Chairman said the Bench would deal leniently with the defendants, taking into consideration that they were civil when the fish were seized and that they had not known that the herrings were unfit for food. They would be fined 30s. (£1.50) each, including costs."

On 3rd October 1894 the Bridgwater Mercury carried a report in their Bridgwater County Petty Sessions column under the heading "Adjourned Licensing Session" concerning two public houses. That part of the report of interest here reads,

"The Bench proceeded again to consider the licence of the Crown Inn, Chedzoy to John Thomas Gregory which had been adjourned because the tenant had not taken out the spirit licence. Mr. P.O.H. Reed appeared for the owner of the house and stated that the full licence would now be taken out. He stated that the reason the spirit licence was not taken out last year was because the Excise suddenly raised the assessment from £11 to £17. He also mentioned that this was the only fully licensed house in Chedzoy. He handed into the Bench two memorials from the parish of Chedzoy, asking that the licence might be renewed, the persons signing it including the vicar, the overseer and the churchwarden of the parish. The Chairman, after a long consultation with his colleagues, said that the Bench had given a great deal of consideration to this case, and they felt they ought to be on the look-out that their licences were not in excess of the requirements of the population. The majority of the Bench had come to the conclusion that as this was the only fully licensed house in the village, the full licence should be granted on this occasion."

Despite the support of the dignitaries of the parish, there were problems with the Crown Inn. In April 1896 the Bridgwater Mercury covered a case of assault.

"Thomas Giles, labourer, appeared in custody on a charge of unlawfully and maliciously wounding John Stone, a labourer. On Saturday evening a little after ten o'clock he was near a blacksmith's shop looking after some sheep when he saw the prisoner Giles who came from the Crown Inn. He was drinky (sic). Prisoner tried to get over the hurdles into the pen but he refused to let him do it, so prisoner fell down in the road and got up again and said to him, 'You —-, you shall have it for this.' Prisoner came to him and held up his hand and cut his (prosecutor's) thumb with a knife. Prosecutor got inside a gate and prisoner said, 'I'll let your heart out with him' - 'him' evidently referring to the knife." John Stone later attended Bridgwater Infirmary and required five stitches to a wound. Emma Stone was upstairs and heard her husband say, "You have stabbed me." "She went outside and said to prisoner, 'You drunken blackguard, you have stabbed him.' Prisoner replied, 'I'll serve you the same.' Prisoner was drinky and excitable." He was later arrested by Superintendent Vowles and committed to the Quarter Sessions in custody pending sureties. Eight weeks later he appeared at that court when he was found not guilty and discharged.

In May 1897 the Bridgwater Mercury reported that

"John Wilkins, labourer, was summoned for having been disorderly and refusing to quit the licensed premises of the Crown Inn. William Joel Blackmore, landlord, stated that the defendant came to the Inn, and shortly afterwards commenced to curse the complainant's wife, but did not know the reason. Witness requested him to leave, but defendant said he should do nothing of the kind and that he intended staying until ten o'clock. Witness did not like to pull him out and came to Superintendent Vowles. There had been two or three little rows before with the defendant, and he thought it was time to stop it. There were several previous convictions against defendant, and he was fined £1 and costs or 21 days."

John Wilkins returned to court later in the year when he was charged with carrying a gun without a licence. He had previously been convicted of a similar offence and on this occasion was fined £2 10s. and costs.

But it was not only customers at the Crown Inn who caused problems. In June 1897 the Mercury carried a report under the headline, "Alleged Inhuman Conduct by a Husband." The important details from this lengthy article were that

"William Joel Blackmore, until recently landlord of the Crown Inn, was summoned by his wife, Elizabeth Ann Blackmore, for being guilty of persistent cruelty towards her, causing her to leave him and live separately from him and she asked for a separation order."

The couple had been married for seven years and had three children, the youngest being 18 months old.

"About Michaelmas last year defendant took the Crown Inn, Chedzoy and up to a few days ago had continued to be the tenant there. Defendant's conduct towards his wife since then, and up to the present time had been - he would use as mild a word as he could - most vile and brutal."

The wife had from time to time had black eyes and been kicked out of bed. The husband got drunk daily, and often threatened to put an end to his wife's life, so she left him. Joel Blackmore went to the United States and sent her just 10s. (50p.) in two months. The case was adjourned for a period and eventually withdrawn as the husband had agreed to a separation on private terms. On 1st September the licence of the Crown Inn was transferred from Joel Blackmore to William Dudderidge.

Trouble continued at the premises. In December 1897 the Mercury reported that

"Henry Jeanes and James Tamlyn (probably a mistake for Tambling), labourers, were charged with being disorderly and refusing to quit the Crown Inn when requested to do so. They pleaded guilty to being disorderly, but not to refusing to quit. Emily Dudderidge, wife of William Dudderidge, landlady of the Crown Inn, said the two defendants were in the house, and were very quiet until one of the defendants knocked the other's hat off and they began quarrelling. She told them to stop or go outside, but they would not, and she went to fetch her husband and they then went away. Fined 5s. and costs."

In January 1898 it was reported that

"James Tambling, mason's labourer, of Chedzoy, was summoned for being unlawfully on the premises of the Crown Inn. P.C. Carter said whilst standing outside he heard someone walking on their toes and a minute afterwards he heard the person coming in the direction of the front door, which was open. Tambling came out and when outside witness asked him what he was doing in the inn. Defendant said his mother was bad, and he came after some brandy for her. When asked to let witness see the brandy, defendant replied he had none. Fined 10s. and costs."

In August the same year,

"John Wilkins, labourer, was summoned for being disorderly on the licensed premises of the Crown Inn on 26th July and a like offence on August 3rd. On 26th July he was under the influence of drink, and the landlord refused to supply him with any, and requested him to leave the house. Defendant refused to do so, and threatened to knock Dudderidge's head off. He remained there about two hours and he was a source of annoyance to the customers. On 3rd August he again came to the Inn and made a great noise and used very objectionable language. Superintendent Vowles intimated there were twelve previous convictions against defendant, including two for being drunk and disorderly and refusing to quit the same house. The man was a pest to the parish, and they were very glad when he was away from the neighbourhood. He had been working in Wales and when he was away they had no rows out there. The Chairman pointed out that there was probably no one with such a record as defendant had, and, having regard to his previous conduct, he would be fined 30s. and costs in each case, or two months' hard labour."

On 18th September 1899 a fire occurred at the inn, and although the fire itself was not reported in the Bridgwater Mercury, events later the same day were given extensive coverage in the court columns.

"James Tamlyn (Tambling), labourer, was charged with being disorderly on licensed premises and refusing to quit when requested to do so by the landlord. On the morning in question defendant came to his house at half past seven o'clock and remained there for an hour. There had been a fire in the house and a lot of people were there. Defendant came in noisy and presently witness saw him strike a man named John Wilkins." After further evidence the defence explained, "There had been a fire at the Crown Inn and there were many people present who had been served with a great deal of drink for services rendered during the fire. The defendant went to the house for the purpose of getting one or two persons in the house to go to work." A struggle then took place. The defence said that, "Several persons on the premises at the time were very drunk, one of them having to be carried away, the landlord lending an overcoat in which the man was wrapped up." John Wilkins complained that, "Defendant struck him between the two eyes, giving him a pair of black 'uns, without any reason."

Tamlyn was convicted of this offence and fined five shillings and costs.

The Bench then heard an application to transfer the licence from William Dudderidge to William Counsell. Referring to the previous case, Mr. P.O.H. Reed explained that the fire

"caused much excitement and a large crowd gathered and assisted in extinguishing the fire. No doubt Dudderidge, not as a licensed victualler, but for the assistance so rendered, gave the people outside some drink. He did not sell it, and apparently those outside the house took more than their share, but Dudderidge informed him that so much excitement prevailed that someone or other in the crowd got into the house and stole some whisky, and with the drink given them and his whisky some drunkenness did take place." The Chairman asked Superintendent Vowles what was the general character of the Crown Inn? "It had been a troublesome house from time to time, but there were a troublesome lot of people living about there." The Chairman concluded, "The house is now on trial and the fresh applicant was on trial as the holder of the licence, and if he permitted any more rows the licence would be taken away."

They agreed to the transfer and renewal of the licence.

The change of licensee did nothing to improve matters. In December 1900,

"Bessie Reed, landlady of the Crown Inn, was charged with having been found drunk on licensed premises. P.C. White said he went into a little room where he saw the defendant. She was drunk. There were three men in the room at the same time - Fry, Brake and Wheeler," who were not further identified. "Fry and Wheeler were under the influence of drink. Witness then spoke to defendant and said, 'Mrs. Reed, this is pretty lively here tonight.' She tried to stand up but fell back in her seat. The defence said it was clear from the policeman's evidence that he did not see Mrs. Reed for any length of time and yet the constable said the landlady was drunk. What were his reasons for coming to such a conclusion? Firstly, because he could not understand what she said and, secondly, because she attempted to rise and fell back again in her seat. The landlady was very exhausted and tired. She only had one glass of porter. She had never been drunk in her life. Fined 10s. and costs."

This report was followed immediately by a second one!

"Sergeant Blacker and P.C. White visited the Crown. Mrs.

Reed was sitting in a chair. She was drunk. The landlady's face was very flushed and she had every appearance of a person who was drunk. P.C. White on 8th December saw the barman, William Thomas. Defendant pressed witness to have some whisky but he refused and told defendant he was drunk. Defendant also apologised to the customers for witness being present. Fined 7s. 6d. and costs."

Village tradition has it that the inn burnt down in the early 1900s and that Rev. Mullens was not sorry to see the demise of the Crown as its proximity to the church led on some occasions to some not altogether desirable behaviour in his congregation. The previous owner, Percy Tucker (1910-1997), who was born in the house, said the inn could not get its licence back because it was too near the church and too noisy, although the "Abstract of Title" shows that the property was sold by Messrs. Starkey, Knight and Ford as it "had become unsuitable for the purpose of the company."

Investigations have failed to substantiate the traditional story and it appears that the fire of village mythology was probably the one which took place in 1899. It seems that all the disorderly behaviour led to the closure. In September 1901 a licence for the inn was refused by the local magistrates. The Bridgwater Mercury reported that the Chairman said,

"We have carefully considered the case, and most of us have heard the cases preferred against the house during the year, and we are of the opinion that the character of the house is so bad that we can't renew the licence. Moreover, we think the population is well enough supplied by having one public house. There is no necessity for this one and therefore we shall not renew the licence."

The cases of the drunkenness of Bessie Reed and the barman were cited as examples of the problems as were the other cases mentioned above.

Before the Bench reached their decision the Clerk had asked Superintendent Vowles, "What is the general character of the house?" to which he replied, "Before the present landlady went there the house was of a disorderly character, but during the time he had been there it has been conducted very orderly and well, and there was not a complaint except at the time it was transferred to Reed." He stated that "There is one beer-house besides this one; this is the only spirit house."

The following month an appeal against this refusal was heard at the Quarter Sessions sitting at Wells. Counsel for the Justices said,

"One after another the licensees had to be got out of the house, and there were a number of convictions with which the house was concerned. The culminating point was reached when the temporary licensee in December 1900, Bessie Reed, was convicted in January for being drunk in the house on 8th December and on 21st December. On the same day William Thomas, Reed's manager, was also convicted of being drunk on the premises on 8th December."

The appeal was dismissed and there were no further press reports of events at the Crown Inn, although in August 1904 the death of Bessie Reed was reported. She had been found dead in her bedroom, but no address was included in the report of the inquest. The cause of death was cancer of the throat exacerbated by self-neglect. Speaking in 1955, Mr. B.T. Jeanes recalled that Fred 'Butcher' Stone claimed the distinction of having been served with the last drink at the Crown Inn "before the licence of that hostelry was surrendered."

Walter Tucker, Percy's father, bought the former inn in 1905 for £205, securing a mortgage of £160. Walter was well known in the district as he used to "walk the entire" - an uncastrated or "entire" stallion - which he owned, taking it from farm to farm in order to service mares. The animal was always walked and not used for drawing a cart. Walter fell foul of the law in September 1906: it would appear that he was goaded into reacting to long-standing provocation. The Mercury reported that

"Walter Tucker of Chedzoy, was charged at Bawdrip with assaulting Felix Peppard and Adolphus Tippetts. There was a cross summons. Peppard and Tippetts and two others were walking in a field. Tucker was drinky and shouted to Peppard, 'I want you, you —-!' Peppard replied, 'What for?' Without explanation Tucker went towards Peppard and struck him in the head twice, knocking him down. Tippetts, seeing Tucker about to strike Peppard again, simply went and took Tucker by the arm and waistcoat and pushed him aside. Tucker alleged that Peppard had been to Mrs. Collins at Pizey and told her that he would not give her more than £10 for a colt. Mr. Aldridge, on behalf of Tucker, said his client had had cause to complain against Peppard who, every time he met him, made use of some insulting remark with regard to a colt belonging to Mrs. Collins. Tucker was fined 2s. 6d. and costs."

The other case was dismissed.

Walter was in trouble again in May 1908 when he appeared before Bridgwater County Magistrates' Court.

"Walter Tucker of Chedzoy was summoned for having been drunk in charge of a horse. P.C. Gard stated he saw the defendant leading an entire horse. Defendant staggered from the horse against two men who were in his company. Witness told defendant that he was drunk and not fit to be in charge of the horse. Defendant replied that he was not drunk. Witness asked him to hand the reins to another man, which he refused to do. Witness took the reins from the defendant who removed his coat and wanted to fight. Day (no Christian name reported) took charge of the horse and defendant went on his way home staggering about the road. Richard Stone of Westonzoyland; Edward Heale (sic), farmer, of Chedzoy; Ernest Haynes, machine owner, of Chedzoy; and Leonard Ashford, farmer's son, of Chedzoy gave evidence, all stating that defendant had a drop to drink. The Bench fined defendant 10s. and costs."

Percy Tucker, Walter's son, could repair almost anything and in 1985, with his brother James 'Jim' Tucker (1898-1986), was responsible for the design and manufacture of the wrought iron gates which now grace the entrance to the churchyard. The gates are a memorial to Edwin 'Ted' Triggol who lived at Frys Farm.

Speaking in 1991, Percy recalled his childhood.

> "You didn't dare stay away from church in those days. One of my friends didn't go to an afternoon service and the vicar, Mr. Mullens, asked him why. He said that his cousin had come to visit but Mr. Mullens said that was no excuse and if he missed another service he could stay away altogether. He never missed another one! Mr. Mullens did a great deal for the village. He gave the hall in 1914 and laid on all sorts of treats for the young people, like tea parties and outings. At the Rectory they had three indoor servants and two gardeners and he used to ride about in a four wheeled coach, driven by a coachman in a top hat. He had six daughters and when they held tennis parties we children used to scramble to collect the balls for them because at the end of the day he always gave us sixpence." One of Percy's favourite stories about Rev. Mullens was that on one occasion the reverend gentlemen saw one of his flock who was rather the worse for drink. "Drunk again?" remarked the Rector, "Yes, vicar, so am I," was the reply!

Percy's sister, Miss Daisy Tucker (1899-1995), played the church organ for 40 years.

> "I learned to play the organ from Mrs. Mullens and I also played the piano for dances in the village hall. When the lads in their boots became too lively Mr. Mullens used to say, 'Stop playing, I don't want the floor damaged!' Everyone went to church in those days and on special occasions I have seen it so full you could hardly move down the aisles."

It seems that Mr. Mullens was also very concerned about the morals of the young people: if he saw a boy kiss a girl at events he would close the village hall for the evening and send everyone home!

Ward Lane

Next to the church, **CHURCH COTTAGE** is also much older than it appears from the exterior, dating from about 1650. Built of cob, the previous owners exposed the beams and an inglenook and revealed a portion of the cob construction for their visitors. In September 1892 the property was sold by auction at the Crown Inn when it was described as being a

> "Desirable double cottage, outbuildings and garden situate on the south side of the churchyard in Chedzoy, numbered 72 on the tithe map of that parish and now in the occupation of Mr. Francis Bennett and Miss Emma Conduit at a gross rental of £6 10s. a year. The property has a good frontage against the roadway and being in the centre of the village will always command tenants."

The sale itself was not reported.

Ben Hooper recalls that in the early years of the 20th Century the cottage was occupied by Fanny Bell (probably Frances Bell, born 1855) who was well known to the children as she kept a parrot as a pet. On one occasion the coalman visited the house and called out, "Any coal today, Missus?" and left without making a delivery after the bird replied, "Not today!"

Fanny Bell was also known to the magistrates and appeared before them in August 1899.

> "Fanny Bell, laundress, was summoned by Amelia Stone, seamstress, for using threats. Since July last year the defendant had been constantly annoying and threatening complainant. In March last complainant was prostrated with a serious attack of diphtheria, and during her illness the defendant went into a public house in Chedzoy and stated that if she (complainant) did not die from diphtheria she would 'do' for her when she became well. The complainant went into her house but defendant came up to her brother, Albert Stone, and in a very filthy manner stated that complainant was discharged from the Bridgwater Infirmary with a disease and if she came out of the door she would knock her —- head off. The Bench dismissed the case, advising the defendant to keep her mouth shut in future."

Possibly the oldest building in the village, apart from the church, and certainly the quaintest, is **MYRTLE COTTAGE**, still with its thatched roof. It is thought to date from the 17th Century. In the late 1960s the cottage was still a shop with a counter and brass scales. It had been a shop since at least the 1910s, where generations of Chedzoy children had bought their sweets and bottles of pop. The floor was cobbled stone and there was at that time a story about a tunnel under the floor but, as with other similar stories, none was found during the deep excavations which were necessary for mains drainage in the village. In those days the cottage was still lit by oil lamps, but shortly afterwards electricity was installed. The cottage was modernised after the death of the last shop keeper, Mrs. Bessie Conduit (1882-1970).

Mrs. Conduit was a witness in a case reported in the Bridgwater Mercury in May 1952.

> "The village blacksmith's dog at Chedzoy bit a little girl as she was leaving a shop, it was alleged at Bridgwater County Magistrates' Court. Percy Tucker of Crown House pleaded not guilty to failing to keep a dangerous dog under proper control. Nine-year old Carol Hooper of Cadbury House, Chedzoy said she was leaving The Stores when a dog rushed from Mr. Tucker's yard and bit her on the leg. Mrs. Bessie Conduit of The Stores, Chedzoy, said she heard the little girl screaming so terribly that she came out of her shop to find out the cause. Mr. Pardoe (for the defence) : 'Have you during

Myrtle Cottage.
This view of the rear was taken in 1971.
Courtesy of Duncan Bouchier.

Myrtle Cottage, November 1991.
Rethatching under way, using Hungarian reed.
Photograph by Muriel Brown.

the past ten years made every complaint possible against Mr. Tucker?' 'No, I have not.' When the witness admitted not being on speaking terms with defendant, Mr. Pardoe asked, 'Is it because you are not on speaking terms that you do everything possible to annoy him?' Witness replied that she did not. P.C. Bradley said there were two small puncture wounds with bruising on the little girl's knee. Defendant told him, 'It is not true she was bitten. Mrs. Conduit it always complaining about something.' ... Having found the case proved, the magistrates made an order for the dog to be kept under control and ordered payment of £1 1s. 6d. costs."

Just past Church Cottage and Myrtle Cottage, on the left, **WHITE HART COTTAGES** were once a cider house, known as the White Hart, according to Percy Tucker. The brick wall adjoining the churchyard was supposed to have been the wall of the skittle alley. Mr. Tucker said that in about 1801 this had been the site of the rectory, but the present building dates from about 1898. However another source, possibly more authoritative, says that the cottages were built by George Hunt for his daughter, Mrs. Theresa Hook, and her sister. This seems more likely as there was, at one time, a communicating door between the two properties. Hilda Hunt, Theresa's first child, was born in 1892 in White Hart Cottages, so it would seem that the building is older than Mr. Tucker suggested. Mrs. Hook's husband, Ernest, was related to the Hook family in Front Street and also the family of the same name who established the company in Eastover, Bridgwater which still bears the family name.

With his parents and brothers, Ben Hooper moved into No. 2 in about 1909: No. 1 was occupied by the Pinchen family. There was one tap outside and this served as the water supply for both families. Ben's mother, Sophia, used to clean the church for the sum of £1 per year, which was paid to her in sixpence's by Joseph Ashford. Ben's father was a bellringer and also the grave digger and cut hair for the princely sum of 3d. Ben and his three brothers all sang in the church choir until Ben "graduated" to pumping the bellows for the organ.

On leaving school Ben started work as an apprentice with Robert Hanham, builder, of Quantock View: one of his first construction jobs was working on The Bungalow, the wooden building still standing in Ward Lane. Later, in order to double his pay from £1 10s. to £3 per week, Ben left Hanham's to work as a painter and decorator for Henry Pollard in Bridgwater. He was told, "You won't know enough for Pollard's, you won't stay long." The prediction came true as Ben only worked there for the next eighteen years!

A notice of a sale by auction appeared in the Bridgwater Mercury in May 1915 when it was indicated that one of the cottages was occupied by George Bennett: no sale report was published. Half of the property was in the news in April 1963 when it was reported,

"Mr. A.E. Ashford of Croftside, Chedzoy, was granted an order at Bridgwater County Court for possession within six weeks of a cottage. Mr. Ashford told His Honour Judge Paton that he was the tenant of the cottage - at 2 White Hart Cottages, Chedzoy - and he had sub-let it to a Mr. and Mrs. Snowball on condition that Mrs. Snowball worked in the witness's house as a daily help. She did so for a while, but in April 1962 she became ill and stopped work. Mr. Ashford said he had given the Snowballs notice to quit because Mrs. Snowball had a newly born baby. She was unable to work, and there was no one to assist in the farmhouse. He had received 14 or 15 applications for the job but the accommodation was required. Mrs. Snowball, who said she was the mother of five children, said she and her husband had been looking for alternative accommodation. They were willing to move. His Honour advised Mrs. Snowball to take the eviction order to the Housing Department of the Bridgwater

Rural Council."

Opposite White Hart Cottages a corrugated iron fence surrounds an area known as the **SAND PIT**: at one time this was the source of much of the sand used in the village. In their proceedings in 1937 the Somerset Archaeological and Natural History Society noted that "Chedzoy Quarry" had not been used for many years and had been filled in since their previous visit in 1930. It was recorded that the sand went down at least 15 feet (5 metres) below the surface. A learned paper published in 1869 made mention of the occurrence of the remains of hippopotamus and mammoth in a river deposit at Chedzoy, but their subsequent location was unknown. Possibly they had been found in this quarry.

On the 1881 and 1891 Census a family named Bryant was living somewhere in this vicinity, and the following report published in July 1888 would appear to relate to them.

> "Michael Brien (63) of Chedzoy was charged with attempting to commit suicide by hanging himself with his braces. - Frederick Brien (22), labourer, said he lived at Chedzoy with the defendant, who was his father. About quarter to six on Friday morning he (witness) was downstairs and presently heard a scuffle up-stairs. Witness went to the defendant's bedroom, and saw him with his braces around his neck. He was holding up the two ends of the brace to tie to the top of the bed-post. Witness asked, 'What are you about?' and defendant replied, 'I am bound to do it.' That was all he (witness) could get out of him, and he put him back into bed and gave him some cocoa. He knew as a matter of fact that his father had been drinking heavily for the past three days and he never knew the defendant endeavour on any previous occasion to take his life. - Defendant was discharged in his own recognisance to keep the peace for six months, in his own surety of £20 and his son in another surety of a like sum."

After the modern bungalow adjoining White Hart Cottages, the visitor comes upon **CROSS COTTAGE** in whose garden, beside the road, stands a village cross of Ham stone, a listed Grade II monument. In the words of an old guide to crosses of Somerset: one octagonal step raised on masonry, supports a socket, also octagonal with a convex chamfer at its upper edge, into which is fixed a tall tapering square shaft, capped by a cross patée. A zinc plate fixed on the shaft bears this inscription: HANC CRUCEM EREXIT GUIEILVVS STRADLING ARMIGER AD 1818. There are also four shields with Masonic devices in the quatre foils. The step and socket alone are old, probably 15th Century.

The cross is one of the village mysteries. Why is it sited here, not at Cross Tree, which would seem to have been the village centre for many years, if not centuries? It is known that produce was once sold at Crosstree when the plague affected the villages and goods were not allowed to be taken into Bridgwater. However, this may have been a more ancient cross in the lee of the church. Certainly two footpaths, the roads of older times, met near the cross. The Rev. Andrew Paschall, in his account of the Battle of Sedgemoor, mentions the watch set at the village cross.

What happened to the original and why did William Stradling set up a replica or replacement? The William Stradling concerned is almost certainly the 19th Century historian and eccentric who build the "Castle" folly, known as Chilton Polden Priory, on the Polden Hills. He filled his imitation castle home with artefacts and curious objects from the past, some of which may be seen in Taunton Museum. No doubt he wished to prevent the complete loss of the village cross and erected the present one on the older plinth of one long since fallen. The monument was mentioned in a report of Bridgwater Rural District Council proceedings in March 1958:

> "An old stone cross at Parchey, in the parish of Chedzoy, is a potential danger to the public, according to a report by the Public Health Committee. Replying to Mr. A.E. Ashford, the Clerk (Mr. H.G. Blay) said no information had been received that the cross was an ancient monument, and the owner was entitled to remove it if it was in a dangerous state. 'If the parish has any feelings about this cross they should come out in the open and ask the owner to conform to public wishes,' added the Clerk. 'It is not a place of historic or architectural merit, but on private land, and is reported to be in a dangerous condition.' The Chairman said it seemed to be purely a local affair. 'We are informed it is in a dangerous condition, therefore it must be moved or put in a satisfactory condition,' he stated. Mr. Ashford said there was a reference to the cross in the history of Chedzoy, and when someone wanted to buy it and take it away there was 'a bit of a row about it.' The Council decided to refer back the matter to the Public Health Committee with a request to take informal action."

In 1964 the cross was moved to the back garden after falling and threatening the carriageway. At that time the Somerset Archaeological Society indicated that only the base was of the 15th Century, and even this was incomplete. The Parish Council decided against spending £40 on the cross's removal and repair. In 1984 it was moved back to its present and original site by the owner of the cottage.

The cottage itself is 200 years old or more. Francis Lovibond was born here on 18th January 1825, at which time it was owned by William Stradling. It was once two dwellings with peak windows. (Interestingly, a couple are to be seen in Stradling's "castle" on the Poldens.) Legend tells of church silver buried in the garden here or in Myrtle Cottage and, like Myrtle Cottage, Cross Cottage is said to be linked to the church by a tunnel, but none has ever been found. In June 1913 the tenant was Ernest Bell when the property was put up for auction, although sale details were not reported. The roof was raised by four feet immediately before the Second World War, the builder being Charlie Stacey of Westonzoyland. The first occupier after this work was Wyndham Fry. There was once a pump outside with the trough and handle cast with Stradling's name. Over forty years ago an article in the Christian Herald had a picture of an open peat fire in the cottage that had been burning for 20 odd years. The house has no foundation and is built directly on the sand and shingle; part cob, part stone, and part very old hand-made bricks.

The premises were mentioned briefly in a report in the Bridgwater Mercury in October 1949:

> "An order for possession in 28 days, together with rent owing, was made at Bridgwater County Court when Mrs. Mabel Agnes Heal (1875-1957), Doutlings (Doltons) Farm, Chedzoy, applied for possession of Ye Old Cross Cottage, occupied by Seymour Roy Nash. Leslie Charles Heal, Mrs. Heal's son, said that Nash, a single man employed on the farm, left on July 30th without giving notice and had not offered any rent since. The cottage was urgently required for another man as it was the only one they had."

The house next door, **THE COTTAGE**, was once tied to Sibleys Farm. It passed into private hands within living memory, for the princely sum of 36 guineas (£37.80)! **FERNSIDE** looks as though part of it was once a chapel, the ogee-arches of the windows giving it an ecclesiastical air. Its age is unknown, but it is well over 120 years old. An old photograph shows a couple with their three children standing outside the house: between the upper windows is a board, partly obscured by a tree, which appears to read LOVIBOND BOOT & SHOE MAKER. On the 1881 Census Francis Lovibond was 56, his wife, Edith, was 42, and their children were aged 7 and 3 years and eleven months: the children shown in the photograph are about those ages. Four adjoining cottages shown in another photograph, apparently taken at the same time, are no longer there, indeed the shell of a fifth cottage adjoins Fernside, and they appear to have been replaced by Sunnyside and Rose Cottage.

By the 1891 Census the Lovibond family had moved to an address "on Westfield Farm" at Chedzoy Lane. In December 1891, "The dwelling house (formerly two cottages) with the butcher's shop, stable, outbuildings and garden" occupied by Alfred and Eliza Salmon was sold at the Crown Inn: unfortunately the sale price can not be established. For many years, at least from the 1930s, the cottage was the home of Sister Edith Newton (1900-1983), midwife to the village.

In recent years the present owners found the tattered remains of a letter hidden in a daub and wattle wall. It appears to read,

> "Dear William, With the pleasure just to know you are near perhaps I shall be down long that way tonight.
> If I am I will come in. So good bye my dearest William."

Fernside about 1881. Francis and Edith Lovibond with their daughters Bessie, Ada and Ellen. Source unknown, courtesy of Dorothy Kidner.

The letter is signed with many kisses. Who was the mysterious author and why was the letter hidden in the wall? William is unlikely to have been the son of Alfred and Eliza Salmon: he was only eleven years old in 1891. The note was written on the back of a leaflet advertising William Hickman, agent for the Phoenix Insurance Company and Chemist of Bridgwater: could he have been the William to whom it was addressed? We'll never know.

The left end of **SUNNYSIDE** was at one time part of the adjoining butcher's shop and many animal bones were unearthed when improvements were being made to the property. **ROSE COTTAGE** (known as **HORNET**S between 1996 and 1999), was apparently pulled down after the last war and virtually rebuilt. Modernisation commenced after the property was sold for £47,500 in 1996. In 1998 it was again on the market, this time for £81,950, although by early 1999 the asking price had been reduced to £74,000. According to the Bridgwater Mercury, in October 1906 the tenant was Fred Stone, a labourer.

> "While digging a ditch at King Sedgemoor, he made an interesting discovery recently when, about 2 feet below the surface, he discovered, embedded in the earth, a gold coin of King Charles II's period. The finder said he has already been offered £7 for the coin."

Was it the same Fred Stone who was in trouble forty years later? In April 1946 the Bridgwater Mercury reported,

> "An early morning incident at Bridgwater, in which a Police Sergeant fell to the ground with two bicycles on top of him, was described in Bridgwater Borough Magistrates' Court when Frederick George Stone of Rose Cottage, Ward Lane, Chedzoy was fined £4 for riding a cycle without lights during the hours of darkness. P.S. Eaton stated that while on duty in Church Street, Bridgwater at 1.10 a.m., he saw Stone riding a cycle which had neither front nor rear light. Witness stopped defendant and found there was no lamp on the front of his machine. There was a rear light but it was not burning. Stone refused to furnish any particulars about his identity, and failed to describe the cycle. He was told he would be taken to the Police Station.
>
> "Arriving at the Town Bridge, Stone suddenly turned round and rode his cycle without lights towards Monmouth Street. Witness gave chase and Stone suddenly dismounted from his cycle. The machine fell against the one ridden by P.S. Eaton, throwing him to the ground, the two machines falling on top of him. Stone ran along Church Street, but witness caught him and obtained his name and address. Stone said he would pay for any damage. Asked by the Magistrates' Clerk to account for his strange behaviour, defendant replied, 'I suppose I had a drink or two and did not realise what I was doing'."

In September 1968 the property was again in the news:

> "Robbed Meter at Mother's Home. Man Gave Himself up to Police. - As Kenneth Victor Smith (21) waited to appear before Bridgwater County Magistrates he told a police officer 'A prison sentence would mean nothing to me,' and the magistrates adjourned his case for three weeks to get medical reports after the defendant had blamed drink for the two

Ward Lane, around 1881. Only "Fernside" (hidden behind nearest cottage, with the Lovibond family at the gate pillars) is still standing. Source unknown, courtesy of Dorothy Kidner.

offences with which he was charged. Smith, unemployed, and of no fixed address, admitted stealing £12 from his mother's electricity meter at Rose Cottage, Chedzoy. ... The accused later went to Rhyl Police Station where he gave himself up and told a constable, 'I did it - it was a rotten thing to do'."

The outcome of the case was not reported.

THE BUNGALOW, the wooden building on the left, was built about 1923 for Jim Chapple by Robert Hanham, builder, of Chedzoy. In January 1939 it changed hands for £135. **SPRINGFIELD COTTAGES**, also on the left, are probably of mid-Victorian construction. At one time the last one, No. 3, was owned by Sara Ann Day, who bought it for £200. She was an "old maid" and used it as a shop where she sold glasses of ginger beer or peppermint for a penny. It seems that she could not understand how to use scales so, instead, sold sweets by quantity: six Bluebird toffees for one penny. In October 1932 notices appeared in the Bridgwater Mercury to the effect that No. 1 Springfield Cottages was to be sold by auction at the Manor House Inn. The occupier and vendor was simply identified as "Miss Lilly." No report of the sale was published.

One of these cottages was the home of John Wilkins (born c.1864) who is already familiar to readers from his escapades at the Crown Inn. He appeared before the magistrates on numerous occasions. In February 1886,

"John Wilkins and Charles Phillips, labourers, of Chedzoy, were charged with assaulting George James, of the same place. - Complainant said the defendants came to his house and whilst Phillips held him fast, Wilkins, who had a lighted candle in his hand, held it to his (complainant's) face, and burnt part of his whiskers. Defendant had paid him 9s. to settle the case. - The Chairman informed the complainant that he had no right to settle a case of this description. - Defendants were fined 1s. each and costs."

In December 1893 John Wilkins

"was summoned for carrying a gun without a licence. Robert Fry, farmer, said he saw defendant on Mr. John Baker's land in search of game. He was carrying a gun and had a dog with him. The Bench fined defendant 15s. and costs."

He was back again in 1895

"for using obscene language at Chedzoy on December 2nd. P.C. Golledge having proved the case, the Bench imposed a fine of 10 shillings and costs or 14 days."

Two years later his neighbour, William Fry (born c.1852) appeared on a similar charge but was only fined five shillings.

John Wilkins was in trouble again in July 1901:

"John Wilkins, thatcher, was charged with having stolen 10s. 6d., the money of Lot Roe whilst being bailee of the same. Mrs. Sarah Roe sent him to Bridgwater for some goods, giving him 10s. 6d. to pay for them. Prisoner never returned. P.C. Fry proved apprehending prisoner at the Knowle Inn on a warrant. Prisoner, when the warrant was read, said, 'That is right. I had the money and I spent it. I fell in with some girls in Bridgwater. I spent it with them.' Prisoner pleaded guilty and 15 other convictions having been proved, although not one for theft, he was sentenced to 21 days hard labour."

Another resident of Ward Lane was in trouble in November 1948, although a precise address was not reported.

"Mr. Day Cycled at Night. - Percival William Day, farm worker, of War-lane (sic), Chedzoy, summoned at Bridgwater County Magistrates' Court for riding a cycle without a rear light during the hours of darkness, stated in a letter to the magistrates, 'I think one hour on the farm, helping to get food, is worth the two or three hours I shall waste at your Police Court.' He enclosed 10s. with the letter in which he thanked Inspector W.F. Burton 'for doing his duty.' Fined 15s."

Continue past Springfield Cottages and past **EASTFIELD**, built in 1977, which is on your right. Beyond Eastfield on your right is a small piece of overgrown land which was once the garden for Cross Cottage. The sharp right-hand bend is known as Green-in Corner: the wide expanse of grass is relatively new, having been purchased by the Council in 1955 in order to remove a hedge and ditch so as to improve visibility. The unusual name is a corruption of the name by which the adjoining field was known in the early years of the 20th Century: Gree End Half Acre. This and the adjoining field, Cucking Stool, were part of Court Farm until sold in 1917.

Beyond Green-in Corner is another sharp bend, this time to the left, outside **PENWOOD FARM** which was built about 1925, but has been much modernised and extended. Continue along the road, retracing your earlier steps, to cross Parchey Bridge and return to your car. Savour the views of King's Sedgemoor Drain and the surrounding levels before leaving for home.

We hope you have enjoyed your visit to our village: you are welcome back at any time. Thank you for your support. All proceeds from the sale of this book will go towards improvements to Chedzoy Village Hall.

Chedzoy Village Hall. By Maxine Heal.

Appendix I - 1891 CENSUS

This Census, the latest available to the public, took place on Sunday, 5th April 1891 and records that there were 75 inhabited and eight uninhabited buildings in the Parish of Chedzoy. The population of the parish was 315 (160 male, 155 female), of whom 217 were born in Chedzoy. This listing includes property located in Chedzoy Lane and Ruggs Drove - a further 97 people (53 male, 44 female), 31 of whom were born in Chedzoy or Chedzoy Lane.

Although the census form had provision for a house number or name, in most cases only the road is shown but fuller address information from other sources is shown in italics. The numbers shown are "schedule numbers." Unless shown otherwise, relationships to the head of each household (the first person listed) are those of the normal family unit.

	Name (and relationship to head)	Age	Occupation	Born
	Chedzoy Lane			
1	John DOWDEN	79	Mason	Bawdrip
	Mrs. Eliza DOWDEN	75		Westonzoyland
2	Robert PARISH ***(Slape Cross)***	76	Gardener	Chedzoy
	Mrs. Mary A. LOVIBOND (servant)	58	General Servant	Bridgwater
	an uninhabited dwelling			
3	Henry HAINES ***(Temple Farm)***	60	Threshing Machine proprietor	Huntspill
	Mrs. Anna HAINES	52		Middlezoy
	Ernest HAINES	18	Steam Engine Driver	Westonzoyland
	Aida B. HAINES	12	Scholar	Chedzoy
	Sidney HAINES	9	Scholar	Chedzoy
4	John WHEELER ***(Nelson Lodge)***	60	Gardener	Chedzoy
	Mrs. Jane WHEELER	67		Chedzoy
	James WHEELER	31	Agricultural Labourer	Chedzoy
	Charles PHILLIPS (son-in-law)	26	Agricultural Labourer	Chedzoy
	Mrs. Sarah Jane PHILLIPS	33		Chedzoy
5	Leslie ANDREWS	58	Farm Labourer	Chedzoy
	Miss Amelia ANDREWS	15		Chedzoy
	William ANDREWS	12	Scholar	Chedzoy
	Eliza ANDREWS	7	Scholar	Chedzoy
6	Henry J. COLLARD	38	Carter on farm	Fordgate
	Mrs. Caroline COLLARD	38		North Petherton
	Ada Mary COLLARD	13	Scholar	North Petherton
	Edward J. COLLARD	9	Scholar	North Petherton
	Harry COLLARD	4	Scholar	Goathurst
	Ernest Charles COLLARD	2		Goathurst
	Annie COLLARD	2		Goathurst
	William COLLARD	11	Scholar	Goathurst
	Mrs. Hannah COLLARD (mother)	71		Yatton
7	Joseph ASHFORD ***(West End Farm)***	35	Farmer	Wincanton
	Mrs. Jane ASHFORD	33		Shepton Montague
	Austin W. ASHFORD	8	Scholar	Chedzoy

Name (and relationship to head)	Age	Occupation	Born
7 continued			
Lilian M. ASHFORD	7	Scholar	Chedzoy
Amelia J. ASHFORD	5	Scholar	Chedzoy
Florence M. ASHFORD	4		Chedzoy
Edith E. ASHFORD	3		Chedzoy
Winifred F. ASHFORD	2		Chedzoy
Leonard J. ASHFORD	6 months		Chedzoy
an uninhabited dwelling			
8 William CARY ***(Manor Farm)***	34	Farmer	Chedzoy
Mrs. Clara V. CARY	24		Bawdrip
Lucy SALMON (servant)	14	General Servant	Chedzoy
9 Charles GULLY ***(1891 roll Yew Tree Cott)***	64	Agricultural Labourer	Chedzoy
Mrs. Fanny GULLY	52		Upottery, Devon
Rose GULLY	16		Huntspill
10 Joseph LOVIBOND ***(1891 roll Yew Tree Cott)***	42	Agricultural Labourer	Chedzoy
Mrs. Emily LOVIBOND	41		Chedzoy
Charles STONE (nephew)	11	Scholar	Woolavington
11 Mrs. Caroline JEWILL [widow] ***(Quantock View)***	55	Charwoman	Chedzoy
Miss Elizabeth CONDUIT (sister)	47	Poulterer	Chedzoy
Walter BARNSTABLE (lodger)	54	Living on own means	Othery
12 Edward STONE ***(1891 roll Westfield Farm)***	25	Agricultural Labourer	Chedzoy
Mrs. Elizabeth STONE	26		Westonzoyland
Ernest E. STONE	5	Scholar	Chedzoy
Alfred J. STONE	2		Chedzoy
Clifford J. STONE	3 months		Chedzoy
13 Francis LOVIBOND ***(1891 roll Westfield Farm)***	66	Shoe Maker	Chedzoy
Mrs. Edith LOVIBOND	52		Chedzoy
Ada Edith LOVIBOND	13	General Servant	Chedzoy
Francis MILLS (lodger)	62	Agricultural Labourer	Chedzoy
Back Lane (Manor Road)			
14 Mrs. Caroline GILBERT [widow]	58	Grocer	Chedzoy
Frank HOOK (nephew)	15	Servant	Chedzoy
Ernest HOOK (lodger)	25	Tailor	Cossington
Manor House Inn			
15 William PHILLIPS	49	Publican and Thatcher	Over Stowey
Mrs. Caroline PHILLIPS	50		Chedzoy
Thomas PHILLIPS	21	Agricultural Labourer	Chedzoy
Charlotte PHILLIPS	16	Draper's Assistant	Chedzoy
Amelia PHILLIPS	12	Scholar	Chedzoy
Bertie PHILLIPS (grandson)	2		Chedzoy

Name (and relationship to head)	Age	Occupation	Born
Manor House Inn continued			
William MILLS (lodger)	56	Army Pensioner	Chedzoy
George JEANES (lodger)	not known	Agricultural Labourer	Chedzoy
Back Lane (Manor Road)			
16 Charles PONSFORD	85	Pauper	Westonzoyland
Mrs. Harriet PONSFORD	80		Bawdrip
17 Mrs. Ellen BELL	38	Dairywoman	Chedzoy
Charles SPARKS (lodger)	64	Army Pensioner	Brigwater
18 William BENNETT ***(1891 roll Pig Lane Cottage)***	52	Agricultural Labourer	Chedzoy
Mrs. Elizabeth BENNETT	46		Stawell
Oliver BENNETT	20	Agricultural Labourer	Chedzoy
Wallace BENNETT	16	Agricultural Labourer	Chedzoy
George BENNETT	13	Agricultural Labourer	Chedzoy
William BENNETT	7	Scholar	Chedzoy
Alberta BENNETT	7	Scholar	Chedzoy
Pig Lane			
19 Wallace LOVIBOND	22	Agricultural Labourer	Chedzoy
Mrs. Louise LOVIBOND	24		Chedzoy
20 Thomas GILES	29	Agricultural Labourer	Bridgwater
Mrs. Mary Ann GILES	29		Berrow
an uninhabited dwelling			
Parchey			
21 William J. TAMBLING	36	Agricultural Labourer	Cannington
Mrs. Mary Ann TAMBLING	36		Chedzoy
Emily TAMBLING	12	Scholar	Chedzoy
William J. TAMBLING	10	Scholar	Chedzoy
Charles TAMBLIN	8	Scholar	Chedzoy
Ethol (sic) May TAMBLING	5 months		Chedzoy
22 Richard GILES ***(Parchey Cottage 1900)***	40	Agricultural Labourer	Chedzoy
Mrs. Jemima GILES (mother) [widow]	67	Living on own means	Chedzoy
Miss Sarah GILES	21	Dress Maker	Chedzoy
William ADAMS (lodger)	23	Agricultural Labourer	Meare
23 Henry G. GILES	27	Agricultural Labourer	Chedzoy
Mrs. Sarah Jane GILES	26	Chedzoy	
24 Charles FRY	66	Farmer	Chedzoy
Mrs. Elizabeth FRY	65		Middlezoy
Miss Ellen FRY	23	Farmer's daughter	Bawdrip

Name (and relationship to head)	Age	Occupation	Born
Parchey continbued			
25 Edwin E. WILKINS	30	Agricultural Labourer	Chedzoy
Mrs. Lucy Ellen WILKINS	29		Chedzoy
Ward Lane			
26 Mrs. Ann FRY	57	Living on own means	Chedzoy
John WEBBER (lodger)	50	Agricultural Labourer	Winsford
27 Mrs. Emma JEANES [widow]	62	Charwoman	North Petherton
Henry Job JEANES	25	Agricultural Labourer	Chedzoy
28 Thomas WILKINS	60	Agricultural Labourer	Chedzoy
Mrs. Jane WILKINS	61		Chedzoy
John WILKINS	27	Agricultural Labourer	Chedzoy
Miss Sarah Jane WILKINS	17	General Servant	Weston-Super-Mare
Herbert WILKINS (grandson)	2		Weston-Super-Mare
29 Miss Martha FRY	71	Charwoman	Chedzoy
30 William FRY	39	Agricultural Labourer	Chedzoy
Mrs. Jane FRY	38		Chedzoy
Amelia Jane FRY	15	Domestic Servant	Chedzoy
George FRY	9	Scholar	Chedzoy
Ernest FRY	7	Scholar	Chedzoy
Alice FRY	5	Scholar	Chedzoy
James FRY	1		Chedzoy
31 George HUNT	45	Agricultural Labourer	Chedzoy
Mrs. Sarah Ann HUNT	46		Chedzoy
Sidney John HUNT	12	Scholar	Chedzoy
Alfred James HUNT	4	Scholar	Chedzoy
32 Michael BRYANT	65	Agricultural Labourer	Edington
Mrs. Jane BRYANT	55	Charwoman	Chedzoy
Elijah BRYANT	14	Labourer	Chedzoy
an uninhabited dwelling			
33 Mrs. Eliza SALMON ***(Fernside)***	42	Living on own means	East Brent
Emma L. SALMON	17	Pupil Teacher	Bawdrip
William B. SALMON	11	Scholar	Chedzoy
George SALMON	9	Scholar	Chedzoy
Frank SALMON	7	Scholar	Chedzoy
Alfred H. SALMON	5	Scholar	Chedzoy
Eliza J. SALMON	4	Scholar	Chedzoy
Clifford A. SALMON	1		Chedzoy
34 Frederick BRYANT	25	Farm Labourer	Chedzoy
Mrs. Mary Ann BRYANT	23		Westonzoyland
Lily May BRYANT	1		Chedzoy

Name (and relationship to head)	Age	Occupation	Born
an uninhabited dwelling			
35 Mrs. Eliza GILES [widow]	76	Pauper	Enmore
Batch			
36 George WHEELER	26	Agricultural Labourer	Chedzoy
Mrs. Maria A. WHEELER	24	Dress Maker	Chedzoy
John WHEELER	2		Chedzoy
Frederick G. WHEELER	3 months		Chedzoy
37 Mrs. Jane TUCKER [widow]	45	Living on own means	Bawdrip
Walter TUCKER	20	Agricultural Labourer	Chedzoy
Frederick L. TUCKER	1		Chedzoy
38 Mrs. Mary STONE [widow]	77	Laundress	Sutton Mallet
Frederick STONE	40	Agricultural Labourer	Chedzoy
Mrs. Frances BELL (daughter)	36	Laundress	Chedzoy
Ernest BELL (grandson)	9	Scholar	Chedzoy
Ernest BELL (grandson)	8	Scholar	Chedzoy
(the Census shows two Ernest's)			
39 George B. CONDUIT	49	Gardener	Chedzoy
Mrs. Elizabeth CONDUIT	48	Dressmaker	Bridgwater
Thomas B. CONDUIT	19		Chedzoy
John CONDUIT	15	Coach painter apprentice	Chedzoy
40 Mrs. Sarah LOCK	71	Pauper	Chedzoy
41 Frank BENNETT ***(1891 roll "near churchyard")***	46	Labourer	Chedzoy
Mrs. Amelia BENNETT	43	Dressmaker	Chedzoy
Flossie L. BENNETT	6	Scholar	Chedzoy
Clifford L. BENNETT	4	Scholar	Chedzoy
Crown Inn (Crown House)			
42 Thomas SPENCE	41	Publican	County Antrim
Mrs. Amelia A. SPENCE	37		Mark
Hellen M. SPENCE	8	Scholar	Dover
Amelia A. SPENCE	5	Scholar	Dover
Clement SPENCE	2		Chedzoy
John JARVIS (father-in-law)	79	Living on own means	Mark
Elizabeth WELLS (boarder)	25	Dress Maker	Mark
Pound Cottage (Front Street, the area of Rose Bower)			
43 Josiah M. WOODS ***(1891 roll Manor Farm)***	42	Church Sexton	Chilton Polden
Mrs. Rhoda WOODS	43		Chedzoy
Winifred WOODS	13	Scholar	Chedzoy
Philip WOODS	10	Scholar	Chedzoy
Christabel WOODS	8	Scholar	Chedzoy
Mrs. Mary MARTIN (mother) [widow]	86	Pauper	Chedzoy

Name (and relationship to head)	Age	Occupation	Born
Front Street			
44 Miss Emma BENNETT	56	Dress Maker	Chedzoy
an uninhabited dwelling			
45 John STONE	56	Agricultural Labourer	Chedzoy
Mrs. Emma STONE	55		Westonzoyland
Simon G. STONE	13	Agricultural Labourer	Chedzoy
Walter J. STONE	13	Agricultural Labourer	Chedzoy
46 William STONE	30	Agricultural Labourer	Chedzoy
Mrs. Hannah STONE	34		Illogan, Cornwall
Henry George STONE	8	Scholar	Chedzoy
Arthur S. STONE	6	Scholar	Chedzoy
Clara E. STONE	4	Scholar	Chedzoy
Rose E. STONE	4 months		Chedzoy
47 Mrs. Ann GULLY [widow]	44	Laundress	Huntspill
Miss Clara GULLY	18	Laundress	Chedzoy
48 Albert GILBERT [widower]	66	Pauper (blind)	Chedzoy
Edward Ralph GILBERT	44	Agricultural Labourer	High Ham
Miss Hannah GILBERT	34	Charwoman	Chedzoy
an uninhabited dwelling			
Rectory			
49 George O. MULLENS	61	Clerk in Holy Orders	Dalston, Middlesex
Mrs. Marcia F. MULLENS	61		Bridgwater
Miss Mary Ann BROOKS (servant)	30	Servant (cook)	Hungerford, Berks.
Miss Louise CHAPLIN (servant)	19	Servant (parlour maid)	Norton Fitzwarren
Miss Annie CONDUIT	17	Servant (house maid)	Chedzoy
Front Street			
50 Miss Emma CONDUIT	46	General Servant	Chedzoy
Ellen L. LOVIBOND (niece)	10	Scholar	Chedzoy
51 Henry FRY ***(Sibleys Farm)***	42	Farmer	Bawdrip
Mrs. Emily FRY	33		Nailsea
Edwin FRY	10	Scholar	Woolavington
Wyndham FRY	8	Scholar	Woolavington
Harry FRY	6	Scholar	Chedzoy
Beatrice FRY	5	Scholar	Chedzoy
Frederick FRY	3		Chedzoy
Gertrude FRY	1		Chedzoy
52 Joseph BROOKS ***(School House)***	33	Certified Teacher	Breadon, Leics.
Constance BROOKS	6	Scholar	Chedzoy
Flora Ruth BROOKS	4	Scholar	Chedzoy

Name (and relationship to head)	Age	Occupation	Born
School House continued			
Edward Joseph BROOKS	1		Chedzoy
Miss Mary Eliza STONE (servant)	17	Servant (domestic)	Chedzoy
Post Office (Avalon House)			
53 Edward NOAKES	61	Carpenter	Brede, Sussex
Mrs. Louise NOAKES	58		Burwash, Sussex
Miss Flora D. NOAKES	24	Assistant Teacher	Chedzoy
Jane R. BROOKS (granddaughter)	7	Scholar	Chedzoy
Front Street			
54 Mrs. Mary RAINEY [widow]	67	Living on own means	Chedzoy
Miss Amanda RAINEY	22	Dress Maker	Chedzoy
Lucy Mary RAINEY (granddaughter)	2 months		Chedzoy
55 Tom BUTLER ***(site of Village Hall)***	43	Blacksmith	Croscombe
Mrs. Eliza BUTLER	32		Chedzoy
James BUTLER	17	Blacksmith	Chedzoy
56 John GULLY	21	Agricultural Labourer	Chedzoy
Mrs. Louise GULLY	20	Dress Maker	Chedzoy
57 Mrs. Jane HOOK [widow] ***(Cadbury House)***	81	Living on own means	Huntspill
Gertrude H. BENNETT (granddaughter)	11	Scholar	Chedzoy
58 Robert FRY ***(Frys Farm) (1891 roll Cranes Farm)***	35	Farmer	Bawdrip
Mrs. Amelia Jane FRY	32		Bridgwater
Ellen Warry FRY	5	Scholar	London
Clifford Edwin FRY	1		Chedzoy
Albert BAKER (boarder)	23	Butcher	Nailsea
59 Thomas JEANES	30	Agricultural Labourer	Chedzoy
Mrs. Laura L. JEANES	26		Chedzoy
Bertrim (sic) F. (?) JEANES	5	Scholar	Chedzoy
60 William RAINEY [widower]	77	Carpenter	Chedzoy
Levi B. M. RAINEY	37	Farmer	Chedzoy
Miss Sarah A. RAINEY	31	Dress Maker	Chedzoy
an uninhabited dwelling			
61 Mrs. Jane HURLEY [widow]	65	Charwoman	Huntspill
Harriet BENNETT (granddaughter)	12	Scholar	Chedzoy
62 Mrs. Susan NEWTON [widow]	65	Charwoman	Stoke St. Gregory
George NEWTON	36	Agricultural Labourer	Chedzoy
63 William BRAKE ***(Westfield Farm)***	32	Farmer	Bridgwater
Mrs. Betsy BRAKE	31		Wincanton

Name (and relationship to head)	Age	Occupation	Born
Westfield farm continued			
William BRAKE	6	Scholar	Chedzoy
Hester BRAKE	4	Scholar	Chedzoy
Percy BRAKE	1		Chedzoy
Miss Mary BENNETT (servant)	28	Servant (domestic)	North Petherton
64 Theodore H. HOOK	37	Tailor	Chedzoy
Mrs. Mary HOOK	33		Woolavington
Helena M. HOOK	6	Scholar	Chedzoy
Bertram H. HOOK	5	Scholar	Chedzoy
65 Henry WHITFIELD	40	Living on own means	Ringwood, Hants.
Mrs. Mary Ann WHITFIELD	39		Rinstone(?), Dorset
Mabel Mary WHITFIELD	8	Scholar	Swanmore, Hants.
66 William CHAPPEL ***(1891 roll Westfield Farm)***	54	Agricultural Labourer	Chedzoy
Mrs. Anne CHAPPEL	55		Kingston
Henry CHAPPEL	27	Agricultural Labourer	Chedzoy
Richard CHAPPEL	14		Chedzoy
Amelia CHAPPEL	11	Scholar	Chedzoy
67 George DAY ***(1891 roll Westfield Farm)***	60	Agricultural Labourer	South Brent
Mrs. Ann DAY	54		Bridgwater
68 Thomas STOKES	38	Labourer at Great Western Carriage Works	Chedzoy
Mrs. Lucy Ellen STOKES	41	Dress Maker	Chedzoy
Emily Susan STOKES	12	Scholar	Chedzoy
Bessie STOKES	10	Scholar	Chedzoy
Charlie STOKES	8	Scholar	Chedzoy
69 Mrs. Susan STOKES	70	Living on own means	Chedzoy
James STOKES	40	Agricultural Labourer	Chedzoy
William STOKES	26	Agricultural Labourer	Chedzoy
Inkers			
70 Frank NEWTON (Francis: electoral roll)	47	Agricultural Labourer	Chedzoy
Mrs. Jane NEWTON	41		?
Joseph NEWTON	14	Labourer	Chedzoy
William NEWTON	9	Scholar	Chedzoy
Emily NEWTON	8	Scholar	Chedzoy
Ernest NEWTON	5	Scholar	Chedzoy
Harry NEWTON	3		Chedzoy
Frederick NEWTON	11 months		Chedzoy
71 George STONE	72	Agricultural Labourer	Chedzoy
Mrs. Jane STONE	71		Stogursey
72 Charles STONE	49	Agricultural Labourer	Chedzoy
Mrs. Eliza STONE	43		Westonzoyland
George STONE	14	Labourer	Chedzoy
Jane STONE	12	Scholar	Chedzoy

Name (and relationship to head)	Age	Occupation	Born
72 continued			
Susan STONE	12	Scholar	Chedzoy
Alicwe STONE	9	Scholar	Chedzoy
73 Mrs. Mary PALMER [widow]	56	Farm Servant	Chedzoy
William ANDREWS (son)	38	Agricultural Labourer	Chedzoy
Elizabeth ANDREWS (mother)	87	Retired farm servant	Greinton
74 Henry BENNETT	41	Farmer	Chedzoy
Mrs. Jane BENNETT	33		Chedzoy
Elizabeth E. BENNETT	5	Scholar	Chedzoy
Reginald H. BENNETT	3		Chedzoy
Fishers Farm			
75 Edward DERRICK	54	Farmer	Moorlinch
Mrs. Elizabeth DERRICK	54		Goathurst
Miss Alice M. M. TUCKER	21	Servant (domestic)	Chedzoy
Stoles			
76 Joseph POTTER	44	Groom	Chedzoy
Mrs. Caroline POTTER	49		Chedzoy
Fowlers Plot			
77 John BAKER ***(Three Oaks Farm)***	51	Farmer	Burroughbridge (sic)
Mrs. Jane BAKER ***(1891- "Fowlers Plot Farm")***	50		Charlton Mackrell
John BAKER	23	Farmer's son	Chedzoy
Miss Louise BAKER	22	Farmer's daughter	Chedzoy
Sidney SELBY (farm servant)	19	Farm servant	London
Miss Ellen BROWN (servant)	19	Domestic servant	Middlezoy
78 Edward HOOPER	30	Agricultural Labourer	Moorlinch
Mrs. Sophia HOOPER	25		Chedzoy
Alfred HOOPER	5	Scholar	Chedzoy
Lyndye HOOPER	3		Chedzoy
Frederick Leonard HOOPER	8 months		Chedzoy
John PALFREY (lodger) [widower]	80	Living on own means	West Monkton
79 George LEAKER	62	Agricultural Labourer	North Petherton
Mrs. Sarah LEAKER	70		Martock
80 James HOOK	50	Carpenter	Chedzoy
Mrs. Clara HOOK	43		Taunton
Stephen James HOOK (nephew)	20	Farmer	Hunspill
Mabel Bertha BENNETT (niece)	9	Scholar	Chedzoy
81 George WINTER ***(Fowlers Plot Farm)***	68	Farmer	Bedminster
Mrs. Maria WINTER	67		Whitchurch
Miss Elizabeth WINTER	34	Farmer's daughter	Stanton Drew
Benjamin G. WINTER	25	Farmer's son	Chedzoy
Miss Alice BENNETT (servant)	14	Servant (domestic)	Chedzoy

Name (and relationship to head)	Age	Occupation	Born
Chedzoy Lane (Parish of St. John, Bridgwater)			
208 James ANDREWS	32	Labourer	Chedzoy Lane
Mrs. Emily ANDREWS	28		Chedzoy
Florence ANDREWS	8	Scholar	Chedzoy Lane
Tilley ANDREWS	6	Scholar	Chedzoy Lane
Bessie ANDREWS	5	Scholar	Chedzoy Lane
Frederick ANDREWS	3		Chedzoy Lane
209 Joseph STONE	46	General Servant	Chedzoy
Mrs. Mercy STONE	50		Cromhall, Gloucs.
James STONE	19	Navvy	Bridgwater
Sidney TOOGOOD (lodger)	24	Navvy	Lamyatt
Fred TOOGOOD (lodger)	16	Agricultural Labourer	Lamyatt
Herbert TOOGOOD	14	Farm Labourer	North Cadbury
210 Edward G. MERRETT	28	General Dealer	Bridgwater
Mrs. Elizabeth A. MERRETT	21		Bridgwater
Edgar G. MERRETT	3 months		Bridgwater
211 Thomas MERRETT	53	General Labourer	Bridgwater
Mrs. Hannah MERRETT	51		Bridgwater
Thomas W. MERRETT	17	General Labourer	Bridgwater
Walter J. MERRETT	14	General Labourer	Bridgwater
Clara E. MERRETT	11	Scholar	Bridgwater
212 Mrs. Mary A. MERRETT ***(Glencairn)***	45	Living on own means	Reading, Berks.
Edward MERRETT	24	Farm Labourer	South Brent
Henry MERRETT	22	Farm Labourer	Bridgwater
Arthur MERRETT	20	Farm Labourer	Bridgwater
Lewis MERRETT	13	Farm Labourer	Bridgwater
James MERRETT	11	Scholar	Bridgwater
213 Stephen TOOGOOD	25	General Labourer	Lamyatt
Mrs. Sarah A. TOOGOOD	25		Bridgwater
Alice M. TOOGOOD	6		Bridgwater
Mabel J. TOOGOOD	2 months		Bridgwater
214 Frederick PARSONS	73	Agricultural Labourer	Chedzoy Lane
Mrs. Elizabeth PARSONS	71		Chedzoy Lane
215 John LEE	73	Agricultural Labourer	Northleigh, Devon
Mrs. Charity LEE	71		Stockland, Devon
Hunter's Inn, Chedzoy Lane (Parish of St. John, Bridgwater)			
216 Mrs. Emily REED [widow]	42	Licensed Victualer	Woolavington
Mary REED	11	Scholar	Chedzoy Lane

Name (and relationship to head)	Age	Occupation	Born
Chedzoy Lane (Parish of St. John, Bridgwater)			
217 George KEIRL	61	Agricultural Labourer	Huntworth
Mrs. Caroline KEIRL	48		Langport
Lucy PYKE (step daughter)	16	Assistant in housework	Huntworth
218 Benjamin REDDICK	38	Brickyard Labourer	Moorlinch
Mrs. Lucy REDDICK	26		Huntspill
Ernest REDDICK	6	Scholar	Chedzoy Lane
Lily REDDICK	4		Chedzoy Lane
Ethel REDDICK	2		Chedzoy Lane
219 Albert JAMES	32	Agricultural Labourer	Burnham
Mrs. Elizabeth JAMES	30		Westonzoyland
Philip JAMES	5		Chedzoy Lane
Fanny JAMES	3		Chedzoy Lane
Alice M. JAMES	1		Chedzoy Lane
Frederick ANDREWS (boarder)	19	Agricultural Labourer	Chedzoy
220 John ANDREWS	37	Labourer	Westonzoyland
Mrs. Harriet ANDREWS	43		North Petherton
Mary Ann ANDREWS	17	Servant (domestic)	Horsey
Charles ANDREWS	12	Labourer	Bridgwater
Sidney G. ANDREWS	8	Scholar	Bridgwater
Emily G. ANDREWS	6	Scholar	Bridgwater
Fanny ANDREWS	2		Bridgwater
221 William J. DOWDEN	52	Mason	Chedzoy
Mrs. Jane DOWDEN	49		Chedzoy
Ernest A. DOWDEN	13	Agricultural Labourer	Bridgwater
Harriet L. DOWDEN (granddaughter)	4		Bridgwater
222 William M. PARSONS	37	Agricultural Labourer	Bridgwater
Mrs. Elizabeth A. PARSONS	37		Southwick, Mark
William J. PARSONS	17	Agricultural Labourer	Highbridge
Charlotte A. PARSONS	11	Scholar	Bridgwater
Louisa J. PARSONS	9	Scholar	Chedzoy
Joseph A. PARSONS	8	Scholar	Chedzoy
Maria E. PARSONS	6	Scholar	Chedzoy
Robert G. PARSONS	3		Chedzoy
James H. PARSONS	1		Chedzoy
223 John FRY	73	Farmer	Chedzoy
Mrs. Hester FRY	67		East Brent
M. (?) (male) FRY	25	Farmer	Bridgwater
224 Mrs. Eliza GRIFFEN [widow]	6	Living on own means	High Ham
225 Edmond RAINEY	43	Farmer	Chedzoy
Mrs. Susan RAINEY	46		Stawell
George RAINEY	16	Butcher	Chedzoy
Charles RAINEY	14	Agricultural Labouer	Chedzoy
Bessie RAINEY	11	Scholar	Chedzoy

Name (and relationship to head)	Age	Occupation	Born
225 continued			
Henry WILKINS (brother-in-law)	55	Labourer	Stawell
226 Sidney BANWELL (Church Acre)	64	Farmer	Weare
Mrs. Mary BANWELL	62		Wedmore
Robert BANWELL	19	General Labourer	Shepton Montague
Wallace BANWELL	17	General Labourer	Shepton Montague
227 George REED (on double bend)	49	Agricultural Labourer	Middlezoy
Mrs. Sarah REED	44		High Ham
William REED	25	Agricultural Labourer	Middlezoy
James REED	17	Agricultural Labourer	Chedzoy
John REED	14	Agricultural Labourer	Chedzoy
Henry REED	11	Scholar	Dunwear
Caroline REED	9	Scholar	Dunwear

Rug Drove (sic) (Parish of Westonzoyland)

Name (and relationship to head)	Age	Occupation	Born
88 Mrs. Dinah STONE [widow] ***(Ruggs Farm)***	59	Farmer	Bridgwater
Richard STONE	37	Farmer	Westonzoyland
Mrs. Sarah A. STONE (daughter-in-law)	38		Bristol
Albert STONE (grandson)	3	Scholar	Bridgwater

Front Street in the 1950s. Compare the roofline of Avalon House (right) with that shown in the earlier picture on page 159. Photograph by F. Frith and Company, courtesy of Barrie Rollinson.

Appendix 2 - Chedzoy Residents in 1999

The next official census takes place in 2001 and will not be available to the public for 100 years. This listing was compiled with the co-operation of most residents. The former occupations of persons no longer in employment are shown in brackets. The final column shows when the person moved to the village: if they have lived at more than one address, the date shown in brackets is when they moved to their present address. Those lifetime residents show as born elsewhere were born to villagers and have lived here since they were infants. * = particulars declined. There are 167 dwellings in the parish and a further 29 in the "greater village" area. Three houses are at present unoccupied. One new house is under construction, and another is being demolished for rebuilding.

Address	Name	Born	Occupation	Resident Since
BRENTSFIELD LANE				
Three Oaks Cottages,				
1	Hedley A. GRANT	1937, Tiverton	Farm Labourer	1963
	Mrs. Averill A. GRANT	1937, Tiverton		1963
	Miss Susan GRANT	1962, Tiverton	Machine Operator	1963
2	Nigel D. FROST	1963, Taunton	Builder	1989 (1996)
	Mrs. Kay M. FROST	1966, Taunton	Playgroup Assistant	1989 (1996)
	Martin D. FROST	1984, Taunton	Schoolboy	1989 (1996)
	Emma M. FROST	1986, Taunton	Schoolgirl	1989 (1996)
CHEDZOY LANE, Chedzoy				
Applevale	Michael G. DAVEY	1959, Taunton	Field Service Engineer	1994
	Mrs. Teresa DAVEY	1960, Goathurst	Play Group Teacher	1994
	Miss Nashelle L. DAVEY	1980,Taunton	Student	1994
	Lloyd M. DAVEY	1985, Taunton	Schoolboy	1994
Broadway House	Ronald H. (Ron) BOHEE	1932, London	(Radio Mechanic)	1998
	Mrs. Jean E. BARRETT	1939, Tonbridge, Yorks	(Computer Operator)	1998
Conifers	Russell G. HARMES	1950,Woking	Sales Manager	1973
	Mrs. Brenda HARMES	1949,Wellington	(Sales Assistant)	1973
Nelson Lodge (site of Wheelers until c.1910)				
	Michael L. (Mike) ROBBINS	1955, Dover	College Vice-Principal	1996
	Mrs. Sheila M. ROBBINS	1955, Bradford-on-Avon	Student	1996
	Rachael M. ROBBINS	1985, Dover	Schoolgirl	1996
	William L. ROBBINS	1987, Dover	Schoolboy	1996
Old Dairy, The	Robert A. (Bob) WESTON	1951, Watford	Taxi Proprietor	1995
	Mrs. Pamela J. (Pam) WESTON	1952, Bridgwater		1995
	Alison J. WESTON	1974, Bridgwater	Insurance Clerk	1995
	Nicola E. (Nicky) WESTON	1976, Bridgwater	Sales Assistant	1995
Ponsfield	Philip H. (Phil) DENNING	1925, Burtle	Farmer	1948 (1988)
	Mrs. Josephine (Josie) DENNING	1927, Chedzoy	Farmer's wife	Life (1988)

Address	Name	Born	Occupation	Resident Since
Chedzoy Lane continued				
Temple Farm	Andrew R. DENNING	1963, Chedzoy	Farmer	Life
	Mrs. Judith L. DENNING	1969, Butleigh	Farmer's wife	1988
	Jessica C.M. DENNING	1989, Taunton	Schoolgirl	Life
	Samuel P.W. (Sam) DENNING	1993, Chedzoy	Schoolboy	Life
	Megan L.J. DENNING	1996, Bridgwater		Life
1 West End Cottages				
	Mrs. Elaine M. CRANE	1958, Shapwick		1978
	Miss Claire L. CRANE	1981, Taunton	Student	Life
	Natalie G. CRANE	1989, Bridgwater	Schoolgirl	Life
2 West End Cottages				
	Keith D. WARRINGTON	1959, Leigh, Lancs.	Salesman	1997
	Mrs. Susan (Sue) WARRINGTON	1969, Taunton	Medical Representative	1997
	Robert P. WARRINGTON	1995, Middlesbrough	Schoolboy	1997
	James A. WARRINGTON	1998, Taunton		Life
1 West End Court	Mark SMITH	1960, Chipping Norton	Graphic Designer	1997
	Judith A. THOMAS	1956, Midsomer Norton	Area Retail Manager	1997
2 West End Court	Mrs. Maureen (Mo) ROBERTS	1948, Ashington, West Sussex	Clerk	1986
3 West End Court	Michael D. HORROBIN	1954, Teignmouth	Horticulturist	1996
	Mrs. Sandra HORROBIN	1956, Bridgwater	Horticulturist	1996
	Darren M. HORROBIN	1982, Taunton	Apprentice Mechanic	1996
	Mark A. HORROBIN	1984, Bridgwater	Schoolboy	1996
4 West End Court	Mrs. Sylvia ALLEN			
5 West End Court	Raymond W. (Ray) THICKER	1943, Bridgwater	Fire Protection Engineer	1996
	Mrs. Patricia A. (Pat) THICKER	1945, Taunton	(Kitchen Domestic)	1996
West End Farm				
	Roger A. SUTTON	1948, Lichfield	Tax Practitioner	1985
	Mrs. Amanda (Mandy) SUTTON	1953, St Austell	Teacher	1985
	Christopher (Chris) SUTTON	1977, Weymouth	Care Worker	1985
	Alexander R. (Alex) SUTTON	1981, Plymouth	Student	1985
	Nicholas J. (Nick) SUTTON	1985, Plymouth	Schoolboy	1985
	James R. SUTTON	1987, Taunton	Schoolboy	Life
FOWLERS PLOT				
1 Fowlers Plot Cottages				
	Cecil A. HUBBARD	1934,Stoke St. Gregory	(Cowman)	1973
	Mrs. Margaret (Mar) HUBBARD	1939, Wrantage	(Farmer's daughter)	1973
2 Fowlers Plot Cottages				
	Michael J. CLAPP	1963, Bridgwater	Cowman	Life (1997)
	Mrs. Julia CLAPP	1972, Taunton		1988 (1997)
	Hanah L. CLAPP	1989, Taunton	Schoolgirl	Life
	Hayley A. CLAPP	1993, Bridgwater	Schoolgirl	Life
	Holly J. CLAPP	1996, Bridgwater		Life

Address	Name	Born	Occupation	Resident Since
Fowlers Plot continued				
Fowlers Plot Farm				
	Mrs. Kathleen (Kath) HOUSE	1920, Highbridge	Farmer's wife	1955 (1983)
Fowlers Plot Farm Annexe				
	John H. HOUSE	1964, Taunton	Farmer	Life (1983)
	Mrs. Elizabeth (Liz) HOUSE	1966, Bridgwater	Nurse	1983
	Matthew J. HOUSE	1991, Taunton	Schoolboy	Life
	Robert (Bobby) HOUSE	1994, Bridgwater	Schoolboy	Life
Three Oaks Farm				
	Raymond E. (Ray) TRIGGOL	1949, Bridgwater	Farmer	Life (1983)
	Mrs. Amanda TRIGGOL	1956, Wegberg, Germany	Child Minder	1975 (1983)
	Simon J. TRIGGOL	1976, Bridgwater	Agricultural Labourer	Life (1983)
	Miss Claire L. TRIGGOL	1978, Bridgwater	Student	Life (1983)
	Philip E. TRIGGOL	1984, Taunton	Schoolboy	Life

FRONT STREET

Address	Name	Born	Occupation	Resident Since
Allandale	Stephen (Steve) WHITE	1955, Portland	Bank Manager	1994
	Mrs. Susan A. (Sue) WHITE	1959, Minehead	(Bank Clerk)	1994
	Christopher J. (Chris) WHITE	1984, Plymouth	Schoolboy	1994
	David J. (Dave) WHITE	1987, Guildford	Schoolboy	1994
	Alexander E. (Alex) WHITE	1992, Guildford	Schoolboy	1994
Avalon House (The Post Office, 1861 until c.1910)				
	David R. (Dave) CLATWORTHY	1962, Taunton	Plant Operator	1996
	Mrs. Sharon T. CLATWORTHY	1967, Taunton	Debt Collector	1996
	Zoe E. CLATWORTHY	1990, Taunton	Schoolgirl	1996
	Lewis W. CLATWORTHY	1992, Taunton	Schoolboy	1996
Barn, The	Anthony G. (Glynn) ROBERTS	1956, Newcastle	Social Worker	1986
	Mrs. Heather (Kerry) ROBERTS	1958, Chard	Community Carer	1986
	Lindsey J. ROBERTS	1986, Taunton	Schoolgirl	1986
	Harry G. ROBERTS	1989, Taunton	Schoolboy	1986
1 Barn, The	Duncan I.M. CARMICHAEL	1949, Berkshire	Dental Surgeon	1999
	Mrs. Julie-Ellen CARMICHAEL	1957, South Molton	College Lecturer	1999
	Luke CARMICHAEL	1973, Taunton	Student	1999
	Lydia E. CARMICHAEL	1978, Taunton	Student	1999
	Benjamin CARMICHAEL	1981, Taunton	Student	1999
	Tobias CARMICHAEL	1995, Taunton	Schoolboy	1999
Birch House	John JENKINS	1962, Taunton	Plumber	1993
	Mrs. Susan (Sue) JENKINS	1963, Bridgwater	(Machine Operator)	1993
	Jordan JENKINS	1993, Taunton	Schoolboy	Life
Cadbury House (Post Office until 1861 and c.1910 until c.1940)				
	Stephen F. (Steve) MAXWELL	1962, Minehead	Carpenter	1994
	Mrs. Katrina H. MAXWELL	1966, Hammersmith	Personal Assistant	1994
	Cherish M.C. MAXWELL	1988, Taunton	Schoolgirl	1994
	Jamil F. MAXWELL	1991, Taunton	Schoolboy	1994

Address	Name	Born	Occupation	Resident Since
Front Street continued				
Carmond	Ronald T. (Ron) PEPPIN	1954, Bridgwater	Builder	1984
	Mrs. Lesley E. PEPPIN	1956, Puriton	Teacher	1984
	Miss Jodi PEPPIN	1981, Bridgwater	Bank Clerk	1984
	Christopher (Chris) PEPPIN	1985, Taunton	Schoolboy	Life
Court Farm Cottage				
	Peter A.G. HOOPER	1951, Ilminster	Truck Driver	1999
	Mrs. Glynis HOOPER	1964,Chippenham	Aromatherapist	1997
	Sophia A. ANDERSON	1992,Taunton	Schoolgirl	1997
Court Farm Cottage Annexe				
	*	*	*	1990
	*	*	*	1990
Court Farm House				
	Robert D. (Rob) STAMP	1951, Plaistow	Production Engineer	1999
	Mrs. Christine (Chris) STAMP	1951, Edmonton	Head Teacher	1999
	Rory STAMP	1977, Harlow	Student	1999
	Samuel (Sam) STAMP	1979, Welwyn Garden City	Computer Technician	1999
Crayston	Mrs. Beryl COOMBS	*, Watchet		1969
Croftside	Erik ALEXANDER	1932, Carshalton	Heating Engineer	1991
	Mrs. Rosemary ALEXANDER	1928, Carshalton	Heating Engineer	1991
Crown House (the Crown Inn until 1901)				
	Guy J. MARION	1961, Cornwall, Ontario	Efficiency Engineer	1997
	Mrs. Yvonne MARION	1961, Bridgwater		1997
	Miss Claire L.M. MARION	1978, Taunton	Barmaid	1997
	Alex J.M. MARION	1982, Taunton	Student	1997
	Christopher J. (Chris) MARION	1987, Taunton	Schoolboy	1997
Crosstree House	John L. WESTON	1947, Bournemouth	Consultant Engineer	1993
	Mrs. Pamela (Pam) WESTON	1949, Bournemouth	Clerk	1993
Cuckoo's Nest	Paul HUXTABLE	1953, Woolavington	Maintenance Engineer	1989
	Denise C. JAMIESON	1957, Manchester	Accounts Supervisor	1989
	Ian JAMIESON	1982, Bridgwater	Student	1989
Doltons Farm	Leslie C. (Les) HEAL	1918, Chedzoy	(Farmer)	Life
Eastcotte	Robert M. (Bob) TOZER	1953, Catcott	Builder	1988
	Mrs. Susan G. (Sue) TOZER	1957, Burrowbridge	Bank Clerk	1988
	Felicity J. TOZER	1987, Taunton	Schoolgirl	1988
	Samuel R. (Sam) TOZER	1989, Taunton	Schoolboy	Life
1 Fishers Cottages				
	Brian H. GALE	1940, London	Farm Labourer	1975
	Mrs. Jean M. GALE	1934, Williton	Kitchen Hand	1975
	Andrew P. (Andy) GALE	1977, Taunton	Car Valet	Life
2 Fishers Cottages				
	Walter F. (Walt) MAY	1931, Chedzoy	(Blacksmith)	Life (1988)
3 Fishers Cottages				
	Mrs. Tracey C. FORD	1964, Sutton Mallet	Herdsperson	1987

Address	Name	Born	Occupation	Resident Since
Front Street continued				
1 Fishers Farm	Rodney MAY	1965, West Huntspill	(Fork Lift Driver)	1967 (1995)
	Mrs. Tina L. MAY	1968, Taunton	(Care Worker)	1996
	Rebecca J.E. MAY	1985, Taunton	Schoolgirl	1996
	Nikki M.K. MAY	1987, Taunton	Schoolgirl	1996
	Adam J. MAY	1990, Taunton	Schoolboy	1996
	Zac P. COOMBS	1991, Taunton	Schoolboy	1996
	Ellie A. MAY	1992, Taunton	Schoolgirl	1996
	Spirit C. MAY	1997, Taunton		Life
2 Fishers Farm	(vacant)			
Frys Farm	Robert (Bob) MORTIMER	1956, Huddersfield	Civil Servant	1997
	Mrs. Ceri E. MORTIMER	1963, Cardiff	Civil Servant	1997
Gables, The	David J. (Dave) EDMUNDS	1962, Hythe, Hants.	Electrical Engineer	1996
	Mrs. Carole E. EDMUNDS	1964, Taunton	Chartered Accountant	1996
	Peter G. EDMUNDS	1998, Taunton		Life
Glasshouse, The	Nicholas (Nick) TUCKER	1962, Woolavington	Computer Programmer	1992
Glebe House (The Rectory, 1964 until 1978)				
	*	*	*	1978
	*	*	*	1978
Greystones	Stephen P. TROWBRIDGE	1955, Bridgwate	Civil Construction Engineer	1985
	Mrs. Lesley (Les) TROWBRIDGE	1959, Bridgwater	Personal Assistant	1985
	Scott A. TROWBRIDGE	1986, Taunton	Schoolboy	Life
	Samuel L. (Sam) TROWBRIDGE	1988, Taunton	Schoolboy	Life
Homeleigh	Martin R. SELLICK	1965, Bridgwater	Carpenter	1993
	Mrs. Tessa L. (Tess) SELLICK	1963, Clevedon	Hairdresser	1993
	George L. SELLICK	1995, Taunton	Schoolboy	Life
	Daisy E.G. SELLICK	1998, Taunton		Life
Inkers House	Matthew J. COOMBS	1968, Bristol	Media Technician	1969 (1996)
	Miss Nicola L. (Nicky) COE	1973, Lancaster	Health Evaluation Officer	1996
Inkers House (adjoining) under construction				
Jasmin Cottage	Miss Elizabeth (Liz) MULLINEAUX	1965 Burnley	Veterinary Surgeon	1999
Kalina	Jan S. (John) SYMIEC	1926, Herby, Poland	(Process Foreman)	1960
	Mrs. Jill SYMIEC	1932, Bridgwater	(Darkroom Technician)	1960
Middle Barn	Michael A. (Mike) FRASER	1942, Luton	(Company Director)	1990
	Mrs. Lynn D. FRASER	1946, Watford	(Secretary)	1990
Moorsedge (Wester Ross until 1983)				
	Roderick N. (Rod) DIXON	1928, Manchester	Teacher / Consultant	1983
	Mrs. Eleanor M. DIXON	1932, Buenos Aires	Unitarian Lay Pastor	1983
Nine O'Clock Cottage (1 Westfield Cottages until 1984)				
	Martin G. ALLEN	1944, Cheshire	Car Restorer	1984
	Mary L. (Lynne) HYDE	1964, Devizes	Assistant Manager	1984
	Kyle N.J. HYDE	1982, Bridgwater	Schoolboy	1984

Address	Name	Born	Occupation	Resident Since
Front Street continued				
Old Chapel, The (Brierton until c.1990, previously Brierton House and Chapel House)				
	Kenneth T. (Ken) BLEWETT	1923, London	(Advertising Copywriter)	1987
	Mrs. Lorna M. BLEWETT	1930, Bebington, Wirral	Teacher	1987
Old Coach House	L. Adrian WAYGOOD	1946, Swansea	Adult Education	1999
	Mrs. Anita J. WAYGOOD	1937, Weymouth	(Clerical Officer)	1999
Old Farmhouse, The (Frys Farm until 1985)				
	Stephen M. (Steve) SMITH	1960, Sutton	Area Sales Manager	1999
	Mrs. Joanna K. (Jo) CHARRETT	1961, Ealing	Midwife	1999
	Robert O. CHARRETT	1986, Taunton	Schoolboy	1999
	Stephen C. CHARRETT	1988, Taunton	Schoolboy	1999
	Peter A. CHARRETT	1990, Taunton	Schoolboy	1999
	Katherine H. CHARRETT	1992, Taunton	Schoolgirl	1999
Old Post Office, The (Post Office c.1940 until 1976)				
	*	*	*	1984
Old School, The (Chedzoy County Junior School until 1995)				
	Martin P. CHANDLER	1967, Taunton	Painter and Decorator	1997
	Mrs. Laura J. CHANDLER	1968, Ashford, Middlesex	(Waitress)	1997
	Jack M. CHANDLER	1996, Taunton		1997
	Micha S. CHANDLER	1998, Taunton		Life
Palfrey House	David C. (Dave) BOWN	1952, Bawdrip	Production Controller	1989
	Julie H. ARNAK	1955, London	Cleaner	1989
	Paul A. BOWN	1979, Taunton	Student	1989
	Ian R. BOWN	1981, Taunton	Carpenter	1989
	Helen BOWN	1985, Taunton	Schoolgirl	1989
	Peter M. ARNAK	1988, Taunton	Schoolboy	1989
Rose Bower (vacant)				
School House	Andrew S.M. (Andy) LEACH	1963, Aldershot	Engineer	1996
	Mrs. Elke H. LEACH	1967, Meppen, Germany	Translator	1996
	Robin A.M. LEACH	1999, Taunton		Life
Sibleys Farm	Norman F. FRY	1919, Chedzoy	(Farmer)	Life
	Mrs. Valerie D. (Val) FRY	1943, Luton	Farmer's wife	1973
	David J. FRY	1974, Bridgwater	Agricultural Engineer	Life
	Matthew J. FRY	1977, Bridgwater	Agricultural Contractor	Life
	Jonathan P. FRY	1980, Bridgwater	Desktop Publisher	Life
Stoneleigh	David P. BECK	1957, Sheffield	Agricultural Sales Manager	1994
	Mrs. Kathryn M. BECK	1956, Huddersfield	Secretary	1994
	James D. BECK	1984, Doncaster	Schoolboy	1994
	Jonathan R. BECK	1987, Doncaster	Schoolboy	1994
Tower View	Mark A. SPEARING	1959, Bridgwater	Electrical Engineer	1997
	Mrs. Michele F. SPEARING	1958, London	Community Nurse	1997
	Katherine A. SPEARING	1995, Taunton	Schoolgirl	1997
	Cameron A. SPEARING	1997, Taunton		Life

Address	Name	Born	Occupation	Resident Since
Front Street continued				
2 Westfield Cottages				
	John A. HOBBS	1947, Scotland	Motor Mechanic	1996
	Lorraine C. SMITH	1965, Lewisham	Aroma Therapist	1996
	Carlhoun M. SMITH-HOBBS	1997, Chedzoy		Life
Westfield Farm House				
	Richard W. (Dick)CLARKE	1942, Cheam	(Colonel)	1999
	Mrs. Jillian (Jilly) CLARKE	1946, Sutton		1999
Westland House	Malcolm L. FRIEND	1948, Torquay	(Bank Manager)	1984
	Mrs. Linda J. FRIEND	1951, Exeter	Parish Clerk	1984
West View	Mrs. Doris E. BUTT	1914, Bridgwater		1949
Whitecroft	Mrs. Hilda M. BELL	1916, Taunton	(Machine Operator)	1962
FRYS LANE				
Old Rectory, The	(The Rectory until 1964)			
	Norman A. LINHAM	1956, Glastonbury	Local Government Officer	1998
	Dierdre (Dee) KLEIN	1963, Bristol	Local Government Officer	1998
Old Rectory Farm				
	Adam RASSIM	*, Cyprus (North)		1996
	Mrs. Grace I. RASSIM	*, London	School Teacher	1996
Sibleys Barn	Roy J. JASINSKI	1957, Bridgwater	Haulier	1993 (1998)
	Mrs. Jane JASINSKI	1959, Bridgwater	Retailer	1993 (1998)
	Miss Helen M. JASINSKI	1977, Taunton	Clerk	1993 (1998)
	Brodie JASINSKI	1980, Redhill	Car Mechanic	1993 (1998)
Tall Trees	Rudolph (Rudi) PLUMMER	1956, Rossendale, Lancs.	(Social Worker)	1995
	Mrs. Lynn PLUMMER	1960, Rossendale, Lancs.	Social Worker	1995
	Rebecca M. (Becky) PLUMMER	1992, Irvine, Ayrshire	Schoolgirl	1995
	Jack A. PLUMMER	1994, Irvine, Ayrshire	Schoolboy	1995
Woodstock Barn				
	Paul A. JASINSKI	1966, Bridgwater	Salesman	1993 (1998)
	Mrs. Juliet H. JASINSKI	1966, Taunton	Customer Service	1993 (1998)
	Joseph P. JASINSKI	1996, Taunton		Life (1998)
	Oliver JASINSKI	1999, Taunton		Life
HIGHER ROAD				
1	Ian DOWNING	1955, Sheffield	Engineer	1994
	Mrs. Yvonne DOWNING	1958, Greinton	Banana Packer	1965 (1980)
2	Colin HILL	1934, Chedzoy	Farm Labourer	Life (1939)
3	Miss Beryl G. CHAPPELL	1926, Chedzoy		Life (1939)

Address	Name	Born	Occupation	Resident Since
Higher Road continued				
4	Michael J. (Mike) WINN	1941, Bridgwater	Lorry Driver	1971 (1977)
	Mrs. Caroline M. (Carol) WINN	1942, Swindon	Cleaner	1971 (1977)
	Miss Susan M. HENLY	1960, Chippenham	Packer	1973 (1977)
	Mrs. Sarah L. BELL	1964, Chippenham		1973 (1977)
	Kelly M. BELL	1984, Taunton	Schoolgirl	Life
	Michelle L. BELL	1989, Taunton	Schoolgirl	Life
5	Ronald E. (Ron) ROSE	1923, Bristol	(Factory Worker)	1955
	Mrs. Eva M. ROSE	1925, Isles of Scilly		1955
6	Mrs. Margaret A. CHICK	1947, Bridgwater	(Machine Operator)	1953 (1971)
7	Mrs. Muriel B. (Betty) TUCKER	1926, London		1945 (1948)
8	Mrs. D. Grace BUTCHER	1929, Chedzoy	(Publican)	Life (1986)
24	Alan W. SPENCER	1944, Grantham	Marketing Manager	1995
	Mrs. Pauline M. SPENCER	1947, Colchester	Buyer	1995
26	Alan R. JARVIS	1950, Hitchin	Systems Analyst	1978
	Mrs. Anne JARVIS	1949, Wath, Yorks.	College Tutor	1978
	Miss Joanna M. JARVIS	1977, Taunton	Student	1978
	Matthew A. JARVIS	1981, Bridgwater	Student	Life
28	Julian K.L. BISHOP	1956, Sidcup	Video Producer	1998
	Mrs. Heather J. BISHOP	1943, Wolverhampton	Admin. Assistant	1945 (1998)
30	Andrew (Andy) HOLMAN	1967, Bridgwater	Electrician	1996
	Mrs. Susan T. HOLMAN	1968, Bridgwater	Customer Advisor	1996
	Chloe HOLMAN	1998, Taunton		Life
31	William G. (Bill) GRIMSTEAD	1931, Bridgwater	(Farmer)	Life (1976)
	Mrs. Ruth E. GRIMSTEAD	1932, Dorchester		1996
32	Richard J. WOODWARD	*, Gloucestershire	*	1978
	Mrs. Wendy WOODWARD	*, Gloucestershire	*	1978
33	Ian WALLACE	1946, Saffron Walden	Youth Worker	1992
	Mrs. Marilyn WALLACE	1950, Haywards Heath	Teacher	1992
34	Raymond E. (Ben) KIDNER	1926, Bridgwater	(General Labourer)	1951 (1977)
	Mrs. Dorothy J. KIDNER	1930, Chedzoy	(Clerk)	Life (1977)
35	Andrew G. (Andy) OSBORNE	1954, Taunton	Paint Sprayer	1997
	Mrs. Linda D. (Lyn) OSBORNE	1955, Bridgwater	Community Carer	1997
	Victoria (Vicky) OSBORNE	1984, Taunton	Schoolgirl	1997
36	Duncan W. BOUCHIER	1947, Stretford	Nuclear Fuelling Engineer	1976
	Mrs. Mary C. BOUCHIER	1953, Worthing	Charity Worker	1991
	Neil BOUCHIER	1974, Taunton	Agricultural Engineer	1976
	Steven BOUCHIER	1976, Bridgwater	Instrument Mechanic	1976
37	Mrs. Margaret I. COX	1924, Bridgwater	(Nursery Nurse)	1973

Address	Name	Born	Occupation	Resident Since
Higher Road continued				
38	Colin JOYCE	1965, Bridgwater	Aircraft Engineer	1998
	Mrs. Hayley JOYCE	1962, Bridgwater	Shop Assistant	1998
	India A.E. JOYCE	1992, Taunton	Schoolgirl	1998
	Saffron A.J. JOYCE	1995, Taunton	Schoolgirl	1998
	Elliot O.C. JOYCE	1996, Taunton		1998
40	Mrs. Patricia (Pat) DARBY	1919, Fulham	(Wages Clerk)	1984
42	Rodney M. YOUNG	1953, Bridgwater	Highways Department	1987
	Mrs. Janet C. YOUNG	1960, Bawdrip	Information Technology	1987
	Amy M. YOUNG	1987, Taunton	Schoolgirl	Life
	Simon F.R. YOUNG	1991, Taunton	Schoolboy	Life
April Cottage (2 Frys Cottages until 1993)				
	Steven G. (Steve) HEAL	1964, Sutton Mallet	Farmer	1993
	Mrs. Maxine A. HEAL	1964, Taunton	Lawyer	Life (1993)
Banfield Barn	Raymond G. (Ray) CULLIFORD	1940, Street	Company Director	1992
	Mrs. Mary CULLIFORD	1943, Nether Stowey	Company Director	1992
	Miss Denise E. (Dee) CULLIFORD	1970, Bridgwater	Civil Servant	1992
Byways	George B. (Barrie) ROLLINSON	1943, Rotherham	Antique Dealer	1998
	Mrs. Diane ROLLINSON	1947, Leeds		1998
	Miss Katie J. ROLLINSON	1979, Dewsbury	Secretary	1998
	Miss Tracy A. ROLLINSON	1981, Dewsbury	Dental Nurse	1998
Field Barn	Mark S. GASCOIGNE	1956, South Shields	Electronics Service Engineer	1998
	Mrs. Kerry A. GASCOIGNE	1958, Tunstall, Staffs.	Finance Officer	1998
	Jessica L. GASCOIGNE	1986, Taunton	Schoolgirl	1998
	Adam P. GASCOIGNE	1988, Taunton	Schoolboy	1998
1 Frys Cottages	Geoffrey J. (Geoff) SLUMAN	1965, Exeter	Manager, Royal Mail	1994
	Mrs. Catherine H. SLUMAN	1965, Stockport	(Bank Clerk)	1994
	Joseph L. SLUMAN	1989, Exeter	Schoolboy	1994
	George W. SLUMAN	1992, Exeter	Schoolboy	1994
	Molly L. SLUMAN	1995, Taunton	Schoolgirl	Life
3 Frys Cottages	Peter J. SIMONS	1965, Combe Florey	Machinist	1999
	Helen L. CHADWICK	1975, Wellington	Chartered Accountant	1999
4 Frys Cottages	Neil PHILLISKIRK	1959, Bristol	Arborist	1999
	Jane M. LACEY	1960, Bristol	(Accounts Manager)	1999
	Dominic C.H. LACEY	1995, Bristol		1999
Manor Farm	Graham J. COTTEY	1947, Taunton	Postman	1996
	Cora A. REECE	1955, Chilton Polden	(Occupational Therapist)	1996
	Zoe REECE	1980, Taunton	Student	1996
	Ria REECE	1983, Bridgwater	Schoolgirl	1996
	Shonah J. REECE	1998, Taunton		Life
Quantock View	Miss Muriel J.C. BROWN	1925, Street	(Nursing Sister)	1954 (1976)

Address	Name	Born	Occupation	Resident Since
Higher Road continued				
Valentine Cottage (1 Yew Tree Cottages until 1989)				
	Peter D. MATTHEWS	1954, Durham	Production Manager	1991
	Mrs. Christina E. MATTHEWS	1956, Woolavington	Machinist	1991
	Robert J. MATTHEWS	1980, Taunton	Store Manager	1991
Wednesday Cottage				
	Peter J. HARDING	1941, Edgware	Engineer	1998
	Mrs. Kathryn J. (Joy) HARDING	1959, Chesterfield	Nurse	1998
2 Yew Tree Cottages				
	Christopher T. (Chris) SMITH	1965, Birmingham	Scaffolder	1985 (1986)
	Mrs. Jane E. SMITH	1964, Bridgwater	Seamstress	1985 (1986)
	Paul C. SMITH	1986, Taunton	Schoolboy	Life
	Samantha J. (Sam) SMITH	1987, Taunton	Schoolgirl	Life

MANOR DRIVE

Address	Name	Born	Occupation	Resident Since
1	Michael A. (Mike) ROWLEY	1955,London	Retail Manager	1998
	Mrs. Eunice ROWLEY	1964,Renfrewshire		1998
	James M. ROWLEY	1989,Taunton	Schoolboy	1998
	Leanne ROWLEY	1991,Bridgwater	Schoolgirl	1998
2	Frederick (Fred) COX	*, Pontypridd	(Quality Controller)	1950
	Mrs. Gladys V. COX	*, Bawdrip	(Shop Assistant)	1950
3	Mrs. Joyce COLLARD	1921,Bridgwater	(Schools Meals Assistant)	1950
4	Mrs. E. Maureen HARDING	1937,Craven Arms, Shropshire		1984 (1992)
5	Peter J. (Pete) DODGE	1951,Bristol	Foundry Worker	1973 (1987)
	Mrs. Jacqueline (Jacqui) DODGE	1952,Chew Stoke		1973 (1987)
	Miss Tanya J. DODGE	1975,Taunton	Shop worker	Life (1987)
6	Terence (Terry) RUSS	1941,Corsham	Machine Operator	1964 (1968)
	Mrs. Carol A. RUSS	1945,Bridgwater	Care Worker	1964 (1968)
	Jason S. RUSS	1970,Bridgwater	Carpet Fitter	Life
7	Philip C. (Phil) BAKER	1961,Bridgwater	Machine Minder	1997
	Mrs. Toni D. BAKER	1961,Bridgwater	(Shop Manageress)	1997
	Jonathan D. BAKER	1981,Bridgwater	Labourer	1997
	Natalie D. BAKER	1982,Taunton	Schoolgirl	1997
	Alice F. BAKER	1995,Taunton	Schoolgirl	1997
	Lewis A. BAKER	1997,Taunton		Life
8	Mrs. Elsie I. (Rene) TRUNKS	1932,Chewton Mendip	(Domestic)	1963 (1970)

MANOR ROAD

Address	Name	Born	Occupation	Resident Since
1	Terence H. (Terry) PURCHASE	1949,Bridgwater	Warehouse Worker	1985
	Mrs. Pamela (Pam) PURCHASE	1948,Bridgwater	Vineyard Worker	1985
	Andew T. (Andy) PURCHASE	1970,Butleigh	Painter and Decorator	1985
	Deborah (Debbie) PURCHASE	1975,Taunton	Shop Assistant	1985

Address	Name	Born	Occupation	Resident Since
Manor Road continued				
2	George W. MAWSON	1940, Doncaster	(Depot Manager)	1986
	Mrs. Hilary MAWSON	1954, Durham	(Clerk)	1986
	John F. MAWSON	1974, Doncaster	Plumber	1986
	Nicholas G. (Nick) MAWSON	1977, Doncaster	Student	1986
	Christopher (Chris) MAWSON	1983, Doncaster	Schoolboy	1986
3	Graham L. ADAMS	1932, Radstock	(Lorry Driver)	1970
	Mrs. Jean S. ADAMS	1941, Somerton	(Home Help)	1970
4	James SMITH	1966, Solihull	Student Teacher	1993
	Deirdre A. (Dee) McCORMACK	1966, London	(Midwife)	1993
	Sunny C. SMITH	1995, Taunton	Schoolgirl	Life
	Alice Z. SMITH	1997, Exeter		Life
5	Ian J. MORRIS	1954, Craven Arms	Game Farm Worker	1983 (1992)
	Mrs. Lorraine MORRIS	1959, Bridgwater	Banana Packer	1983 (1992)
	Edward P. (Ed) MORRIS	1978, Hereford	Trainee Psychiatric Nurse	1983 (1992)
	Miss Rebecca L. (Becky) MORRIS	1980, Bridgwater	Nursery Nurse	1983 (1992)
	Victoria J. (Vicky) MORRIS	1983, Bridgwater	Trainee Dog Beautician	1983 (1992)
	Thomas J. (Tom) MORRIS	1988, Bridgwater	Schoolboy	1992
6	Paul M. BUTCHER	1949, Bridgwater	Painter and Decorator	1989
	Mrs. Susan E. (Sue) BUTCHER	1952, Bridgwater	Seamstress	1989
	Mark P. BUTCHER	1975, Bridgwater	Painter and Decorator	1989
14	Anthony J.W. (John) WEEKS	1943, Finedon, N'hants.	(Detective Constable)	1972
	Mrs. Maureen Weeks	1944, Bengeo, Hertford	(Midwife)	1972
16	Wavell W. (Wave) DERRY	1941, Lichfield	Mechanical Engineer	1980
	Mrs. Sandra DERRY	1944, Merthyr Tydfil	School Secretary	1980
18	Sydney C. (Syd) REDDING	1927, Bridgwater	(Dispatch Manager)	1972
	Mrs. Irene M. (Rene) REDDING	1925, Merridge	(Shop Assistant)	1972
20	David J. (Dave) BROMME	1964, Bridgwater	Design Manager	1989
	Mrs. Suzanne V. BROMME	1965, Bridgwater	Commercial Officer	1989
	James D. BROMME	1990, Taunton	Schoolboy	Life
	Joanna L. BROMME	1992, Bridgwater	Schoolgirl	Life
Barn, The	Ian T. FRY	1944, Wokingham	Warehouseman	1988 (1991)
	Mrs. Susan M. (Sue) FRY	1945, Reading	Cook	1988 (1991)
Byre, The	Parweez (Peter) LATIF	1965, Birmingham	Shop Proprietor	1999
	Mrs. Susan J. (Sue) LATIF	1965, Birmingham	Shop Proprietor	1999
	Ajaib (Ajay) LATIF	1988, Birmingham	Schoolboy	1999
	Sameerah LATIF	1990, Birmingham	Schoolgirl	1999
Field View	Derek A. GROWTAGE	1934, Bridgwater	(Insurance Representative)	1967 (1976)
	Mrs. G. Eileen GROWTAGE	1929, Warrington	(Hairdresser)	1967 (1976)
Laburnum House	Nicholas J. (Nick) ROWE	1965, Taunton	Training Manager	1993
	Mrs. Rhena I. ROWE	1965, Uxbridge	(Florist/Confectioner)	1993
	Lucy E. ROWE	1995, Taunton	Schoolgirl	Life
	Annie L. ROWE	1999, Taunton		Life

Address	Name	Born	Occupation	Resident Since
Manor Road continued				
Little Barn	Mrs. Margaret (Peggy) FROST	1927, Angersleigh	Charity Worker	1997
Manor Barn	Nicholas P. (Nick) EDMONDS	1964, Taunton	Company Director	1990 (1997)
	Mrs. Vanessa J. EDMONDS	1963, Radstock	Teaching Coordinator	1990 (1997)
	Sam W.N. EDMONDS	1989, Taunton	Schoolboy	1990 (1997)
	Harriet E.C. EDMONDS	1991, Taunton	Schoolgirl	Life (1997)
Manor House Inn				
	Mrs. Elaine K. WHITE	1937, Dawlish	Publican	1963
	Michael R. WHITE	1968, Chedzoy		Life
Manor Villa	Kenneth (Ken) SUMNER	1921, Portsmouth	(Engineer)	1981
	Mrs. Hilda B. SUMNER	1928, Frome	(Baker's Assistant)	1981
Moggs Farm	Jonathan S. (Jon) HUGHES	1965, Swansea	Team Leader	1995
	Mrs. Sarah J. HUGHES	1966, Neath	Technical Assistant	1995
	Nicholas J. HUGHES	1995, Taunton	Schoolboy	Life
	David S. HUGHES	1996, Taunton		Life
	Matthew J. HUGHES	1998, Taunton		Life
Pennard	Ian C. MEDLAND	1957, Woking	Police Sergeant	1983
	Mrs. Gillian (Gill) MEDLAND	1957, Wimbledon	Caterer	1983
	Kate (Katie) MEDLAND	1984, Taunton	Schoolgirl	Life
	Danielle (Ellie) MEDLAND	1988, Taunton	Schoolgirl	Life
Woodlands (Charmante until 1970)				
	Gareth M. DAVIES	1959, Taunton	Computer Consultant	1988
	Mrs. Patricia C. (Pat) DAVIES	1959, Wellington		1988
	Martyn G. DAVIES	1989, Taunton	Schoolboy	Life
	Ceri M. DAVIES	1992, Taunton	Schoolgirl	Life
	Bethany R. DAVIES	1994, Taunton	Schoolgirl	Life

PARCHEY

Address	Name	Born	Occupation	Resident Since
Parchey Cottage	Terence A. (Terry) WILLIAMS	1940, Solihull	Swimming Pool Engineer	1990
	Mrs. Margaret J. (Jo) WILLIAMS	1940, Derby	Feng Shui Director	1990
	Miss Elizabeth (Liz) WILLIAMS	1968, Rugeley, Staffs.	Executive Consultant	1990
Parchey House	Robin S. (Rob) WILLIAMS	1943, West Hatch	New Car Dealer	1980
	Mrs. Cynthia R. WILLIAMS	1943, Penrhiwceiber, Glam.	New Car Dealer	1980
	Leigh G. WILLIAMS	1974, West Hatch	Professional Motocross Rider	1980
Parchey View	Ashley MEADOWS	1959, Chilton Polden	Motor Mechanic	1984
	Mrs. Susan M. (Sue) MEADOWS	1960, Street	(Milk Recorder)	1984
	Ella L. MEADOWS	1987, Taunton	Schoolgirl	Life
	Lucas O. MEADOWS	1989, Taunton	Schoolboy	Life
	Chloe F. MEADOWS	1993, Taunton	Schoolgirl	Life
	Harrison J. MEADOWS	1996, Taunton		Life
Penwood Farm	Ernest F. (Jim) CLAPP	1936, Chedzoy	Warehouseman	Life
	Mrs. Pauline M. CLAPP	1937, Lambeth	(Head Teacher)	1968 (1972)
	Ronald (Ron) CLAPP	1937, Chedzoy	Farm Labourer	Life

Address	Name	Born	Occupation	Resident Since
Parchey continued				
West Moor House (formerly Parchey Farm)				
	Jonathan R. (Jon) MASON	1964, Taunton	General Manager	1996
	Mrs. Samantha (Sam) MASON	1966, Tunbridge Wells	Sales Coordinator	1996
	Jessica K. MASON	1988, Canterbury	Schoolgirl	1996
	Alexandra H. (Alex) MASON	1990, Canterbury	Schoolgirl	1996
	Harriet L. (Hattie) MASON	1993, Canterbury	Schoolgirl	1996
PIG LANE				
Knowle View	George O. BENNETT	1905, Chedzoy	(Publican)	Life (1963)
Koz-e-Kot	Allan STOKES	1940, Chedzoy	Builder	Life (1995)
	Mrs. Carol A. STOKES	1944, Broomfield	Personal Assistant	1972 (1995)
ST. MARY'S CLOSE				
1	Richard S. LENNARD	1936, Northampton	Marketing Manager	1979
	Mrs. Patricia L. (Pat) LENNARD	*, Rhymney, Gwent	Health Visitor	1979
2	Stephen R. (Steve) HILL	1951, Bridgwater	Electrical Engineer	1987
	Mrs. Jacqueline (Jacqui) HILL	1950, Tredegar	(Radiographer)	1987
	Elizabeth A. HILL	1989, Taunton	Schoolgirl	Life
	Jonathan W. HILL	1994, Taunton	Schoolboy	Life
WARD LANE				
Anchorage, The (Asafa until 1985)				
	J. Howard GOODISSON	1953, Sheffield	School Teacher	1986
	Mrs. Anne GOODISON	1955, Dartford, Kent	School Teacher	1986
	Hannah GOODISON	1987, Taunton	Pupil	Life
	Sarah GOODISON	1990, Taunton	Schoolgirl	Life
Bungalow, The (vacant)				
Church Cottage	Alastair R.T. (Rob) JUDGE	1964, Worcester	Technical Sales Representative	1998
	Mrs. Zoë JUDGE	1966, Spalding	Primary School Teacher	1998
	Benjamain E. JUDGE	1993, Northampton	Schoolboy	1998
	Thomas H. JUDGE	1996, Northampton		1998
Cottage, The	Klaus VETTER	1955, Eschollbrücken, Germany	Engineer	1996
	Helene LAGORD	1969, Bagneux, France	Student	1996
Cross Cottage	Mrs. S. Cherry MORGAN	1949, Woking	Florist	1985
	Miss Zoe C. MORGAN	1979, Bristol	Nursery Nurse	1985
Eastfield Farm	Mrs. Audrey FRY	1931, Middlezoy	Farmer	1965 (1979)
Fernside	Mrs. Linda M. MARKEY	1950, Cheltenham	Pharmacy Assistant	1989
	Luke T. MARKEY	1981, Newport, I.o.W.	Student	1989
Myrtle Cottage	Mrs. Bridie BAKER	1946, Birmingham	Assistant Lecturer	1976

Address	Name	Born	Occupation	Resident Since
Ward Lane continued				
Rose Cottage (Hornets from 1996 to 1999)				
	James D. BUNNEY	1975, Melton Mowbray	Product Manager	1999
	Sarah L. HOPE	1975, Plymouth	Environmental Monitor	1999
1 Springfield Cottages				
	Mrs. Fanny L. DYER	1904, Stogursey	(Domestic)	1958
	Frederick A. (Fred) DYER	1927, Moorlinch	(Factory Worker)	1958
2 Springfield Cottages				
	Laurence CUMBERS	1959, Woking	Maintenance Engineer	1990
3 Springfield Cottage				
	Michael W. (Mike) BUTTIGIEG	1961, Benfleet	(Carpenter and Joiner)	1989
	Jane E. BARNETT	1963, Lytham St. Annes	Teacher	1989
	Imogen R. BARNETT	1991, Taunton	Schoolgirl	Life
	Lydia R. BARNETT	1995, Chedzoy	Schoolgirl	Life
Sunnyside	Terrance A. (Terry) OXMAN	1947, Sutton Mallet	Carpet Fitter	1948
	Mrs. Eileen M. OXMAN	1950, Bawdrip	Clerical Assistant	1970
	Miss Sarah J.L. OXMAN	1981, Taunton	Customer Services	Life
1 White Hart Cottages				
	Mrs. Gladys A. (Glad) PRIOR	1918, Southampton	(Domestic Servant)	1964
	Robert N. (Bob) PRIOR	1950, Alton, Hants.	Council Worker	1964
2 White Hart Cottages				
	Charles ROWLAND	1923, London	(Accountant)	1966
	Mrs. Katrina R. ROWLAND	1926, Novosjolovka, Ukraine	(Head Teacher)	1966

WILLOW GREEN

Bramley	*	*	*	1985
	*	*	*	1985
Cherry Lea	*	*	*	1972
	*	*	*	1982
Cranley	Walter J. PADFIELD	1921, Chilcompton	(Sub-postmaster)	1983
	Mrs. Marjorie PADFIELD	1923, Bradford	(Hairdresser)	1983

CHEDZOY LANE (Bridgwater Without Parish)

1	William G. PALMER	1930, Bridgwater	(Fork Lift Driver)	1954
2	David R. QUINT	1963, Exeter	Teacher	1999
	Angela B. QUINT	1962, Glasgow	Flight Attendant	1999
	Bradley D. QUINT	1994, Taunton	Schoolboy	1999
3	Wilfred COOPER	1951, Taunton		1998
	Mrs. Susan (Sue) COOPER	1955, Taunton		1998
	Miss Priscilla (Cilla) COOPER	1973, Taunton		1998

Address	Name	Born	Occupation	Resident Since
Chedzoy Lane (Bridgwater Without) continued				
4	David A. (Dave) BUTT	1940, Winscombe	Machine Setter	1941 (1986)
	Mrs. Jeannette A. BUTT	1938, Gloucester	Care Supervisor	1970 (1986)
Combe Dingle	Paul A. COX	1946, Taunton	Commercial Vehicles Saleman	1999
	Mrs. Pamela R. (Pam) COX	1959, Watchet	Computer Sales	1999
	Miss Rachel L. COX	1982, Taunton	Student	1999
Crossway House	Mrs. Ivy I. PRIDDLE	1922, Burrowbridge	(Withy Worker)	1964
Glencairn	Mrs. Eileen R. BARROW	1938, East Huntspill	Car Valet	1975
Glynswood	Anthony J. (Tony) ELLICOTT	1943, Bridgwater	Farmer	1970
	Mrs. Susan E. (Sue) ELLICOTT	1951, Chedzoy	Farmer's wife	Life (1970)
	Michael J. ELLICOTT	1975, Bridgwater	Farmer	Life
Greens Farm	Mrs. Audrey F. FRENCH	1921, Chedzoy	Farmer's wife	Life (1947)
Hunters Lodge	David D. (Dave) WARD	1949, London	Garage Proprietor	1997
	Mrs. Jacqueline (Jacqui) WARD	1952, Leicester	Garage Proprietor	1997
	Amy WARD	1992, Torquay	Schoolgirl	1997
Marstan	Douglas R. (Doug) PURCHASE	1940, Crewkerne	(Charge Hand)	1970
	Mrs. Gillian (Gill) PURCHASE	1945, Holloway	(Hairdresser)	1970
Meadowland	Kenneth H. (Ken) BROWN	1951, Bridgwater	Geologist	1998
	Patricia (Trish) FRENCH	1941, Oxford	Secretary	1998
Meads Farm	Robert A. (Bob) BUTCHER	1956, Chedzoy	Motor Mechanic	Life (1987)
	Mrs. Wendy J. BUTCHER	1960, Bridgwater	School Assistant	1984 (1987)
	Miss Carrie L. BUTCHER	1982, Taunton	Student	1984 (1987)
	Laura J. BUTCHER	1983, Taunton	Schoolgirl	1984 (1987)
	Alex R. BUTCHER	1990, Taunton	Schoolboy	Life
Medway Farm	Alan G. HOUSE	1953, Purtion	Driver	1999
	Mrs. Janet E. HOUSE	1956, Chedzoy	Sales Manager	Life (1999)
	Lorna J. HOUSE	1979, Taunton	Racehorse Groom	1999
	Christopher W. (Chris) HOUSE	1984, Taunton	Schoolboy	1999
Newhaven	Trevor J. HILL	1943, Bridgwater	(Engineering Manager)	1987
	Mrs. Shirley A. HILL	1944, Dorchester	(Charge Hand)	1987
Pencroft	Mrs. Julie A. NEWMAN	1956, Barnet	(Police Officer)	1998
	Hannah L.M. NEWMAN	1986, Enfield	Schoolgirl	1998
	Andrew E.A. NEWMAN	1989, Enfield	Schoolboy	1998
	Marie A.C. NEWMAN	1994, Enfield	Schoolgirl	1998
Poseidon	Douglas A. (Doug) BAKER	1932, Bridgwater	(Garage Proprietor)	1961
	Mrs. Ellen J. (Joey) BAKER	1933, Wick St. Lawrence		1961
Rose View (Zilnim until mid-1970s)				
	Roy M. FISHER	1951, Burnham-on-Sea	Maintenance Fitter	1978
	Mrs. Susan C. (Sue) FISHER	1954, Bridgwater	School Caretaker	1978
	Darren M. FISHER	1977, Taunton	Warehouse Operative	1978
	Miss Kathryn FISHER	1979, Taunton	Student	Life

Address	Name	Born	Occupation	Resident Since
Chedzoy Lane (Bridgwater Without) continued				
Rowan Cottage (Devonia until 1983)				
	William J. (Jim) COX	1931, Chilton Polden	Gardener	1983
	Mrs. Joyce COX	1932, West Ham	(Receptionist)	1983
Slape Cross Cottage				
	Paul GIBBS	1960, Croxley Green	Computer Engineer	1999
	Mrs. Kim GIBBS	1968, Pudsey, Yorks.	Computer Engineer	1999
	Ashley J.L. GIBBS	1988, Leeds	Schoolboy	1999
	Karl GIBBS	1988, Watford	Schoolboy	1999
	Matthew GIBBS	1990, Watford	Schoolboy	1999
	Rebecca GIBBS	1990, Leeds	Schoolgirl	1999
Slape Farm	Demolished in October 1999 prior to rebuilding			
Southside	Clifford (Charlie) CHAPLIN	1933, Yeovil	(Milkman)	1948 (1961)
	Mrs. Betty R. CHAPLIN	1935, Chedzoy	(Machine Operator)	Life
Southside Caravan				
	Brian R. WILLIAMS	1947, Cannington	Retail Delivery Driver	1983
	Mrs. Elizabeth (Sally) WILLIAMS	1959, Chedzoy	Kitchen Domestic	Life (1983)
	Lucy R.I. WILLIAMS	1986, Taunton	Schoolgirl	Life
	Alice M.E. WILLIAMS	1991, Taunton	Schoolgirl	Life
Woodland	Arthur E. (Bob) TAYLOR	1926, Lewisham	(Farmer)	1960
	Mrs. Dinah J. (Di) TAYLOR	1930, Chedzoy	(Farmer's wife)	Life (1960)
CROW LANE (Bridgwater Without Parish)				
East Side Farm	Malcolm A. YOUNG	1932, Moorlinch	Farmer	1976
	Mrs. Muriel D. YOUNG	1933, Bridgwater	Farmer's wife	1976
Greenacres	Trevor HAWKES	1938, Bridgwater	Bricklayer	1985
	Mrs. Janet M. HAWKES	1937, Stogursey	(Hospital Domestic)	1985
RUGGS DROVE (Westonzoyland Parish)				
Ruggs Cottage	Joseph A. (Tony) KENNY	1951, Bridgwater	Plumber	1985 (1985)
	Mrs. Vera C. (Christine) KENNY	1953, Donyatt	Book Keeper	1985 (1985)
	Miss Sarah L. KENNY	1980, Taunton	Student	1985 (1985)
	James M. KENNY	1983, Taunton	Schoolboy	1985 (1985)
Ruggs Farm	Peter J. (Pete) CLAPP	1939, Chedzoy	Farmer Labourer	Life (1968)
	Mrs. Shirley CLAPP	1939, Bridgwater		1958 (1968)
New Barn Bungalow (Bridgwater Without Parish)				
	James A. (Jim) BAGNALL	1947, Colchester	Nurse	1997
	Mrs. Christine BAGNALL	1944, London	Social Worker	1997
NON-RESIDENTS				
Westonzoyland	Rev. Peter J. RICHMOND	1954, Portsmouth	Priest-in-charge	1995
Bridgwater	Mrs. Sally F. LACY	1949, Cardon, Venezuela	Curate	1996
Bridgwater	Peter J. (Pete) BELL	1941, Bridgwater	Postman	1995
Cannington	Andrew J. (Andy) BARRON	1965, Taunton	Police Constable	1999

Appendix 3 - Chedzoy War Memorial

The following persons are recorded on the memorial tablet in St. Mary's Church, Chedzoy as having given their lives in the service of their country during two world wars. Most of these details have been provided by the Commonwealth War Graves Commission.

1914 - 1918

Leonard Joseph Ashford was a Private with the 15th Battalion, 3rd Infantry Brigade, Australian Imperial Forces, and died at the age of 24 years on 10th May 1915 as a result of wounds received in Gallipoli. He was the son of Joseph and Jane Ashford of West End Farm, Chedzoy and had emigrated to Australia in 1913. He was buried at sea off Cape Kabatepe [Gaba Tepe], Gelibolu [Gallipoli], Turkey and his name is recorded on the Lone Pine Memorial between Kabatepe and Chunuk Bair.

William Brooks was a Private serving in the 2nd Battalion, Devonshire Regiment, who died on 12th March 1915. His age is not recorded. He was the son of James and Ellen Brooks of Knowle, Bawdrip. His name is recorded on panels 8 and 9 of the Le Touret Memorial near Béthune, Pas de Calais, France. This memorial records the names of over 13,000 men who fell in the area before 25th September 1915 and who have no known grave. His association with Chedzoy has not been ascertained.

Harold William Cary was 26 years old and serving in the Royal Navy as an Engine Room Artificer 3rd Class on submarine D6 when he was killed in action on 24th June 1918 off the coast of Northern Ireland. He was the son of William and Clara Cary of Manor Farm, Chedzoy. His name is recorded on the Royal Naval Memorial at Chatham, Kent.

Lance Corporal Arthur Denning of the 1st West Somerset Yeomanry died on 7th July 1916 at the age of 19 years and was buried in the Cairo War Memorial Cemetery in Egypt. Records do not include his parents details, but he was born in Taunton and enlisted in North Petherton. It is known that he lived at Three Oaks Farm, Chedzoy and Monmouth Street, Bridgwater.

Ernest Fry was a Sergeant with the King's Company, 1st Battalion, Grenadier Guards and was killed on 29th October 1914 at Ypres, Belgium whilst commanding a section during a counter attack. He was 31 years old and the son of William and Jane Fry of Ward Lane, Chedzoy, but had left the village to serve in the Metropolitan Police. He was a reservist who had been recalled to the colours on 26th September 1914. The school log book has an entry dated 19th November 1914 that "The sad news that one of our 'old boys' - Ernest Fry - has been killed 'at the front,' reached the village this morning." His name is recorded on Addenda Panel 57 of the Ypres Memorial (the Menin Gate) at Ieper, Belgium.

Edward Reginald Hooper served as a Private with the 12th Battalion, Devonshire Regiment and died at the age of 23 years on 17th March 1917 as a result of his wounds. He was the son of Edward and Sophia Hooper of Chedzoy. He was buried at Doullens Communal Cemetery Extension No. 1, twenty miles north of Amiens, Somme, France.

Walter S. Radford was a Rifleman with the 1st Battalion, Royal Irish Rifles and was 19 years old when he died at King George's Hospital, Waterloo, London on 26th November 1918. He had been wounded on 22nd August 1918 at Bullecourt, near Cambrai. He was buried on 2nd December 1918 in St. Mary's churchyard, Chedzoy. He was the son of Mr. and Mrs. W. Radford of Bathpool, but had lived most of his life with grandparents in Chedzoy and worked for the Ashford family.

George Sloman died of his wounds on 12th April 1918 at the age of 38 years. He was a Private in "B" Company, 16th Battalion, Lancashire Fusiliers. He was the son of John and Jane Sloman of Halse, Somerset. His connection with Chedzoy is not certain, but he used to work for the Rev. G.R. Mullens. He was buried at Boisguillaume Communal Cemetery Extension near Rouen, Seine-Maritime, France.

Clifford James Stokes was 22 when he was killed on 9th April 1917 while serving as a Corporal with the 1st Battalion, The Rifle Brigade. He was the son of James and Alice Stokes of Chedzoy. His details are recorded on the memorial at Arras, Pas de Calais, France. According to a report in the Bridgwater Mercury he enlisted in the first week of September 1914, being the first lad from the village to do so. Before enlisting he had been employed "on the land."

Samuel Woolley was a Private in the 8th Battalion, Somerset Light Infantry and died on 1st July 1916. His details are recorded on the memorial at Thipval, Somme, France. The Commonwealth War Graves Commission records do not include his age, but he was born in Puriton and enlisted in Chedzoy.

In addition to those recorded on the memorial tablet, contemporary reports indicate that fifty Chedzoy men joined the forces during the First World War.

1939 - 1945

Ronald Edwin Collard was a Convoy Signalman serving on Arctic convoys with the Royal Navy aboard S.S. Benalbanach when he was killed on 7th January 1943 at the age of 20 years. He was the son of Harry and Charlotte Collard of Chedzoy. His name appears on the Royal Naval Memorial at Chatham, Kent.

Clifford David Stone was also 20 years old when he was killed on 8th June 1944 when serving as a Sapper with 59 Section, 136 Mechanical Equipment Company, Royal Engineers. He was the son of Ernest and Katie Stone of Rose Cottage, Chedzoy. He was buried in the Bayeux War Cemetery in Normandy, France.

Appendix 4 - Old Somerset Recipes

Recipes from Eileen Growtage

Somerset Herb Cheese

8ozs Cheddar cheese
6 tablespoons of cream
2 tablespoons of chopped chives and parsley

Grate the cheese and with the other ingredients render it down in a double saucepan, stirring all the time for maximum creaminess. Pour into small pots and cool. The herbs make it a delicate green/blue colour.

Porlock Farm Cake

12ozs of flour
1Oz butter
2oz raisins
half teaspoon mixed spice
pinch of cinnamon or nutmeg
pinch of salt
2oz caster sugar
1oz lard
2ozs currants
1 egg
1 tablespoon milk
1oz candied peel

Mix the salt with the flour and rub in the fats. Add spices, sugar, currants, raisins and sliced candied peel. Mix well. Add the well-beaten egg and milk to produce a rather stiff dough. Roll out this dough into a flat, round cake 2 inches thick. Place in a greased baking tray, and bake in a moderate heat for about half an hour.

Dunkery Lemonade

4lbs of sugar
1oz citric acid
1oz tartaric acid
Rind of 4 lemons
juice of 6 lemons
3 pints of water

Mix together and pour the three pints of boiling water. In use it will dilute.

Index

ACKNOWLEDGEMENTS

Margaret Alsford - Brooks/Noakes family
Duncan Bouchier - photographs
Muriel Brown - Cecil Cary's photographs
Jeannette & Dave Butt - Coronation poster
Pauline Clapp - School minutes & log book
Linda Friend - Parish Council minutes
Audrey Fry
Eileen and Derek Growtage
Valerie and Norman Fry
Les Heal
Helen Hunt - Church Acre poster and William Bennett's account ledger
Dorothy Kidner - Francis Lovibond's diary
Pat Lennard - Parochial Church Council minutes
Peter Parrish - Wilton Gaol records
Colin Powney - Methodist Chapel records
Rev. Peter Richmond - Parochial records
Carol & Allan Stokes - SWEB poster
Amy Young

BIBLIOGRAPHY

The following have been consulted and will provide further information :

Chedzoy Candle Auction	R.W. Patton	"Folklore," Spring 1971
Aspects of Somerset History	T.J. Hunt & R.R. Sellman	Somerset County Council
Avalon and Sedgemoor	Desmond Hawkins	David and Charles
Bridgwater Alfred		(1831-1833)
Bridgwater Independent		(1907-1928)
Brigwater Mercury		(1857-1999)
Bridgwater Standard		(1861-1870)
Bridgewater Times		(1846-1861)
Domesday Book (Somerset)		Phillmore Press
The Draining of the Somerset Levels	Michael Williams	Cambridge University
Experiments and Observations	Dr. Robert Hooke	W. Derman, F.R.S.
Kings and Queens of England	Antonia Fraser	Weidenfeld and Nicholson
The Monmouth Rebellion	Robert Dunning	Dovecote Press
The Monouth Rebels	W. McDonald Wigfield	Alan Sutton Publishing
The Natural History of the Somerset Levels	Bernard Storer	Dovecote Press
Sedgemoor, Its History & Natural History	Bernard Storer	David and Charles
Somerset at War, 1939-1945	Mac Hawkins	Hawk Editions
Somerset Legends	Berta Lawrence	David and Charles
Somerset, the Complete Guide	Robin Bush	Dovecote Press
The Story of Somersetshire	W.R. Richmond	Wake and Dean
The Victorian History of Somerset	Institute of Historical Research	Oxford University Press
Wildlife of the Somerset Levels	S. Davies and R. Jarman	R.S.P.B. booklet

Chedzoy Village Hall

Addendum

With the help of grants from Somerset County Council, Sedgemoor District Council the National Lottery Community Fund, Wyvern Environmental Trust (administrators of the Land Fill Tax) and Chedzoy Parish Council, plus the raising of some £10,000 within the village by means of various fund raising events, the hall has now been modernised.

Work commenced on the first phase of the work in March 2002. This consisted of the gutting of the toilet block in order that modern facilities, including those for the disabled, could be installed. A new kitchen, refreshment area and storage facilities were constructed to the rear of the main building. This phase of the work was officially opened on the afternoon of Golden Jubilee Day, 2002 when Norman Fry unveiled a commemorative plaque in "The Jubilee Room". On the same day games were provided for the children in the afternoon and in the evening a pig roast with live entertainment was provided for many of the residents. Jubilee mugs were manufactured for the Parish Council and presented to every child in the village as a souvenir of this important occasion.

Following some difficulties, the second stage of the modernisation was undertaken in May 2003: this entailed the removal of the old kitchen so as to enlarge the main hall, the insulation of the roof and the modernisation of the heating and electrical system.

The hall now has all the facilities which are expected in the 21st Century whilst retaining its essential character and is now at the heart of many activities in the village.

Slape Farm was demolished in 1999 and a new property, Sycamore House, built on the site. Rose Bower, adjoining the church, was demolished in 2003 and a new house built in its place. Inkers Farmhouse has been extensively modernised.

Chedzoy has now established linked with Middlezoy and Westonzoyland to form the Zoy Villages Association and twinning links have been established with the villages of Val d'Ille, Brittany. The formal twinning ceremony took place in Guipel, France in April 2003.

Life in the village continues much as in the past but we look forward to the future with confidence that our community still retains that spirit which has been lost in so many of England's villages.

Once again, thank you for your support: proceeds from the sale of this book now go directly to maintaining the fabric of the hall and the provision of further equipment.

John Weeks May 2003